Drama Essentials

An Anthology of Plays

Matthew Roudané
Georgia State University

Australia • Brazil • Japan • Korea • Mexico • Singapore • Spain • United Kingdom • United States

Drama Essentials: An Anthology of Plays
Matthew Roudané

Executive Publisher: Patricia Coryell
Editor-in-Chief: Carrie Brandon
Senior Marketing Manager: Tom Ziolkowski
Development Editor: Bruce Cantley
Project Editor: Aimee Chevrette
Art and Design Manager: Jill Haber
Cover Design Director: Tony Saizon
Senior Photo Editor: Jennifer Meyer Dare
Senior Composition Buyer: Chuck Dutton
New Title Project Manager: Susan Peltier
Editorial Assistant: Daisuke Yasutake
Marketing Assistant: Bettina Chiu

Cover image: Children in Halloween costumes running together with their hands on the person in front of them. 1960, Westport.
Credit: George Silk / Time & Life Pictures / Getty Images

Text Credits continue on page 707, which constitute an extension of the copyright page.

Library of Congress Control Number: 2007934923

ISBN-13: 978-0-618-47477-6

ISBN-10: 0-618-47477-3

Wadsworth Cengage Learning
20 Davis Drive
Belmont, CA 94002-3098
USA

Cengage Learning is a leading provider of customized learning solutions with office locations around the globe, including Singapore, the United Kingdom, Australia, Mexico, Brazil, and Japan. Locate your local office at **www.cengage.com/global**

Cengage Learning products are represented in Canada by Nelson Education, Ltd.

To learn more about Wadsworth, visit **www.cengage.com/wadsworth**

Purchase any of our products at your local college store or at our preferred online store **www.cengagebrain.com**

Printed in the United States of America
2 3 4 5 6 22 21 20 19 18

CONTENTS

THE PLAYS

APPENDIXES

PREFACE

The title of this collection of 12 plays suggests its scope and range. The contents of *Drama Essentials: An Anthology of Plays* range from Sophocles' ancient Greek *Antigonê*, to William Shakespeare's *Hamlet*, to nineteenth- and twentieth-century classics such as Henrik Ibsen's *A Doll House*, Susan Glaspell's *Trifles*, Arthur Miller's *Death of a Salesman*, and Tennessee Williams' *The Glass Menagerie*—plays that theatergoers and readers of drama have come to regard as essential works of the stage. In addition to the acknowledged classics, this collection also includes a number of essential works of the contemporary stage, including Paula Vogel's *How I Learned to Drive*, Gao Xingjian's *Dialogue and Rebuttal*, and Suzan-Lori Parks' *Top Dog/Underdog*, all of which demonstrate the versatility and continuing vitality of drama in the twenty-first century.

Whether they are acknowledged classics or new to the drama canon, all of the plays in this anthology are entertaining, enlightening, and challenging. While they are beautifully constructed, brimming with wonderful dialogue and poetry, and simply enjoyable on a pure entertainment level, they also tell us something significant about ourselves and about the culture we inhabit. Arthur Miller once articulated the social significance of drama when he told me about the influence of Shakespeare on the contemporary stage: "See how the plays that we call great have made us somehow more civilized. The great Shakespearean plays set up structures of order which became part of our mental equipment. In the immense love stories, the wonderful comedies, there's all sorts of color. But back of these great plays is a civic function. The author was really a poet-philosopher." The works in this anthology embody the specific qualities Miller mentioned. Most would agree that these plays are moving largely because of their sheer theatrical energy—because they radiate such intense action. In terms of time, place, setting, and characters, these plays stage the particulars of men and women in a specific time and place. But their power lies in something far beyond surface action. They also have a timelessness and universality. For example, while exploring the details of Peter and Jerry's fatal encounter in *The Zoo Story,* Edward Albee also illuminates larger issues of alienation, aloneness, and death in ways that resonate as much today as they did in the late 1950s, when the play premiered. The same is true of a play as ancient as *Antigonê,* in which themes such as conflicts between family and state and between the human and the cosmic are not simply reflective of life in ancient Greece, but also evoke instantly recognizable feelings in us today. Each play reveals important traces of the identity, politics, spirit, mores, and morals of the time and place the play was written and the audience for whom it was written.

In short, the selection of plays in this anthology serves two primary purposes: to introduce students to the essential—and most teachable—plays both in the canon and on the contemporary stage, and to demonstrate the universal, timeless relevance of drama as an art form that illuminates the human condition. In addition to anthologizing the essential plays in an affordable, compact format, *Drama Essentials* also provides a thorough introduction to the language of drama via its wide range of special features. These features demonstrate how to approach drama in its historical context, in the context of writing about drama, in the biographical context of individual playwrights, and in the context of dramatic terminology. The special features are outlined in more detail below.

SPECIAL FEATURES

* **A Brief Overview of World Theater** Whether used as a primary text for an introduction to drama course or as a supplementary text in a multi-genre literature course, *Drama Essentials* may be the first drama text most college students have ever used. Therefore, to prepare students for this complex subject, this anthology begins with a brief but wide-ranging introduction to drama from its origins to the present. To demonstrate that the theater is not exclusively a Western invention (even though most of the plays in this anthology are, in fact, Western), this introduction outlines the history of both the Western tradition and the Eastern theatrical traditions of China, Japan, and India. To help students grasp the drama terminology by necessity woven throughout this introduction, any terminology that may be new to students appears in boldface type on its first occurrence as a cue to consult the Glossary of Dramatic Terms in the end matter for further clarification.

* **Reading and Writing About Drama (with sample annotated student paper)** Written by my colleague Pearl McHaney, this introduction provides a clear methodology that prepares students for the often

daunting process of writing papers about drama. From getting prepared; to developing a thesis statement; to considering theme, text, context, and audience; to choosing a focus; and finally to using proper paper and MLA citation format; this introduction eases students into the process. The essay concludes with an annotated sample research paper written by one of McHaney's students, with further commentary following the paper. As in the Brief Overview, all drama terminology is rendered in bold upon first occurrence and defined in the Glossary.

* **SELECTION OF PLAYS** Within the limitations of a mostly canonical anthology of 12 plays, I have attempted to provide as much diversity of voice in the selection of plays as possible. Because until recently drama has historically been a genre dominated by male writers—more so even than in the fiction and poetry genres—the anthology is inevitably weighted toward canonical male playwrights such as Shakespeare, Ibsen, Williams, Miller, Pinter, etc. However, I have made a concerted effort to tip the gender balance by including an early classic by a woman playwright (Susan Glaspell's *Trifles*), and two contemporary plays by woman playwrights, *How I Learned to Drive* by Paula Vogel and *Top Dog/Underdog* by Suzan-Lori Parks, the latter also representing the emergence of a powerful African American voice on the contemporary scene. In addition, although most canonical plays taught in drama courses today are by Western playwrights, I have provided one contemporary Eastern play to tip the balance slightly, *Dialogue and Rebuttal* by Chinese playwright Gao Xingjian. Ideally, as the drama canon expands to include more woman playwrights, opens itself up to include a greater range of racially and ethnically diverse voices, and becomes more receptive to the teaching of the great Eastern traditions, imbalances in primarily canonical tables of contents such as this one will disappear.

* **AUTHOR HEADNOTES** Each play is preceded by an informative headnote that provides the birth and (if applicable) death date of the playwright, includes biographical background on the playwright, introduces the themes of the play (while avoiding giving away the ending or prescribing how students should approach the play), and contextualizes the play's importance in world theater.

* **FOOTNOTES** Most drama anthologies provide footnotes only for ancient plays and Shakespeare. However, because plays usually include at least a few references that may be linguistically, culturally, or historically obscure to readers, I have scoured each play carefully and provided footnotes wherever I felt students might find clarification helpful.

* **Appendixes** *Glossary of Dramatic Terms* Dramatic terms introduced and appearing in boldface in the introductory material are fully defined in this extensive appendix.

Selected Audio and Video Resources In keeping with the performance nature of drama, this appendix provides a list of films and audio reenactments of the plays in this anthology.

Selected Bibliography To get students started on the research process, this appendix provides an extensive bibliography of secondary works, organized by playwright.

ACKNOWLEDGMENTS

Within Houghton Mifflin Company, I would like to extend my thanks to Michael Gillespie, who originally took on this anthology for publication; Suzanne Phelps Weir, who oversaw the signing process; Senior Sponsoring Editor Lisa Kimball and Editor-in-Chief Carrie Brandon, who oversaw the project during development; Development Editor Bruce Cantley, whose editorial advice and perseverance ensured the completion of the anthology; Project Editor Aimee Chevrette, who carried the book through copyediting, design, proof, and printing; Editorial Assistant Kaitlin Crowley, who kept the project on track and assembled the final manuscript; and Tom Ziolkowski, Senior Marketing Manager, who handled all aspects of marketing this book.

Outside of Houghton Mifflin, I would like to thank my colleagues Anna Cavallarin, Laura Barbáran, Isabel Durán, Kerin Flatley, James Hirsh, and Ana Antón Pacheco. And last, but certainly not least, I would like to thank the proposal and manuscript reviewers who helped shape this book through their insightful comments and thoughtful suggestions: Audrey Bilger at Claremont McKenna College, Joan DelFattore at The University of Delaware, Eileen Kearney at Texas A&M University, Elizabeth Nelson at St. Peter's College, Tony Stuart Stelly at The Pennsylvania State University–York, and Russell Vandenbroucke at The University of Louisville.

Matthew Roudané

INTRODUCTORY MATERIALS

A BRIEF OVERVIEW OF WORLD THEATER

The Origins of Theater

The exact origins of theater remain unknown. However, most theater historians agree that, whether staged in ancient Egypt, Greece, or in countries in the Far East, the earliest drama probably emerged from religious activities and ceremonies, as did most art forms. For instance, the earliest surviving examples of sculpture from around the world typically depict ancient gods or the Buddha, and most ancient hieroglyphics (from the Greek terms for "sacred" and "writing"), which were an early form of both storytelling and illustration, were religious in nature and inscribed on temple and tomb walls. Although we have less archaeological proof of the origins of theater than of the visual arts, it is not too fanciful to suggest that dramas in the ancient world were enacted through tribal rituals. Originating with dances and chants, religious rituals were eventually embellished with costumed performers and then further developed into enactments of stories, fables, and myths.

Surely song, dance, music, spectacle, storytelling, sacred chants, and so on developed, at times simultaneously, on a truly global scale. But as drama matured in the ancient world, a few noteworthy cultures played pivotal roles.

Eastern Drama

China

One powerful Eastern theatrical tradition was Chinese drama, whose origins can be traced to 1500 BC. Over the centuries, Chinese drama became increasingly sophisticated, moving from musical and acrobatic entertainments, to increasingly complex forms of shadow puppetry developed during the Tang dynasty (600s to 900s AD), to multi-act plays performed during the Yuan dynasty (1200s and 1300s AD), to refined operas that combined drama, poetry, music, and dance during the Ming dynasty (later 1300s to 1600s), and finally to the **Peking Opera**[1], which emerged during the 1800s as a major and popular art form. The Peking Opera stage is noted for its simplicity, but the actors, elaborately and colorfully costumed and made up, sing, dance, speak, and perform acrobatics, with a haunting clarity that is based on well-established Chinese traditions. Inspired by myth and romance, folklore and history, these operas proved to be immensely popular and continue to be performed frequently and internationally today, along with contemporary forms of drama.

Japan

Traditional Japanese theater consists of four types of performance, the **Noh, Kyogen, Kabuki,** and **Bunraku.** The Noh theater, which originated in the 1300s, was the outgrowth of a combination and refinement of various ancient folk entertainments. Noh performances are akin to staged poems, suffused with Buddhist and Shintoist religious meaning. Featuring spoken word, dance, and music, these compact, brief plays feature some actors wearing masks. Noh drama is a tightly controlled and sophisticated form of theater, with exacting attention paid to each gesture and spoken word. As such, it appealed mostly to the cultural elite. Often, Kyogen, or brief, humorous performances (whose tradition dates back to the fifth century) will be enacted during the intermission of a Noh play. First appearing in the 1600s and still a popular form of theater today, the Kabuki play was developed in opposition to the historical focus and highly controlled nature of the Noh theater. Kabuki plays focused on contemporary, ordinary themes, which sparked their popularity among ordinary Japanese citizens. Eventually, however, Kabuki too became a highly stylized form like the Noh. By the 1600s and 1700s the Japanese Bunraku, or puppet theater, developed. In a Bunraku play, the puppeteers work in full view of the audience, operating the nearly four-foot-tall puppets, whose eyes, eyebrows, mouth, and other joints move realistically while a speaker reads the script and conveys the puppet's psychological and emotional state to the audience. Today, all of the above theatrical traditions continue to exist, alongside modern forms of theater that have developed since the late nineteenth and early twentieth centuries, when Japan first began to industrialize.

India

Another great Eastern theatrical tradition developed in India. Its precise beginnings are not known, but most believe that as early as 2000 BC,

---

[1]Words in **bold** typeface are included in the Glossary of Dramatic Terms that begins on page 685 of this anthology.

during the Aryan Civilization, the Indians performed their first dramas. Somewhere between the fifth and second centuries BC, Bharata Muni composed an important document entitled *Natyasastra,* which systematically outlined the fundamentals of Indian drama with regard to costumes, acting styles, dance, and so on. Plays from this era, known as **Sanskrit drama** because of the language in which they were written, were epic plays that explored a variety of human emotions and moods, and they always ended on a positive note. The key play of the era is *Skakuntala* (circa 400 AD), written by Kalidasa, India's greatest dramatist from this era. Because of India's long history of conquest by outside forces, Indian drama took on many forms through the centuries. During the Middle Ages, Bhavabuti is considered to have been India's most important dramatist, and much later, during India's occupation by Great Britain (which lasted until 1947), many plays took the form of social protest. Today, Indian theater is as thriving and modern as that of any other region in the world.

Western Drama

In the Western world, ancient theater developed independently from the theater of the East, first in Greece and then in Rome. Over time, the oral and dance traditions of theater were complemented by written texts.

Greece

Many theater historians believe that drama as a codified art form first developed in ancient Greece. As early as 600 BC, festivals were held celebrating **Dionysus,** the god of fertility and wine, and featuring performances filled with song and dance. These festivals were known as the **City Dionysia.** Soon the Greeks created contests for writing tragedies (circa 534 BC), which were staged in Athens. A man named Thespis won the first contest and is considered by many to have been the first true playwright and theatrical actor. Hence the contemporary use of the word **thespian,** meaning "of or related to drama." These dramatic festivals, mixing religion with entertainment, were full-blown cultural celebrations. The drama contests became both increasingly popular and increasingly competitive, resulting in tragedies and comedies that by the 400s BC had become quite sophisticated and meaningful. Ancient Greek plays were often staged in massive outdoor amphitheaters. The Theater of Dionysus, situated on a hill below the

Acropolis in Athens, could seat approximately 14,000 spectators. The stage itself must have been impressive, with the audience wrapped partially around the orchestra, a round acting area where the action took place, and a large stage house, called a skene, where actors would change costumes.

The plays, for the ancient audience, functioned as more than mere entertainments that could be enjoyed and forgotten shortly thereafter. They served as models of community and of citizenship. They were, as noted twentieth-century rhetorician Kenneth Burke might say, "equipment for living." On a personal and social level, the plays taught people something about themselves, about their friends and family, about their village or city, and about how to conduct themselves within society. On a political level the plays critiqued the laws and rulers of the land. On an aesthetic level, the plays were inspiring works of art that ennobled the human spirit. Above all, on a religious level, for most spectators these plays were sacred texts, dramatizing the secular world while addressing broader spiritual issues.

The ancient Greeks were particularly attracted to the **tragedy,** or a play that is serious and ends on a sorrowful note. Although hundreds of tragedies were composed, only just over thirty of these plays are known today. Of those playwrights whose works have survived, three dramatists in particular stand out as embodying the greatest achievements in Greek tragedy: Aeschylus (who is considered the father of Greek tragedy and whose plays including the *Oresteia* trilogy, *The Persians,* and *Seven Against Thebes* are the oldest surviving Greek plays), Sophocles (perhaps the most famous Greek playwright, whose most well-known plays are *Oedipus the King, Oedipus at Colonus,* and *Antigonê*), and Euripides (whose most famous plays include *The Bacchae, Media,* and *Electra*).

Although the Greeks enjoyed tragedies, they also developed the **comedy,** a play that is intended to amuse the audience. One form of comedy, the **satyr play,** was a brief comic parody of a popular Greek myth, which provided audiences with comic relief from the seriousness of the tragedies. Another form of comedy, the **Old Comedy,** was an often-rowdy, satiric, and humorous play criticizing the current state of affairs in the world. The most famous example of an Old Comedy is Aristophanes' *Lysistrata.* In contrast to the Old Comedy, the **New Comedy** focused on more private, domestic concerns of everyday Athenians, rather than on politics. Meander's *The Grouch* is a great example of a New Comedy.

Much of the theater terminology we still use today was invented by the ancient Greeks. It was the Greeks (particularly the philosopher

Aristotle in his work *The Poetics*) who identified and codified such theatrical concepts as the **elements of drama (theme, plot, characterization, diction, melody,** and **spectacle**), **catharsis** (the extreme emotional purge that audiences feel during the height of a tragic play), **deus ex machina** (the device of solving the play's problems by introducing a new, improbable situation), **mimesis** (the way in which art imitates nature), and many others.

Greek drama began to lose its luster after 200 BC, while the dramatic tradition in Rome grew in strength and stature. In Rome, farce and comedy were more popular than tragedy, and audiences, drawn by free admission to shows, often found themselves immersed in a party-like atmosphere at the theater. Today the only known comedies from this period of Roman history are by Plautus (whose surviving plays include *Miles Gloriosus* and *Pseudolus*) and Terence (whose surviving plays include *Adelphoe: The Brothers, Eunuchus,* and *Hechyra: The Mother-in-Law*), and their works were essentially takeoffs of the New Comedy from Greece. Theirs were vigorous plays, featuring comic twists, deceptions, farce, and character types whose quirky mannerisms delighted Roman audiences. Plautus' and Terence's plays also featured song and music. In addition to Plautus' and Terence's comedies, a brief, funny, and bawdy form of comic play, called a **mime,** was also popular, as were pieces in which one actor, listening to a choral narrative and music, silently played out the stories. This type of play was known as a **pantomime.**

Rome

While the Romans gravitated toward comedy, they still appreciated the tragic mode. Livius Andronicus ushered in the first tragic performances in approximately 240 BC, but Lucius Annaeus Seneca is the best-known Roman tragedian. Seneca's best-known play, *Phaedra,* is still performed today. Seneca's unique use of ornate language, popularization of the five-act form, deployment of ghosts and magic, and development of the revenge tragedy provided subsequent playwrights, especially during the Renaissance, with fresh ideas for creating their plays.

As the Roman Empire declined, so did its theater, and scholars believe that the last theatrical performances in ancient Rome occurred in 533 AD, after which very little cultural achievement occurred until about 900 AD (hence the term the "Dark Ages" used to describe the period between the fall of Rome and the revitalization of culture that began around the turn of the first millennium).

The Middle Ages

During the Middle Ages or medieval period, from about 900 AD through the 1500s, Western drama, often religious in nature, re-emerged. This is not to say that drama did not exist during the Dark Ages, only that it most likely existed as a popular form and was largely not recorded for posterity. In addition, the Roman Catholic church had banned most forms of drama during the Dark Ages, in an effort to curtail what were perceived as the excesses of the Roman Empire. But starting around 900 AD, as part of worship services, priests and choirboys began acting in brief plays, spoken in Latin, which became known as **liturgical drama,** some of which survive in written form today. Based on key biblical events, these performances signaled the move out of the Dark Ages and the cultural reintroduction of drama as an important part of life in Europe. By around the 1200s, the **mystery play** appeared. Mystery plays were verse dramas meant to teach Christianity to the people. They were often performed with a comic flair, with the Biblical characters behaving exactly like living contemporaries of the congregation. By the 1300s, many mystery plays were staged by non-religious theater troupes, and these brief plays were often clustered together as a group of dramas known as a **cycle** of plays. These cycles dramatized the Christian experience, from the Creation to the Crucifixion. Such cycles were popular in France, Italy, and other countries such as Spain and England, where plays were performed on pageant wagons that could be moved from town to town. Later in the Middle Ages, two new forms, the **morality play** and the **miracle play,** became popular. Morality plays focused on the lives and plights of the Virgin Mary and the saints (the most famous surviving example of this is the play *Everyman,* whose author is unknown), while miracle plays were less overtly about religion but were filled with moral warnings and guidelines. Secular plays also existed during this time, but little recorded evidence of these plays remains today.

The Renaissance

Following the slow reinvigoration of theater during the Middle Ages, a period of vast cultural reawakening of the arts, known as the Renaissance, occurred between approximately the fourteenth and sixteenth centuries, resulting in remarkable theatrical works by playwrights such as William Shakespeare in England, Pedro Calderón de la Barca in Spain, and Molière in France.

England

Shakespeare is usually credited for elevating the art of drama to its greatest form. Shakespeare created an eloquence, ambiguity, and depth in drama that few—if any—other playwrights have matched. Scholars contend that Shakespeare's plays and poems were written between 1586 and 1612, during which time he created an astounding body of work. His plays are generally broken into four stylistic categories: the tragedies (serious fictional plays, including *Hamlet, Othello, King Lear, Romeo and Juliet,* and *Macbeth*), the comedies (fictional plays often involving mistaken identity, including *Much Ado about Nothing, The Taming of the Shrew, Love's Labors Lost,* and *The Comedy of Errors*), the histories (plays that focus on real historical figures, including *Henry IV, Parts I, II, and III, Richard III,* and *Henry V*), and the romances (lyrical plays that often involve fantastical elements, including *A Winter's Tale, The Tempest,* and *Cymbeline*). Some critics have added a fifth category, known as the "problem plays," which deal with contemporary social problems, mix tragedy and comedy in equal portions, and tend to have ambiguous endings (as opposed to straightforward happy or sad endings). Examples of Shakespearean problem plays include the comedies *As You Like It, Measure for Measure,* and *Troilus and Cressida,* often categorized as comedies, but darker in tone than Shakespeare's lighter comedies. While the authorship of some of Shakespeare's plays is debated, his greatest plays are clearly recognizable by their brilliant verse, rich characterizations, and ability to capture the richness and complexity of human existence within the confines of the dramatic form.

By 1660, thanks to Shakespeare's influence and the Restoration (the reunification of England, Ireland, and Scotland by King Charles II, which marked the end of the English Civil War and allowed culture to flourish), the British theater once again emerged as an important genre. Slowly at first, but with an emerging popularity, the theater began to reassert itself as part of the national culture. More quality plays were being written than ever before, sets became increasingly elaborate, a form of popular play known as the **masque** (and its opposite, the **antimasque**) became popular, and women actors began to appear on stage for the first time. Restoration and eighteenth-century British drama, thanks to the pioneering work of such playwrights as William Wycherley, William Congreve, Richard Brinsley Sheridan, John Dryden, and Aphra Behn, ensured that the British stage regained the vitality that had been so pronounced during Shakespeare's day. Their comedies of manners, heroic dramas, and satires remain important works to this day.

Spain

Meanwhile, Spain was enjoying its own Golden Age of drama from the mid-1500s through the 1600s. After a long period of wars involving a number of small, independent states, Spain became a unified kingdom in 1469. The new Kingdom of Spain was a Christian one, and drama began to play an important religious function in the country, allowing the Christian church to reassert its presence. "Autos sacrementales," or religious plays, were morality dramas meant to reinforce Christian doctrinal ethics. Often in the form of **allegory**, with characters with names such as Sin and Pleasure, the plays proved to be enormously popular. The plays staged in Madrid were enacted on "carros," which were tall wagons, one carrying props and scenery and a second serving as a stage. As in other European countries, mobile theater companies toured the country, stopping at one city after another and performing in open markets. Not until 1579 did the first permanent theater house opened in Madrid. At this time, playwrights such as Lope de Vega and Pedro Calderón de la Barca grew in prominence as the two greatest playwrights of the era. De Vega, who wrote more than 1800 plays, 400 of which survive today, interwove religion, history, and myth in his works, as did de la Barca, whose plays were often philosophical and exotic.

France

In France, as in Spain and many other European countries, the Renaissance theater had its genesis in religious plays staged during the medieval period. In the 1400s the *Confrérie de la Passion,* a theater guild, set up one of the first theaters in Paris, and by the early 1600s Alexandre Hardy had written many extremely popular plays that were performed there. The influence of classical Greek and Roman theater on French drama of the 1600s is best seen in Pierre Corneille's play, *Le Cid.* Jean Racine was also a major figure of the era. The most widely recognized playwright of this period was Molière, whose satiric plays, particularly his 1666 comedy, *The Misanthrope,* remain popular and are often performed today. With the passing of Corneille, Racine, and Molière, French drama became a paler version of its former self. However, playwrights such as Denis Diderot and Pierre Marivaux were important later figures who influenced the French stage in the 1700s and 1800s.

During the Renaissance and thereafter, theater thrived in other European countries as well. In Italy, for example, the **commedia dell'arte** was an extremely popular form in the 1700s, and, for many, Carlo Goldoni was the most important Italian dramatist of the era. By the early 1800s, two German playwrights, Johann Wolfgang von Goethe and Friedrich Schiller, had written great tragic and romantic works. But it wasn't until the modem period (roughly after 1850) that theater became a truly international phenomenon.

The Modern Period

As a result of the industrial revolution, by the 1850s what we think of as "modern drama" had begun to evolve throughout the world: in Africa, in Asia, in Europe, in Australia, and in the Americas. Increasingly, plays were seen as representations of national thinking. For instance, in Chile, Argentina, and emerging African nations, nineteenth-century playwrights composed dramas to celebrate their newly won national independence. Some of the most important and influential playwrights to emerge in the nineteenth century were Henrik Ibsen, August Strindberg, Anton Chekhov, George Bernard Shaw, and Oscar Wilde, all of whom tackled social issues.

Norwegian playwright Henrik Ibsen, considered by many to be the father of modern drama, wrote great dramas that raised important social questions of the day. Ibsen wrote extremely realistic plays whose moral seriousness demonstrated that the theater could have a powerful influence on public debate. In his plays, Ibsen tackled such controversial topics as the role of women in modern society, the need to deal with sexually transmitted diseases more responsibly, and the debate over the origins of the human species, in response to Charles Darwin's then recently published theory of human evolution. *A Doll's House, Ghosts, Hedda Gabler, The Master Builder,* and *When We Dead Awaken,* works premiering between 1879 and 1900, certify Ibsen's place as an important social commentator and theatrical innovator of the school of **realism.**

The same could be said of Ibsen's Swedish contemporary, August Strindberg, who similarly wrote realist plays early in his career and tackled social topics of the day in plays such as *Miss Julie.* Later, he moved away from realistic plays to more abstract, symbolic works (known as theatrical **expressionism**), such as *A Dream Play.*

During this same era, Russian playwright and short story author Anton Chekhov wrote groundbreaking plays that realistically explored the psychology of his characters while simultaneously commenting upon the character of the Russian people as a whole. Although he was primarily a short story author and only wrote a handful of plays, five of these plays—*Ivanov, Uncle Vanya, The Seagull, The Three Sisters,* and *The Cherry Orchard*—broke new ground in psychological realism and are regularly performed today.

In England, George Bernard Shaw and Oscar Wilde both wrote provocative plays that mixed comedy with harsh critique of English traditions. Wilde's most famous plays include *The Importance of Being Earnest, An Ideal Husband,* and *A Woman of No Importance,* while Shaw is best remembered for the social comedies *Arms and the Man, Major Barbara, Pygmalion,* and *Man and Superman.*

By the early twentieth century, even after movies had become a more sophisticated and popular medium, the theater was a major draw for audiences in nearly every industrialized country in the world, particularly in Europe. In Ireland, Dublin's Abbey Theatre showcased the brilliance of playwrights such as Lady Gregory, Sean O'Casey, John Millington Synge, and William Butler Yeats. In Italy, Luigi Pirandello, with his play *Six Characters in Search of an Author,* provided the modern stage with a wonderful sense of experimentalism. In France, playwrights such as Jean Cocteau, Jean Giraudoux, and Jean Anouilh explored a sense of the absurd.

Contemporary Drama

After World War II a host of other dramatists envisioned the modern stage as an ideal site to contest the reigning values, mores, and morals of the day. Samuel Beckett's 1953 play *Waiting for Godot* revolutionized the modern stage and became part of what we now call the **Theater of the Absurd,** which was characterized by a politicized sense of futility and meaninglessness in a world constantly under the threat of war and nuclear annihilation. Absurdist theater calls into question traditional forms of narration, plot, language, character, and resolution. In addition to Beckett, practitioners of the Theater of the Absurd included the Romanian Eugène Ionesco, the Czech Václav Havel, and the Germans Friedrich Dürrenmatt, Heiner Müller, and Peter Weiss, all of whom carried on the politicized tradition of Bertolt Brecht, whose **Epic Theater** in the 1920s through 1940s focused on the intense social issues Germans were experiencing at that time. Later, in England, such talents as John Osborne, Harold Pinter, Edward Bond, Caryl Churchill, David Hare, Tom Stoppard, and Sarah Kane, inspired by the absurdists' politicized theater, tackled and today continue to write about the political realities of post-World-War-II Great Britain.

What these post-World-War-II playwrights all brought forth in their art, regardless of their national origins, was a commitment to exploring the social, political, and intellectual issues of their respective eras. This remains true for such contemporary dramatists as Wole Soyinka of Nigeria, Dario Fo of Italy, Athol Fugard of South Africa, Derek Walcott of the West

Indies, Leilah Assumpçáo, Consuelo de Castro, and Plínio Marcos of Brazil, and Gao Xingjian of China (whose *Dialogue and Rebuttal* is included in this anthology). The theater, after all, like the novel and the poem, is not only about the values, desires, inadequacies, and triumphs of individuals, but also about these same aspects of society. Long the most public of the arts, the theater is naturally placed to be a barometer of public as well as private sentiments.

As American poet Ezra Pound said, artists are always seeking ways to "make it new," exploring new techniques, forms, languages, and resolutions. After World War II, an enhanced interest in exploring social issues was one way to "make it new." So was an increased impulse to experiment with dramatic form. Although playwrights have always experimented with form to a degree, an overt experimentalism, or pushing of the boundaries of what we traditionally think of as theater, begun prior to World War II by such playwrights as Spain's Frederico García Lorca, Italy's Luigi Pirandello, and France's Antonin Artaud, an iconoclastic director.

In the United States, Eugene O'Neill, Tennessee Williams, and Arthur Miller sought to tell primal stories in new ways, and this approach was taken up by later writers such as Edward Albee, Sam Shepard, David Mamet, Adrienne Kennedy, Paula Vogel, August Wilson, and many others. Meanwhile, numerous new **avant-garde** and **alternative theater** troupes, who staged plays that involved improvisation, audience participation, and radical politics, emerged. Some of the more innovative of the alternative theater groups included the Living Theatre, the Bread and Puppet Theatre, and the Open Theatre in the United States.

Since the 1960s, especially in the United States, women playwrights increased their presence in the theater, staging feminist works that drew attention to female concerns. Adrienne Kennedy, Megan Terry, Marsha Norman, Wendy Wasserstein, and Maria Irene Fornés are but a few who have created distinctly female protagonists whose struggles and triumphs animate their stages. African American drama, too, continued to mature with such playwrights as August Wilson and Suzan-Lori Parks earning Pulitzer Prizes for their work. Latino/a theater, performance art, and gay theater also emerged since the 1960s as a powerful presence within the American stage. The musical remains enormously popular with audiences here and abroad. While it seems that Broadway will never return to the glory days of the mid-twentieth century when the works of Eugene O'Neill, Tennessee Williams, and Arthur Miller were first produced, regional and alternative theaters have flourished throughout the United States.

In the twenty-first century, world theater continues to thrive by embracing the rich traditions of the past and seeking ways to renew the genre. As ever, theater continues to be a powerful avenue for personal exploration, experimentation, and social commentary. The world stage continues to thrive because the theater, the most public of the arts, continues to tackle emerging public issues and private concerns.

READING AND WRITING ABOUT DRAMA

Reading Drama Effectively

By Matthew Roudané

Reading dramatic literature is both rewarding and challenging. It is rewarding because, like reading a good novel, reading a successful dramatic text brings the reader into a world of narrative twists and turns, unexpected ironies, fated heroes, often violent climaxes, and intriguing endings. The process of reading drama is also challenging because for many, a play visually looks quite different from a novel—one turns the page of a play and sees pure **dialogue**[1], often without the familiar and richly detailed descriptions of landscapes or individuals one finds in a Toni Morrison or William Faulkner novel, for example.

Because plays consist mostly of dialogue, many find it useful to read any prefatory material written by the playwright to get information about time, place, and visual aspects (such as how the characters look and move) that the dialogue doesn't provide. In pre-twentieth-century drama—a category that includes most Classical Greek and Roman, as well as Renaissance productions—the spoken word itself, the dialogue, carried forth the action, and the playwrights provided little or no background information. In modern and contemporary drama, however, we have witnessed the ascendancy of the "side text," the non-verbal but important secondary text whose presence in written drama and absence in live stage performance is quite noteworthy. The "side text" is also referred to as the **stage directions.** These stage directions, often found at the beginning of many modern plays as well as within the plays, provide foreground for much of what is to follow by supplying rich character descriptions, notes on the set and setting, and information about the characters' body language. In addition, stage directions often, as in Arthur Miller's *Death of a Salesman,* allude to the play's major

[1]Words in **bold** typeface are included in the Glossary of Dramatic Terms that begins on page 685 of this anthology.

themes. George Bernard Shaw's prefaces are as textured and as entertaining as the plays themselves. It would be impossible to stage Eugene O'Neill's *The Hairy Ape* or *Long Day's Journey into Night* without coming to terms with these plays' stage directions. And some of Tennessee Williams's stage directions, functioning at times like a narrator in a novel or short story, read like stories themselves. In live performance the stage directions, even though they remain invisible, nonetheless can provide viewers with background information they may need, because the actors, director, set designers, costume workers, light technicians, and others will have brought these directions to life during the performance. Readers of modern dramatic literature need not be in the dark about background information either, because they have the benefit of stage directions to help them better understand plays outside of performance, as they appear on the written page.

When I worked with the legendary actor, playwright, and director Joseph Chaikin on his last professional directing effort before his death—a production of Arthur Miller's *Broken Glass* in 2004—at the very first rehearsal, after the actors had signed their contracts and other business details were taken care of, the entire cast and crew sat around a table and *read* the play. We talked about the characters, what the spirit of the production should be like, the language of the script, the set and setting, and more—much of which was to be found in the stage directions.

One's careful reading of both the play's dialogue and the stage directions enables the reader to produce a more carefully considered oral or written conversation about the significance of a play than could be obtained by reading the dialogue alone and skipping the stage directions. So, before writing about a play, as will be discussed in detail by Pearl McHaney below, make the most of the reading experience first. Carefully consider how dialogue and stage directions work together to create the totality of the play.

Writing About Drama

By Pearl McHaney

Writing about drama is similar to writing about novels, short stories, or poems in that the subject of your essay is literature, or imaginative prose. Your essay in response to a play that you have read in this anthology, for example, will emanate from the literature itself: the reading, discussion, study, analysis, understanding, and enjoyment of the work.

Before I discuss the specifics of writing about drama, I want to first make an important distinction between the terms "drama" and "theater." The basic definition of **drama**—a play written in prose or verse that tells a story through dialogue and actions performed by actors impersonating the characters of the story—implies a few of the genre's conventions: story (**conflict** and **plot** with **characters**), **dialogue, action,** and actors. The primary difference between drama and **theater** is that drama refers to the written text of the play and theater refers to that play in live performance.

Now to the specifics of writing about drama: In this introduction, I will say a few words about writing effectively; preparing to write; writing your hypothesis and thesis statement; writing the essay with a consideration of author, text, context, and audience; focusing on characterization, staging, structure, or theme; using proper form; and citing sources correctly using MLA style. The concluding section of this introduction will feature a student essay with evaluative comments.

Writing Effectively

The purpose of writing about drama is to communicate effectively your ideas concerning some aspect of the play or plays that you have read, discussed, and studied. In a nutshell, the best ways to write effectively about drama are to write about what you know, to care about your ideas, to re-read your drafts once they are down on paper, and to revise your drafts in order to sharpen the organization, diction, and syntax of your essay. In addition, your essay will be enriched by quoting key lines from the play or plays (this brings both the playwright's and the characters' voices into the argument, letting them, in effect, speak for themselves), and avoiding clichéd expressions (they are overused and prevent you from digging deeply into the text), academic jargon (words and phrases aimed solely at pleasing the teacher will probably have the opposite effect), generalizations (they are unconvincing and again, prevent you from digging deeply into the text), and repetition (of words or ideas or sentence type—including only compound sentences joined by "and" makes the essay boring, for example).

Getting Prepared

Within the parameters of the assignment, the most important starting point is to select a topic and a play/character/theme about which you are excited. Effective writing in many ways grows out of a genuine interest in the subject matter. Choose a play that particularly interests you: that is, one that intrigued you while you were reading it; one that led to an interesting class discussion; one that led you to ask more questions, think of new ideas, or change your initial opinions; one for which you felt **empathy** or sympathy for one of the characters; or one for which you were drawn into the play's paradoxes, ironies, ambiguities, **conflicts, characterizations,** or **actions.** Choose a play that you are eager to re-read. Write down as many questions as you can think of regarding the play and the essay topic. Gather your class notes and study notes related to the play or plays about which you want to write. Skim the "Glossary of Dramatic Terms" at the end of this anthology to better familiarize yourself with drama terminology that you can incorporate into your essay, and write down a list of terms relevant to your essay. When you re-read the play, or at minimum the scenes pertinent to your topic, keep in mind the topic and questions you wish to address in your essay, look for key actions and portions of dialogue that will contribute to the topic you are exploring, and write them down.

Creating Your Hypothesis and Thesis Statement

Having prepared your questions, class and study notes, list of relevant quotations to use, and list of dramatic terms to incorporate into the essay, you will be ready to draft a hypothesis, or working thesis statement. Given your topic and your knowledge of the play, what idea might you want to prove or argue? For example, if your topic is death in *Hamlet,* what does Shakespeare's play illustrate about death? That death is inevitable, yet must be fought against? That death is less important than life? That a death (of someone else) as a means to an end is justifiable? That death is a satisfactory and satisfying escape from seemingly insurmountable problems? "Death" (or another subject like sanity, familial loyalty, power, illusion, education, society, governance, etc.) as a topic would be much too general (and too broad) to cover in an essay, but a more narrow topic, such as what one character in *Hamlet* demonstrates about death, can lead to a fascinating essay. To draft your hypothesis, begin with a stock sentence such as "William Shakespeare's *Hamlet* illustrates that. . . ." or "In William Shakespeare's tragedy *Hamlet,* Hamlet demonstrates that. . . ." A hypothesis can serve as a roadmap to guide you as you write and to keep you focused on your goal of successfully proving your point. After you have organized your ideas and created a first draft of your essay to prove your hypothesis, you can transform your hypothesis into a thesis statement, or a more carefully worded version of the hypothesis, that will guide your readers through your argument.

Considering Author, Text, Context, and Audience

Most writing about literature can be approached by considering four basic aspects of a given literary work: the author, the text, the context, and the audience. These four areas offer opportunities for asking questions about the work that support your thesis statement. Consider the following sentences that I might write in an essay about *Hamlet*:

> Shakespeare was surely aware of the convention of the Chorus in Greek tragedy, which provided an avenue for the playwright to not only comment upon his characters' motivations but also to comment upon the play itself. In *Hamlet*, one opportunity Shakespeare creates to comment upon both his characters' motivations and upon his own work is the play within a play that Prince Hamlet devises to shock his uncle, King Claudius, into a confession of murder. When Hamlet sets his plan in motion and wryly concludes, "the play's the thing/Wherein I'll catch the conscience of the King" (2.2.604–605), as is so often the case in his work, Shakespeare winks to the audience about the effect plays, including his own play, can have on people.

These few sentences include pieces of evidence that I have written my essay on *Hamlet* with author, text, context, and audience all kept firmly in mind.

First, I indicate that Shakespeare is the author, and discuss Shakespeare's intentions, thereby pointing out that I understand that the author cannot be separated from the work, that authorial intentions have a strong impact upon one's interpretation of the author's work.

Second, I discuss the text in some detail, pointing out that Prince Hamlet and King Claudius are two of the characters; that the Prince thinks his uncle is a murderer (this suggests something about the conflict); and that it seems that the Prince will write a play to trick the King—the play will act as a sort of mouse trap. I even directly quote a couplet from the text. In doing so, I demonstrate that the text itself is the support for my argument, and I avoid the trap many essay writers fall into: losing track of the evidence to be found within the text itself.

Third, I demonstrate that I understand the importance of context. Plays, even those written by geniuses like Shakespeare, are not written in a vacuum, that is, they are not written in complete isolation from outside forces. Playwrights are influenced not only by social, historical, and other exterior forces, but also by the work of other playwrights and existing play conventions—in other words, the material surrounding the play that affects what it is, or the context. Of course, an essay writer must contextualize his or her arguments as accurately as possible. For instance, making an argument that Shakespeare was influenced by modern self-referencing films like *Adaptation* and *Eternal Sunshine of the Spotless Mind* would not make any contextual sense because these films were simply not part of the context in which Shakespeare worked, but it does make sense to argue, as I do above, that Shakespeare would have been aware of the self-referential aspects of Greek tragedies when writing his own tragedies, and incorporated those aspects into *Hamlet.*

Finally, I indicate that I am aware of the importance of audience when making my argument. As Shakespeare's "wink" to his audience makes especially clear in this case, plays, like all works of art, are created to have an effect on an audience. Keeping the playwright's audience in mind as you support your argument for *your* audience is yet another way to support your arguments.

You may be asking yourself a number of questions at this point, such as "How am I supposed to know what the author was really like or meant to convey?" "How do I know if I am looking at the right portions of the text or interpreting them properly?" "How can I really understand the context in which the author worked?" and "What do I know about the original audience for the author's plays or what the author expected to get across to them?" These are all valid and complex questions, but don't let yourself be dragged into quicksand by them. You may not be able to answer all of these questions fully, but neither can the innumerable scholars who have been debating the works of Shakespeare (and many other playwrights, poets, novelists, painters, sculptors, historians, etc.) for centuries. As mentioned in this anthology's "A Brief Overview of World Theater," there is even considerable debate about whether or not Shakespeare wrote many of the plays that are attributed to him. The best general advice I can offer is to use common sense, do background research when necessary (particularly in terms of working with author and context questions, but research can also help you with text and audience questions), and support your arguments with evidence from that research or from the text you're interpreting. Following is some more detailed advice.

Questions about the author of a play and about that author's probable intentions can be answered first by reading the information provided in the anthology you are using, such as in this anthology's "A Brief Overview of World Theater" and the headnotes at the beginning of each play. Birth and death dates provide you with a historical reference that might lead to a better understanding of the author's style, subject, or audience. The author's biography will also suggest the ideas the author preferred to write about in his or her body of work, and how the particular play you are interpreting fits within that author's body of work. One might ask other questions regarding the author: What subjects did he or she frequently dramatize? What historical events occurred during the author's lifetime or would have influenced the author for other reasons? Where did the author live (urban, suburban, or rural location) and what local dialects and customs were common in that place and may have influenced the author's work? What traditions and innovations are customarily evident in the author's writing? Biographical criticism leads us to ask how the author's life is reflected in his or her writing. For instance, consider how the fact that Arthur Miller's father was bankrupted by the Great Depression might have affected Miller's writing of *Death of a Salesman,* a play that is ultimately about a father's failure. Or when reading *The Glass Menagerie,* consider the fact that Tennessee Williams's birth name was Tom and that Williams always felt remorseful about his fragile sister Rose's lobotomy and hospitalization, biographical details that come to life in the play. Consulting your anthology's introductory materials and headnotes will give you a good start. If you are writing a lengthier, more complex essay, such as a research paper, you will also need to consult library and Internet resources for further information about the author.

The text offers itself as the resource for inquiry, but to properly ask questions about the text of a play, you need to know about the elements of drama and how the text of a play works. For instance, you need to be able to analyze the plot of the play, to identify the conflicts occurring within the play, to establish who the protagonist(s) and antagonist(s) are and the relationships between these characters, to understand how language reflects both characters and actions, and to decipher how characters, plot, and dialogue all work together to contribute to the dramatization of life that is a play. You will learn these skills in the drama classroom, and you can explore further by familiarizing yourself with dramatic terms and conventions. As discussed earlier, this text features a "Glossary of Dramatic Terms" providing definitions of important terms such as **plot** (and the parts that make up a plot), **characterization, antagonist/protagonist, act** and **scene, irony,** and **symbolism.** In addition to understanding the elements of drama, terminology, and dramatic conventions, an intelligent close reading of the text will be enhanced by background information and research around such topics as when the play was written, when and where it was first produced, what earlier drafts or formats (a one-act, a short story, a journal entry) preceded the play's premiere, what references to historical people, places, or events appear within the play, what allusions to other literary works or other works of art are significant in the play, in what form the play is written (verse, prose, or a combination of the two), in what way the play is structured (one act, several acts), what types of special dramatic "tricks" appear within the play (**dialogues, soliloquies, asides,** a **play-within-the-play,** etc.), what symbols or images recur throughout the play, and so on. Paying special attention to a close reading of all aspects of the text is known as explication, a term invented by literary critics Cleanth Brooks and Robert Penn Warren.

In thinking about the context of a play, background information and research will again enhance your arguments. As with author and textual background information, one place to start (apart from information you learn in the classroom) is to consult materials provided in the anthology you are using. In this anthology, clues to these literary contexts of the play or plays you choose to interpret can be found in "A Brief Overview of World Theater" and in the headnotes that precede each play. To inquire further about the context of a play is to research the cultural and other factors that gave rise to that play and the ideas contained within the play. For instance: What were the cultural mores that determined Creon's and Antigonê's actions in Sophocles's *Antigonê*? What was the role of women during the period depicted in Glaspell's *Trifles*, and how did it influence the conflicts and ideas present within that play? What are some recent historical events in China and what is life like in China today, as depicted in Xingjian's *Dialogue and Rebuttal*? When thinking about the context of a play, it may also be helpful to have a basic understanding of such schools of critical thought as Cultural Theory (deciphering literature in terms of the social landscape from which it emerged), New Historicism (looking at literature through the lens of history), Marxist Theory (examining literature in terms of class and economic issues), Postcolonial Theory (analyzing literature from formerly colonized regions of the world in terms of the experience of colonization), Multicultural Theory (understanding literature in terms of the influence of racial and ethnic concerns), Gay and Lesbian Theory (interpreting literature in terms of the influence of gay and lesbian concerns), Feminist Theory (approaching literature in terms of the influence of women's concerns) and others. For example, Marxist Theory's concerns about social and economic class are relevant to both David Mamet's *Glengarry Glen Ross* and Suzan-Lori Parks's *Topdog/Underdog,* whereas questions from Feminist Theory about women's roles and patriarchal systems may lead to interesting analyses of Sophocles' *Antigonê,* Susan Glaspell's *Trifles,* and Paula Vogel's *How I Learned to Drive.* Often, questions that are less often asked of a play are startlingly revelatory: for example, as a woman of her era, what powers does Linda have, not have, use, or not use in *Death of a Salesman*? Or, in what ways are Nora and Torvald Helmer's choices in Henrik Ibsen's *A Doll House* driven by the economics of their lives?

Audience is a particularly challenging consideration when writing about drama in written form rather than in staged performance. When thinking about audience as you read a dramatic work, consider the audience to be you, the reader. How do you respond to the play? As the reader/audience, you walk away from reading a play with two different types of responses to the play, which interact with one another, and which were identified by Louise Rosenblatt. One type of response is the efferent response (from the Latin *efferre* meaning "to carry away"), and it involves what you have learned from the play—not necessarily factual information you have learned (though you may walk away from the play having learned about a historical era, a social issue, etc.), but also what you learned about relationships, conflicts, and anything else you didn't go into the play knowing in quite the same way. The other type of response is the aesthetic response, which concerns how you feel, how you react, and how you empathize or sympathize with the character(s) or situation(s) presented in the play. An aesthetic response emanates from your personal identification with what you have read. Considering these two types of audience response as you write your paper will lead you to determine how the play taught you certain information or how it made you feel certain emotions. Failing to consider yourself, the audience/reader, as you write your essay would leave you without an intellectual or emotional perspective from which to present your arguments. So, for instance, you may want to consider how you feel about the moral dilemmas presented in *Glengarry Glen Ross,* or what you think about feminist concerns and how they are presented in *Trifles, Topdog/Underdog,* and *How I Learned to Drive.*

Focusing on Characterization, Staging, Structure, or Theme

Having chosen a play and topic that interests you and having kept the considerations of authorship, text, context, and audience in mind when interpreting one or more aspects of a play or plays, it may be helpful to keep your essay from meandering into too many areas by focusing on one of the following aspects: **characterization, staging, structure,** or **theme.**

If you choose to focus your essay on characterization, keep in mind what Russian theater and acting innovator Konstantin Stanislavsky called the character's "spine." What is the character like physically, psychologically, or spiritually? What is the character's worldview? What might we know about the character's past? What body language and facial expressions does the character exhibit? What significant relationships does this character have with other characters? What does the character want from life? What prevents the character from getting what he or she wants from life? How free or trapped is the character? In short, what is revealed by what the character says and does, what others say about him or her, and what the playwright tells us about the character? For instance, reading *Antigonê,* what do we learn about Ismene when she says to her sister, "I still maintain that we two share the guilt"? When the Chorus says "It's very important/To keep women strictly disciplined"? When Antigonê hangs herself? Consider also the metaphoric or symbolic qualities of characters' names: Wingfield (*The Glass Menagerie*), or Lincoln and Booth (*Topdog/Underdog*). When you prepare to write about a character, identify key lines from the play, lines that reveal something telling about the character's spine.

To choose to write about the staging of a play in your essay is to consider such audiovisual aspects of the play as the stage itself, the set(s), the lights, the music, and the costumes, all the context prepared for the viewing audience by the play's cast and crew, but delivered to the reader through the playwright's stage directions, the characters' actions and dialogue, and the reader's own imagination. To help my students visualize staging (when they read a play rather than view a play in performance), I often suggest that they close their eyes to simulate the darkened theater at the moment the house lights go out and to open their eyes when, metaphorically, the stage lights go on (and perhaps a curtain goes up or opens). What stands out about the stage when, in the mind's eye if not in the theater itself, one settles into his or her seat? How do the lighting and sound help create a particular atmosphere? Are special effects in use and if so, to what end? Is music part of the play? If so, how might the music reinforce some of the major plot developments, or reflect something about a character's state of mind? In some plays, the set itself becomes a kind of actor, visually signifying to the audience something about the characters and even themes of the play. So, when writing about staging, you should ask yourself questions about the set. Is it a highly realistic set or a bizarre or surreal set? Is the set open and expansive or small and claustrophobic? Actors' costumes also convey meaning and reveal thematic information. Therefore, costuming should be taken into consideration when writing an essay from the standpoint of staging. Are the costumes fancy, plain, or tattered? Are the costumes true to the play's time period? Do the costumes reveal something about the characters' personalities? What function does nudity serve in the play, if there is any nudity? If the stage directions don't reveal much information about staging, it may be instructive, and entertaining, to write your essay about staging from the perspective of a stage director. If you were the stage director, what contemporary music would be analogous to the themes and actions of the play, and how would you "sell" your idea to the playwright? Imagine how you would program the light board. What colors, intensities, fadeouts, and movements would you suggest to augment the emotions and actions of the characters? Imagine yourself as the set designer. How open or cramped would the stage look, and what types of props would you use in various scenes?

A focus on the structure of the play entails careful analysis of the plot, attention to the play's construction into scenes and acts, and a consideration of how the play fits into genre conventions. Critiquing the plot is not synonymous with summarizing the plot's action, but instead requires you to evaluate the **exposition,** the causes and initiation of the **conflict,** the **complications** and **rising action,** leading to a **climax** (or **anticlimax**), the **falling action,** and the **dénouement** (and **epilogue,** if there is one). Along the way, you also need to identify the **subplots,** asides, or ironies that contribute to an effective analysis of the structure. To analyze the construction of the play is also to evaluate how the play is subdivided into **acts** and **scenes.** If the play is organized into scenes only, why does the playwright choose not to use act divisions? What is it that leads to a break in the action and consequently a new scene or act? A focus on genre conventions means identifying first if the play is a **tragedy** or **comedy** and if one or the other, what kind of tragedy or comedy? Is it a typical example of a **domestic tragedy** or a **revenge tragedy**? Is it a **comedy of manners, a black comedy,** or a **farce**? Or is it a combination of the two genres, a **tragicomedy**? In addition, one should consider if the play is a **well-made play**. If not, how does the play vary from a defined subgenre; what innovations does it bring to the subgenre?

Finally, if you choose to focus on theme, keep in mind that, contrary to what you may have heard, a play's theme or themes are rarely actually "hidden" from the reader/audience's view, as if a play were a puzzle that needed to be put together by clever audience members. Literature is not supposed to be elusive, but illuminating (unless a particular playwright is trying to make some commentary and deliberately writes an indecipherable play). Rather, the theme or themes of a play are the central ideas that a playwright brings to life through the actions, dialogue, conflicts, staging, and setting of the play. A play may deal with a variety of themes. For instance, a play could simultaneously be about family dynamics, spiritual loss, and redemption. If that is the case, you may want to focus on one of the play's central themes.

Using Proper Form and Citing Sources Correctly

Although the form of your essay may seem like a mundane topic, it is actually an important part of engaging your reader(s) and presenting your argument.

Your essay should begin with a title that makes its topic clear. Don't begin with a title such as "*Topdog/Underdog*" and leave it at that. This title is insufficient, because it names only the play as the subject of the essay without providing any clue as to the topic or thesis. Instead, create a clear title that illustrates both the subject and the focus of the essay, such as "*Topdog/Underdog:* A Structure of Power."

The introduction to your essay should be one or more paragraphs, depending upon the overall length of the paper, and it should conclude with your thesis statement. The introduction provides a context for the discussion to follow, then focuses on the particular argument that you intend to make. You want to interest the reader in your topic first and then narrow the topic down via your thesis statement. Your thesis statement should not be too narrow or too general, as discussed earlier.

The length of your paper is determined by the parameters of the assignment and by the amount of evidence you will need to provide to argue your thesis. Each new paragraph indicates that you are turning to a new discussion of some aspect of your presentation of evidence, argument, or illustration. You should link your essay's paragraphs with transitional words, phrases, or ideas so that readers are able to follow your argument and see where it is moving next. Were you to cut the essay apart paragraph by paragraph and jumble the pieces, good transitions would enable you to easily reconstruct your essay. If you are in doubt about an appropriate transition, read the paragraph preceding the transition and the paragraph following the transition and think about why one paragraph follows the other. Nearly always, you can discover a natural transition, an inherent reason for the argument of the second paragraph to follow the first.

The conclusion of your essay is not simply a rephrasing of your introduction. It offers the opportunity to gather together the ideas you have presented earlier and to answer the rhetorical question, "So what?" In the conclusion, explain why your thesis and your argument are significant, interesting, and possibly inventive. You have analyzed an important idea about a play that you have studied, and the conclusion is the final opportunity to clarify your thesis and all the evidence that you have assembled. Below is the conclusion of "Characterization: Lee and Austin's Naturalistic Descent in *True West*" by Georgia State University student Tristram Hayes, in which he successfully answers the "So what?" question:

> The identity conflict that Austin and Lee experience forces them to descend into naturalistic animal states. The initial characterizations of the brothers shows that they have clear differences, but as the play progresses, they become similar in their savagery. Their inability to avoid the violence that ends the play is the result of past and present influences that they cannot escape. Lee attempts to leave his wild past behind but is forced back to it by Austin, while Austin decides that he wants the freedom of the desert but is prevented by Lee from realizing this change. The two characters are inseparable because of their envious views of each other's lives. Austin and Lee fail to successfully mimic each other's lives and are ultimately forced toward a chaotic violent end.

In addition to following the essay format outlined above, try to integrate quotations from the play or from secondary sources (if the assignment calls for the use of secondary sources) to support your argument. When doing so, remember that direct quotations, paraphrases, and summaries from secondary sources must be cited. This means that material that is not your original idea must be credited to its author. Direct quotations must be identified with quotation marks, but you need not cite a complete sentence if you wish to quote only a phrase or a clause. Cite directly those lines that are particularly pithy or appropriate. Paraphrases must be cited also, but are not indicated by quotation marks. Citations from classical plays that have act, scene, and line numbers should use Arabic numbers separated by periods, as in (*Hamlet* 1.5.36). Modern Language Association (MLA) style, which is the preferred documentation style for literary essays, requires that you cite the source internally (within the sentence) rather than in a footnote or an endnote. If the author's name is included in your sentence or if it is clearly understood that you are writing about a particular play, then you need cite only the page number or numbers; for example: "When the glass unicorn breaks, Laura replies, 'Now it is just like the other horses' (24)." If the author's name is not included in the sentence, yet is needed for clarity, the citation must include the author's last name and the page number(s) without a comma; for example: "In some dramas, 'a dream rises out of reality' (Miller 24)." If an author has two or more entries in the Works Cited, then you will use the author's last name and a short title followed by a comma, and the page number; for instance: "A playwright wants to 'cure a raging imbalance' (Mamet *Three,* 51)." If the author is named within your sentence, use just the short title and the page number in the citation; for example: "Mamet says that a playwright wants to 'cure a raging imbalance' (*Three* 51)." The end punctuation for the sentence follows the parenthesis of the citation to clearly indicate that the citation belongs to that sentence: (Ibsen 110).

In addition to internal citations, an essay using MLA documentation style should include a Work Cited (if you cite only the play itself) or Works Cited (if you cite the play and secondary sources) list at the end of the paper. Each entry in a Works Cited list is organized by author's last name, author's first name, title, and publication information. The Works Cited is titled thusly and is organized alphabetically by the first word of each entry (typically the author's last name) with a hanging indentation. It should begin following the end of the essay, not on a separate page. Following is a sample Works Cited list with a variety of resources that you might use following the MLA style.

Essay in a scholarly journal

Internet resource

Play in this anthology

Separately published play

Critical book by a single author; in this case, Mamet, the same author as above, thus the use of three connected dashes to indicate repetition of his name

Multiple authors of an essay in an edited book

Interview

Class lecture

Works Cited

Carpenter, Charles A. "The Absurdity of Dread: Pinter's *Dumb Waiter*." *Modern Drama* 16 (1973): 279–83.

Hampton, Wilborn. "Review/Theater: Reason Battles Instinct in Calderon's 'Dream.'" *New York Times* 16 Dec. 1989. 8 Nov. 2006. http://www.nytimes.com.

Ibsen, Henrik. *A Doll House.* 1879. *Drama Essentials.* Ed. Matthew Roudané. Boston: Houghton Mifflin, 2009.

Mamet, David. *Glengarry Glen Ross.* 1982. New York: Grove Press, 1984.

———. *Three Uses of the Knife.* New York: Columbia UP, 1998.

Martin, Robert A., and Richard D. Meyer. "Arthur Miller on Plays and Playwriting." *Conversations with Arthur Miller.* Ed. Matthew C. Roudané. Jackson: University Press of Mississippi, 1987. 262–72.

Roudané, Matthew. Interview with the author. October 31, 2006. Atlanta, GA.

Smith, Laura. Lecture on *The Dumb Waiter*. Engl 3506—American Drama. Success University, Anytown, MA. 6 Nov. 2006.

Sample Student Essay in Response to a Play

Below is Georgia State University student King Mengert's essay written in the Summer of 2006. Conventions of the upper division undergraduate Twentieth-Century American Drama class for which it was written as well as a textbook that King was using are evident. Even an essay that receives a high evaluation can be improved upon through rereading, rethinking, and revising.

1

Arthur Miller's Staging Innovations in *Death of a Salesman*

This clause announces the specific direction of the essay.

Long Day's Journey Into Night, The Glass Menagerie, Who's Afraid of Virginia Woolf?

I might comment on the questionable diction of the phrase "tricky business," but King may also be making a punning allusion to Tom Wingfield's opening lines in The Glass Menagerie*: "Yes, I have tricks in my pocket, I have things up my sleeve."*

Note King's care to admit that he is not an expert and to frame his comments as an analysis based on his close reading and study.

In no other play that we have read thus far are the playwright's set descriptions and stage directions as integral to the purpose and meaning of the work as in Arthur Miller's *Death of a Salesman*. In each of the other plays, the thematic thrust is carried by characterization and language, event and dialogue. In *Salesman,* Miller uses the set in such a way as to underscore the thematic content and to enhance the characterization of Willy Loman. The first steps towards making such use of staging (at least in American drama) were taken by Tennessee Williams, who broke with the staging conventions of realism. Miller, though, made use of scenery and staging in such a way that they became intrinsic to the very sense of the play. As I have never witnessed a theatrical production of either *Death of a Salesman* or Williams's *The Glass Menagerie,* it is a somewhat tricky business to analyze their staging. Staging, one might argue, is more an aspect of production than of text. I contend, however, that in their meticulous stage notes

2

Typically, one should maintain a consistent order of subjects: Miller and then Williams. As his essay is about Miller's play Death of a Salesman, King references Miller first. Here, however, King mentions Williams before Miller to indicate that Williams's The Glass Menagerie was composed prior to Death of a Salesman.

both Williams and Miller presented visions and conceptions of the plays' ideal productions that are precise enough to substantiate an analysis of staging.

This should be the thesis of the essay, but King includes both Williams and Miller here; whereas, his title suggests that the essay is about Death of a Salesman only. As the writing is interesting and I can easily follow his argument, I continue reading to see how he will use Williams. At the same time, I hope that he does not digress too far.

Tennessee Williams, in the stage notes preceding the opening scene of *The Glass Menagerie,* offered a somewhat elaborate description of that play's scenery as he envisioned it. In his introductory "Production Notes," Williams detailed the nature and function of music and lighting in the play and even explained his conception of the screen device, which was jettisoned from the play's original written version during production. Significantly, the notes include this testimony: "These remarks are not meant as a preface only to this particular play. They have to do with a conception of a new, plastic theater which must take the place of the exhausted theater of realistic conventions if the theater is to resume vitality as a part of our culture". And indeed, his experimental approach to staging and spectacle was hugely influential upon other American dramatists, Arthur Miller perhaps most notably.

This is a small point to make, but I might question King's choice of "spectacular" because the word references things that can be seen, yet here, he uses the term to describe sounds (music) as well as sights (lighting and set). A more accurate word might be "suggestive" to remark upon the allusive qualities of the staging or "marvelous" if he wishes to call attention to the innovative nature of the staging. He uses "suggestive" in the next sentence, however, so that choice would lead to repetitiveness.

Miller, in fact, took the experimental use of scenery a step further. While the scenic devices employed in *The Glass Menagerie* were evocative and new, and broke with the conventional techniques of dramatic realism, they remained, finally, atmospheric flourishes. Such spectacular aspects as music, lighting, and set were utilized to define the mood and tone of the play. They were suggestive elements, providing a conducive context wherein the play's themes and action

A diction/word choice question arises here also with the alliterative "conducive context." When you are writing, you must take care to insure that repetition, alliteration, and all word choice contribute your intentional meaning rather than distracting the reader from your point.

might most effectively unfold. In *Death of a Salesman,* Miller conceives of the set in such a way that it becomes an essential thematic element in itself.

Clear thesis statement.

In order to fully grasp the thematic implications of Miller's stage descriptions, it is necessary to know his early conceptions of the play and its set. Miller's original title was *The Inside of His Head* (Roudané). "The first image that occurred to me which was to result in *Death of a Salesman*," Miller claimed, "was of an enormous face the height of the proscenium arch which would appear and then open up, and we would see the inside of a man's head" (Introduction 155). While the use of such overtly emblematic scenery was abandoned, the setting described by Miller at the beginning of act one retains a related symbolic significance to that original conception: "In a way, the setup of the stage [for the first production] respected Miller's original plan, but instead of portraying a cross-section of Willy's head, it presented a metaphor for a cross-section of his life. The audience was not looking in on just a living room, as in the nineteenth-century Ibsenist approach, but on an entire house and an entire life" (Jacobus 1128). This is a perceptive assessment of the significance of the play's set. It would seem that the metaphorical weight of the set was, in fact, increased by replacing "a cross-section of Willy's head" with "a cross-section of his life" (Jacobus 1128). In its later incarnation, the visible scenery, the house, represents not just Willy Loman's mental space, but his life in its

4

entirety. It is a dramatic arena which serves as much more than merely the physical space containing the characters and action of the play. It is, as well, a psychological, emotional, and spiritual space, a terrain encompassing the distances of past and present, Willy's remembered experiences, his delusions, fears, and longings.

The set's transparency, as Miller described in the act one stage notes, further enables the "plastic," nonrealistic use of staging in the play (342). Many earlier-written plays made use of invisible or implied scenery: walls, windows, doors, etc. The presence of such scenic elements is suggested to the audience largely by the characters' careful observance of their imagined presence. Thus, the audience accepts both the presence of and the constraints of a certain physical space. Drama is, after all, an imaginative medium. Most early theater, including Shakespeare's Elizabethan theater, relied entirely on the imagination of the players and the audience for setting. The characters in *Salesman,* however, periodically disregard imaginary walls and doors in order to establish fluid shifts in temporal representation. Miller explicitly describes this staging device in the opening stage notes: "Whenever the action is in the present the actors observe the imaginary wall-lines, entering the house only through its door at the left. But in the scenes of the past these boundaries are broken, and characters enter or leave a room by stepping 'through' a wall onto the forestage" (342). It is as though the physical

Whenever you quote directly from a published text, you must double check to be certain that you quote exactly including punctuation. Here, note the single quotation marks inside the double quotation marks in keeping with Miller's text.

5

space of the present (as suggested by the players' treatment of the stage-space) melts away as the action is transported to a memory space in which surroundings are transformed. Thus, again, the set and staging reflect Willy's own internal condition. As he fades out of the present moment into reminiscence, the corporeal context dissolves. Walls disappear, and the action is transported to some past scene. But, importantly, the visual remainder of Willy's house, his life, the sum of his human experience, remains always on the stage.

I might ask King to expand his conclusion by identifying the specific aspects of the Willy Loman character that are dramatized by the staging that King has described.

With his staging innovations in *Death of a Salesman,* Arthur Miller completed the break with realistic staging conventions that Williams began. He created a stage space inseparable from the character and action of his play. The stage set, here, is not a mere structure, not a backdrop against which the play develops. The set and the players' various positions and movements upon it are inextricably connected with the character of Willy Loman and, hence, with the play itself.

Works Cited

Jacobus, Lee A., ed. *The Bedford Introduction to Drama.* 5th ed. Boston: Bedford/St. Martin's, 2005.

Miller, Arthur. *Death of a Salesman.* 1949. *Drama Essentials.* Ed. Matthew Roudané. Boston: Houghton Mifflin, 2007. 341–430.

———. Introduction to *Collected Plays.* Rpt. in *Arthur Miller:* Death of a Salesman: *Text and Criticism,* ed. Gerald Weales. New York: Penguin, 1977. 155–171.

6

Roudané, Matthew. Guest lecture on *Death of a Salesman.* Engl 3860—Twentieth-Century American Drama. Georgia State University, Atlanta, GA. 27 June 2006.

Williams, Tennessee. *The Glass Menagerie*. 1944. *Drama Essentials*. Ed. Matthew Roudané. Boston: Houghton Mifflin, 2009. 281–340.

———.“Production Notes.” *The Glass Menagerie* New York: New Directions, 1999. xix–xii.

King Mengert

June 29, 2006

I ask my students to write their names on the back of the last page of the essay only. This aids me in making an objective evaluation of the essay.

Additional Commentary on the Student Paper

King's essay met the required length of the assignment, even though he did not develop his thesis as much as I would have wished. Before his conclusion, King might have inserted an additional paragraph or two in which he analyzed several specific scenes that illustrate the movement between present and past and how the staging enhances the understanding of the force of the past upon Willy Loman's present actions. He should clarify the "essential thematic element" that the set "becomes," as stated in his thesis. Also, the introduction is a bit long for the length of the essay. These weaknesses are counterbalanced by clear writing, interesting ideas, and an obvious understanding of the staging of the play. Therefore, it is a mostly successful essay that just needs some further revision.

In revising the essay, King might consider shortening the long introduction and discussion of Williams's staging. Or, he might change the title and the thesis statement in order to write a comparative essay in which he analyzes the staging and the effects of the staging in both *The Glass Menagerie* and *Death of a Salesman.* However, since such an essay was not within the parameters of the original assignment, King used *The Glass Menagerie* only as a framing device to prepare the reader for a discussion of the innovative staging of *Death of a Salesman.*

When a reader is delighted and educated by an essay, she or he wants to read more and wants to encourage the student to write further about the play that intrigues them both. This is a means of having a conversation about the play itself, of continuing the pleasure derived from studying an outstanding play. Whatever you write, for whatever reader, you should aim to write about that which you enjoy, that play or character or idea about which you feel passionate. In this way, you bring the play to life.

THE PLAYS

Antigonê SOPHOCLES

Translated by Dudley Fitts and Robert Fitzgerald

Sophocles (ca. 496–406 BC) wrote more than 100 plays, of which only seven survive. Along with his predecessor Aeschylus and his contemporary Euripides, Sophocles is considered to be one of the greatest tragedians ever to have written for the Greek stage. Indeed, Sophocles was partially responsible for defining the Golden Age of Greece.

Antigonê (441 BC) reflects the full force and magnificence of its time. In her determination to defy King Kreon's edict, Antigonê emerges as a supreme tragic heroine in whose actions we see the conflict between family and state, between genuine love and man-made laws, and between human choice and cosmic fate.

Sophocles' dramatization of human frailty, hubris, and complexity set the trajectory for all Western drama to follow. When he died, Sophocles was considered a national hero, one who depicted the always tricky relationship between the individual and the state. This relationship lies at the heart of *Antigonê*.

CHARACTERS

ANTIGONÊ
ISMENÊ
EURYDICÊ
KREON
HAIMON
TEIRESIAS
A SENTRY
A MESSENGER
CHORUS

SCENE. *Before the palace of* KREON, *King of Thebes. A central double door, and two lateral doors. A platform extends the length of the façade, and from this platform three steps lead down into the "orchestra," or chorus-ground.*

TIME. *Dawn of the day after the repulse of the Argive army from the assault on Thebes.*

Prologue

(ANTIGONÊ *and* ISMENÊ *enter from the central door of the palace.*)

ANTIGONÊ: Ismenê, dear sister,
You would think that we had already suffered enough
For the curse on Oedipus.
I cannot imagine any grief

That you and I have not gone through. And now—
Have they told you of the new decree of our King Kreon?

ISMENÊ: I have heard nothing: I know
That two sisters lost two brothers, a double death
In a single hour; and I know that the Argive army
Fled in the night; but beyond this, nothing.

ANTIGONÊ: I thought so. And that is why I wanted you
To come out here with me. There is something we must do.

ISMENÊ: Why do you speak so strangely?

ANTIGONÊ: Listen, Ismenê:
Kreon buried our brother Eteoclês
With military honors, gave him a soldier's funeral,
And it was right that he should; but Polyneicês,
Who fought as bravely and died as miserably,—
They say that Kreon has sworn
No one shall bury him, no one mourn for him,
But his body must lie in the fields, a sweet treasure
For carrion birds to find as they search for food.
That is what they say, and our good Kreon is coming here
To announce it publicly; and the penalty—
Stoning to death in the public square!
There it is,
And now you can prove what you are:
A true sister, or a traitor to your family.

ISMENÊ: Antigonê, you are mad! What could I possibly do?

ANTIGONÊ: You must decide whether you will help me or not.

ISMENÊ: I do not understand you. Help you in what?

ANTIGONÊ: Ismenê, I am going to bury him. Will you come?

ISMENÊ: Bury him! You have just said the new law forbids it.

ANTIGONÊ: He is my brother. And he is your brother, too.

ISMENÊ: But think of the danger! Think what Kreon will do!

ANTIGONÊ: Kreon is not strong enough to stand in my way.

ISMENÊ: Ah, sister!
Oedipus died, everyone hating him
For what his own search brought to light, his eyes
Ripped out by his own hand; and Iokastê died,
His mother and wife at once: she twisted the cords
That strangled her life; and our two brothers died,
Each killed by the other's sword. And we are left:
But oh, Antigonê,

Think how much more terrible than these
Our own death would be if we should go against Kreon
And do what he has forbidden! We are only women,
We cannot fight with men, Antigonê!
The law is strong, we must give in to the law
In this thing, and in worse. I beg the Dead
To forgive me, but I am helpless: I must yield
To those in authority. And I think it is dangerous business
To be always meddling.

ANTIGONÊ: If that is what you think,
I should not want you, even if you asked to come.
You have made your choice, you can be what you want to be.
But I will bury him; and if I must die,
I say that this crime is holy: I shall lie down
With him in death, and I shall be as dear
To him as he to me.
It is the dead,
Not the living, who make the longest demands:
We die for ever . . .
You may do as you like,
Since apparently the laws of the gods mean nothing to you.

ISMENÊ: They mean a great deal to me; but I have no strength
To break laws that were made for the public good.

ANTIGONÊ: That must be your excuse, I suppose. But as for me,
I will bury the brother I love.

ISMENÊ: Antigonê,
I am so afraid for you!

ANTIGONÊ: You need not be:
You have yourself to consider, after all.

ISMENÊ: But no one must hear of this, you must tell no one!
I will keep it a secret, I promise!

ANTIGONÊ: O tell it! Tell everyone!
Think how they'll hate you when it all comes out
If they learn that you knew about it all the time!

ISMENÊ: So fiery! You should be cold with fear.

ANTIGONÊ: Perhaps. But I am doing only what I must.

ISMENÊ: But can you do it? I say that you cannot.

ANTIGONÊ: Very well: when my strength gives out,
I shall do no more.

ISMENÊ: Impossible things should not be tried at all.

ANTIGONÊ: Go away, Ismenê:
I shall be hating you soon, and the dead will too,
For your words are hateful. Leave me my foolish plan:
I am not afraid of the danger; if it means death,
It will not be the worst of deaths—death without honor.
ISMENÊ: Go then, if you feel that you must.
You are unwise,
But a loyal friend indeed to those who love you.

(*Exit into the palace.* ANTIGONÊ *goes off, left. Enter the* CHORUS.)

Párodos

Strophe I

CHORUS: Now the long blade of the sun, lying
Level east to west, touches with glory
Thebes of the Seven Gates. Open, unlidded
Eye of golden day! O marching light
Across the eddy and rush of Dircê's stream,[1]
Striking the white shields of the enemy
Thrown headlong backward from the blaze of morning!
CHORAGOS:[2] Polyneicês their commander
Roused them with windy phrases,
He the wild eagle screaming
Insults above our land,
His wings their shields of snow,
His crest their marshalled helms.

Antistrophe I

CHORUS: Against our seven gates in a yawning ring
The famished spears came onward in the night;
But before his jaws were sated with our blood,
Or pinefire took the garland of our towers,
He was thrown back; and as he turned, great Thebes—
No tender victim for his noisy power—
Rose like a dragon behind him, shouting war.

[1]a stream to the west of Thebes [2]the leader of the Chorus

CHORAGOS: For God hates utterly
The bray of bragging tongues;
And when he beheld their smiling,
Their swagger of golden helms,
The frown of his thunder blasted
Their first man from our walls.

Strophe 2

CHORUS: We heard his shout of triumph high in the air
Turn to a scream; far out in a flaming arc
He fell with his windy torch, and the earth struck him.
And others storming in fury no less than his
Found shock of death in the dusty joy of battle.
CHORAGOS: Seven captains at seven gates
Yielded their clanging arms to the god
That bends the battle-line and breaks it.
These two only, brothers in blood,
Face to face in matchless rage,
Mirroring each the other's death,
Clashed in long combat.

Antistrophe 2

CHORUS: But now in the beautiful morning of victory
Let Thebes of the many chariots sing for joy!
With hearts for dancing we'll take leave of war:
Our temples shall be sweet with hymns of praise,
And the long nights shall echo with our chorus.

Scene I

CHORAGOS: But now at last our new King is coming:
Kreon of Thebes, Menoikeus' son.
In this auspicious dawn of his rein
What are the new complexities
That shifting Fate has woven for him?
What is his counsel? Why has he summoned
The old men to hear him?

(*Enter* KREON *from the palace, center. He addresses the* CHORUS *from the top step.*)

KREON: Gentlemen: I have the honor to inform you that our Ship of State, which recent storms have threatened to destroy, has come safely to harbor at last, guided by the merciful wisdom of Heaven. I have summoned you here this morning because I know that I can depend upon you: your devotion to King Laïos was absolute; you never hesitated in your duty to our late ruler Oedipus; and when Oedipus died, your loyalty was transferred to his children. Unfortunately, as you know, his two sons, the princes Eteoclês and Polyneicês, have killed each other in battle; and I, as the next in blood, have succeeded to the full power of the throne.

I am aware, of course, that no Ruler can expect complete loyalty from his subjects until he has been tested in office. Nevertheless, I say to you at the very outset that I have nothing but contempt for the kind of Governor who is afraid, for whatever reason, to follow the course that he knows is best for the State; and as for the man who sets private friendship above the public welfare,—I have no use for him, either. I call God to witness that if I saw my country headed for ruin, I should not be afraid to speak out plainly; and I need hardly remind you that I would never have any dealings with an enemy of the people. No one values friendship more highly than I; but we must remember that friends made at the risk of wrecking our Ship are not real friends at all.

These are my principles, at any rate, and that is why I have made the following decision concerning the sons of Oedipus: Eteoclês, who died as a man should die, fighting for his country, is to be buried with full military honors, with all the ceremony that is usual when the greatest heroes die; but his brother Polyneicês, who broke his exile to come back with fire and sword against his native city and the shrines of his fathers' gods, whose one idea was to spill the blood of his blood and sell his own people into slavery—Polyneicês, I say, is to have no burial: no man is to touch him or say the least prayer for him; he shall lie on the plain, unburied; and the birds and the scavenging dogs can do with him whatever they like.

This is my command, and you can see the wisdom behind it. As long as I am King, no traitor is going to be honored with the loyal man. But whoever shows by word and deed that he is on the side of the State,—he shall have my respect while he is living and my reverence when he is dead.

CHORAGOS: If that is your will, Kreon son of Menoikeus,
You have the right to enforce it: we are yours.

KREON: That is my will. Take care that you do your part.

CHORAGOS: We are old men: let the younger ones carry it out.

KREON: I do not mean that: the sentries have been appointed.

CHORAGOS: Then what is it that you would have us do?

KREON: You will give no support to whoever breaks this law.

CHORAGOS: Only a crazy man is in love with death!

KREON: And death it is; yet money talks, and the wisest
Have sometimes been known to count a few coins too many.

(*Enter* SENTRY *from left.*)

SENTRY: I'll not say that I'm out of breath from running, King, because every time I stopped to think about what I have to tell you, I felt like going back. And all the time a voice kept saying, "You fool, don't you know you're walking straight into trouble?"; and then another voice: "Yes, but if you let somebody else get the news to Kreon first, it will be even worse than that for you!" But good sense won out, at least I hope it was good sense, and here I am with a story that makes no sense at all; but I'll tell it anyhow, because, as they say, what's going to happen's going to happen and—

KREON: Come to the point. What have you to say?

SENTRY: I did not do it. I did not see who did it. You must not punish me for what someone else has done.

KREON: A comprehensive defense! More effective, perhaps,
If I knew its purpose. Come: what is it?

SENTRY: A dreadful thing . . . I don't know how to put it—

KREON: Out with it!

SENTRY: Well, then;
The dead man—
Polyneicês—

(*Pause. The* SENTRY *is overcome, fumbles for words.* KREON *waits impassively.*)

out there—
someone,—
New dust on the slimy flesh!

(*Pause. No sign from* KREON.)

Someone has given it burial that way, and
Gone . . .

(*Long pause.* KREON *finally speaks with deadly control.*)

KREON: And the man who dared do this?
SENTRY: I swear I
Do not know! You must believe me!
Listen:
The ground was dry, not a sign of digging, no,
Not a wheeltrack in the dust, no trace of anyone.
It was when they relieved us this morning: and one of them,
The corporal, pointed to it.
There it was,
The strangest—
Look:
The body, just mounded over with light dust: you see?
Not buried really, but as if they'd covered it
Just enough for the ghost's peace. And no sign
Of dogs or any wild animal that had been there.

And then what a scene there was! Every man of us
Accusing the other: we all proved the other man did it,
We all had proof that we could not have done it.
We were ready to take hot iron in our hands,
Walk through fire, swear by all the gods,
It was not I!
I do not know who it was, but it was not I!

(KREON'*s rage has been mounting steadily, but the* SENTRY *is too intent upon his story to notice it.*)

And then, when this came to nothing, someone said
A thing that silenced us and made us stare
Down at the ground: you had to be told the news,
And one of us had to do it! We threw the dice,
And the bad luck fell to me. So here I am,
No happier to be here than you are to have me:
Nobody likes the man who brings bad news.
CHORAGOS: I have been wondering, King: can it be that the gods have done this?
KREON (*furiously*): Stop!
Must you doddering wrecks
Go out of your heads entirely? "The gods"!
Intolerable!
The gods favor this corpse? Why? How had he served them?
Tried to loot their temples, burn their images,

Yes, and the whole State, and its laws with it!
Is it your senile opinion that the gods love to honor bad men?
A pious thought!—
No, from the very beginning
There have been those who have whispered together,
Stiff-necked anarchists, putting their heads together,
Scheming against me in alleys. These are the men,
And they have bribed my own guard to do this thing.
(*sententiously*) Money!
There's nothing in the world so demoralizing as money.
Down go your cities,
Homes gone, men gone, honest hearts corrupted,
Crookedness of all kinds, and all for money!
(*to* SENTRY) But you—!
I swear by God and by the throne of God,
The man who has done this thing shall pay for it!
Find that man, bring him here to me, or your death
Will be the least of your problems: I'll string you up
Alive, and there will be certain ways to make you
Discover your employer before you die;
And the process may teach you a lesson you seem to have missed:
The dearest profit is sometimes all too dear:
That depends on the source. Do you understand me?
A fortune won is often misfortune.

SENTRY: King, may I speak?

KREON: Your very voice distresses me.

SENTRY: Are you sure that it is my voice, and not your conscience?

KREON: By God, he wants to analyze me now!

SENTRY: It is not what I say, but what has been done, that hurts you.

KREON: You talk too much.

SENTRY: Maybe; but I've done nothing.

KREON: Sold your soul for some silver: that's all you've done.

SENTRY: How dreadful it is when the right judge judges wrong!

KREON: Your figures of speech
May entertain you now; but unless you bring me the man,
You will get little profit from them in the end.

(*Exit* KREON *into the palace.*)

SENTRY: "Bring me the man"—!
I'd like nothing better than bringing him the man!

But bring him or not, you have seen the last of me here. At any rate, I am safe!

(*Exit* SENTRY.)

Ode I

Strophe 1

CHORUS: Numberless are the world's wonders, but none
More wonderful than man; the stormgray sea
Yields to his prows, the huge crests bear him high;
Earth, holy and inexhaustible, is graven
With shining furrows where his plows have gone
Year after year, the timeless labor of stallions.

Antistrophe 1

The lightboned birds and beasts that cling to cover,
The lithe fish lighting their reaches of dim water,
All are taken, tamed in the net of his mind;
The lion on the hill, the wild horse windy-maned,
Resign to him; and his blunt yoke has broken
The sultry shoulders of the mountain bull.

Strophe 2

Words also, and thought as rapid as air,
He fashions to his good use; statecraft is his,
And his the skill that deflects the arrows of snow,
The spears of winter rain: from every wind
He has made himself secure—from all but one:
In the late wind of death he cannot stand.

Antistrophe 2

O clear intelligence, force beyond all measure!
O fate of man, working both good and evil!
When the laws are kept, how proudly his city stands!
When the laws are broken, what of his city then?
Never may the anárchic man find rest at my hearth,
Never be it said that my thoughts are his thoughts.

Scene II

(*Reenter* SENTRY *leading* ANTIGONÊ.)

CHORAGOS: What does this mean? Surely this captive woman
Is the Princess, Antigonê. Why should she be taken?
SENTRY: Here is the one who did it! We caught her
In the very act of burying him.—Where is Kreon?
CHORAGOS: Just coming from the house.

(*Enter* KREON, *center*.)

KREON: What has happened?
Why have you come back so soon?
SENTRY (*expansively*): O King,
A man should never be too sure of anything:
I would have sworn
That you'd not see me here again: your anger
Frightened me so, and the things you threatened me with;
But how could I tell then
That I'd be able to solve the case so soon?
No dice-throwing this time: I was only too glad to come!
Here is this woman. She is the guilty one:
We found her trying to bury him.
Take her, then; question her; judge her as you will.
I am through with the whole thing now, and glad of it.
KREON: But this is Antigonê! Why have you brought her here?
SENTRY: She was burying him, I tell you!
KREON (*severely*): Is this the truth?
SENTRY: I saw her with my own eyes. Can I say more?
KREON: The details: come, tell me quickly!
SENTRY: It was like this:
After those terrible threats of yours, King,
We went back and brushed the dust away from the body.
The flesh was soft by now, and stinking,
So we sat on a hill to windward and kept guard.
No napping this time! We kept each other awake.
But nothing happened until the white round sun
Whirled in the center of the round sky over us:
Then, suddenly,
A storm of dust roared up from the earth, and the sky
Went out, the plain vanished with all its trees
In the stinging dark. We closed our eyes and endured it.

The whirlwind lasted a long time, but it passed;
And then we looked, and there was Antigonê!
I have seen
A mother bird come back to a stripped nest, heard
Her crying bitterly a broken note or two
For the young ones stolen. Just so, when this girl
Found the bare corpse, and all her love's work wasted,
She wept, and cried on heaven to damn the hands
That had done this thing.
And then she brought more dust
And sprinkled wine three times for her brother's ghost.

We ran and took her at once. She was not afraid,
Not even when we charged her with what she had done.
She denied nothing.
And this was a comfort to me,
And some uneasiness: for it is a good thing
To escape from death, but it is no great pleasure
To bring death to a friend.
Yet I always say
There is nothing so comfortable as your own safe skin!

KREON (*slowly, dangerously*): And you, Antigonê,
You with your head hanging,—do you confess this thing?

ANTIGONÊ: I do. I deny nothing.

KREON (*to* SENTRY): You may go.

(*Exit* SENTRY.)

(*to* ANTIGONÊ) Tell me, tell me briefly:
Had you heard my proclamation touching this matter?

ANTIGONÊ: It was public. Could I help hearing it?

KREON: And yet you dared defy the law.

ANTIGONÊ: I dared.
It was not God's proclamation. That final Justice
That rules the world below makes no such laws.

Your edict, King, was strong,
But all your strength is weakness itself against
The immortal unrecorded laws of God.
They are not merely now: they were, and shall be,
Operative for ever, beyond man utterly.

I knew I must die, even without your decree:

I am only mortal. And if I must die
Now, before it is my time to die,
Surely this is no hardship: can anyone
Living, as I live, with evil all about me,
Think Death less than a friend? This death of mine
Is of no importance; but if I had left my brother
Lying in death unburied, I should have suffered.
Now I do not.
You smile at me. Ah Kreon,
Think me a fool, if you like; but it may well be
That a fool convicts me of folly.

CHORAGOS: Like father, like daughter: both headstrong, deaf to reason!
She has never learned to yield:

KREON: She has much to learn.
The inflexible heart breaks first, the toughest iron
Cracks first, and the wildest horses bend their necks
At the pull of the smallest curb.
Pride? In a slave?
This girl is guilty of a double insolence,
Breaking the given laws and boasting of it.
Who is the man here,
She or I, if this crime goes unpunished?
Sister's child, or more than sister's child,
Or closer yet in blood—she and her sister
Win bitter death for this!
(*to* SERVANTS) GO, some of you,
Arrest Ismenê. I accuse her equally.
Bring her: you will find her sniffling in the house there.

Her mind's a traitor: crimes kept in the dark
Cry for light, and the guardian brain shudders;
But how much worse than this
Is brazen boasting of barefaced anarchy!

ANTIGONÊ: Kreon, what more do you want than my death?

KREON: Nothing.
That gives me everything.

ANTIGONÊ: Then I beg you: kill me.
This talking is a great weariness: your words
Are distasteful to me, and I am sure that mine

Seem so to you. And yet they should not seem so:
I should have praise and honor for what I have done.
All these men here would praise me
Were their lips not frozen shut with fear of you.
(*bitterly*) Ah the good fortune of kings,
Licensed to say and do whatever they please!

KREON: You are alone here in that opinion.

ANTIGONÊ: No, they are with me. But they keep their tongues in leash.

KREON: Maybe. But you are guilty, and they are not.

ANTIGONÊ: There is no guilt in reverence for the dead.

KREON: But Eteoclês—was he not your brother too?

ANTIGONÊ: My brother too.

KREON: And you insult his memory?

ANTIGONÊ (*softly*): The dead man would not say that I insult it.

KREON: He would: for you honor a traitor as much as him.

ANTIGONÊ: His own brother, traitor or not, and equal in blood.

KREON: He made war on his country. Eteoclês defended it.

ANTIGONÊ: Nevertheless, there are honors due all the dead.

KREON: But not the same for the wicked as for the just.

ANTIGONÊ: Ah Kreon, Kreon,
Which of us can say what the gods hold wicked?

KREON: An enemy is an enemy, even dead.

ANTIGONÊ: It is my nature to join in love, not hate.

KREON (*finally losing patience*): Go join them then; if you must have your love,
Find it in hell!

CHORAGOS: But see, Ismenê comes:

(*Enter* ISMENÊ, *guarded.*)

Those tears are sisterly, the cloud
That shadows her eyes rains down gentle sorrow.

KREON: You too, Ismenê,
Snake in my ordered house, sucking my blood
Stealthily—and all the time I never knew
That these two sisters were aiming at my throne!
Ismenê
Do you confess your share in this crime, or deny it?
Answer me.

ISMENÊ: Yes, if she will let me say so. I am guilty.

ANTIGONÊ (*coldly*): No, Ismenê. You have no right to say so.

You would not help me, and I will not have you help me.
ISMENÊ: But now I know what you meant; and I am here
To join you, to take my share of punishment.
ANTIGONÊ: The dead man and the gods who rule the dead
Know whose act this was. Words are not friends.
ISMENÊ: Do you refuse me, Antigonê? I want to die with you:
I too have a duty that I must discharge to the dead.
ANTIGONÊ: You shall not lessen my death by sharing it.
ISMENÊ: What do I care for life when you are dead?
ANTIGONÊ: Ask Kreon. You're always hanging on his opinions.
ISMENÊ: You are laughing at me. Why, Antigonê?
ANTIGONÊ: It's a joyless laughter, Ismenê.
ISMENÊ: But can I do nothing?
ANTIGONÊ: Yes. Save yourself. I shall not envy you.
There are those who will praise you; I shall have honor, too.
ISMENÊ: But we are equally guilty!
ANTIGONÊ: No more, Ismenê.
You are alive, but I belong to Death.
KREON (*to the* CHORUS): Gentlemen, I beg you to observe these girls:
One has just now lost her mind; the other,
It seems, has never had a mind at all.
ISMENÊ: Grief teaches the steadiest minds to waver, King.
KREON: Yours certainly did, when you assumed guilt with the guilty!
ISMENÊ: But how could I go on living without her?
KREON: You are.
She is already dead.
ISMENÊ: But your own son's bride!
KREON: There are places enough for him to push his plow.
I want no wicked women for my sons!
ISMENÊ: O dearest Haimon, how your father wrongs you!
KREON: I've had enough of your childish talk of marriage!
CHORAGOS: Do you really intend to steal this girl from your son?
KREON: No; Death will do that for me.
CHORAGOS: Then she must die?
KREON (*ironically*): You dazzle me.
—But enough of this talk!
(*to* GUARDS) You, there, take them away and guard them well:
For they are but women, and even brave men run
When they see Death coming.

(*Exeunt* ISMENÊ, ANTIGONÊ, *and* GUARDS.)

Ode II

Strophe I

CHORUS: Fortunate is the man who has never tasted God's vengeance!
Where once the anger of heaven has struck, that house is shaken
For ever: damnation rises behind each child
Like a wave cresting out of the black northeast,
When the long darkness under sea roars up
And bursts drumming death upon the windwhipped sand.

Antistrophe I

I have seen this gathering sorrow from time long past
Loom upon Oedipus' children: generation from generation
Takes the compulsive rage of the enemy god.
So lately this last flower of Oedipus' line
Drank the sunlight; but now a passionate word
And a handful of dust have closed up all its beauty.

Strophe 2

What mortal arrogance
Transcends the wrath of Zeus?
Sleep cannot lull him nor the effortless long months
Of the timeless gods: but he is young for ever,
And his house is the shining day of high Olympos.
All that is and shall be,
And all the past, is his.
No pride on earth is free of the curse of heaven.

Antistrophe 2

The straying dreams of men
May bring them ghosts of joy:
But as they drowse, the waking embers burn them;
Or they walk with fixed eyes, as blind men walk.
But the ancient wisdom speaks for our own time:
Fate works most for woe
With Folly's fairest show.
Man's little pleasure is the spring of sorrow.

Scene III

CHORAGOS: But here is Haimon, King, the last of all your sons.
Is it grief for Antigonê that brings him here,
And bitterness at being robbed of his bride?

(*Enter* HAIMON.)

KREON: We shall soon see, and no need of diviners.
—Son,
You have heard my final judgment on that girl:
Have you come here hating me, or have you come
With deference and with love, whatever I do?
HAIMON: I am your son, father. You are my guide.
You make things clear for me, and I obey you.
No marriage means more to me than your continuing wisdom.
KREON: Good. That is the way to behave: subordinate
Everything else, my son, to your father's will.
This is what a man prays for, that he may get
Sons attentive and dutiful in his house,
Each one hating his father's enemies,
Honoring his father's friends. But if his sons
Fail him, if they turn out unprofitably,
What has he fathered but trouble for himself
And amusement for the malicious?
So you are right
Not to lose your head over this woman.
Your pleasure with her would soon grow cold, Haimon,
And then you'd have a hellcat in bed and elsewhere.
Let her find her husband in Hell!
Of all the people in this city, only she
Has had contempt for my law and broken it.

Do you want me to show myself weak before the people?
Or to break my sworn word? No, and I will not.
The woman dies.
I suppose she'll plead "family ties." Well, let her.
If I permit my own family to rebel,
How shall I earn the world's obedience?
Show me the man who keeps his house in hand,
He's fit for public authority.
I'll have no dealings

With lawbreakers, critics of the government:
Whoever is chosen to govern should be obeyed—
Must be obeyed, in all things, great and small,
Just and unjust! O Haimon,
The man who knows how to obey, and that man only,
Knows how to give commands when the time comes.
You can depend on him, no matter how fast
The spears come: he's a good soldier, he'll stick it out.

Anarchy, anarchy! Show me a greater evil!
This is why cities tumble and the great houses rain down,
This is what scatters armies!
No, no: good lives are made so by discipline.
We keep the laws then, and the lawmakers,
And no woman shall seduce us. If we must lose,
Let's lose to a man, at least! Is a woman stronger than we?

CHORAGOS: Unless time has rusted my wits,
What you say, King, is said with point and dignity.

HAIMON (*boyishly earnest*): Father:
Reason is God's crowning gift to man, and you are right
To warn me against losing mine. I cannot say—
I hope that I shall never want to say!—that you
Have reasoned badly. Yet there are other men
Who can reason, too; and their opinions might be helpful.
You are not in a position to know everything
That people say or do, or what they feel:
Your temper terrifies—everyone
Will tell you only what you like to hear.
But I, at any rate, can listen; and I have heard them
Muttering and whispering in the dark about this girl.
They say no woman has ever, so unreasonably,
Died so shameful a death for a generous act:
"She covered her brother's body. Is this indecent?
She kept him from dogs and vultures. Is this a crime?
Death?—She should have all the honor that we can give her!"

This is the way they talk out there in the city.

You must believe me:
Nothing is closer to me than your happiness.

What could be closer? Must not any son
Value his father's fortune as his father does his?
I beg you, do not be unchangeable:
Do not believe that you alone can be right.
The man who thinks that,
The man who maintains that only he has the power
To reason correctly, the gift to speak, the soul—
A man like that, when you know him, turns out empty.

It is not reason never to yield to reason!

In flood time you can see how some trees bend,
And because they bend, even their twigs are safe,
While stubborn trees are torn up, roots and all.
And the same thing happens in sailing:
Make your sheet fast, never slacken,—and over you go,
Head over heels and under: and there's your voyage.
Forget you are angry! Let yourself be moved!
I know I am young; but please let me say this:
The ideal condition
Would be, I admit, that men should be right by instinct;
But since we are all too likely to go astray,
The reasonable thing is to learn from those who can teach.

CHORAGOS: You will do well to listen to him, King,
If what he says is sensible. And you, Haimon,
Must listen to your father.—Both speak well.

KREON: You consider it right for a man of my years and experience
To go to school to a boy?

HAIMON: It is not right
If I am wrong. But if I am young, and right,
What does my age matter?

KREON: You think it right to stand up for an anarchist?

HAIMON: Not at all. I pay no respect to criminals.

KREON: Then she is not a criminal?

HAIMON: The City would deny it, to a man.

KREON: And the City proposes to teach me how to rule?

HAIMON: Ah. Who is it that's talking like a boy now?

KREON: My voice is the one voice giving orders in this City!

HAIMON: It is no City if it takes orders from one voice.

KREON: The State is the King!
HAIMON: Yes, if the State is a desert.

(*Pause.*)

KREON: This boy, it seems, has sold out to a woman.
HAIMON: If you are a woman: my concern is only for you.
KREON: So? Your "concern"! In a public brawl with your father!
HAIMON: How about you, in a public brawl with justice?
KREON: With justice, when all that I do is within my rights?
HAIMON: You have no right to trample on God's right.
KREON (*completely out of control*): Fool, adolescent fool! Taken in by a woman!
HAIMON: You'll never see me taken in by anything vile.
KREON: Every word you say is for her!
HAIMON (*quietly, darkly*): And for you.
And for me. And for the gods under the earth.
KREON: You'll never marry her while she lives.
HAIMON: Then she must die.—But her death will cause another.
KREON: Another?
Have you lost your senses? Is this an open threat?
HAIMON: There is no threat in speaking to emptiness.
KREON: I swear you'll regret this superior tone of yours!
You are the empty one!
HAIMON: If you were not my father,
I'd say you were perverse.
KREON: You girlstruck fool, don't play at words with me!
HAIMON: I am sorry. You prefer silence.
KREON: Now, by God—!
I swear, by all the gods in heaven above us,
You'll watch it, I swear you shall!
(*to the* SERVANTS) Bring her out!
Bring the woman out! Let her die before his eyes!
Here, this instant, with her bridegroom beside her!
HAIMON: Not here, no; she will not die here, King.
And you will never see my face again.
Go on raving as long as you've a friend to endure you.

(*Exit* HAIMON.)

CHORAGOS: Gone, gone.
Kreon, a young man in a rage is dangerous!

KREON: Let him do, or dream to do, more than a man can.
He shall not save these girls from death.
CHORAGOS: These girls?
You have sentenced them both?
KREON: No, you are right.
I will not kill the one whose hands are clean.
CHORAGOS: But Antigonê?
KREON (*somberly*): I will carry her far away
Out there in the wilderness, and lock her
Living in a vault of stone. She shall have food,
As the custom is, to absolve the State of her death.
And there let her pray to the gods of hell:
They are her only gods:
Perhaps they will show her an escape from death,
Or she may learn,
though late,
That piety shown the dead is pity in vain.

(*Exit* KREON.)

Ode III

Strophe

CHORUS: Love, unconquerable
Waster of rich men, keeper
Of warm lights and all-night vigil
In the soft face of a girl:
Sea-wanderer, forest-visitor!
Even the pure Immortals cannot escape you,
And mortal man, in his one day's dusk,
Trembles before your glory.

Antistrophe

Surely you swerve upon ruin
The just man's consenting heart,
As here you have made bright anger
Strike between father and son—
And none has conquered but Love!
A girl's glance working the will of heaven:

Pleasure to her alone who mocks us,
Merciless Aphroditê.[3]

Scene IV

CHORAGOS (*as* ANTIGONÊ *enters guarded*): But I can no longer stand in awe of this,
Nor, seeing what I see, keep back my tears.
Here is Antigonê, passing to that chamber
Where all find sleep at last.

Strophe I

ANTIGONÊ: Look upon me, friends, and pity me
Turning back at the night's edge to say
Good-by to the sun that shines for me no longer;
Now sleepy Death
Summons me down to Acheron,[4] that cold shore:
There is no bridesong there, nor any music.
CHORUS: Yet not unpraised, not without a kind of honor,
You walk at last into the underworld;
Untouched by sickness, broken by no sword.
What woman has ever found your way to death?

Antistrophe I

ANTIGONÊ: How often I have heard the story of Niobê,[5]
Tantalos' wretched daughter, how the stone
Clung fast about her, ivy-close: and they say
The rain falls endlessly
And sifting soft snow; her tears are never done.
I feel the loneliness of her death in mine.
CHORUS: But she was born of heaven, and you
Are woman, woman-born. If her death is yours,
A mortal woman's, is this not for you
Glory in our world and in the world beyond?

[3]goddess of love [4]a river in the underworld [5]Niobê, the daughter of Tantalos, was turned into a stone on Mount Sipylus while bemoaning the destruction of her many children by Leto, the mother of Apollo.

Strophe 2

ANTIGONÊ: You laugh at me. Ah, friends, friends,
Can you not wait until I am dead? O Thebes,
O men many-charioted, in love with Fortune,
Dear springs of Dircê, sacred Theban grove,
Be witnesses for me, denied all pity,
Unjustly judged! and think a word of love
For her whose path turns
Under dark earth, where there are no more tears.

CHORUS: You have passed beyond human daring and come at last
Into a place of stone where Justice sits.
I cannot tell
What shape of your father's guilt appears in this.

Antistrophe 2

ANTIGONÊ: You have touched it at last:
that bridal bed
Unspeakable, horror of son and mother mingling:
Their crime, infection of all our family!
O Oedipus, father and brother!
Your marriage strikes from the grave to murder mine.
I have been a stranger here in my own land:
All my life
The blasphemy of my birth has followed me.

CHORUS: Reverence is a virtue, but strength
Lives in established law: that must prevail.
You have made your choice,
Your death is the doing of your conscious hand.

Epode

ANTIGONÊ: Then let me go, since all your words are bitter,
And the very light of the sun is cold to me.
Lead me to my vigil, where I must have
Neither love nor lamentation; no song, but silence.

(KREON *interrupts impatiently.*)

KREON: If dirges and planned lamentations could put off death,

Men would be singing for ever.
(to *the* SERVANTS) Take her, go!
You know your orders: take her to the vault
And leave her alone there. And if she lives or dies,
That's her affair, not ours: our hands are clean.

ANTIGONÊ: O tomb, vaulted bride-bed in eternal rock,
Soon I shall be with my own again
Where Persephonê[6] welcomes the thin ghosts
underground:
And I shall see my father again, and you, mother,
And dearest Polyneicês—
dearest indeed
To me, since it was my hand
That washed him clean and poured the ritual wine:
And my reward is death before my time!

And yet, as men's hearts know, I have done no wrong,
I have not sinned before God. Or if I have,
I shall know the truth in death. But if the guilt
Lies upon Kreon who judged me, then, I pray,
May his punishment equal my own.

CHORAGOS: O passionate heart,
Unyielding, tormented still by the same winds!

KREON: Her guards shall have good cause to regret their delaying.

ANTIGONÊ: Ah! That voice is like the voice of death!

KREON: I can give you no reason to think you are mistaken.

ANTIGONÊ: Thebes, and you my fathers' gods,
And rulers of Thebes, you see me now, the last
Unhappy daughter of a line of kings,
Your kings, led away to death. You will remember
What things I suffer, and at what men's hands,
Because I would not transgress the laws of heaven.
(*to the* GUARDS, *simply*) Come: let us wait no longer.

(*Exit* ANTIGONÊ, *left, guarded.*)

---

[6]queen of the underworld

Ode IV

Strophe 1

CHORUS: All Danaê's[7] beauty was locked away
In a brazen cell where the sunlight could not come:
A small room still as any grave, enclosed her.
Yet she was a princess too,
And Zeus in a rain of gold poured love upon her.
O child, child,
No power in wealth or war
Or tough sea-blackened ships
Can prevail against untiring Destiny!

Antistrophe 1

And Dryas' son[8] also, that furious king,
Bore the god's prisoning anger for his pride:
Sealed up by Dionysos in deaf stone,
His madness died among echoes.
So at the last he learned what dreadful power
His tongue had mocked:
For he had profaned the revels,
And fired the wrath of the nine
Implacable Sisters[9] that love the sound of the flute.

Strophe 2

And old men tell a half-remembered tale
Of horror where a dark ledge splits the sea
And a double surf beats on the gráy shóres:
How a king's new woman,[10] sick
With hatred for the queen he had imprisoned,
Ripped out his two sons' eyes with her bloody hands
While grinning Arês[11] watched the shuttle plunge
Four times: four blind wounds crying for revenge.

---

[7]the mother of Perseus by Zeus, who visited her during her imprisonment in the form of a golden rain [8]Lycurgus, king of Thrace [9]the Muses [10]Eidothea, King Phineus' second wife, blinded her stepsons. [11]god of war

Antistrophe 2

Crying, tears and blood mingled.—Piteously born,
Those sons whose mother was of heavenly birth!
Her father was the god of the North Wind
And she was cradled by gales,
She raced with young colts on the glittering hills
And walked untrammeled in the open light:
But in her marriage deathless Fate found means
To build a tomb like yours for all her joy.

Scene V

(*Enter blind* TEIRESIAS, *led by a boy. The opening speeches of* TEIRESIAS *should be in singsong contrast to the realistic lines of* KREON.)

TEIRESIAS: This is the way the blind man comes, Princes, Princes,
Lock-step, two heads lit by the eyes of one.
KREON: What new thing have you to tell us, old Teiresias?
TEIRESIAS: I have much to tell you: listen to the prophet, Kreon.
KREON: I am not aware that I have ever failed to listen.
TEIRESIAS: Then you have done wisely, King, and ruled well.
KREON: I admit my debt to you. But what have you to say?
TEIRESIAS: This, Kreon: you stand once more on the edge of fate.
KREON: What do you mean? Your words are a kind of dread.
TEIRESIAS: Listen, Kreon:
I was sitting in my chair of augury, at the place
Where the birds gather about me. They were all a-chatter,
As is their habit, when suddenly I heard
A strange note in their jangling, a scream, a
Whirring fury; I knew that they were fighting,
Tearing each other, dying
In a whirlwind of wings clashing. And I was afraid.
I began the rites of burnt-offering at the altar,
But Hephaistos[12] failed me: instead of bright flame,
There was only the sputtering slime of the fat thigh-flesh
Melting: the entrails dissolved in gray smoke,
The bare bone burst from the welter. And no blaze!

[12]god of fire

This was a sign from heaven. My boy described it,
Seeing for me as I see for others.

I tell you, Kreon, you yourself have brought
This new calamity upon us. Our hearths and altars
Are stained with the corruption of dogs and carrion birds
That glut themselves on the corpse of Oedipus' son.
The gods are deaf when we pray to them, their fire
Recoils from our offering, their birds of omen
Have no cry of comfort, for they are gorged
With the thick blood of the dead.
O my son,
These are no trifles! Think: all men make mistakes,
But a good man yields when he knows his course is wrong,
And repairs the evil. The only crime is pride.

Give in to the dead man, then: do not fight with a corpse—
What glory is it to kill a man who is dead?
Think, I beg you:
It is for your own good that I speak as I do.
You should be able to yield for your own good.

KREON: It seems that prophets have made me their especial province.
All my life long
I have been a kind of butt for the dull arrows
Of doddering fortune-tellers!
No, Teiresias:
If your birds—if the great eagles of God himself
Should carry him stinking bit by bit to heaven,
I would not yield. I am not afraid of pollution:
No man can defile the gods.
Do what you will,
Go into business, make money, speculate
In India gold or that synthetic gold from Sardis,
Get rich otherwise than by my consent to bury him.
Teiresias, it is a sorry thing when a wise man
Sells his wisdom, lets out his words for hire!

TEIRESIAS: Ah Kreon! Is there no man left in the world—

KREON: To do what?—Come, let's have the aphorism!

TEIRESIAS: No man who knows that wisdom outweighs any wealth?

KREON: As surely as bribes are baser than any baseness.

TEIRESIAS: You are sick, Kreon! You are deathly sick!
KREON: As you say: it is not my place to challenge a prophet.
TEIRESIAS: Yet you have said my prophecy is for sale.
KREON: The generation of prophets has always loved gold.
TEIRESIAS: The generation of kings has always loved brass.
KREON: You forget yourself! You are speaking to your King.
TEIRESIAS: I know it. You are a king because of me.
KREON: You have a certain skill; but you have sold out.
TEIRESIAS: King, you will drive me to words that—
KREON: Say them, say them!
Only remember: I will not pay you for them.
TEIRESIAS: No, you will find them too costly.
KREON: No doubt. Speak:
Whatever you say, you will not change my will.
TEIRESIAS: Then take this, and take it to heart!
The time is not far off when you shall pay back
Corpse for corpse, flesh of your own flesh.
You have thrust the child of this world into living night,
You have kept from the gods below the child that is theirs:
The one in a grave before her death, the other,
Dead, denied the grave. This is your crime:
And the Furies and the dark gods of Hell
Are swift with terrible punishment for you.
Do you want to buy me now, Kreon?

Not many days,
And your house will be full of men and women weeping,
And curses will be hurled at you from far
Cities grieving for sons unburied, left to rot
Before the walls of Thebes.

These are my arrows, Kreon: they are all for you.

(*To* BOY.) But come, child: lead me home.
Let him waste his fine anger upon younger men.
Maybe he will learn at last
To control a wiser tongue in a better head.

(*Exit* TEIRESIAS.)

CHORAGOS: The old man has gone, King, but his words

Remain to plague us. I am old, too,
But I cannot remember that he was ever false.

KREON: That is true. . . . It troubles me.
Oh it is hard to give in! but it is worse
To risk everything for stubborn pride.

CHORAGOS: Kreon: take my advice.

KREON: What shall I do?

CHORAGOS: Go quickly: free Antigonê from her vault
And build a tomb for the body of Polyneicês.

KREON: You would have me do this!

CHORAGOS: Kreon, yes!
And it must be done at once: God moves
Swiftly to cancel the folly of stubborn men.

KREON: It is hard to deny the heart! But I
Will do it: I will not fight with destiny.

CHORAGOS: You must go yourself, you cannot leave it to others.

KREON: I will go.
—Bring axes, servants:
Come with me to the tomb. I buried her, I
Will set her free.
Oh quickly!
My mind misgives—
The laws of the gods are mighty, and a man must serve them
To the last day of his life!

(*Exit* KREON.)

Paean[13]

Strophe I

CHORAGOS: God of many names

CHORUS: O Iacchos[14]
son
of Kadmeian Sémelê[15]
O born of the Thunder!
Guardian of the West
Regent

[13]a hymn of praise [14]another name for Dionysos (Bacchus) [15]the daughter of Kadmos, the founder of Thebes

of Eleusis' plain
O Prince of maenad Thebes
and the Dragon Field by rippling Ismenós:[16]

Antistrophe 1

CHORAGOS: God of many names
CHORUS: the flame of torches
flares on our hills
the nymphs of Iacchos
dance at the spring of Castalia:[17]
from the vine-close mountain
come ah come in ivy:
Evohé evohé! sings through the streets of Thebes

Strophe 2

CHORAGOS: God of many names
CHORUS: Iacchos of Thebes
heavenly Child
of Sémelê bride of the Thunderer!
The shadow of plague is upon us:
come
with clement feet
oh come from Parnasos
down the long slopes
across the lamenting water

Antistrophe 2

CHORAGOS: Iô Fire! Chorister of the throbbing stars!
O purest among the voices of the night!
Thou son of God, blaze for us!
CHORUS: Come with choric rapture of circling Maenads[18]
Who cry *Iô Iacche!*
God of many names!

---

[16]a river east of Thebes; the ancestors of the Theban nobility sprang from dragon's teeth sown by the Ismenós. [17]a spring on Mount Parnasos [18]the worshippers of Dionysos

Exodos

(*Enter* MESSENGER *from left.*)

MESSENGER: Men of the line of Kadmos, you who live
Near Amphion's citadel,[19]
I cannot say
Of any condition of human life "This is fixed,
This is clearly good, or bad" Fate raises up,
And Fate casts down the happy and unhappy alike:
No man can foretell his Fate.
Take the case of Kreon:
Kreon was happy once, as I count happiness:
Victorious in battle, sole governor of the land,
Fortunate father of children nobly born.
And now it has all gone from him! Who can say
That a man is still alive when his life's joy fails?
He is a walking dead man. Grant him rich,
Let him live like a king in his great house:
If his pleasure is gone, I would not give
So much as the shadow of smoke for all he owns.

CHORAGOS: Your words hint at sorrow: what is your news for us?

MESSENGER: They are dead. The living are guilty of their death.

CHORAGOS: Who is guilty? Who is dead? Speak!

MESSENGER: Haimon.
Haimon is dead; and the hand that killed him
Is his own hand.

CHORAGOS: His father's? or his own?

MESSENGER: His own, driven mad by the murder his father had done.

CHORAGOS: Teiresias, Teiresias, how clearly you saw it all!

MESSENGER: This is my news: you must draw what conclusions you can from it.

CHORAGOS: But look: Eurydicê, our Queen:
Has she overheard us?

(*Enter* EURYDICÊ *from the palace, center.*)

[19]Amphion used the music of his magic lyre to lure stones to form a wall around Thebes.

EURYDICÊ: I have heard something, friends:
As I was unlocking the gate of Pallas'[20] shrine,
For I needed her help today, I heard a voice
Telling of some new sorrow. And I fainted
There at the temple all my maidens about me.
But speak again: whatever it is, I can bear it:
Grief and I are no strangers.

MESSENGER: Dearest Lady,
I will tell you plainly all that I have seen.
I shall not try to comfort you: what is the use,
Since comfort could lie only in what is not true?
The truth is always best.
I went with Kreon
To the outer plain where Polyneicês was lying,
No friend to pity him, his body shredded by dogs.
We made our prayers in that place to Hecatê
And Pluto,[21] that they would be merciful. And we bathed
The corpse with holy water, and we brought
Fresh-broken branches to burn what was left of it,
And upon the urn we heaped up a towering barrow
Of the earth of his own land.
When we were done, we ran
To the vault where Antigonê lay on her couch of stone.
One of the servants had gone ahead,
And while he was yet far off he heard a voice
Grieving within the chamber, and he came back
And told Kreon. And as the King went closer,
The air was full of wailing, the words lost,
And he begged us to make all haste. "Am I a prophet?"
He said, weeping, "And must I walk this road,
The saddest of all that I have gone before?
My son's voice calls me on. Oh quickly, quickly!
Look through the crevice there, and tell me
If it is Haimon, or some deception of the gods!"

We obeyed; and in the cavern's farthest corner
We saw her lying:
She had made a noose of her fine linen veil

[20]Pallas Athena, the goddess of wisdom [21]*Hecatê . . . Pluto* the ruling deities of the underworld

And hanged herself. Haimon lay beside her,
His arms about her waist, lamenting her,
His love lost under ground, crying out
That his father had stolen her away from him.

When Kreon saw him the tears rushed to his eyes
And he called to him: "What have you done, child?
Speak to me.
What are you thinking that makes your eyes so strange?
O my son, my son, I come to you on my knees!"
But Haimon spat in his face. He said not a word,
Staring—
And suddenly drew his sword
And lunged. Kreon shrank back, the blade missed; and the boy,
Desperate against himself, drove it half its length
Into his own side, and fell. And as he died
He gathered Antigonê close in his arms again,
Choking, his blood bright red on her white cheek.
And now he lies dead with the dead, and she is his
At last, his bride in the house of the dead.

(*Exit* EURYDICÊ *into the palace.*)

CHORAGOS: She has left us without a word. What can this mean?
MESSENGER: It troubles me, too; yet she knows what is best,
Her grief is too great for public lamentation,
And doubtless she has gone to her chamber to weep
For her dead son, leading her maidens in his dirge.

(*Pause.*)

CHORAGOS: It may be so: but I fear this deep silence.
MESSENGER: I will see what she is doing. I will go in.

(*Exit* MESSENGER *into the palace. Enter* KREON *with attendants, bearing* HAIMON'S *body.*)

CHORAGOS: But here is the king himself: oh look at him,
Bearing his own damnation in his arms.
KREON: Nothing you say can touch me any more.
My own blind heart has brought me
From darkness to final darkness. Here you see
The father murdering, the murdered son—
And all my civic wisdom!

Haimon my son, so young, so young to die,
I was the fool, not you; and you died for me.
CHORAGOS: That is the truth; but you were late in learning it.
KREON: This truth is hard to bear. Surely a god
Has crushed me beneath the hugest weight of heaven,
And driven me headlong a barbaric way
To trample out the thing I held most dear.

The pains that men will take to come to pain!

(*Enter* MESSENGER *from the palace.*)

MESSENGER: The burden you carry in your hands is heavy,
But it is not all: you will find more in your house.
KREON: What burden worse than this shall I find there?
MESSENGER: The Queen is dead.
KREON: O port of death, deaf world,
Is there no pity for me? And you, Angel of evil,
I was dead, and your words are death again.
Is it true, boy? Can it be true?
Is my wife dead? Has death bred death?
MESSENGER: You can see for yourself.

(*The doors are opened and the body of* EURYDICÊ is *disclosed within.*)

KREON: Oh pity!
All true, all true, and more than I can bear!
O my wife, my son!
MESSENGER: She stood before the altar, and her heart
Welcomed the knife her own hand guided,
And a great cry burst from her lips for Megareus[22] dead,
And for Haimon dead, her sons; and her last breath
Was a curse for their father, the murderer of her sons.
And she fell, and the dark flowed in through her closing eyes.
KREON: O God, I am sick with fear.
Are there no swords here? Has no one a blow for me?
MESSENGER: Her curse is upon you for the deaths of both.
KREON: It is right that it should be. I alone am guilty.
I know it, and I say it. Lead me in,

[22]Megareus, brother of Haimon, had died in the assault on Thebes.

Quickly, friends.
I have neither life nor substance. Lead me in.
CHORAGOS: You are right, if there can be right in so much wrong.
The briefest way is best in a world of sorrow.
KREON: Let it come,
Let death come quickly, and be kind to me.
I would not ever see the sun again.
CHORAGOS: All that will come when it will; but we, meanwhile,
Have much to do. Leave the future to itself.
KREON: All my heart was in that prayer!
CHORAGOS: Then do not pray any more: the sky is deaf.
KREON: Lead me away. I have been rash and foolish.
I have killed my son and my wife.
I look for comfort; my comfort lies here dead.
Whatever my hands have touched has come to nothing.
Fate has brought all my pride to a thought of dust.

(*As* KREON *is being led into the house, the* CHORAGOS *advances and speaks directly to the audience.*)

CHORAGOS: There is no happiness where there is no wisdom;
No wisdom but in submission to the gods.
Big words are always punished,
And proud men in old age learn to be wise.

Hamlet, Prince of Denmark WILLIAM SHAKESPEARE

William Shakespeare (1564–1616) wrote a play that remains, for many, the greatest tragedy ever written: *Hamlet* (ca. 1601). No play has attracted as much critical attention as this particular tragedy. It is filled with mystery, twists of plot, clever and witty dialogues, some of Shakespeare's greatest soliloquies, and memorable and numerous characters, including a ghost. It is a great murder mystery, a revenge tragedy whose philosophic underpinnings complement the action. The play is a remarkable study of human desires, ambitions, and frailties.

Hamlet himself lies at the nerve center of the play, drawing our attention to his inherent contradictions, the very ambiguous nature of his being. He is a man who is savagely divided against himself. Guilt, shame, and honor plague him, and while he knows he should take action, he procrastinates, allowing a shocking series of tragedies to occur. By the final curtain, Shakespeare has staged a fully developed tragedy whose themes and resolutions resonate as much in the twenty-first century as they did when the play was first performed on the Elizabethan stage. To this day, *Hamlet* continues to attract the world's most accomplished actors and to fascinate audiences around the world.

DRAMATIS PERSONAE

CLAUDIUS, *King of Denmark*
HAMLET, *son to the late King Hamlet, and nephew to the present King*
POLONIUS, *Lord Chamberlain*
HORATIO, *friend to Hamlet*
LAERTES, *son to Polonius*
VOLTEMAND, CORNELIUS, ROSENCRANTZ, GUILDENSTERN, OSRIC, GENTLEMAN — *courtiers*
MARCELLUS, BARNARDO — *officers*
FRANCISCO, *a soldier*
REYNALDO, *servant to Polonius*
FORTINBRAS, *Prince of Norway*
NORWEGIAN CAPTAIN
DOCTOR OF DIVINITY

PLAYERS
Two CLOWNS, *grave-diggers*
ENGLISH AMBASSADORS

GERTRUDE, *Queen of Denmark, and mother to Hamlet*
OPHELIA, *daughter to Polonius*

GHOST *of Hamlet's Father*
LORDS, LADIES, OFFICERS, SOLDIERS, SAILORS, MESSENGERS, *and* ATTENDANTS

SCENE: *Denmark*

Act I

Scene I

Enter BARNARDO *and* FRANCISCO, *two sentinels,* [*meeting*].

BAR: Who's there?
FRAN: Nay, answer me. Stand and unfold yourself.
BAR: Long live the King!
FRAN: Barnardo.
BAR: He.
FRAN: You come most carefully upon your hour.
BAR: 'Tis now strook twelf. Get thee to bed, Francisco.
FRAN: For this relief much thanks. 'Tis bitter cold,
And I am sick at heart.
BAR: Have you had quiet guard?
FRAN: Not a mouse stirring.
BAR: Well, good night.
If you do meet Horatio and Marcellus,
The rivals of my watch, bid them make haste.

Enter HORATIO *and* MARCELLUS.

FRAN: I think I hear them. Stand ho! Who is there?
HOR: Friends to this ground.

Words and passages enclosed in square brackets in the text above are either emendations of the copy-text or additions to it.

I.i. Location: Elsinore. A guard-platform of the castle. 2. **answer me:** i.e. *you* answer *me.* Francisco is on watch; Barnardo has come to relieve him. **unfold yourself:** make known who you are. 3. **Long . . . King.** Perhaps a password, perhaps simply an utterance to allow the voice to be recognized. 7. **strook twelf:** struck twelve. 9. **sick at heart:** in low spirits. 14. **rivals:** partners.

MAR: And liegemen to the Dane.
FRAN: Give you good night.
MAR: O, farewell, honest [soldier].
Who hath reliev'd you?
FRAN: Barnardo hath my place.
Give you good night. *Exit* FRANCISCO.
MAR: Holla, Barnardo!
BAR: Say—
What, is Horatio there?
HOR: A piece of him.
BAR: Welcome, Horatio, welcome, good Marcellus.
HOR: What, has this thing appear'd again to-night?
BAR: I have seen nothing.
MAR: Horatio says 'tis but our fantasy,
And will not let belief take hold of him
Touching this dreaded sight twice seen of us;
Therefore I have entreated him along,
With us to watch the minutes of this night,
That if again this apparition come,
He may approve our eyes and speak to it.
HOR: Tush, tush, 'twill not appear.
BAR: Sit down a while,
And let us once again assail your ears,
That are so fortified against our story,
What we have two nights seen.
HOR: Well, sit we down,
And let us hear Barnardo speak of this.
BAR: Last night of all,
When yond same star that's westward from the pole
Had made his course t' illume that part of heaven
Where now it burns, Marcellus and myself,
The bell then beating one—

Enter GHOST.

MAR: Peace, break thee off! Look where it comes again!
BAR: In the same figure like the King that's dead.

---

17. **liegemen . . . Dane:** loyal subjects to the King of Denmark. 18. **Give:** God give. 30. **fantasy:** imagination. 36. **approve:** corroborate. 45. **pole:** pole star. 46. **his:** its (the commonest form of the neuter possessive singular in Shakespeare's day). 50. **like:** in the likeness of.

MAR: Thou art a scholar, speak to it, Horatio.
BAR: Looks 'a not like the King? Mark it, Horatio.
HOR: Most like; it [harrows] me with fear and wonder.
BAR: It would be spoke to.
MAR: Speak to it, Horatio.
HOR: What art thou that usurp'st this time of night,
Together with that fair and warlike form
In which the majesty of buried Denmark
Did sometimes march? By heaven I charge thee speak!
MAR: It is offended.
BAR: See, it stalks away!
HOR: Stay! Speak, speak, I charge thee speak!

Exit GHOST.

MAR: 'Tis gone, and will not answer.
BAR: How now, Horatio? you tremble and look pale.
Is not this something more than fantasy?
What think you on't?
HOR: Before my God, I might not this believe
Without the sensible and true avouch
Of mine own eyes.
MAR: Is it not like the King?
HOR: As thou art to thyself.
Such was the very armor he had on
When he the ambitious Norway combated.
So frown'd he once when in an angry parle
He smote the sledded [Polacks] on the ice.
'Tis strange.
MAR: Thus twice before, and jump at this dead hour,
With martial stalk hath he gone by our watch.
HOR: In what particular thought to work I know not,
But in the gross and scope of mine opinion,
This bodes some strange eruption to our state.

---

51. **a scholar:** i.e. one who knows how best to address it. 52. **'a:** he. 54. **It . . . to.** A ghost had to be spoken to before it could speak. 56. **usurp'st.** The ghost, a supernatural being, has invaded the realm of nature. 58. **majesty . . . Denmark:** late King of Denmark. 59. **sometimes:** formerly. 68. **sensible:** relating to the senses. **avouch:** guarantee. 73. **Norway:** King of Norway. 74. **parle:** parley. 75. **sledded:** using sleds or sledges. **Polacks:** Poles. 77. **jump:** precisely. 79–80. **In . . . opinion:** while I have no precise theory about it, my general feeling is that. *Gross* = wholeness, totality; *scope* = range. 81. **eruption:** upheaval.

MAR: Good now, sit down, and tell me, he that knows,
Why this same strict and most observant watch
So nightly toils the subject of the land,
And [why] such daily [cast] of brazen cannon,
And foreign mart for implements of war,
Why such impress of shipwrights, whose sore task
Does not divide the Sunday from the week,
What might be toward, that this sweaty haste
Doth make the night joint-laborer with the day:
Who is't that can inform me?

HOR: That can I,
At least the whisper goes so: our last king,
Whose image even but now appear'd to us,
Was, as you know, by Fortinbras of Norway,
Thereto prick'd on by a most emulate pride,
Dar'd to the combat; in which our valiant Hamlet
(For so this side of our known world esteem'd him)
Did slay this Fortinbras, who, by a seal'd compact
Well ratified by law and heraldy,
Did forfeit (with his life) all [those] his lands
Which he stood seiz'd of, to the conqueror;
Against the which a moi'ty competent
Was gaged by our king, which had [return'd]
To the inheritance of Fortinbras,
Had he been vanquisher; as by the same comart
And carriage of the article [design'd],
His fell to Hamlet. Now, sir, young Fortinbras,
Of unimproved mettle hot and full,
Hath in the skirts of Norway here and there
Shark'd up a list of lawless resolutes
For food and diet to some enterprise

---

84. **toils:** causes to work. **subject:** subjects. 86. **foreign mart:** dealing with foreign markets. 87. **impress:** forced service. 89. **toward:** in preparation. 96. **emulate:** emulous, proceeding from rivalry. 100. **law and heraldy:** heraldic law (governing combat). *Heraldy* is a variant of *heraldry.* 102. **seiz'd of:** possessed of. 103. **moi'ty:** portion. **competent:** adequate, i.e. equivalent. 104. **gaged:** pledged. **had:** would have. 105. **inheritance:** possession. 106. **comart:** bargain. 107. **carriage:** tenor. **design'd:** drawn up. 109. **unimproved:** untried (?) or not directed to any useful end (?). 110. **skirts:** outlying territories. 111. **Shark'd up:** gathered up hastily and indiscriminately.

That hath a stomach in't, which is no other,
As it doth well appear unto our state,
But to recover of us, by strong hand
And terms compulsatory, those foresaid lands
So by his father lost; and this, I take it,
Is the main motive of our preparations,
The source of this our watch, and the chief head
Of this post-haste and romage in the land.

BAR: I think it be no other but e'en so.
Well may it sort that this portentous figure
Comes armed through our watch so like the King
That was and is the question of these wars

HOR: A mote it is to trouble the mind's eye.
In the most high and palmy state of Rome,
A little ere the mightiest Julius fell,
The graves stood [tenantless] and the sheeted dead
Did squeak and gibber in the Roman streets.
As stars with trains of fire, and dews of blood,
Disasters in the sun; and the moist star
Upon whose influence Neptune's empire stands
Was sick almost to doomsday with eclipse.
And even the like precurse of [fear'd] events,
As harbingers preceding still the fates
And prologue to the omen coming on,
Have heaven and earth together demonstrated
Unto our climatures and countrymen.

Enter GHOST.

But soft, behold! lo where it comes again!

---

113. **stomach:** relish of danger (?) or demand for courage (?). 119. **head:** source. 120. **romage:** rummage, bustling activity. 122. **sort:** fit. **portentous:** ominous. 129. One or more lines may have been lost between this line and the next. 131. **Disasters:** ominous signs. **moist star:** moon. 132. **Neptune's empire stands:** the seas are dependent. 133. **sick . . . doomsday:** i.e. almost totally darkened. When the Day of Judgment is imminent, says Matthew 24:29, "the moon shall not give her light." **eclipse.** There were a solar and two total lunar eclipses visible in England in 1598; they caused gloomy speculation. 134. **precurse:** foreshadowing. 135. **harbingers:** advance messengers. **still:** always. 136. **omen:** i.e. the events portended. 138. **climatures:** regions.

It spreads his arms.

I'll cross it though it blast me. Stay, illusion!
If thou hast any sound or use of voice,
Speak to me.
If there be any good thing to be done
That may to thee do ease, and grace to me,
Speak to me.
If thou art privy to thy country's fate,
Which happily foreknowing may avoid,
O speak!
Or if thou hast uphoarded in thy life
Extorted treasure in the womb of earth,
For which, they say, your spirits oft walk in death,
Speak of it, stay and speak! (*The cock crows.*) Stop it,
Marcellus.

MAR: Shall I strike it with my partisan?

HOR: Do, if it will not stand.

BAR: 'Tis here!

HOR: 'Tis here!

MAR: 'Tis gone! [*Exit* GHOST.]
We do it wrong, being so majestical,
To offer it the show of violence,
For it is as the air, invulnerable,
And our vain blows malicious mockery.

BAR: It was about to speak when the cock crew.

HOR: And then it started like a guilty thing
Upon a fearful summons. I have heard
The cock, that is the trumpet to the morn,
Doth with his lofty and shrill-sounding throat
Awake the god of day, and at his warning,
Whether in sea or fire, in earth or air,
Th' extravagant and erring spirit hies
To his confine; and of the truth herein

---

139. s.d. **his:** its. 140. **cross it:** cross its path, confront it directly. **blast:** wither (by supernatural means). 147. **happily:** haply, perhaps. 151. **your:** Colloquial and impersonal; cf. I.v.167, IV.iii.21, 23. Most editors adopt *you* from F1. 154. **partisan:** long-handled spear. 162. **malicious mockery:** mockery of malice, i.e. empty pretenses of harming it. 166. **trumpet:** trumpeter. 170. **extravagant:** wandering outside its proper bounds. **erring:** wandering abroad. **hies:** hastens.

This present object made probation.
MAR: It faded on the crowing of the cock.
Some say that ever 'gainst that season comes
Wherein our Saviour's birth is celebrated,
This bird of dawning singeth all night long,
And then they say no spirit dare stir abroad,
The nights are wholesome, then no planets strike,
No fairy takes, nor witch hath power to charm,
So hallowed, and so gracious, is that time.
HOR: So have I heard and do in part believe it.
But look, the morn in russet mantle clad
Walks o'er the dew of yon high eastward hill.
Break we our watch up, and by my advice
Let us impart what we have seen to-night
Unto young Hamlet, for, upon my life,
This spirit, dumb to us, will speak to him.
Do you consent we shall acquaint him with it,
As needful in our loves, fitting our duty?
MAR: Let's do't, I pray, and I this morning know
Where we shall find him most convenient.

Exeunt.

Scene II

Flourish. Enter CLAUDIUS, KING OF DENMARK, GERTRUDE THE QUEEN; COUNCIL: *as* POLONIUS; *and his son* LAERTES, HAMLET, *cum aliis* [*including* VOLTEMAND *and* CORNELIUS].

KING: Though yet of Hamlet our dear brother's death
The memory be green, and that it us befitted
To bear our hearts in grief, and our whole kingdom
To be contracted in one brow of woe,
Yet so far hath discretion fought with nature
That we with wisest sorrow think on him
Together with remembrance of ourselves.

---

172. **object:** sight. **probation:** proof. 174. **'gainst:** just before. 178. **strike:** exert malevolent influence. 179. **takes:** bewitches, charms. 180. **gracious:** blessed. 182. **russet:** coarse greyish-brown cloth.

I.ii. Location: The castle. o.s.d. **Flourish:** trumpet fanfare. **cum aliis:** with others. 2. **befitted:** would befit. 4. **contracted in:** (1) reduced to; (2) knit or wrinkled in. **brow of woe:** mournful brow.

Therefore our sometime sister, now our queen,
Th' imperial jointress to this warlike state,
Have we, as 'twere with a defeated joy,
With an auspicious, and a dropping eye,
With mirth in funeral, and with dirge in marriage,
In equal scale weighing delight and dole,
Taken to wife; nor have we herein barr'd
Your better wisdoms, which have freely gone
With this affair along. For all, our thanks.
Now follows that you know young Fortinbras,
Holding a weak supposal of our worth,
Or thinking by our late dear brother's death
Our state to be disjoint and out of frame,
Co-leagued with this dream of his advantage,
He hath not fail'd to pester us with message
Importing the surrender of those lands
Lost by his father, with all bands of law,
To our most valiant brother. So much for him.
Now for ourself, and for this time of meeting,
Thus much the business is: we have here writ
To Norway, uncle of young Fortinbras—
Who, impotent and bedred, scarcely hears
Of this his nephew's purpose—to suppress
His further gait herein, in that the levies,
The lists, and full proportions are all made
Out of his subject; and we here dispatch
You, good Cornelius, and you, Voltemand,
For bearers of this greeting to old Norway,
Giving to you no further personal power
To business with the King, more than the scope
Of these delated articles allow. [*Giving a paper.*]
Farewell, and let your haste commend your duty.

COR., VOL: In that, and all things, will we show our duty.

---

9. **jointress:** joint holder. 10. **defeated:** impaired. 11. **auspicious . . . dropping:** cheerful . . . weeping. 15. **freely:** fully, without reservation. 17. **know:** be informed, learn. 18. **supposal:** conjecture, estimate. 21. **Co-leagued:** joined. 22. **pester . . . message:** trouble me with persistent messages (the original sense of *pester* is "overcrowd"). 23. **Importing:** having as import. 24. **bands:** bonds, binding terms. 29. **impotent and bedred:** feeble and bedridden. 31. **gait:** proceeding. 31–33. **in . . . subject:** since the troops are all drawn from his subjects. 38. **delated:** extended, detailed (a variant of *dilated*).

KING: We doubt it nothing; heartily farewell.

[*Exeunt* VOLTEMAND *and* CORNELIUS.]

And now, Laertes, what's the news with you?
You told us of some suit, what is't, Laertes?
You cannot speak of reason to the Dane
And lose your voice. What wouldst thou beg, Laertes,
That shall not be my offer, not thy asking?
The head is not more native to the heart,
The hand more instrumental to the mouth,
Than is the throne of Denmark to thy father.
What wouldst thou have, Laertes?

LAER: My dread lord,
Your leave and favor to return to France,
From whence though willingly I came to Denmark
To show my duty in your coronation,
Yet now I must confess, that duty done,
My thoughts and wishes bend again toward France,
And bow them to your gracious leave and pardon.

KING: Have you your father's leave? What says Polonius?

POL: H'ath, my lord, wrung from me my slow leave
By laborsome petition, and at last
Upon his will I seal'd my hard consent.
I do beseech you give him leave to go.

KING: Take thy fair hour, Laertes, time be thine,
And thy best graces spend it at thy will!
But now, my cousin Hamlet, and my son—

HAM [*Aside.*]: A little more than kin, and less than kind.

KING: How is it that the clouds still hang on you?

HAM: Not so, my lord, I am too much in the sun.

QUEEN: Good Hamlet, cast thy nighted color off,
And let thine eye look like a friend on Denmark.
Do not for ever with thy vailed lids
Seek for thy noble father in the dust.

---

41. **nothing:** not at all. 45. **lose:** waste. 47. **native:** closely related. 48. **instrumental:** serviceable. 52. **leave and favor:** gracious permission. 57. **pardon:** permission to depart. 59. **H'ath:** he hath. 61. **hard:** reluctant. 65. **cousin:** kinsman (used in familiar address to any collateral relative more distant than a brother or sister; here to a nephew). 66. **A little . . . kind:** closer than a nephew, since you are my mother's husband; yet more distant than a son, too (and not well disposed to you). 68. **sun:** With obvious quibble on *son.* 71. **vailed:** downcast.

Thou know'st 'tis common, all that lives must die,
Passing through nature to eternity.
HAM: Ay, madam, it is common.
QUEEN: If it be,
Why seems it so particular with thee?
HAM: Seems, madam? nay, it is, I know not "seems."
'Tis not alone my inky cloak, [good] mother,
Nor customary suits of solemn black,
Nor windy suspiration of forc'd breath,
No, nor the fruitful river in the eye,
Nor the dejected havior of the visage,
Together with all forms, moods, [shapes] of grief,
That can [denote] me truly. These indeed seem,
For they are actions that a man might play,
But I have that within which passes show,
These but the trappings and the suits of woe.
KING: 'Tis sweet and commendable in your nature, Hamlet,
To give these mourning duties to your father.
But you must know your father lost a father,
That father lost, lost his, and the survivor bound
In filial obligation for some term
To do obsequious sorrow. But to persever
In obstinate condolement is a course
Of impious stubbornness, 'tis unmanly grief,
It shows a will most incorrect to heaven,
A heart unfortified, or mind impatient,
An understanding simple and unschool'd:
For what we know must be, and is as common
As any the most vulgar thing to sense,
Why should we in our peevish opposition
Take it to heart? Fie, 'tis a fault to heaven,
A fault against the dead, a fault to nature,
To reason most absurd, whose common theme
Is death of fathers, and who still hath cried,
From the first corse till he that died to-day,
"This must be so." We pray you throw to earth
This unprevailing woe, and think of us

---

73. **common:** general, universal. 77. **particular:** individual, personal. 82. **fruitful:** copious. 94. **obsequious:** proper to obsequies. 95. **condolement:** grief 97. **incorrect:** unsubmissive. 101. **any . . . sense:** what is perceived to be commonest. 103. **to:** against. 105. **absurd:** contrary. 109. **unprevailing:** unavailing.

As of a father, for let the world take note
You are the most immediate to our throne,
And with no less nobility of love
Than that which dearest father bears his son
Do I impart toward you. For your intent
In going back to school in Wittenberg,
It is most retrograde to our desire,
And we beseech you bend you to remain
Here in the cheer and comfort of our eye,
Our chiefest courtier, cousin, and our son.

QUEEN: Let not thy mother lose her prayers, Hamlet,
I pray thee stay with us, go not to Wittenberg.

HAM: I shall in all my best obey you, madam.

KING: Why, 'tis a loving and a fair reply.
Be as ourself in Denmark. Madam, come.
This gentle and unforc'd accord of Hamlet
Sits smiling to my heart, in grace whereof,
No jocund health that Denmark drinks to-day,
But the great cannon to the clouds shall tell,
And the King's rouse the heaven shall bruit again,
Respeaking earthly thunder. Come away.

Flourish. Exeunt all but HAMLET.

HAM: O that this too too sallied flesh would melt,
Thaw, and resolve itself into a dew!
Or that the Everlasting had not fix'd
His canon 'gainst [self-]slaughter! O God, God,
How [weary], stale, flat, and unprofitable
Seem to me all the uses of this world!
Fie on't, ah fie! 'tis an unweeded garden
That grows to seed, things rank and gross in nature
Possess it merely. That it should come [to this]!
But two months dead, nay, not so much, not two.
So excellent a king, that was to this
Hyperion to a satyr, so loving to my mother
That he might not beteem the winds of heaven
Visit her face too roughly. Heaven and earth,

---

113. **dearest:** most loving. 114. **impart:** i.e. impart love. 129. **rouse:** bumper, drink. **bruit:** loudly declare. 131. **sallied:** sullied. Many editors prefer the F1 reading, *solid,* 134. **canon:** law. 136. **uses:** customs. 139. **merely:** utterly. 141. **to:** in comparison with. 142. **Hyperion:** the sun-god. 143. **beteem:** allow.

Must I remember? Why, she should hang on him
As if increase of appetite had grown
By what it fed on, and yet, within a month—
Let me not think on't! Frailty, thy name is woman!—
A little month, or ere those shoes were old
With which she followed my poor father's body,
Like Niobe, all tears—why, she, [even she]—
O God, a beast that wants discourse of reason
Would have mourn'd longer—married with my uncle,
My father's brother, but no more like my father
Than I to Hercules. Within a month,
Ere yet the salt of most unrighteous tears
Had left the flushing in her galled eyes,
She married—O most wicked speed: to post
With such dexterity to incestious sheets,
It is not, nor it cannot come to good,
But break my heart, for I must hold my tongue.

Enter HORATIO, MARCELLUS, *and* BARNARDO.

HOR: Hail to your lordship!
HAM: I am glad to see you well.
Horatio—or I do forget myself.
HOR: The same, my lord, and your poor servant ever.
HAM: Sir, my good friend—I'll change that name with you.
And what make you from Wittenberg, Horatio? Marcellus.
MAR: My good lord.
HAM: I am very glad to see you. [*To* BARNARDO.]
Good even, sir.—
But what, in faith, make you from Wittenberg?
HOR: A truant disposition, good my lord.
HAM: I would not hear your enemy say so,
Nor shall you do my ear that violence
To make it truster of your own report

---

149. **or ere:** before. 151. **Niobe.** She wept endlessly for her children, whom Apollo and Artemis had killed. 152. **wants . . . reason:** lacks the power of reason (which distinguishes men from beasts). 156. **unrighteous:** i.e. hypocritical. 157. **flushing:** redness. **galled:** inflamed. 159. **incestious:** incestuous. The marriage of a man to his brother's widow was so regarded until long after Shakespeare's day. 166. **change:** exchange. 167. **what . . . from:** what are you doing away from. 170. **truant disposition:** inclination to play truant.

Against yourself. I know you are no truant.
But what is your affair in Elsinore?
We'll teach you to drink [deep] ere you depart.
HOR: My lord, I came to see your father's funeral.
HAM: I prithee do not mock me, fellow studient,
I think it was to [see] my mother's wedding.
HOR: Indeed, my lord, it followed hard upon.
HAM: Thrift, thrift, Horatio, the funeral bak'd-meats
Did coldly furnish forth the marriage tables.
Would I had met my dearest foe in heaven
Or ever I had seen that day, Horatio!
My father—methinks I see my father.
HOR: Where, my lord?
HAM: In my mind's eye, Horatio.
HOR: I saw him once, 'a was a goodly king.
HAM: 'A was a man, take him for all in all,
I shall not look upon his like again.
HOR: My lord, I think I saw him yesternight.
HAM: Saw, who?
HOR: My lord, the King your father.
HAM: The King my father?
HOR: Season your admiration for a while
With an attent ear, till I may deliver,
Upon the witness of these gentlemen,
This marvel to you.
HAM: For God's love let me hear!
HOR: Two nights together had these gentlemen,
Marcellus and Barnardo, on their watch,
In the dead waste and middle of the night,
Been thus encount'red: a figure like your father,
Armed at point exactly, cap-a-pe,
Appears before them, and with solemn march
Goes slow and stately by them; thrice he walk'd
By their oppress'd and fear-surprised eyes
Within his truncheon's length, whilst they, distill'd

178. **studient:** student 182. **coldly:** when cold. 183. **dearest:** most intensely hated. 184. **Or:** ere, before. 195. **Season:** temper. **admiration:** wonder. 196. **deliver:** report. 202. **waste:** empty expanse. 204. **at point exactly:** in every particular. **cap-a-pe:** from head to foot. 207. **fear-surprised:** overwhelmed by fear. 208. **truncheon:** short staff carried as a symbol of military command.

Almost to jelly with the act of fear,
Stand dumb and speak not to him. This to me
In dreadful secrecy impart they did,
And I with them the third night kept the watch,
Where, as they had delivered, both in time,
Form of the thing, each word made true and good,
The apparition comes. I knew your father,
These hands are not more like.

HAM: But where was this?

MAR: My lord, upon the platform where we watch.

HAM: Did you not speak to it?

HOR: My lord, I did,
But answer made it none. Yet once methought
It lifted up it head and did address
Itself to motion like as it would speak;
But even then the morning cock crew loud,
And at the sound it shrunk in haste away
And vanish'd from our sight.

HAM: 'Tis very strange.

HOR: As I do live, my honor'd lord, 'tis true,
And we did think it writ down in our duty
To let you know of it.

HAM: Indeed, [indeed,] sirs. But this troubles me.
Hold you the watch to-night?

[MAR., BAR.] We do, my lord.

HAM: Arm'd, say you?

[MAR., BAR.] Arm'd, my lord.

HAM: From top to toe?

[MAR., BAR.] My lord, from head to foot.

HAM: Then saw you not his face.

HOR: O yes, my lord, he wore his beaver up.

HAM: What, look'd he frowningly?

HOR: A countenance more
In sorrow than in anger.

HAM: Pale, or red?

HOR: Nay, very pale.

---

209. **act:** action, operation. 211. **dreadful:** held in awe, i.e. solemnly sworn. 216. **are . . . like:** i.e. do not resemble each other more closely than the apparition resembled him. 222. **it:** its. 222–223. **address . . . motion:** begin to make a gesture. 239. **beaver:** visor.

HAM: And fix'd his eyes upon you?
HOR: Most constantly.
HAM: I would I had been there.
HOR: It would have much amaz'd you.
HAM: Very like, [very like]. Stay'd it long?
HOR: While one with moderate haste might tell a hundreth.
Both [MAR., BAR.]. Longer, longer.
HOR: Not when I saw't.
HAM: His beard was grisl'd, no?
HOR: It was, as I have seen it in his life,
A sable silver'd.
HAM: I will watch to-night,
Perchance 'twill walk again.
HOR: I warr'nt it will.
HAM: If it assume my noble father's person,
I'll speak to it though hell itself should gape
And bid me hold my peace. I pray you all,
If you have hitherto conceal'd this sight,
Let it be tenable in your silence still,
And whatsomever else shall hap to-night,
Give it an understanding but no tongue.
I will requite your loves. So fare you well.
Upon the platform 'twixt aleven and twelf
I'll visit you.
All. Our duty to your honor.
HAM: Your loves, as mine to you; farewell.
Exeunt [*all but* HAMLET].

My father's spirit—in arms! All is not well,
I doubt some foul play. Would the night were come!
Till then sit still, my soul. [Foul] deeds will rise,
Though all the earth o'erwhelm them, to men's eyes.
Exit.

Scene III

Enter LAERTES *and* OPHELIA, *his sister.*

LAER: My necessaries are inbark'd. Farewell.

---

250. **tell a hundreth:** count a hundred. 253. **grisl'd:** grizzled, mixed with grey. 263. **tenable:** held close. 267. **aleven:** eleven. 272. **doubt:** suspect.

I.iii. Location: Polonius' quarters in the castle. 1. **inbark'd:** embarked, abroad.

And, sister, as the winds give benefit
And convey [is] assistant, do not sleep,
But let me hear from you.
OPH: Do you doubt that?
LAER: For Hamlet, and the trifling of his favor,
Hold it a fashion and a toy in blood,
A violet in the youth of primy nature,
Forward, not permanent, sweet, not lasting,
The perfume and suppliance of a minute—
No more.
OPH: No more but so?
LAER: Think it no more:
For nature crescent does not grow alone
In thews and [bulk], but as this temple waxes,
The inward service of the mind and soul
Grows wide withal. Perhaps he loves you now,
And now no soil nor cautel doth besmirch
The virtue of his will, but you must fear,
His greatness weigh'd, his will is not his own,
[For he himself is subject to his birth:]
He may not, as unvalued persons do,
Carve for himself, for on his choice depends
The safety and health of this whole state,
And therefore must his choice be circumscrib'd
Unto the voice and yielding of that body
Whereof he is the head. Then if he says he loves you,
It fits your wisdom so far to believe it
As he in his particular act and place
May give his saying deed, which is no further
Than the main voice of Denmark goes withal.

---

3. **convey is assistant:** means of transport is available. 7. **a fashion:** i.e. standard behavior for a young man. **toy in blood:** idle fancy of youthful passion. 8. **primy:** springlike. 9. **Forward:** early of growth. 10. **suppliance:** pastime. 13. **crescent:** growing, increasing. 15. **thews:** muscles, sinews. 15–17. **as . . . withal:** as the body develops, the powers of mind and spirit grow along with it. 18. **soil:** stain. **cautel:** deceit. 19. **will:** desire. 20. **His greatness weigh'd:** considering his princely status. 22. **unvalued:** of low rank. 23. **Carve for himself:** indulge his own wishes. 26. **voice:** vote, approval. **yielding:** consent. **that body:** i.e. the state. 29. **in . . . place:** i.e. acting as he must act in the position he occupies. 31. **main:** general. **goes withal:** accord with.

Then weigh what loss your honor may sustain
If with too credent ear you list his songs,
Or lose your heart, or your chaste treasure open
To his unmast'red importunity.
Fear it, Ophelia, fear it, my dear sister,
And keep you in the rear of your affection,
Out of the shot and danger of desire.
The chariest maid is prodigal enough
If she unmask her beauty to the moon.
Virtue itself scapes not calumnious strokes.
The canker galls the infants of the spring
Too oft before their buttons be disclos'd,
And in the morn and liquid dew of youth
Contagious blastments are most imminent.
Be wary then, best safety lies in fear:
Youth to itself rebels, though none else near.

OPH: I shall the effect of this good lesson keep
As watchman to my heart. But, good my brother,
Do not, as some ungracious pastors do,
Show me the steep and thorny way to heaven,
Whiles, [like] a puff'd and reckless libertine,
Himself the primrose path of dalliance treads,
And reaks not his own rede.

LAER: O, fear me not.

Enter POLONIUS.

I stay too long—but here my father comes.
A double blessing is a double grace,
Occasion smiles upon a second leave.

POL: Yet here, Laertes? Aboard, aboard, for shame!
The wind sits in the shoulder of your sail,
And you are stay'd for. There—[*laying his hand on* LAERTES' *head*]
my blessing with thee!
And these few precepts in thy memory
Look thou character. Give thy thoughts no tongue,

---

33. **credent:** credulous. 38. **shot:** range. 42. **canker:** canker-worm. 43. **buttons:** buds. **disclos'd:** opened. 45. **blastments:** withering blights, 47. **to:** of. 50. **ungracious:** graceless. 52. **puff'd:** bloated. 54. **reaks:** recks, heeds. **rede:** advice. **fear me not:** don't worry about me. 58. **Occasion:** opportunity (here personified, as often). **smiles upon:** i.e. graciously bestows. 63. **character:** inscribe

Nor any unproportion'd thought his act.
Be thou familiar, but by no means vulgar:
Those friends thou hast, and their adoption tried,
Grapple them unto thy soul with hoops of steel,
But do not dull thy palm with entertainment
Of each new-hatch'd, unfledg'd courage. Beware
Of entrance to a quarrel, but being in,
Bear't that th' opposed may beware of thee.
Give every man thy ear, but few thy voice,
Take each man's censure, but reserve thy judgment.
Costly thy habit as thy purse can buy,
But not express'd in fancy, rich, not gaudy,
For the apparel oft proclaims the man,
And they in France of the best rank and station
[Are] of a most select and generous chief in that.
Neither a borrower nor a lender [be],
For [loan] oft loses both itself and friend,
And borrowing dulleth [th'] edge of husbandry.
This above all: to thine own self be true,
And it must follow, as the night the day,
Thou canst not then be false to any man.
Farewell, my blessing season this in thee!

LAER: Most humbly do I take my leave, my lord.

POL: The time invests you, go, your servants tend.

LAER: Farewell, Ophelia, and remember well
What I have said to you.

OPH: 'Tis in my memory lock'd,
And you yourself shall keep the key of it.

LAER: Farewell. *Exit* LAERTES

POL: What is't, Ophelia, he hath said to you?

OPH: So please you, something touching the Lord Hamlet.

POL: Marry, well bethought.
'Tis told me, he hath very oft of late

---

65. **unproportion'd:** unfitting. 66. **familiar:** affable, sociable. **vulgar:** friendly with everybody. 67. **their adoption tried:** their association with you tested and proved. 70. **courage:** spirited, young blood. 72. **Bear't that:** manage it in such a way that. 74. **Take:** listen to. **censure:** opinion. 79. **generous:** noble, **chief:** eminence (?). But the line is probably corrupt. Perhaps *of a* is intrusive, in which case *chief* = chiefly. 82. **husbandry:** thrift. 86. **season:** preserve (?) or ripen, make fruitful (?). 88. **invests:** besieges. **tend:** wait. 95. **Marry:** indeed (originally the name of the Virgin Mary used as an oath).

Given private time to you, and you yourself
Have of your audience been most free and bounteous.
If it be so—as so 'tis put on me,
And that in way of caution—I must tell you,
You do not understand yourself so clearly
As it behooves my daughter and your honor.
What is between you? Give me up the truth.

OPH: He hath, my lord, of late made many tenders
Of his affection to me.

POL: Affection, puh! You speak like a green girl,
Unsifted in such perilous circumstance.
Do you believe his tenders, as you call them?

OPH: I do not know, my lord, what I should think.

POL: Marry, I will teach you: think yourself a baby
That you have ta'en these tenders for true pay,
Which are not sterling. Tender yourself more dearly,
Or (not to crack the wind of the poor phrase,
[Wringing] it thus) you'll tender me a fool.

OPH: My lord, he hath importun'd me with love
In honorable fashion.

POL: Ay, fashion you may call it. Go to, go to.

OPH: And hath given countenance to his speech, my lord,
With almost all the holy vows of heaven.

POL: Ay, springes to catch woodcocks. I do know,
When the blood burns, how prodigal the soul
Lends the tongue vows. These blazes, daughter,
Giving more light than heat, extinct in both
Even in their promise, as it is a-making,
You must not take for fire. From this time
Be something scanter of your maiden presence,
Set your entreatments at a higher rate
Than a command to parle. For Lord Hamlet,

---

99. **put on:** told to. 104. **tenders:** offers. 107. **Unsifted:** untried. 111. **tenders.** With play on the sense "money offered in payment" (as in *legal tender*). 112. **Tender:** hold, value. 114. **Wringing:** straining, forcing to the limit. **tender . . . fool:** (1) show me that you are a fool; (2) make me look like a fool; (3) present me with a (bastard) grandchild. 117. **fashion.** See note on line 7. 118. **countenance:** authority. 120. **springes:** snares. **woodcocks.** Proverbially gullible birds. 127–128. **Set . . . parle:** place a higher value on your favors; do not grant interviews simply because he asks for them. Polonius uses a military figure: *entreatments* = negotiations for surrender; *parle* = parley, discuss terms.

Believe so much in him, that he is young,
And with a larger teder may he walk
Than may be given you. In few, Ophelia,
Do not believe his vows, for they are brokers,
Not of that dye which their investments show,
But mere [implorators] of unholy suits,
Breathing like sanctified and pious bonds,
The better to [beguile]. This is for all:
I would not, in plain terms, from this time forth
Have you so slander any moment leisure
As to give words or talk with the Lord Hamlet.
Look to't, I charge you. Come your ways.
OPH: I shall obey, my lord. *Exeunt.*

Scene IV

Enter HAMLET, HORATIO, *and* MARCELLUS.

HAM: The air bites shrowdly, it is very cold.
HOR: It is [a] nipping and an eager air.
HAM: What hour now?
HOR: I think it lacks of twelf.
MAR: No, it is strook.
HOR: Indeed? I heard it not. It then draws near the season
Wherein the spirit held his wont to walk.

A flourish of trumpets, and two pieces goes off [*within*].

What does this mean, my lord?
HAM: The King doth wake to-night and takes his rouse,
Keeps wassail, and the swagg'ring up-spring reels;
And as he drains his draughts of Rhenish down,
The kettle-drum and trumpet thus bray out

---

129. **so . . . him:** no more than this with respect to him. 130. **larger teder:** longer tether. 132. **brokers:** procuers. 133. **Not . . . show:** not of the color that their garments (*investments*) exhibit, i.e. not what they seem. 134. **mere:** out-and-out. 135. **bonds:** (lover's) vows or assurances. Many editors follow Theobald in reading *bawds.* 138. **slander:** disgrace. **moment:** momentary. 140. **Come your ways:** come along.

I.iv. Location: The guard-platform of the castle. 1. **shrowdly:** shrewdly, wickedly. 2. **eager:** sharp. 8. s.d. **pieces:** cannon. 9. **doth . . . rouse:** i.e. holds revels far into the night. 10. **wassail:** carousal, **up-spring:** wild dance. 11. **Rhenish:** Rhine wine.

The triumph of his pledge.
HOR: Is it a custom?
HAM: Ay, marry, is't,
But to my mind, though I am native here
And to the manner born, it is a custom
More honor'd in the breach than the observance.
This heavy-headed revel east and west
Makes us traduc'd and tax'd of other nations.
They clip us drunkards, and with swinish phrase
Soil our addition, and indeed it takes
From our achievements, though perform'd at height,
The pith and marrow of our attribute.
So, oft it chances in particular men,
That for some vicious mole of nature in them,
As in their birth, wherein they are not guilty
(Since nature cannot choose his origin),
By their o'ergrowth of some complexion
Oft breaking down the pales and forts of reason,
Or by some habit, that too much o'er-leavens
The form of plausive manners—that these men,
Carrying, I say, the stamp of one defect,
Being nature's livery, or fortune's star,
His virtues else, be they as pure as grace,
As infinite as man may undergo,
Shall in the general censure take corruption
From that particular fault: the dram of [ev'l]
Doth all the noble substance of a doubt

---

13. **triumph . . . pledge:** accomplishment of his toast (by draining his cup at a single draught). 17. **manner:** custom (of carousing). 18. **More . . . observance:** which it is more honorable to break than to observe. 20. **tax'd of:** censured by. 21. **clip:** clepe, call. 22. **addition:** titles of honor. 23. **at height:** most excellently. 24. **attribute:** reputation. 25. **particular:** individual. 26. **vicious . . . nature:** small natural blemish. 28. **his:** its. 29. **By . . . complexion:** by the excess of some one of the humors (which were thought to govern the disposition). 30. **pales:** fences. 31. **o'er-leavens:** makes itself felt throughout (as leaven works in the whole mass of dough). 32. **plausive:** pleasing. 34. **Being . . . star:** i.e. whether they were born with it, or got it by misfortune. *Star* means "blemish," 36. **undergo:** carry the weight of, sustain. 37. **general censure:** popular opinion. 38. **dram:** minute amount. **ev'l:** evil, with a pun on *eale,* "yeast" (cf. *o'er-leavens* in line 31). 39. **of a doubt.** A famous crux, for which many emendations have been suggested, the most widely accepted being Steevens' *often dout* (i.e. extinguish).

To his own scandal.

Enter GHOST.

HOR: Look, my lord, it comes!
HAM: Angels and ministers of grace defend us!
Be thou a spirit of health, or goblin damn'd,
Bring with thee airs from heaven, or blasts from hell,
Be thy intents wicked, or charitable,
Thou com'st in such a questionable shape
That I will speak to thee. I'll call thee Hamlet,
King, father, royal Dane. O, answer me!
Let me not burst in ignorance, but tell
Why thy canoniz'd bones, hearsed in death,
Have burst their cerements; why the sepulchre,
Wherein we saw thee quietly [inurn'd,]
Hath op'd his ponderous and marble jaws
To cast thee up again. What may this mean,
That thou, dead corse, again in complete steel
Revisits thus the glimpses of the moon,
Making night hideous, and we fools of nature
So horridly to shake our disposition
With thoughts beyond the reaches of our souls?
Say why is this? wherefore? what should we do?

[GHOST] *beckons* [HAMLET].

HOR: It beckons you to go away with it,
As if it some impartment did desire
To you alone.
MAR: Look with what courteous action
It waves you to a more removed ground,
But do not go with it.
HOR: No, by no means.
HAM: It will not speak, then I will follow it.
HOR: Do not, my lord.

---

40. **To . . . scandal:** i.e. so that it all shares in the disgrace. 43. **of health:** wholesome, good. 46. **questionable:** inviting talk. 50. **canoniz'd:** buried with the prescribed rites. 51. **cerements:** grave-clothes. 55. **complete steel:** full armor. 56. **Revisits.** The *-s* ending in the second person singular is common. 57. **fools of nature:** the children (or the dupes) of a purely natural order, baffled by the supernatural. 58. **disposition:** nature. 62. **impartment:** communication.

HAM: Why, what should be the fear?
I do not set my life at a pin's fee,
And for my soul, what can it do to that,
Being a thing immortal as itself?
It waves me forth again, I'll follow it.
HOR: What if it tempt you toward the flood, my lord,
Or to the dreadful summit of the cliff
That beetles o'er his base into the sea,
And there assume some other horrible form
Which might deprive your sovereignty of reason,
And draw you into madness? Think of it.
The very place puts toys of desperation,
Without more motive, into every brain
That looks so many fadoms to the sea
And hears it roar beneath.
HAM: It waves me still.—
Go on, I'll follow thee.
MAR: You shall not go, my lord.
HAM: Hold off your hands.
HOR: Be rul'd, you shall not go.
HAM: My fate cries out,
And makes each petty artere in this body
As hardy as the Nemean lion's nerve.
Still am I call'd. Unhand me, gentlemen.
By heaven, I'll make a ghost of him that lets me!
I say away!—Go on, I'll follow thee.

Exeunt GHOST *and* HAMLET.

HOR: He waxes desperate with [imagination].
MAR: Let's follow. 'Tis not fit thus to obey him.
HOR: Have after. To what issue will this come?
MAR: Something is rotten in the state of Denmark.
HOR: Heaven will direct it.
MAR: Nay, let's follow him. *Exeunt.*

---

70. **fee:** worth. 79. **deprive . . . reason:** unseat reason from the rule of your mind. 81. **toys of desperation:** fancies of desperate action, i.e inclinations to jump off. 83. **fadoms:** fathoms. 91. **artere:** variant spelling of *artery;* here, ligament, sinew. 92. **Nemean lion**. Slain by Hercules as one of his twelve labors. **nerve:** sinew. 94. **lets:** hinders. 100. **it:** i.e. the issue.

Scene V

Enter Ghost *and* Hamlet.

HAM: Whither wilt thou lead me? Speak, I'll go no further.
GHOST: Mark me.
HAM: I will.
GHOST: My hour is almost come
When I to sulph'rous and tormenting flames
Must render up myself.
HAM: Alas, poor ghost!
GHOST: Pity me not, but lend thy serious hearing
To what I shall unfold.
HAM: Speak, I am bound to hear.
GHOST: So art thou to revenge, when thou shalt hear.
HAM: What?
GHOST: I am thy father's spirit,
Doom'd for a certain term to walk the night,
And for the day confin'd to fast in fires,
Till the foul crimes done in my days of nature
Are burnt and purg'd away. But that I am forbid
To tell the secrets of my prison-house,
I could a tale unfold whose lightest word
Would harrow up thy soul, freeze thy young blood,
Make thy two eyes like stars start from their spheres,
Thy knotted and combined locks to part,
And each particular hair to stand an end,
Like quills upon the fearful porpentine.
But this eternal blazon must not be
To ears of flesh and blood. List, list, O, list!
If thou didst ever thy dear father love—
HAM: O God!
GHOST: Revenge his foul and most unnatural murther.
HAM: Murther!
GHOST: Murther most foul, as in the best it is,
But this most foul, strange, and unnatural.
HAM: Haste me to know't, that I with wings as swift

I.v. Location: On the battlements of the castle.

15. **fast:** do penance. 16. **crimes:** sins. 21. **spheres:** eye-sockets; with allusion to the revolving spheres in which, according to the Ptolemaic astronomy, the stars were fixed. 23. **an end:** on end. 24. **fearful porpentine:** frightened porcupine. 25. **eternal blazon:** revelation of eternal things.

As meditation, or the thoughts of love,
May sweep to my revenge.
GHOST: I find thee apt,
And duller shouldst thou be than the fat weed
That roots itself in ease on Lethe wharf,
Wouldst thou not stir in this. Now, Hamlet, hear:
'Tis given out that, sleeping in my orchard,
A serpent stung me, so the whole ear of Denmark
Is by a forged process of my death
Rankly abus'd; but know, thou noble youth,
The serpent that did sting thy father's life
Now wears his crown.
HAM: O my prophetic soul!
My uncle?
GHOST: Ay, that incestuous, that adulterate beast,
With witchcraft of his wits, with traitorous gifts—
O wicked wit and gifts that have the power
So to seduce!—won to his shameful lust
The will of my most seeming virtuous queen.
O Hamlet, what [a] falling-off was there
From me, whose love was of that dignity
That it went hand in hand even with the vow
I made to her in marriage, and to decline
Upon a wretch whose natural gifts were poor
To those of mine!
But virtue, as it never will be moved,
Though lewdness court it in a shape of heaven,
So [lust], though to a radiant angel link'd,
Will [sate] itself in a celestial bed
And prey on garbage.
But soft, methinks I scent the morning air,
Brief let me be. Sleeping within my orchard,
My custom always of the afternoon,
Upon my secure hour thy uncle stole,
With juice of cursed hebona in a vial,

---

34. **meditation:** thought. 38. **Lethe:** river of Hades, the water of which made the drinker forget the past. **wharf:** bank. 40. **orchard:** garden. 42. **forged process:** false account. 43. **abus'd:** deceived. 48. **adulterate:** adulterous. 60. **shape of heaven:** angelic form. 67. **secure:** carefree. 68. **hebona:** ebony (which Shakespeare, following a literary tradition, and perhaps also associating the word with *henbane,* thought the name of a poison).

And in the porches of my ears did pour
The leprous distillment, whose effect
Holds such an enmity with blood of man
That swift as quicksilver it courses through
The natural gates and alleys of the body,
And with a sudden vigor it doth [posset]
And curd, like eager droppings into milk,
The thin and wholesome blood. So did it mine,
And a most instant tetter bark'd about,
Most lazar-like, with vile and loathsome crust
All my smooth body.
Thus was I, sleeping, by a brother's hand
Of life, of crown, of queen, at once dispatch'd,
Cut off even in the blossoms of my sin,
Unhous'led, disappointed, unanel'd,
No reck'ning made, but sent to my account
With all my imperfections on my head.
O, horrible, O, horrible, most horrible!
If thou hast nature in thee, bear it not,
Let not the royal bed of Denmark be
A couch for luxury and damned incest.
But howsomever thou pursues this act,
Taint not thy mind, nor let thy soul contrive
Against thy mother aught. Leave her to heaven,
And to those thorns that in her bosom lodge
To prick and sting her. Fare thee well at once!
The glow-worm shows the matin to be near,
And gins to pale his uneffectual fire.
Adieu, adieu, adieu! remember me. [*Exit.*]

HAM: O all you host of heaven! O earth! What else?
And shall I couple hell? O fie, hold, hold, my heart,
And you, my sinows, grow not instant old,
But bear me [stiffly] up. Remember thee!
Ay, thou poor ghost, whiles memory holds a seat
In this distracted globe. Remember thee!

---

74. **posset:** curdle. 75. **eager:** sour. 77. **tetter:** scabby eruption. **bark'd:** formed a hard covering, like bark on a tree. 78. **lazar-like:** leper-like. 81. **at once:** all at the same time. **dispatch'd:** deprived. 83. **Unhous'led:** without the Eucharist. **disappointed:** without (spiritual) preparation. **unanel'd:** unanointed, without extreme unction. 87. **nature:** natural feeling. 89. **luxury:** lust. 95. **matin:** morning. 96. **gins:** begins. 100. **sinows:** sinews. 103. **globe:** head.

Yea, from the table of my memory
I'll wipe away all trivial fond records,
All saws of books, all forms, all pressures past
That youth and observation copied there,
And thy commandement all alone shall live
Within the book and volume of my brain,
Unmix'd with baser matter. Yes, by heaven!
O most pernicious woman!
O villain, villain, smiling, damned villain!
My tables—meet it is I set it down
That one may smile, and smile, and be a villain!
At least I am sure it may be so in Denmark.

[*He writes.*]

So, uncle, there you are. Now to my word:
It is "Adieu, adieu! remember me."
I have sworn't.

HOR [*Within.*]: My lord, my lord!
MAR [*Within.*]: Lord Hamlet!

Enter HORATIO *and* MARCELLUS.

HOR: Heavens secure him!
HAM: So be it!
MAR: Illo, ho, ho, my lord!
HAM: Hillo, ho, ho, boy! Come, [bird,] come.
MAR: How is't, my noble lord?
HOR: What news, my lord?
HAM: O, wonderful!
HOR: Good my lord, tell it.
HAM: No, you will reveal it.
HOR: Not I, my lord, by heaven.
MAR: Nor I, my lord.
HAM: How say you then, would heart of man once think it?—
But you'll be secret?
Both [HOR., MAR.]: Ay, by heaven, [my lord].
HAM: There's never a villain dwelling in all Denmark
But he's an arrant knave.

---

104. **table:** writing tablet. 105. **fond:** foolish. 106. **saws:** wise sayings. **forms:** shapes, images. **pressures:** impressions. 116. **word:** i.e. word of command from the Ghost. 124. **Hillo . . . come.** Hamlet answers Marcellus' halloo with a falconer's cry.

HOR: There needs no ghost, my lord, come from the grave
To tell us this.
HAM: Why, right, you are in the right,
And so, without more circumstance at all,
I hold it fit that we shake hands and part,
You, as your business and desire shall point you,
For every man hath business and desire,
Such as it is, and for my own poor part,
I will go pray.
HOR: These are but wild and whirling words, my lord.
HAM: I am sorry they offend you, heartily,
Yes, faith, heartily.
HOR: There's no offense, my lord.
HAM: Yes, by Saint Patrick, but there is, Horatio,
And much offense too. Touching this vision here,
It is an honest ghost, that let me tell you.
For your desire to know what is between us,
O'ermaster't as you may. And now, good friends,
As you are friends, scholars, and soldiers,
Give me one poor request.
HOR: What is't, my lord, we will.
HAM: Never make known what you have seen tonight.
Both [HOR., MAR.]: My lord, we will not.
HAM: Nay, but swear't.
HOR: In faith,
My lord, not I.
MAR: Nor I, my lord, in faith.
HAM: Upon my sword.
MAR: We have sworn, my lord, already.
HAM: Indeed, upon my sword, indeed.

GHOST *cries under the stage.*

GHOST: Swear.
HAM: Ha, ha, boy, say'st thou so? Art thou there, truepenny?
Come on, you hear this fellow in the cellarage,
Consent to swear.
HOR: Propose the oath, my lord.

---

140. **circumstance:** ceremony. 152. **honest:** true, genuine. 157. **What is't:** whatever it is. 164. **Upon my sword:** i.e. on the cross formed by the hilt. 168. **truepenny:** trusty fellow.

HAM: Never to speak of this that you have seen,
Swear by my sword.
GHOST [*Beneath.*]: Swear.
HAM: *Hic et ubique?* Then we'll shift our ground.
Come hither, gentlemen,
And lay your hands again upon my sword.
Swear by my sword
Never to speak of this that you have heard.
GHOST [*Beneath.*]: Swear by his sword.
HAM: Well said, old mole, canst work i' th' earth so fast?
A worthy pioner! Once more remove, good friends.
HOR: O day and night, but this is wondrous strange!
HAM: And therefore as a stranger give it welcome.
There are more things in heaven and earth, Horatio,
Than are dreamt of in your philosophy.
But come—
Here, as before, never, so help you mercy,
How strange or odd some'er I bear myself—
As I perchance hereafter shall think meet
To put an antic disposition on—
That you, at such times seeing me, never shall,
With arms encumb'red thus, or this headshake,
Or by pronouncing of some doubtful phrase,
As "Well, well, we know," or "We could, and if we would,"
Or "If we list to speak," or "There be, and if they might,"
Or such ambiguous giving out, to note
That you know aught of me—this do swear,
So grace and mercy at your most need help you.
GHOST [*Beneath.*]: Swear. [*They swear.*]
HAM: Rest, rest, perturbed spirit! So, gentlemen,
With all my love I do commend me to you,
And what so poor a man as Hamlet is
May do t' express his love and friending to you,
God willing, shall not lack. Let us go in together,
And still your fingers on your lips, I pray.

---

175. **Hic et ubique:** here and everywhere. 182. **pioner:** digger, miner (variant of *pioneer*). 184. **as . . . welcome:** give it the welcome due in courtesy to strangers. 186. **your.** See note on I.i. 151. **philosophy:** i.e. natural philosophy, science. 191. **put . . . on:** behave in some fantastic manner, act like a madman. 193. **encumb'red:** folded. 195. **and if:** if. 196. **list:** cared, had a mind. 197. **note:** indicate. 206. **still:** always.

The time is out of joint—O cursed spite,
That ever I was born to set it right!
Nay, come, let's go together. *Exeunt.*

Act II

Scene I

Enter old POLONIUS *with his man* [REYNALDO].

POL: Give him this money and these notes, Reynaldo.
REY: I will, my lord.
POL: You shall do marvell's wisely, good Reynaldo,
Before you visit him, to make inquire
Of his behavior.
REY: My lord, I did intend it.
POL: Marry, well said, very well said. Look you, sir,
Inquire me first what Danskers are in Paris,
And how, and who, what means, and where they keep,
What company, at what expense, and finding
By this encompassment and drift of question
That they do know my son, come you more nearer
Than your particular demands will touch it.
Take you as 'twere some distant knowledge of him,
As thus, "I know his father and his friends,
And in part him." Do you mark this, Reynaldo?
REY: Ay, very well, my lord.
POL: "And in part him—but," you may say, "not well.
But if't be he I mean, he's very wild,
Addicted so and so," and there put on him
What forgeries you please: marry, none so rank
As may dishonor him, take heed of that,
But, sir, such wanton, wild, and usual slips
As are companions noted and most known
To youth and liberty.
REY: As gaming, my lord.
POL: Ay, or drinking, fencing, swearing, quarrelling,
Drabbing—you may go so far.

---

209. **Nay . . . together.** They are holding back to let him go first.

II.i. Location: Polonius' quarters in the castle. 3. **marvell's:** marvellous(ly). 7. **Danskers:** Danes. 8. **keep:** lodge. 10. **encompassment:** circuitousness. **drift of question:** directing of the conversation. 12. **particular demands:** direct questions. 20. **forgeries:** invented charges. 22. **wanton:** sportive. 27. **Drabbing:** whoring.

REY: My lord, that would dishonor him.
POL: Faith, as you may season it in the charge:
You must not put another scandal on him,
That he is open to incontinency—
That's not my meaning. But breathe his faults so quaintly
That they may seem the taints of liberty,
The flash and outbreak of a fiery mind,
A savageness in unreclaimed blood,
Of general assault.
REY: But, my good lord—
POL: Wherefore should you do this?
REY: Ay, my lord,
I would know that.
POL: Marry, sir, here's my drift,
And I believe it is a fetch of wit:
You laying these slight sallies on my son,
As 'twere a thing a little soil'd [wi' th'] working,
Mark you,
Your party in converse, him you would sound,
Having ever seen in the prenominate crimes
The youth you breathe of guilty, be assur'd
He closes with you in this consequence:
"Good sir," or so, or "friend," or "gentleman,"
According to the phrase or the addition
Of man and country.
REY: Very good, my lord.
POL: And then, sir, does 'a this—'a does—what was
I about to say?
By the mass, I was about to say something.
Where did I leave?
REY: At "closes in the consequence."
POL: At "closes in the consequence," ay, marry.
He closes thus: "I know the gentleman.
I saw him yesterday, or th' other day,

---

29. **Faith.** Most editors read *Faith, no,* this makes easier sense. **season:** qualify, temper. 31. **open to incontinency:** habitually profligate. 32. **quaintly:** artfully. 35. **unreclaimed:** untamed. 36. **Of general assault:** i.e. to which young men are generally subject. 42. **fetch of wit:** ingenious device. 43. **sallies:** sullies, blemishes. 44. **soil'd . . . working:** i.e. shopworn. 47. **Having:** if he has. **prenominate crimes:** aforementioned faults. 49. **closes:** falls in. **in this consequence:** as follows. 51. **addition:** style of address.

Or then, or then, with such or such, and as you say,
There was 'a gaming, there o'ertook in 's rouse,
There falling out at tennis"; or, perchance,
"I saw him enter such a house of sale,"
Videlicet, a brothel, or so forth. See you now,
Your bait of falsehood take this carp of truth,
And thus do we of wisdom and of reach,
With windlasses and with assays of bias,
By indirections find directions out;
So by my former lecture and advice
Shall you my son. You have me, have you not?

REY: My lord, I have.

POL: God buy ye, fare ye well.

REY: Good my lord.

POL: Observe his inclination in yourself.

REY: I shall, my lord.

POL: And let him ply his music.

REY: Well, my lord.

POL: Farewell. *Exit* REYNALDO.

Enter OPHELIA.

How now, Ophelia, what's the matter?

OPH. O my lord, my lord, I have been so affrighted!

POL: With what, i' th' name of God?

OPH. My lord, as I was sewing in my closet,
Lord Hamlet, with his doublet all unbrac'd,
No hat upon his head, his stockins fouled,
Ungart'red, and down-gyved to his ankle,
Pale as his shirt, his knees knocking each other,
And with a look so piteous in purport
As if he had been loosed out of hell
To speak of horrors—he comes before me.

---

63. **o'ertook in 's rouse:** overcome by drink. 68. **reach:** capacity, understanding. 69. **windlasses:** roundabout methods. **assays of bias:** indirect attempts (a figure from the game of bowls, in which the player must make allowance for the curving course his bowl will take toward its mark). 70. **directions:** the way things are going. 72. **have me:** understand me. 74. **God buy ye:** good-bye (a contraction of *God be with you*). 76. **in:** by. Polonius asks him to observe Laertes directly, as well as making inquiries. 78. **let him ply:** see that he goes on with. 84. **closet:** private room. 85. **unbrac'd:** unlaced. 86. **stockins fouled:** stockings dirty. 87. **down-gyved:** hanging down like fetters on a prisoner's legs.

POL: Mad for thy love?
OPH: My lord, I do not know,
But truly I do fear it.
POL: What said he?
OPH: He took me by the wrist, and held me hard,
Then goes he to the length of all his arm,
And with his other hand thus o'er his brow,
He falls to such perusal of my face
As 'a would draw it. Long stay'd he so.
At last, a little shaking of mine arm,
And thrice his head thus waving up and down,
He rais'd a sigh so piteous and profound
As it did seem to shatter all his bulk
And end his being. That done, he lets me go,
And with his head over his shoulder turn'd,
He seem'd to find his way without his eyes,
For out a' doors he went without their helps,
And to the last bended their light on me.
POL: Come, go with me. I will go seek the King.
This is the very ecstasy of love,
Whose violent property fordoes itself,
And leads the will to desperate undertakings
As oft as any passions under heaven
That does afflict our natures. I am sorry—
What, have you given him any hard words of late?
OPH: No, my good lord, but as you did command
I did repel his letters, and denied
His access to me.
POL: That hath made him mad.
I am sorry that with better heed and judgment
I had not coted him. I fear'd he did but trifle
And meant to wrack thee, but beshrow my jealousy!
By heaven, it is as proper to our age
To cast beyond ourselves in our opinions,
As it is common for the younger sort
To lack discretion. Come, go we to the King.

---

104. **bulk:** body. 111. **ecstasy:** madness. 112. **property:** quality. **fordoes:** destroys. 122. **coted:** observed. 123. **beshrow:** beshrew, plague take. **jealousy:** suspicious mind. 124. **proper . . . age:** characteristic of men of my age. 125. **cast beyond ourselves:** overshoot, go too far (by way of caution).

This must be known, which, being kept close, might move
More grief to hide, than hate to utter love.
Come. *Exeunt.*

Scene II

Flourish. Enter KING *and* QUEEN, ROSENCRANTZ *and* GUILDENSTERN [*cum aliis*].

KING: Welcome, dear Rosencrantz and Guildenstern!
Moreover that we much did long to see you,
The need we have to use you did provoke
Our hasty sending. Something have you heard
Of Hamlet's transformation; so call it,
Sith nor th' exterior nor the inward man
Resembles that it was. What it should be,
More than his father's death, that thus hath put him
So much from th' understanding of himself,
I cannot dream of. I entreat you both
That, being of so young days brought up with him,
And sith so neighbored to his youth and havior,
That you voutsafe your rest here in our court
Some little time, so by your companies
To draw him on to pleasures, and to gather
So much as from occasion you may glean,
Whether aught to us unknown afflicts him thus,
That, open'd, lies within our remedy.
QUEEN: Good gentlemen, he hath much talk'd of you,
And sure I am two men there is not living
To whom he more adheres. If it will please you
To show us so much gentry and good will
As to expend your time with us a while
For the supply and profit of our hope,
Your visitation shall receive such thanks
As fits a king's remembrance.
ROS: Both your Majesties
Might, by the sovereign power you have of us,

---

128. **close:** secret. 128–129. **move . . . love:** cause more grievous consequences by its concealment than we shall incur displeasure by making it known.

II.ii. Location: The castle. 2. **Moreover . . . you:** besides the fact that we wanted to see you for your own sakes. 6. **Sith:** since. 11. **of:** from. 13. **voutsafe your rest:** vouchsafe to remain. 21. **more adheres:** is more attached. 22. **gentry:** courtesy. 24. **supply and profit:** support and advancement.

Put your dread pleasures more into command
Than to entreaty.

GUIL: But we both obey,
And here give up ourselves, in the full bent,
To lay our service freely at your feet,
To be commanded.

KING: Thanks, Rosencrantz and gentle Guildenstern.

QUEEN: Thanks, Guildenstern and gentle Rosencrantz.
And I beseech you instantly to visit
My too much changed son. Go some of you
And bring these gentlemen where Hamlet is.

GUIL: Heavens make our presence and our practices
Pleasant and helpful to him!

QUEEN: Ay, amen!

Exeunt ROSENCRANTZ *and* GUILDENSTERN [*with some Attendants*].

Enter POLONIUS.

POL: Th' embassadors from Norway, my good lord,
Are joyfully return'd.

KING: Thou still hast been the father of good news.

POL: Have I, my lord? I assure my good liege
I hold my duty as I hold my soul,
Both to my God and to my gracious king;
And I do think, or else this brain of mine
Hunts not the trail of policy so sure
As it hath us'd to do, that I have found
The very cause of Hamlet's lunacy.

KING: O, speak of that, that do I long to hear.

POL: Give first admittance to th' embassadors;
My news shall be the fruit to that great feast.

KING: Thyself do grace to them, and bring them in. [*Exit* POLONIUS.]
He tells me, my dear Gertrude, he hath found
The head and source of all your son's distemper.

QUEEN: I doubt it is no other but the main,
His father's death and our [o'erhasry] marriage.

Enter [POLONIUS *with* VOLTEMAND *and* CORNELIUS, *the*] *Embassadors.*

---

32. **in . . . bent:** to our utmost. 43. **embassadors:** ambassador. 45. **still:** always. 46. **liege:** sovereign. 50. **policy:** statecraft. 55. **fruit:** dessert. 58. **head.** Synonymous with *source.* **distemper:** (mental) illness. 59. **doubt:** suspect. **main:** main cause.

KING: Well, we shall sift him.—Welcome, my good friends!
Say, Voltemand, what from our brother Norway?
VOL: Most fair return of greetings and desires.
Upon our first, he sent out to suppress
His nephew's levies, which to him appear'd
To be a preparation 'gainst the Polack;
But better look'd into, he truly found
It was against your Highness. Whereat griev'd,
That so his sickness, age, and impotence
Was falsely borne in hand, sends out arrests
On Fortinbras, which he, in brief, obeys,
Receives rebuke from Norway, and in fine,
Makes vow before his uncle never more
To give th' assay of arms against your Majesty.
Whereon old Norway, overcome with joy,
Gives him three thousand crowns in annual fee,
And his commission to employ those soldiers,
So levied, as before, against the Polack,
With an entreaty, herein further shown,

[*Giving a paper.*]

That it might please you to give quiet pass
Through your dominions for this enterprise,
On such regards of safety and allowance
As therein are set down.
KING: It likes us well,
And at our more considered time we'll read,
Answer, and think upon this business.
Mean time, we thank you for your well-took labor.
Go to your rest, at night we'll feast together.
Most welcome home!

Exeunt Embassadors [*and Attendants*].

POL: This business is well ended.
My liege, and madam, to expostulate
What majesty should be, what duty is,
Why day is day, night night, and time is time,

---

64. **Upon our first:** at our first representation. 68. **griev'd:** aggrieved, offended. 70. **borne in hand:** taken advantage of. 72. **in fine:** in the end. 74. **assay:** trial. 82. **On . . . allowance:** with such safeguards and provisos, 84. **likes:** pleases. 85. **consider'd:** suitable for consideration. 91. **expostulate:** expound.

Were nothing but to waste night, day, and time,
Therefore, [since] brevity is the soul of wit,
And tediousness the limbs and outward flourishes,
I will be brief. Your noble son is mad:
Mad call I it, for to define true madness,
What is't but to be nothing else but mad?
But let that go.

QUEEN: More matter with less art.

POL: Madam, I swear I use no art at all.
That he's mad, 'tis true, 'tis true 'tis pity,
And pity 'tis 'tis true—a foolish figure,
But farewell it, for I will use no art.
Mad let us grant him then, and now remains
That we find out the cause of this effect,
Or rather say, the cause of this defect,
For this effect defective comes by cause:
Thus it remains, and the remainder thus.
Perpend.
I have a daughter—have while she is mine—
Who in her duty and obedience, mark,
Hath given me this. Now gather, and surmise.

[*Reads the salutation of the letter.*]

"To the celestial and my soul's idol, the most beautified Ophelia"—
That's an ill phrase, a vile phrase, "beautified" is a vile phrase.
But you shall hear. Thus:
"In her excellent white bosom, these, etc."

QUEEN: Came this from Hamlet to her?

POL: Good madam, stay awhile. I will be faithful.

[*Reads the*] *letter.*

"Doubt thou the stars are fire,
Doubt that the sun doth move,
Doubt truth to be a liar,
But never doubt I love.
O dear Ophelia, I am ill at these numbers. I have not

---

95. **wit:** understanding, wisdom. 101. **art:** i.e. rhetorical art, 104. **figure:** figure of speech. 109. **For . . . cause:** for this effect (which shows as a defect in Hamlet's reason) is not merely accidental, and has a cause we may trace. 111. **Perpend:** consider. 115–16. **beautified:** beautiful (not an uncommon usage). 121. **Doubt:** suspect. 125. **ill . . . numbers:** bad at versifying.

art to reckon my groans, but that I love thee best, O
most best, believe it. Adieu.
Thine evermore, most dear lady,
whilst this machine is to him, Hamlet."
This in obedience hath my daughter shown me,
And more [above], hath his solicitings,
As they fell out by time, by means, and place,
All given to mine ear.

KING: But how hath she
Receiv'd his love?

POL: What do you think of me?

KING: As of a man faithful and honorable.

POL: I would fain prove so. But what might you think,
When I had seen this hot love on the wing—
As I percciv'd it (I must tell you that)
Before my daughter told me—what might you,
Or my dear Majesty your queen here, think,
If I had play'd the desk or table-book,
Or given my heart a [winking,] mute and dumb,
Or look'd upon this love with idle sight,
What might you think? No, I went round to work,
And my young mistress thus I did bespeak:
"Lord Hamlet is a prince out of thy star;
This must not be"; and then I prescripts gave her,
That she should lock herself from [his] resort,
Admit no messengers, receive no tokens.
Which done, she took the fruits of my advice;
And he repell'd, a short tale to make,
Fell into a sadness, then into a fast,
Thence to a watch, thence into a weakness,
Thence to [a] lightness, and by this declension,
Into the madness wherein now he raves,
And all we mourn for.

KING: Do you think ['tis] this?

QUEEN: It may be, very like.

---

126. **reckon:** count (with a quibble on *numbers*). 129. **machine:** body. 131. **more above:** furthermore. 138. **fain:** willingly, gladly. 143. **play'd . . . table-book:** i.e. noted the matter secretly. 144. **winking:** closing of the eyes. 145. **idle sight:** noncomprehending eyes. 146. **round:** straightforwardly. 147. **bespeak:** address. 148. **star:** i.e. sphere, lot in life. 152. **took . . . of:** profited by, i.e. carried out. 153. **repell'd:** repulsed. 155. **watch:** sleeplessness. 156. **lightness:** lightheadedness.

POL: Hath there been such a time—I would fain know that—
That I have positively said, " 'Tis so,"
When it prov'd otherwise?
KING: Not that I know.
POL [*Points to his head and shoulder.*]: Take this from this, if this be otherwise.
If circumstances lead me, I will find
Where truth is hid, though it were hid indeed
Within the centre.
KING: How may we try it further?
POL: You know sometimes he walks four hours together
Here in the lobby.
QUEEN: So he does indeed.
POL: At such a time I'll loose my daughter to him.
Be you and I behind an arras then,
Mark the encounter: if he love her not,
And be not from his reason fall'n thereon,
Let me be no assistant for a state,
But keep a farm and carters.
KING: We will try it.

Enter HAMLET [*reading on a book*].

QUEEN: But look where sadly the poor wretch comes reading.
POL: Away, I do beseech you, both away.
I'll board him presently.

Exeunt KING *and* QUEEN.

O, give me leave,
How does my good Lord Hamlet?
HAM: Well, God-a-mercy.
POL: Do you know me, my lord?
HAM: Excellent well, you are a fishmonger.
POL: Not I, my lord.
HAM: Then I would you were so honest a man.
POL: Honest, my lord?
HAM: Ay, sir, to be honest, as this world goes, is to be one man pick'd out of ten thousand.

---

169. **centre:** i.e. of the earth (which in the Ptolemaic system is also the centre of the universe). 175. **arras:** hanging tapestry. 177. **thereon:** because of that. 183. **board:** accost. **presently:** at once. 186. **God-a-mercy:** thank you. 188. **fishmonger.** Usually explained as slang for "bawd," but no evidence has been produced for such a usage in Shakespeare's day.

POL: That's very true, my lord.

HAM: For if the sun breed maggots in a dead dog, being a good kissing carrion—Have you a daughter?

POL: I have, my lord.

HAM: Let her not walk i' th' sun. Conception is a blessing, but as your daughter may conceive, friend, look to't.

POL [*Aside.*]: How say you by that? still harping on my daughter. Yet he knew me not at first, 'a said I was a fishmonger. 'A is far gone. And truly in my youth I suff'red much extremity for love—very near this. I'll speak to him again.—What do you read, my lord?

HAM: Words, words, words.

POL: What is the matter, my lord?

HAM: Between who?

POL: I mean, the matter that you read, my lord.

HAM: Slanders, sir; for the satirical rogue says here that old men have grey beards, that their faces are wrinkled, their eyes purging thick amber and plum-tree gum, and that they have a plentiful lack of wit, together with most weak hams; all which, sir, though I most powerfully and potently believe, yet I hold it not honesty to have it thus set down, for yourself, sir, shall grow old as I am, if like a crab you could go backward.

POL [*Aside.*]: Though this be madness, yet there is method in't.—Will you walk out of the air, my lord?

HAM: Into my grave.

POL: Indeed that's out of the air. [*Aside.*] How pregnant sometimes his replies are! a happiness that often madness hits on, which reason and [sanity] could not so prosperously be deliver'd of. I will leave him, [and suddenly contrive the means of meeting between him] and my daughter.—My lord, I will take my leave of you.

HAM: You cannot take from me any thing that I will not more willingly part withal—except my life, except my life, except my life.

POL: Fare you well, my lord.

HAM: These tedious old fools!

Enter GUILDENSTERN *and* ROSENCRANTZ.

---

196. **good kissing carrion:** flesh good enough for the sun to kiss. 198. **Conception:** understanding (with following play on the sense "conceiving a child"). 205. **matter:** subject; but Hamlet replies as if he had understood Polonius to mean "cause for a quarrel." 212. **honesty:** a fitting thing. 215. **method:** orderly arrangement, sequence of ideas. 216. **out . . . air.** Outdoor air was thought to be bad for invalids. 218. **pregnant:** apt. 221. **suddenly:** at once.

POL: You go to seek the Lord Hamlet, there he is.

ROS [*To Polonius.*]: God save you, sir!

[*Exit* POLONIUS.]

GUIL: My honor'd lord!

ROS: My most dear lord!

HAM: My [excellent] good friends! How dost thou, Guildenstern? Ah, Rosencrantz! Good lads, how do you both?

ROS: As the indifferent children of the earth.

GUIL: Happy, in that we are not [over-]happy, on Fortune's [cap] we are not the very button.

HAM: Nor the soles of her shoe?

ROS: Neither, my lord.

HAM: Then you live about her waist, or in the middle of her favors?

GUIL: Faith, her privates we.

HAM: In the secret parts of Fortune? O, most true, she is a strumpet. What news?

ROS: None, my lord, but the world's grown honest.

HAM: Then is doomsday near. But your news is not true. Let me question more in particular. What have you, my good friends, deserv'd at the hands of Fortune, that she sends you to prison hither?

GUIL: Prison, my lord?

HAM: Denmark's a prison.

ROS: Then is the world one.

HAM: A goodly one, in which there are many confines, wards, and dungeons, Denmark being one o' th' worst.

ROS: We think not so, my lord.

HAM: Why then 'tis none to you; for there is nothing either good or bad, but thinking makes it so. To me it is a prison.

ROS: Why then your ambition makes it one. 'Tis too narrow for your mind.

HAM: O God, I could be bounded in a nutshell, and count myself a king of infinite space—were it not that I have bad dreams.

GUIL: Which dreams indeed are ambition, for the very substance of the ambitious is merely the shadow of a dream.

HAM: A dream itself is but a shadow.

ROS: Truly, and I hold ambition of so airy and light a quality that it is but a shadow's shadow.

---

233. **indifferent:** average. 239. **privates:** (1) intimate friends; (2) genitalia. 240. **strumpet.** A common epithet for Fortune, because she grants favors to all men. 249. **wards:** cells.

HAM: Then are our beggars bodies, and our monarchs and outstretch'd heroes the beggars' shadows. Shall we to th' court? for, by my fay, I cannot reason.

Both [ROS., GUIL.]: We'll wait upon you.

HAM: No such matter. I will not sort you with the rest of my servants; for to speak to you like an honest man, I am most dreadfully attended. But in the beaten way of friendship, what make you at Elsinore?

ROS: To visit you, my lord, no other occasion.

HAM: Beggar that I am, I am [even] poor in thanks—but I thank you, and sure, dear friends, my thanks are too dear a halfpenny. Were you not sent for? is it your own inclining? is it a free visitation? Come, come, deal justly with me. Come, come—nay, speak.

GUIL: What should we say, my lord?

HAM: Any thing but to th' purpose. You were sent for, and there is a kind of confession in your looks, which your modesties have not craft enough to color. I know the good King and Queen have sent for you.

ROS: To what end, my lord?

HAM: That you must teach me. But let me conjure you, by the rights of our fellowship, by the consonancy of our youth, by the obligation of our ever-preserv'd love, and by what more dear a better proposer can charge you withal, be even and direct with me, whether you were sent for or no!

ROS [*Aside to Guildenstern.*]: What say you?

HAM [*Aside.*]: Nay then I have an eye of you!—If you love me, hold not off.

GUIL: My lord, we were sent for.

HAM: I will tell you why, so shall my anticipation prevent your discovery, and your secrecy to the King and Queen moult no feather.

---

263. **bodies:** i.e. not shadows (since they lack ambition). **outstretch'd:** i.e. with their ambition extended to the utmost (and hence producing stretched-out or elongated shadows). 264. **fay:** faith. 266. **wait upon you:** attend you thither. 267. **sort:** associate. 268. **dreadfully:** execrably. 273. **too . . . halfpenny:** too expensive priced at a halfpenny, i.e. not worth much. 275. **justly:** honestly. 277. **but.** Ordinarily punctuated with a comma preceding, to give the sense "provided that it is"; but Hamlet may intend, or include, the sense "except." 278. **modesties:** sense of shame. 283. **consonancy . . . youth:** similarity of our ages. 285. **charge:** urge, adjure. **even:** frank, honest (cf. modern "level with me"). 288. **of:** on. 291. **prevent your discovery:** forestall your disclosure (of what the King and Queen have said to you in confidence). 292. **moult no feather:** not be impaired in the least.

I have of late—but wherefore I know not—lost all my mirth, forgone all custom of exercises; and indeed it goes so heavily with my disposition, that this goodly frame, the earth, seems to me a sterile promontory; this most excellent canopy, the air, look you, this brave o'erhanging firmament, this majestical roof fretted with golden fire, why, it appeareth nothing to me but a foul and pestilent congregation of vapors. What [a] piece of work is a man, how noble in reason, how infinite in faculties, in form and moving, how express and admirable in action, how like an angel in apprehension, how like a god! the beauty of the world; the paragon of animals; and yet to me what is this quintessence of dust? Man delights not me—nor women neither, though by your smiling you seem to say so.

ROS: My lord, there was no such stuff in my thoughts.

HAM: Why did ye laugh then, when I said, "Man delights not me"?

ROS: To think, my lord, if you delight not in man, what lenten entertainment the players shall receive from you. We coted them on the way, and hither are they coming to offer you service.

HAM: He that plays the king shall be welcome—his Majesty shall have tribute on me, the adventerous knight shall use his foil and target, the lover shall not sigh gratis, the humorous man shall end his part in peace, [the clown shall make those laugh whose lungs are [tickle] a' th' sere,] and the lady shall say her mind freely, or the [blank] verse shall halt for't. What players are they?

ROS: Even those you were wont to take such delight in, the tragedians of the city.

HAM: How chances it they travel? Their residence, both in reputation and profit, was better both ways.

---

294. **custom of exercises:** my usual athletic activities. 296. **brave:** splendid. 297. **fretted:** ornamented as with fretwork. 299. **piece of work:** masterpiece. 300. **express:** exact. 303. **quintessence:** finest and purest extract. 307. **lenten entertainment:** meagre reception. 308. **coted:** outstripped. 311. **on:** of, from. 311. **adventerous:** adventurous, i.e. wandering in search of adventure. **foil and target:** light fencing sword and small shield. 312. **gratis:** without reward. **humorous:** dominated by some eccentric trait (like the melancholy Jaques in *As You Like It*). 313–314. **tickle . . . sere:** i.e. easily made to laugh (literally, describing a gun that goes off easily; *sere* = a catch in the gunlock; *tickle* = easily affected, highly sensitive to stimulus). 315. **halt:** limp, come off lamely (the verse will not scan if she omits indecent words).

ROS: I think their inhibition comes by the means of the late innovation.

HAM: Do they hold the same estimation they did when I was in the city? Are they so follow'd?

ROS: No indeed are they not.

HAM: How comes it? do they grow rusty?

ROS: Nay, their endeavor keeps in the wonted pace; but there is, sir, an aery of children, little eyases, that cry out on the top of question, and are most tyrannically clapp'd for't. These are now the fashion, and so [berattle] the common stages—so they call them—that many wearing rapiers are afraid of goose-quills and dare scarce come thither.

HAM: What, are they children? Who maintains 'em? How are they escoted? Will they pursue the quality no longer than they can sing? Will they not say afterwards, if they should grow themselves to common players (as it is [most like], if their means are [no] better), their writers do them wrong, to make them exclaim against their own succession?

ROS: Faith, there has been much to do on both sides, and the nation holds it no sin to tarre them to controversy. There was for a while no money bid for argument, unless the poet and the player went to cuffs in the question.

---

320. **inhibition:** hindrance (to playing in the city). The word could be used of an official prohibition. See next note. 321. **innovation.** Shakespeare elsewhere uses this word of a political uprising or revolt, and lines 320–21 are often explained as meaning that the company had been forbidden to play in the city as the result of some disturbance. It is commonly conjectured that the allusion is to the Essex rebellion of 1601, but it is known that Shakespeare's company, though to some extent involved on account of the special performance of *Richard II* they were commissioned to give on the eve of the rising, were not in fact punished by inhibition. A second interpretation explains *innovation* as referring to the new theatrical vogue described in lines 326 ff., and conjectures that *inhibition* may allude to a Privy Council order of 1600 restricting the number of London playhouses to two and the number of performances to two a week. 325–45. **How . . . too.** This passage refers topically to the "War of the Theatres" between the child actors and their poet Jonson on the one side, and on the other the adults, with Dekker, Marston, and possibly Shakespeare as spokesmen, in 1600–1601. 327. **aery:** nest. **eyases:** unfledged hawks. 327. **cry . . . question:** cry shrilly above others in controversy. 328. **tyrannically:** outrageously. 329. **berattle:** cry down, satirize. **common stages:** public theatres (the children played at the Blackfriars, a private theatre). 330. **goose-quills:** pens (of satirical playwrights). 333. **escoted:** supported. **quality:** profession (of acting). **no . . . sing:** i.e. only until their voices change. 337. **succession:** future. 338. **to do:** ado. 339. **tarre:** incite. 340. **argument:** plot of a play. 341. **in the question:** i.e. as part of the script.

HAM: Is't possible?

GUIL: O, there has been much throwing about of brains.

HAM: Do the boys carry it away?

ROS: Ay, that they do, my lord—Hercules and his load too.]

HAM: It is not very strange, for my uncle is King of Denmark, and those that would make mouths at him while my father liv'd, give twenty, forty, fifty, a hundred ducats a-piece for his picture in little. 'Sblood, there is something in this more than natural, if philosophy could find it out.

A flourish [for the PLAYERS].

GUIL: There are the players.

HAM: Gentlemen, you are welcome to Elsinore. Your hands, come then: th' appurtenance of welcome is fashion and ceremony. Let me comply with you in this garb, [lest my] extent to the players, which, I tell you, must show fairly outwards, should more appear like entertainment than yours. You are welcome; but my uncle-father and aunt-mother are deceiv'd.

GUIL: In what, my dear lord?

HAM: I am but mad north-north-west. When the wind is southerly I know a hawk from a hand-saw.

Enter POLONIUS.

POL: Well be with you, gentlemen!

HAM [*Aside to them.*]: Hark you, Guildenstern, and you too—at each ear a hearer—that great baby you see there is not yet out of his swaddling-clouts.

ROS: Happily he is the second time come to them, for they say an old man is twice a child.

HAM: I will prophesy, he comes to tell me of the players, mark it. [*Aloud.*] You say right, sir, a' Monday morning, 'twas then indeed.

---

344. **carry it away:** win. 345. **Hercules . . . too.** Hercules in the course of one of his twelve labors supported the world for Atlas; the children do better, for they carry away the world and Hercules as well. There is an allusion to the Globe playhouse, which reportedly had for its sign the figure of Hercules upholding the world. 347. **mouths:** derisive faces. 348. **'Sblood:** by God's (Christ's) blood. 353. **comply:** observe the formalities. 354. **garb:** fashion, manner. **my extent:** i.e. the degree of courtesy I show. 355–56. **more . . . yours:** seem to be a warmer reception than I have given you. 360. **hawk, hand-saw.** Both cutting-tools; but also both birds, if *hand-saw* quibbles on *hernshaw,* "heron," a bird preyed upon by the hawk. 364. **swaddling-clouts:** swaddling clothes. 365. **Happily:** haply, perhaps. 366. **twice:** i.e. for the second time.

POL: My lord, I have news to tell you.

HAM: My lord, I have news to tell you. When Roscius was an actor in Rome—

POL: The actors are come hither, my lord.

HAM: Buzz, buzz!

POL: Upon my honor—

HAM: "Then came each actor on his ass"—

POL: The best actors in the world, either for tragedy, comedy, history, pastoral, pastoral-comical, historical-pastoral, [tragical-historical, tragical-comical-historical-pastoral,] scene individable, or poem unlimited; Seneca cannot be too heavy, nor Plautus too light, for the law of writ and the liberty: these are the only men.

HAM: O Jephthah, judge of Israel, what a treasure hadst thou!

POL: What a treasure had he, my lord?

HAM: Why—
"One fair daughter, and no more,
    The which he loved passing well."

POL [*Aside.*]: Still on my daughter.

HAM: Am I not i' th' right, old Jephthah?

POL: If you call me Jephthah, my lord, I have a daughter that I love passing well.

HAM: Nay, that follows not.

POL: What follows then, my lord?

HAM: Why—
        "As by lot, God wot,"
and then, yon know,
    "It came to pass, as most like it was"—
the first row of the pious chanson will show you more, for look where my abridgment comes.

---

370. **Roscius:** the most famous of Roman actors (died 62 B.C.). News about him would be stale news indeed. 373. **Buzz:** exclamation of impatience at someone who tells news already known. 378. **scene individable:** play observing the unity of place. 378–79. **poem unlimited:** play ignoring rules such as the three unities. 379. **Seneca:** Roman writer of tragedies. **Plautus:** Roman writer of comedies. 379–80. **for . . . liberty:** for strict observance of the rules, or for freedom from them (with possible allusion to the location of playhouses, which were not built in properties under city jurisdiction, but in the "liberties"—land once monastic and now outside the jurisdiction of the city authorities). 380. **only:** very best (a frequent use). 381. **Jephthah . . . Israel:** title of a ballad, from which Hamlet goes on to quote. For the story of Jephthah and his daughter, see Judges 11. 396. **row:** stanza. **chanson:** song ballad, 397. **abridgment:** (1) interruption; (2) pastime.

Enter the PLAYERS, [*four or five*].

You are welcome, masters, welcome all. I am glad to see thee well. Welcome, good friends. O, old friend! why, thy face is valanc'd since I saw thee last; com'st thou to beard me in Denmark? What, my young lady and mistress! by' lady, your ladyship is nearer to heaven than when I saw you last, by the altitude of a chopine. Pray God your voice, like a piece of uncurrent gold, be not crack'd within the ring. Masters, you are all welcome. We'll e'en to't like [French] falc'ners—fly at any thing we see; we'll have a speech straight. Come give us a taste of your quality, come, a passionate speech.

[*1.*] PLAY: What speech, my good lord?

HAM: I heard thee speak me a speech once, but it was never acted, or if it was, not above once; for the play, I remember, pleas'd not the million, 'twas caviary to the general, but it was—as I receiv'd it, and others, whose judgments in such matters cried in the top of mine—an excellent play, well digested in the scenes, set down with as much modesty as cunning. I remember one said there were no sallets in the lines to make the matter savory, nor no matter in the phrase that might indict the author of affection, but call'd it an honest method, as wholesome as sweet, and by very much more handsome than fine. One speech in't I chiefly lov'd, 'twas Aeneas' [tale] to Dido, and thereabout of it especially when he speaks of Priam's slaughter. If it live in your memory, begin at this line—let me see, let me see:
"The rugged Pyrrhus, like th' Hyrcanian beast—"
'Tis not so, it begins with Pyrrhus:
"The rugged Pyrrhus, he whose sable arms,

399. **valanc'd:** fringed, i.e. bearded. 400. **beard:** confront boldly (with obvious pun). 401. **by' lady:** by Our Lady. 402. **chopine:** thick-soled shoe. 403. **crack'd . . . ring:** i.e. broken to the point where you can no longer play female roles. A coin with a crack extending far enough in from the edge to cross the circle surrounding the stamp of the sovereign's head was unacceptable in exchange (*uncurrent*). 405. **straight:** straightway. **quality:** professional skill. 410. **caviary . . . general:** caviare to the common people, i.e. too choice for the multitude. 411. **cried . . . of:** were louder than, i.e. carried more authority than. 413. **sallets:** salads, i.e. spicy jokes. 414. **savory:** zesty. 415. **affection:** affectation. 416. **fine:** showily dressed (in language). 418. **Priam's slaughter:** the slaying of Priam (at the fall of Troy). 420. **Pyrrhus:** another name for, Neoptolemus Achilles' son. **Hyrcanian beast**. Hyrcania in the Caucasus was notorious for its tigers. 422. **sable arms.** The Greeks within the Trojan horse had blackened their skin so as to be inconspicuous when they emerged at night.

Black as his purpose, did the night resemble
When he lay couched in th' ominous horse,
Hath now this dread and black complexion smear'd
With heraldy more dismal: head to foot
Now is he total gules, horridly trick'd
With blood of fathers, mothers, daughters, sons,
Bak'd and impasted with the parching streets,
That lend a tyrannous and a damned light
To their lord's murther. Roasted in wrath and fire,
And thus o'er-sized with coagulate gore,
With eyes like carbuncles, the hellish Pyrrhus
Old grandsire Priam seeks."
So proceed you.

POL: 'Fore God, my lord, well spoken, with good accent and good discretion.

[*1.*] PLAY: "Anon he finds him
Striking too short at Greeks. His antique sword,
Rebellious to his arm, lies where it falls,
Repugnant to command. Unequal match'd,
Pyrrhus at Priam drives, in rage strikes wide,
But with the whiff and wind of his fell sword
Th' unnerved father falls. [Then senseless Ilium,]
Seeming to feel this blow, with flaming top
Stoops to his base, and with a hideous crash
Takes prisoner Pyrrhus' ear; for lo his sword,
Which was declining on the milky head
Of reverent Priam, seem'd i' th' air to stick.
So as a painted tyrant Pyrrhus stood
[And,] like a neutral to his will and matter,
Did nothing.
But as we often see, against some storm,
A silence in the heavens, the rack stand still,

---

426. **heraldy:** heraldry. **dismal:** ill-boding. 427. **gules:** red (heraldic term). **trick'd:** adorned. 429. **Bak'd:** caked. **impasted:** crusted. **with . . . streets:** i.e. by the heat from the burning streets. 432. **o'er-sized:** covered over as with a coat of sizing. 433. **carbuncles:** jewels believed to shine in the dark. 441. **Repugnant:** resistant, hostile. 443. **fell:** cruel. 444. **unnerved:** drained of strength. **senseless:** insensible. **Ilium:** the citadel of Troy. 449. **reverent:** reverend, aged. 451. **like . . . matter:** i.e. poised midway between intention and performance. 453. **against:** just before. 454. **rack:** cloud-mass.

The bold winds speechless, and the orb below
As hush as death, anon the dreadful thunder
Doth rend the region; so after Pyrrhus' pause,
A roused vengeance sets him new a-work,
And never did the Cyclops' hammers fall
On Mars's armor forg'd for proof eterne
With less remorse than Pyrrhus' bleeding sword
Now falls on Priam.
Out, out, thou strumpet Fortune! All you gods,
In general synod take away her power!
Break all the spokes and [fellies] from her wheel,
And bowl the round nave down the hill of heaven
As low as to the fiends!"

POL: This is too long.

HAM: It shall to the barber's with your beard. Prithee say on, he's for a jig or a tale of bawdry, or he sleeps. Say on, come to Hecuba.

[*1.*] PLAY: "But who, ah woe, had seen the mobled queen"—

HAM: "The mobled queen"?

POL: That's good, ["[mobled] queen" is good].

[*1.*] PLAY: "Run barefoot up and down, threat'ning the flames
With bisson rheum, a clout upon that head
Where late the diadem stood, and for a robe,
About her lank and all o'er-teemed loins,
A blanket, in the alarm of fear caught up—
Who this had seen, with tongue in venom steep'd,
'Gainst Fortune's state would treason have pronounc'd.
But if the gods themselves did see her then,
When she saw Pyrrhus make malicious sport
In mincing with his sword her [husband's] limbs,
The instant burst of clamor that she made,
Unless things mortal move them not at all,
Would have made milch the burning eyes of heaven,
And passion in the gods."

---

457. **region:** i.e. air. 479. **Cyclops:** giants who worked in Vulcan's smithy, where armor was made for the gods. 460. **proof eterne:** eternal endurance. 461. **remorse:** pity. 465. **fellies:** rims. 466. **nave:** hub. 470. **jig:** song-and-dance entertainment performed after the main play. 472. **mobled:** muffled. 475. **bisson rheum:** blinding tears. **clout:** cloth. 477. **o'er-teemed:** worn out by childbearing. 480. **state:** rule, government. 486. **milch:** moist (literally, milky). 487. **passion:** grief.

POL: Look whe'er he has not turn'd his color and has tears in 's eyes. Prithee no more.

HAM: 'Tis well, I'll have thee speak out the rest of this soon. Good my lord, will you see the players well bestow'd? Do you hear, let them be well us'd, for they are the abstract and brief chronicles of the time. After your death you were better have a bad epitaph than their ill report while you live.

POL: My lord, I will use them according to their desert.

HAM: God's bodkin, man, much better: use every man after his desert, and who shall scape whipping? Use them after your own honor and dignity—the less they deserve, the more merit is in your bounty. Take them in.

POL: Come, sirs. [*Exit.*]

HAM: Follow him, friends, we'll hear a play to morrow. [*Exeunt all the Players but the First.*] Dost thou hear me, old friend? Can you play "The Murther of Gonzago"?

[*1.*] PLAY: Ay, my lord.

HAM: We'll ha't to-morrow night. You could for need study a speech of some dozen or sixteen lines, which I would set down and insert in't, could you not?

[*1.*] PLAY: Ay, my lord.

HAM: Very well. Follow that lord, and look you mock him not. [*Exit First Player.*] My good friends, I'll leave you [till] night. You are welcome to Elsinore.

ROS: Good my lord!

HAM: Ay so, God buy to you.

Exeunt [ROSENCRANTZ *and* GUILDENSTERN].

Now I am alone.

O, what a rogue and peasant slave am I!
Is it not monstrous that this player here,
But in a fiction, in a dream of passion,
Could force his soul so to his own conceit
That from her working all the visage wann'd,
Tears in his eyes, distraction in his aspect,
A broken voice, an' his whole function suiting

---

488. **Look . . . not:** i.e. note how he has. 491. **bestow'd:** lodged. 492. **us'd:** treated. 496. **God's bodkin:** by God's (Christ's) little body. 505. **for need:** if necessary. 518. **conceit:** imaginative conception. 521. **his whole function:** the operation of his whole body.

With forms to his conceit? And all for nothing,
For Hecuba!
What's Hecuba to him, or he to [Hecuba],
That he should weep for her? What would he do
Had he the motive and [the cue] for passion
That I have? He would drown the stage with tears,
And cleave the general ear with horrid speech,
Make mad the guilty, and appall the free,
Confound the ignorant, and amaze indeed
The very faculties of eyes and ears. Yet I,
A dull and muddy-mettled rascal, peak
Like John-a-dreams, unpregnant of my cause,
And can say nothing; no, not for a king,
Upon whose property and most dear life
A damn'd defeat was made. Am I a coward?
Who calls me villain, breaks my pate across,
Plucks off my beard and blows it in my face,
Tweaks me by the nose, gives me the lie i' th' throat
As deep as to the lungs? Who does me this?
Hah, 'swounds, I should take it; for it cannot be
But I am pigeon-liver'd, and lack gall
To make oppression bitter, or ere this
I should 'a' fatted all the region kites
With this slave's offal. Bloody, bawdy villain!
Remorseless, treacherous, lecherous, kindless villain!
Why, what an ass am I! This is most brave,
That I, the son of a dear [father] murthered,
Prompted to my revenge by heaven and hell,
Must like a whore unpack my heart with words,
And fall a-cursing like a very drab,
A stallion. Fie upon't, foh!

---

522. **forms:** actions, expressions. 529. **free:** innocent. 530. **amaze:** confound. 532. **muddy-mettled:** dull-spirited. **peak:** mope. 533. **John-a-dreams:** a sleepy fellow. **unpregnant of:** unquickened by. 536. **defeat:** destruction. 539–40. **gives . . . lungs:** calls me a liar in the extremest degree. 541. **'swounds:** by God's (Christ's) wounds. **should:** would certainly. 542. **am . . . gall:** i.e. am constitutionally incapable of resentment. That doves were mild because they had no gall was a popular belief. 544. **region kites:** kites of the air. 545. **offal:** entrails. 546. **kindless:** unnatural. 552. **stallion:** male whore.

About, my brains! Hum—I have heard
That guilty creatures sitting at a play
Have by the very cunning of the scene
Been strook so to the soul, that presently
They have proclaim'd their malefactions:
For murther, though it have no tongue, will speak
With most miraculous organ. I'll have these players
Play something like the murther of my father
Before mine uncle. I'll observe his looks,
I'll tent him to the quick. If 'a do blench,
I know my course. The spirit that I have seen
May be a [dev'l], and the [dev'l] hath power
T' assume a pleasing shape, yea, and perhaps,
Out of my weakness and my melancholy,
As he is very potent with such spirits,
Abuses me to damn me. I'll have grounds
More relative than this—the play's the thing
Wherein I'll catch the conscience of the King *Exit.*

Act III

Scene I

Enter KING, QUEEN, POLONIUS, OPHELIA, ROSENCRANTZ, GUILDENSTERN, LORDS.

KING: An' can you by no drift of conference
Get from him why he puts on this confusion,
Grating so harshly all his days of quiet
With turbulent and dangerous lunacy?
ROS: He does confess he feels himself distracted,
But from what cause 'a will by no means speak.
GUIL: Nor do we find him forward to be sounded,
But with a crafty madness keeps aloof
When we would bring him on to some confession
Of his true state.

---

553. **About:** to work. 556. **presently:** at once, then and there. 562. **tent:** probe. **blench:** flinch. 567. **spirits:** states of temperament. 568. **Abuses:** deludes. 569. **relative:** closely related (to fact), i.e. conclusive.

III.i Location: The castle. 1. **An':** and. **drift of conference:** leading on of conversation. 7. **forward:** readily willing. **sounded:** plumbed, probed. 8. **crafty madness:** i.e. mad craftiness, the shrewdness that mad people sometimes exhibit.

QUEEN: Did he receive you well?
ROS: Most like a gentleman.
GUIL: But with much forcing of his disposition.
ROS: Niggard of question, but of our demands
Most free in his reply.
QUEEN: Did you assay him
To any pastime?
ROS: Madam, it so fell out that certain players
We o'erraught on the way; of these we told him,
And there did seem in him a kind of joy
To hear of it. They are here about the court,
And as I think, they have already order
This night to play before him.
POL: 'Tis most true,
And he beseech'd me to entreat your Majesties
To hear and see the matter.
KING: With all my heart, and it doth much content me
To hear him so inclin'd.
Good gentlemen, give him a further edge,
And drive his purpose into these delights.
ROS: We shall, my lord.

Exeunt ROSENCRANTZ *and* GUILDENSTERN.

KING: Sweet Gertrude, leave us two,
For we have closely sent for Hamlet hither,
That he, as 'twere by accident, may here
Affront Ophelia. Her father and myself,
We'll so bestow ourselves that, seeing unseen,
We may of their encounter frankly judge,
And gather by him, as he is behav'd,
If't be th' affliction of his love or no
That thus he suffers for.
QUEEN: I shall obey you.
And for your part, Ophelia, I do wish
That your good beauties be the happy cause
Of Hamlet's wildness. So shall I hope your virtues
Will bring him to his wonted way again,

---

13. **disposition:** inclination. 14. **question:** conversation. **demands:** questions. 16. **assay:** attempt to win. 19. **o'erraught:** passed (literally, overreached). 29. **edge:** stimulus. 30. **into:** on to. 33. **closely:** privately. 35. **Affront:** meet. 37. **frankly:** freely.

To both your honors.
OPH: Madam, I wish it may. [*Exit* QUEEN.]
POL: Ophelia, walk you here.—Gracious, so please you,
We will bestow ourselves. [*To* OPHELIA.] Read on this book,
That show of such an exercise may color
Your [loneliness]. We are oft to blame in this—
'Tis too much prov'd—that with devotion's visage
And pious action we do sugar o'er
The devil himself.
KING: [*Aside.*] O, 'tis too true!
How smart a lash that speech doth give my conscience!
The harlot's cheek, beautied with plast'ring art,
Is not more ugly to the thing that helps it
Than is my deed to my most painted word.
O heavy burthen!
POL: I hear him coming. Withdraw, my lord.

[*Exeunt* KING *and* POLONIUS.]

Enter HAMLET.

HAM: To be, or not to be, that is the question:
Whether 'tis nobler in the mind to suffer
The slings and arrows of outrageous fortune,
Or to take arms against a sea of troubles,
And by opposing, end them. To die, to sleep—
No more, and by a sleep to say we end
The heart-ache and the thousand natural shocks
That flesh is heir to; 'tis a consummation
Devoutly to be wish'd. To die, to sleep—
To sleep, perchance to dream—ay, there's the rub,
For in that sleep of death what dreams may come,
When we have shuffled off this mortal coil,
Must give us pause; there's the respect
That makes calamity of so long life:
For who would bear the whips and scorns of time,

---

50. **exercise:** i.e. religious exercise (as the next sentence makes clear). 50–51. **color Your loneliness:** make your solitude seem natural. 52. **too much prov'd:** too often proved true. 53. **action:** demeanor. 58. **to . . . it:** in comparison with the paint that makes it look beautiful. 63. **suffer:** submit to, endure patiently. 69. **consummation:** completion, end. 71. **rub:** obstacle (a term from the game of bowls). 73. **shuffled off:** freed ourselves from. **this mortal coil:** the turmoil of this mortal life. 74. **respect:** consideration. 75. **of . . . life:** so long-lived. 76. **time:** the world.

Th' oppressor's wrong, the proud man's contumely,
The pangs of despis'd love, the law's delay,
The insolence of office, and the spurns
That patient merit of th' unworthy takes,
When he himself might his quietus make
With a bare bodkin; who would fardels bear,
To grunt and sweat under a weary life,
But that the dread of something after death,
The undiscover'd country, from whose bourn
No traveller returns, puzzles the will,
And makes us rather bear those ills we have,
Than fly to others that we know not of?
Thus conscience does make cowards [of us all],
And thus the native hue of resolution
Is sicklied o'er with the pale cast of thought,
And enterprises of great pitch and moment
With this regard their currents turn awry,
And lose the name of action.—Soft you now,
The fair Ophelia. Nymph, in thy orisons
Be all my sins rememb'red.

OPH: Good my lord,
How does your honor for this many a day?

HAM: I humbly thank you, well, [well, well]

OPH: My lord, I have remembrances of yours
That I have longed long to redeliver.
I pray you now receive them.

HAM: No, not I,
I never gave you aught.

OPH: My honor'd lord, you know right well you did,
And with them words of so sweet breath compos'd
As made these things more rich. Their perfume lost,
Take these again, for to the noble mind
Rich gifts wax poor when givers prove unkind.

---

81. **his quietus make:** write paid to his account. 82. **bare bodkin:** mere dagger. **fardels:** burdens. 85. **undiscover'd:** not disclosed to knowledge; about which men have no information. **bourn:** boundary, i.e. region. 86. **puzzles:** paralyzes. 89. **conscience:** reflection (but with some of the modern sense, too). 90. **native hue:** natural (ruddy) complexion. 91. **pale cast:** pallor. **thought:** i.e. melancholy thought, brooding. 92. **pitch:** loftiness (a term from falconry, signifying the highest point of a hawk's flight). 95. **orisons:** prayers.

There, my lord.

HAM: Ha, ha! are you honest?

OPH: My lord?

HAM: Are you fair?

OPH: What means your lordship?

HAM: That if you be honest and fair, [your honesty] should admit no discourse to your beauty.

OPH: Could beauty, my lord, have better commerce than with honesty?

HAM: Ay, truly, for the power of beauty will sooner transform honesty from what it is to a bawd than the force of honesty can translate beauty into his likeness. This was sometime a paradox, but now the time gives it proof. I did love you once.

OPH: Indeed, my lord, you made me believe so.

HAM: You should not have believ'd me, for virtue cannot so [inoculate] our old stock but we shall relish of it. I lov'd you not.

OPH: I was the more deceiv'd.

HAM: Get thee [to] a nunn'ry, why wouldst thou be a breeder of sinners? I am myself indifferent honest, but yet I could accuse me of such things that it were better my mother had not borne me: I am very proud, revengeful, ambitious, with more offenses at my beck than I have thoughts to put them in, imagination to give them shape, or time to act them in. What should such fellows as I do crawling between earth and heaven? We are arrant knaves, believe none of us. Go thy ways to a nunn'ry. Where's your father?

OPH: At home, my lord.

HAM: Let the doors be shut upon him, that he may play the fool no where but in 's own house. Farewell.

OPH: O, help him, you sweet heavens!

HAM: If thou dost marry, I'll give thee this plague for thy dowry: be thou as chaste as ice, as pure as snow, thou shalt not escape calumny. Get thee to a nunn'ry, farewell. Or if thou wilt needs marry, marry a fool, for wise men know well enough what monsters you make of them. To a nunn'ry, go, and quickly too. Farewell.

OPH: Heavenly powers, restore him!

---

111. **honest:** chaste. 121. **sometime:** formerly. **paradox:** tenet contrary to accepted belief. 124–25. **virtue . . . it:** virtue, engrafted on our old stock (of viciousness), cannot so change the nature of the plant that no trace of the original will remain. 128. **indifferent honest:** tolerably virtuous. 142. **monsters:** Alluding to the notion that the husbands of unfaithful wives grew horns. **you:** you women.

HAM: I have heard of your paintings, well enough. God hath given you one face, and you make yourselves another. You jig and amble, and you [lisp,] you nickname God's creatures and make your wantonness [your] ignorance. Go to, I'll no more on't, it hath made me mad. I say we will have no moe marriage. Those that are married already (all but one) shall live, the rest shall keep as they are. To a nunn'ry, go.

Exit.

OPH: O, what a noble mind is here o'erthrown!
The courtier's, soldier's, scholar's, eye, tongue, sword,
Th' expectation and rose of the fair state,
The glass of fashion and the mould of form,
Th' observ'd of all observers, quite, quite down!
And I, of ladies most deject and wretched,
That suck'd the honey of his [music] vows,
Now see [that] noble and most sovereign reason
Like sweet bells jangled out of time, and harsh;
That unmatch'd form and stature of blown youth
Blasted with ecstasy. O, woe is me
T' have seen what I have seen, see what I see!

[OPHELIA *withdraws.*]

Enter KING *and* POLONIUS.

KING: Love? his affections do not that way tend,
Nor what he spake, though it lack'd form a little,
Was not like madness. There's something in his soul
O'er which his melancholy sits on brood,
And I do doubt the hatch and the disclose
Will be some danger; which for to prevent,
I have in quick determination
Thus set it down: he shall with speed to England
For the demand of our neglected tribute.
Haply the seas, and countries different,

146–47. **You . . . creatures:** i.e. you walk and talk affectedly. 147–48. **make . . . ignorance:** excuse your affectation as ignorance. 149. **moe:** more. 154. **expectation:** hope. **rose:** ornament. **fair.** Probably proleptic: "(the kingdom) made fair by his presence." 155. **glass:** mirror. **mould of form:** pattern of (courtly) behavior. 156. **observ'd . . . observers.** Shakespeare uses *observe* to mean not only "behold, mark attentively" but also "pay honor to." 161. **blown:** in full bloom. 162. **Blasted:** withered. **ecstasy:** madness. 164. **affections:** inclinations, feelings. 168. **doubt:** fear. **disclose.** Synonymous with *hatch;* see also V.i.271.

With variable objects, shall expel
This something-settled matter in his heart,
Whereon his brains still beating puts him thus
From fashion of himself. What think you on't?

POL: It shall do well; but yet do I believe
The origin and commencement of his grief
Sprung from neglected love. [OPHELIA *comes forward.*]
How now, Ophelia?
You need not tell us what Lord Hamlet said,
We heard it all. My lord, do as you please,
But if you hold it fit, after the play
Let his queen-mother all alone entreat him
To show his grief. Let her be round with him,
And I'll be plac'd (so please you) in the ear
Of all their conference. If she find him not,
To England send him, or confine him where
Your wisdom best shall think.

KING: It shall be so.
Madness in great ones must not [unwatch'd] go.

Exeunt.

Scene II

Enter HAMLET *and three of the* PLAYERS.

HAM: Speak the speech, I pray you, as I pronounc'd it to you, trippingly on the tongue, but if you mouth it, as many of our players do, I had as live the town-crier spoke my lines. Nor do not saw the air too much with your hand, thus, but use all gently, for in the very torrent, tempest, and, as I may say, whirlwind of your passion, you must acquire and beget a temperance that may give it smoothness. O, it offends me to the soul to hear a robustious periwig-pated fellow tear a passion to totters, to very rags, to spleet the ears of the groundlings, who for the most part are capable of nothing but

---

180. **neglected:** unrequited. 186. **his grief:** what is troubling him. **round:** blunt, outspoken. 187. **find him:** learn the truth about him.

III.ii. Location: The castle. 2. **mouth:** pronounce with exaggerated distinctness or declamatory effect. 3. **live:** lief, willingly. 8. **totters:** tatters. **spleet:** split. 9. **groundlings:** those who paid the lowest admission price and stood on the ground in the "yard" or pit of the theatre. **capable of:** able to take in.

inexplicable dumb shows and noise. I would have such a fellow whipt for o'erdoing Termagant, it out-Herods Herod, pray you avoid it.

[*1.*] PLAY: I warrant your honor.

HAM: Be not too tame neither, but let your own discretion be your tutor. Suit the action to the word, the word to the action, with this special observance, that you o'erstep not the modesty of nature: for any thing so o'erdone is from the purpose of playing, whose end, both at the first and now, was and is, to hold as 'twere the mirror up to nature; to show virtue her feature, scorn her own image, and the very age and body of the time his form and pressure. Now this overdone, or come tardy off, though it makes the unskillful laugh, cannot but make the judicious grieve; the censure of which one must in your allowance o'erweigh a whole theatre of others. O, there be players that I have seen play—and heard others [praise], and that highly—not to speak it profanely, that, neither having th' accent of Christians nor the gait of Christian, pagan, nor man, have so strutted and bellow'd that I have thought some of Nature's journeymen had made men, and not made them well, they imitated humanity so abominably.

[*1.*] PLAY: I hope we have reform'd that indifferently with us, [sir].

HAM: O, reform it altogether. And let those that play your clowns speak no more than is set down for them, for there be of them that will themselves laugh to set on some quantity of barren spectators to laugh too, though in the mean time some necessary question of the play be then to be consider'd. That's villainous, and shows a most pitiful ambition in the fool that uses it. Go make you ready.

[*Exeunt* PLAYERS.]

---

11. **Termagant:** a supposed god of the Saracens, whose role in medieval drama, like that of Herod (line 11), was noisy and violent. 16. **modesty:** moderation. 17. **from:** contrary to. 19. **scorn:** i.e. that which is worthy of scorn. 21. **pressure:** impression (as of a seal), exact image. **tardy:** inadequately. 23. **censure:** judgment. **which one:** (even) one of whom. **allowance:** estimation. 26. **profanely:** irreverently. 28–30. **some . . . abominably:** i.e. they were so unlike men that it seemed Nature had not made them herself, but had delegated the task to mediocre assistants. 31. **indifferently:** pretty well. 35. **of them:** some of them. 39. **fool:** (1) stupid person; (2) actor playing a fool's role.

Enter POLONIUS, GUILDENSTERN, *and* ROSENCRANTZ.

How now, my lord? Will the King hear this piece of work?
POL: And the Queen too, and that presently.
HAM: Bid the players make haste. [*Exit* POLONIUS.]
Will you two help to hasten them?
ROS: Ay, my lord. *Exeunt they two.*
HAM: What ho, Horatio!

Enter HORATIO.

HOR: Here, sweet lord, at your service.
HAM: Horatio, thou art e'en as just a man
As e'er my conversation cop'd withal.
HOR: O my dear lord—
HAM: Nay, do not think I flatter,
For what advancement may I hope from thee
That no revenue hast but thy good spirits
To feed and clothe thee? Why should the poor be flatter'd?
No, let the candied tongue lick absurd pomp,
And crook the pregnant hinges of the knee
Where thrift may follow fawning. Dost thou hear?
Since my dear soul was mistress of her choice
And could of men distinguish her election,
Sh' hath seal'd thee for herself, for thou hast been
As one in suff'ring all that suffers nothing,
A man that Fortune's buffets and rewards
Hast ta'en with equal thanks; and blest are those
Whose blood and judgment are so well co-meddled,
That they are not a pipe for Fortune's finger
To sound what stop she please. Give me that man
That is not passion's slave, and I will wear him
In my heart's core, ay, in my heart of heart,
As I do thee. Something too much of this.
There is a play to-night before the King,
One scene of it comes near the circumstance
Which I have told thee of my father's death.

---

40. **piece of work:** masterpiece (said jocularly). 41. **presently:** at once. 47. **thou . . . man:** i.e. you come as close to being what a man should be (*just* = exact, precise). 48. **my . . . withal:** my association with people has brought me into contact with. 54. **candied:** sugared, i.e. flattering. **absurd:** tasteless (Latin sense). 55. **pregnant:** moving readily. 56. **thrift:** thriving, profit. 63. **blood:** passions. **co-meddled:** mixed, blended. 67. **my heart of heart:** the heart of my heart.

I prithee, when thou seest that act afoot,
Even with the very comment of thy soul
Observe my uncle. If his occulted guilt
Do not itself unkennel in one speech,
It is a damned ghost that we have seen,
And my imaginations are as foul
As Vulcan's stithy. Give him heedful note,
For I mine eyes will rivet to his face,
And after we will both our judgments join
In censure of his seeming.

HOR: Well, my lord.
If' a steal aught the whilst this play is playing,
And scape [detecting], I will pay the theft.

[*Sound a flourish. Danish march.*] *Enter Trumpets and Kettle-drums,* KING, QUEEN, POLONIUS, OPHELIA, [ROSENCRANTZ, GUILDENSTERN, *and other* LORDS *attendant, with his* GUARD *carrying torches*].

HAM: They are coming to the play. I must be idle;
Get you a place.

KING: How fares our cousin Hamlet?

HAM: Excellent, i' faith, of the chameleon's dish: I eat the air, promise-cramm'd—you cannot feed capons so.

KING: I have nothing with this answer, Hamlet, these words are not mine.

HAM: No, nor mine now. [*To* POLONIUS.] My lord, you play'd once i' th' university, you say?

POL: That did I, my lord, and was accounted a good actor.

HAM: What did you enact?

POL: I did enact Julius Caesar. I was kill'd i' th' Capitol; Brutus kill'd me.

HAM: It was a brute part of him to kill so capital a calf there. Be the players ready?

ROS: Ay, my lord, they stay upon your patience.

---

73. **very . . . soul:** your most intense critical observation. 74. **occulted:** hidden. 75. **unkennel:** bring into the open. 76. **damned ghost:** evil spirit, devil. 78. **stithy:** forge. 81. **censure . . . seeming:** reaching a verdict on his behavior. 85. **be idle:** act foolish, pretend to be crazy. 87. **fares:** Hamlet takes up this word in another sense. 88. **chameleon's dish:** Chameleons were thought to feed on air. Hamlet says that he subsists on an equally nourishing diet, the promise of succession. There is probably a pun on *air/heir.* 90. **have nothing with:** do not understand. 91. **mine:** i.e. an answer to my question. 98. **part:** action.

QUEEN: Come hither, my dear Hamlet, sit by me.

HAM: No, good mother, here's metal more attractive.

[*Lying down at* OPHELIA' *s feet.*]

POL: [*To the* KING.] O ho, do you mark that?

HAM: Lady, shall I lie in your lap?

OPH: No, my lord.

[HAM: I mean, my head upon your lap?

OPH: Ay, my lord.]

HAM: Do you think I meant country matters?

OPH: I think nothing, my lord.

HAM: That's a fair thought to lie between maids' legs.

OPH: What is, my lord?

HAM: Nothing.

OPH: You are merry, my lord.

HAM: Who, I?

OPH: Ay, my lord.

HAM: O God, your only jig-maker. What should a man do but be merry, for look you how cheerfully my mother looks, and my father died within 's two hours.

OPH: Nay, 'tis twice two months, my lord.

HAM: So long? Nay then let the dev'l wear black, for I'll have a suit of sables. O heavens, die two months ago, and not forgotten yet? Then there's hope a great man's memory may outlive his life half a year, but, by'r lady, 'a must build churches then, or else shall 'a suffer not thinking on, with the hobby-horse, whose epitaph is, "For O, for O, the hobby-horse is forgot."

The trumpets sounds. Dumb show follows.

Enter a King and a Queen [*very lovingly*], *the Queen embracing him and he her.* [*She kneels and makes show of protestation unto him.*] *He takes her up and declines his head upon her neck. He lies him down upon a bank of flowers. She, seeing him asleep, leaves him. Anon come in another man, takes off his crown, kisses it, pours poison in the sleeper's ears, and leaves him. The*

---

108. **country matters:** indecency. 116. **only:** very best. **jig-maker:** one who composed or played in the farcical song-and-dance entertainments that followed plays. 118. **'s:** this. 121–21. **let . . . sables:** i.e. to the devil with my garments; after so long a time I am ready for the old man's garb of sables (fine fur). 124. **not thinking on:** not being thought of, i.e. being forgotten. 124–25. **For . . . forgot:** line from a popular ballad lamenting puritanical suppression of such country sports as the May-games, in which the hobby-horse, a character costumed to resemble a horse, traditionally appeared.

Queen returns, finds the King dead, makes passionate action. The pois'ner with some three or four [mutes] come in again, seem to condole with her. The dead body is carried away. The pois'ner woos the Queen with gifts; she seems harsh [and unwilling] awhile, but in the end accepts love.

[*Exeunt.*]

OPH: What means this, my lord?

HAM: Marry, this' [miching] mallecho, it means mischief.

OPH: Belike this show imports the argument of the play.

Enter PROLOGUE.

HAM: We shall know by this fellow. The players cannot keep [counsel], they'll tell all.

OPH: Will 'a tell us what this show meant?

HAM: Ay, or any show that you will show him. Be not you asham'd to show, he'll not shame to tell you what it means.

OPH: You are naught, you are naught. I'll mark the play.

PRO: For us, and for our tragedy,
Here stooping to your clemency,
We beg your hearing patiently. [*Exit.*]

HAM: Is this a prologue, or the posy of a ring?

OPH: 'Tis brief, my lord.

HAM: As woman's love.

Enter [two Players,] KING *and* QUEEN.

[*P.*] KING: Full thirty times hath Phoebus' cart gone round
Neptune's salt wash and Tellus' orbed ground,
And thirty dozen moons with borrowed sheen
About the world have times twelve thirties been,
Since love our hearts and Hymen did our hands
Unite comutual in most sacred bands.

[*P.*] QUEEN: So many journeys may the sun and moon
Make us again count o'er ere love be done!
But woe is me, you are so sick of late,
So far from cheer and from [your] former state,
That I distrust you. Yet though I distrust,
Discomfort you, my lord, it nothing must,

---

127. **this' miching mallecho:** this is sneaking mischief. 128. **argument:** subject, plot. 129. **counsel.** secrets. 132. **Be not you:** if you are not. 134. **naught:** wicked. 138. **posy . . . ring:** verse motto inscribed in a ring (necessarily short). 141. **Phoebus' cart:** the sun-god's chariot. 142. **Tellus:** goddess of the earth. 145. **Hymen:** god of marriage. 146. **bands:** bonds. 151. **distrust:** fear for.

[For] women's fear and love hold quantity,
In neither aught, or in extremity.
Now what my [love] is, proof hath made you know,
And as my love is siz'd, my fear is so.
Where love is great, the littlest doubts are fear;
Where little fears grow great, great love grows there.
[*P.*] KING: Faith, I must leave thee, love, and shortly too;
My operant powers their functions leave to do,
And thou shalt live in this fair world behind,
Honor'd, belov'd, and haply one as kind
For husband shalt thou—
[*P.*] QUEEN: O, confound the rest!
Such love must needs be treason in my breast.
In second husband let me be accurs'd!
None wed the second but who kill'd the first.
HAM [*Aside.*]: That's wormwood!
[*P.* QUEEN.] The instances that second marriage move
Are base respects of thrift, but none of love.
A second time I kill my husband dead,
When second husband kisses me in bed.
[*P.*] KING: I do believe you think what now you speak,
But what we do determine, oft we break.
Purpose is but the slave to memory,
Of violent birth, but poor validity,
Which now, the fruit unripe, sticks on the tree,
But fall unshaken when they mellow be.
Most necessary 'tis that we forget
To pay ourselves what to ourselves is debt.
What to ourselves in passion we propose,
The passion ending, doth the purpose lose.
The violence of either grief or joy
Their own enactures with themselves destroy.

---

153. **hold quantity:** are related in direct proportion. 155. **proof:** experience. 160. **operant:** active, vital. **leave to do:** cease to perform. 164. **confound the rest:** may destruction befall what you are about to speak of—a second marriage on my part. 169. **instances:** motives. **move:** give rise to. 170. **respects of thrift:** considerations of advantage. 176. **validity:** strength, power to last. 179–80. **Most . . . debt:** i.e. such resolutions are debts we owe to ourselves, and it would be foolish to pay such debts. 181. **passion:** violent emotion. 183–84. **The violence . . . destroy:** i.e. both violent grief and violent joy fail of their intended acts because they destroy themselves by their very violence.

Where joy most revels, grief doth most lament;
Grief [joys], joy grieves, on slender accident.
This world is not for aye, nor 'tis not strange
That even our loves should with our fortunes change:
For 'tis a question left us yet to prove,
Whether love lead fortune, or else fortune love.
The great man down, you mark his favorite flies,
The poor advanc'd makes friends of enemies.
And hitherto doth love on fortune tend,
For who not needs shall never lack a friend,
And who in want a hollow friend doth try,
Directly seasons him his enemy.
But orderly to end where I begun,
Our wills and fates do so contrary run
That our devices still are overthrown,
Our thoughts are ours, their ends none of our own:
So think thou wilt no second husband wed,
But die thy thoughts when thy first lord is dead.

[*P.*] QUEEN: Nor earth to me give food, nor heaven light,
Sport and repose lock from me day and night,
To desperation turn my trust and hope,
[An] anchor's cheer in prison be my scope!
Each opposite that blanks the face of joy
Meet what I would have well and it destroy!
Both here and hence pursue me lasting strife,
If once a widow, ever I be wife!

HAM: If she should break it now!

[*P.*] KING: 'Tis deeply sworn. Sweet, leave me here a while,
My spirits grow dull, and fain I would beguile
The tedious day with sleep. [*Sleeps.*]

[*P.*] QUEEN: Sleep rock thy brain,
And never come mischance between us twain! *Exit.*

HAM: Madam, how like you this play?

QUEEN: The lady doth protest too much, methinks.

HAM: O but she'll keep her word.

KING: Have you heard the argument? is there no offense in't?

---

186. **slender accident:** slight occasion. 196. **seasons:** ripens, converts into. 199. **devices:** devisings, intentions. **still:** always. 206. **anchor's cheer:** hermit's fare. **my scope:** the extent of my comforts. 207. **blanks:** blanches, makes pale (a symptom of grief). 220. **offense:** offensive matter (but Hamlet quibbles on the sense "crime").

HAM: No, no, they do but jest, poison in jest—no offense i' th' world.

KING: What do you call the play?

HAM: "The Mouse-trap." Marry, how? tropically: this play is the image of a murther done in Vienna; Gonzago is the duke's name, his wife, Baptista. You shall see anon. 'Tis a knavish piece of work, but what of that? Your Majesty, and we that have free souls, it touches us not. Let the gall'd jade winch, our withers are unwrung.

Enter LUCIANUS.

This is one Lucianus, nephew to the king.

OPH: You are as good as a chorus, my lord.

HAM: I could interpret between you and your love, if I could see the puppets dallying.

OPH: You are keen, my lord, you are keen.

HAM: It would cost you a groaning to take off mine edge.

OPH: Still better, and worse.

HAM: So you mistake your husbands. Begin, murtherer, leave thy damnable faces and begin. Come, the croaking raven doth bellow for revenge.

LUC: Thoughts black, hands apt, drugs fit, and time agreeing,
[Confederate] season, else no creature seeing,
Thou mixture rank, of midnight weeds collected,
With Hecat's ban thrice blasted, thrice [infected],
Thy natural magic and dire property
On wholesome life usurps immediately.

[*Pours the poison in his ears.*]

HAM: 'A poisons him i' th' garden for his estate. His name's Gonzago, the story is extant, and written in very choice Italian. You shall see anon how the murtherer gets the love of Gonzago's wife.

---

221. **jest:** i.e. pretend. 223. **tropically:** figuratively **image:** representation. 226. **free souls:** clear consciences. 227. **gall'd jade:** chafed horse. **winch:** wince. **withers:** ridge between a horse's shoulders. **unwrung:** not rubbed sore. 229. **chorus:** i.e. one who explains the forthcoming action. 230–31. **I . . . dallying:** I could speak the dialogue between you and your lover like a puppet-master (with an indecent jest). 232. **keen:** bitter, sharp. 234. **better, and worse:** i.e. more pointed and less decent. 235. **So:** i.e. "for better, for worse," in the words of the marriage service. **mistake:** i.e. mis-take, take wrongfully. Their vows, Hamlet suggests, prove false. 236. **faces:** facial expressions. 236–37. **the croaking . . . revenge.** Misquoted from an old play. *The True Tragedy of Richard III.* 239. **Confederate season:** the time being my ally. 241. **Hecat's ban:** the curse of Hecate, goddess of witchcraft.

OPH: The King rises.
[HAM: What, frighted with false fire?]
QUEEN: How fares my lord?
POL: Give o'er the play.
KING: Give me some light. Away!
POL: Lights, lights, lights!

Exeunt all but HAMLET *and* HORATIO.

HAM: "Why, let the strooken deer go weep,
The hart ungalled play,
For some must watch while some must sleep,
Thus runs the world away."
Would not this, sir, and a forest of feathers—if the rest of my fortunes turn Turk with me—with [two] Provincial roses on my raz'd shoes, get me a fellowship in a cry of players?
HOR: Half a share.
HAM: A whole one, I.
"For thou dost know, O Damon dear,
This realm dismantled was
Of Jove himself, and now reigns here
A very, very"—pajock.
HOR: You might have rhym'd.
HAM: O good Horatio, I'll take the ghost's word for a thousand pound. Didst perceive?
HOR: Very well, my lord.
HAM: Upon the talk of the pois'ning?
HOR: I did very well note him.
HAM: Ah, ha! Come, some music! Come, the recorders!
For if the King like not the comedy,
Why then belike he likes it not, perdy.
Come, some music!

Enter ROSENCRANTZ *and* GUILDENSTERN.

GUIL: Good my lord, voutsafe me a word with you.

---

248. **false fire:** i.e. a blank cartridge. 253. **strooken:** struck, i.e. wounded. 254. **ungalled:** unwounded. 255. **watch:** stay awake. 257. **feathers:** the plumes worn by tragic actors. 258. **turn Turk:** i.e. go to the bad. **Provincial roses:** rosettes designed to look like a variety of French rose. **raz'd:** with decorating slashing. 259. **fellowship:** partnership. 259. **cry:** company. 263. **dismantled:** divested, deprived. 265. **pajock:** peacock (substituting for the rhyme-word *ass*). The natural history of the time attributed many vicious qualities to the peacock. 274. **perdy:** assuredly (French *pardieu*, "by God").

HAM: Sir, a whole history.

GUIL: The King, sir—

HAM: Ay, sir, what of him?

GUIL: Is in his retirement marvellous distemp'red.

HAM: With drink, sir?

GUIL: No, my lord, with choler.

HAM: Your wisdom should show itself more richer to signify this to the doctor, for for me to put him to his purgation would perhaps plunge him into more choler.

GUIL: Good my lord, put your discourse into some frame, and [start] not so wildly from my affair.

HAM: I am tame, sir. Pronounce.

GUIL: The Queen, your mother, in most great affliction of spirit, hath sent me to you.

HAM: You are welcome.

GUIL: Nay, good my lord, this courtesy is not of the right breed. If it shall please you to make me a wholesome answer, I will do your mother's commandement; if not, your pardon and my return shall be the end of [my] business.

HAM: Sir, I cannot.

ROS: What, my lord?

HAM: Make you a wholesome answer—my wit's diseas'd. But, sir, such answer as I can make, you shall command, or rather, as you say, my mother.
Therefore no more, but to the matter: my mother, you say—

ROS: Then thus she says: your behavior hath strook her into amazement and admiration.

HAM: O wonderful son, that can so stonish a mother! But is there no sequel at the heels of this mother's admiration? Impart.

ROS: She desires to speak with you in her closet ere you go to bed.

HAM: We shall obey, were she ten times our mother. Have you any further trade with us?

ROS: My lord, you once did love me.

HAM: And do still, by these pickers and stealers.

---

282. **choler:** anger (but Hamlet willfully takes up the word in the sense "biliousness"). 284. **put . . . purgation:** i.e. prescribe for what's wrong with him. 286. **frame:** logical structure 293. **wholesome:** sensible, rational. 294. **pardon:** permission for departure. 302–3. **amazement and admiration:** bewilderment and wonder. 304. **stonish:** astound. 306. **closet:** private room. 310. **pickers and stealers:** hands; which, as the Catechism says, we must keep "from picking and stealing."

ROS: Good my lord, what is your cause of distemper? You do surely bar the door upon your own liberty if you deny your griefs to your friend.

HAM: Sir, I lack advancement.

ROS: How can that be, when you have the voice of the King himself for your succession in Denmark?

HAM: Ay, sir, but "While the grass grows"—the proverb is something musty.

Enter the PLAYERS *with recorders.*

O, the recorders! Let me see one.—To withdraw with you—why do you go about to recover the wind of me, as if you would drive me into a toil?

GUIL: O my lord, if my duty be too bold, my love is too unmannerly.

HAM: I do not well understand that. Will you play upon this pipe?

GUIL: My lord, I cannot.

HAM: I pray you.

GUIL: Believe me, I cannot.

HAM: I do beseech you.

GUIL: I know no touch of it, my lord.

HAM: It is as easy as lying. Govern these ventages with your fingers and [thumbs], give it breath with your mouth, and it will discourse most eloquent music. Look you, these are the stops.

GUIL: But these cannot I command to any utt'rance of harmony. I have not the skill.

HAM: Why, look you now, how unworthy a thing you make of me! You would play upon me, you would seem to know my stops, you would pluck out the heart of my mystery, you would sound me from my lowest note to [the top of] my compass; and there is much music, excellent voice, in this little organ, yet cannot you make it speak. 'Sblood, do you think I am easier to be play'd on than a pipe? Call me what instrument you will, though you fret me, [yet] you cannot play upon me.

Enter POLONIUS.

God bless you, sir.

POL: My lord, the Queen would speak with you, and presently.

---

317. **proverb:** i.e. "While the grass grows, the steed starves." 317–18. **something musty:** somewhat stale. 320. **recover the wind:** get to windward. **toil:** snare. 328. **ventages:** stops. 337. **organ:** instrument. 339. **fret:** (1) finger (an instrument); (2) vex. 342. **presently:** at once.

HAM: Do you see yonder cloud that's almost in shape of a camel?
POL: By th' mass and 'tis, like a camel indeed.
HAM: Methinks it is like a weasel.
POL: It is back'd like a weasel.
HAM: Or like a whale.
POL: Very like a whale.
HAM: Then I will come to my mother by and by. [*Aside.*] They fool me to the top of my bent.—I will come by and by.
[POL.] I will say so. [*Exit.*]
HAM: "By and by" is easily said. Leave me, friends.

[*Exeunt all but* HAMLET.]

'Tis now the very witching time of night,
When churchyards yawn and hell itself [breathes] out
Contagion to this world. Now could I drink hot blood,
And do such [bitter business as the] day
Would quake to look on. Soft, now to my mother.
O heart, lose not thy nature! let not ever
The soul of Nero enter this firm bosom,
Let me be cruel, not unnatural;
I will speak [daggers] to her, but use none.
My tongue and soul in this be hypocrites—
How in my words somever she be shent,
To give them seals never my soul consent! *Exit.*

Scene III

Enter KING, ROSENCRANTZ, *and* GUILDENSTERN.

KING: I like him not, nor stands it safe with us
To let his madness range. Therefore prepare you.
I your commission will forthwith dispatch,
And he to England shall along with you.
The terms of our estate may not endure
Hazard so near 's as doth hourly grow
Out of his brows.

349–50. **They...bent:** they make me play the fool to the limit of my ability. 350. **by and by:** at once. 353. **witching:** i.e. when the powers of evil are at large. 358. **nature:** natural affection, filial feeling. 359. **Nero.** Murderer of his mother. 363. **shent:** rebuked. 364. **give them seals:** confirm them by deeds.

III.iii. Location: The castle. 1. **him:** i.e. his state of mind, his behavior. 3. **dispatch:** have drawn up. 5. **terms:** conditions, nature. **our estate:** my position (as king). 7. **his brows:** the madness visible in his face (?).

GUIL: We will ourselves provide.
Most holy and religious fear it is
To keep those many many bodies safe
That live and feed upon your Majesty.
ROS: The single and peculiar life is bound
With all the strength and armor of the mind
To keep itself from noyance, but much more
That spirit upon whose weal depends and rests
The lives of many. The cess of majesty
Dies not alone, but like a gulf doth draw
What's near it with it. Or it is a massy wheel
Fix'd on the summit of the highest mount,
To whose [huge] spokes ten thousand lesser things
Are mortis'd and adjoin'd, which when it falls,
Each small annexment, petty consequence,
Attends the boist'rous [ruin]. Never alone
Did the King sigh, but [with] a general groan.
KING: Arm you, I pray you, to this speedy viage,
For we will fetters put about this fear,
Which now goes too free-footed.
ROS: We will haste us.

Exeunt Gentlemen [ROSENCRANTZ *and* GUILDENSTERN].

Enter POLONIUS.

POL: My lord, he's going to his mother's closet.
Behind the arras I'll convey myself
To hear the process. I'll warrant she'll tax him home,
And as you said, and wisely was it said,
'Tis meet that some more audience than a mother,
Since nature makes them partial, should o'erhear
The speech, of vantage. Fare you well, my liege,
I'll call upon you ere you go to bed,
And tell you what I know.
KING: Thanks, dear my lord.

Exit [POLONIUS].

---

9. **fear:** concern. 12. **single and peculiar:** individual and private. 14. **noyance:** injury. 16. **cess:** cessation, death. 17. **gulf:** whirlpool. 21. **mortis'd:** fixed. 23. **Attends:** accompanies. **ruin:** fall. 25. **Arm:** prepare. **viage:** voyage. 26. **fear:** object of fear. 31. **process:** course of the talk. **tax him home:** take him severely to task. 35. **of vantage:** from an advantageous position (?) or in addition (?).

O, my offense is rank, it smells to heaven,
It hath the primal eldest curse upon't,
A brother's murther. Pray can I not,
Though inclination be as sharp as will.
My stronger guilt defeats my strong intent,
And, like a man to double business bound,
I stand in pause where I shall first begin,
And both neglect. What if this cursed hand
Were thicker than itself with brother's blood,
Is there not rain enough in the sweet heavens
To wash it white as snow? Whereto serves mercy
But to confront the visage of offense?
And what's in prayer but this twofold force,
To be forestalled ere we come to fall,
Or [pardon'd] being down? then I'll look up.
My fault is past, but, O, what form of prayer
Can serve my turn? "Forgive me my foul murther"?
That cannot be, since I am still possess'd
Of those effects for which I did the murther:
My crown, mine own ambition, and my queen.
May one be pardon'd and retain th' offense?
In the corrupted currents of this world
Offense's gilded hand may [shove] by justice,
And oft 'tis seen the wicked prize itself
Buys out the law, but 'tis not so above:
There is no shuffling, there the action lies
In his true nature, and we ourselves compell'd,
Even to the teeth and forehead of our faults,
To give in evidence. What then? What rests?
Try what repentance can. What can it not?
Yet what can it, when one can not repent?
O wretched state! O bosom black as death!

---

40. **primal eldest curse:** i.e. God's curse on Cain, who also slew his brother. 42. **Though . . . will:** though my desire is as strong as my resolve to do so. 44. **bound:** committed. 46. **neglect:** omit. 49–50. **Whereto . . . offense:** i.e. what function has mercy except when there has been sin. 59. **th' offense:** i.e. the "effects" or fruits of the offense. 60. **currents:** courses. 61. **gilded:** i.e. bribing. 62. **wicked prize:** rewards of vice. 64. **shuffling:** evasion. **the action lies:** the charge comes for legal consideration. 66. **Even . . . forehead:** i.e. fully recognizing their features, extenuating nothing. 67. **rests:** remains.

O limed soul, that struggling to be free
Art more engag'd! Help, angels! Make assay,
Bow, stubborn knees, and heart, with strings of steel,
Be soft as sinews of the new-born babe!
All may be well. [*He kneels.*]

Enter HAMLET.

HAM: Now might I do it [pat], now 'a is a-praying;
And now I'll do't—and so 'a goes to heaven,
And so am I [reveng'd]. That would be scann'd:
A villain kills my father, and for that
I, his sole son, do this same villain send
To heaven.
Why, this is [hire and salary], not revenge.
'A took my father grossly, full of bread,
With all his crimes broad blown, as flush as May,
And how his audit stands who knows save heaven?
But in our circumstance and course of thought
'Tis heavy with him. And am I then revenged,
To take him in the purging of his soul,
When he is fit and season'd for his passage?
No!
Up, sword, and know thou a more horrid hent:
When he is drunk asleep, or in his rage,
Or in th' incestious pleasure of his bed,
At game a-swearing, or about some act
That has no relish of salvation in't—.
Then trip him, that his heels may kick at heaven,
And that his soul may be as damn'd and black
As hell, whereto it goes. My mother stays,
This physic but prolongs thy sickly days. *Exit.*

KING: [*Rising.*] My words fly up, my thoughts remain below:
Words without thoughts never to heaven go. *Exit.*

---

71. **limed:** caught (as in birdlime, a sticky substance used for catching birds). 72. **engag'd:** entangled. 78. **would be scann'd:** must be carefully considered. 83. **grossly:** in a gross state; not spiritually prepared. 84. **crimes:** sins. **broad blown:** in full bloom. **flush:** lusty, vigorous. 85. **audit:** account. 86. **in . . . thought:** i.e. to the best of our knowledge and belief. 91. **Up:** into the sheath. **know . . . bent:** be grasped at a more dreadful time. 95. **relish:** trace. 99. **physic:** (attempted) remedy, i.e. prayer.

Scene IV

Enter [QUEEN] GERTRUDE *and* POLONIUS.

POL: 'A will come straight. Look you lay home to him.
Tell him his pranks have been too broad to bear with,
And that your Grace hath screen'd and stood between
Much heat and him. I'll silence me even here;
Pray you be round [with him].

QUEEN: I'll [warr'nt] you, fear me not. Withdraw,
I hear him coming. [POLONIUS *hides behind the arras.*]

Enter HAMLET.

HAM: Now, mother, what's the matter?

QUEEN: Hamlet, thou hast thy father much offended.

HAM: Mother, you have my father much offended.

QUEEN: Come, come, you answer with an idle tongue.

HAM: Go, go, you question with a wicked tongue.

QUEEN: Why, how now, Hamlet?

HAM: What's the matter now?

QUEEN: Have you forgot me?

HAM: No, by the rood, not so:
You are the Queen, your husband's brother's wife,
And would it were not so, you are my mother.

QUEEN: Nay, then I'll set those to you that can speak.

HAM: Come, come, and sit you down, you shall not boudge;
You go not till I set you up a glass
Where you may see the [inmost] part of you.

QUEEN: What wilt thou do? Thou wilt not murther me?
Help ho!

POL [*Behind.*]: What ho, help!

HAM [*Drawing.*]: How now? A rat? Dead, for a ducat, dead! [*Kills* POLONIUS *through the arras.*]

POL [*Behind.*]: O, I am slain.

QUEEN: O me, what hast thou done?

HAM: Nay, I know not, is it the King?

QUEEN: O, what a rash and bloody deed is this!

III.iv. Location: The Queen's closet in the castle. 1. **lay . . . him:** reprove him severely. 2. **broad:** unrestrained. 5. **round:** plain-spoken. 6. **fear me not:** have no fears about my handling of the situation. 11. **idle:** foolish. 16. **rood:** cross. 20. **boudge:** budge. 26. **for a ducat:** I'll wager a ducat.

HAM: A bloody deed! almost as bad, good mother,
As kill a king, and marry with his brother.
QUEEN: As kill a king!
HAM: Ay, lady, it was my word.

[*Parts the arras and discovers* POLONIUS.]

Thou wretched, rash, intruding fool, farewell!
I took thee for thy better. Take thy fortune;
Thou find'st to be too busy is some danger.—
Leave wringing of your hands. Peace, sit you down,
And let me wring your heart, for so I shall
If it be made of penetrable stuff,
If damned custom have not brass'd it so
That it be proof and bulwark against sense.
QUEEN: What have I done, that thou dar'st wag thy tongue
In noise so rude against me?
HAM: Such an act
That blurs the grace and blush of modesty,
Calls virtue hypocrite, takes off the rose
From the fair forehead of an innocent love
And sets a blister there, makes marriage vows
As false as dicers' oaths, O, such a deed
As from the body of contraction plucks
The very soul, and sweet religion makes
A rhapsody of words. Heaven's face does glow
O'er this solidity and compound mass
With heated visage, as against the doom;
Is thought-sick at the act.
QUEEN: Ay me, what act,
That roars so loud and thunders in the index?
HAM: Look here upon this picture, and on this,
The counterfeit presentment of two brothers.
See what a grace was seated on this brow:

---

37. **busy:** officious, meddlesome. 41. **damned custom:** i.e. the habit of ill-doing. **brass'd:** hardened, literally, plated with brass. 42. **proof:** armor. **sense:** feeling. 49. **blister:** brand of shame. 51. **contraction:** the making of contracts, i.e. the assuming of solemn obligation. 52. **religion:** i.e. sacred vows. 53. **rhapsody:** miscellaneous collection, jumble. **glow:** i.e. with anger. 54. **this . . . mass:** i.e. the earth. *Compound* = compounded of the four elements. 55. **as . . . doom:** as if for Judgment Day. 58. **index:** i.e. table of contents. The index was formerly placed at the beginning of a book. 60. **counterfeit presentment:** painted likenesses.

Hyperion's curls, the front of Jove himself,
An eye like Mars, to threaten and command,
A station like the herald Mercury
New lighted on a [heaven-]kissing hill,
A combination and a form indeed,
Where every god did seem to set his seal
To give the world assurance of a man.
This was your husband. Look you now what follows:
Here is your husband, like a mildewed ear,
Blasting his wholesome brother. Have you eyes?
Could you on this fair mountain leave to feed,
And batten on this moor? ha, have you eyes?
You cannot call it love, for at your age
The heyday in the blood is tame, it's humble,
And waits upon the judgment, and what judgment
Would step from this to this? Sense sure you have,
Else could you not have motion, but sure that sense
Is apoplex'd, for madness would not err,
Nor sense to ecstasy was ne'er so thrall'd
But it reserv'd some quantity of choice
To serve in such a difference. What devil was't
That thus hath cozen'd you at hoodman-blind?
Eyes without feeling, feeling without sight,
Ears without hands or eyes, smelling sans all,
Or but a sickly part of one true sense
Could not so mope. O shame, where is thy blush?
Rebellious hell,
If thou canst mutine in a matron's bones,
To flaming youth let virtue be as wax
And melt in her own fire. Proclaim no shame
When the compulsive ardure gives the charge,
Since frost itself as actively doth burn,
And reason [panders] will.

---

62. **Hyperion's:** the sun-god's. **front:** forehead. 64. **station:** bearing. 70. **ear:** i.e. of grain. 73. **batten:** gorge. 75. **heyday:** excitement. 77. **Sense:** sense perception, the five senses. 79. **apoplex'd:** paralyzed. 79–82. **madness . . . difference:** i.e. madness itself could not go so far astray, nor were the senses ever so enslaved by lunacy that they did not retain the power to make so obvious a distinction. 83. **cozen'd:** cheated. **hoodman-blind:** blindman's bluff. 85. **sans:** without. 87. **mope:** be dazed. 89. **mutine:** rebel. 91–94. **Proclaim . . . will:** do not call it sin when the hot blood of youth is responsible for lechery, since here we see people of calmer age on fire for it; and reason acts as procurer for desire, instead of restraining it. *Ardure* = ardor.

QUEEN: O Hamlet, speak no more!
Thou turn'st my [eyes into my very] soul,
And there I see such black and [grained] spots
As will [not] leave their tinct.
HAM: Nay, but to live
In the rank sweat of an enseamed bed,
Stew'd in corruption, honeying and making love
Over the nasty sty!
QUEEN: O, speak to me no more!
These words like daggers enter in my ears.
No more, sweet Hamlet!
HAM: A murtherer and a villain!
A slave that is not twentith part the [tithe]
Of your precedent lord, a Vice of kings,
A cutpurse of the empire and the rule,
That from a shelf the precious diadem stole,
And put it in his pocket—
QUEEN: No more!

Enter GHOST [*in his night-gown*].

HAM: A king of shreds and patches—
Save me, and hover o'er me with your wings,
You heavenly guards! What would your gracious figure?
QUEEN: Alas, he's mad!
HAM: Do you not come your tardy son to chide,
That, laps'd in time and passion, lets go by
Th' important acting of your dread command?
O, say!
GHOST: Do not forget! This visitation
Is but to whet thy almost blunted purpose.
But look, amazement on thy mother sits,
O, step between her and her fighting soul.
Conceit in weakest bodies strongest works,
Speak to her, Hamlet.
HAM: How is it with you, lady?

---

97. **grained:** fast-dyed, indelible. 98. **leave their tinct:** lose their color. 100. **enseamed:** greasy. 107. **twentith:** twentieth. 108. **precedent:** former. **Vice:** buffoon (like the Vice of the morality plays). 112. s.d. **night-gown:** dressing gown. 113. **of . . . patches:** clownish (alluding to the motley worn by jesters) (?) or patched-up, beggarly (?). 118. **laps'd . . . passion:** "having suffered time to slip and passion to cool" (Johnson). 119. **important:** urgent. 123. **amazement:** utter bewilderment. 125. **Conceit:** imagination.

QUEEN: Alas, how is't with you,
That you do bend your eye on vacancy,
And with th' incorporal air do hold discourse?
Forth at your eyes your spirits wildly peep,
And as the sleeping soldiers in th' alarm,
Your bedded hair, like life in excrements,
Start up and stand an end. O gentle son,
Upon the heat and flame of thy distemper
Sprinkle cool patience. Whereon do you look?
HAM: On him, on him! look you how pale he glares!
His form and cause conjoin'd, preaching to stones,
Would make them capable.—Do not look upon me,
Lest with this piteous action you convert
My stern effects, then what I have to do
Will want true color—tears perchance for blood.
QUEEN: To whom do you speak this?
HAM: Do you see nothing there?
QUEEN: Nothing at all, yet all that is I see.
HAM: Nor did you nothing hear?
QUEEN: No, nothing but ourselves.
HAM: Why, look you there, look how it steals away!
My father, in his habit as he lived!
Look where he goes, even now, out at the portal!

Exit GHOST.

QUEEN: This is the very coinage of your brain,
This bodiless creation ecstasy
Is very cunning in.
HAM: [Ecstasy?]
My pulse as yours doth temperately keep time,
And makes as healthful music. It is not madness
That I have utt'red. Bring me to the test,
And [I] the matter will reword, which madness
Would gambol from. Mother, for love of grace,
Lay not that flattering unction to your soul,

---

132. **in th' alarm:** when the call to arms is sounded. 133. **excrements:** outgrowths; here, hair (also used of nails). 134. **an end:** on end. 136. **patience:** self-control. 138. **His . . . cause:** his appearance and what he has to say. 139. **capable:** sensitive, receptive. 140. **convert:** alter. 141. **effects:** (purposed) actions. 142. **want true color:** lack its proper appearance. 149. **habit:** dress. 152. **ecstasy:** madness. 158. **gambol:** start, jerk away. 159. **flattering unction:** soothing ointment.

That not your trespass but my madness speaks;
It will but skin and film the ulcerous place,
Whiles rank corruption, mining all within,
Infects unseen. Confess yourself to heaven,
Repent what's past, avoid what is to come,
And do not spread the compost on the weeds
To make them ranker. Forgive me this my virtue,
For in the fatness of these pursy times
Virtue itself of vice must pardon beg,
Yea, curb and woo for leave to do him good.

QUEEN: O Hamlet, thou hast cleft my heart in twain.

HAM: O, throw away the worser part of it,
And [live] the purer with the other half.
Good night, but go not to my uncle's bed—
Assume a virtue, if you have it not.
That monster custom, who all sense doth eat,
Of habits devil, is angel yet in this,
That to the use of actions fair and good
He likewise gives a frock or livery
That aptly is put on. Refrain [to-]night,
And that shall lend a kind of easiness
To the next abstinence, the next more easy;
For use almost can change the stamp of nature,
And either [. . . .] the devil or throw him out
With wondrous potency. Once more good night,
And when you are desirous to be blest,
I'll blessing beg of you. For this same lord,

[*Pointing to* POLONIUS.]

I do repent; but heaven hath pleas'd it so
To punish me with this, and this with me,
That I must be their scourge and minister.

---

165. **compost:** manure. 167. **pursy:** puffy, out of condition. 169. **curb and woo:** bow and entreat. 175. **all . . . eat:** wears away all natural feeling. 176. **Of habits devil:** i.e. though it acts like a devil in establishing bad habits. Most editors read (in lines 175–76) *eat / Of habits evil*, following Theobald. 178–79. **frock . . . on:** i.e. a "habit" or customary garment, readily put on without need of any decision. 182. **use:** habit. 183. A word seems to be wanting after *either* 185. **desirous . . . blest:** i.e. repentant. 189. **scourge and minister:** the agent of heavenly justice against human crime. *Scourge* suggests a permissive cruelty (Tamburlaine was the "scourge of God"), but "woe to him by whom the offense cometh"; the scourge most suffer for the evil it performs.

I will bestow him, and will answer well
The death I gave him. So again good night.
I must be cruel only to be kind.
This bad begins and worse remains behind.
One word more, good lady.
QUEEN: What shall I do?
HAM: Not this, by no means, that I bid you do:
Let the bloat king tempt you again to bed,
Pinch wanton on your cheek, call you his mouse,
And let him, for a pair of reechy kisses,
Or paddling in your neck with his damn'd fingers,
Make you to ravel all this matter out,
That I essentially am not in madness,
But mad in craft. 'Twere good you let him know,
For who that's but a queen, fair, sober, wise,
Would from a paddock, from a bat, a gib,
Such dear concernings hide? Who would do so?
No, in despite of sense and secrecy,
Unpeg the basket on the house's top,
Let the birds fly, and like the famous ape,
To try conclusions in the basket creep,
And break your own neck down.
QUEEN: Be thou assur'd, if words be made of breath,
And breath of life, I have no life to breathe
What thou hast said to me.
HAM: I must to England, you know that?
QUEEN: Alack,
I had forgot. 'Tis so concluded on.
HAM: There's letters seal'd, and my two schoolfellows,
Whom I will trust as I will adders fang'd,
They bear the mandate, they must sweep my way
And marshal me to knavery. Let it work,
For 'tis the sport to have the enginer
Hoist with his own petar, an't shall go hard

---

190. **bestow:** dispose of. **answer:** answer for. 193. **behind:** to come. 199. **reechy:** filthy. 205. **paddock:** toad. **gib:** tom-cat. 206. **dear concernings:** matters of intense concern. 208. **Unpeg the basket:** open the door of the cage. 209. **famous ape.** The actual story has been lost. 210. **conclusions:** experiments (to see whether he too can fly if he enters the cage and then leaps out). 211. **down:** by the fall. 221. **knavery:** some knavish scheme against me. 222. **enginer:** deviser of military "engines" or contrivances. 223. **Hoist with:** blown up by. **petar:** petard, bomb.

But I will delve one yard below their mines,
And blow them at the moon. O, 'tis most sweet
When in one line two crafts directly meet.
This man shall set me packing;
I'll lug the guts into the neighbor room.
Mother, good night indeed. This counsellor
Is now most still, most secret, and most grave,
Who was in life a foolish prating knave.
Come, sir, to draw toward an end with you.
Good night, mother.

Exeunt [*severally,* HAMLET *tugging in* POLONIUS].

Act IV

Scene I

Enter KING *and* QUEEN *with* ROSENCRANTZ *and* GUILDENSTERN.

KING: There's matter in these sighs, these profound heaves—
You must translate, 'tis fit we understand them.
Where is your son?
QUEEN: Bestow this place on us a little while.

[*Exeunt* ROSENCRANTZ *and* GUILDENSTERN.]

Ah, mine own lord, what have I seen to-night!
KING: What, Gertrude? How does Hamlet?
QUEEN: Mad as the sea and wind when both contend
Which is the mightier. In his lawless fit,
Behind the arras hearing something stir,
Whips out his rapier, cries, "A rat, a rat!"
And in this brainish apprehension kills
The unseen good old man.
KING: O heavy deed!
It had been so with us had we been there.
His liberty is full of threats to all,
To you yourself, to us, to every one.
Alas, how shall this bloody deed be answer'd?

---

226. **crafts:** plots. 227. **packing:** (1) taking on a load; (2) leaving in a hurry. 232. **draw... end:** finish my conversation.

IV.i. Location: The castle. 11. **brainish apprehension:** crazy notion. 17. **answer'd:** i.e. satisfactorily accounted for to the public.

It will be laid to us, whose providence
Should have kept short, restrain'd, and out of haunt
This mad young man; but so much was our love,
We would not understand what was most fit,
But like the owner of a foul disease,
To keep it from divulging, let it feed
Even on the pith of life. Where is he gone?

QUEEN: To draw apart the body he hath kill'd,
O'er whom his very madness, like some ore
Among a mineral of metals base,
Shows itself pure: 'a weeps for what is done.

KING: O Gertrude, come away!
The sun no sooner shall the mountains touch,
But we will ship him hence, and this vile deed
We must with all our majesty and skill
Both countenance and excuse. Ho, Guildenstern!

Enter ROSENCRANTZ *and* GUILDENSTERN.

Friends both, go join you with some further aid:
Hamlet in madness hath Polonius slain,
And from his mother's closet hath he dragg'd him.
Go seek him out, speak fair, and bring the body
Into the chapel. I pray you haste in this.

[*Exeunt* ROSENCRANTZ *and* GUILDENSTERN.]

Come, Gertrude, we'll call up our wisest friends
And let them know both what we mean to do
And what's untimely done, [. . . .]
Whose whisper o'er the world's diameter,
As level as the cannon to his blank,
Transports his pois'ned shot, may miss our name,
And hit the woundless air. O, come away!
My soul is full of discord and dismay. *Exeunt.*

---

18. **providence:** foresight. 19. **short:** on a short leash. **out of haunt:** away from other people. 23. **divulging:** being revealed. 26. **ore:** vein of gold. 27. **mineral:** mine. 41. Some words are wanting at the end of the line. Capell's conjecture, *so, haply, slander,* probably indicates the intended sense of the passage. 43. **As level:** with aim as good. **blank:** target. 45. **woundless:** incapable of being hurt.

Scene II

Enter HAMLET.

HAM: Safely stow'd.

[GENTLEMEN. (*Within.*) Hamlet! Lord Hamlet!]

[HAM:] But soft, what noise? Who calls on Hamlet? O, here they come.

Enter ROSENCRANTZ *and* [GUILDENSTERN].

ROS: What have you done, my lord, with the dead body?

HAM: [Compounded] it with dust, whereto 'tis kin.

ROS: Tell us where 'tis, that we may take it thence, And bear it to the chapel.

HAM: Do not believe it.

ROS: Believe what?

HAM: That I can keep your counsel and not mine own. Besides, to be demanded of a spunge, what replication should be made by the son of a king?

ROS: Take you me for a spunge, my lord?

HAM: Ay, sir, that soaks up the King's countenance, his rewards, his authorities. But such officers do the King best service in the end: he keeps them, like [an ape] an apple, in the corner of his jaw, first mouth'd, to be last swallow'd. When he needs what you have glean'd, it is but squeezing you, and, spunge, you shall be dry again.

ROS: I understand you not, my lord.

HAM: I am glad of it, a knavish speech sleeps in a foolish ear.

ROS: My lord, you must tell us where the body is, and go with us to the King.

HAM: The body is with the King, but the King is not with the body. The King is a thing—

GUIL: A thing, my lord?

HAM: Of nothing, bring me to him. [Hide fox, and all after.]

Exeunt.

IV.ii. Location: The castle. 11. **demanded of:** questioned by. **spunge:** sponge. **replication:** reply. 14. **countenance:** favor. 20. **sleeps:** is meaningless. 23. **The body... the body.** Possibly alluding to the legal fiction that the king's dignity is separate from his mortal body. 26. **Of nothing:** of no account. Cf. "Man is like a thing of nought, his time passeth away like a shadow" (Psalm 144:4 in the Prayer Book version). "Hamlet at once insults the King and hints that his days are numbered" (Dover Wilson). 26. **Hide... after.** Probably a cry in some game resembling hide-and-seek.

Scene III

Enter KING *and two or three.*

KING: I have sent to seek him, and to find the body.
How dangerous is it that this man goes loose!
Yet must not we put the strong law on him.
He's lov'd of the distracted multitude,
Who like not in their judgment, but their eyes,
And where 'tis so, th' offender's scourge is weigh'd,
But never the offense. To bear all smooth and even,
This sudden sending him away must seem
Deliberate pause. Diseases desperate grown
By desperate appliance are reliev'd,
Or not at all.

Enter ROSENCRANTZ.

How now, what hath befall'n?
ROS: Where the dead body is bestow'd, my lord,
We cannot get from him.
KING: But where is he?
ROS: Without, my lord, guarded, to know your pleasure.
KING: Bring him before us.
ROS: Ho, bring in the lord.

They [HAMLET *and* GUILDENSTERN] *enter.*

KING: Now, Hamlet, where's Polonius?
HAM: At supper.
KING: At supper? where?
HAM: Not where he eats, but where 'a is eaten; a certain convocation of politic worms are e'en at him. Your worm is your only emperor for diet: we fat all creatures else to fat us, and we fat ourselves for maggots; your fat king and your lean beggar is but variable service, two dishes, but to one table—that's the end.
KING: Alas, alas!
HAM: A man may fish with the worm that hath eat of a king, and eat of the fish that hath fed of that worm.

IV.iii. Location: The castle. 4. **distracted:** unstable. 6. **scourge:** i.e. punishment. 7. **bear:** manage. 8–9. **must . . . pause:** i.e. must be represented as a maturely considered decision. 23. **politic:** crafty, prying; "such worms as might breed in a politician's corpse" (Dowden). **e'en:** even now. 24. **for diet:** with respect to what it eats. 25. **variable service:** different courses of a meal.

KING: What dost thou mean by this?

HAM: Nothing but to show you how a king may go a progress through the guts of a beggar.

KING: Where is Polonius?

HAM: In heaven, send thither to see; if your messenger find him not there, seek him i' th' other place yourself. But if indeed you find him not within this month, you shall nose him as you go up the stairs into the lobby.

KING [*To Attendants.*]: Go seek him there.

HAM: 'A will stay till you come.

[*Exeunt* ATTENDANTS.]

KING: Hamlet, this deed, for thine especial safety—
Which we do tender, as we dearly grieve
For that which thou hast done—must send thee hence
[With fiery quickness]; therefore prepare thyself,
The bark is ready, and the wind at help,
Th' associates tend, and every thing is bent
For England.

HAM: For England.

KING: Ay, Hamlet.

HAM: Good.

KING: So is it, if thou knew'st our purposes.

HAM: I see a cherub that sees them. But come, for England! Farewell, dear mother.

KING: Thy loving father, Hamlet.

HAM: My mother: father and mother is man and wife, man and wife is one flesh—so, my mother.
Come, for England! *Exit.*

KING: Follow him at foot, tempt him with speed aboard.
Delay it not, I'll have him hence to-night.
Away, for every thing is seal'd and done
That else leans on th' affair. Pray you make haste.

[*Exeunt* ROSENCRANTZ *and* GUILDENSTERN.]

And, England, if my love thou hold'st at aught—
As my great power thereof may give thee sense,

---

31. **progress:** royal journey of state. 41. **tender:** regard with tenderness, hold dear. **dearly:** with intense feeling. 44. **at help:** favorable. 45. **Th':** thy. **tend:** await. **bent:** made ready. 48. **I . . . them:** i.e. heaven sees them. 54. **at foot:** at his heels, close behind. 60. **leans on:** relates to. 61. **England:** King of England.

Since yet thy cicatrice looks raw and red
After the Danish sword, and thy free awe
Pays homage to us—thou mayst not coldly set
Our sovereign process, which imports at full,
By letters congruing to that effect,
The present death of Hamlet. Do it, England,
For like the hectic in my blood he rages,
And thou must cure me. Till I know 'tis done,
How e'er my haps, my joys [were] ne'er [begun]. *Exit.*

Scene IV

Enter FORTINBRAS *with his army over the stage.*

FORT: Go, captain, from me greet the Danish king.
Tell him that by his license Fortinbras
Craves the conveyance of a promis'd march
Over his kingdom. You know the rendezvous.
If that his Majesty would aught with us,
We shall express our duty in his eye,
And let him know so.

CAP: I will do't, my lord.

FORT: Go softly on. [*Exeunt all but the* CAPTAIN.]

Enter HAMLET, ROSENCRANTZ, [GUILDENSTERN,] *etc.*

HAM: Good sir, whose powers are these?

CAP: They are of Norway, sir.

HAM: How purpos'd, sir, I pray you?

CAP: Against some part of Poland.

HAM: Who commands them, sir?

CAP: The nephew to old Norway, Fortinbras.

HAM: Goes it against the main of Poland, sir,
Or for some frontier?

CAP: Truly to speak, and with no addition,

---

63. **cicatrice:** scar. 64–65. **thy . . . Pays:** your fear makes you pay voluntarily. 65. **coldly set:** undervalue, disregard. 66. **process:** command. 67. **congruing to:** in accord with. 68. **present:** immediate. 69. **hectic:** continuous fever. 71. **haps:** fortunes.

IV.iv. Location: The Danish coast, near the castle. 3. **conveyance of:** escort for. 6. **eye:** presence. 9. **softly:** slowly. 10. **powers:** forces. 16. **main:** main territory.

We go to gain a little patch of ground
That hath in it no profit but the name.
To pay five ducats, five, I would not farm it;
Nor will it yield to Norway or the Pole
A ranker rate, should it be sold in fee.

HAM: Why then the Polack never will defend it.

CAP: Yes, it is already garrison'd.

HAM: Two thousand souls and twenty thousand ducats
Will not debate the question of this straw.
This is th' imposthume of much wealth and peace,
That inward breaks, and shows no cause without
Why the man dies. I humbly thank you, sir.

CAP: God buy you, sir. [*Exit.*]

ROS: Will't please you go, my lord?

HAM: I'll be with you straight—go a little before.

[*Exeunt all but* HAMLET.]

How all occasions do inform against me,
And spur my dull revenge! What is a man,
If his chief good and market of his time
Be but to sleep and feed? a beast, no more.
Sure He that made us with such large discourse,
Looking before and after, gave us not
That capability and godlike reason
To fust in us unus'd. Now whether it be
Bestial oblivion, or some craven scruple
Of thinking too precisely on th' event—
A thought which quarter'd hath but one part wisdom
And ever three parts coward—I do not know
Why yet I live to say, "This thing's to do,"
Sith I have cause, and will, and strength, and means
To do't. Examples gross as earth exhort me:
Witness this army of such mass and charge,
Led by a delicate and tender prince,

---

21. **To pay:** i.e. for an annual rent of. **farm:** lease. 23. **ranker:** higher. **in fee:** outright. 27. **Will not debate:** i.e. will scarcely be enough to fight out. 28. **imposthume:** abscess. 34. **inform against:** denounce, accuse. 36. **market:** purchase, profit. 38. **discourse:** reasoning power. 41. **fust:** grow mouldy. 42. **oblivion:** forgetfulness. 43. **event:** outcome. 48. **gross:** large, obvious. 49. **mass and charge:** size and expense.

Whose spirit with divine ambition puff'd
Makes mouths at the invisible event,
Exposing what is mortal and unsure
To all that fortune, death, and danger dare,
Even for an egg-shell. Rightly to be great
Is not to stir without great argument,
But greatly to find quarrel in a straw
When honor's at the stake. How stand I then,
That have a father kill'd, a mother stain'd,
Excitements of my reason and my blood,
And let all sleep, while to my shame I see
The imminent death of twenty thousand men,
That for a fantasy and trick of fame
Go to their graves like beds, fight for a plot
Whereon the numbers cannot try the cause,
Which is not tomb enough and continent
To hide the slain? O, from this time forth,
My thoughts be bloody, or be nothing worth! *Exit.*

Scene V

Enter HORATIO, [QUEEN] GERTRUDE, *and a* GENTLEMAN.

QUEEN: I will not speak with her.
GENT: She is importunate, indeed distract.
Her mood will needs be pitied.
QUEEN: What would she have?
GENT: She speaks much of her father, says she hears
There's tricks i' th' world, and hems, and beats her heart,
Spurns enviously at straws, speaks things in doubt
That carry but half sense. Her speech is nothing,
Yet the unshaped use of it doth move
The hearers to collection; they yawn at it,

52. **Makes mouths at:** treats scornfully. **invisible:** i.e. unforeseeable. 56. **Is not to:** i.e. is *not* not to. **argument:** cause. 57. **greatly:** nobly. 60. **Excitements of:** urgings by. 63. **fantasy:** caprice. **trick:** trifle. 65. **Whereon . . . cause:** which isn't large enough to let the opposing armies engage upon it. 66. **continent:** container.

IV.v. Location: The castle. 7. **Spurns . . . straws:** spitefully takes offense at trifles. **in doubt:** obscurely. 8. **Her speech:** what she says. 9. **unshaped use:** distracted manner. 10. **collection:** attempts to gather the meaning. **yawn at:** gape eagerly (as if to swallow). Most editors adopt the F1 reading *aim at.*

And botch the words up fit to their own thoughts,
Which as her winks and nods and gestures yield them,
Indeed would make one think there might be thought,
Though nothing sure, yet much unhappily.
HOR: 'Twere good she were spoken with, for she may strew
Dangerous conjectures in ill-breeding minds.
[QUEEN.] Let her come in. [*Exit* GENTLEMAN.]
[*Aside.*] To my sick soul, as sin's true nature is,
Each toy seems prologue to some great amiss,
So full of artless jealousy is guilt,
It spills itself in fearing to be spilt.

Enter OPHELIA [*distracted, with her hair down, playing an a lute*].

OPH: Where is the beauteous majesty of Denmark?
QUEEN: How now, Ophelia?
OPH: "How should I your true-love know *She sings.*
From another one?
By his cockle hat and staff,
And his sandal shoon."
QUEEN: Alas, sweet lady, what imports this song?
OPH: Say you? Nay, pray you mark.
"He is dead and gone, lady, *Song.*
He is dead and gone,
At his head a grass-green turf,
At his heels a stone."
O ho!
QUEEN: Nay, but, Ophelia—
OPH: Pray you mark.

[Sings.] "White his shroud as the mountain snow"—

Enter KING.

11. **botch:** patch. 12. **Which:** i.e. the words. 13. **thought:** inferred, conjectured. 16. **ill-breeding:** conceiving ill thoughts, prone to think the worst. 19. **toy:** trifle. **amiss:** calamity. 20. **artless jealousy:** uncontrolled suspicion. 21. **spills:** destroys. 24–25. These lines resemble a passage in an earlier ballad beginning "As you came from the holy land / Of Walsingham." Probably all the song fragments sung by Ophelia were familiar to the Globe audience, but only one other line (187) is from a ballad still extant. 26. **cockle hat:** hat bearing a cockle shell, the badge of a pilgrim to the shrine of St. James of Compostela in Spain. **staff.** Another mark of a pilgrim. 27. **shoon:** shoes (already an archaic form in Shakespeare's day).

QUEEN: Alas, look here, my lord.
OPH: "Larded all with sweet flowers, *Song.*
Which bewept to the ground did not go
With true-love showers."

KING: How do you, pretty lady?

OPH: Well, God dild you! They say the owl was a baker's daughter. Lord, we know what we are, but know not what we may be. God be at your table!

KING: Conceit upon her father.

OPH: Pray let's have no words of this, but when they ask you what it means, say you this:
"To-morrow is Saint Valentine's day, *Song.*
All in the morning betime,
And I a maid at your window,
To be your Valentine.

"Then up he rose and donn'd his clo'es,
And dupp'd the chamber-door,
Let in the maid, that out a maid
Never departed more."

KING: Pretty Ophelia!

OPH: Indeed without an oath I'll make an end on't,
[*Sings.*] "By Gis, and by Saint Charity,
Alack, and fie for shame!
Young men will do't if they come to't,
By Cock, they are to blame.

"Quoth she, 'Before you tumbled me,
You promis'd me to wed.'"
(He answers.)
"'So would I 'a' done, by yonder sun,
And thou hadst not come to my bed.'"

KING: How long hath she been thus?

OPH: I hope all will be well. We must be patient,

---

38. **Larded:** adorned. 39. **not.** Contrary to the expected sense, and unmetrical; explained as Ophelia's alteration of the line to accord with the facts of Polonius' burial (see line 82). 42. **dild:** yield, reward. **owl.** Alluding to the legend of a baker's daughter whom Jesus turned into an owl because she did not respond generously to his request for bread. 45. **Conceit:** fanciful brooding. 53. **dupp'd:** opened. 58. **Gis:** contraction of *Jesus.* 61. **Cock:** corruption of *God.* 65. **And:** if.

but I cannot choose but weep to think they would lay him i' th' cold ground. My brother shall know of it, and so I thank you for your good counsel. Come, my coach! Good night, ladies, good night. Sweet ladies, good night, good night. [*Exit.*]

KING: Follow her close, give her good watch, I pray you.

[*Exit* HORATIO.]

O, this is the poison of deep grief, it springs
All from her father's death—and now behold!
O Gertrude, Gertrude,
When sorrows come, they come not single spies,
But in battalions: first, her father slain;
Next, your son gone, and he most violent author
Of his own just remove; the people muddied,
Thick and unwholesome in [their] thoughts and whispers
For good Polonius' death; and we have done but greenly
In hugger-mugger to inter him; poor Ophelia
Divided from herself and her fair judgment,
Without the which we are pictures, or mere beasts;
Last, and as much containing as all these,
Her brother is in secret come from France,
Feeds on this wonder, keeps himself in clouds,
And wants not buzzers to infect his ear
With pestilent speeches of his father's death,
Wherein necessity, of matter beggar'd,
Will nothing stick our person to arraign
In ear and ear. O my dear Gertrude, this,
Like to a murd'ring-piece, in many places
Gives me superfluous death. *A noise within.*

[QUEEN: Alack, what noise is this?]

KING: Attend!
Where is my Swissers? Let them guard the door.

Enter a MESSENGER.

What is the matter?

76. **spies:** i.e. soldiers sent ahead of the main force to reconnoiter, scouts. 79. **muddied:** confused. 81. **greenly:** unwisely. 82. **In hugger-mugger:** secretly and hastily. 87. **in clouds:** i.e. in cloudy surmise and suspicion (rather than the light of fact). 88. **wants:** lacks. **buzzers:** whispering informers. 90. **of matter beggar'd:** destitute of facts 91. **nothing . . . arraign:** scruple not at all to charge me with the crime. 93. **murd'ring-piece:** cannon firing a scattering charge. 97. **Swissers:** Swiss guards.

MESS. Save yourself, my lord!
The ocean, overpeering of his list,
Eats not the flats with more impiteous haste
Than young Laertes, in a riotous head,
O'erbears your officers. The rabble call him lord,
And as the world were now but to begin,
Antiquity forgot, custom not known,
The ratifiers and props of every word,
[They] cry, "Choose we, Laertes shall be king!"
Caps, hands, and tongues applaud it to the clouds,
"Laertes shall be king, Laertes king!" *A noise within.*

QUEEN: How cheerfully on the false trail they cry!
O, this is counter, you false Danish dogs!

Enter LAERTES *with others.*

KING: The doors are broke.

LAER: Where is this king? Sirs, stand you all without.

ALL: No, let's come in.

LAER: I pray you give me leave.

ALL: We will, we will.

LAER: I thank you, keep the door. [*Exeunt* LAERTES' *followers.*]
O thou vile king,
Give me my father!

QUEEN: Calmly, good Laertes.

LAER: That drop of blood that's calm proclaims me bastard,
Cries cuckold to my father, brands the harlot
Even here between the chaste unsmirched brow
Of my true mother.

KING: What is the cause, Laertes,
That thy rebellion looks so giant-like?
Let him go, Gertrude, do not fear our person:
There's such divinity doth hedge a king
That treason can but peep to what it would,
Acts little of his will. Tell me, Laertes,
Why thou art thus incens'd. Let him go, Gertrude.
Speak, man.

---

100. **overpeering . . . list:** rising higher than its shores. 102. **in . . . head:** with a rebellious force. 104. **as:** as if. 106. **word:** pledge, promise. 111. **counter:** on the wrong scent (literally, following the scent backward). 127. **fear:** fear for. 129. **would:** i.e. would like to do.

LAER: Where is my father?
KING: Dead.
QUEEN: But not by him.
KING: Let him demand his fill.
LAER: How came he dead? I'll not be juggled with.
To hell, allegiance! vows, to the blackest devil!
Conscience and grace, to the profoundest pit!
I dare damnation. To this point I stand,
That both the worlds I give to negligence,
Let come what comes, only I'll be reveng'd
Most throughly for my father.
KING: Who shall stay you?
LAER: My will, not all the world's:
And for my means, I'll husband them so well,
They shall go far with little.
KING: Good Laertes,
If you desire to know the certainty
Of your dear father, is't writ in your revenge
That, swoopstake, you will draw both friend and foe,
Winner and loser?
LAER: None but his enemies.
KING: Will you know them then?
LAER: To his good friends thus wide I'll ope my arms,
And like the kind life-rend'ring pelican,
Repast them with my blood.
KING: Why, now you speak
Like a good child and a true gentleman.
That I am guiltless of your father's death,
And am most sensibly in grief for it,
It shall as level to your judgment 'pear
As day does to your eye.
A noise within: "Let her come in!"
LAER: How now, what noise is that?
Enter OPHELIA.

---

141. **both . . . negligence:** i.e. I don't care what the consequences are in this world or in the next. 143. **throughly:** thoroughly. 145. **world's:** i.e. world's will. 151. **swoopstake:** sweeping up everything without discrimination (modern *sweepstake*). 156. **pelican.** The female pelican was believed to draw blood from her own breast to nourish her young. 159. **good child:** faithful son. 161. **sensibly:** feelingly. 162. **level:** plain.

O heat, dry up my brains! tears seven times salt
Burn out the sense and virtue of mine eye!
By heaven, thy madness shall be paid with weight
[Till] our scale turn the beam. O rose of May!
Dear maid, kind sister, sweet Ophelia!
O heavens, is't possible a young maid's wits
Should be as mortal as [an old] man's life?
[Nature is fine in love, and where 'tis fine,
It sends some precious instance of itself
After the thing it loves.]

OPH: "They bore him barefac'd on the bier, *Song.*
[Hey non nonny, nonny, hey nonny,]
And in his grave rain'd many a tear"—
Fare you well, my dove!

LAER: Hadst thou thy wits and didst persuade revenge,
It could not move thus.

OPH: You must sing, "A-down, a-down," and you call him a-down-a. O how the wheel becomes it! It is the false steward, that stole his master's daughter.

LAER: This nothing's more than matter.

OPH: There's rosemary, that's for remembrance; pray you, love, remember. And there is pansies, that's for thoughts.

LAER: A document in madness, thoughts and remembrance fitted.

OPH [*To* CLAUDIUS.]: There's fennel for you, and columbines. [*To* GERTRUDE.] There's rue for you, and here's some for me; we may call it herb of grace a' Sundays. You may wear your rue with a difference. There's a daisy. I would give you some violets, but they wither'd all when my father died. They say 'a made a good end—

---

167. **virtue:** faculty. 173. **fine in:** refined or spiritualized by. 174. **instance:** proof, token. So delicate is Ophelia's love for her father that her sanity has pursued him into the grave. 180. **persuade:** argue logically for. 182–83. **and . . . . a-down-a:** "if he indeed agrees that Polonius is 'a-down,' i.e. fallen low" (Dover Wilson). 183. **wheel:** refrain (?) or spinning-wheel, at which women sang ballads (?). 185. **matter:** lucid speech. 187. **A document in madness:** a lesson contained in mad talk. 189. **fennel, columbines.** Symbols respectively of flattery and ingratitude. 190. **rue.** Symbolic of sorrow and repentance. 192. **with a difference:** i.e. to represent a different cause of sorrow. *Difference* is a term from heraldry, meaning a variation in a coat of arms made to distinguish different members of a family. 192–93. **daisy, violets.** Symbolic respectively of dissembling and faithfulness. It is not clear who are the recipients of these.

[*Sings.*] "For bonny sweet Robin is all my joy."
LAER: Thought and afflictions, passion, hell itself,
She turns to favor and to prettiness.
OPH: "And will 'a not come again? *Song.*
"And will 'a not come again?
No, no, he is dead,
Go to thy death-bed,
He never will come again.

"His beard was as white as snow,
[All] flaxen was his pole,
He is gone, he is gone,
And we cast away moan,
God 'a' mercy on his soul!"
And of all Christians' souls, [I pray God]. God buy you.
[*Exit.*]
LAER: Do you [see] this, O God?
KING: Laertes, I must commune with your grief,
Or you deny me right. Go but apart,
Make choice of whom your wisest friends you will,
And they shall hear and judge 'twixt you and me.
If by direct or by collateral hand
They find us touch'd, we will our kingdom give,
Our crown, our life, and all that we call ours,
To you in satisfaction; but if not,
Be you content to lend your patience to us,
And we shall jointly labor with your soul
To give it due content.
LAER: Let this be so.
His means of death, his obscure funeral—
No trophy, sword, nor hatchment o'er his bones,
No noble rite nor formal ostentation—
Cry to be heard, as 'twere from heaven to earth,
That I must call't in question.
KING: So you shall,
And where th' offense is, let the great axe fall.
I pray you go with me. *Exeunt.*

---

196. **Thought:** melancholy. 197. **favor:** grace, charm. 204. **flaxen:** white. **pole:** poll, head. 214. **collateral:** i.e. indirect. 215. **touch'd:** guilty. 223. **trophy:** memorial. **hatchment:** heraldic memorial tablet. 224. **formal ostentation:** fitting and customary ceremony. 226. **That:** so that.

Scene VI

Enter HORATIO *and others.*

HOR: What are they that would speak with me?

GENTLEMAN: Sea-faring men, sir. They say they have letters for you.

HOR: Let them come in. [*Exit* GENTLEMAN.]

I do not know from what part of the world
I should be greeted, if not from Lord Hamlet.

Enter SAILORS.

[*1.*] SAIL: God bless you, sir.

HOR: Let him bless thee too.

[*1.*] SAIL: 'A shall, sir, and['t] please him. There's a letter for you, sir—it came from th' embassador that was bound for England—if your name be Horatio, as I am let to know it is.

HOR [Reads.]: "Horatio, when thou shalt have overlook'd this, give these fellows some means to the King, they have letters for him. Ere we were two days old at sea, a pirate of very warlike appointment gave us chase. Finding ourselves too slow of sail, we put on a compell'd valor, and in the grapple I boarded them. On the instant they got clear of our ship, so I alone became their prisoner. They have dealt with me like thieves of mercy, but they knew what they did: I am to do a [good] turn for them. Let the King have the letters I have sent, and repair thou to me with as much speed as thou wouldest fly death. I have words to speak in thine ear will make thee dumb, yet are they much too light for the [bore] of the matter. These good fellows will bring thee where I am. Rosencrantz and Guildenstern hold their course for England, of them I have much to tell thee. Farewell.

[He] that thou knowest thine,

Hamlet."

Come, I will [give] you way for these your letters,
And do't the speedier that you may direct me
To him from whom you brought them. *Exeunt.*

IV.vi. Location: The castle. 17. **thieves of mercy:** merciful thieves. 21. **bore:** calibre, size (gunnery term).

Scene VII

Enter KING *and* LAERTES.

KING: Now must your conscience my acquittance seal,
And you must put me in your heart for friend,
Sith you have heard, and with a knowing ear,
That he which hath your noble father slain
Pursued my life.
LAER: It well appears. But tell me
Why you [proceeded] not against these feats
So criminal and so capital in nature,
As by your safety, greatness, wisdom, all things else
You mainly were stirr'd up.
KING: O, for two special reasons,
Which may to you perhaps seem much unsinow'd,
But yet to me th' are strong. The Queen his mother
Lives almost by his looks, and for myself—
My virtue or my plague, be it either which—
She is so [conjunctive] to my life and soul,
That, as the star moves not but in his sphere,
I could not but by her. The other motive,
Why to a public count I might not go,
Is the great love the general gender bear him,
Who, dipping all his faults in their affection,
Work like the spring that turneth wood to stone,
Convert his gyves to graces, so that my arrows,
Too slightly timber'd for so [loud a wind],
Would have reverted to my bow again,
But not where I have aim'd them.
LAER: And so have I a noble father lost,
A sister driven into desp'rate terms,
Whose worth, if praises may go back again,
Stood challenger on mount of all the age
For her perfections—but my revenge will come.

IV.vii. Location: The castle. 1. **my acquittance seal:** ratify my acquittal, i.e. acknowledge my innocence in Polonius' death. 7. **feats:** acts. 9. **safety:** i.e. regard for your own safety. 10. **mainly:** powerfully. 12. **unsinow'd:** unsinewed, i.e. weak. 15. **either which:** one or the other. 16. **conjunctive:** closely joined. 17. **in his sphere:** by the movement of the sphere in which it is fixed (as the Ptolemaic astronomy taught). 19. **count:** reckoning. 20. **the general gender:** everybody. 23. **gyves:** fetters. 28. **terms:** condition. 29. **go back again:** i.e. refer to what she was before she went mad. 30. **on mount:** pre-eminent.

KING: Break not your sleeps for that. You must not think
That we are made of stuff so flat and dull
That we can let our beard be shook with danger
And think it pastime. You shortly shall hear more.
I lov'd your father, and we love ourself,
And that, I hope, will teach you to imagine—

Enter a MESSENGER *with letters.*

[How now? What news?
MESS: Letters, my lord, from Hamlet:]
These to your Majesty, this to the Queen.
KING: From Hamlet? Who brought them?
MESS: Sailors, my lord, they say, I saw them not.
They were given me by Claudio. He receiv'd them
Of him that brought them.
KING: Laertes, you shall hear them.
—Leave us. [*Exit* MESSENGER.]

[*Reads.*] "High and mighty, You shall know I am set naked on your kingdom. To-morrow shall I beg leave to see your kingly eyes, when I shall, first asking you pardon thereunto, recount the occasion of my sudden [and more strange] return.
[Hamlet.]"

What should this mean? Are all the rest come back?
Or is it some abuse, and no such thing?
LAER: Know you the hand?
KING: 'Tis Hamlet's character. "Naked"!
And in a postscript here he says "alone."
Can you devise me?
LAER: I am lost in it, my lord. But let him come,
It warms the very sickness in my heart
That I [shall] live and tell him to his teeth,
"Thus didst thou."

---

32. **for that:** i.e. for fear of losing your revenge. 33. **flat:** spiritless. 34. **let . . . shook.** To ruffle or tweak a man's beard was an act of insolent defiance that he could not disregard without loss of honor. Cf. II.ii.538. **with:** by. 47. **naked:** destitute. 49. **pardon thereunto:** permission to do so. 52. **abuse:** deceit. 54. **character:** handwriting. 56. **devise me:** explain it to me.

KING: If it be so, Laertes—
As how should it be so? how otherwise?—
Will you be rul'd by me?
LAER: Ay, my lord,
So you will not o'errule me to a peace.
KING: To thine own peace. If he be now returned
As [checking] at his voyage, and that he means
No more to undertake it, I will work him
To an exploit, now ripe in my device,
Under the which he shall not choose but fall;
And for his death no wind of blame shall breathe,
But even his mother shall uncharge the practice,
And call it accident.
LAER: My lord, I will be rul'd,
The rather if you could devise it so
That I might be the organ.
KING: It falls right.
You have been talk'd of since your travel much,
And that in Hamlet's hearing, for a quality
Wherein they say you shine. Your sum of parts
Did not together pluck such envy from him
As did that one, and that, in my regard,
Of the unworthiest siege.
LAER: What part is that, my lord?
KING: A very riband in the cap of youth,
Yet needful too, for youth no less becomes
The light and careless livery that it wears
Than settled age his sables and his weeds,
Importing health and graveness. Two months since
Here was a gentleman of Normandy:
I have seen myself, and serv'd against, the French,
And they can well on horseback, but this gallant

---

62. **As . . . otherwise:** How can he have come back? Yet he obviously has. 65. **So:** provided that. 67. **checking at:** turning from (like a falcon diverted from its quarry by other prey). 72. **uncharge the practice:** adjudge the plot no plot, i.e. fail to see the plot. 76. **organ:** instrument, agent. 79. **quality:** skill. 80. **Your . . . parts:** all your (other) accomplishments put together. 83. **unworthiest:** i.e. least important (with no implication of unsuitableness). **siege:** status, position. 88. **weeds:** (characteristic) garb. 89. **Importing . . . graveness:** signifying prosperity and dignity. 92. **can . . . horseback:** are excellent riders.

Had witchcraft in't, he grew unto his seat,
And to such wondrous doing brought his horse,
As had he been incorps'd and demi-natur'd
With the brave beast. So far he topp'd [my] thought,
That I in forgery of shapes and tricks
Come short of what he did.

LAER: A Norman was't?

KING: A Norman.

LAER: Upon my life, Lamord.

KING: The very same.

LAER: I know him well. He is the brooch indeed
And gem of all the nation.

KING: He made confession of you,
And gave you such a masterly report
For art and exercise in your defense,
And for your rapier most especial,
That he cried out 'twould be a sight indeed
If one could match you. The scrimers of their nation
He swore had neither motion, guard, nor eye,
If you oppos'd them. Sir, this report of his
Did Hamlet so envenom with his envy
That he could nothing do but wish and beg
Your sudden coming o'er to play with you.
Now, out of this—

LAER: What out of this, my lord?

KING: Laertes, was your father dear to you?
Or are you like the painting of a sorrow,
A face without a heart?

LAER: Why ask you this?

KING: Not that I think you did not love your father,
But that I know love is begun by time,
And that I see, in passages of proof,
Time qualifies the spark and fire of it.
There lives within the very flame of love

---

95. **incorps'd:** made one body. **demi-natur'd:** i.e. become half of a composite animal. 97. **forgery:** mere imagining. 103. **brooch:** ornament (worn in the hat). 105. **made . . . you:** acknowledged your excellence. 110. **scrimers:** fencers. 115. **sudden:** speedy. 123. **time:** i.e. a particular set of circumstances. 124. **in . . . proof:** i.e. by the test of experience, by actual examples. 125. **qualifies:** moderates.

A kind of week or snuff that will abate it,
And nothing is at a like goodness still,
For goodness, growing to a plurisy,
Dies in his own too much. That we would do,
We should do when we would; for this "would" changes,
And hath abatements and delays as many
As there are tongues, are hands, are accidents,
And then this "should" is like a spendthrift's sigh,
That hurts by easing. But to the quick of th' ulcer:
Hamlet comes back. What would you undertake
To show yourself indeed your father's son
More than in words?

LAER: To cut his throat i' th' church.

KING: No place indeed should murther sanctuarize,
Revenge should have no bounds. But, good Laertes,
Will you do this, keep close within your chamber.
Hamlet return'd shall know you are come home.
We'll put on those shall praise your excellence,
And set a double varnish on the fame
The Frenchman gave you, bring you in fine together,
And wager o'er your heads. He, being remiss,
Most generous, and free from all contriving,
Will not peruse the foils, so that with ease,
Or with a little shuffling, you may choose
A sword unbated, and in a [pass] of practice
Requite him for your father.

LAER: I will do't,
And for [that] purpose I'll anoint my sword.
I bought an unction of a mountebank,

---

127. **week:** wick. 128. **nothing . . . still:** nothing remains forever at the same pitch of perfection. 129. **plurisy:** plethora (a variant spelling of *pleurisy*, which was erroneously related to *plus*, stem *plur-*, "more, overmuch." 130. **too much:** excess. 134. **spendthrift's sigh.** A sigh was supposed to draw blood from the heart. 135. **hurts by easing:** injures us at the same time that it gives us relief. 140. **sanctuarize:** offer asylum to. 142. **Will . . . this:** if you want to undertake this. 144. **put on those:** incite those who. 145. **double varnish:** second coat of varnish. 146. **in fine:** finally. 147. **remiss:** careless, overtrustful. 148. **generous:** noble-minded. **free . . . contriving:** innocent of sharp practices. 149. **peruse:** examine. 150. **shuffling:** cunning exchange. 151. **unbated:** not blunted. **pass of practice:** tricky thrust. 155. **unction:** ointment. **mountebank:** travelling quack-doctor.

So mortal that, but dip a knife in it,
Where it draws blood, no cataplasm so rare,
Collected from all simples that have virtue
Under the moon, can save the thing from death
That is but scratch'd withal. I'll touch my point
With this contagion, that if I gall him slightly,
It may be death.

KING: Let's further think of this,
Weigh what convenience both of time and means
May fit us to our shape. If this should fail,
And that our drift look through our bad performance,
'Twere better not assay'd; therefore this project
Should have a back or second, that might hold
If this did blast in proof. Soft, let me see.
We'll make a solemn wager on your cunnings—
I ha't!
When in your motion you are hot and dry—
As make your bouts more violent to that end—
And that he calls for drink, I'll have preferr'd him
A chalice for the nonce, whereon but sipping,
If he by chance escape your venom'd stuck,
Our purpose may hold there. But stay, what noise?

Enter QUEEN.

QUEEN: One woe doth tread upon another's heel,
So fast they follow. Your sister's drown'd, Laertes.

LAER: Drown'd! O, where?

QUEEN: There is a willow grows askaunt the brook,
That shows his hoary leaves in the glassy stream,
Therewith fantastic garlands did she make
Of crow-flowers, nettles, daisies, and long purples
That liberal shepherds give a grosser name,

---

156. **mortal:** deadly. 157. **cataplasm:** poultice. 158. **simples:** medicinal herbs. **virtue:** curative power. 161. **gall:** graze. 165. **fit . . . shape:** i.e. suit our purposes best. 166. **drift:** purpose. **look through:** become visible, be detected. 168. **back or second:** i.e. a second plot in reserve for emergency. 169. **blast in proof:** blow up while being tried (an image from gunnery). 173. **As:** i.e. and you should. 174. **preferr'd:** offered to. 175. **nonce:** occasion. 176. **stuck:** thrust (from *stoccado,* a fencing term). 181. **askaunt:** sideways over. 182. **hoary:** grey-white. 183. **Therewith:** i.e. with willow branches. 184. **long purples:** wild orchids. 185. **liberal:** free-spoken.

But our cull-cold maids do dead men's fingers call them.
There on the pendant boughs her crownet weeds
Clamb'ring to hang, an envious sliver broke,
When down her weedy trophies and herself
Fell in the weeping brook. Her clothes spread wide,
And mermaid-like awhile they bore her up,
Which time she chaunted snatches of old lauds,
As one incapable of her own distress,
Or like a creature native and indued
Unto that element. But long it could not be
Till that her garments, heavy with their drink,
Pull'd the poor wretch from her melodious lay
To muddy death.

LAER: Alas, then she is drown'd?

QUEEN: Drown'd, drown'd.

LAER: Too much of water hast thou, poor Ophelia,
And therefore I forbid my tears; but yet
It is our trick, Nature her custom holds,
Let shame say what it will; when these are gone,
The woman will be out. Adieu, my lord,
I have a speech a' fire that fain would blaze,
But that this folly drowns it. *Exit.*

KING: Let's follow, Gertrude.
How much I had to do to calm his rage!
Now fear I this will give it start again,
Therefore let's follow. *Exeunt.*

Act V

Scene I

Enter two CLOWNS [*with spades and mattocks*].

1. CLO: Is she to be buried in Christian burial when she willfully seeks her own salvation?

---

186. **cull-cold:** chaste. 187. **crownet:** made into coronets. 188. **envious sliver:** malicious branch. 192. **lauds:** hymns. 193. **incapable:** insensible. 194. **indued:** habituated. 203. **It:** i.e. weeping. **trick:** natural way. 204. **these:** these tears. 205. **The woman . . . out:** my womanish traits will be gone for good.

V.i. Location: A churchyard. o.s.d. **Clowns:** rustics.

2. CLO: I tell thee she is, therefore make her grave straight. The crowner hath sate on her, and finds it Christian burial.

1. CLO: How can that be, unless she drown'd herself in her own defense?

2. CLO: Why, 'tis found so.

1. CLO: It must be [*se offendendo*], it cannot be else. For here lies the point: if I drown myself wittingly, it argues an act, and an act hath three branches—it is to act, to do, to perform; [argal], she drown'd herself wittingly.

2. CLO: Nay, but hear you, goodman delver—

1. CLO: Give me leave. Here lies the water; good. Here stands the man; good. If the man go to this water and drown himself, it is, will he, nill he, he goes, mark you that. But if the water come to him and drown him, he drowns not himself; argal, he that is not guilty of his own death shortens not his own life.

2. CLO: But is this law?

1. CLO: Ay, marry, is't—crowner's quest law.

2. CLO: Will you ha' the truth an't? If this had not been a gentlewoman, she should have been buried out a' Christian burial.

1. CLO: Why, there thou say'st, and the more pity that great folk should have count'nance in this world to drown or hang themselves, more than their even-Christen. Come, my spade. There is no ancient gentlemen but gard'ners, ditchers, and grave-makers; they hold up Adam's profession.

2. CLO: Was he a gentleman?

1. CLO: 'A was the first that ever bore arms.

[2. CLO: Why, he had none.

1. CLO: What, art a heathen? How dost thou understand the Scripture? The Scripture says Adam digg'd; could he dig without arms?] I'll put another question to thee. If thou answerest me not to the purpose, confess thyself—

---

3. **straight:** immediately. 4. **crowner:** coroner. 8. **se offendendo:** blunder for *se defendendo,* "in self-defense." 11. **argal:** blunder for *ergo,* "therefore." 13–17. **Here . . . life.** Alluding to a very famous suicide case, that of Sir James Hales, a judge who drowned himself in 1554; it was long cited in the courts. The clown gives a garbled account of the defense summing-up and the verdict. 15. **nill he:** will be not. 19. **quest:** inquest. 24. **even-Christen:** fellow-Christians. 29. **none:** i.e. no coat of arms.

2. CLO: Go to.

1. CLO: What is he that builds stronger than either the mason, the shipwright, or the carpenter?

2. CLO: The gallows-maker, for that outlives a thousand tenants.

1. CLO: I like thy wit well, in good faith. The gallows does well; but how does it well? It does well to those that do ill. Now thou dost ill to say the gallows is built stronger than the church; argal, the gallows may do well to thee. To't again, come.

2. CLO: Who builds stronger than a mason, a shipwright, or a carpenter?

1. CLO: Ay, tell me that, and unyoke.

2. CLO: Marry, now I can tell.

1. CLO: To't.

2. CLO: Mass, I cannot tell.

Enter HAMLET *and* HORATIO [*afar off*].

1. CLO: Cudgel thy brains no more about it, for your dull ass will not mend his pace with beating, and when you are ask'd this question next. say "a gravemaker": the houses he makes lasts till doomsday. Go get thee in, and fetch me a sup of liquor.

[*Exit Second Clown. First Clown digs.*]

"In youth when I did love, did love, *Song.*
Methought it was very sweet,
To contract—O—the time for—a—my behove,
O, methought there—a—was nothing—a—meet."

HAM: Has this fellow no feeling of his business? 'a sings in grave-making.

HOR: Custom hath made it in him a property of easiness.

HAM: 'Tis e'en so, the hand of little employment hath the daintier sense.

1. CLO: "But age with his stealing steps *Song.*
Hath clawed me in his clutch,

---

44. **unyoke:** i.e. cease to labor, call it a day. 47. **Mass:** by the mass. 54. **contract . . . behove:** shorten, i.e. spend agreeably . . . advantage. The song, punctuated by the grunts of the clown as he digs, is a garbled version of a poem by Thomas Lord Vaux. entitled "The Aged Lover Renounceth Love." 58. **Custom:** habit. 58. **a property of easiness:** i.e. a thing he can do with complete ease of mind. 59–60. **daintier sense:** more delicate sensitivity.

And hath shipped me into the land,
As if I had never been such."

[*Throws up a shovelful of earth with a skull in it.*]

HAM: That skull had a tongue in it, and could sing once. How the knave jowls it to the ground, as if 'twere Cain's jaw-bone, that did the first murder! This might be the pate of a politician, which this ass now o'erreaches, one that would circumvent God, might it not?

HOR: It might, my lord.

HAM: Or of a courtier, which could say, "Good morrow, sweet lord! How dost thou, sweet lord?" This might be my Lord Such-a-one, that prais'd my Lord Such-a-one's horse when 'a [meant] to beg it, might it not?

HOR: Ay, my lord.

HAM: Why, e'en so, and now my Lady Worm's, chopless, and knock'd about the [mazzard] with a sexton's spade. Here's fine revolution, and we had the trick to see't. Did these bones cost no more the breeding, but to play at loggats with them? Mine ache to think on't.

1. CLO: "A pickaxe and a spade, a spade, *Song.*
For and a shrouding sheet:
O, a pit of clay for to be made
For such a guest is meet."

[*Throws up another skull.*]

HAM: There's another. Why may not that be the skull of a lawyer? Where be his quiddities now, his quillities, his cases, his tenures, and his tricks? Why does he suffer this mad knave now to knock him about the sconce with a dirty shovel, and will not tell him of his action of battery? Hum! This fellow might be in 's time a great buyer of land, with his statutes, his recognizances, his fines, his double vouchers, his recoveries. [Is this the fine of his fines,

66. **jowls:** dashes. 67. **politician:** schemer, intriguer. 68. **o'erreaches:** gets the better of (with play on the literal sense). 68–69. **circumvent God:** bypass God's law. 76. **chopless:** lacking the lower jaw. 77. **mazzard:** head. **revolution:** change. 78. **and:** if. **trick:** knack, ability. **Did . . . cost:** were . . . worth. 89. **loggats:** a game in which blocks of wood were thrown at a stake. 86. **quiddities:** subtleties, quibbles. **quillities:** fine distinctions. **tenures:** titles to real estate. 88. **sconce:** head. 90. **statutes, recognizances:** bonds securing debts by attaching land and property.

and the recovery of his recoveries,] to have his fine pate full of fine dirt? Will [his] vouchers vouch him no more of his purchases, and [double ones too], than the length and breadth of a pair of indentures? The very conveyances of his lands will scarcely lie in this box, and must th' inheritor himself have no more, ha?

HOR: Not a jot more, my lord.

HAM: Is not parchment made of sheep-skins?

HOR: Ay, my lord, and of calves'-skins too.

HAM: They are sheep and calves which seek out assurance in that. I will speak to this fellow. Whose grave's this, sirrah?

1. CLO: Mine, sir.

[*Sings.*] "[O], a pit of clay for to be made
[For such a guest is meet]."

HAM: I think it be thine indeed, for thou liest in't.

1. CLO: You lie out on't, sir, and therefore 'tis not yours; for my part, I do not lie in't, yet it is mine.

HAM: Thou dost lie in't, to be in't and say it is thine. 'Tis for the dead, not for the quick; therefore thou liest.

1. CLO: 'Tis a quick lie, sir, 'twill away again from me to you.

HAM: What man dost thou dig it for?

1. CLO: For no man, sir.

HAM: What woman then?

1. CLO: For none neither.

HAM: Who is to be buried in't?

1. CLO: One that was a woman, sir, but, rest her soul, she's dead.

HAM: How absolute the knave is! we must speak by the card, or equivocation will undo us. By the Lord, Horatio, this three years I have took note of it: the age is grown so pick'd that the toe of the peasant comes so near the heel of the courtier, he galls his kibe. How long hast thou been grave-maker?

90–91. **fines, recoveries:** procedures for converting an entailed estate to freehold. 91. **double vouchers:** documents guaranteeing title to real estate, signed by two persons. 91. **fine:** end. 95. **pair of indentures:** legal document cut into two parts which fitted together on a serrated edge. Perhaps Hamlet thus refers to the two rows of teeth in the skull, or to the bone sutures. 95. **conveyances:** documents relating to transfer of property. 96. **this box:** i.e. the skull itself. **inheritor:** owner. 102. **sirrah:** term of address to inferiors. 118. **absolute:** positive. **by the card:** by the compass, i.e. punctiliously. 119. **equivocation:** ambiguity. 120. **pick'd:** refined. 122. **galls his kibe:** rubs the courtier's chilblain.

1. CLO: Of [all] the days i' th' year, I came to't that day that our last king Hamlet overcame Fortinbras.

HAM: How long is that since?

1. CLO: Cannot you tell that? Every fool can tell that. It was that very day that young Hamlet was born—he that is mad, and sent into England.

HAM: Ay, marry, why was he sent into England?

1. CLO: Why, because 'a was mad. 'A shall recover his wits there, or if 'a do not, 'tis no great matter there.

HAM: Why?

1. CLO: 'Twill not be seen in him there, there the men are as mad as he.

HAM: How came he mad?

1. CLO: Very strangely, they say.

HAM: How strangely?

1. CLO: Faith, e'en with losing his wits.

HAM: Upon what ground?

1. CLO: Why, here in Denmark. I have been sexton here, man and boy, thirty years.

HAM: How long will a man lie i' th' earth ere he rot?

1. CLO: Faith, if 'a be not rotten before 'a die—as we have many pocky corses, that will scarce hold the laying in—'a will last you some eight year or nine year. A tanner will last you nine year.

HAM: Why he more than another?

1. CLO: Why, sir, his hide is so tann'd with his trade that 'a will keep out water a great while, and your water is a sore decayer of your whoreson dead body. Here's a skull now hath lien you i' th' earth three and twenty years.

HAM: Whose was it?

1. CLO: A whoreson mad fellow's it was. Whose do you think it was?

HAM: Nay, I know not.

1. CLO: A pestilence on him for a mad rogue! 'a pour'd a flagon of Rhenish on my head once. This same skull, sir, was, sir, Yorick's skull, the King's jester.

HAM: This? [*Takes the skull.*]

1. CLO: E'en that.

---

144. **pocky:** rotten with venereal disease. **hold . . . in:** last out the burial.

HAM: Alas, poor Yorick! I knew him, Horatio, a fellow of infinite jest, of most excellent fancy. He hath bore me on his back a thousand times, and now how abhorr'd in my imagination it is! my gorge rises at it. Here hung those lips that I have kiss'd I know not how oft. Where be your gibes now, your gambols, your songs, your flashes of merriment, that were wont to set the table on a roar? Not one now to mock your own grinning—quite chop-fall'n. Now get you to my lady's [chamber], and tell her, let her paint an inch thick, to this favor she must come; make her laugh at that. Prithee, Horatio, tell me one thing.

HOR: What's that, my lord?

HAM: Dost thou think Alexander look'd a' this fashion i' th' earth?

HOR: E'en so.

HAM: And smelt so? pah! [*Puts down the skull.*]

HOR: E'en so, my lord.

HAM: To what base uses we may return, Horatio! Why may not imagination trace the noble dust of Alexander, till 'a find it stopping a bunghole?

HOR: 'Twere to consider too curiously, to consider so.

HAM: No, faith, not a jot, but to follow him thither with modesty enough and likelihood to lead it: Alexander died, Alexander was buried, Alexander returneth to dust, the dust is earth, of earth we make loam, and why of that loam whereto he was converted might they not stop a beer-barrel?
Imperious Caesar, dead and turn'd to clay,
Might stop a hole to keep the wind away.
O that that earth which kept the world in awe
Should patch a wall t' expel the [winter's] flaw!
But soft, but soft awhile, here comes the King,

Enter KING, QUEEN, LAERTES, *and* [*a* DOCTOR OF DIVINITY, *following*] *the corse,* [*with* LORDS *attendant*].

The Queen, the courtiers. Who is this they follow?
And with such maimed rites? This doth betoken

---

168. **chop-fall'n:** (1) lacking the lower jaw; (2) downcast. 169. **favor:** appearance. 181. **curiously:** closely, minutely. 182. **modesty:** moderation. 185. **loam:** a mixture of moistened clay with sand, straw, etc. 187. **Imperious:** imperial. 190. **flaw:** gust. 193. **maimed rites:** lack of customary ceremony.

The corse they follow did with desp'rate hand
Foredo it own life. 'Twas of some estate.
Couch we a while and mark. [*Retiring with* HORATIO.]

LAER: What ceremony else?

HAM: That is Laertes, a very noble youth. Mark.

LAER: What ceremony else?

DOCTOR: Her obsequies have been as far enlarg'd
As we have warranty. Her death was doubtful,
And but that great command o'ersways the order,
She should in ground unsanctified been lodg'd
Till the last trumpet; for charitable prayers,
[Shards,] flints, and pebbles should be thrown on her.
Yet here she is allow'd her virgin crants,
Her maiden strewments, and the bringing home
Of bell and burial.

LAER: Must there no more be done?

DOCTOR: No more be done:
We should profane the service of the dead
To sing a requiem and such rest to her
As to peace-parted souls.

LAER: Lay her i' th' earth,
And from her fair and unpolluted flesh
May violets spring! I tell thee, churlish priest,
A minist'ring angel shall my sister be
When thou liest howling.

HAM: What, the fair Ophelia!

QUEEN [*Scattering flowers.*]: Sweets to the sweet,
farewell!
I hop'd thou shouldst have been my Hamlet's wife.
I thought thy bride-bed to have deck'd, sweet maid,
And not have strew'd thy grave.

LAER: O, treble woe
Fall ten times [treble] on that cursed head
Whose wicked deed thy most ingenious sense

---

195. **Foredo:** fordo, destroy. **it:** its. **estate:** rank. 196. **Couch we:** let us conceal ourselves. 201. **doubtful:** i.e. the subject of an "open verdict." 202. **order:** customary procedure. 203. **should:** would certainly. 204. **for:** instead of. 206. **crants:** garland. 207. **maiden strewments:** flowers scattered on the grave of an unmarried girl. 207–8. **bringing . . . burial:** i.e. burial in consecrated ground, with the bell tolling. 212. **requiem:** dirge. 220. **Sweets:** flowers. 227. **ingenious:** intelligent.

Depriv'd thee of! Hold off the earth a while,
Till I have caught her once more in mine arms.

[*Leaps in the grave.*]

Now pile your dust upon the quick and dead,
Till of this flat a mountain you have made
T'o'ertop old Pelion, or the skyish head
Of blue Olympus.

HAM [*Coming forward.*]: What is he whose grief
Bears such an emphasis, whose phrase of sorrow
Conjures the wand'ring stars and makes them stand
Like wonder-wounded hearers? This is I,
Hamlet the Dane! [HAMLET *leaps in after* LAERTES.]

LAER: The devil take thy soul!

[*Grappling with him.*]

HAM: Thou pray'st not well.
I prithee take thy fingers from my throat.
For though I am not splenitive [and] rash,
Yet have I in me something dangerous,
Which let thy wisdom fear. Hold off thy hand!

KING: Pluck them asunder

QUEEN: Hamlet, Hamlet!

ALL: Gentlemen!

HOR: Good my lord, be quiet.

[*The* ATTENDANTS *part them, and they come out of the grave.*]

HAM: Why, I will fight with him upon this theme
Until my eyelids will no longer wag.

QUEEN: O my son, what theme?

HAM: I lov'd Ophelia. Forty thousand brothers
Could not with all their quantity of love
Make up my sum. What wilt thou do for her?

KING: O, he is mad, Laertes.

QUEEN: For love of God, forbear him.

HAM: 'Swounds, show me what thou't do.
Woo't weep, woo't fight, woo't fast, woo't tear thyself?

232–33. **Pelion, Olympus:** mountains in northeastern Greece. 235. **emphasis, phrase:** Rhetorical terms, here used in disparaging reference to Laertes' inflated language. 236. **Conjures:** puts a spell upon. **wand'ring stars:** planets. 238. **the Dane.** This title normally signifies the King. 242. **splenitive:** impetuous. 257. **thou't:** thou wilt. 258. **Woo't:** will thou.

Woo't drink up eisel, eat a crocadile?
I'll do't. Dost [thou] come here to whine?
To outface me with leaping in her grrave?
Be buried quick with her, and so will I.
And if thou prate of mountains, let them throw
Millions of acres on us, till our ground,
Singeing his pate against the burning zone,
Make Ossa like a wart! Nay, and thou'lt mouth,
I'll rant as well as thou.

QUEEN: This is mere madness,
And [thus] a while the fit will work on him;
Anon, as patient as the female dove,
When that her golden couplets are disclosed,
His silence will sit drooping.

HAM: Hear you, sir,
What is the reason that you use me thus?
I lov'd you ever. But it is no matter.
Let Hercules himself do what he may,
The cat will mew, and dog will have his day.

Exit HAMLET.

KING: I pray thee, good Horatio, wait upon him.

[*Exit*] HORATIO.

[*To* LAERTES.] Strengthen your patience in our last night's speech,
We'll put the matter to the present push.—
Good Gertrude, set some watch over your son.
This grave shall have a living monument.
An hour of quiet [shortly] shall we see,
Till then in patience our proceeding be. *Exeunt.*

---

259. **eisel:** vinegar. **crocadile:** crocodile. 263. **if . . . mountains.** Referring to lines 230–33. 265. **burning zone:** sphere of the sun. 266. **Ossa:** another mountain in Greece, near Pelion and Olympus. **mouth:** talk bombast (synonymous with *rant* in the next line). 268. **mere:** utter. 270. **patient:** calm. 271. **golden couplets:** pair of baby birds, covered with yellow down. **disclosed:** hatched. 276–77. **Let . . . day:** i.e. nobody can prevent another from making the scenes he feels he has a right to. 279. **in:** i.e. by recalling. 280. **present push:** immediate test **living:** enduring (?) or in the form of a lifelike effigy (?).

Scene II

Enter HAMLET *and* HORATIO.

HAM: So much for this, sir, now shall you see the other—
You do remember all the circumstance?
HOR: Remember it, my lord!
HAM: Sir, in my heart there was a kind of fighting
That would not let me sleep. [Methought] I lay
Worse than the mutines in the [bilboes]. Rashly—
And prais'd be rashness for it—let us know
Our indiscretion sometime serves us well
When our deep plots do pall, and that should learn us
There's a divinity that shapes our ends,
Rough-hew them how we will—
HOR: That is most certain.
HAM: Up from my cabin,
My sea-gown scarf'd about me, in the dark
Grop'd I to find out them, had my desire,
Finger'd their packet, and in fine withdrew
To mine own room again, making so bold,
My fears forgetting manners, to [unseal]
Their grand commission; where I found, Horatio—
Ah, royal knavery!—an exact command,
Larded with many several sorts of reasons,
Importing Denmark's health and England's too,
With, ho, such bugs and goblins in my life,
That, on the supervise, no leisure bated,
No, not to stay the grinding of the axe,
My head should be strook off.
HOR: Is't possible?

V.ii. Location: The castle. 1. **see the other:** i.e. hear the other news I have to tell you (hinted at in the letter to Horatio, IV.vi.20–21). 6. **mutines:** mutineers (but the term *mutiny* was in Shakespeare's day used of almost any act of rebellion against authority). **bilboes:** fetters attached to a heavy iron bar. **Rashly:** on impulse. 7. **know:** recognize, acknowledge. 9. **pall:** lose force, come to nothing. **learn:** teach. 10. **shapes our ends:** gives final shape to our designs. 11. **Rough-hew them:** block them out in initial form. 16. **Finger'd:** filched, "pinched." 21. **Larded:** garnished. 22. **Importing:** relating to. 23. **bugs . . . life:** terrifying things in prospect if I were permitted to remain alive. *Bugs* = bugaboos. 24. **supervise:** perusal. **bated:** deducted (from the stipulated speediness). 25. **stay:** wait for.

HAM: Here's the commission, read it at more leisure.
But wilt thou hear now how I did proceed?
HOR: I beseech you.
HAM: Being thus benetted round with [villainies],
Or I could make a prologue to my brains,
They had begun the play. I sat me down,
Devis'd a new commission, wrote it fair.
I once did hold it, as our statists do,
A baseness to write fair, and labor'd much
How to forget that learning, but, sir, now
It did me yeman's service. Wilt thou know
Th' effect of what I wrote?
HOR: Ay, good my lord.
HAM: An earnest conjuration from the King,
As England was his faithful tributary,
As love between them like the palm might flourish,
As peace should still her wheaten garland wear
And stand a comma 'tween their amities,
And many such-like [as's] of great charge,
That on the view and knowing of these contents,
Without debatement further, more or less,
He should those bearers put to sudden death,
Not shriving time allow'd.
HOR: How was this seal'd?
HAM: Why, even in that was heaven ordinant.
I had my father's signet in my purse,
Which was the model of that Danish seal;
Folded the writ up in the form of th' other,
[Subscrib'd] it, gave't th' impression, plac'd it safely,
The changeling never known. Now the next day
Was our sea-fight, and what to this was sequent
Thou knowest already.

---

32. **Or:** before. 34. **fair:** i.e. in a beautiful hand (such as a professional scribe would use). 35. **statists:** statesmen, public officials. 36. **A baseness:** i.e. a skill befitting men of low rank. 38. **yeman's:** yeoman's, i.e. solid, substantial. 39. **effect:** purport, gist. 45. **comma:** connective, link. 46. **as's . . . charge:** (1) weighty clauses beginning with *as;* (2) asses with heavy loads. 50. **shriving time:** time for confession and absolution. 52. **ordinant:** in charge, guiding. 54. **model:** small copy. 56. **Subscrib'd:** signed. 57. **changeling:** i.e. Hamlet's letter, substituted secretly for the genuine letter, as fairies substituted their children for human children. **never known:** never recognized as a substitution (unlike the fairies' changelings).

HOR: So Guildenstern and Rosencrantz go to't.
HAM: [Why, man, they did make love to this employment,]
They are not near my conscience. Their defeat
Does by their own insinuation grow.
'Tis dangerous when the baser nature comes
Between the pass and fell incensed points
Of mighty opposites.
HOR: Why, what a king is this!
HAM: Does it not, think thee, stand me now upon—
He that hath kill'd my king and whor'd my mother,
Popp'd in between th' election and my hopes,
Thrown out his angle for my proper life,
And with such coz'nage— is't not perfect conscience
[To quit him with this arm? And is't not to be damn'd,
To let this canker of our nature come
In further evil?
HOR: It must be shortly known to him from England
What is the issue of the business there.
HAM: It will be short; the interim's mine,
And a man's life's no more than to say "one."
But I am very sorry, good Horatio,
That to Laertes I forgot myself,
For by the image of my cause I see
The portraiture of his. I'll [court] his favors.
But sure the bravery of his grief did put me
Into a tow'ring passion.
HOR: Peace, who comes here?]

Enter [young OSRIC,] *a courtier.*

OSR: Your lordship is right welcome back to Denmark.
HAM: I [humbly] thank you, sir.—Dost know this water-fly?
HOR: No, my good lord.

60. **go to't:** i.e. are going to their death. 62. **defeat:** ruin, overthrow. 63. **insinuation:** winding their way into the affair. 64. **baser:** inferior. 65. **pass:** thrust. **fell:** fierce. 68. **stand . . . upon:** i.e. rest upon me as a duty. 70. **election:** i.e. as King of Denmark. 71. **angle:** hook and line. **proper:** very. 72. **coz'nage:** trickery. 73. **quit him:** pay him back. 74. **canker:** cancerous sore. 74–75. **come In:** grow into. 79. **a man's . . . more:** i.e. to kill a man takes no more time. **say "one."** Perhaps this is equivalent to "deliver one sword thrust"; see line 245 below, where Hamlet says "One" as he makes the first hit. 82. **image:** likeness. 84. **bravery:** ostentatious expression. 88. **water-fly:** i.e. tiny, vainly agitated creature.

HAM: Thy state is the more gracious, for 'tis a vice to know him. He hath much land, and fertile; let a beast be lord of beasts, and his crib shall stand at the King's mess. 'Tis a chough, but, as I say, spacious in the possession of dirt.

OSR: Sweet lord, if your lordship were at leisure, I should impart a thing to you from his Majesty.

HAM: I will receive it, sir, with all diligence of spirit. [Put] your bonnet to his right use, 'tis for the head.

OSR: I thank your lordship, it is very hot.

HAM: No, believe me, 'tis very cold, the wind is northerly.

OSR: It is indifferent cold, my lord, indeed.

HAM: But yet methinks it is very [sultry] and hot [for] my complexion.

OSR: Exceedingly, my lord, it is very sultry—as 'twere—I cannot tell how. My lord, his Majesty bade me signify to you that 'a has laid a great wager on your head. Sir, this is the matter—

HAM: I beseech you remember.

[HAMLET *moves him to put on his hat.*]

OSR: Nay, good my lord, for my ease, in good faith. Sir, here is newly come to court Laertes, believe me, an absolute [gentleman], full of most excellent differences, of very soft society, and great showing; indeed, to speak sellingly of him, he is the card or calendar of gentry; for you shall find in him the continent of what part a gentleman would see.

HAM: Sir, his definement suffers no perdition in you, though I know to divide him inventorially would dozy th' arithmetic of memory, and yet but yaw neither in respect of his quick sail; but in the verity of extolment, I take him to be a soul of great article, and his infusion

---

90. **gracious:** virtuous. 91–92. **let . . . mess:** i.e. if a beast owned as many cattle as Osric, he could feast with the King. 92. **chough:** jackdaw, a bird that could be taught to speak. 96. **bonnet:** hat. 100. **indifferent:** somewhat. 101. **complexion:** temperament. 106. **for my ease:** i.e. I am really more comfortable with my hat off (a polite insistence on maintaining ceremony). 107. **absolute:** complete, possessing every quality a gentleman should have. 108. **differences:** distinguishing characteristics, personal qualities. **soft:** agreeable. **great showing:** splendid appearance. 109. **sellingly:** i.e. like a seller to a prospective buyer; in a fashion to do full justice. **card or calendar:** chart or register, i.e. compendious guide. 109. **gentry:** gentlemanly behavior. 110. **the continent . . . part:** one who contains every quality. 112. **perdition:** loss. 113. **dozy:** make dizzy. 114. **yaw:** keep deviating erratically from its course (said of a ship). **neither:** for all that. **in respect of:** compared with. 114–15. **in . . . extolment:** to praise him truly. 115. **article:** scope (?) or importance (?). **infusion:** essence, quality.

of such dearth and rareness as, to make true diction of him, his semblable is his mirror, and who else would trace him, his umbrage, nothing more.

OSR: Your lordship speaks most infallibly of him.

HAM: The concernancy, sir? Why do we wrap the gentleman in our more rawer breath?

OSR: Sir?

HOR: Is't not possible to understand in another tongue? You will to't, sir, really.

HAM: What imports the nomination of this gentleman?

OSR: Of Laertes?

HOR: His purse is empty already: all 's golden words are spent.

HAM: Of him, sir.

OSR: I know you are not ignorant—

HAM: I would you did, sir, yet, in faith, if you did, it would not much approve me. Well, sir?

OSR: You are not ignorant of what excellence Laertes is—

HAM: I dare not confess that, lest I should compare with him in excellence, but to know a man well were to know himself.

OSR: I mean, sir, for [his] weapon, but in the imputation laid on him by them, in his meed he's unfellow'd.

HAM: What's his weapon?

OSR: Rapier and dagger.

HAM: That's two of his weapons—but well.

OSR: The King, sir, hath wager'd with him six Barbary horses, against the which he has impawn'd, as I take it, six French rapiers and poniards, with their assigns, as girdle, [hangers], and so. Three of the carriages, in faith, are very dear to fancy, very responsive to the hilts, most delicate carriages, and of very liberal conceit.

---

116. **dearth:** scarceness. **make true diction:** speak truly. **his semblable:** his only likeness or equal. 117. **who...him:** anyone else who tries to follow him. **umbrage:** shadow. 120. **concernancy:** relevance. 121. **more rawer breath:** i.e. words too crude to describe him properly. 123. **in another tongue:** i.e. when someone else is the speaker. 123–124. **You...really:** i.e. you can do it if you try. 125. **nomination:** naming, mention. 130. **approve:** commend. 133. **compare . . . excellence:** i.e. seem to claim the same degree of excellence for myself. 133. **but.** The sense seems to require *for.* 134. **himself:** i.e. oneself. 135. **in . . . them:** i.e. in popular estimation. 136. **meed:** merit. 141. **impawn'd:** staked. 142. **assigns:** appurtenances. **hangers:** straps on which the swords hang from the girdle. 143. **carriages:** properly, gun-carriages; here used affectedly in place of *hangers.* **fancy:** taste. 143. **very responsive to:** matching well. 144. **liberal conceit:** elegant design.

HAM: What call you the carriages?

HOR: I knew you must be edified by the margent ere you had done.

OSR: The [carriages], sir, are the hangers.

HAM: The phrase would be more germane to the matter if we could carry a cannon by our sides; I would it [might be] hangers till then. But on: six Barb'ry horses against six French swords, their assigns, and three liberal-conceited carriages; that's the French bet against the Danish. Why is this all [impawn'd, as] you call it?

OSR: The King, sir, hath laid, sir, that in a dozen passes between yourself and him, he shall not exceed you three hits; he hath laid on twelve for nine; and it would come to immediate trial, if your lordship would vouchsafe the answer.

HAM: How if I answer no?

OSR: I mean, my lord, the opposition of your person in trial.

HAM: Sir, I will walk here in the hall. If it please his Majesty, it is the breathing time of day with me. Let the foils be brought, the gentleman willing, and the King hold his purpose, I will win for him and I can; if not, I will gain nothing but my shame and the odd hits.

OSR: Shall I deliver you so?

HAM: To this effect, sir—after what flourish your nature will.

OSR: I commend my duty to your lordship.

HAM: Yours. [*Exit* OSRIC.] ['A] does well to commend it himself, there are no tongues else for 's turn.

HOR: This lapwing runs away with the shell on his head.

HAM: 'A did [comply], sir, with his dug before 'a suck'd it. Thus has he, and many more of the same breed that I know the drossy age

---

146. **must . . . margent:** would require enlightenment from a marginal note. 154. **laid:** wagered. 155. **he . . . hits.** Laertes must win by at least eight to four (if none of the "passes" or bouts are draws), since at seven to five he would be only two up. 155-56. **he . . . nine.** Not satisfactorily explained despite much discussion. One suggestion is that Laertes has raised the odds against himself by wagering that out of twelve bouts he will win nine. 157. **answer:** encounter (as Hamlet's following quibble forces Osric to explain in his next speech). 161. **breathing . . . me:** my usual hour for exercise. 166. **after what flourish:** with whatever embellishment of language. 167. **commend my duty:** offer my dutiful respects (but Hamlet picks up the phrase in the sense "praise my manner of bowing"). 170. **lapwing:** a foolish bird which upon hatching was supposed to run with part of the eggshell still over its head. (Osric has put his hat on at last.) 171. **comply . . . dug:** bow politely to his mother's nipple. 172. **drossy:** i.e. worthless.

dotes on, only got the tune of the time, and out of an habit of encounter, a kind of [yesty] collection, which carries them through and through the most [profound] and [winnow'd] opinions, and do but blow them to their trial, the bubbles are out.

Enter a LORD.

LORD: My lord, his Majesty commended him to you by young Osric, who brings back to him that you attend him in the hall. He sends to know if your pleasure hold to play with Laertes, or that you will take longer time.

HAM: I am constant to my purposes, they follow the King's pleasure. If his fitness speaks, mine is ready; now or whensoever, provided I be so able as now.

LORD: The King and Queen and all are coming down.

HAM: In happy time.

LORD: The Queen desires you to use some gentle entertainment to Laertes before you fall to play.

HAM: She well instructs me. [*Exit* LORD.]

HOR: You will lose, my lord.

HAM: I do not think so; since he went into France I have been in continual practice. I shall win at the odds. Thou wouldst not think how ill all's here about my heart—but it is no matter.

HOR: Nay, good my lord—

HAM: It is but foolery, but it is such a kind of [gain-]giving, as would perhaps trouble a woman.

HOR: If your mind dislike any thing, obey it. I will forestall their repair hither, and say you are not fit.

HAM: Not a whit, we defy augury. There is special providence in the fall of a sparrow. If it be [now], 'tis not to come; if it be not to come, it will be now; if it be not now, yet it [will] come—the readiness is all. Since no man, of aught he leaves, knows what is't to leave betimes, let be.

---

173. **tune . . . time:** i.e. fashionable ways of talk. 173–174. **habit of encounter:** mode of social intercourse. 174. **yesty:** yeasty, frothy. **collection:** i.e. anthology of fine phrases. 175. **winnow'd:** sifted, choice. 176. **opinions:** judgments. **blow . . . trial:** test them by blowing on them, i.e. make even the least demanding trial of them. 176. **out:** blown away (?) or at an end, done for (?). 182. **If . . . ready:** i.e. if this is a good moment for him, it is for me also. 186. **gentle entertainment:** courteous greeting. 194. **gain-giving:** misgiving, 198–99. **special . . . sparrow.** See Matthew 10:29. 201. **of aught:** i.e. whatever. **knows . . . betimes:** knows what is the best time to leave it.

A table prepar'd, [*and flagons of wine on it. Enter*] *Trumpets, Drums, and Officers with cushions, foils, daggers;* KING, QUEEN, LAERTES, [OSRIC,] *and all the State.*

KING: Come, Hamlet, come, and take this hand from me.

[*The* KING *puts* LAERTES' *hand into* HAMLET'S.]

HAM: Give me your pardon, sir. I have done you wrong,
But pardon't as you are a gentleman.
This presence knows,
And you must needs have heard, how I am punish'd
With a sore distraction. What I have done
That might your nature, honor, and exception
Roughly awake, I here proclaim was madness.
Was't Hamlet wrong'd Laertes? Never Hamlet!
If Hamlet from himself be ta'en away,
And when he's not himself does wrong Laertes,
Then Hamlet does it not, Hamlet denies it.
Who does it then? His madness. If't be so,
Hamlet is of the faction that is wronged,
His madness is poor Hamlet's enemy.
[Sir, in this audience,]
Let my disclaiming from a purpos'd evil
Free me so far in your most generous thoughts,
That I have shot my arrow o'er the house
And hurt my brother.

LAER: I am satisfied in nature,
Whose motive in this case should stir me most
To my revenge, but in my terms of honor
I stand aloof, and will no reconcilement
Till by some elder masters of known honor
I have a voice and president of peace
To [keep] my name ungor'd. But [till] that time
I do receive your offer'd love like love,
And will not wrong it.

HAM: I embrace it freely,

---

206. s.d. **State:** nobles. 206. **presence:** assembled court. 207. **punish'd:** afflicted. 209. **exception:** objection. 219. **my . . . evil:** my declaration that I intended no harm. 220. **Free:** absolve. 223. **in nature:** so far as my personal feelings are concerned. 225. **in . . . honor:** i.e. as a man governed by an established code of honor. 228–29. **have . . . ungor'd:** can secure an opinion backed by precedent that I can make peace with you without injury to my reputation.

And will this brothers' wager frankly play.
Give us the foils. [Come on.]

LAER: Come, one for me.

HAM: I'll be your foil, Laertes; in mine ignorance
Your skill shall like a star i' th' darkest night
Stick fiery off indeed.

LAER: You mock me, sir.

HAM: No, by this hand.

KING: Give them the foils, young Osric. Cousin Hamlet,
You know the wager?

HAM: Very well, my lord.
Your Grace has laid the odds a' th' weaker side.

KING: I do not fear it, I have seen you both;
But since he is [better'd], we have therefore odds.

LAER: This is too heavy; let me see another.

HAM: This likes me well. These foils have all a length?

[*Prepare to play.*]

OSR: Ay, my good lord.

KING: Set me the stoups of wine upon that table.
If Hamlet give the first or second hit,
Or quit in answer of the third exchange,
Let all the battlements their ord'nance fire.
The King shall drink to Hamlet's better breath,
And in the cup an [union] shall he throw,
Richer than that which four successive kings
In Denmark's crown have worn. Give me the cups,
And let the kettle to the trumpet speak,
The trumpet to the cannoneer without,
The cannons to the heavens, the heaven to earth,
"Now the King drinks to Hamlet." Come begin;

Trumpets the while.

And you, the judges, bear a wary eye.

---

233. **brothers':** i.e. amicable, as if between brothers. **frankly:** freely, without constraint. 236. **foil:** thin sheet of metal placed behind a jewel to set it off. 238. **Stick . . . off:** blaze out in contrast. 244. **laid the odds:** i.e. wagered a higher stake (horses to rapiers). 246. **is better'd:** has perfected his skill. **odds:** i.e. the arrangement that Laertes must take more bouts than Hamlet to win. 248. **likes:** pleases. **a length:** the same length. 250. **stoups:** tankards. 252. **quit . . . exchange:** pays back wins by Laertes in the first and second bouts by taking the third. 255. **union:** an especially fine pearl. 258. **kettle:** kettle-drum.

HAM: Come on, sir.

LAER: Come, my lord.

[*They play and* HAMLET *scores a hit.*]

HAM: One.

LAER: No.

HAM: Judgment.

OSR: A hit, a very palpable hit.

LAER: Well, again.

KING: Stay, give me drink. Hamlet, this pearl is thine,
Here's to thy health! Give him the cup.

Drum, trumpets [*sound*] *flourish. A piece goes off* [*within*].

HAM: I'll play this bout first, set it by a while.
Come. [*They play again.*] Another hit; what say you?

LAER: [A touch, a touch,] I do confess't.

KING: Our son shall win.

QUEEN: He's fat, and scant of breath.
Here, Hamlet, take my napkin, rub thy brows.
The Queen carouses to thy fortune, Hamlet.

HAM: Good madam!

KING: Gertrude, do not drink.

QUEEN: I will, my lord, I pray you pardon me.

KING [*Aside.*]: It is the pois'ned cup, it is too late.

HAM: I dare not drink yet, madam; by and by.

QUEEN: Come, let me wipe thy face.

LAER: My lord, I'll hit him now.

KING: I do not think't.

LAER [*Aside.*]: And yet it is almost against my conscience.

HAM: Come, for the third, Laertes, you do but dally.
I pray you pass with your best violence;
I am sure you make a wanton of me.

LAER: Say you so? Come on. [*They play.*]

OSR: Nothing, neither way.

LAER: Have at you now!

---

276. **fat:** sweaty. 278. **carouses:** drinks a toast. 290. **make... me:** i.e. are holding back in order to let me win, as one does with a spoiled child (*wanton*).

[LAERTES *wounds* HAMLET; *then, in scuffling, they change rapiers.*]

KING: Part them, they are incens'd.
HAM: Nay, come again.

[HAMLET *wounds* LAERTES. *The* QUEEN *falls.*]

OSR: Look to the Queen there ho!
HOR: They bleed on both sides. How is it, my lord?
OSR: How is't, Laertes?
LAER: Why, as a woodcock to mine own springe, Osric:
I am justly kill'd with mine own treachery.
HAM: How does the Queen?
KING: She sounds to see them bleed.
QUEEN: No, no, the drink, the drink—O my dear Hamlet—
The drink, the drink! I am pois'ned. [*Dies.*]
HAM: O villainy! Ho, let the door be lock'd!
Treachery! Seek it out.
LAER: It is here, Hamlet. [Hamlet,] thou art slain.
No med'cine in the world can do thee good;
In thee there is not half an hour's life.
The treacherous instrument is in [thy] hand,
Unbated and envenom'd. The foul practice
Hath turn'd itself on me. Lo here I lie,
Never to rise again. Thy mother's pois'ned
I can no more—the King, the King's to blame.
HAM: The point envenom'd too!
Then, venom, to thy work. [*Hurts the* KING.]
ALL: Treason! treason!
KING: O, yet defend me, friends, I am but hurt.
HAM: Here, thou incestious, [murd'rous], damned Dane,
Drink [off] this potion! Is [thy union] here?
Follow my mother! [KING *dies.*]
LAER: He is justly served,
It is a poison temper'd by himself.
Exchange forgiveness with me, noble Hamlet.
Mine and my father's death come not upon thee,
Nor thine on me! [*Dies.*]

---

299. **springe:** snare. 302. **sounds:** swoons. 311. **Unbated:** not blunted. **foul practice:** vile plot. 316. s.d. **Hurts:** wounds. 323. **temper'd:** mixed.

HAM: Heaven make thee free of it! I follow thee.
I am dead, Horatio. Wretched queen, adieu!
You that look pale, and tremble at this chance,
That are but mutes or audience to this act,
Had I but time—as this fell sergeant, Death,
Is strict in his arrest—O, I could tell you—
But let it be. Horatio, I am dead,
Thou livest. Report me and my cause aright
To the unsatisfied.
HOR: Never believe it;
I am more an antique Roman than a Dane.
Here's yet some liquor left.
HAM: As th' art a man,
Give me the cup. Let go! By heaven, I'll ha't!
O God, Horatio, what a wounded name,
Things standing thus unknown, shall I leave behind me!
If thou didst ever hold me in thy heart,
Absent thee from felicity a while,
And in this harsh world draw thy breath in pain
To tell my story. *A march afar off* [*and a shot within*].
What warlike noise is this?

[OSRIC *goes to the door and returns.*]

OSR: Young Fortinbras, with conquest come from Poland,
To th' embassadors of England gives
This warlike volley.
HAM: O, I die, Horatio,
The potent poison quite o'er-crows my spirit.
I cannot live to hear the news from England,
But I do prophesy th' election lights
On Fortinbras, he has my dying voice.
So tell him, with th' occurrents more and less
Which have solicited—the rest is silence. [*Dies.*]
HOR: Now cracks a noble heart. Good night, sweet prince,
And flights of angels sing thee to thy rest!

---

327. **make thee free:** absolve you. 330. **mutes or audience:** silent spectators. 331. **fell:** cruel. **sergeant:** sheriff's officer. 337. **antique Roman:** i.e. one who will commit suicide on such an occasion. 352. **o'er-crows:** triumphs over (a term derived from cockfighting). **spirit:** vital energy. 355. **voice:** vote. 356. **occurrents:** occurrences. 357. **solicited:** instigated.

[*March within.*]

Why does the drum come hither?

Enter FORTINBRAS *with the* [ENGLISH] EMBASSADORS, [*with Drum, Colors, and* ATTENDANTS].

FORT: Where is this sight?
HOR: What is it you would see?
If aught of woe or wonder, cease your search.
FORT: This quarry cries on havoc. O proud death,
What feast is toward in thine eternal cell,
That thou so many princes at a shot
So bloodily hast strook?
[1.] EMB: The sight is dismal,
And our affairs from England come too late.
The ears are senseless that should give us hearing,
To tell him his commandment is fulfill'd,
That Rosencrantz and Guildenstern are dead.
Where should we have our thanks?
HOR: Not from his mouth,
Had it th' ability of life to thank you.
He never gave commandement for their death.
But since so jump upon this bloody question,
You from the Polack wars, and you from England,
Are here arrived, give order that these bodies
High on a stage be placed to the view,
And let me speak to [th'] yet unknowing world
How these things came about. So shall you hear
Of carnal, bloody, and unnatural acts,
Of accidental judgments, casual slaughters,
Of deaths put on by cunning and [forc'd] cause,
And in this upshot, purposes mistook
Fall'n on th' inventors' heads: all this can I
Truly deliver.
FORT: Let us haste to hear it,
And call the noblest to the audience.

---

364. **This . . . havoc:** this heap of corpses proclaims a massacre. 365. **toward:** in preparation 374. **his:** i.e. the King's. 377. **jump:** precisely, pat. **question:** matter. 380. **stage:** platform. 384. **judgments:** retributions. **casual:** happening by chance. 385. **put on:** instigated.

For me, with sorrow I embrace my fortune.
I have some rights, of memory in this kingdom,
Which now to claim my vantage doth invite me.
HOR: Of that I shall have also cause to speak,
And from his mouth whose voice will draw [on] more.
But let this same be presently perform'd
Even while men's minds are wild, lest more mischance
On plots and errors happen.
FORT: Let four captains
Bear Hamlet like a soldier to the stage,
For he was likely, had he been put on,
To have prov'd most royal; and for his passage,
The soldiers' music and the rite of war
Speak loudly for him.
Take up the bodies. Such a sight as this
Becomes the field, but here shows much amiss.
Go bid the soldiers shoot.

Exeunt [*marching; after the which a peal of ordinance are shot off*].

392. **of memory:** unforgotten. 393. **my vantage:** i.e. my opportune presence at a moment when the throne is empty. 395. **his . . . more:** the mouth of one (Hamlet) whose vote will induce others to support your claim. 396. **presently:** at once. 397. **wild:** distraught. 401. **put on:** put to the test (by becoming king). 402. **passage:** death. 406. **Becomes . . . amiss:** befits the battlefield, but appears very much out of place here.

Susan Glaspell (1876–1948) staged *Trifles* in 1916 as part of a twin bill with a play by the then-unknown Eugene O'Neill. On the surface, Glaspell's play seems to be a rather trite murder mystery, its narrative revolving around the murder of Minnie Foster Wright's husband. As the play develops, however, we see that Glaspell has worked carefully to stage a play that also raises issues of the subjugation of women, especially as seen in the female characters' responses to the male authority figures' reactions.

It is also a play animated by various forms of murder. The most obvious murder, of course, occurs before the play begins—within minutes into the action, we learn that John Wright had been strangled in his sleep. While Glaspell sparks audience interest by immediately involving us in the mystery of John Wright's murder, our real interest lies elsewhere: in the various symbolic forms of murder that gradually reveal themselves as the drama unfolds. Some of Glaspell's larger themes beyond female intuition versus male investigation concern the severance of human communication, the death of Minnie and John's love, and, significantly, the murder of Minnie Foster Wright's spirit. Thus while the physical death plays an important part within the play, the symbolic deaths give Glaspell's work its anything but trifling energy.

Glaspell, an accomplished journalist who based the play on an actual murder, went on to win the Pulitzer Prize for *Alison's House* (1930), a play inspired by the life of Emily Dickinson. While Glaspell's theater reputation slowly faded after World War II, her plays and life have attracted a great deal of critical interest and appreciation in recent years.

SCENE: *The kitchen in the now abandoned farmhouse of* JOHN WRIGHT, *a gloomy kitchen, and left without having been put in order—the walls covered with a faded wallpaper.* D. R. *is a door leading to the parlor. On the* R. *wall above this door is a built-in kitchen cupboard with shelves in the upper portion and drawers below. In the rear wall at* R., *up two steps is a door opening onto stairs leading to the second floor. In the rear wall at* L. *is a door to the shed and from there to the outside. Between these two doors is an old-fashioned black iron stove. Running along the* L. *wall from the shed door is an old iron sink and sink shelf, in which is set a hand pump. Downstage of the sink is an uncurtained window. Near the window is an old wooden rocker. Center stage is an unpainted wooden kitchen table with straight chairs on either side. There is a small chair* D. R. *Unwashed pans under the sink, a loaf of bread outside the breadbox, a dish towel on the table—other signs of incompleted work. At the rear the shed door opens and the* SHERIFF *comes in followed by the* COUNTY ATTORNEY *and* HALE. *The* SHERIFF *and* HALE *are men in middle life, the* COUNTY ATTORNEY *is a young man; all are much bundled up and go at once to the stove. They are followed by the two women—the* SHERIFF'S *wife,* MRS. PETERS, *first;*

she is a slight wiry woman, a thin nervous face. MRS. HALE *is larger and would ordinarily be called more comfortable looking, but she is disturbed now and looks fearfully about as she enters. The women have come in slowly, and stand close together near the door.*

COUNTY ATTORNEY (*at stove rubbing his hands*): This feels good. Come up to the fire, ladies.

MRS. PETERS (*after taking a step forward*): I'm not—cold.

SHERIFF (*unbuttoning his overcoat and stepping away from the stove to right of table as if to mark the beginning of official business*): Now, Mr. Hale, before we move things about, you explain to Mr. Henderson just what you saw when you came here yesterday morning.

COUNTY ATTORNEY (*crossing down to left of the table*): By the way, has anything been moved? Are things just as you left them yesterday?

SHERIFF (*looking about*): It's just the same. When it dropped below zero last night I thought I'd better send Frank out this morning to make a fire for us—(*sits right of center table*) no use getting pneumonia with a big case on, but I told him not to touch anything except the stove—and you know Frank.

COUNTY ATTORNEY: Somebody should have been left here yesterday.

SHERIFF: Oh—yesterday. When I had to send Frank to Morris Center for that man who went crazy—I want you to know I had my hands full yesterday. I knew you could get back from Omaha by today and as long as I went over everything here myself——

COUNTY ATTORNEY: Well, Mr. Hale, tell just what happened when you came here yesterday morning.

HALE (*crossing down to above table*): Harry and I had started to town with a load of potatoes. We came along the road from my place and as I got here I said, "I' m going to see if I can't get John Wright to go in with me on a party telephone." I spoke to Wright about it once before and he put me off, saying folks talked too much anyway, and all he asked was peace and quiet—I guess you know about how much he talked himself; but I thought maybe if I went to the house and talked about it before his wife, though I said to Harry that I didn't know as what his wife wanted made much difference to John——

COUNTY ATTORNEY: Let's talk about that later, Mr. Hale. I do want to talk about that, but tell now just what happened when you got to the house.

HALE: I didn't hear or see anything; I knocked at the door, and still it was all quiet inside. I knew they must be up, it was past eight o'clock. So I knocked again, and I thought I heard somebody say, "Come in." I wasn't sure, I'm not sure yet, but I opened the door—this door (*indicating the door by which the two women are still standing*) and there in that rocker—(*pointing to it*) sat Mrs. Wright. (*They all look at the rocker* D. L.)

COUNTY ATTORNEY: What—was she doing?

HALE: She was rockin' back and forth. She had her apron in her hand and was kind of—pleating it.

COUNTY ATTORNEY: And how did she—look?

HALE: Well, she looked queer.

COUNTY ATTORNEY: How do you mean—queer?

HALE: Well, as if she didn't know what she was going to do next. And kind of done up.

COUNTY ATTORNEY (*takes out notebook and pencil and sits left of center table*): How did she seem to feel about your coming?

HALE: Why, I don't think she minded—one way or other. She didn't pay much attention. I said, "How do, Mrs. Wright, it's cold, ain't it?" And she said, "Is it?"—and went on kind of pleating at her apron. Well, I was surprised; she didn't ask me to come up to the stove, or to set down, but just sat there, not even looking at me, so I said, "I want to see John." And then she—laughed. I guess you would call it a laugh. I thought of Harry and the team outside, so I said a little sharp: "Can't I see John?" "No," she says, kind o' dull like. "Ain't he home?" says I. "Yes," says she, "he's home." "Then why can't I see him?" I asked her, out of patience. "Cause he's dead," says she. "*Dead?*" says I. She just nodded her head, not getting a bit excited, but rockin' back and forth. "Why—where is he?" says I, not knowing what to say. She just pointed upstairs—like that (*Himself pointing to the room above*). I started for the stairs, with the idea of going up there. I walked from there to here—then I says, "Why, what did he die of?" "He died of a rope round his neck," says she, and just went on pleatin' at her apron. Well, I went out and called Harry. I thought I might—need help. We went upstairs and there he was lyin'—.

COUNTY ATTORNEY: I think I'd rather have you go into that upstairs, where you can point it all out. Just go on now with the rest of the story.

HALE: Well, my first thought was to get that rope off. It looked . . . (*stops, his face twitches*) . . . but Harry, he went up to him, and he said, "No, he's dead all right, and we'd better not touch anything." So we went back downstairs. She was still sitting that same way. "Has anybody been notified?" I asked. "No," says she, unconcerned. "Who did this, Mrs. Wright?" said Harry. He said it businesslike—and she stopped pleatin' of her apron. "I don't know," she says. "You don't *know*?" says Harry. "No," says she. "Weren't you sleepin' in the bed with him?" says Harry. "Yes," says she, "but I was on the inside." "Somebody slipped a rope round his neck and strangled him and you didn't wake up?" says Harry. "I didn't wake up," she said after him. We must 'a' looked as if we didn't see how that could be, for after a minute she said, "I sleep sound." Harry was going to ask her more questions but I said maybe we ought to let her tell her story first to the coroner, or the sheriff, so Harry went fast as he could to Rivers' place, where there's a telephone.

COUNTY ATTORNEY: And what did Mrs. Wright do when she knew that you had gone for the coroner?

HALE: She moved from the rocker to that chair over there (*pointing to a small chair in the* D. R. *corner*) and just sat there with her hands held together and looking down. I got a feeling that I ought to make some conversation, so I said I had come in to see if John wanted to put in a telephone, and at that she started to laugh, and then she stopped and looked at me—scared (*The* COUNTY ATTORNEY, *who has had his notebook out, makes a note*). I dunno, maybe it wasn't scared. I wouldn't like to say it was. Soon Harry got back, and then Dr. Lloyd came, and you, Mr. Peters, and so I guess that's all I know that you don't.

COUNTY ATTORNEY (*rising and looking around*): I guess we'll go upstairs first—and then out to the barn and around there. (*To the* SHERIFF). You're convinced that there was nothing important here—nothing that would point to any motive?

SHERIFF: Nothing here but kitchen things. (*The* COUNTY ATTORNEY, *after again looking around the kitchen, opens the door of a cupboard closet in* R. *wall. He brings a small chair from* R.—*gets up on it and looks on a shelf. Pulls his hand away, sticky.*)

COUNTY ATTORNEY: Here's a nice mess. (*The women draw nearer* U. C.)

MRS. PETERS (*to the other woman*): Oh, her fruit; it did freeze. (*To the* LAWYER). She worried about that when it turned so cold. She said the fire'd go out and her jars would break.

SHERIFF (*rises*): Well, can you beat the women! Held for murder and worryin' about her preserves.

COUNTY ATTORNEY (*getting down from chair*): I guess before we're through she may have something more serious than preserves to worry about. (*Crosses down* R. C.)

HALE: Well, women are used to worrying over trifles. (*The two women move a little closer together.*)

COUNTY ATTORNEY (*with the gallantry of a young politician*): And yet, for all their worries, what would we do without the ladies? (*The women do not unbend. He goes below the center table to the sink, takes a dipperful of water from the pail and pouring it into a basin, washes his hands. While he is doing this the* SHERIFF *and* HALE *cross to cupboard, which they inspect. The* COUNTY ATTORNEY *starts to wipe his hands on the roller towel, turns it for a cleaner place*). Dirty towels! (*Kicks his foot against the pans under the sink*). Not much of a housekeeper, would you say, ladies?

MRS. HALE (*stiffly*): There's a great deal of work to be done on a farm.

COUNTY ATTORNEY: To be sure. And yet (*with a little bow to her*) I know there are some Dickson County farmhouses which do not have such roller towels. (*He gives it a pull to expose its full length again.*)

MRS. HALE: Those towels get dirty awful quick. Men's hands aren't always as clean as they might be.

COUNTY ATTORNEY: Ah, loyal to your sex, I see. But you and Mrs. Wright were neighbors. I suppose you were friends, too.

MRS. HALE (*shaking her head*): I've not seen much of her of late years. I've not been in this house—it's more than a year.

COUNTY ATTORNEY (*crossing to women* U. C.): And why was that? You didn't like her?

MRS. HALE: I liked her all well enough. Farmers' wives have their hands full, Mr. Henderson. And then——

COUNTY ATTORNEY: Yes——?

MRS. HALE (*looking about*): It never seemed a very cheerful place.

COUNTY ATTORNEY: No—it's not cheerful. I shouldn't say she had the homemaking instinct.

MRS. HALE: Well, I don't know as Wright had, either.

COUNTY ATTORNEY: You mean that they didn't get on very well?

MRS. HALE: No, I don't mean anything. But I don't think a place'd be any cheerfuller for John Wright's being in it.

COUNTY ATTORNEY: I'd like to talk more of that a little later. I want to get the lay of things upstairs now. (*He goes past the women to* U. R. *where steps lead to a stair door.*)

SHERIFF: I suppose anything Mrs. Peters does'll be all right. She was to take in some clothes for her, you know, and a few little things. We left in such a hurry yesterday.

COUNTY ATTORNEY: Yes, but I would like to see what you take, Mrs. Peters, and keep an eye out for anything that might be of use to us.

MRS. PETERS: Yes, Mr. Henderson. (*The men leave by* U. R. *door to stairs. The women listen to the men's steps on the stairs, then look about the kitchen.*)

MRS. HALE (*crossing* L. *to sink*): I'd hate to have men coming into my kitchen, snooping around and criticizing. (*She arranges the pans under sink which the* LAWYER *had shoved out of place.*)

MRS. PETERS: Of course it's no more than their duty. (*Crosses to cupboard* U. R.)

MRS. HALE: Duty's all right, but I guess that deputy sheriff that came out to make the fire might have got a little of this on. (*Gives the roller towel a pull*). Wish I'd thought of that sooner. Seems mean to talk about her for not having things slicked up when she had to come away in such a hurry. (*Crosses* R. *to* MRS. PETERS *at cupboard.*)

MRS. PETERS (*who has been looking through cupboard, lifts one end of a towel that covers a pan*): She had bread set. (*Stands still.*)

MRS. HALE (*eyes fixed on a loaf of bread beside the breadbox, which is on a low shelf of the cupboard*): She was going to put this in there. (*Picks up loaf, then abruptly drops it. In a manner of returning to familiar things*). It's a shame about her fruit. I wonder if it's all gone. (*Gets up on the chair and looks*). I think there's some here that's all right, Mrs. Peters. Yes—here; (*holding it toward the window*) this is cherries, too. (*Looking again*). I declare I believe that's the only one. (*Gets down, jar in her hand. Goes to the sink and wipes it off on the outside*). She'll feel awful bad after all her hard work in the hot weather. I remember the afternoon I put up my cherries last summer. (*She puts the jar on the big kitchen table, center of the room. With a sigh, is about to sit down in the rocking chair. Before she is seated realizes what chair it is; with a slow look *at it, steps back. The chair which she has touched rocks back and forth.* MRS. PETERS *moves to center table and they both watch the chair rock for a moment or two.*)

MRS. PETERS (*shaking off the mood which the empty rocking chair has evoked. Now in a businesslike manner she speaks*): Well, I must get those things from the front room closet. (*She goes to the door at the* R., *but, after looking into the other room, steps back*). You coming with me, Mrs. Hale? You could help me carry them. (*They go in the other room; reappear,* MRS. PETERS *carrying a dress, petticoat and skirt,* MRS. HALE *following with a pair of shoes*). My, it's cold in there. (*She puts the clothes on the big table, and hurries to the stove.*)

MRS. HALE (*right of center table examining the skirt*): Wright was close. I think maybe that's why she kept so much to herself. She didn't even belong to the Ladies' Aid. I suppose she felt she couldn't do her part, and then you don't enjoy things when you feel shabby. I heard she used to wear pretty clothes and be lively, when she was Minnie Foster, one of the town girls singing in the choir. But that—oh, that was thirty years ago. This all you was to take in?

MRS. PETERS: She said she wanted an apron. Funny thing to want, for there isn't much to get you dirty in jail, goodness knows. But I suppose just to make her feel more natural. (*Crosses to cupboard*). She said they was in the top drawer in this cupboard. Yes, here. And then her little shawl that always hung behind the door. (*Opens stair door and looks*). Yes, here it is. (*Quickly shuts door leading upstairs.*)

MRS. HALE (*abruptly moving toward her*): Mrs. Peters?

MRS. PETERS: Yes, Mrs. Hale? (*At* U. R. *door.*)

MRS. HALE: Do you think she did it?

MRS. PETERS (*in a frightened voice*): Oh, I don't know.

MRS. HALE: Well, I don't think she did. Asking for an apron and her little shawl. Worrying about her fruit.

MRS. PETERS (*starts to speak, glances up, where footsteps are heard in the room above. In a low voice*): Mr. Peters says it looks bad for her. Mr. Henderson is awful sarcastic in a speech and he'll make fun of her sayin' she didn't wake up.

MRS. HALE: Well, I guess John Wright didn't wake when they was slipping that rope under his neck.

MRS. PETERS (*crossing slowly to table and placing shawl and apron on table with other clothing*): No, it's strange. It must have been done awful crafty and still. They say it was such a—funny way to kill a man, rigging it all up like that.

MRS. HALE (*crossing to left of* MRS. PETERS *at table*): That's just what Mr. Hale said. There was a gun in the house. He says that's what he can't understand.

MRS. PETERS: Mr. Henderson said coming out that what was needed for the case was a motive; something to show anger, or—sudden feeling.

MRS. HALE (*who is standing by the table*): Well, I don't see any signs of anger around here. (*She puts her hand on the dish towel which lies on the table, stands looking down at table, one-half of which is clean, the other half messy*). It's wiped to here. (*Makes a move as if to finish work, then turns and looks at loaf of bread outside the breadbox. Drops towel. In that voice of coming back to familiar things*). Wonder how they are finding things upstairs. (*Crossing below table to* D. R.). I hope she had it a little more red-up[1] up there. You know, it seems kind of *sneaking*. Locking her up in town and then coming out here and trying to get her own house to turn against her!

MRS. PETERS: But, Mrs. Hale, the law is the law.

MRS. HALE: I s'pose 'tis. (*Unbuttoning her coat*). Better loosen up your things, Mrs. Peters. You won't feel them when you go out. (MRS. PETERS *takes off her fur tippet, goes to hang it on chair back left of table, stands looking at the work basket on floor near* D. L. *window.*)

MRS. PETERS: She was piecing a quilt. (*She brings the large sewing basket to the center table and they look at the bright pieces,* MRS. HALE *above the table and* MRS. PETERS *left of it.*)

MRS. HALE: It's a log cabin pattern. Pretty, isn't it? I wonder if she was goin' to quilt it or just knot it? (*Footsteps have been heard coming down the stairs. The* SHERIFF *enters followed by* HALE *and the* COUNTY ATTORNEY.)

SHERIFF: They wonder if she was going to quilt it or just knot it! (*The men laugh, the women look abashed.*)

COUNTY ATTORNEY (*rubbing his hands over the stove*): Frank's fire didn't do much up there, did it? Well, let's go out to the barn and get that cleared up. (*The men go outside by* U. L. *door.*)

MRS. HALE (*resentfully*): I don't know as there's anything so strange, our takin' up our time with little things while we're waiting for them to get the evidence. (*She sits in chair right of table smoothing out a block with decision*). I don't see as it's anything to laugh about.

---

[1]**red-up:** slang term for "ready for company"

MRS. PETERS (*apologetically*): Of course they've got awful important things on their minds. (*Pulls up a chair and joins* MRS. HALE *at the left of the table.*)

MRS. HALE (*examining another block*): Mrs. Peters, look at this one. Here, this is the one she was working on, and look at the sewing! All the rest of it has been so nice and even. And look at this! It's all over the place! Why, it looks as if she didn't know what she was about! (*After she has said this they look at each other, then start to glance back at the door. After an instant* MRS. HALE *has pulled at a knot and ripped the sewing.*)

MRS. PETERS: Oh, what are you doing, Mrs. Hale?

MRS. HALE (*mildly*): Just pulling out a stitch or two that's not sewed very good. (*Threading a needle*). Bad sewing always made me fidgety.

MRS. PETERS (*with a glance at door, nervously*): I don't think we ought to touch things.

MRS. HALE: I'll just finish up this end. (*Suddenly stopping and leaning forward*). Mrs. Peters?

MRS. PETERS: Yes, Mrs. Hale?

MRS. HALE: What do you suppose she was so nervous about?

MRS. PETERS: Oh—I don't know. I don't know as she was nervous. I sometimes sew awful queer when I'm just tired. (MRS. HALE *starts to say something, looks at* MRS. PETERS *then goes on sewing*). Well, I must get these things wrapped up. They may be through sooner than we think. (*Putting apron and other things together*). I wonder where I can find a piece of paper, and string. (*Rises.*)

MRS. HALE: In that cupboard, maybe.

MRS. PETERS (*crosses* R. *looking in cupboard*): Why, here's a bird-cage. (*Holds it up*). Did she have a bird, Mrs. Hale?

MRS. HALE: Why, I don't know whether she did or not—I've not been here for so long. There was a man around last year selling canaries cheap, but I don't know as she took one; maybe she did. She used to sing real pretty herself.

MRS. PETERS (*glancing around*): Seems funny to think of a bird here. But she must have had one, or why would she have a cage? I wonder what happened to it?

MRS. HALE: I s'pose maybe the cat got it.

MRS. PETERS: No, she didn't have a cat. She's got that feeling some people have about cats—being afraid of them. My cat got in her room and she was real upset and asked me to take it out.

MRS. HALE: My sister Bessie was like that. Queer, ain't it?

MRS. PETERS (*examining the cage*): Why, look at this door. It's broke. One hinge is pulled apart. (*Takes a step down to* MRS. HALE'S *right.*)

MRS. HALE (*looking too*): Looks as if someone must have been rough with it.

MRS. PETERS: Why, yes. (*She brings the cage forward and puts it on the table.*)

MRS. HALE (*glancing toward* U. L. *door*): I wish if they're going to find any evidence they'd be about it. I don't like this place.

MRS. PETERS: But I'm awful glad you came with me, Mrs. Hale. It would be lonesome for me sitting here alone.

MRS. HALE: It would, wouldn't it? (*Dropping her sewing*). But I tell you what I do wish, Mrs. Peters. I wish I had come over sometimes when she was here. I—(*looking around the room*)—wish I had.

MRS. PETERS: But of course you were awful busy, Mrs. Hale—your house and your children.

MRS. HALE (*rises and crosses* L.): I could've come. I stayed away because it weren't cheerful—and that's why I ought to have come. I—(*looking out* L. *window*)—I've never liked this place. Maybe because it's down in a hollow and you don't see the road. I dunno what it is, but it's a lonesome place and always was. I wish I had come over to see Minnie Foster sometimes. I can see now——(*Shakes her head.*)

MRS. PETERS (*left of table and above it*): Well, you mustn't reproach yourself, Mrs. Hale. Somehow we just don't see how it is with other folks until—something turns up.

MRS. HALE: Not having children makes less work—but it makes a quiet house, and Wright out to work all day, and no company when he did come in. (*Turning from window*). Did you know John Wright, Mrs. Peters?

MRS. PETERS: Not to know him; I've seen him in town. They say he was a good man.

MRS. HALE: Yes—good; he didn't drink, and kept his word as well as most, I guess, and paid his debts. But he was a hard man, Mrs. Peters. Just to pass the time of day with him——(*Shivers*). Like a raw wind that gets to the bone. (*Pauses, her eye falling on the cage*). I should think she would 'a' wanted a bird. But what do you suppose went with it?

MRS. PETERS: I don't know, unless it got sick and died. (*She reaches over and swings the broken door, swings it again, both women watch it.*)

MRS. HALE: You weren't raised round here, were you? (MRS. PETERS *shakes her head*). You didn't know—her?

MRS. PETERS: Not till they brought her yesterday.

MRS. HALE: She—come to think of it, she was kind of like a bird herself—real sweet and pretty, but kind of timid and—fluttery. How—she—did—change. (*Silence; then as if struck by a happy thought and relieved to get back to everyday things. Crosses* R. *above* MRS. PETERS *to cupboard, replaces small chair used to stand on to its original place* D. R.). Tell you what, Mrs. Peters, why don't you take the quilt in with you? It might take up her mind.

MRS. PETERS: Why, I think that's a real nice idea, Mrs. Hale. There couldn't possibly be any objection to it, could there? Now, just what would I take? I wonder if her patches are in here—and her things. (*They look in the sewing basket.*)

MRS. HALE (*crosses to right of table*): Here's some red. I expect this has got sewing things in it. (*Brings out a fancy box*). What a pretty box. Looks like something somebody would give you. Maybe her scissors are in here. (*Opens box. Suddenly puts her hand to her nose*). Why—(MRS. PETERS *bends nearer, then turns her face away*). There's something wrapped up in this piece of silk.

MRS. PETERS: Why, this isn't her scissors

MRS. HALE (*lifting the silk*): Oh, Mrs. Peters—it's—(MRS. PETERS *bends closer.*)

MRS. PETERS: It's the bird.

MRS. HALE: But, Mrs. Peters—look at it! Its neck! Look at its neck! It's all—other side to.

MRS. PETERS: Somebody—wrung—its—neck. (*Their eyes meet. A look of growing comprehension, of horror. Steps are heard outside.* MRS. HALE *slips box under quilt pieces, and sinks into her chair. Enter* SHERIFF *and* COUNTY ATTORNEY. MRS. PETERS *steps* D. L. *and stands looking out of window.*)

COUNTY ATTORNEY (*as one turning from serious things to little pleasantries*). Well, ladies, have you decided whether she was going to quilt it or knot it? (*Crosses to* C. *above table.*)

MRS. PETERS: We think she was going to—knot it (SHERIFF *crosses to right of stove, lifts stove lid and glances at fire, then stands warming hands at stove.*)

COUNTY ATTORNEY: Well, that's interesting, I'm sure. (*Seeing the birdcage*). Has the bird flown?

MRS. HALE (*putting more quilt pieces over the box*): We think the—cat got it.

COUNTY ATTORNEY (*preoccupied*): Is there a cat? (MRS. HALE *glances in a quick covert way at* MRS. PETERS.)

MRS. PETERS (*turning from window takes a step in*): Well, not *now.* They're superstitious, you know. They leave.

COUNTY ATTORNEY (*to* SHERIFF PETERS, *continuing an interrupted conversation*): No sign at all of anyone having come from the outside. Their own rope. Now let's go up again and go over it piece by piece. (*They start upstairs*). It would have to have been someone who knew just the——(MRS. PETERS *sits down left of table. The two women sit there not looking at one another, but as if peering into something and at the same time holding back. When they talk now it is in the manner of feeling their way over strange ground, as if afraid of what they are saying, but as if they cannot help saying it.*)

MRS. HALE (*hesitatively and in hushed voice*): She liked the bird. She was going to bury it in that pretty box.

MRS. PETERS (*in a whisper*): When I was a girl—my kitten—there was a boy took a hatchet, and before my eyes—and before I could get there—(*Covers her face an instant*). If they hadn't held me back I would have—(*catches herself, looks upstairs where steps are heard, falters weakly*)—hurt him.

MRS. HALE (*with a slow look around her*): I wonder how it would seem never to have had any children around. (*Pause*). No, Wright wouldn't like the bird—a thing that sang. She used to sing. He killed that, too.

MRS. PETERS (*moving uneasily*): We don't know who killed the bird.

MRS. HALE: I knew John Wright.

MRS. PETERS: It was an awful thing was done in this house that night, Mrs. Hale. Killing a man while he slept, slipping a rope around his neck that choked the life out of him.

MRS. HALE: His neck. Choked the life out of him. (*Her hand goes out and rests on the bird-cage.*)

MRS. PETERS (*with rising voice*): We don't know who killed him. We don't know.

MRS. HALE (*her own feeling not interrupted*): If there'd been years and years of nothing, then a bird to sing to you, it would be awful—still, after the bird was still.

MRS. PETERS (*something within her speaking*): I know what stillness is. When we homesteaded in Dakota, and my first baby died—after he was two years old, and me with no other then——

MRS. HALE (*moving*): How soon do you suppose they'll be through looking for the evidence?

MRS. PETERS: I know what stillness is. (*Pulling herself back*). The law has got to punish crime, Mrs. Hale.

MRS. HALE (*not as if answering that*): I wish you'd seen Minnie Foster when she wore a white dress with blue ribbons and stood up there in the choir and sang. (*A look around the room*). Oh, I *wish* I'd come over here once in a while! That was a crime! That was a crime! Who's going to punish that?

MRS. PETERS (*looking upstairs*): We mustn't—take on.

MRS. HALE: I might have known she needed help! I know how things can be—for women. I tell you, it's queer, Mrs. Peters. We live close together and we live far apart. We all go through the same things—it's all just a different kind of the same thing. (*Brushes her eyes, noticing the jar of fruit, reaches out for it*). If I was you I wouldn't tell her her fruit was gone. Tell her it *ain't*. Tell her it's all right Take this in to prove it to her. She—she may never know whether it was broke or not.

MRS. PETERS (*takes the jar, looks about for something to wrap it in; takes petticoat from the clothes brought from the other room, very nervously begins winding this around the jar. In a false voice*): My, it's a good thing the men couldn't hear us. Wouldn't they just laugh! Getting all stirred up over a little thing like a—dead canary. As if that could have anything to do with—with—wouldn't they *laugh!* (*The men are heard coming downstairs.*)

MRS. HALE (*under her breath*): Maybe they would—maybe they wouldn't.

COUNTY ATTORNEY: No, Peters, it's all perfectly clear except a reason for doing it. But you know juries when it comes to women. If there was some definite thing. (*Crosses slowly to above table,* SHERIFF *crosses* D. R. MRS. HALE *and* MRS. PETERS *remain seated at either side of table*). Something to show—something to make a story about—a thing that would connect up with this strange way of doing it——(*The women's eyes meet for an instant. Enter* HALE *from outer door.*)

HALE (*remaining* U. L. *by door*): Well, I've got the team around. Pretty cold out there.

COUNTY ATTORNEY: I'm going to stay awhile by myself. (To *the* SHERIFF). You can send Frank out for me, can't you? I want to go over everything. I'm not satisfied that we can't do better.

SHERIFF: Do you want to see what Mrs. Peters is going to take in? (*The* LAWYER *picks up the apron, laughs.*)

COUNTY ATTORNEY: Oh, I guess they're not very dangerous things the ladies have picked out. (*Moves a few things about, disturbing the quilt pieces which cover the box. Steps back*). No, Mrs. Peters doesn't need supervising. For that matter a sheriff's wife is married to the law. Ever think of it that way, Mrs. Peters?

MRS. PETERS: Not—just that way.

SHERIFF (*chuckling*): Married to the law. (*Moves to* D. R. *door to the other room*). I just want you to come in here a minute, George. We ought to take a look at these windows.

COUNTY ATTORNEY (*scoffingly*): Oh, windows!

SHERIFF: We'll be right out, Mr. Hale, (HALE *goes outside. The* SHERIFF *follows the* COUNTY ATTORNEY *into the other room. Then* MRS. HALE *rises, hands tight together, looking intensely at* MRS. PETERS, *whose eyes make a slow turn, finally meeting* MRS. HALE'S. *A moment* MRS. HALE *holds her, then her own eyes point the way to where the box is concealed. Suddenly* MRS. PETERS *throws back quilt pieces and tries to put the box in the bag she is carrying. It is too big. She opens box, starts to take bird out, cannot touch it, goes to pieces, stands there helpless. Sound of a knob turning in the other room.* MRS. HALE *snatches the box and puts it in the pocket of her big coat. Enter* COUNTY ATTORNEY *and* SHERIFF, *who remains* D. R.)

COUNTY ATTORNEY (*crosses to* U. L. *door facetiously*): Well, Henry, at least we found out that she was not going to quilt it. She was going to—what is it you call it, ladies?

MRS. HALE: (*standing* C. *below table facing front, her hand against her pocket*).

We call it—knot it, Mr. Henderson.

CURTAIN

A Doll House — HENRIK IBSEN

Translated by Rolf Fjelde

The Norwegian playwright Henrik Ibsen (1828–1906) is often called the "father" of modern drama. It is a fitting title, in that he was one of the first playwrights to write compelling plays about controversial and important topics such as women's rights in the latter part of the nineteenth century.

A Doll House is considered one of the true classics of the Western stage. With its concern for the status of women, their education, and their autonomy, the play was considered shocking when it premiered in 1879, and it still rings as true today as it did then. The central character, Nora, overwhelmed by her selfish and domineering husband, Torvald, gains heroic stature by play's end, for she displays immense courage, insight, and self-awareness in her actions, despite a future filled with uncertainty.

Ibsen was a master of the then-new mode of playwriting known as realism. After struggling to gain public recognition through the 1850s and 1860s he finally achieved it with his plays *The Pillars of Society* (1877) and *A Doll House* (1879). By the time he finished his other great plays *An Enemy of the People* (1882), *The Wild Duck* (1884), *Hedda Gabler* (1890), *The Master Builder* (1892), and *John Gabriel Borkman* (1896), Ibsen had reinvented the modern stage. Most considered him at the time of his death to be the most important dramatist in the Western world.

THE CHARACTERS

TORVALD HELMER, *a lawyer*
NORA, *his wife*
DR. RANK
MRS. LINDE
NILS KROGSTAD, *a bank clerk*
THE HELMERS' THREE SMALL CHILDREN
ANNE-MARIE, *their nurse*
HELENE, *a maid*
A DELIVERY BOY

The action takes place in Helmer's residence.

Act I

(A comfortable room, tastefully but not expensively furnished. A door to the right in the back wall leads to the entryway; another to the left leads to Helmer's study. Between these doors, a piano. Midway in the left-hand wall a door, and further back a window. Near the window a round table with an armchair and a small sofa. In the right-hand wall, toward the rear, a door, and nearer the foreground a porcelain stove with two armchairs and a rocking chair beside it. Between the stove and the side door, a small table. Engravings on the walls. An étagère[1] *with china figures and other small art objects; a small bookcase with richly bound books; the floor carpeted; a fire burning in the stove. It is a winter day.)*

(A bell rings in the entryway; shortly after we hear the door being unlocked. Nora comes into the room, humming happily to herself; she is wearing street clothes and carries an armload of packages, which she puts down on the table to the right. She has left the hall door open, and through it a DELIVERY BOY *is seen holding a Christmas tree and a basket, which he gives to the Maid who let them in.)*

NORA: Hide the tree well, Helene. The children mustn't get a glimpse of it till this evening, after it's trimmed. (*To the* DELIVERY BOY, *taking out her purse.*) How much?

DELIVERY BOY: Fifty, ma'am.

NORA: There's a crown. No, keep the change. (*The* BOY *thanks her and leaves. Nora shuts the door. She laughs softly to herself while taking off her street things. Drawing a bag of macaroons from her pocket, she eats a couple, then steals over and listens at her husband's study door.*) Yes, he's home. (*Hums again as she moves to the table right.*)

HELMER (*from the study*): Is that my little lark twittering out there?

NORA (*busy opening some packages*): Yes, it is.

HELMER: Is that my squirrel rummaging around?

NORA: Yes!

HELMER: When did my squirrel get in?

NORA: Just now. (*Putting the macaroon bag in her pocket and wiping her mouth.*) Do come in, Torvald, and see what I've bought.

HELMER: Can't be disturbed. (*After a moment he opens the door and peers in, pen in hand.*) Bought, you say? All that there? Has the little spendthrift been out throwing money around again?

NORA: Oh, but Torvald, this year we really should let ourselves go a bit. It's the first Christmas we haven't had to economize.

HELMER: But you know we can't go squandering.

---

[1]**étagère:** French term for a cabinet with shelves

NORA: Oh yes, Torvald, we can squander a little now. Can't we? Just a tiny, wee bit. Now that you've got a big salary and are going to make piles and piles of money.

HELMER: Yes—starting New Year's. But then it's a full three months till the raise comes through.

NORA: Pooh! We can borrow that long.

HELMER: Nora! (*Goes over and playfully takes her by the ear.*) Are your scatterbrains off again? What if today I borrowed a thousand crowns, and you squandered them over Christmas week, and then on New Year's Eve a roof tile fell on my head, and I lay there—

NORA (*putting her hand on his mouth*): Oh! Don't say such things!

HELMER: Yes, but what if it happened—then what?

NORA: If anything so awful happened, then it just wouldn't matter if I had debts or not.

HELMER: Well, but the people I'd borrowed from?

NORA: Them? Who cares about them! They're strangers.

HELMER: Nora, Nora, how like a woman! No, but seriously, Nora, you know what I think about that. No debts! Never borrow! Something of freedom's lost—and something of beauty, too—from a home that's founded on borrowing and debt. We've made a brave stand up to now, the two of us; and we'll go right on like that the little while we have to.

NORA (*going toward the stove*): Yes, whatever you say, Torvald.

HELMER (*following her*): Now, now, the little lark's wings mustn't droop. Come on, don't be a sulky squirrel. (*Taking out his wallet.*) Nora, guess what I have here.

NORA (*turning quickly*): Money!

HELMER: There, see. (*Hands her some notes.*) Good grief, I know how costs go up in a house at Christmastime.

NORA: Ten—twenty—thirty—forty. Oh, thank you, Torvald; I can manage no end on this.

HELMER: You really will have to.

NORA: Oh yes, I promise I will! But come here so I can show you everything I bought. And so cheap! Look, new clothes for Ivar here—and a sword. Here a horse and a trumpet for Bob. And a doll and a doll's bed here for Emmy; they're nothing much, but she'll tear them to bits in no time anyway. And here I have dress material and handkerchiefs for the maids. Old Anne-Marie really deserves something more.

HELMER: And what's in that package there?

NORA (*with a cry*): Torvald, no! You can't see that till tonight!

HELMER: I see. But tell me now, you little prodigal, what have you thought of for yourself?

NORA: For myself? Oh, I don't want anything at all.

HELMER: Of course you do. Tell me just what—within reason—you'd most like to have.

NORA: I honestly don't know. Oh, listen, Torvald—

HELMER: Well?

NORA (*fumbling at his coat buttons, without looking at him*): If you want to give me something, then maybe you could—you could—

HELMER: Come on, out with it.

NORA (*hurriedly*): You could give me money, Torvald. No more than you think you can spare; then one of these days I'll buy something with it.

HELMER: But Nora—

NORA: Oh, please, Torvald darling, do that! I beg you, please. Then I could hang the bills in pretty gilt paper on the Christmas tree. Wouldn't that be fun?

HELMER: What are those little birds called that always fly through their fortunes?

NORA: Oh yes, spendthrifts; I know all that. But let's do as I say, Torvald; then I'll have time to decide what I really need most. That's very sensible, isn't it?

HELMER (*smiling*): Yes, very—that is, if you actually hung onto the money I give you, and you actually used it to buy yourself something. But it goes for the house and for all sorts of foolish things, and then I only have to lay out some more.

NORA: Oh, but Torvald—

HELMER: Don't deny it, my dear little Nora. (*Putting his arm around her waist.*) Spendthrifts are sweet, but they use up a frightful amount of money. It's incredible what it costs a man to feed such birds.

NORA: Oh, how can you say that! Really, I save everything I can.

HELMER (*laughing*): Yes, that's the truth. Everything you can. But that's nothing at all.

NORA (*humming, with a smile of quiet satisfaction*): Hm, if you only knew what expenses we larks and squirrels have, Torvald.

HELMER: You're an odd little one. Exactly the way your father was. You're never at a loss for scaring up money; but the moment you have it, it runs right out through your fingers; you never know what you've done with it. Well, one takes you as you are. It's deep in your blood. Yes, these things are hereditary, Nora.

NORA: Ah, I could wish I'd inherited many of Papa's qualities.

HELMER: And I couldn't wish you anything but just what you are, my sweet little lark. But wait; it seems to me you have a very—what should I call it?—a very suspicious look today—

NORA: I do?

HELMER: You certainly do. Look me straight in the eye.

NORA (*looking at him*): Well?

HELMER (*shaking an admonitory finger*): Surely my sweet tooth hasn't been running riot in town today, has she?

NORA: No. Why do you imagine that?

HELMER: My sweet tooth really didn't make a little detour through the confectioner's?

NORA: No, I assure you, Torvald—

HELMER: Hasn't nibbled some pastry?

NORA: No, not at all.

HELMER: Not even munched a macaroon or two?

NORA: No, Torvald, I assure you, really—

HELMER: There, there now. Of course I'm only joking.

NORA (*going to the table, right*): You know I could never think of going against you.

HELMER: No, I understand that; and you *have* given me your word. (*Going over to her.*) Well, you keep your little Christmas secrets to yourself, Nora darling. I expect they'll come to light this evening, when the tree is lit.

NORA: Did you remember to ask Dr. Rank?

HELMER: No. But there's no need for that, it's assumed he'll be dining with us. All the same, I'll ask him when he stops by here this morning. I've ordered some fine wine. Nora, you can't imagine how I'm looking forward to this evening.

NORA: So am I. And what fun for the children, Torvald!

HELMER: Ah, it's so gratifying to know that one's gotten a safe, secure job, and with a comfortable salary. It's a great satisfaction, isn't it?

NORA: Oh, it's wonderful!

HELMER: Remember last Christmas? Three whole weeks before, you shut yourself in every evening till long after midnight, making flowers for the Christmas tree, and all the other decorations to surprise us. Ugh, that was the dullest time I've ever lived through.

NORA: It wasn't at all dull for me.

HELMER (*smiling*): But the outcome *was* pretty sorry, Nora.

NORA: Oh, don't tease me with that again. How could I help it that the cat came in and tore everything to shreds.

HELMER: No, poor thing, you certainly couldn't. You wanted so much to please us all, and that's what counts. But it's just as well that the hard times are past.

NORA: Yes, it's really wonderful.

HELMER: Now I don't have to sit here alone, boring myself, and you don't have to tire your precious eyes and your fair little delicate hands—

NORA (*clapping her hands*): No, is it really true, Torvald, I don't have to? Oh, how wonderfully lovely to hear! (*Taking his arm.*) Now I'll tell you just how I've thought we should plan things. Right after Christmas—(*The doorbell rings.*) Oh, the bell. (*Straightening the room up a bit.*) Somebody would have to come. What a bore!

HELMER: I'm not at home to visitors, don't forget.

MAID (*from the hall doorway*): Ma'am, a lady to see you—

NORA: All right, let her come in.

MAID (*to Helmer*): And the doctor's just come too.

HELMER: Did he go right to my study?

MAID: Yes, he did.

(HELMER *goes into his room. The* MAID *shows in* MRS. LINDE, *dressed in traveling clothes, and shuts the door after her.*)

MRS. LINDE (*in a dispirited and somewhat hesitant voice*): Hello, Nora.

NORA (*uncertain*): Hello—

MRS. LINDE: You don't recognize me.

NORA: No, I don't know—but wait, I think—(*Exclaiming.*) What! Kristine! Is it really you?

MRS. LINDE: Yes, it's me.

NORA: Kristine! To think I didn't recognize you. But then, how could I? (*More quietly.*) How you've changed, Kristine!

MRS. LINDE: Yes, no doubt I have. In nine—ten long years.

NORA: Is it so long since we met! Yes, it's all of that. Oh, these last eight years have been a happy time, believe me. And so now you've come in to town, too. Made the long trip in the winter. That took courage.

MRS. LINDE: I just got here by ship this morning.

NORA: To enjoy yourself over Christmas, of course. Oh, how lovely! Yes, enjoy ourselves, we'll do that. But take your coat off. You're not still cold? (*Helping her.*) There now, let's get cozy here by the stove. No, the easy chair there! I'll take the rocker here. (*Seizing her hands.*) Yes, now you have your old look again; it was only in that first moment. You're a bit more pale, Kristine—and maybe a bit thinner.

MRS. LINDE: And much, much older, Nora.

NORA: Yes, perhaps a bit older; a tiny, tiny bit; not much at all. (*Stopping short; suddenly serious.*) Oh, but thoughtless me, to sit here, chattering away. Sweet, good Kristine, can you forgive me?

MRS. LINDE: What do you mean, Nora?

NORA (*softly*): Poor Kristine, you've become a widow.

MRS. LLNDE: Yes, three years ago.

NORA: Oh, I knew it, of course; I read it in the papers. Oh, Kristine, you must believe me; I often thought of writing you then, but I kept postponing it, and something always interfered.

MRS. LINDE: Nora dear, I understand completely.

NORA: No, it was awful of me, Kristine. You poor thing, how much you must have gone through. And he left you nothing?

MRS. LINDE: No.

NORA: And no children?

MRS. LINDE: No.

NORA: Nothing at all, then?

MRS. LINDE: Not even a sense of loss to feed on.

NORA (*looking incredulously at her.*): But Kristine, how could that be?

MRS. LINDE (*smiling wearily and smoothing her hair*): Oh, sometimes it happens, Nora.

NORA: So completely alone. How terribly hard that must be for you. I have three lovely children. You can't see them now; they're out with the maid. But now you must tell me everything—

MRS. LINDE: No, no, no, tell me about yourself.

NORA: No, you begin. Today I don't want to be selfish. I want to think only of you today. But there is something I must tell you. Did you hear of the wonderful luck we had recently?

MRS. LINDE: No, what's that?

NORA: My husband's been made manager in the bank, just think!

MRS. LINDE: Your husband? How marvelous!

NORA: Isn't it? Being a lawyer is such an uncertain living, you know, especially if one won't touch any cases that aren't clean and decent. And of course Torvald would never do that, and I'm with him completely there. Oh, we're simply delighted, believe me! He'll join the bank right after New Year's and start getting a huge salary and lots of commissions. From now on we can live quite differently—just as we want. Oh, Kristine, I feel so light and happy! Won't it be lovely to have stacks of money and not a care in the world?

MRS. LINDE: Well, anyway, it would be lovely to have enough for necessities.

NORA: No, not just for necessities, but stacks and stacks of money!

MRS. LINDE (*smiling*): Nora, Nora, aren't you sensible yet? Back in school you were such a free spender.

NORA (*with a quiet laugh*): Yes, that's what Torvald still says. (*Shaking her finger.*) But "Nora, Nora" isn't as silly as you all think. Really, we've been in no position for me to go squandering. We've had to work, both of us.

MRS. LINDE: You too?

NORA: Yes, at odd jobs—needlework, crocheting, embroidery, and such—(*casually*) and other things too. You remember that Torvald left the department when we were married? There was no chance of promotion in his office, and of course he needed to earn more money. But that first year he drove himself terribly. He took on all kinds of extra work that kept him going morning and night. It wore him down, and then he fell deathly ill. The doctors said it was essential for him to travel south.

MRS. LINDE: Yes, didn't you spend a whole year in Italy?

NORA: That's right. It wasn't easy to get away, you know. Ivar had just been born. But of course we had to go. Oh, that was a beautiful trip, and it saved Torvald's life. But it cost a frightful sum, Kristine.

MRS. LINDE: I can well imagine.

NORA: Four thousand, eight hundred crowns it cost. That's really a lot of money.

MRS. LINDE: But it's lucky you had it when you needed it.

NORA: Well, as it was, we got it from Papa.

MRS. LINDE: I see. It was just about the time your father died.

NORA: Yes, just about then. And, you know, I couldn't make that trip out to nurse him. I had to stay here, expecting Ivar any moment, and with my poor sick Torvald to care for. Dearest Papa, I never saw him again, Kristine. Oh, that was the worst time I've known in all my marriage.

MRS. LINDE: I know how you loved him. And then you went off to Italy?

NORA: Yes. We had the means now, and the doctors urged us. So we left a month after.

MRS. LINDE: And your husband came back completely cured?

NORA: Sound as a drum!

MRS. LINDE: But—the doctor?

NORA: Who?

MRS. LINDE: I thought the maid said he was a doctor, the man who came in with me.

NORA: Yes, that was Dr. Rank—but he's not making a sick call. He's our closest friend, and he stops by at least once a day. No, Torvald hasn't had a sick moment since, and the children are fit and strong, and I am, too. (*Jumping up and clapping her hands.*) Oh, dear God, Kristine, what a lovely thing to live and be happy! But how disgusting of me—I'm talking of nothing but my own affairs. (*Sits on a stool close by Kristine, arms resting across her knees.*) Oh, don't be angry with me! Tell me, is it really true that you weren't in love with your husband? Why did you marry him, then?

MRS. LINDE: My mother was still alive, but bedridden and helpless—and I had my two younger brothers to look after. In all conscience, I didn't think I could turn him down.

NORA: No, you were right there. But was he rich at the time?

MRS. LINDE: He was very well off, I'd say. But the business was shaky, Nora. When he died, it all fell apart, and nothing was left.

NORA: And then—?

MRS. LINDE: Yes, so I had to scrape up a living with a little shop and a little teaching and whatever else I could find. The last three years have been like one endless workday without a rest for me. Now, it's over, Nora. My poor mother doesn't need me, for she's passed on. Nor the boys, either; they're working now and can take care of themselves.

NORA: How free you must feel—

MRS. LINDE: No—only unspeakably empty. Nothing to live for now. (*Standing up anxiously.*) That's why I couldn't take it any longer out in that desolate hole. Maybe here it'll be easier to find something to do and keep my mind occupied. If I could only be lucky enough to get a steady job, some office work—

NORA: Oh, but Kristine, that's so dreadfully tiring, and you already look so tired. It would be much better for you if you could go off to a bathing resort.

MRS. LINDE (*going toward the window*): I have no father to give me travel money, Nora.

NORA (*rising*): Oh, don't be angry with me.

MRS. LINDE (*going to her*): Nora dear, don't you be angry with me. The worst of my kind of situation is all the bitterness that's stored away. No one to work for, and yet you're always having to snap up your opportunities. You have to live; and so you grow selfish. When you told me the happy change in your lot, do you know I was delighted less for your sakes than for mine?

NORA: How so? Oh, I see. You think maybe Torvald could do something for you.

MRS. LLNDE: Yes, that's what I thought.

NORA: And he will, Kristine! Just leave it to me; I'll bring it up so delicately—find something attractive to humor him with. Oh, I'm so eager to help you.

MRS. LINDE: How very kind of you, Nora, to be so concerned over me—doubly kind, considering you really know so little of life's burdens yourself.

NORA: I—? I know so little—?

MRS. LINDE (*smiling*): Well, my heavens—a little needlework and such—Nora, you're just a child.

NORA (*tossing her head and pacing the floor*): You don't have to act so superior.

MRS. LINDE: Oh?

NORA: You're just like the others. You all think I'm incapable of anything serious—

MRS. LINDE: Come now—

NORA: That I've never had to face the raw world.

MRS. LINDE: Nora dear, you've just been telling me all your troubles.

NORA: Hm! Trivial! (*Quietly.*) I haven't told you the big thing.

MRS. LINDE: Big thing? What do you mean?

NORA: You look down on me so, Kristine, but you shouldn't. You're proud that you worked so long and hard for your mother.

MRS. LINDE: I don't look down on a soul. But it is true: I'm proud—and happy, too—to think it was given to me to make my mother's last days almost free of care.

NORA: And you're also proud thinking of what you've done for your brothers.

MRS. LINDE: I feel I've a right to be.

NORA: I agree. But listen to this, Kristine—I've also got something to be proud and happy for.

MRS. LINDE: I don't doubt it. But whatever do you mean?

NORA: Not so loud. What if Torvald heard! He mustn't, not for anything in the world. Nobody must know, Kristine. No one but you.

MRS. LINDE: But what is it, then?

NORA: Come here. (*Drawing her down beside her on the sofa.*) It's true—I've also got something to be proud and happy for. I'm the one who saved Torvald's life.

MRS. LINDE: Saved—? Saved how?

NORA: I told you about the trip to Italy. Torvald never would have lived if he hadn't gone south—

MRS. LINDE: Of course; your father gave you the means—

NORA (*smiling*): That's what Torvald and all the rest think, but—

MRS. LINDE: But—?

NORA: Papa didn't give us a pin. I was the one who raised the money.

MRS. LINDE: You? That whole amount?

NORA: Four thousand, eight hundred crowns. What do you say to that?

MRS. LINDE: But Nora, how was it possible? Did you win the lottery?

NORA (*disdainfully*): The lottery? Pooh! No art to that.

MRS. LINDE: But where did you get it from then?

NORA (*humming, with a mysterious smile*): Hmm, tra-la-la-la.

MRS. LINDE: Because you couldn't have borrowed it.

NORA: No? Why not?

MRS. LINDE: A wife can't borrow without her husband's consent.

NORA (*tossing her head*): Oh, but a wife with a little business sense, a wife who knows how to manage—

MRS. LINDE: Nora, I simply don't understand—

NORA: You don't have to. Whoever said I *borrowed* the money? I could have gotten it other ways. (*Throwing herself back on the sofa.*) I could have gotten it from some admirer or other. After all, a girl with my ravishing appeal—

MRS. LINDE: You lunatic.

NORA: I'll bet you're eaten up with curiosity, Kristine.

MRS. LINDE: Now listen here, Nora—you haven't done something indiscreet?

NORA (*sitting up again*): Is it indiscreet to save your husband's life?

MRS. LINDE: I think it's indiscreet that without his knowledge you—

NORA: But that's the point: He mustn't know! My Lord, can't you understand? He mustn't ever know the close call he had. It was to *me* the doctors came to say his life was in danger—that nothing could save him but a stay in the south. Didn't I try strategy then! I began talking about how lovely it would be for me to travel abroad like other young wives; I begged and I cried; I told him please to remember my condition, to be kind and indulge me; and then I dropped a hint that he could easily take out a loan. But at that, Kristine, he nearly exploded. He said I was frivolous, and it was his duty as man of the house not to indulge me in whims and fancies—as I think he called them. Aha, I thought, now you'll just have to be saved—and that's when I saw my chance.

MRS. LINDE: And your father never told Torvald the money wasn't from him?

NORA: No, never. Papa died right about then. I'd considered bringing him into my secret and begging him never to tell. But he was too sick at the time—and then, sadly, it didn't matter.

MRS. LINDE: And you've never confided in your husband since?

NORA: For heaven's sake, no! Are you serious? He's so strict on that subject. Besides—Torvald, with all his masculine pride—how painfully humiliating for him if he ever found out he was in debt to me. That would just ruin our relationship. Our beautiful, happy home would never be the same.

MRS. LINDE: Won't you ever tell him?

NORA (*thoughtfully, half smiling*): Yes—maybe sometime years from now, when I'm no longer so attractive. Don't laugh! I only mean when Torvald loves me less than now, when he stops enjoying my dancing and dressing up and reciting for him. Then it might be wise to have something in reserve—(*Breaking off.*) How ridiculous! That'll never happen—Well, Kristine, what do you think of my big secret? I'm capable of something too, hm? You can imagine, of course, how this thing hangs over me. It really hasn't been easy meeting the payments on time. In the business world there's what they call quarterly interest and what they call amortization, and these are always so terribly hard to manage. I've had to skimp a little here and there, wherever I could, you know. I could hardly spare anything from my house allowance, because Torvald has to live well. I couldn't let the children go poorly dressed; whatever I got for them, I felt I had to use up completely—the darlings!

MRS. LINDE: Poor Nora, so it had to come out of your own budget, then?

NORA: Yes, of course. But I was the one most responsible, too. Every time Torvald gave me money for new clothes and such, I never used more than half; always bought the simplest, cheapest outfits. It was a godsend that everything looks so well on me that Torvald never noticed. But it did weigh me down at times, Kristine. It *is* such a joy to wear fine things. You understand.

MRS. LINDE: Oh, of course.

NORA: And then I found other ways of making money. Last winter I was lucky enough to get a lot of copying to do. I locked myself in and sat writing every evening till late in the night. Ah, I was tired so often, dead tired. But still it was wonderful fun, sitting and working like that, earning money. It was almost like being a man.

MRS. LINDE: But how much have you paid off this way so far?

NORA: That's hard to say, exactly. These accounts, you know, aren't easy to figure. I only know that I've paid out all I could scrape together. Time and again I haven't known where to turn. (*Smiling.*) Then I'd sit here dreaming of a rich old gentleman who had fallen in love with me—

MRS. LINDE: What! Who is he?

NORA: Oh, really! And that he'd died, and when his will was opened, there in big letters it said, "All my fortune shall be paid over in cash, immediately, to that enchanting Mrs. Nora Helmer."

MRS. LINDE: But Nora dear—who *was* this gentleman?

NORA: Good grief, can't you understand? The old man never existed; that was only something I'd dream up time and again whenever I was at my wits' end for money. But it makes no difference now; the old fossil can go where he pleases for all I care; I don't need him or his will—because now I'm free. (*Jumping up.*) Oh, how lovely to think of that, Kristine! Carefree! To know you're carefree, utterly carefree; to be able to romp and play with the children, and to keep up a beautiful, charming home—everything just the way Torvald likes it! And think, spring is coming, with big blue skies. Maybe we can travel a little then. Maybe I'll see the ocean again. Oh yes, it *is* so marvelous to live and be happy!

(*The front doorbell rings.*)

MRS. LINDE (*rising*): There's the bell. It's probably best that I go.

NORA: No, stay. No one's expected. It must be for Torvald.

MAID (*from the hall doorway*): Excuse me, ma'am—there's a gentleman here to see Mr. Helmer, but I didn't know—since the doctor's with him—

NORA: Who is the gentleman?

KROGSTAD (*from the doorway*): It's me, Mrs. Helmer.

(MRS. LINDE *starts and turns away toward the window.*)

NORA (*stepping toward him, tense, her voice a whisper*): You? What is it? Why do you want to speak to my husband?

KROGSTAD: Bank business—after a fashion. I have a small job in the investment bank, and I hear now your husband is going to be our chief—

NORA: In other words, it's—

KROGSTAD: Just dry business, Mrs. Helmer. Nothing but that.

NORA: Yes, then please be good enough to step into the study. (*She nods indifferently as she sees him out by the hall door, then returns and begins stirring up the stove.*)

MRS. LINDE: Nora—who was that man?

NORA: That was a Mr. Krogstad—a lawyer.

MRS. LINDE: Then it really was him.

NORA: Do you know that person?

MRS. LINDE: I did once—many years ago. For a time he was a law clerk in our town.

NORA: Yes, he's been that.

MRS. LINDE: How he's changed.

NORA: I understand he had a very unhappy marriage.

MRS. LINDE: He's a widower now.

NORA: With a number of children. There now, it's burning. (*She closes the stove door and moves the rocker a bit to one side.*)

MRS. LINDE: They say he has a hand in all kinds of business.

NORA: Oh? That may be true; I wouldn't know. But let's not think about business. It's so dull.

(DR. RANK *enters from* HELMER'S *study.*)

RANK (*still in the doorway*): No, no, really—I don't want to intrude, I'd just as soon talk a little while with your wife. (*Shuts the door, then notices* MRS. LINDE.) Oh, beg pardon. I'm intruding here too.

NORA: No, not at all. (*Introducing him.*) Dr. Rank, Mrs. Linde.

RANK: Well now, that's a name much heard in this house. I believe I passed the lady on the stairs as I came.

MRS. LINDE: Yes, I take the stairs very slowly. They're rather hard on me.

RANK: Uh-hm, some touch of internal weakness?

MRS. LINDE: More overexertion, I'd say.

RANK: Nothing else? Then you're probably here in town to rest up in a round of parties?

MRS. LINDE: I'm here to look for work.

RANK: Is that the best cure for overexertion?

MRS. LINDE: One has to live, Doctor.

RANK: Yes, there's a common prejudice to that effect.

NORA: Oh, come on, Dr. Rank—you really do want to live yourself.

RANK: Yes, I really do. Wretched as I am, I'll gladly prolong my torment indefinitely. All my patients feel like that. And it's quite the same, too, with the morally sick. Right at this moment there's one of those moral invalids in there with Helmer—

MRS. LINDE (*softly*): Ah!

NORA: Who do you mean?

RANK: Oh, it's a lawyer, Krogstad, a type you wouldn't know. His character is rotten to the root—but even he began chattering all-importantly about how he had to *live*.

NORA: Oh? What did he want to talk to Torvald about?

RANK: I really don't know. I only heard something about the bank.

NORA: I didn't know that Krog—that this man Krogstad had anything to do with the bank.

RANK: Yes, he's gotten some kind of berth down there. (*To* MRS. LINDE.) I don't know if you also have, in your neck of the woods, a type of person who scuttles about breathlessly, sniffing out hints of moral corruption, and then maneuvers his victim into some sort of key position where he can keep an eye on him. It's the healthy these days that are out in the cold.

MRS. LINDE: All the same, it's the sick who most need to be taken in.

RANK (*with a shrug*): Yes, there we have it. That's the concept that's turning society into a sanatorium.

(NORA, *lost in her thoughts, breaks out into quiet laughter and claps her hands.*)

RANK: Why do you laugh at that? Do you have any real idea of what society is?

NORA: What do I care about dreary old society? I was laughing at something quite different—something terribly funny. Tell me, Doctor—is everyone who works in the bank dependent now on Torvald?

RANK: Is that what you find so terribly funny?

NORA (*smiling and humming*): Never mind, never mind! (*Pacing the floor.*) Yes, that's really immensely amusing: that we—that Torvald has so much power now over all those people. (*Taking the bag out of her pocket.*) Dr. Rank, a little macaroon on that?

RANK: See here, macaroons! I thought they were contraband here.

NORA: Yes, but these are some that Kristine gave me.

MRS. LINDE: What? I—?

NORA: Now, now, don't be afraid. You couldn't possibly know that Torvald had forbidden them. You see, he's worried they'll ruin my teeth. But hmp! Just this once! Isn't that so, Dr. Rank? Help yourself! (*Puts a macaroon in his mouth.*) And you too, Kristine. And I'll also have one, only a little one—or two, at the most. (*Walking about again.*) Now I'm really tremendously happy. Now's there's just one last thing in the world that I have an enormous desire to do.

RANK: Well! And what's that?

NORA: It's something I have such a consuming desire to say so Torvald could hear.

RANK: And why can't you say it?

NORA: I don't dare. It's quite shocking.

MRS. LINDE: Shocking?

RANK: Well, then it isn't advisable. But in front of us you certainly can. What do you have such a desire to say so Torvald could hear?

NORA: I have such a huge desire to say—to hell and be damned!

RANK: Are you crazy?

MRS. LINDE: My goodness, Nora!

RANK: Go on, say it. Here he is.

NORA (*hiding the macaroon bag*): Shh, shh, shh!

(HELMER *comes in from his study, hat in hand, overcoat over his arm.*)

NORA (*going toward him*): Well, Torvald dear, are you through with him?

HELMER: Yes, he just left.

NORA: Let me introduce you—this is Kristine, who's arrived here in town.

HELMER: Kristine—? I'm sorry, but I don't know—

NORA: Mrs. Linde, Torvald dear. Mrs. Kristine Linde.

HELMER: Of course. A childhood friend of my wife's, no doubt?

MRS. LINDE: Yes, we knew each other in those days.

NORA: And just think, she made the long trip down here in order to talk with you.

HELMER: What's this?

MRS. LINDE: Well, not exactly—

NORA: You see, Kristine is remarkably clever in office work, and so she's terribly eager to come under a capable man's supervision and add more to what she already knows—

HELMER: Very wise, Mrs. Linde.

NORA: And then when she heard that you'd become a bank manager—the story was wired out to the papers—then she came in as fast as she could and—Really, Torvald, for my sake you can do a little something for Kristine, can't you?

HELMER: Yes, it's not at all impossible. Mrs. Linde, I suppose you're a widow?

MRS. LINDE: Yes.

HELMER: Any experience in office work?

MRS. LINDE: Yes, a good deal.

HELMER: Well, it's quite likely that I can make an opening for you—

NORA (*clapping her hands*): You see, you see!

HELMER: You've come at a lucky moment, Mrs. Linde.

MRS. LINDE: Oh, how can I thank you?

HELMER: Not necessary. (*Putting his overcoat on.*) But today you'll have to excuse me—

RANK: Wait, I'll go with you. (*He fetches his coat from the hall and warms it at the stove.*)

NORA: Don't stay out long, dear.

HELMER: An hour; no more.

NORA: Are you going too, Kristine?

MRS. LINDE (*putting on her winter garments*): Yes, I have to see about a room now.

HELMER: Then perhaps we can all walk together.

NORA (*helping her*): What a shame we're so cramped here, but it's quite impossible for us to—

MRS. LINDE: Oh, don't even think, of it! Good-bye, Nora dear, and thanks for everything.

NORA: Good-bye for now. Of course you'll be back this evening. And you too, Dr. Rank. What? If you're well enough? Oh, you've got to be! Wrap up tight now.

(*In a ripple of small talk the company moves out into the hall; children's voices are heard outside on the steps.*)

NORA: There they are! There they are! (*She runs to open the door.* THE CHILDREN *come in with their nurse,* ANNE-MARIE.) Come in, come in! (*Bends down and kisses them.*) Oh, you darlings—! Look at them, Kristine. Aren't they lovely!

RANK: No loitering in the draft here.

HELMER: Come, Mrs. Linde—this place is unbearable now for anyone but mothers.

(DR. RANK, HELMER, *and* MRS. LINDE *go down the stairs.* ANNE-MARIE *goes into the living room with* THE CHILDREN. NORA *follows, after closing the hall door.*)

NORA: How fresh and strong you look. Oh, such red cheeks you have! Like apples and roses. (THE CHILDREN *interrupt her throughout the following.*) And it was so much fun? That's wonderful. Really? You pulled both Emmy and Bob on the sled? Imagine, all together! Yes, you're a clever boy, Ivar. Oh, let me hold her a bit, Anne-Marie. My sweet little doll baby! (*Takes the smallest from the nurse and dances with her.*) Yes, yes, Mama will dance with Bob as well. What? Did you throw snowballs? Oh, if I'd only been there! No, don't bother, Anne-Marie—I'll undress them myself. Oh yes, let me. It's such fun. Go in and rest; you look half frozen. There's hot coffee waiting for you on the stove. (*The nurse goes into the room to the left.* NORA *takes the children's winter things off, throwing them about, while the children talk to her all at once.*) Is that so? A big dog chased you? But it didn't bite? No, dogs never bite little, lovely doll babies. Don't peek in the packages, Ivar! What is it? Yes, wouldn't you like to know. No, no, it's an ugly something. Well? Shall we play? What shall we play? Hide-and-seek? Yes, let's play hide-and-seek. Bob must hide first. I must? Yes, let me hide first. (*Laughing and shouting, she and the children play in and out of the living room and the adjoining room to the right. At last* NORA *hides under the table. The children come storming in, search, but cannot find her, then hear her muffled laughter, dash over to the table, lift the cloth up and find her. Wild shouting. She creeps forward as if to scare them. More shouts. Meanwhile, a knock at the hall door; no one has noticed it. Now the door half opens, and* KROGSTAD *appears. He waits a moment; the game goes on.*)

KROGSTAD: Beg pardon, Mrs. Helmer—

NORA (*with a strangled cry, turning and scrambling to her knees*): Oh! What do you want?

KROGSTAD: Excuse me. The outer door was ajar; it must be someone forgot to shut it—

NORA (*rising*): My husband isn't home, Mr. Krogstad.

KROGSTAD: I know that.

NORA: Yes—then what do you want here?

KROGSTAD: A word with you.

NORA: With—? (*To the children, quietly.*) Go in to Anne-Marie. What? No, the strange man won't hurt Mama. When he's gone, we'll play some more. (*She leads the children into the room to the left and shuts the door after them. Then, tense and nervous:*) You want to speak to me?

KROGSTAD: Yes, I want to.

NORA: Today? But it's not yet the first of the month—

KROGSTAD: No, it's Christmas Eve. It's going to be up to you how merry a Christmas you have.

NORA: What is it you want? Today I absolutely can't—

KROGSTAD: We won't talk about that till later. This is something else. You do have a moment to spare, I suppose?

NORA: Oh yes, of course—I do, except—

KROGSTAD: Good. I was sitting over at Olsen's Restaurant when I saw your husband go down the street—

NORA: Yes?

KROGSTAD: With a lady.

NORA: Yes. So?

KROGSTAD: If you'll pardon my asking: Wasn't that lady a Mrs. Linde?

NORA: Yes.

KROGSTAD: Just now come into town?

NORA: Yes, today.

KROGSTAD: She's a good friend of yours?

NORA: Yes, she is. But I don't see—

KROGSTAD: I also knew her once.

NORA: I'm aware of that.

KROGSTAD: Oh? You know all about it. I thought so. Well, then let me ask you short and sweet: Is Mrs. Linde getting a job in the bank?

NORA: What makes you think you can cross-examine me, Mr. Krogstad—you, one of my husband's employees? But since you ask, you might as well know—yes, Mrs. Linde's going to be taken on at the bank. And I'm the one who spoke for her Mr. Krogstad. Now you know.

KROGSTAD: So I guessed right.

NORA (*pacing up and down*): Oh, one does have a tiny bit of influence, I should hope. Just because I am a woman, don't think it means that—When one has a subordinate position, Mr. Krogstad, one really ought to be careful about pushing somebody who—hm—

KROGSTAD: Who has influence?

NORA: That's right.

KROGSTAD (*in a different tone*): Mrs. Helmer, would you be good enough to use your influence on my behalf?

NORA: What? What do you mean?

KROGSTAD: Would you please make sure that I keep my subordinate position in the bank?

NORA: What does that mean? Who's thinking of taking away your position?

KROGSTAD: Oh, don't play the innocent with me. I'm quite aware that your friend would hardly relish the chance of running into me again; and I'm also aware now whom I can thank for being turned out.

NORA: But I promise you—

KROGSTAD: Yes, yes, yes, to the point: There's still time, and I'm advising you to use your influence to prevent it.

NORA: But Mr. Krogstad, I have absolutely no influence.

KROGSTAD: You haven't? I thought you were just saying—

NORA: You shouldn't take me so literally. I! How can you believe that I have any such influence over my husband?

KROGSTAD: Oh, I've known your husband from our student days. I don't think the great bank manager's more steadfast than any other married man.

NORA: You speak insolently about my husband, and I'll show you the door.

KROGSTAD: The lady has spirit.

NORA: I'm not afraid of you any longer. After New Year's, I'll soon be done with the whole business.

KROGSTAD (*restraining himself*): Now listen to me, Mrs. Helmer. If necessary, I'll fight for my little job in the bank as if it were life itself.

NORA: Yes, so it seems.

KROGSTAD: It's not just a matter of income; that's the least of it. It's something else—All right, out with it! Look, this is the thing. You know, just like all the others, of course, that once, a good many years ago, I did something rather rash.

NORA: I've heard rumors to that effect.

KROGSTAD: The case never got into court; but all the same, every door was closed in my face from then on. So I took up those various activities you know about. I had to grab hold somewhere; and I dare say I haven't been among the worst. But now I want to drop all that. My boys are growing up. For their sakes, I'll have to win back as much respect as possible here in town. That job in the bank was like the first rung in my ladder. And now your husband wants to kick me right back down in the mud again.

NORA: But for heaven's sake, Mr. Krogstad, it's simply not in my power to help you.

KROGSTAD: That's because you haven't the will to—but I have the means to make you.

NORA: You certainly won't tell my husband that I owe you money?

KROGSTAD: Hm—what if I told him that?

NORA: That would be shameful of you. (*Nearly in tears.*) This secret—my joy and my pride—that he should learn it in such a crude and disgusting way—learn it from you. You'd expose me to the most horrible unpleasantness—

KROGSTAD: Only unpleasantness?

NORA (*vehemently*): But go on and try. It'll turn out the worse for you, because then my husband will really see what a crook you are, and then you'll never be able to hold your job.

KROGSTAD: I asked if it was just domestic unpleasantness you were afraid of?

NORA: If my husband finds out, then of course he'll pay what I owe at once, and then we'd be through with you for good.

KROGSTAD (*a step closer*): Listen, Mrs. Helmer—you've either got a very bad memory, or else no head at all for business. I'd better put you a little more in touch with the facts.

NORA: What do you mean?

KROGSTAD: When your husband was sick, you came to me for a loan of four thousand, eight hundred crowns.

NORA: Where else could I go?

KROGSTAD: I promised to get you that sum—

NORA: And you got it.

KROGSTAD: I promised to get you that sum, on certain conditions. You were so involved in your husband's illness, and so eager to finance your trip, that I guess you didn't think out all the details. It might just be a good idea to remind you. I promised you the money on the strength of a note I drew up.

NORA: Yes, and that I signed.

KROGSTAD: Right. But at the bottom I added some lines for your father to guarantee the loan. He was supposed to sign down there.

NORA: Supposed to? He did sign.

KROGSTAD: I left the date blank. In other words, your father would have dated his signature himself. Do you remember that?

NORA: Yes, I think—

KROGSTAD: Then I gave you the note for you to mail to your father. Isn't that so?

NORA: Yes.

KROGSTAD: And naturally you sent it at once—because only some five, six days later you brought me the note, properly signed. And with that, the money was yours.

NORA: Well, then; I've made my payments regularly, haven't I?

KROGSTAD: More or less. But—getting back to the point—those were hard times for you then, Mrs. Helmer.

NORA: Yes, they were.

KROGSTAD: Your father was very ill, I believe.

NORA: He was near the end.

KROGSTAD: He died soon after?

NORA: Yes.

KROGSTAD: Tell me, Mrs. Helmer, do you happen to recall the date of your father's death? The day of the month, I mean.

NORA: Papa died the twenty-ninth of September.

KROGSTAD: That's quite correct; I've already looked into that. And now we come to a curious thing—(*taking out a paper*) which I simply cannot comprehend.

NORA: Curious thing? I don't know—

KROGSTAD: This is the curious thing: that your father co-signed the note for your loan three days after his death.

NORA: How—? I don't understand.

KROGSTAD: Your father died the twenty-ninth of September. But look. Here your father dated his signature October second. Isn't that curious, Mrs. Helmer? (NORA *is silent.*) Can you explain it to me? (NORA *remains silent.*) It's also remarkable that the words "October second" and the year aren't written in your father's hand, but rather in one that I think I know. Well, it's easy to understand. Your father forgot perhaps to date his signature, and then someone or other added it, a bit sloppily, before anyone knew of his death. There's nothing wrong in that. It all comes down to the signature. And there's no question about *that,* Mrs. Helmer. It really *was* your father who signed his own name here, wasn't it?

NORA (*after a short silence, throwing her head back and looking squarely at him*): No, it wasn't. *I* signed Papa's name.

KROGSTAD: Wait, now—are you fully aware that this is a dangerous confession?

NORA: Why? You'll soon get your money.

KROGSTAD: Let me ask you a question—why didn't you send the paper to your father?

NORA: That was impossible. Papa was so sick. If I'd asked him for his signature, I also would have had to tell him what the money was for. But I couldn't tell him, sick as he was, that my husband's life was in danger. That was just impossible.

KROGSTAD: Then it would have been better if you'd given up the trip abroad.

NORA: I couldn't possibly. The trip was to save my husband's life. I couldn't give that up.

KROGSTAD: But didn't you ever consider that this was a fraud against me?

NORA: I couldn't let myself be bothered by that. You weren't any concern of mine. I couldn't stand you, with all those cold complications you made, even though you knew how badly off my husband was.

KROGSTAD: Mrs. Helmer, obviously you haven't the vaguest idea of what you've involved yourself in. But I can tell you this: It was nothing more and nothing worse that I once did—and it wrecked my whole reputation.

NORA: You? Do you expect me to believe that you ever acted bravely to save your wife's life?

KROGSTAD: Laws don't inquire into motives.

NORA: Then they must be very poor laws.

KROGSTAD: Poor or not—if I introduce this paper in court, you'll be judged according to law.

NORA: This I refuse to believe. A daughter hasn't a right to protect her dying father from anxiety and care? A wife hasn't a right to save her husband's life? I don't know much about laws, but I'm sure that somewhere in the books these things are allowed. And you don't know anything about it—you who practice the law? You must be an awful lawyer, Mr. Krogstad.

KROGSTAD: Could be. But business—the kind of business we two are mixed up in—don't you think I know about that? All right. Do what you want now. But I'm telling you *this:* If I get shoved down a second time, you're going to keep me company. (*He bows and goes out through the hall.*)

NORA (*pensive for a moment, then tossing her head*): Oh, really! Trying to frighten me! I'm not so silly as all that. (*Begins gathering up the children's clothes, but soon stops.*) But—? No, but that's impossible! I did it out of love.

THE CHILDREN (*in the doorway, left*): Mama, that strange man's gone out the door.

NORA: Yes, yes, I know it. But don't tell anyone about the strange man. Do you hear? Not even Papa!

THE CHILDREN: No, Mama. But now will you play again?

NORA: No, not now.

THE CHILDREN: Oh, but Mama, you promised.

NORA: Yes, but I can't now. Go inside; I have too much to do. Go in, go in, my sweet darlings. (*She herds them gently back in the room and shuts the door after them. Settling on the sofa, she takes up a piece of embroidery and makes some stitches, but soon stops abruptly.*) No! (*Throws the work aside, rises, goes to the hall door and calls out.*) Helene! Let me have the tree in here. (*Goes to the table, left, opens the table drawer, and stops again.*) No, but that's utterly impossible!

MAID (*with the Christmas tree*): Where should I put it, ma'am?

NORA: There. The middle of the floor.

MAID: Should I bring anything else?

NORA: No, thanks. I have what I need.

(*The* MAID, *who has set the tree down, goes out.*)

NORA (*absorbed in trimming the tree*): Candles here—and flowers here. That terrible creature! Talk, talk, talk! There's nothing to it at all. The tree's going to be lovely. I'll do anything to please you Torvald. I'll sing for you, dance for you—

(HELMER *comes in from the hall, with a sheaf of papers under his arm.*)

NORA: Oh! You're back so soon?

HELMER: Yes. Has anyone been here?

NORA: Here? No.

HELMER: That's odd. I saw Krogstad leaving the front door.

NORA: So? Oh yes, that's true. Krogstad was here a moment.

HELMER: Nora, I can see by your face that he's been here, begging you to put in a good word for him.

NORA: Yes.

HELMER: And it was supposed to seem like your own idea? You were to hide it from me that he'd been here. He asked you that, too, didn't he?

NORA: Yes, Torvald, but—

HELMER: Nora, Nora, and you could fall for that? Talk with that sort of person and promise him anything? And then in the bargain, tell me an untruth.

NORA: An untruth—?

HELMER: Didn't you say that no one had been here? (*Wagging his finger.*) My little songbird must never do that again. A songbird needs a clean beak to warble with. No false notes. (*Putting his arm about her waist.*) That's the way it should be, isn't it? Yes, I'm sure of it. (*Releasing her.*) And so, enough of that. (*Sitting by the stove.*) Ah, how snug and cozy it is here. (*Leafing among his papers.*)

NORA (*busy with the tree, after a short pause*): Torvald!

HELMER: Yes.

NORA: I'm so much looking forward to the Stenborgs' costume party, day after tomorrow

HELMER: And I can't wait to see what you'll surprise me with.

NORA: Oh, that stupid business!

HELMER: What?

NORA: I can't find anything that's right. Everything seems so ridiculous, so inane.

HELMER: So my little Nora's come to *that* recognition?

NORA (*going behind his chair, her arms resting on its back*): Are you very busy, Torvald?

HELMER: Oh—

NORA: What papers are those?

HELMER: Bank matters.

NORA: Already?

HELMER: I've gotten full authority from the retiring management to make all necessary changes in personnel and procedure. I'll need Christmas week for that. I want to have everything in order by New Year's.

NORA: So that was the reason this poor Krogstad—

HELMER: Hm.

NORA (*still leaning on the chair and slowly stroking the nape of his neck*): If you weren't so very busy, I would have asked you an enormous favor, Torvald.

HELMER: Let's hear. What is it?

NORA: You know, there isn't anyone who has your good taste—and I want so much to look well at the costume party. Torvald, couldn't you take over and decide what I should be and plan my costume?

HELMER: Ah, is my stubborn little creature calling for a lifeguard?

NORA: Yes, Torvald, I can't get anywhere without your help.

HELMER: All right—I'll think it over. We'll hit on something.

NORA: Oh, how sweet of you. (*Goes to the tree again. Pause.*) Aren't the red flowers pretty—? But tell me, was it really such a crime that this Krogstad committed?

HELMER: Forgery. Do you have any idea what that means?

NORA: Couldn't he have done it out of need?

HELMER: Yes, or thoughtlessness, like so many others. I'm not so heartless that I'd condemn a man categorically for just one mistake.

NORA: No, of course not, Torvald!

HELMER: Plenty of men have redeemed themselves by openly confessing their crimes and taking their punishment.

NORA: Punishment—?

HELMER: But now Krogstad didn't go that way. He got himself out by sharp practices, and that's the real cause of his moral breakdown.

NORA: Do you really think that would—?

HELMER: Just imagine how a man with that sort of guilt in him has to lie and cheat and deceive on all sides, has to wear a mask even with the nearest and dearest he has, even with his own wife and children. And with the children, Nora—that's where it's most horrible.

NORA: Why?

HELMER: Because that kind of atmosphere of lies infects the whole life of a home. Every breath the children take in is filled with the germs of something degenerate.

NORA (*coming closer behind him*): Are you sure of that?

HELMER: Oh, I've seen it often enough as a lawyer. Almost everyone who goes bad early in life has a mother who's a chronic liar.

NORA: Why just—the mother?

HELMER: It's usually the mother's influence that's dominant, but the father's works in the same way, of course. Every lawyer is quite familiar with it. And still this Krogstad's been going home year in, year out, poisoning his own children with lies and pretense; that's why I call him morally lost. (*Reaching his hands out toward her.*) So my sweet little Nora must promise me never to plead his cause. Your hand on it. Come, come, what's this? Give me your hand. There, now. All settled. I can tell you it'd be impossible for me to work alongside of him. I literally feel physically revolted when I'm anywhere near such a person.

NORA (*withdraws her hand and goes to the other side of the Christmas tree*): How hot it is here! And I've got so much to do.

HELMER (*getting up and gathering his papers*): Yes, and I have to think about getting some of these read through before dinner. I'll think about your costume, too. And something to hang on the tree in gilt paper, I may even see about that. (*Putting his hand on her head.*) Oh you, my darling little songbird. (*He goes into his study and closes the door after him.*)

NORA (*softly, after a silence*): Oh, really! It isn't so. It's impossible. It must be impossible.

ANNE-MARIE (*in the doorway left*): The children are begging so hard to come in to Mama.

NORA: No, no, no, don't let them in to me! You stay with them, Anne-Marie.

ANNE-MARIE: Of course, ma'am. (*Closes the door.*)

NORA (*pale with terror*): Hurt my children—! Poison my home? (*A moment's pause; then she tosses her head.*) That's not true. Never. Never in all the world.

Act II

(Same room. Beside the piano the Christmas tree now stands stripped of ornament, burned-down candle stubs on its ragged branches. NORA'S *street clothes lie on the sofa.* NORA, *alone in the room, moves restlessly about; at last she stops at the sofa and picks up her coat.)*

NORA (*dropping the coat again*): Someone's coming! (*Goes toward the door, listens.*) No—there's no one. Of course—nobody's coming today, Christmas Day—or tomorrow, either. But maybe—(*Opens the door and looks out.*) No, nothing in the mailbox. Quite empty. (*Coming forward.*) What nonsense! He won't do anything serious. Nothing terrible could happen. It's impossible. Why, I have three small children.

(ANNE-MARIE, *with a large carton, comes in from the room to the left.*)

ANNE-MARIE: Well, at last I found the box with the masquerade clothes.

NORA: Thanks. Put it on the table.

ANNE-MARIE (*does so*): But they're all pretty much of a mess.

NORA: Ahh! I'd love to rip them in a million pieces!

ANNE-MARIE: Oh, mercy, they can be fixed right up. Just a little patience.

NORA: Yes, I'll go get Mrs. Linde to help me.

ANNE-MARIE: Out again now? In this nasty weather? Miss Nora will catch cold—get sick.

NORA: Oh, worse things could happen—How are the children?

ANNE-MARIE: The poor mites are playing with their Christmas presents, but—

NORA: Do they ask for me much?

ANNE-MARIE: They're so used to having Mama around, you know.

NORA: Yes, but Anne-Marie, I *can't* be together with them as much as I was.

ANNE-MARIE: Well, small children get used to anything.

NORA: You think so? Do you think they'd forget their mother if she was gone for good?

ANNE-MARIE: Oh, mercy—gone for good!

NORA: Wait, tell me. Anne-Marie—I've wondered so often—how could you ever have the heart to give your child over to strangers?

ANNE-MARIE: But I had to, you know, to become little Nora's nurse.

NORA: Yes, but how could you *do* it?

ANNE-MARIE: When I could get such a good place? A girl who's poor and who's gotten in trouble is glad enough for that. Because that slippery fish, he didn't do a thing for me, you know.

NORA: But your daughter's surely forgotten you.

ANNE-MARIE: Oh, she certainly has not. She's written to me, both when she was confirmed and when she was married.

NORA (*clasping her about the neck*): You old Anne-Marie, you were a good mother for me when I was little.

ANNE-MARIE: Poor little Nora, with no other mother but me.

NORA: And if the babies didn't have one, then I know that you'd—What silly talk! (*Opening the carton.*) Go in to them. Now I'll have to—Tomorrow you can see how lovely I'll look.

ANNE-MARIE: Oh, there won't be anyone at the party as lovely as Miss Nora. (*She goes off into the room, left.*)

NORA (*begins unpacking the box, but soon throws it aside*): Oh, if I dared to go out. If only nobody would come. If only nothing would happen here while I'm out. What craziness—nobody's coming. Just don't think. This muff—needs a brushing. Beautiful gloves, beautiful gloves. Let it go. Let it go! One, two, three, four, five, six—(*With a cry.*) Oh, there they are! (*Poises to move toward the door, but remains irresolutely standing. Mrs. Linde enters from the hall, where she has removed her street clothes.*)

NORA: Oh, it's you, Kristine. There's no one else our there? How good that you've come.

MRS. LINDE: I hear you were up asking for me.

NORA: Yes, I just stopped by. There's something you really can help me with. Let's get settled on the sofa. Look, there's going to be a costume party tomorrow evening at the Stenborgs' right above us, and now Torvald wants me to go as a Neapolitan peasant girl and dance the tarantella that I learned in Capri.

MRS. LINDE: Really, are you giving a whole performance?

NORA: Torvald says yes, I should. See, here's the dress. Torvald had it made for me down there; but now it's all so tattered that I just don't know—

MRS. LINDE: Oh, we'll fix that up in no time. It's nothing more than the trimmings—they're a bit loose here and there. Needle and thread? Good, now we have what we need.

NORA: Oh, how sweet of you!

MRS. LINDE (*sewing*): So you'll be in disguise tomorrow, Nora. You know what? I'll stop by then for a moment and have a look at you all dressed up. But listen, I've absolutely forgotten to thank you for that pleasant evening yesterday.

NORA (*getting up and walking about*): I don't think it was as pleasant as usual yesterday. You should have come to town a bit sooner, Kristine—Yes, Torvald really knows how to give a home elegance and charm.

MRS. LINDE: And you do, too, if you ask me. You're not your father's daughter for nothing. But tell me, is Dr. Rank always so down in the mouth as yesterday?

NORA: No, that was quite an exception. But he goes around critically ill all the time—tuberculosis of the spine, poor man. You know, his father was a disgusting thing who kept mistresses and so on—and that's why the son's been sickly from birth.

MRS. LINDE (*lets her sewing fall to her lap*): But my dearest Nora, how do you know about such things?

NORA (*walking more jauntily*): Hmp! When you've had three children, then you've had a few visits from—from women who know something of medicine, and they tell you this and that.

MRS. LINDE (*resumes sewing; a short pause*): Does Dr. Rank come here every day?

NORA: Every blessed day. He's Torvald's best friend from childhood, and *my* good friend, too. Dr. Rank almost belongs to this house.

MRS. LINDE: But tell me—is he quite sincere? I mean, doesn't he rather enjoy flattering people?

NORA: Just the opposite. Why do you think that?

MRS. LINDE: When you introduced us yesterday, he was proclaiming that he'd often heard my name in this house; but later I noticed that your husband hadn't the slightest idea who I really was. So how could Dr. Rank—?

NORA: But it's all true, Kristine. You see, Torvald loves me beyond words, and, as he puts it, he'd like to keep me all to himself. For a long time he'd almost be jealous if I even mentioned any of my old friends back home. So of course I dropped that. But with Dr. Rank I talk a lot about such things because he likes hearing about them.

MRS. LINDE: Now listen, Nora; in many ways you're still like a child. I'm a good deal older than you, with a little more experience. I'll tell you something: You ought to put an end to all this with Dr. Rank.

NORA: What should I put an end to?

MRS. LINDE: Both parts of it, I think. Yesterday you said something about a rich admirer who'd provide you with money—

NORA: Yes, one who doesn't exist—worse luck. So?

MRS. LINDE: Is Dr. Rank well off?

NORA: Yes, he is.

MRS. LINDE: With no dependents?

NORA: No, no one. But—

MRS. LINDE: And he's over here every day?

NORA: Yes, I told you that.

MRS. LINDE: How can a man of such refinement be so grasping?

NORA: I don't follow you at all.

MRS. LINDE: Now don't try to hide it, Nora. You think I can't guess who loaned you the forty-eight hundred crowns?

NORA: Are you out of your mind? How could you think such a thing! A friend of ours, who comes here every single day. What an intolerable situation that would have been!

MRS. LINDE: Then it really wasn't him.

NORA: No, absolutely not. It never even crossed my mind for a moment—And he had nothing to lend in those days; his inheritance came later.

MRS. LINDE: Well, I think that was a stroke of luck for you, Nora dear.

NORA: No, it never would have occurred to me to ask Dr. Rank—Still, I'm quite sure that if I had asked him—

MRS. LINDE: Which you won't, of course.

NORA: No, of course not. I can't see that I'd ever need to. But I'm quite positive that if I talked to Dr. Rank—

MRS. LINDE: Behind your husband's back?

NORA: I've got to clear up this other thing; *that's* also behind his back. I've *got* to clear it all up.

MRS. LINDE: Yes, I was saying that yesterday, but—

NORA (*pacing up and down*): A man handles these problems so much better than a woman—

MRS. LINDE: One's husband does, yes.

NORA: Nonsense. (*Stopping.*) When you pay everything you owe, then you get your note back, right?

MRS. LINDE: Yes, naturally.

NORA: And can rip it into a million pieces and burn it up—that filthy scrap of paper!

MRS. LINDE (*looking hard at her, laying her sewing aside, and rising slowly*): Nora, you're hiding something from me.

NORA: You can see it in my face?

MRS. LINDE: Something's happened to you since yesterday morning. Nora, what is it?

NORA (*hurrying toward her*): Kristine! (*Listening.*) Shh! Torvald's home. Look, go in with the children a while. Torvald can't bear all this snipping and stitching. Let Anne-Marie help you.

MRS. LINDE (*gathering up some of the things*): All right, but I'm not leaving here until we've talked this out. (*She disappears into the room, left, as* TORVALD *enters from the hall.*)

NORA: Oh, how I've been waiting for you, Torvald dear.

HELMER: Was that the dressmaker?

NORA: No, that was Kristine. She's helping me fix up my costume. You know, it's going to be quite attractive.

HELMER: Yes, wasn't that a bright idea I had?

NORA: Brilliant! But then wasn't I good as well to give in to you?

HELMER: Good—because you give in to your husband's judgment? All right, you little goose, I know you didn't mean it like that. But I won't disturb you. You'll want to have a fitting, I suppose.

NORA: And you'll be working?

HELMER: Yes. (*Indicating a bundle of papers.*) See. I've been down to the bank. (*Starts toward his study.*)

NORA: Torvald.

HELMER (*stops*): Yes.

NORA: If your little squirrel begged you, with all her heart and soul, for something—?

HELMER: What's that?

NORA: Then would you do it?

HELMER: First, naturally, I'd have to know what it was.

NORA: Your squirrel would scamper about and do tricks, if you'd only be sweet and give in.

HELMER: Out with it.

NORA: Your lark would be singing high and low in every room—

HELMER: Come on, she does that anyway.

NORA: I'd be a wood nymph and dance for you in the moonlight.

HELMER: Nora—don't tell me it's that same business from this morning?

NORA (*coming closer*): Yes, Torvald, I beg you, please!

HELMER: And you actually have the nerve to drag that up again?

NORA: Yes, yes, you've got to give in to me; you *have* to let Krogstad keep his job in the bank.

HELMER: My dear Nora, I've slated his job for Mrs. Linde.

NORA: That's awfully kind of you. But you could just fire another clerk instead of Krogstad.

HELMER: This is the most incredible stubbornness! Because you go and give an impulsive promise to speak up for him, I'm expected to—

NORA: That's not the reason, Torvald. It's for your own sake. That man does writing for the worst papers; you said it yourself. He could do you any amount of harm. I'm scared to death of him—

HELMER: Ah, I understand. It's the old memories haunting you.

NORA: What do you mean by that?

HELMER: Of course, you're thinking about your father.

NORA: Yes, all right. Just remember how those nasty gossips wrote in the papers about Papa and slandered him so cruelly. I think they'd have had him dismissed if the department hadn't sent you up to investigate, and if you hadn't been so kind and open-minded toward him.

HELMER: My dear Nora, there's a notable difference between your father and me. Your father's official career was hardly above reproach. But mine is; and I hope it'll stay that way as long as I hold my position.

NORA: Oh, who can ever tell what vicious minds can invent? We could be so snug and happy now in our quiet, carefree home—you and I and the children, Torvald! That's why I'm pleading with you so—

HELMER: And just by pleading for him you make it impossible for me to keep him on. It's already known at the bank that I'm firing Krogstad. What if it's rumored around now that the new bank manager was vetoed by his wife—

NORA: Yes, what then—?

HELMER: Oh yes—as long as our little bundle of stubbornness gets her way—! I should go and make myself ridiculous in front of the whole office—give people the idea I can be swayed by all kinds of outside pressure. Oh, you can bet I'd feel the effects of that soon enough! Besides—there's something that rules Krogstad right out at the bank as long as I'm the manager.

NORA: What's that?

HELMER: His moral failings I could maybe overlook if I had to—

NORA: Yes, Torvald, why not?

HELMER: And I hear he's quire efficient on the job. But he was a crony of mine back in my teens—one of those rash friendships that crop up again and again to embarrass you later in life. Well, I might as well say it straight out: We're on a first-name basis. And that tactless fool makes no effort at all to hide it in front of others. Quite the contrary—he thinks that entitles him to take a familiar air around me, and so every other second he comes booming out with his, "Yes, Torvald!" and "Sure thing, Torvald!" I tell you, it's been excruciating for me. He's out to make my place in the bank unbearable.

NORA: Torvald, you can't be serious about all this.

HELMER: Oh no? Why not?

NORA: Because these are such petty considerations.

HELMER: What are you saying? Petty? You think I'm petty!

NORA: No, just the opposite, Torvald dear. That's exactly why—

HELMER: Never mind. You call my motives petty; then I might as well be just that. Petty! All right! We'll put a stop to this for good. (*Goes to the hall door and calls.*) Helene!

NORA: What do you want?

HELMER (*searching among his papers*): A decision. (*The* MAID *comes in.*) Look here; take this letter; go out with it at once. Get hold of a messenger and have him deliver it. Quick now. It's already addressed. Wait, here's some money.

MAID: Yes, sir. (*She leaves with the letter.*)

HELMER (*straightening his papers*): There, now, little Miss Willful.

NORA (*breathlessly*): Torvald, what was that letter?

HELMER: Krogstad's notice.

NORA: Call it back, Torvald! There's still time. Oh, Torvald, call it back! Do it for my sake—for your sake, for the children's sake! Do you hear, Torvald; do it! You don't know how this can harm us.

HELMER: Too late.

NORA: Yes, too late.

HELMER: Nora, dear, I can forgive you this panic, even though basically you're insulting me. Yes, you are! Or isn't it an insult to think that *I* should be afraid of a courtroom hack's revenge? But I forgive you anyway, because this shows so beautifully how much you love me. (*Takes her in his arms.*) This is the way it should be, my darling Nora. Whatever comes, you'll see: When it really counts, I have strength and courage enough as a man to take on the whole weight myself.

NORA (*terrified*): What do you mean by that?

HELMER: The whole weight, I said.

NORA (*resolutely*): No, never in all the world.

HELMER: Good. So we'll share it, Nora, as man and wife. That's as it should be. (*Fondling her.*) Are you happy now? There, there, there—not these frightened dove's eyes. It's nothing at all but empty fantasies—Now you should run through your tarantella and practice your tambourine. I'll go to the inner office, and shut both doors, so I won't hear a thing; you can make all the noise you like. (*Turning in the doorway.*) And when Rank comes, just tell him where he can find me. (*He nods to her and goes with his papers into the study, closing the door.*)

NORA (*standing as though rooted, dazed with fright, in a whisper*): He really could do it. He will do it. He'll do it in spite of everything. No, not that, never, never! Anything but that! Escape! A way out—(*The doorbell rings.*) Dr. Rank! Anything but that! *Anything*, whatever it is! (*Her hands pass over her face, smoothing it; she pulls herself together, goes over and opens the hall door.* DR. RANK *stands outside, hanging his fur coat up. During the following scene, it begins getting dark.*)

NORA: Hello, Dr. Rank. I recognized your ring. But you mustn't go in to Torvald yet; I believe he's working.

RANK: And you?

NORA: For you, I always have an hour to spare—you know that. (*He has entered, and she shuts the door after him.*)

RANK: Many thanks. I'll make use of these hours while I can.

NORA: What do you mean by that? While you can?

RANK: Does that disturb you?

NORA: Well, it's such an odd phrase. Is anything going to happen?

RANK: What's going to happen is what I've been expecting so long—but I honestly didn't think it would come so soon.

NORA (*gripping his arm*): What is it you've found out? Dr. Rank, you have to tell me!

RANK (*sitting by the stove*): It's all over with me. There's nothing to be done about it.

NORA (*breathing easier*): Is it you—then—?

RANK: Who else? There's no point in lying to one's self. I'm the most miserable of all my patients, Mrs. Helmer. These past few days I've been auditing my internal accounts. Bankrupt! Within a month I'll probably be laid out and rotting in the churchyard.

NORA: Oh, what a horrible thing to say.

RANK: The thing itself is horrible. But the worst of it is all the other horror before it's over. There's only one final examination left; when I'm finished with that, I'll know about when my disintegration will begin. There's something I want to say. Helmer with his sensitivity has such a sharp distaste for anything ugly. I don't want him near my sickroom.

NORA: Oh, but Dr. Rank—

RANK: I won't have him in there. Under no condition. I'll lock my door to him—As soon as I'm completely sure of the worst, I'll send you my calling card marked with a black cross, and you'll know then the wreck has started to come apart.

NORA: No, today you're completely unreasonable. And I wanted you so much to be in a really good humor.

RANK: With death up my sleeve? And then to suffer this way for somebody else's sins. Is there any justice in that? And in every single family, in some way or another, this inevitable retribution of nature goes on—

NORA (*her hands pressed over her ears*): Oh, stuff! Cheer up! Please—be gay!

RANK: Yes, I'd just as soon laugh at it all. My poor, innocent spine, serving time for my father's gay army days.

NORA (*by the table, left*): He was so infatuated with asparagus tips and pâté de foie gras, wasn't that it?

RANK: Yes—and with truffles.

NORA: Truffles, yes. And then with oysters, I suppose?

RANK: Yes, tons of oysters, naturally.

NORA: And then the port and champagne to go with it. It's so sad that all these delectable things have to strike at our bones.

RANK: Especially when they strike at the unhappy bones that never shared in the fun.

NORA: Ah, that's the saddest of all.

RANK (*looks searchingly at her*): Hm.

NORA (*after a moment*): Why did you smile?

RANK: No, it was you who laughed.

NORA: No, it was you who smiled, Dr. Rank!

RANK (*getting up*): You're even a bigger tease than I'd thought.

NORA: I'm full of wild ideas today.

RANK: That's obvious.

NORA (*putting both hands on his shoulders*): Dear, dear Dr. Rank, you'll never die for Torvald and me.

RANK: Oh, that loss you'll easily get over. Those who go away are soon forgotten.

NORA (*looks fearfully at him*): You believe that?

RANK: One makes new connections, and then—

NORA: Who makes new connections?

RANK: Both you and Torvald will when I'm gone. I'd say you're well under way already. What was that Mrs. Linde doing here last evening?

NORA: Oh, come—you can't be jealous of poor Kristine?

RANK: Oh yes, I am. She'll be my successor here in the house. When I'm down under, that woman will probably—

NORA: Shh! Not so loud. She's right in there.

RANK: Today as well. So you see.

NORA: Only to sew on my dress. Good gracious, how unreasonable you are. (*Sitting on the sofa.*) Be nice now, Dr. Rank. Tomorrow you'll see how beautifully I'll dance; and you can imagine then that I'm dancing only for you—yes, and of course for Torvald, too—that's understood. (*Takes various items out of the carton.*) Dr. Rank, sit over here and I'll show you something.

RANK (*sitting*): What's that?

NORA: Look here. Look.

RANK: Silk stockings.

NORA: Flesh-colored. Aren't they lovely? Now it's so dark here, but tomorrow—No, no, no, just look at the feet. Oh well, you might as well look at the rest.

RANK: Hm—

NORA: Why do you look so critical? Don't you believe they'll fit?

RANK: I've never had any chance to form an opinion on that.

NORA (*glancing at him a moment*): Shame on you. (*Hits him lightly on the ear with the stockings.*) That's for you. (*Puts them away again.*)

RANK: And what other splendors am I going to see now?

NORA: Not the least bit more, because you've been naughty. (*She hunts a little and rummages among her things.*)

RANK (*after a short silence*): When I sit here together with you like this, completely easy and open, then I don't know—I simply can't imagine—whatever would have become of me if I'd never come into this house.

NORA (*smiling*): Yes, I really think you feel completely at ease with us.

RANK (*more quietly, staring straight ahead*): And then to have to go away from it all—

NORA: Nonsense, you're not going away.

RANK (*his voice unchanged*): —and not even be able to leave some poor show of gratitude behind, scarcely a fleeting regret—no more than a vacant place that anyone can fill.

NORA: And if I asked you now for—No—

RANK: For what?

NORA: For a great proof of your friendship—

RANK: Yes, yes?

NORA: No, I mean—for an exceptionally big favor—

RANK: Would you really, for once, make me so happy?

NORA: Oh, you haven't the vaguest idea what it is.

RANK: All right, then tell me.

NORA: No, but I can't, Dr. Rank—it's all out of reason. It's advice and help, too—and a favor—

RANK: So much the better. I can't fathom what you're hinting at. Just speak out. Don't you trust me?

NORA: Of course. More than anyone else. You're my best and truest friend, I'm sure. That's why I want to talk to you. All right, then, Dr. Rank: There's something you can help me prevent. You know how deeply, how inexpressibly dearly Torvald loves me; he'd never hesitate a second to give up his life for me.

RANK (*leaning close to her*): Nora—do you think he's the only one—

NORA (*with a slight start*): Who—?

RANK: Who'd gladly give up his life for you.

NORA (*heavily*): I see.

RANK: I swore to myself you should know this before I'm gone. I'll never find a better chance. Yes, Nora, now you know. And also you know now that you can trust me beyond anyone else.

NORA (*rising, natural and calm*): Let me by.

RANK (*making room for her, but still sitting*): Nora—

NORA (*in the hall doorway*): Helene, bring the lamp in. (*Goes over to the stove.*) Ah, dear Dr. Rank, that was really mean of you.

RANK (*getting up*): That I've loved you just as deeply as somebody else? Was *that* mean?

NORA: No, but that you came out and told me. That was quite unnecessary—

RANK: What do you mean? Have you known—?

(*The* MAID *comes in with the lamp, sets it on the table, and goes out again.*)

RANK: Nora—Mrs. Helmer—I'm asking you: Have you known about it?

NORA: Oh, how can I tell what I know or don't know? Really, I don't know what to say—Why did you have to be so clumsy, Dr. Rank! Everything was so good.

RANK: Well, in any case, you now have the knowledge that my body and soul are at your command. So won't you speak out?

NORA (*looking at him*): After that?

RANK: Please, just let me know what it is.

NORA: You can't know anything now.

RANK: I have to. You mustn't punish me like this. Give me the chance to do whatever is humanly possible for you.

NORA: Now there's nothing you can do for me. Besides, actually, I don't need any help. You'll see—it's only my fantasies. That's what it is. Of course! (*Sits in the rocker, looks at him, and smiles.*) What a nice one you are, Dr. Rank. Aren't you a little bit ashamed, now that the lamp is here?

RANK: No, not exactly. But perhaps I'd better go—for good?

NORA: No, you certainly can't do that. You must come here just as you always have. You know Torvald can't do without you.

RANK: Yes, but *you?*

NORA: You know how much I enjoy it when you're here.

RANK: That's precisely what threw me off. You're a mystery to me. So many times I've felt you'd almost rather be with me than with Helmer.

NORA: Yes—you see, there are some people that one loves most and other people that one would almost prefer being with.

RANK: Yes, there's something to that.

NORA: When I was back home, of course I loved Papa most. But I always thought it was so much fun when I could sneak down to the maids' quarters, because they never tried to improve me, and it was always so amusing, the way they talked to each other.

RANK: Aha, so it's their place that I've filled.

NORA (*jumping up and going to him*): Oh, dear, sweet Dr. Rank, that's not what I meant at all. But you can understand that with Torvald it's just the same as with Papa—

(*The* MAID *enters from the hall.*)

MAID: Ma'am—please! (*She whispers to* NORA *and hands her a calling card.*)

NORA (*glancing at the card*): Ah! (*Slips it into her pocket.*)

RANK: Anything wrong?

NORA: No, no, not at all. It's only some—it's my new dress—

RANK: Really? But—there's your dress.

NORA: Oh, that. But this is another one—I ordered it—Torvald mustn't know—

RANK: Ah, now we have the big secret.

NORA: That's right. Just go in with him—he's back in the inner study. Keep him there as long as—

RANK: Don't worry. He won't get away. (*Goes into the study.*)

NORA (*to the* MAID): And he's standing waiting in the kitchen?

MAID: Yes, he came up by the back stairs.

NORA: But didn't you tell him somebody was here?

MAID: Yes, but that didn't do any good.

NORA: He won't leave?

MAID: No, he won't go till he's talked with you, ma'am.

NORA: Let him come in, then—but quietly. Helene, don't breathe a word about this. It's a surprise for my husband.

MAID: Yes, yes, I understand—(*Goes out.*)

NORA: This horror—it's going to happen. No, no, no, it can't happen, it mustn't. (*She goes and bolts* HELMER'S *door. The* MAID *opens the hall door for Krogstad and shuts it behind him. He is dressed for travel in a fur coat, boots, and a fur cap.*)

NORA (*going toward him*): Talk softly. My husband's home.

KROGSTAD: Well, good for him.

NORA: What do you want?

KROGSTAD: Some information.

NORA: Hurry up, then. What is it?

KROGSTAD: You know, of course, that I got my notice.

NORA: I couldn't prevent it, Mr. Krogstad. I fought for you to the bitter end, but nothing worked.

KROGSTAD: Does your husband's love for you run so thin? He knows everything I can expose you to, and all the same he dares to—

NORA: How can you imagine he knows anything about this?

KROGSTAD: Ah, no—I can't imagine it either, now. It's not at all like my fine Torvald Helmer to have so much guts—

NORA: Mr. Krogstad, I demand respect for my husband!

KROGSTAD: Why, of course—all due respect. But since the lady's keeping it so carefully hidden, may I presume to ask if you're also a bit better informed than yesterday about what you've actually done?

NORA: More than you ever could teach me.

KROGSTAD: Yes, I *am* such an awful lawyer.

NORA: What is it you want from me?

KROGSTAD: Just a glimpse of how you are, Mrs. Helmer. I've been thinking about you all day long. A cashier, a night-court scribbler, a—well, a type like me also has a little of what they call a heart, you know.

NORA: Then show it. Think of my children.

KROGSTAD: Did you or your husband ever think of mine? But never mind. I simply wanted to tell you that you don't need to take this thing too seriously. For the present, I'm not proceeding with any action.

NORA: Oh no, really! Well—I knew that.

KROGSTAD: Everything can be settled in a friendly spirit. It doesn't have to get around town at all; it can stay just among us three.

NORA: My husband must never know anything of this.

KROGSTAD: How can you manage that? Perhaps you can pay me the balance?

NORA: No, not right now.

KROGSTAD: Or you know some way of raising the money in a day or two?

NORA: No way that I'm willing to use.

KROGSTAD: Well, it wouldn't have done you any good, anyway. If you stood in front of me with a fistful of bills, you still couldn't buy your signature back.

NORA: Then tell me what you're going to do with it.

KROGSTAD: I'll just hold onto it—keep it on file. There's no outsider who'll even get wind of it. So if you've been thinking of taking some desperate step—

NORA: I have.

KROGSTAD: Been thinking of running away from home—

NORA: I have!

KROGSTAD: Or even of something worse—

NORA: How could you guess that?

KROGSTAD: You can drop those thoughts.

NORA: How could you guess I was thinking of *that*?

KROGSTAD: Most of us think about *that* at first. I thought about it too, but I discovered I hadn't the courage—

NORA (*lifelessly*): I don't either.

KROGSTAD (*relieved*): That's true, you haven't the courage? You too?

NORA: I don't have it—I don't have it.

KROGSTAD: It would be terribly stupid, anyway. After that first storm at home blows out, why, then—I have here in my pocket a letter for your husband—

NORA: Telling everything?

KROGSTAD: As charitably as possible.

NORA (*quickly*): He mustn't ever get that letter. Tear it up. I'll find some way to get money.

KROGSTAD: Beg pardon, Mrs. Helmer, but I think I just told you—

NORA: Oh, I don't mean the money I owe you. Let me know how much you want from my husband, and I'll manage it.

KROGSTAD: I don't want any money from your husband.

NORA: What do you want, then?

KROGSTAD: I'll tell you what. I want to recoup, Mrs. Helmer; I want to get on in the world—and there's where your husband can help me. For a year and a half I've kept myself clean of anything disreputable—all that time struggling with the worst conditions; but I was satisfied, working my way up step by step. Now I've been written right off, and I'm just not in the mood to come crawling back. I tell you, I want to move on. I want to get back in the bank—in a better position. Your husband can set up a job for me—

NORA: He'll never do that!

KROGSTAD: He'll do it. I know him. He won't dare breathe a word of protest. And once I'm in there together with him, you just wait and see! Inside of a year, I'll be the manager's right-hand man. It'll be Nils Krogstad, not Torvald Helmer, who runs the bank.

NORA: You'll never see the day!

KROGSTAD: Maybe you think you can—

NORA: I have the courage now—for *that.*

KROGSTAD: Oh, you don't scare me. A smart, spoiled lady like you—

NORA: You'll see; you'll see!

KROGSTAD: Under the ice, maybe? Down in the freezing, coal-black water? There, till you float up in the spring, ugly, unrecognizable, with your hair falling out—

NORA: You don't frighten me.

KROGSTAD: Nor do you frighten me. One doesn't do these things, Mrs. Helmer. Besides what good would it be? I'd still have him safe in my pocket.

NORA: Afterwards? When I'm no longer—?

KROGSTAD: Are you forgetting that *I'll* be in control then over your final reputation? (NORA *stands speechless, staring at him.*) Good; now I've warned you. Don't do anything stupid. When Helmer's read my letter, I'll be waiting for his reply. And bear in mind that it's your husband himself who's forced me back to my old ways. I'll never forgive him for that. Good-bye, Mrs. Helmer. (*He goes out through the hall.*)

NORA (*goes to the hall door, opens it a crack, and listens*): He's gone. Didn't leave the letter. Oh no, no, that's impossible too! (*Opening the door more and more.*) What's that? He's standing outside—not going downstairs. He's thinking it over? Maybe he'll—? (*A letter falls in the mailbox; then Krogstad's footsteps are heard, dying away down a flight of stairs.* NORA *gives a muffled cry and runs over toward the sofa table. A short pause.*) In the mailbox. (*Slips warily over to the hall door.*) It's lying there. Torvald, Torvald—now we're lost!

MRS. LINDE (*entering with the costume from the room, left*): There now, I can't see anything else to mend. Perhaps you'd like to try—

NORA (*in a hoarse whisper*): Kristine, come here.

MRS. LINDE (*tossing the dress on the sofa*): What's wrong? You look upset.

NORA: Come here. See that letter? There! Look—through the glass in the mailbox.

MRS. LINDE: Yes, yes, I see it.

NORA: That letter's from Krogstad—

MRS. LINDE: Nora—it's Krogstad who loaned you the money!

NORA: Yes, and now Torvald will find out everything.

MRS. LINDE: Believe me, Nora, it's best for both of you.

NORA: There's more you don't know. I forged a name.

MRS. LINDE: But for heaven's sake—?

NORA: I only want to tell you that, Kristine, so that you can be my witness.

MRS. LINDE: Witness? Why should I—?

NORA: If I should go out of my mind—it could easily happen—

MRS. LINDE: Nora!

NORA: Or anything else occurred—so I couldn't be present here—

MRS. LINDE: Nora, Nora, you aren't yourself at all!

NORA: And someone should try to take on the whole weight, all of the guilt, you follow me—

MRS. LINDE: Yes, of course, but why do you think—?

NORA: Then you're the witness that it isn't true, Kristine. I'm very much myself; my mind right now is perfectly clear; and I'm telling you: Nobody else has known about this; I alone did everything. Remember that.

MRS. LINDE: I will. But I don't understand all this.

NORA: Oh, how could you ever understand it? It's the miracle now that's going to take place.

MRS. LINDE: The miracle?

NORA: Yes, the miracle. But it's so awful, Kristine. It mustn't take place, not for anything in the world.

MRS. LINDE: I'm going right over and talk with Krogstad.

NORA: Don't go near him; he'll do you some terrible harm!

MRS. LINDE: There was a time once when he'd gladly have done anything for me.

NORA: He?

MRS. LINDE: Where does he live?

NORA: Oh, how do I know? Yes. (*Searches in her pocket.*) Here's his card. But the letter, the letter—!

HELMER (*from the study, knocking on the door*): Nora!

NORA (*with a cry of fear*): Oh! What is it? What do you want?

HELMER: Now, now, don't be so frightened. We're not coming in. You locked the door—are you trying on the dress?

NORA: Yes, I'm trying it. I'll look just beautiful, Torvald.

MRS. LINDE (*who has read the card*): He's living right around the corner.

NORA: Yes, but what's the use? We're lost. The letter's in the box.

MRS. LINDE: And your husband has the key?

NORA: Yes, always.

MRS. LINDE: Krogstad can ask for his letter back unread; he can find some excuse—

NORA: But it's just this time that Torvald usually—

MRS. LINDE: Stall him. Keep him in there. I'll be back as quick as I can. (*She hurries out through the hall entrance.*)

NORA (*goes to Helmer's door, opens it, and peers in*): Torvald!

HELMER (*from the inner study*): Well—does one dare set foot in one's own living room at last? Come on, Rank, now we'll get a look—(*In the doorway.*) But what's this?

NORA: What, Torvald dear?

HELMER: Rank had me expecting some grand masquerade.

RANK (*in the doorway*): That was my impression, but I must have been wrong.

NORA: No one can admire me in my splendor—not till tomorrow.

HELMER: But Nora dear, you look so exhausted. Have you practiced too hard?

NORA: No, I haven't practiced at all yet.

HELMER: You know, it's necessary—

NORA: Oh, it's absolutely necessary, Torvald. But I can't get anywhere without your help. I've forgotten the whole thing completely.

HELMER: Ah, we'll soon take care of that.

NORA: Yes, take care of me, Torvald, please! Promise me that? Oh, I'm so nervous. That big party—You must give up everything this evening for me. No business—don't even touch your pen. Yes? Dear Torvald, promise?

HELMER: It's a promise. Tonight I'm totally at your service—you little helpless thing. Hm—but first there's one thing I want to—(*Goes toward the hall door.*)

NORA: What are you looking for?

HELMER: Just to see if there's any mail.

NORA: No, no, don't do that, Torvald!

HELMER: Now what?

NORA: Torvald, please. There isn't any.

HELMER: Let me look, though. (*Starts out.* NORA, *at the piano, strikes the first notes of the tarantella.* HELMER, *at the door, stops.*) Aha!

NORA: I can't dance tomorrow if I don't practice with you.

HELMER (*going over to her*): Nora dear, are you really so frightened?

NORA: Yes, so terribly frightened. Let me practice right now; there's still time before dinner. Oh, sit down and play for me, Torvald. Direct me. Teach me, the way you always have.

HELMER: Gladly, if it's what you want. (*Sits at the piano.*)

NORA (*snatches the tambourine up from the box, then a long, varicolored shawl, which she throws around herself, whereupon she springs forward and cries out*): Play for me now! Now I'll dance!

(HELMER *plays and* NORA *dances.* RANK *stands behind* HELMER *at the piano and looks on.*)

HELMER (*as he plays*): Slower. Slow down.

NORA: Can't change it.

HELMER: Not so violent, Nora!

NORA: Has to be just like this.

HELMER (*stopping*): No, no, that won't do at all.

NORA (*laughing and swinging her tambourine*): Isn't that what I told you?

RANK: Let me play for her.

HELMER (*getting up*): Yes, go on. I can teach her more easily then.

(RANK *sits at the piano and plays,* NORA *dances more and more wildly.* HELMER *has stationed himself by the stove and repeatedly gives her directions; she seems not to hear them; her hair loosens and falls over her shoulders; she does not notice, but goes on dancing.* MRS. LINDE *enters.*)

MRS. LINDE (*standing dumbfounded at the door*): Ah—!

NORA (*still dancing*): See what fun, Kristine!

HELMER: But Nora darling, you dance as if your life were at stake.

NORA: And it is.

HELMER: Rank, stop! This is pure madness. Stop it, I say!

(RANK *breaks off playing, and* NORA *halts abruptly*).

HELMER (*going over to her*): I never would have believed it. You've forgotten everything I taught you.

NORA (*throwing away the tambourine*): You see for yourself.

HELMER: Well, there's certainly room for instruction here.

NORA: Yes, you see how important it is. You've got to teach me to the very last minute. Promise me that, Torvald?

HELMER: You can bet on it.

NORA: You mustn't, either today or tomorrow, think about anything else but me; you mustn't open any letters—or the mailbox—

HELMER: Ah, it's still the fear of that man—

NORA: Oh yes, yes, that too.

HELMER: Nora, it's written all over you—there's already a letter from him out there.

NORA: I don't know. I guess so. But you mustn't read such things now; there mustn't be anything ugly between us before it's all over.

RANK (*quietly to* HELMER): You shouldn't deny her.

HELMER (*putting his arm around her*): The child can have her way. But tomorrow night, after you've danced—

NORA: Then you'll be free.

MAID (*in the doorway, right*): Ma'am, dinner is served.

NORA: We'll be wanting champagne, Helene.

MAID: Very good, ma'am. (*Goes out.*)

HELMER: So—a regular banquet, hm?

NORA: Yes, a banquet—champagne till daybreak! (*Calling out.*) And some macaroons, Helene. Heaps of them—just this once.

HELMER (*taking her hands*): Now, now, now—no hysterics. Be my own little lark again.

NORA: Oh, I will soon enough. But go on in—and you, Dr. Rank. Kristine, help me put up my hair.

RANK (*whispering, as they go*): There's nothing wrong—really wrong, is there?

HELMER: Oh, of course not. It's nothing more than this childish anxiety I was telling you about. (*They go out, right.*)

NORA: Well?

MRS. LINDE: Left town.

NORA: I could see by your face.

MRS. LINDE: He'll be home tomorrow evening. I wrote him a note.

NORA: You shouldn't have. Don't try to stop anything now. After all, it's a wonderful joy, this waiting here for the miracle.

MRS. LINDE: What is it you're waiting for?

NORA: Oh, you can't understand that. Go in to them; I'll be along in a moment.

(MRS. LINDE *goes into the dining room.* NORA *stands a short while as if composing herself; then she looks at her watch.*)

NORA: Five. Seven hours to midnight. Twenty-four hours to the midnight after, and then the tarantella's done. Seven and twenty-four? Thirty-one hours to live.

HELMER (*in the doorway, right*): What's become of the little lark?

NORA (*going toward him with open arms*): Here's your lark!

Act III

(*Same scene. The table, with chairs around it, has been moved to the center of the room. A lamp on the table is lit. The hall door stands open. Dance music drifts down from the floor above.* MRS. LINDE *sits at the table, absently paging through a book, trying to read, but apparently unable to focus her thoughts. Once or twice she pauses, tensely listening for a sound at the outer entrance.*)

MRS. LINDE (*glancing at her watch*): Not yet—and there's hardly any time left. If only he's not—(*Listening again.*) Ah, there it is. (*She goes out in the hall and cautiously opens the outer door. Quiet footsteps are heard on the stairs. She whispers.*) Come in. Nobody's here.

KROGSTAD (*in the doorway*): I found a note from you at home. What's back of all this?

MRS. LINDE: I just *had* to talk to you.

KROGSTAD: Oh? And it just *had* to be here in this house?

MRS. LINDE: At my place it was impossible; my room hasn't a private entrance. Come in, we're all alone. The maid's asleep, and the Helmers are at the dance upstairs.

KROGSTAD (*entering the room*): Well, well, the Helmers are dancing tonight? Really?

MRS. LINDE: Yes, why not?

KROGSTAD: How true—why not?

MRS. LINDE: All right, Krogstad, let's talk.

KROGSTAD: Do we two have anything more to talk about?

MRS. LINDE: We have a great deal to talk about.

KROGSTAD: I wouldn't have thought so.

MRS. LINDE: No, because you've never understood me, really.

KROGSTAD: Was there anything more to understand—except what's all too common in life? A calculating woman throws over a man the moment a better catch comes by.

MRS. LINDE: You think I'm so thoroughly calculating? You think I broke it off lightly?

KROGSTAD: Didn't you?

MRS. LINDE: Nils—is that what you really thought?

KROGSTAD: If you cared, then why did you write me the way you did?

MRS. LINDE: What else could I do? If I had to break off with you, then it was my job as well to root out everything you felt for me.

KROGSTAD (*wringing his hands*): So that was it. And this—all this, simply for money!

MRS. LINDE: Don't forget I had a helpless mother and two small brothers. We couldn't wait for you, Nils; you had such a long road ahead of you then.

KROGSTAD: That may be; but you still hadn't the right to abandon me for somebody else's sake.

MRS. LINDE: Yes—I don't know. So many, many times I've asked myself if I did have that right.

KROGSTAD (*more softly*): When I lost you, it was as if all the solid ground dissolved from under my feet. Look at me; I'm a half-drowned man now, hanging onto a wreck.

MRS. LINDE: Help may be near.

KROGSTAD: It was near—but then you came and blocked it off.

MRS. LINDE: Without my knowing it, Nils. Today for the first time I learned that it's you I'm replacing at the bank.

KROGSTAD: All right—I believe you. But now that you know, will you step aside?

MRS. LINDE: No, because that wouldn't benefit you in the slightest.

KROGSTAD: Not "benefit" me, hm! I'd step aside anyway.

MRS. LINDE: I've learned to be realistic. Life and hard, bitter necessity have taught me that.

KROGSTAD: And life's taught me never to trust fine phrases.

MRS. LINDE: Then life's taught you a very sound thing. But you do have to trust in actions, don't you?

KROGSTAD: What does that mean?

MRS. LINDE: You said you were hanging on like a half-drowned man to a wreck.

KROGSTAD: I've good reason to say that.

MRS. LINDE: I'm also like a half-drowned woman on a wreck. No one to suffer with; no one to care for.

KROGSTAD: You made your choice.

MRS. LINDE: There wasn't any choice then.

KROGSTAD: So—what of it?

MRS. LINDE: Nils, if only we two shipwrecked people could reach across to each other.

KROGSTAD: What are you saying?

MRS. LINDE: Two on one wreck are at least better off than each on his own.

KROGSTAD: Kristine!

MRS. LINDE: Why do you think I came into town?

KROGSTAD: Did you really have some thought of me?

MRS. LINDE: I have to work to go on living. All my born days, as long as I can remember, I've worked, and it's been my best and my only joy. But now I'm completely alone in the world; it frightens me to be so empty and lost. To work for yourself—there's no joy in that. Nils, give me something—someone to work for.

KROGSTAD: I don't believe all this. It's just some hysterical feminine urge to go out and make a noble sacrifice.

MRS. LINDE: Have you ever found me to be hysterical?

KROGSTAD: Can you honestly mean this? Tell me—do you know everything about my past?

MRS. LINDE: Yes.

KROGSTAD: And you know what they think I'm worth around here.

MRS. LINDE: From what you were saying before, it would seem that with me you could have been another person.

KROGSTAD: I'm positive of that.

MRS. LINDE: Couldn't it happen still?

KROGSTAD: Kristine—you're saying this in all seriousness? Yes, you are! I can see it in you. And do you really have the courage, then—?

MRS. LINDE: I need to have someone to care for, and your children need a mother. We both need each other. Nils, I have faith that you're good at heart—I'll risk everything together with you.

KROGSTAD (*gripping her hands*): Kristine, thank you, thank you—Now I know I can win back a place in their eyes. Yes—but I forgot—

MRS. LINDE (*listening*): Shh! The tarantella. Go now! Go on!

KROGSTAD: Why? What is it?

MRS. LINDE: Hear the dance up there? When that's over, they'll be coming down.

KROGSTAD: Oh, then I'll go. But—it's all pointless. Of course, you don't know the move I made against the Helmers.

MRS. LINDE: Yes, Nils, I know.

KROGSTAD: And all the same, you have the courage to—?

MRS. LINDE: I know how far despair can drive a man like you.

KROGSTAD: Oh, if I only could take it all back.

MRS. LINDE: You easily could—your letter's still lying in the mailbox.

KROGSTAD: Are you sure of that?

MRS. LINDE: Positive. But—

KROGSTAD (*looks at her searchingly*): Is that the meaning of it, then? You'll save your friend at any price. Tell me straight out. Is that it?

MRS. LINDE: Nils—anyone who's sold herself for somebody else once isn't going to do it again.

KROGSTAD: I'll demand my letter back.

MRS. LINDE: No, no.

KROGSTAD: Yes, of course. I'll stay here till Helmer comes down; I'll tell him to give me my letter again—that it only involves my dismissal—that he shouldn't read it—

MRS. LINDE: No, Nils, don't call the letter back.

KROGSTAD: But wasn't that exactly why you wrote me to come here?

MRS. LINDE: Yes, in that first panic. But it's been a whole day and night since then, and in that time I've seen such incredible things in this house. Helmer's got to learn everything; this dreadful secret has to be aired; those two have to come to a full understanding; all these lies and evasions can't go on.

KROGSTAD: Well, then, if you want to chance it. But at least there's one thing I can do, and do right away—

MRS. LINDE (*listening*): Go now, go, quick! The dance is over. We're not safe another second.

KROGSTAD: I'll wait for you downstairs.

MRS. LINDE: Yes, please do; take me home.

KROGSTAD: I can't believe it; I've never been so happy. (*He leaves by way of the outer door; the door between the room and the hall stays open.*)

MRS. LINDE (*straightening up a bit and getting together her street clothes*): How different now! How different! Someone to work for, to live for—a home to build. Well, it is worth the try! Oh, if they'd only come! (*Listening.*) Ah, there they are. Bundle up. (*She picks up her hat and coat.* NORA'S *and* HELMER'S *voices can be heard outside; a key turns in the lock, and* HELMER *brings* NORA *into the hall almost by force. She is wearing the Italian costume with a large black shawl about her; he has on evening dress, with a black domino open over it.*)

NORA (*struggling in the doorway*): No, no, no, not inside! I'm going up again. I don't want to leave so soon.

HELMER: But Nora dear—

NORA: Oh, I beg you, please, Torvald. From the bottom of my heart, *please*—only an hour more!

HELMER: Not a single minute, Nora darling. You know our agreement. Come on, in we go; you'll catch cold out here. (*In spite of her resistance, he gently draws her into the room.*)

MRS. LINDE: Good evening.

NORA: Kristine!

HELMER: Why, Mrs. Linde—are you here so late?

MRS. LINDE: Yes, I'm sorry, but I did want to see Nora in costume.

NORA: Have you been sitting here, waiting for me?

MRS. LINDE: Yes. I didn't come early enough; you were all upstairs; and then I thought I really couldn't leave without seeing you.

HELMER (*removing* NORA'S *shawl*): Yes, take a good look. She's worth looking at, I can tell you that, Mrs. Linde. Isn't she lovely?

MRS. LINDE: Yes, I should say—

HELMER: A dream of loveliness, isn't she? That's what everyone thought at the party, too. But she's horribly stubborn—this sweet little thing. What's to be done with her? Can you imagine, I almost had to use force to pry her away.

NORA: Oh, Torvald, you're going to regret you didn't indulge me, even for just a half hour more.

HELMER: There, you see. She danced her tarantella and got a tumultuous hand—which was well earned, although the performance may have been a bit too naturalistic—I mean it rather overstepped the proprieties of art. But never mind—what's important is, she made a success, an overwhelming success. You think I could let her stay on after that and spoil the effect? Oh no; I took my lovely little Capri girl—my capricious little Capri girl, I should say—took her under my arm; one quick tour of the ballroom, a curtsy to every side, and then—as they say in novels—the beautiful vision disappeared. An exit should always be effective, Mrs. Linde, but that's what I can't get Nora to grasp. Phew, it's hot in here. (*Flings the domino on a chair and opens the door to his room.*) Why's it dark in here? Oh yes, of course. Excuse me. (*He goes in and lights a couple of candles.*)

NORA (*in a sharp, breathless whisper*): So?

MRS. LINDE (*quietly*): I talked with him.

NORA: And—?

MRS. LINDE: Nora—you must tell your husband everything.

NORA (*dully*): I knew it.

MRS. LINDE: You've got nothing to fear from Krogstad, but you have to speak out.

NORA: I won't tell.

MRS. LINDE: Then the letter will.

NORA: Thanks, Kristine. I know now what's to be done. Shh!

HELMER (*reentering*): Well, then, Mrs. Linde—have you admired her?

MRS. LINDE: Yes, and now I'll say good night.

HELMER: Oh, come, so soon? Is this yours, this knitting?

MRS. LINDE: Yes, thanks. I nearly forgot it.

HELMER: Do you knit, then?

MRS. LINDE: Oh yes.

HELMER: You know what? You should embroider instead.

MRS. LINDE: Really? Why?

HELMER: Yes, because it's a lot prettier. See here, one holds the embroidery so, in the left hand, and then one guides the needle with the right—so—in an easy, sweeping curve—right?

MRS. LINDE: Yes, I guess that's—

HELMER: But, on the other hand, knitting—it can never be anything but ugly. Look, see here, the arms tucked in, the knitting needles going up and down—there's something Chinese about it. Ah, that was really a glorious champagne they served.

MRS. LINDE: Yes, good night, Nora, and don't be stubborn anymore.

HELMER: Well put, Mrs. Linde!

MRS. LINDE: Good night, Mr. Helmer.

HELMER (*accompanying her to the door*): Good night, good night. I hope you get home all right. I'd be very happy to—but you don't have far to go. Good night, good night. (*She leaves. He shuts the door after her and returns.*) There, now, at last we got her out the door. She's a deadly bore, that creature.

NORA: Aren't you pretty tired, Torvald?

HELMER: No, not a bit.

NORA: You're not sleepy?

HELMER: Not at all. On the contrary, I'm feeling quite exhilarated. But you? Yes, you really look tired and sleepy.

NORA: Yes, I'm very tired. Soon now I'll sleep.

HELMER: See! You see! I was right all along that we shouldn't stay longer.

NORA: Whatever you do is always right.

HELMER (*kissing her brow*): Now my little lark talks sense. Say, did you notice what a time Rank was having tonight?

NORA: Oh, was he? I didn't get to speak with him.

HELMER: I scarcely did either, but it's a long time since I've seen him in such high spirits. (*Gazes at her a moment, then comes nearer her.*) Hm—it's marvelous, though, to be back home again—to be completely alone with you. Oh, you bewitchingly lovely young woman!

NORA: Torvald, don't look at me like that!

HELMER: Can't I look at my richest treasure? At all that beauty that's mine, mine alone—completely and utterly.

NORA (*moving around to the other side of the table*): You mustn't talk to me that way tonight.

HELMER (*following her*): The tarantella is still in your blood. I can see—and it makes you even more enticing. Listen. The guests are beginning to go. (*Dropping his voice.*) Nora—it'll soon be quiet through this whole house.

NORA: Yes, I hope so.

HELMER: You do, don't you, my love? Do you realize—when I'm out at a party like this with you—do you know why I talk to you so little, and keep such a distance away; just send you a stolen look now and then—you know why I do it? It's because I'm imagining then that you're my secret darling, my secret young bride-to-be, and that no one suspects there's anything between us.

NORA: Yes, yes; oh, yes, I know you're always thinking of me.

HELMER: And then when we leave and I place the shawl over those fine young rounded shoulders—over that wonderful curving neck—then I pretend that you're my young bride, that we're just coming from the wedding, that for the first time I'm bringing you into my house—that for the first time I'm alone with you—completely alone with you, your trembling young beauty! All this evening I've longed for nothing but you. When I saw you turn and sway in the tarantella—my blood was pounding till I couldn't stand it—that's why I brought you down here so early—

NORA: Go away, Torvald! Leave me alone. I don't want all this.

HELMER: What do you mean? Nora, you're teasing me. You will, won't you? Aren't I your husband—?

(*A knock at the outside door.*)

NORA (*startled*): What's that?

HELMER (*going toward the hall*): Who is it?

RANK (*outside*): It's me. May I come in a moment?

HELMER (*with quiet irritation*): Oh, what does he want now? (*Aloud.*) Hold on. (*Goes and opens the door.*) Oh, how nice that you didn't just pass us by!

RANK: I thought I heard your voice, and then I wanted so badly to have a look in. (*Lightly glancing about.*) Ah, me, these old familiar haunts. You have it snug and cozy in here, you two.

HELMER: You seemed to be having it pretty cozy upstairs, too.

RANK: Absolutely. Why shouldn't I? Why not take in everything in life? As much as you can, anyway, and as long as you can. The wine was superb—

HELMER: The champagne especially.

RANK: You noticed that too? It's amazing how much I could guzzle down.

NORA: Torvald also drank a lot of champagne this evening.

RANK: Oh?

NORA: Yes, and that always makes him so entertaining.

RANK: Well, why shouldn't one have a pleasant evening after a well-spent day?

HELMER: Well spent? I'm afraid I can't claim that.

RANK (*slapping him on the back*): But I can, you see!

NORA: Dr. Rank, you must have done some scientific research today.

RANK: Quite so.

HELMER: Come now—little Nora talking about scientific research!

NORA: And can I congratulate you on the results?

RANK: Indeed you may.

NORA: Then they were good?

RANK: The best possible for both doctor and patient—certainty.

NORA (*quickly and searchingly*): Certainty?

RANK: Complete certainty. So don't I owe myself a gay evening afterwards?

NORA: Yes, you're right, Dr. Rank.

HELMER: I'm with you—just so long as you don't have to suffer for it in the morning.

RANK: Well, one never gets something for nothing in life.

NORA: Dr. Rank—are you very fond of masquerade parties?

RANK: Yes, if there's a good array of odd disguises—

NORA: Tell me, what should we two go as at the next masquerade?

HELMER: You little featherhead—already thinking of the next!

RANK: We two? I'll tell you what: You must go as Charmed Life—

HELMER: Yes, but find a costume for that!

RANK: Your wife can appear just as she looks every day.

HELMER: That was nicely put. But don't you know what you're going to be?

RANK: Yes, Helmer, I've made up my mind.

HELMER: Well?

RANK: At the next masquerade I'm going to be invisible.

HELMER: That's a funny idea.

RANK: They say there's a hat—black, huge—have you never heard of the hat that makes you invisible? You put it on, and then no one on earth can see you.

HELMER (*suppressing a smile*): Ah, of course.

RANK: But I'm quite forgetting what I came for. Helmer, give me a cigar, one of the dark Havanas.

HELMER: With the greatest pleasure. (*Holds out his case.*)

RANK: Thanks. (*Takes one and cuts off the tip.*)

NORA (*striking a match*): Let me give you a light.

RANK: Thank you. (*She holds the match for him; he lights the cigar.*) And now good-bye.

HELMER: Good-bye, good-bye, old friend.

NORA: Sleep well, Doctor.

RANK: Thanks for that wish.

NORA: Wish me the same.

RANK: You? All right, if you like—Sleep well. And thanks for the light. (*He nods to them both and leaves.*)

HELMER (*his voice subdued*): He's been drinking heavily.

NORA (*absently*): Could be. (HELMER *takes his keys from his pocket and goes out in the hall.*) Torvald—what are you after?

HELMER: Got to empty the mailbox; it's nearly full. There won't be room for the morning papers.

NORA: Are you working tonight?

HELMER: You know I'm not. Why—what's this? Someone's been at the lock.

NORA: At the lock—?

HELMER: Yes, I'm positive. What do you suppose—? I can't imagine one of the maids—? Here's a broken hairpin. Nora, it's yours—

NORA (*quickly*): Then it must be the children—

HELMER: You'd better break them of that. Hm, hm—well, opened it after all. (*Takes the contents out and calls into the kitchen.*) Helene! Helene, would you put out the lamp in the hall. (*He returns to the *room, shutting the hall door, then displays the handful of mail*) Look how it's piled up. (*Sorting through them.*) Now what's this?

NORA (*at the window*): The letter! Oh, Torvald, no!

HELMER: Two calling cards—from Rank.

NORA: From Dr. Rank?

HELMER (*examining them*): "Dr. Rank, Consulting Physician." They were on top. He must have dropped them in as he left.

NORA: Is there anything on them?

HELMER: There's a black cross over the name. See? That's a gruesome notion. He could almost be announcing his own death.

NORA: That's just what he's doing.

HELMER: What! You've heard something? Something he's told you?

NORA: Yes. That when those cards came, he'd be taking his leave of us. He'll shut himself in now and die.

HELMER: Ah, my poor friend! Of course I knew he wouldn't be here much longer. But so soon—And then to hide himself away like a wounded animal.

NORA: If it has to happen, then it's best it happens in silence—don't you think so, Torvald?

HELMER (*pacing up and down*): He's grown right into our lives. I simply can't imagine him gone. He with his suffering and loneliness—like a dark cloud setting off our sunlit happiness. Well, maybe it's best this way. For him, at least. (*Standing still.*) And maybe for us too, Nora. Now we're thrown back on each other, completely. (*Embracing her,*) Oh you, my darling wife, how can I hold you close enough? You know what, Nora—time and again I've wished you were in some terrible danger, just so I could stake my life and soul and everything, for your sake.

NORA (*tearing herself away, her voice firm and decisive*): Now you must read your mail, Torvald.

HELMER: No, no, not tonight. I want to stay with you, dearest.

NORA: With a dying friend on your mind?

HELMER: You're right. We've both had a shock. There's ugliness between us—these thoughts of death and corruption. We'll have to get free of them first. Until then—we'll stay apart.

NORA (*clinging about his neck*): Torvald—good night! Good night!

HELMER (*kissing her on the cheek*): Good night, little songbird. Sleep well, Nora I'll be reading my mail now. (*He takes the letters into his room and shuts the door after him.*)

NORA (*with bewildered glances, groping about, seizing Helmers domino, throwing it around her, and speaking in short, hoarse, broken whispers*): Never see him again. Never, never. (*Putting her shawl over her head.*) Never see the children either—them, too. Never, never. Oh, the freezing black water! The depths—down—Oh, I wish it were over—He has it now; he's reading it—now. Oh no, no, not yet. Torvald, good-bye, you and the children—(*She starts for the hall; as she does, Helmer throws open his door and stands with an open letter in his hand.*)

HELMER: Nora!

NORA (*screams*): Oh—!

HELMER: What is this? You know what's in this letter?

NORA: Yes, I know. Let me go! Let me out!

HELMER (*holding her back*): Where are you going?

NORA (*struggling to break loose*): You can't save me, Torvald!

HELMER (*slumping back*): True! Then it's true what he writes? How horrible! No, no, it's impossible—it can't be true.

NORA: It *is* true. I've loved you more than all this world.

HELMER: Ah, none of your slippery tricks.

NORA (*taking one step toward him*): Torvald—!

HELMER: What *is* this you've blundered into!

NORA: Just let me loose. You're not going to suffer for my sake. You're not going to take on my guilt.

HELMER: No more playacting. (*Locks the hall door.*) You stay right here and give me a reckoning. You understand what you've done? Answer! You understand?

NORA (*looking squarely at him, her face hardening*): Yes. I'm beginning to understand everything now.

HELMER (*striding about*): Oh, what an awful awakening! In all these eight years—she who was my pride and joy—a hypocrite, a liar—worse, worse—a criminal! How infinitely disgusting it all is! The shame! (NORA *says nothing and goes on looking straight at him. He stops in front of her.*) I should have suspected something of the kind. I should have known. All your father's flimsy values—Be still! All your father's flimsy values have come out in you. No religion, no morals, no sense of duty—Oh, how I'm punished for letting him off! I did it for your sake, and you repay me like this.

NORA: Yes, like this.

HELMER: Now you've wrecked all my happiness—ruined my whole future. Oh, it's awful to think of. I'm in a cheap little grafter's hands; he can do anything he wants with me, ask for anything, play with me like a puppet—and I can't breathe a word. I'll be swept down miserably into the depths on account of a featherbrained woman.

NORA: When I'm gone from this world, you'll be free.

HELMER: Oh, quit posing. Your father had a mess of those speeches too. What good would that ever do me if you were gone from this world, as you say? Not the slightest. He can still make the whole thing known; and if he does, I could be falsely suspected as your accomplice. They might even think that I was behind it—that I put you up to it. And all that I can thank you for—you that I've coddled the whole of our marriage. Can you see now what you've done to me?

NORA (*icily calm*): Yes.

HELMER: It's so incredible, I just can't grasp it. But we'll have to patch up whatever we can. Take off the shawl. I said, take it off! I've got to appease him somehow or other. The thing has to be hushed up at any cost. And as for you and me, it's got to seem like everything between us is just as it was—to the outside world, that is. You'll go right on living in this house, of course. But you can't be allowed to bring up the children; I don't dare trust you with them—Oh, to have to say this to someone I've loved so much! Well, that's done with. From now on happiness doesn't matter; all that matters is saving the bits and pieces, the appearance—(*The doorbell rings.* HELMER *starts.*) What's that? And so late. Maybe the worst—? You think he'd—? Hide, Nora! Say you're sick. (NORA *remains standing motionless.* HELMER *goes and opens the door.*)

MAID (*half dressed, in the hall*): A letter for Mrs. Helmer.

HELMER: I'll take it. (*Snatches the letter and shuts the door.*) Yes, it's from him. You don't get it; I'm reading it myself.

NORA: Then read it.

HELMER (*by the lamp*): I hardly dare. We may be ruined, you and I. But—I've got to know. (*Rips open the letter, skims through a few lines, glances at an enclosure, then cries out joyfully.*) Nora! (NORA *looks inquiringly at him.*) Nora! Wait—better check it again—Yes, yes, it's true. I'm saved. Nora, I'm saved!

NORA: And I?

HELMER: You too, of course. We're both saved, both of us. Look. He's sent back your note. He says he's sorry and ashamed—that a happy development in his life—oh, who cares what he says! Nora, we're saved! No one can hurt you. Oh, Nora, Nora—but first, this ugliness all has to go. Let me see—(*Takes a look at the note.*) No, I don't want to see it; I want the whole thing to fade like a dream. (*Tears the note and both letters to pieces, throws them into the stove and watches them burn.*) There—now there's nothing left—He wrote that since Christmas Eve you—Oh, they must have been three terrible days for you, Nora.

NORA: I fought a hard fight.

HELMER: And suffered pain and saw no escape but—No, we're not going to dwell on anything unpleasant. We'll just be grateful and keep on repeating: It's over now, it's over! You hear me, Nora? You don't seem to realize—it's over. What's it mean—that frozen look? Oh, poor little Nora, I understand. You can't believe I've forgiven you. But I have, Nora; I swear I have. I know that what you did, you did out of love for me.

NORA: That's true.

HELMER: You loved me the way a wife ought to love her husband. It's simply the means that you couldn't judge. But you think I love you any the less for not knowing how to handle your affairs? No, no—just lean on me; I'll guide you and teach you. I wouldn't be a man if this feminine helplessness didn't make you twice as attractive to me. You mustn't mind those sharp words I said—that was all in the first confusion of thinking my world had collapsed. I've forgiven you, Nora; I swear I've forgiven you.

NORA: My thanks for your forgiveness. (*She goes out through the door, right.*)

HELMER: No, wait—(*Peers in.*) What are you doing in there?

NORA (*inside*): Getting out of my costume.

HELMER (*by the open door*): Yes, do that. Try to calm yourself and collect your thoughts again, my frightened little songbird. You can rest easy now; I've got wide wings to shelter you with. (*Walking about close by the door.*) How snug and nice our home is, Nora. You're safe here; I'll keep you like a hunted dove I've rescued out of a hawk's claws. I'll bring peace to your poor, shuddering heart. Gradually it'll happen, Nora; you'll see. Tomorrow all this will look different to you; then everything will be as it was. I won't have to go on repeating I forgive you; you'll feel it for yourself. How can you imagine I'd ever conceivably want to disown you—or even blame you in any way? Ah, you don't know a man's heart, Nora. For a man there's something indescribably sweet and satisfying in knowing he's forgiven his wife—and forgiven her out of a full and open heart. It's as if she belongs to him in two ways now: In a sense he's given her fresh into the world again, and she's become his wife and his child as well. From now on that's what you'll be to me—you little, bewildered, helpless thing. Don't be afraid of anything, Nora; just open your heart to me, and I'll be conscience and will to you both—(NORA *enters in her regular clothes.*) What's this? Not in bed? You've changed your dress?

NORA: Yes, Torvald, I've changed my dress.

HELMER: But why now, so late?

NORA: Tonight I'm not sleeping.

HELMER: But Nora dear—

NORA (*looking at her watch*): It's still not so very late. Sit down, Torvald; we have a lot to talk over. (*She sits at one side of the table.*)

HELMER: Nora—what is this? That hard expression—

NORA: Sit down. This'll take some time. I have a lot to say.

HELMER (*sitting at the table directly opposite her*): You worry me, Nora. And I don't understand you.

NORA: No, that's exactly it. You don't understand me. And I've never understood you either—until tonight. No, don't interrupt. You can just listen to what I say. We're closing out accounts, Torvald.

HELMER: How do you mean that?

NORA (*after a short pause*): Doesn't anything strike you about our sitting here like this?

HELMER: What's that?

NORA: We've been married now eight years. Doesn't it occur to you that this is the first time we two, you and I, man and wife, have ever talked seriously together?

HELMER: What do you mean—seriously?

NORA: In eight whole years—longer even—right from our first acquaintance, we've never exchanged a serious word on any serious thing.

HELMER: You mean I should constantly go and involve you in problems you couldn't possibly help me with?

NORA: I'm not talking of problems. I'm saying that we've never sat down seriously together and tried to get to the bottom of anything.

HELMER: But dearest, what good would that ever do you?

NORA: That's the point right there: You've never understood me. I've been wronged greatly, Torvald—first by Papa, and then by you.

HELMER: What! By us—the two people who've loved you more than anyone else?

NORA (*shaking her head*): You never loved me. You've thought it fun to be in love with me, that's all.

HELMER: Nora, what a thing to say!

NORA: Yes, it's true now, Torvald. When I lived at home with Papa, he told me all his opinions, so I had the same ones too; or if they were different I hid them, since he wouldn't have cared for that. He used to call me his doll-child, and he played with me the way I played with my dolls. Then I came into your house—

HELMER: How can you speak of our marriage like that?

NORA (*unperturbed*): I mean, then I went from Papa's hands into yours. You arranged everything to your own taste, and so I got the same taste as you—or I pretended to; I can't remember. I guess a little of both, first one, then the other. Now when I look back, it seems as if I'd lived here like a beggar—just from hand to mouth. I've lived by doing tricks for you, Torvald. But that's the way you wanted it. It's a great sin what you and Papa did to me. You're to blame that nothing's become of me.

HELMER: Nora, how unfair and ungrateful you are! Haven't you been happy here?

NORA: No, never. I thought so—but I never have.

HELMER: Not—not happy!

NORA: No, only lighthearted. And you've always been so kind to me. But our home's been nothing but a playpen. I've been your doll-wife here, just as at home I was Papa's doll-child. And in turn the children have been my dolls. I thought it was fun when you played with me, just as they thought it fun when I played with them. That's been our marriage, Torvald.

HELMER: There's some truth in what you're saying—under all the raving exaggeration. But it'll all be different after this. Playtime's over; now for the schooling.

NORA: Whose schooling—mine or the children's?

HELMER: Both yours and the children's, dearest.

NORA: Oh, Torvald, you're not the man to teach me to be a good wife to you.

HELMER: And you can say that?

NORA: And I—how am I equipped to bring up children?

HELMER: Nora!

NORA: Didn't you say a moment ago that that was no job to trust me with?

HELMER: In a flare of temper! Why fasten on that?

NORA: Yes, but you were so very right. I'm not up to the job. There's another job I have to do first. I have to try to educate myself. You can't help me with that. I've got to do it alone. And that's why I'm leaving you now.

HELMER (*jumping up*): What's that?

NORA: I have to stand completely alone, if I'm ever going to discover myself and the world out there. So I can't go on living with you.

HELMER: Nora, Nora!

NORA: I want to leave right away. Kristine should put me up for the night—

HELMER: You're insane! You've no right! I forbid you!

NORA: From here on, there's no use forbidding me anything. I'll take with me whatever is mine. I don't want a thing from you, either now or later.

HELMER: What kind of madness is this!

NORA: Tomorrow I'm going home—I mean, home where I came from. It'll be easier up there to find something to do.

HELMER: Oh, you blind, incompetent child!

NORA: I must learn to be competent, Torvald.

HELMER: Abandon your home, your husband, your children! And you're not even thinking what people will say.

NORA: I can't be concerned about that. I only know how essential this is.

HELMER: Oh, it's outrageous. So you'll run out like this on your most sacred vows.

NORA: What do you think are my most sacred vows?

HELMER: And I have to tell you that! Aren't they your duties to your husband and children?

NORA: I have other duties equally sacred.

HELMER: That isn't true. What duties are they?

NORA: Duties to myself.

HELMER: Before all else, you're a wife and a mother.

NORA: I don't believe in that anymore. I believe that before all else, I'm a human being, no less than you—or anyway, I ought to try to become one. I know the majority thinks you're right, Torvald, and plenty of books agree with you, too. But I can't go on believing what the majority says, or what's written in books. I have to think over these things myself and try to understand them.

HELMER: Why can't you understand your place in your own home? On a point like that, isn't there one everlasting guide you can turn to? Where's your religion?

NORA: Oh, Torvald, I'm really not sure what religion is.

HELMER: What—?

NORA: I only know what the minister said when I was confirmed. He told me religion was this thing and that. When I get clear and away by myself, I'll go into that problem too. I'll see if what the minister said was right, or, in any case, if it's right for me.

HELMER: A young woman your age shouldn't talk like that. If religion can't move you, I can try to rouse your conscience. You do have some moral feeling? Or, tell me—has that gone too?

NORA: It's not easy to answer that, Torvald. I simply don't know. I'm all confused about these things. I just know I see them so differently from you. I find out for one thing, that the law's not at all what I'd thought—but I can't get it through my head that the law is fair. A woman hasn't a right to protect her dying father or save her husband's life! I can't believe that.

HELMER: You talk like a child. You don't know anything of the world you live in.

NORA: No, I don't. But now I'll begin to learn for myself. I'll try to discover who's right, the world or I.

HELMER: Nora, you're sick; you've got a fever. I almost think you're out of your head.

NORA: I've never felt more clearheaded and sure in my life.

HELMER: And—clearheaded and sure—you're leaving your husband and children?

NORA: Yes.

HELMER: Then there's only one possible reason.

NORA: What?

HELMER: You no longer love me.

NORA: No. That's exactly it.

HELMER: Nora! You can't be serious!

NORA: Oh, this is so hard, Torvald—you've been so kind to me always. But I can't help it. I don't love you anymore.

HELMER (*struggling for composure*): Are you also clearheaded and sure about that?

NORA: Yes, completely. That's why I can't go on staying here.

HELMER: Can you tell me what I did to lose your love?

NORA: Yes, I can tell you. It was this evening when the miraculous thing didn't come—then I knew you weren't the man I'd imagined.

HELMER: Be more explicit; I don't follow you.

NORA: I've waited now so patiently eight long years—for, my Lord, I know miracles don't come every day. Then this crisis broke over me, and such a certainty filled me: *Now* the miraculous event would occur. While Krogstad's letter was lying out there, I never for an instant dreamed that you could give in to his terms. I was so utterly sure you'd say to him: Go on, tell your tale to the whole wide world. And when he'd done that—

HELMER: Yes, what then? When I'd delivered my own wife into shame and disgrace—!

NORA: When he'd done that, I was so utterly sure that you'd step forward, take the blame on yourself and say: I am the guilty one.

HELMER: Nora—!

NORA: You're thinking I'd never accept such a sacrifice from you? No, of course not. But what good would my protests be against you? That was the miracle I was waiting for, in terror and hope. And to stave that off, I would have taken my life.

HELMER: I'd gladly work for you day and night, Nora—and take on pain and deprivation. But there's no one who gives up honor for love.

NORA: Millions of women have done just that.

HELMER: Oh, you think and talk like a silly child.

NORA: Perhaps. But you neither think nor talk like the man I could join myself to. When your big fright was over—and it wasn't from any threat against me, only for what might damage you—when all the danger was past, for you it was just as if nothing had happened. I was exactly the same, your little lark, your doll, that you'd have to handle with double care now that I'd turned out so brittle and frail. (*Gets up.*) Torvald—in that instant it dawned on me that for eight years I've been living here with a stranger, and that I'd even conceived three children—oh, I can't stand the thought of it! I could tear myself to bits.

HELMER (*heavily*): I see. There's a gulf that's opened between us—that's clear. Oh, but Nora, can't we bridge it somehow?

NORA: The way I am now, I'm no wife for you.

HELMER: I have the strength to make myself over.

NORA: Maybe—if your doll gets taken away.

HELMER: But to part! To part from you! No, Nora, no—I can't imagine it.

NORA (*going out, right*): All the more reason why it has to be. (*She reenters with her coat and a small overnight bag, which she puts on a chair by the table.*)

HELMER: Nora, Nora, not now! Wait till tomorrow.

NORA: I can't spend the night in a strange man's room.

HELMER: But couldn't we live here like brother and sister—

NORA: You know very well how long that would last. (*Throws her shawl about her.*) Good-bye, Torvald. I won't look in on the children. I know they're in better hands than mine. The way I am now, I'm no use to them.

HELMER: But someday, Nora—someday—?

NORA: How can I tell? I haven't the least idea what'll become of me.

HELMER: But you're my wife, now and wherever you go.

NORA: Listen, Torvald—I've heard that when a wife deserts her husband's house just as I'm doing, then the law frees him from all responsibility. In any case, I'm freeing you from being responsible. Don't feel yourself bound, any more than I will. There has to be absolute freedom for us both. Here, take your ring back. Give me mine.

HELMER: That too?

NORA: That too.

HELMER: There it is.

NORA: Good. Well, now it's all over. I'm putting the keys here. The maids know all about keeping up the house—better than I do. Tomorrow, after I've left town, Kristine will stop by to pack up everything that's mine from home. I'd like those things shipped up to me.

HELMER: Over! All over! Nora, won't you ever think about me?

NORA: I'm sure I'll think of you often, and about the children and the house here.

HELMER: May I write you?

NORA: No—never. You're not to do that.

HELMER: Oh, but let me send you—

NORA: Nothing. Nothing.

HELMER: Or help you if you need it.

NORA: No. I accept nothing from strangers.

HELMER: Nora—can I never be more than a stranger to you?

NORA (*picking up the overnight bag*): Ah, Torvald—it would take the greatest miracle of all—

HELMER: Tell me the greatest miracle!

NORA: You and I both would have to transform ourselves to the point that—Oh, Torvald, I've stopped believing in miracles.

HELMER: But I'll believe. Tell me! Transform ourselves to the point that—?

NORA: That our living together could be a true marriage. (*She goes out down the hall.*)

HELMER (*sinks down on a chair by the door, face buried in his hands*): Nora! Nora! (*Looking about and rising.*) Empty. She's gone. (*A sudden hope leaps in him.*) The greatest miracle—?

(*From below, the sound of a door slamming shut.*)

The Glass Menagerie TENNESSEE WILLIAMS

The Glass Menagerie, which was first staged in Chicago in December of 1944 and made its Broadway debut in the spring of 1945, was Tennessee Williams's (1911–1983) first great success. It announced the arrival of a fresh voice for the American stage. With a few notable exceptions, such as Eugene O'Neill's *The Hairy Ape,* Sophie Treadwell's *Machinal,* and Elmer Rice's *The Adding Machine,* most American drama in the first half of the twentieth century was exceedingly realistic in nature. Williams forever altered this realistic tradition by writing a play whose poetic textures and its use of lighting and sounds deployed a new kind of language, one that moved audiences deeply.

The Glass Menagerie is, as Williams reminds us, a memory play, a drama recalled through the troubled consciousness of Tom Wingfield. It is a play about the Wingfield family—Amanda, the well-meaning but ever-hovering mother; Laura, the timid daughter who has withdrawn into her glass menagerie world; and Tom, a poet trapped in a dead-end job at the warehouse. At times too sentimental, *The Glass Menagerie* nonetheless succeeds in its poignant depiction of a family lost within both a problematic social world and their own self-generated mythical world.

With such plays as *A Streetcar Named Desire* (1947), *Cat on a Hot Tin Roof* (1955), and *Night of the Iguana* (1961), Williams brought worldwide attention to himself and to the American theater. Today he remains one of the most popular of all American playwrights, and his works continue to attract favorable attention throughout the world.

CHARACTERS

AMANDA WINGFIELD, *the mother.*

A little woman of great but confused vitality clinging frantically to another time and place. Her characterization must be carefully created, not copied from type. She is not paranoiac, but her life is paranoia. There is much to admire in AMANDA, *and as much to love and pity as there is to laugh at. Certainly she has endurance and a kind of heroism, and though her foolishness makes her unwittingly cruel at times, there is tenderness in her slight person.*

LAURA WINGFIELD, *her daughter.*

AMANDA, *having failed to establish contact with reality, continues to live vitally in her illusions, but* LAURA'S *situation is even graver. A childhood illness has left her crippled, one leg slightly shorter than the other, and held in a brace. This defect need not be more than suggested on the stage. Stemming from this,* LAURA'S *separation increases till she is like a piece of her own glass collection, too exquisitely fragile to move from the shelf.*

TOM WINGFIELD, *her son, and the narrator of the play.*
A poet with a job in a warehouse. His nature is not remorseless, but to escape from a trap he has to act without pity.

JIM O'CONNOR, *the gentleman caller.*
A nice, ordinary, young man.

SCENE: *An alley in St. Louis.*

PART I: *Preparation for a Gentleman Caller.*

PART II: *The Gentleman Calls.*

TIME: *Now and the Past.*

Scene I

The Wingfield apartment is in the rear of the building, one of those vast hive-like conglomerations of cellular living-units that flower as warty growths in overcrowded urban centers of lower middle-class population and are symptomatic of the impulse of this largest and fundamentally enslaved section of American society to avoid fluidity and differentiation and to exist and function as one interfused mass of automatism.

The apartment faces an alley and is entered by a fire-escape, a structure whose name is a touch of accidental poetic truth, for all of these huge buildings are always burning with the slow and implacable fires of human desperation. The fire-escape is included in the set—that is, the landing of it and steps descending from it.

The scene is memory and is therefore nonrealistic. Memory takes a lot of poetic license. It omits some details; others are exaggerated, according to the emotional value of the articles it touches, for memory is seated predominantly in the heart. The interior is therefore rather dim and poetic.

At the rise of the curtain, the audience is faced with the dark, grim rear wall of the Wingfield tenement. This building, which runs parallel to the footlights, is flanked on both sides by dark, narrow alleys which run into murky canyons of tangled clotheslines, garbage cans and the sinister latticework of neighboring fire-escapes. It is up and down these side alleys that exterior entrances and exits are made, during the play. At the end of TOM'S *opening commentary, the dark tenement wall slowly reveals (by means of a transparency) the interior of the ground floor Wingfield apartment.*

Downstage is the living room, which also serves as a sleeping room for LAURA, *the sofa unfolding to make her bed. Upstage, center, and divided by a wide arch or second proscenium with transparent faded portieres (or second curtain), is the dining room. In an old-fashioned what-not in the living room are seen scores of transparent glass animals. A blown-up photograph of the father hangs on the wall of the living room, facing the audience, to the left of the archway. It is the face of a very handsome young man in a doughboy's First World War cap. He is gallantly smiling, ineluctably smiling, as if to say, "I will be smiling forever."*

The audience hears and sees the opening scene in the dining room through both the transparent fourth wall of the building and the transparent gauze portieres of the dining-room arch. It is during this revealing scene that the fourth wall slowly ascends, out of sight. This transparent exterior wall is not brought down again until the very end of the play, during TOM'S *final speech.*

The narrator is an undisguised convention of the play. He takes whatever license with dramatic convention as is convenient to his purposes.

TOM *enters dressed as a merchant sailor from alley, stage left, and strolls across the front of the stage to the fire-escape. There he stops and lights a cigarette. He addresses the audience.*

TOM: Yes, I have tricks in my pocket, I have things up my sleeve. But I am the opposite of a stage magician. He gives you illusion that has the appearance of truth. I give you truth in the pleasant disguise of illusion. To begin with, I turn back time. I reverse it to that quaint period, the thirties, when the huge middle class of America was matriculating in a school for the blind. Their eyes had failed them, or they had failed their eyes, and so they were having their fingers pressed forcibly down by the fiery Braille alphabet of a dissolving economy. In Spain there was revolution. Here there was only shouting and confusion. In Spain there was Guernica. Here there were disturbances of labor, sometimes pretty violent, in otherwise peaceful cities such as Chicago, Cleveland, Saint Louis. . . . This is the social background of the play.

(*Music.*)

The play is memory. Being a memory play, it is dimly lighted, it is sentimental, it is not realistic. In memory everything seems to happen to music. That explains the fiddle in the wings. I am the narrator of the play, and also a character in it. The other characters are my mother, Amanda, my sister, Laura, and a gentleman caller who appears in the final scenes. He is the most realistic character in the play, being an emissary from a world of reality that we were somehow set apart from. But since I have a poet's weakness for symbols, I am using this character also as a symbol; he is the long delayed but always expected something that we live for. There is a fifth character in the play who doesn't appear except in this larger-than-life photograph over the mantel. This is our father who left us a long time ago. He was a telephone man who fell in love with long distances; he gave up his job with the telephone company and skipped the light fantastic out of town . . . The last we heard of him was a picture post-card from Mazatlan, on the Pacific coast of Mexico, containing a message of two words—"Hello—Goodbye!" and an address. I think the rest of the play will explain itself. . . .

(*Amanda's voice becomes audible through the portieres.*)

(*Legend on screen: "Où sont les neiges".*)

(*He divides the portieres and enters the upstage area.*

AMANDA *and* LAURA *are seated at a drop-leaf table. Eating is indicated by gestures without food or utensils.* AMANDA *faces the audience.* TOM *and* LAURA *are seated in profile.*

The interior has lit up softly and through the scrim we see AMANDA *and* LAURA *seated at the table in the upstage area.*)

AMANDA (*calling*): Tom?

TOM: Yes, Mother.

AMANDA: We can't say grace until you come to the table!

TOM: Coming, Mother. (*He bows slightly and withdraws, reappearing a few moments later in his place at the table.*)

AMANDA (*to her son*): Honey, don't *push* with your *fingers.* If you have to push with something, the thing to push with is a crust of bread. And chew—chew! Animals have sections in their stomachs which enable them to digest food without mastication, but human beings are supposed to chew their food before they swallow it down. Eat food leisurely, son, and really enjoy it. A well-cooked meal has lots of delicate flavors that have to be held in the mouth for appreciation. So chew your food and give your salivary glands a chance to function!

(TOM *deliberately lays his imaginary fork down and pushes his chair back from the table.*)

TOM: I haven't enjoyed one bite of this dinner because of your constant directions on how to eat it. It's you that makes me rush through meals with your hawk-like attention to every bite I take.

Sickening—spoils my appetite—all this discussion of animals' secretion—salivary glands—mastication!

AMANDA (*lightly*): Temperament like a Metropolitan star! (*He rises and crosses downstage.*) You're not excused from the table.

TOM: I am getting a cigarette.

AMANDA: You smoke too much.

(LAURA *rises.*)

LAURA: I'll bring in the blanc mange.

(*He remains standing with his cigarette by the portieres during the following.*)

AMANDA (*rising*): No, sister, no, sister—you be the lady this time and I'll be the darky.

LAURA: I'm already up.

AMANDA: Resume your seat, little sister—I want you to stay fresh and pretty—for gentlemen callers!

LAURA: I'm not expecting any gentlemen callers.

AMANDA (*crossing out to kitchenette; airily*): Sometimes they come when they are least expected! Why, I remember one Sunday afternoon in Blue Mountain—(*enters kitchenette*)

TOM: I know what's coming!

LAURA: Yes. But let her tell it.

TOM: Again?

LAURA: She loves to tell it.

(AMANDA *returns with bowl of dessert.*)

AMANDA: One Sunday afternoon in Blue Mountain—your mother received—*seventeen!*—gentlemen callers! Why, sometimes there weren't chairs enough to accommodate them all. We had to send the nigger over to bring in folding chairs from the parish house.

TOM (*remaining at portieres*): How did you entertain those gentlemen callers?

AMANDA: I understood the art of conversation!

TOM: I bet you could talk.

AMANDA: Girls in those days *knew* how to talk, I can tell you.

TOM: Yes?

(*Image:* AMANDA *as a girl on a porch greeting callers.*)

AMANDA: They knew how to entertain their gentlemen callers. It wasn't enough for a girl to be possessed of a pretty face and a graceful figure—although I wasn't slighted in either respect. She also needed to have a nimble wit and a tongue to meet all occasions.

TOM: What did you talk about?

AMANDA: Things of importance going on in the world! Never anything coarse or common or vulgar. (*She addresses* TOM as *though he were seated in the vacant chair at the table though he remains by portieres. He plays this scene as though he held the book.*) My callers were gentlemen—all! Among my callers were some of the most prominent young planters of the Mississippi Delta—planters and sons of planters!

(TOM *motions for music and a spot of light on* AMANDA. *Her eyes lift, her face glows, her voice becomes rich and elegiac.*)

(*Screen legend: "Où sont les neiges."*)[1]

There was young Champ Laughlin who later became vice-president of the Delta Planters Bank. Hadley Stevenson who was drowned in Moon Lake and left his widow one hundred and fifty thousand in Government bonds. There were the Cutrere brothers, Wesley and Bates. Bates was one of my bright particular beaux! He got in a quarrel with that wild Wainright boy. They shot it out on the floor of Moon Lake Casino. Bates was shot through the stomach. Died in the ambulance on his way to Memphis. His widow was also well-provided for, came into eight or ten thousand acres, that's all. She married him on the rebound—never loved her—carried my picture on him the night he died! And there was that boy that every girl in the Delta had set her cap for! That beautiful, brilliant young Fitzhugh boy from Green County!

TOM: What did he leave his widow?

AMANDA: He never married! Gracious, you talk as though all of my old admirers had turned up their toes to the daisies!

TOM: Isn't this the first you mentioned that still survives?

AMANDA: That Fitzhugh boy went North and made a fortune—came to be known as the Wolf of Wall Street! He had the Midas touch, whatever he touched turned to gold! And I could have been Mrs. Duncan J. Fitzhugh, mind you! But—I picked your *father!*

LAURA (*rising*): Mother, let me clear the table.

AMANDA: No, dear, you go in front and study your typewriter chart. Or practice your shorthand a little. Stay fresh and pretty—It's almost

[1]**Où sont les neiges:** French for "Where are the snows [from the past]?"

time for our gentlemen callers to start arriving. (*She flounces girlishly toward the kitchenette.*) How many do you suppose we're going to entertain this afternoon?

(TOM *throws down the paper and jumps up with a groan.*)

LAURA (*alone in the dining room*): I don't believe we're going to receive any, Mother.

AMANDA (*reappearing, airily*): What? No one—not one? You must be joking! (LAURA *nervously echoes her laugh. She slips in a fugitive manner through the half-open portieres and draws them gently behind her. A shaft of very clear light is thrown on her face against the faded tapestry of the curtains. Music: "The Glass Menagerie" under faintly; lightly.*) Not one gentleman caller? It can't be true! There must be a flood, there must have been a tornado!

LAURA: It isn't a flood, it's not a tornado, Mother. I'm just not popular like you were in Blue Mountain. . . . (TOM *utters another groan.* LAURA *glances at him with a faint, apologetic smile; her voice catching a little.*) Mother's afraid I'm going to be an old maid.

(*The scene dims out with "Glass Menagerie" music.*)

Scene II

("LAURA, *Haven't You Ever Liked Some Boy?*")

On the dark stage the screen is lighted with the image of blue roses.

Gradually LAURA'S *figure becomes apparent and the screen goes out.*

The music subsides.

LAURA *is seated in the delicate ivory chair at the small clawfoot table.*

She wears a dress of soft violet material for a kimono—her hair tied back from her forehead with a ribbon.

She is washing and polishing her collection of glass.

AMANDA *appears on the fire-escape steps. At the sound of her ascent,* LAURA *catches her breath, thrusts the bowl of ornaments away and seats herself stiffly before the diagram of the typewriter keyboard as though it held her spellbound. Something has happened to* AMANDA. *It is written in her face as she climbs to the landing: a look that is grim and hopeless and a little absurd.*

She has on one of those cheap or imitation velvety-looking cloth coats with imitation fur collar. Her hat is five or six years old, one of those dreadful cloche hats that were worn in the late twenties and she is clasping an enormous black patent-leather pocket-book with nickel clasp and initials. This is her full-dress outfit, the one she usually wears to the D.A.R.[2]

Before entering she looks through the door.

She purses her lips, opens her eyes wide, rolls them upward, and shakes her head.

Then she slowly lets herself in the door. Seeing her mother's expression LAURA *touches her lips with a nervous gesture.*

LAURA: Hello, Mother, I was—(*She makes a nervous gesture toward the chart on the wall.* AMANDA *leans against the shut door and stares at* LAURA *with a martyred look.*)

AMANDA: Deception? Deception? (*She slowly removes her hat and gloves, continuing the swift suffering stare. She lets the hat and gloves fall on the floor—a bit of acting.*)

LAURA (*shakily*): How was the D.A.R. meeting? (AMANDA *slowly opens her purse and removes a dainty white handkerchief which she shakes out delicately and delicately touches to her lips and nostrils.*) Didn't you go to the D.A.R. meeting, Mother?

AMANDA (*faintly, almost inaudibly*): —No.—No. (*then more forcibly*) I did not have the strength—to go to the D.A.R. In fact, I did not have the courage! I wanted to find a hole in the ground and hide myself in it forever! (*She crosses slowly to the wall and removes the diagram of the typewriter keyboard. She holds it in front of her for a second, staring at it sweetly and sorrowfully—then bites her lips and tears it in two pieces.*)

LAURA (*faintly*): Why did you do that, Mother? (AMANDA *repeats the same procedure with the chart of the Gregg Alphabet.*) Why are you—

AMANDA: Why? Why? How old are you, Laura?

LAURA: Mother, you know my age.

AMANDA: I thought that you were an adult; it seems that I was mistaken. (*She crosses slowly to the sofa and sinks down and stares at* LAURA.)

LAURA: Please don't stare at me, Mother.

(AMANDA *closes her eyes and lowers her head. Count ten.*)

AMANDA: What are we going to do, what is going to become of us, what is the future?

(*Count ten.*)

---

[2]**D.A.R.:** Daughters of the American Revolution, a patriotic women's organization

LAURA: Has something happened, Mother? (AMANDA *draws a long breath and takes out the handkerchief again; dabbing process.*) Mother, has—something happened?

AMANDA: I'll be all right in a minute. I'm just bewildered—(*Count five.*)—by life. . . .

LAURA: Mother, I wish that you would tell me what's happened.

AMANDA: As you know, I was supposed to be inducted into my office at the D.A.R. this afternoon, (IMAGE: A SWARM OF TYPEWRITERS.) But I stopped off at Rubicam's Business College to speak to your teachers about your having a cold and ask them what progress they thought you were making down there.

LAURA: Oh. . . .

AMANDA: I went to the typing instructor and introduced myself as your mother. She didn't know who you were. Wingfield, she said. We don't have any such student enrolled at the school! I assured her she did, that you had been going to classes since early in January. "I wonder," she said, "if you could be talking about that terribly shy little girl who dropped out of school after only a few days' attendance?" "No," I said, "Laura, my daughter, has been going to school every day for the past six weeks!" "Excuse me," she said. She took the attendance book out and there was your name, unmistakably printed, and all the dates you were absent until they decided that you had dropped out of school. I still said, "No, there must have been some mistake! There must have been some mix-up in the records!" And she said, "No—I remember her perfectly now. Her hand shook so that she couldn't hit the right keys! The first time we gave a speed-test, she broke down completely—was sick at the stomach and almost had to be carried into the wash-room! After that morning she never showed up any more. We phoned the house but never got any answer—while I was working at Famous and Barr, I suppose, demonstrating those—Oh!" I felt so weak I could barely keep on my feet! I had to sit down while they got me a glass of water! Fifty dollars' tuition, all of our plans—my hopes and ambitions for you—just gone up the spout, just gone up the spout like that. (LAURA *draws a long breath and gets awkwardly to her feet. She crosses to the victrola and winds it up.*) What are you doing?

LAURA: Oh! (*She releases the handle and returns to her seat.*)

AMANDA: Laura, where have you been going when you've gone out pretending that you were going to business college?

LAURA: I've just been going out walking.

AMANDA: That's not true.

LAURA: It is. I just went walking.

AMANDA: Walking? Walking? In winter? Deliberately courting pneumonia in that light coat? Where did you walk to, Laura?

LAURA: All sorts of places—mostly in the park.

AMANDA: Even after you'd started catching that cold?

LAURA: It was the lesser of two evils, Mother. (IMAGE: WINTER SCENE IN PARK.) I couldn't go back up. I—threw up—on the floor!

AMANDA: From half past seven till after five every day you mean to tell me you walked around in the park, because you wanted to make me think that you were still going to Rubicam's Business College?

LAURA: It wasn't as bad as it sounds. I went inside places to get warmed up.

AMANDA: Inside where?

LAURA: I went in the art museum and the bird-houses at the Zoo. I visited the penguins every day! Sometimes I did without lunch and went to the movies. Lately I've been spending most of my afternoons in the Jewel-box, that big glass house where they raise the tropical flowers.

AMANDA: You did all this to deceive me, just for the deception? (LAURA *looks down.*) Why?

LAURA: Mother, when you're disappointed, you get that awful suffering look on your face, like the picture of Jesus' mother in the museum!

AMANDA: Hush!

LAURA: I couldn't face it.

(*Pause. A whisper of strings.*)

(*Legend: "The crust of humility."*)

AMANDA (*hopelessly fingering the huge pocketbook*): So what are we going to do the rest of our lives? Stay home and watch the parades go by? Amuse ourselves with the glass menagerie, darling? Eternally play those worn-out phonograph records your father left as a painful reminder of him? We won't have a business career—we've given that up because it gave us nervous indigestion! (*laughs wearily*) What is there left but dependency all our lives? I know so well what becomes of unmarried women who aren't prepared to occupy a position. I've seen such pitiful cases in the South—barely tolerated spinsters living upon the grudging patronage of sister's husband or brother's wife!—stuck away in some little mouse-trap of a room—encouraged by one in-law to visit another—little birdlike women without any nest—eating the crust of humility all their life! Is that the future that we've mapped out for ourselves? I swear it's the only alternative I can think of! It isn't a very pleasant alternative, is it? Of course—some girls *do marry.* (LAURA *twists her hands nervously.*) Haven't you ever liked some boy?

LAURA: Yes. I liked one once. (*rises*) I came across his picture a while ago.

AMANDA (*with some interest*): He gave you his picture?

LAURA: No, it's in the year-book.

AMANDA (*disappointed*): Oh—a high-school boy.

(*Screen image: Jim as a high-school hero bearing a silver cup.*)

LAURA: Yes. His name was Jim. (LAURA *lifts the heavy annual from the claw-foot table.*) Here he is in *The Pirates of Penzance.*

AMANDA (*absently*): The what?

LAURA: The operetta the senior class put on. He had a wonderful voice and we sat across the aisle from each other Mondays, Wednesdays and Fridays in the Aud. Here he is with the silver cup for debating! See his grin?

AMANDA (*absently*): He must have had a jolly disposition.

LAURA: He used to call me—Blue Roses.

(*Image: Blue roses.*)

AMANDA: Why did he call you such a name as that?

LAURA: When I had that attack of pleurosis—he asked me what was the matter when I came back. I said pleurosis—he thought that I said Blue Roses! So that's what he always called me after that. Whenever he saw me, he'd holler, "Hello, Blue Roses!" I didn't care for the girl that he went out with. Emily Meisenbach. Emily was the best-dressed girl at Soldan. She never struck me, though, as being sincere . . . It says in the Personal Section—they're engaged. That's—six years ago! They must be married by now.

AMANDA: Girls that aren't cut out for business careers usually wind up married to some nice man. (*gets up with a spark of revival*) Sister, that's what you'll do!

(LAURA *utters a startled, doubtful laugh. She reaches quickly for a piece of glass.*)

LAURA: But, Mother—

AMANDA: Yes? (*crossing to photograph*)

LAURA (*in a tone of frightened apology*): I'm—crippled!

(*Image: Screen.*)

AMANDA: Nonsense! Laura, I've told you never, never to use that word. Why, you're not crippled, you just have a little defect—hardly noticeable, even! When people have some slight disadvantage like that, they cultivate other things to make up for it—develop charm—and vivacity—and—*charm!* That's all you have to do! (*She turns again to the photograph.*) One thing your father had *plenty of*—was *charm!*

(TOM *motions to the fiddle in the wings.*)

(*The scene fades out with music.*)

Scene III

(*Legend on screen: "After the fiasco—"*)

TOM *speaks from the fire-escape landing.*

TOM: After the fiasco at Rubicam's Business College, the idea of getting a gentleman caller for Laura began to play a more important part in Mother's calculations. It became an obsession. Like some archetype of the universal unconscious, the image of the gentleman caller haunted our small apartment. . . . (IMAGE: YOUNG MAN AT DOOR WITH FLOWERS.) An evening at home rarely passed without some allusion to this image, this spectre, this hope. . . . Even when he wasn't mentioned, his presence hung in Mother's preoccupied look and in my sister's frightened, apologetic manner—hung like a sentence passed upon the Wingfields! Mother was a woman of action as well as words. She began to take logical steps in the planned direction. Late that winter and in the early spring—realizing that extra money would be needed to properly feather the nest and plume the bird—she conducted a vigorous campaign on the telephone, roping in subscribers to one of those magazines for matrons called *The Home-maker's Companion,* the type of journal that features the serialized sublimations of ladies of letters who think in terms of delicate cup-like breasts, slim, tapering waists, rich, creamy thighs, eyes like wood-smoke in autumn, fingers that soothe and caress like strains of music, bodies as powerful as Etruscan sculpture.

(*Screen image: Glamour magazine cover.*)

(AMANDA *enters with phone on long extension cord. She is spotted in the dim stage.*)

AMANDA: Ida Scott? This is Amanda Wingfield! We *missed* you at the D.A.R. last Monday! I said to myself: She's probably suffering with that sinus condition! How is that sinus condition? Horrors! Heaven have mercy!—You're a Christian martyr, yes, that's what you are, a Christian martyr! Well, I just now happened to notice that your subscription to the *Companion*'s about to expire! Yes, it expires with the next issue, honey!—just when that wonderful new serial by Bessie Mae Hopper is getting off to such an exciting start. Oh, honey, it's something that you can't miss! You remember how *Gone With the Wind* took everybody by storm? You simply couldn't go out if you hadn't read it. All everybody *talked* was Scarlett O'Hara. Well, this is a book that critics already compare to *Gone With the Wind.* It's the *Gone With the Wind* of the post-World War generation!—What?—Burning?—Oh, honey, don't let them burn, go take a look in the oven and I'll hold the wire! Heavens—I think she's hung up!

(*Dim out.*)

(*Legend on screen: "You think I'm in love with Continental Shoemakers?"*)

(*Before the stage is lighted, the violent voices of* TOM *and* AMANDA *are heard.*

They are quarreling behind the portieres. In front of them stands LAURA *with clenched hands and panicky expression.*

A clear pool of light on her figure throughout this scene.)

TOM: What in Christ's name am I—

AMANDA (*shrilly*): Don't you use that—

TOM: Supposed to do!

AMANDA: Expression! Not in my—

TOM: Ohhh!

AMANDA: Presence! Have you gone out of your senses?

TOM: I have, that's true, *driven* out!

AMANDA: What is the matter with you, you—big—big—IDIOT!

TOM: Look—I've got *no thing,* no single thing—

AMANDA: Lower your voice!

TOM: In my life here that I can call my OWN! Everything is—

AMANDA: Stop that shouting!

TOM: Yesterday you confiscated my books! You had the nerve to—

AMANDA: I took that horrible novel back to the library—yes! That hideous book by that insane Mr. Lawrence. (TOM *laughs wildly.*) I cannot control the output of diseased minds or people who cater to them—(TOM *laughs still more wildly.*) BUT I WON'T ALLOW SUCH FILTH BROUGHT INTO MY HOUSE! No, no, no, no, no!

TOM: House, house! Who pays rent on it, who makes a slave of himself to—

AMANDA (*fairly screeching*): Don't you DARE to—

TOM: No, no, *I* mustn't say things! *I've* got to just—

AMANDA: Let me tell you—

TOM: I don't want to hear any more! (*He tears the portieres open. The upstage area is lit with a turgid smoky red glow.*)

(AMANDA'S *hair is in metal curlers and she wears a very old bathrobe, much too large for her slight figure, a relic of the faithless Mr. Wingfield.*

An upright typewriter and a wild disarray of manuscripts is on the dropleaf table. The quarrel was probably precipitated by AMANDA'S *interruption of his creative labor. A chair lying overthrown on the floor.*

Their gesticulating shadows are cast on the ceiling by the fiery glow.)

AMANDA: You *will* hear more, you—

TOM: No, I won't hear more, I'm going out!

AMANDA: You come right back in—

TOM: Out, out out! Because I'm—

AMANDA: Come back here, Tom Wingfield! I'm not through talking to you!

TOM: Oh, go—

LAURA (*desperately*): —Tom!

AMANDA: You're going to listen, and no more insolence from you! I'm at the end of my patience! (*He comes back toward her.*)

TOM: What do you think I'm at? Aren't I supposed to have any patience to reach the end of, Mother? I know, I know. It seems unimportant to you, what I'm *doing*—what I *want* to do—having a little *difference* between them! You don't think that—

AMANDA: I think you've been doing things that you're ashamed of. That's why you act like this. I don't believe that you go every night to the movies. Nobody goes to the movies night after night. Nobody in their right minds goes to the movies as often as you pretend to. People don't go to the movies at nearly midnight, and movies don't let out at two A.M. Come in stumbling. Muttering to yourself like a maniac! You get three hours sleep and then go to work. Oh, I can picture the way you're doing down there. Moping, doping, because you're in no condition.

TOM (*wildly*): No, I'm in no condition!

AMANDA: What right have you got to jeopardize your job? Jeopardize the security of us all? How do you think we'd manage if you were—

TOM: Listen! You think I'm crazy *about* the *warehouse?* (*He bends fiercely toward her slight figure.*) You think I'm in love with the Continental Shoemakers? You think I want to spend fifty-five *years* down there in that—*celotex interior!* with—*fluorescent*—*tubes!* Look! I'd rather somebody picked up a crowbar and battered out my brains—than go back mornings! I *go!* Every time you come in yelling that God damn *"Rise and Shine!" "Rise and Shine!"* I say to myself "How *lucky dead* people are!" But I get up. I *go!* For sixty-five dollars a month I give up all that I dream of doing and being *ever!* And you say self—*self's* all I ever think of. Why, listen, if self is what I thought of, Mother, I'd be where he is—GONE! (*pointing to father's picture*) As far as the system of transportation reaches! (*He starts past her. She grabs his arm.*) Don't grab me, Mother!

AMANDA: Where are you going?

TOM: I'm going to the *movies!*

AMANDA: I don't believe that lie!

TOM (*crouching toward her, overtowering her tiny figure. She backs away, gasping.*): I'm going to opium dens! Yes, opium dens, dens of vice and criminals' hangouts, Mother. I've joined the Hogan gang, I'm a hired assassin, I carry a tommy-gun in a violin case! I run a string of cat-houses in the Valley! They call me Killer, Killer Wingfield, I'm leading a double-life, a simple, honest warehouse worker by day, by night, a dynamic *czar* of the *underworld, Mother.* I go to gambling casinos, I spin away fortunes on the roulette table! I wear a patch over one eye and a false mustache, sometimes I put on green whiskers. On those occasions they call me—*El Diablo!* Oh, I could tell you things to make you sleepless! My enemies plan to dynamite this place. They're going to blow us all sky-high some night! I'll be glad, very happy, and so will you! You'll go up, up on a broomstick, over Blue Mountain with seventeen gentlemen callers! You ugly—babbling old—*witch....* (*He goes through a series of violent, clumsy movements, seizing his overcoat, lunging to the door, pulling it fiercely open. The women watch him, aghast. His arm catches in the sleeve of the coat as he struggles to pull it on. For a moment he is pinioned by the bulky garment. With an outraged groan he tears the coat off again, splitting the shoulders of it, and hurls it across the room. It strikes against the shelf of* LAURA*'s glass collection, there is a tinkle of shattering glass.* LAURA *cries out as if wounded.*)

(*Music legend: "The Glass Menagerie."*)

LAURA (*shrilly*): *My glass!*—menagerie. . . . (*She covers her face and turns away.*)

(*But* AMANDA *is still stunned and stupefied by the "ugly witch" so that she barely notices this occurrence. Now she recovers her speech.*)

AMANDA (*in an awful voice*): I won't speak to you—until you apologize! (*She crosses through portieres and draws them together behind her.* TOM *is left with* LAURA. LAURA *clings weakly to the mantel with her face averted.* TOM *stares at her stupidly for a moment. Then he crosses to shelf. Drops awkwardly to his knees to collect the fallen glass, glancing at* LAURA *as if he would speak but couldn't.*)

"The Glass Menagerie" steals in as

(*The scene dims out.*)

Scene IV

The interior is dark. Faint light in the alley.

A deep-voiced bell in a church is tolling the hour of five as the scene commences.

TOM *appears at the top of the alley. After each solemn boom of the bell in the tower, he shakes a little noise-maker or rattle as if to express the tiny spasm of man in contrast to the sustained power and dignity of the Almighty. This and the unsteadiness of his advance make it evident that he has been drinking.*

As he climbs the few steps to the fire-escape landing light steals up inside. LAURA *appears in night-dress, observing* TOM*'s empty bed in the front room.*

TOM *fishes in his pockets for the door-key, removing a motley assortment of articles in the search, including a perfect shower of movie-ticket stubs and an empty bottle. At last he finds the key, but just as he is about to insert it, it slips from his fingers. He strikes a match and crouches below the door.*

TOM (*bitterly*): One crack—and it falls through!

(LAURA *opens the door.*)

LAURA: Tom! Tom, what are you doing?

TOM: Looking for a door-key.

LAURA: Where have you been all this time?

TOM: I have been to the movies.

LAURA: All this time at the movies?

TOM: There was a very long program. There was a Garbo picture and a Mickey Mouse and a travelogue and a newsreel and a preview of coming attractions. And there was an organ solo and a collection for the milk-fund—simultaneously—which ended up in a terrible fight between a fat lady and an usher!

LAURA (*innocently*): Did you have to stay through everything?

TOM: Of course! And, oh, I forgot! There was a big stage show! The headliner on this stage show was Malvolio the Magician. He performed wonderful tricks, many of them, such as pouring water back and forth between pitchers. First it turned to wine and then it turned to beer and then it turned to whiskey. I know it was whiskey it finally turned into because he needed somebody to come up out of the audience to help him, and I came up—both shows! It was Kentucky Straight Bourbon. A very generous fellow, he gave souvenirs. (*He pulls from his back pocket a shimmering rainbow-colored scarf.*) He gave me this. This is his magic scarf. You can have it, Laura. You wave it over a canary cage and you get a bowl of gold-fish. You wave it over the gold-fish bowl and they fly away canaries. . . . But the wonderfullest trick of all was the coffin trick. We nailed him into a coffin and he got out of the coffin without removing one nail. (*He has come inside.*) There is a trick that would come in handy for me—get me out of this 2 by 4 situation! (*flops onto bed and starts removing shoes*)

LAURA: Tom—Shhh!

TOM: What you shushing me for?

LAURA: You'll wake up Mother.

TOM: Goody, goody! Pay 'er back for all those "Rise an' Shines." (*lies down, groaning*) You know it don't take much intelligence to get yourself into a nailed-up coffin, Laura. But who in hell ever got himself out of one without removing one nail?

(*As if in answer, the father's grinning photograph lights up.*)

(*Scene dims out.*)

(*Immediately following: The church bell is heard striking six. At the sixth stroke the alarm clock goes off in* AMANDA*'s room, and after a few moments we hear her calling: "Rise and Shine! Rise and Shine! Laura, go tell your brother to rise and shine!"*)

TOM (*sitting up slowly*): I'll rise—but I won't shine.

(*The light increases.*)

AMANDA: Laura, tell your brother his coffee is ready.

(LAURA *slips into front room.*)

LAURA: Tom! it's nearly seven. Don't make Mother nervous. (*He stares at her stupidly, beseechingly.*) Tom, speak to Mother this morning. Make up with her, apologize, speak to her!

TOM: She won't to me. It's her that started not speaking.

LAURA: If you just say you're sorry she'll start speaking.

TOM: Her not speaking—is that such a tragedy?

LAURA: Please—please!

AMANDA (*calling from kitchenette*): Laura, are you going to do what I asked you to do, or do I have to get dressed and go out myself?

LAURA: Going, going—soon as I get on my coat! (*She pulls on a shapeless felt hat with nervous, jerky movement, pleadingly glancing at* TOM. *Rushes awkwardly for coat. The coat is one of* AMANDA*'s, inaccurately made-over, the sleeves too short for* LAURA.) Butter and what else?

AMANDA (*entering upstage*): Just butter. Tell them to charge it.

LAURA: Mother, they make such faces when I do that.

AMANDA: Sticks and stones may break my bones, but the expression on Mr. Garfinkel's face won't harm us! Tell your brother his coffee is getting cold.

LAURA (*at door*): Do what I asked you, will you, will you, Tom?

(*He looks sullenly away.*)

AMANDA: Laura, go now or just don't go at all!

LAURA (*rushing out*): Going—going! (*A second later she cries out.* TOM *springs up and crosses to the door.* AMANDA *rushes anxiously in.* TOM *opens the door.*)

TOM: Laura?

LAURA: I'm all right. I slipped, but I'm all right.

AMANDA (*peering anxiously after her*): If anyone breaks a leg on those fire-escape steps, the landlord ought to be sued for every cent he possesses! (*She shuts door, remembers she isn't speaking, and returns to other room.*)

(*As* TOM *enters listlessly for his coffee, she turns her back to him and stands rigidly facing the window on the gloomy gray vault of the areaway. Its light on her face with its aged but childish features is cruelly sharp, satirical as a Daumier print.*)

(*Music under: "Ave Maria."*)

(TOM *glances sheepishly but sullenly at her averted figure and slumps at the table. The coffee is scalding hot; he sips it and gasps and spits it back in the cup. At his gasp,* AMANDA *catches her breath and half turns. Then catches herself and turns back to window.*

TOM *blows on his coffee, glancing sidewise at his mother. She clears her throat.* TOM *clears his. He starts to rise. Sinks back down again, scratches his head, clears his throat again.* AMANDA *coughs.* TOM *raises his cup in both hands to blow on it, his eyes staring over the rim of it at his mother for several moments. Then he slowly sets the cup down and awkwardly and hesitantly rises from the chair.*)

TOM (*hoarsely*): Mother. I—I apologize. Mother. (AMANDA *draws a quick, shuddering breath. Her face works grotesquely. She breaks into childlike tears.*) I'm sorry for what I said, for everything that I said, I didn't mean it.

AMANDA (*sobbingly*): My devotion has made me a witch and so I make myself hateful to my children!

TOM: No, you *don't.*

AMANDA: I worry so much, don't sleep, it makes me nervous!

TOM (*gently*): I understand that.

AMANDA: I've had to put up a solitary battle all these years. But you're my right-hand bower! Don't fall down, don't fail!

TOM (*gently*): I try, Mother.

AMANDA (*with great enthusiasm*): Try and you will SUCCEED! (*The notion makes her breathless.*) Why, you—you're just *full* of natural endowments! Both of my children—they're *unusual* children! Don't you think I know it? I'm so—*proud!* Happy and—feel I've—so much to be thankful for but—Promise me one thing, son!

TOM: What, Mother?

AMANDA: Promise, son, you'll—never be a drunkard!

TOM (*turns to her grinning*): I will never be a drunkard, Mother.

AMANDA: That's what frightened me so, that you'd be drinking! Eat a bowl of Purina!

TOM: Just coffee, Mother.

AMANDA: Shredded wheat biscuit?

TOM: No. No, Mother, just coffee.

AMANDA: You can't put in a day's work on an empty stomach. You've got ten minutes—don't gulp! Drinking too-hot liquids makes cancer of the stomach. . . . Put cream in.

TOM: No, thank you.

AMANDA: To cool it.

TOM: No! No, thank you, I want it black.

AMANDA: I know, but it's not good for you. We have to do all that we can to build ourselves up. In these trying times we live in, all that we have to cling to is—each other. . . . That's why it's so important to—Tom, I—I sent out your sister so I could discuss something with you. If you hadn't spoken I would have spoken to you. (*sits down*)

TOM (*gently*): What is it, Mother, that you want to discuss?

AMANDA: Laura!

(TOM *puts his cup down slowly.*)

(*Legend on screen: "Laura".*)

(*Music: "The Glass Menagerie".*)

TOM: —Oh.—Laura . . .

AMANDA (*touching his sleeve*): You know how Laura is. So quiet but—still water runs deep! She notices things and I think she—broods about them. (TOM *looks up.*) A few days ago I came in and she was crying.

TOM: What about?

AMANDA: You.

TOM: Me?

AMANDA: She has an idea that you're not happy here.

TOM: What gave her that idea?

AMANDA: What gives her any idea? However, you do act strangely. I—I'm not criticizing, understand *that!* I know your ambitions do not lie in the warehouse, that like everybody in the whole wide world—you've had to—make sacrifices, but—Tom—Tom—life's not easy, it calls for—Spartan endurance! There's so many things in my heart that I cannot describe to you! I've never told you but I—*loved* your father. . . .

TOM (*gently*): I know that, Mother.

AMANDA: And you—when I see you taking after his ways! Staying out late—and—well, you *had* been drinking the night you were in that—terrifying condition! Laura says that you hate the apartment and that you go out nights to get away from it! Is that true, Tom?

TOM: No. You say there's so much in your heart that you can't describe to me. That's true of me, too. There's so much in my heart that I can't describe to *you!* So let's respect each other's—

AMANDA: But, why—*why,* Tom—are you always so *restless?* Where do you go to, nights?

TOM: I—go to the movies.

AMANDA: Why do you go to the movies so much, Tom?

TOM: I go to the movies because—I like adventure. Adventure is something I don't have much of at work, so I go to the movies.

AMANDA: But, Tom, you go to the movies *entirely* too *much!*

TOM: I like a lot of adventure.

(AMANDA *looks baffled, then hurt. As the familiar inquisition resumes he becomes hard and impatient again.* AMANDA *slips back into her querulous attitude toward him.*)

(*Image on screen: Sailing vessel with Jolly Roger.*)[3]

AMANDA: Most young men find adventure in their careers.

TOM: Then most young men are not employed in a warehouse.

AMANDA: The world is full of young men employed in warehouses and offices and factories.

TOM: Do all of them find adventure in their careers?

AMANDA: They do or they do without it! Not everybody has a craze for adventure.

TOM: Man is by instinct a lover, a hunter, a fighter, and none of those instincts are given much play at the warehouse!

AMANDA: Man is by instinct! Don't quote instinct to me! Instinct is something that people have got away from! It belongs to animals! Christian adults don't want it!

TOM: What do Christian adults want, then, Mother?

AMANDA: Superior things! Things of the mind and the spirit! Only animals have to satisfy instincts! Surely your aims are somewhat higher than theirs! Than monkeys—pigs—

TOM: I reckon they're not.

AMANDA: You're joking. However, that isn't what I wanted to discuss.

TOM (*rising*): I haven't much time.

AMANDA (*pushing his shoulders*): Sit down.

TOM: You want me to punch in red at the warehouse, Mother?

AMANDA: You have five minutes. I want to talk about Laura.

---

[3]**Jolly Roger:** a black flag with skull and crossbones favored by pirates

(*Legend: "Plans and provisions."*)

TOM: All right! What about Laura?

AMANDA: We have to be making plans and provisions for her. She's older than you, two years, and nothing has happened. She just drifts along doing nothing. It frightens me terribly how she just drifts along.

TOM: I guess she's the type that people call home girls.

AMANDA: There's no such type, and if there is, it's a pity! That is unless the home is hers, with a husband!

TOM: What?

AMANDA: Oh, I can see the handwriting on the wall as plain as I see the nose in front of my face! It's terrifying! More and more you remind me of your father! He was out all hours without explanation—Then *left! Goodbye!* And me with a bag to hold. I saw that letter you got from the Merchant Marine. I know what you're dreaming of. I'm not standing here blindfolded. Very well, then. Then *do* it! But not till there's somebody to take your place.

TOM: What do you mean?

AMANDA: I mean that as soon as Laura has got somebody to take care of her, married, a home of her own, independent—why, then you'll be free to go wherever you please, on land, on sea, whichever way the wind blows! But until that time you've got to look out for your sister. I don't say me because I'm old and don't matter! I say for your sister because she's young and dependent. I put her in business college—a dismal failure! Frightened her so it made her sick to her stomach. I took her over to the Young People's League at the church. Another fiasco. She spoke to nobody, nobody spoke to her. Now all she does is fool with those pieces of glass and play those worn-out records. What kind of life is that for a girl to lead?

TOM: What can I do about it?

AMANDA: Overcome selfishness! Self, self, self is all that you ever think of! (TOM *springs up and crosses to get his coat. It is ugly and bulky. He pulls on a cap with earmuffs.*) Where is your muffler? Put your wool muffler on! (*He snatches it angrily from the closet and tosses it around his neck and pulls both ends tight.*) Tom! I haven't said what I had in mind to ask you.

TOM: I'm too late to—

AMANDA (*catching his arm—very importunately; then shyly:*): Down at the warehouse, aren't there some—nice young men?

TOM: No!

AMANDA: There *must* be—*some* . . .

TOM: Mother—

(*Gesture.*)

AMANDA: Find out one that's clean-living—doesn't drink and—ask him out for sister!

TOM: What?

AMANDA: For *sister!* To *meet!* Get *acquainted!*

TOM (*stamping to door*): Oh, my *go-osh!*

AMANDA: Will you? (*He opens door; imploringly:*) Will you? (*He starts down.*) Will you? *Will* you, dear?

TOM (*calling back*): YES!

(AMANDA *closes the door hesitantly and with a troubled but faintly hopeful expression.*)

(*Screen image: Glamour magazine cover.*)

(*Spot* AMANDA *at phone.*)

AMANDA: Ella Cartwright? This is Amanda Wingfield! How are you, honey? How is that kidney condition? (*Count five.*) *Horrors!* (*Count five.*) You're a Christian martyr, yes, honey, that's what you are, a Christian martyr! Well, I just happened to notice in my little red book that your subscription to the *Companion* has just run out! I knew that you wouldn't want to miss out on the wonderful serial starting in this new issue. It's by Bessie Mae Hopper, the first thing she's written since *Honeymoon for Three.* Wasn't that a strange and interesting story? Well, this one is even lovelier, I believe. It has a sophisticated society background. It's all about the horsey set on Long Island!

(*Fade out.*)

Scene V

(*Legend on screen: "Annunciation."*)

Fade with music.

It is early dusk of a spring evening. Supper has just been finished in the Wingfield apartment. AMANDA *and* LAURA *in light colored dresses are removing dishes from the table, in the upstage area, which is shadowy, their movements formalized almost as a dance or ritual, their moving forms as pale and silent as moths.*

Tom, in white shirt and trousers, rises from the table and crosses toward the fire escape.

AMANDA (*as he passes her*): Son, will you do me a favor?

TOM: What?

AMANDA: Comb your hair! You look so pretty when your hair is combed! (TOM *slouches on sofa with evening paper; enormous caption "Franco Triumphs."*) There is only one respect in which I would like you to emulate your father.

TOM: What respect is that?

AMANDA: The care he always took of his appearance. He never allowed himself to look untidy. (*He throws down the paper and crosses to fire escape.*) Where are you going?

TOM: I'm going out to smoke.

AMANDA: You smoke too much. A pack a day at fifteen cents a pack. How much would that amount to in a month? Thirty times fifteen is how much, Tom? Figure it out and you will be astounded at what you could save. Enough to give you a night-school course in accounting at Washington U! Just think what a wonderful thing that would be for you, son!

(TOM *is unmoved by the thought.*)

TOM: I'd rather smoke. (*He steps out on landing, letting the screen door slam.*)

AMANDA: (*sharply*) I know! That's the tragedy of it. . . . (*Alone, she turns to look at her husband's picture.*)

(*Dance music: "All the world is waiting for the sunrise!"*)

TOM (*to the audience*): Across the alley from us was the Paradise Dance Hall. On evenings in spring the windows and doors were open and the music came outdoors. Sometimes the lights were turned out except for a large glass sphere that hung from the ceiling. It would turn slowly about and filter the dusk with delicate rainbow colors. Then the orchestra played a waltz or a tango, something that had a slow and sensuous rhythm. Couples would come outside, to the relative privacy of the alley. You could see them kissing behind ashpits and telephone poles. This was the compensation for lives that passed like mine, without any change or adventure. Adventure and change were imminent in this year. They were waiting around the corner for all these kids. Suspended in the mist over Berchtesgaden, caught in the folds of Chamberlain's umbrella—In Spain there was

Guernica![4] But here there was only hot swing music and liquor, dance halls, bars, and movies, and sex that hung in the gloom like a chandelier and flooded the world with brief, deceptive rainbows. . . . All the world was waiting for bombardments!

(AMANDA *turns from the picture and comes outside.*)

AMANDA (*sighing*): A fire-escape landing's a poor excuse for a porch. (*She spreads a newspaper on a step and sits down, gracefully and demurely as if she were settling into a swing on a Mississippi veranda.*) What are you looking at?

TOM: The moon.

AMANDA: Is there a moon this evening?

TOM: It's rising over Garfinkel's Delicatessen.

AMANDA: So it is! A little silver slipper of a moon. Have you made a wish on it yet?

TOM: Um-hum.

AMANDA: What did you wish for?

TOM: That's a secret.

AMANDA: A secret, huh? Well, I won't tell mine either. I will be just as mysterious as you.

TOM: I bet I can guess what yours is.

AMANDA: Is my head so transparent?

TOM: You're not a sphinx.

AMANDA: No, I don't have secrets. I'll tell you what I wished for on the moon. Success and happiness for my precious children! I wish for that whenever there's a moon, and when there isn't a moon, I wish for it, too.

TOM: I thought perhaps you wished for a gentleman caller.

AMANDA: Why do you say that?

TOM: Don't you remember asking me to fetch one?

AMANDA: I remember suggesting that it would be nice for your sister if you brought home some nice young man from the warehouse. I think I've made that suggestion more than once.

TOM: Yes, you have made it repeatedly.

---

[4]**Berchtesgaden . . . Chamberlain . . . Guernica:** These three terms are allusions to World War II. Berchtesgaden was the summer home of Adolf Hitler. Chamberlain refers to Neville Chamberlain, the Prime Minister of England, who signed the Munich Pact—a signing that the allies regard as a political victory for Hitler. Guernica was a Spanish town annihilated by German bombing raids in the late 1930s, which Pablo Picasso depicted in his famous painting of the same name.

AMANDA: Well?

TOM: We are going to have one.

AMANDA: *What?*

TOM: A gentleman caller!

(*The annunciation is celebrated with music.*)

(AMANDA *rises.*)

(*Image on screen: Caller with bouquet.*)

AMANDA: You mean you have asked some nice young man to come over?

TOM: Yep. I've asked him to dinner.

AMANDA: You really did?

TOM: I did!

AMANDA: You did, and did he—*accept?*

TOM: He did!

AMANDA: Well, well—well, well! That's—lovely!

TOM: I thought that you would be pleased.

AMANDA: It's definite, then?

TOM: Very definite.

AMANDA: Soon?

TOM: Very soon.

AMANDA: For heaven's sake, stop putting on and tell me some things, will you?

TOM: What things do you want me to tell you?

AMANDA: *Naturally* I would like to know when he's *coming!*

TOM: He's coming tomorrow.

AMANDA: *Tomorrow?*

TOM: Yep. Tomorrow.

AMANDA: But, Tom!

TOM: Yes, Mother?

AMANDA: Tomorrow gives me no time!

TOM: Time for what?

AMANDA: Preparations! Why didn't you phone me at once, as soon as you asked him, the minute that he accepted? Then, don't you see, I could have been getting ready!

TOM: You don't have to make any fuss.

AMANDA: Oh, Tom, Tom, Tom, of course I have to make a fuss! I want things nice, not sloppy! Not thrown together. I'll certainly have to do some fast thinking, won't I?

TOM: I don't see why you have to think at all.

AMANDA: You just don't know. We can't have a gentleman caller in a pig-sty! All my wedding silver has to be polished, the monogrammed table linen ought to be laundered! The windows have to be washed and fresh curtains put up. And how about clothes? We have to *wear* something, don't we?

TOM: Mother, this boy is no one to make a fuss over!

AMANDA: Do you realize he's the first young man we've introduced to your sister? It's terrible, dreadful, disgraceful that poor little sister has never received a single gentleman caller! Tom, come inside! (*She opens the screen door.*)

TOM: What for?

AMANDA: I want to ask you some things.

TOM: If you're going to make such a fuss, I'll call it off, I'll tell him not to come.

AMANDA: You certainly won't do anything of the kind. Nothing offends people worse than broken engagements. It simply means I'll have to work like a Turk! We won't be brilliant, but we'll pass inspection. Come on inside. (TOM *follows, groaning.*) Sit down.

TOM: Any particular place you would like me to sit?

AMANDA: Thank heavens I've got that new sofa! I'm also making payments on a floor lamp I'll have sent out! And put the chintz covers on, they'll brighten things up! Of course I'd hoped to have these walls re-papered.... What is the young man's name?

TOM: His name is O'Connor.

AMANDA: That, of course, means fish—tomorrow is Friday! I'll have that salmon loaf—with Durkee's dressing! What does he do? He works at the warehouse?

TOM: Of course! How else would I—

AMANDA: Tom, he—doesn't drink?

TOM: Why do you ask me that?

AMANDA: Your father *did!*

TOM: Don't get started on that!

AMANDA: He *does* drink, then?

TOM: Not that I know of!

AMANDA: Make sure, be certain! The last thing I want for my daughter's a boy who drinks!

TOM: Aren't you being a little premature? Mr. O'Connor has not yet appeared on the scene!

AMANDA: But will tomorrow. To meet your sister, and what do I know about this character? Nothing! Old maids are better off than wives of drunkards!

TOM: Oh, my God!

AMANDA: Be still!

TOM (*leaning forward to whisper*): Lots of fellows meet girls whom they don't marry!

AMANDA: Oh, talk sensibly, Tom—and don't be sarcastic! (*She has gotten a hairbrush.*)

TOM: What are you doing?

AMANDA: I'm brushing that cow-lick down! What is this young man's position at the warehouse?

TOM (*submitting grimly to the brush and the interrogation*): This young man's position is that of a shipping clerk, Mother.

AMANDA: Sounds to me like a fairly responsible job, the sort of a job *you* would be in if you just had more *get-up*. What is his salary? Have you got any idea?

TOM: I would judge it to be approximately eighty-five dollars a month.

AMANDA: Well—not princely, but—

TOM: Twenty more than I make.

AMANDA: Yes, how well I know! But for a family man, eighty-five dollars a month is not much more than you can just get by on....

TOM: Yes, but Mr. O'Connor is not a family man.

AMANDA: He might be, mightn't he? Some time in the future?

TOM: I see. Plans and provisions.

AMANDA: You are the only young man that I know of who ignores the fact that the future becomes the present, the present the past, and the past turns into everlasting regret if you don't plan for it!

TOM: I will think that over and see what I can make of it.

AMANDA: Don't be supercilious with your mother! Tell me some more about this—what do you call him?

TOM: James D. O'Connor. The D. is for Delaney.

AMANDA: Irish on *both* sides! *Gracious!* And doesn't drink?

TOM: Shall I call him up and ask him right this minute?

AMANDA: The only way to find out about those things is to make discreet inquiries at the proper moment. When I was a girl in Blue Mountain and it was suspected that a young man drank, the girl whose attentions he had been receiving, if any girl *was*, would sometimes speak to the minister of his church, or rather her father would if her father was living, and sort of feel him out on the young man's character. That is the way such things are discreetly handled to keep a young woman from making a tragic mistake!

TOM: Then how did you happen to make a tragic mistake?

AMANDA: That innocent look of your father's had everyone fooled! He *smiled*—the world was *enchanted!* No girl can do worse than put herself at the mercy of a handsome appearance! I hope that Mr. O'Connor is not too good-looking.

TOM: No, he's not too good-looking. He's covered with freckles and hasn't too much of a nose.

AMANDA: He's not right-down homely, though?

TOM: Not right-down homely. Just medium homely. I'd say.

AMANDA: Character's what to look for in a man.

TOM: That's what I've always said, Mother.

AMANDA: You've never said anything of the kind and I suspect you would never give it a thought.

TOM: Don't be suspicious of me.

AMANDA: At least I hope he's the type that's up and coming.

TOM: I think he really goes in for self-improvement.

AMANDA: What reason have you to think so?

TOM: He goes to night school.

AMANDA (*beaming*): Splendid! What does he do, I mean study?

TOM: Radio engineering and public speaking!

AMANDA: Then he has visions of being advanced in the world! Any young man who studies public speaking is aiming to have an executive job some day! And radio engineering? A thing for the future! Both of these facts are very illuminating. Those are the sort of things that a mother should know concerning any young man who comes to call on her daughter. Seriously or—not.

TOM: One little warning. He doesn't know about Laura. I didn't let on that we had dark ulterior motives. I just said, why don't you come have dinner with us? He said okay and that was the whole conversation.

AMANDA: I bet it was! You're eloquent as an oyster. However, he'll know about Laura when he gets here. When he sees how lovely and sweet and pretty she is, he'll thank his lucky stars he was asked to dinner.

TOM: Mother, you mustn't expect too much of Laura.

AMANDA: What do you mean?

TOM: Laura seems all those things to you and me because she's ours and we love her. We don't even notice she's crippled any more.

AMANDA: Don't say crippled! You know that I never allow that word to be used!

TOM: But face facts, Mother. She is and—that's not all—

AMANDA: What do you mean "not all"?

TOM: Laura is very different from other girls.

AMANDA: I think the difference is all to her advantage.

TOM: Not quite all—in the eyes of others—strangers—she's terribly shy and lives in a world of her own and those things make her seem a little peculiar to people outside the house.

AMANDA: Don't say peculiar.

TOM: Face the facts. She is.

(*The dance-hall music changes to a tango that has a minor and somewhat ominous tone.*)

AMANDA: In what was is she peculiar—may I ask?

TOM (*gently*): She lives in a world of her own—a world of—little glass ornaments, Mother. . . . (*Gets up.* AMANDA *remains holding brush, looking at him, troubled.*) She plays old phonograph records and—that's about all—(*He glances at himself in the mirror and crosses to door.*)

AMANDA (*sharply*): Where are you going?

TOM: I'm going to the movies. (*out screen door*)

AMANDA: Not to the movies, every night to the movies! (*follows quickly to screen door*) I don't believe you always go to the movies! (*He is gone.* AMANDA *looks worriedly after him for a moment. Then vitality and optimism return and she turns from the door, crossing to portieres.*) Laura! Laura! (LAURA *answers from kitchenette.*)

LAURA: Yes, Mother.

AMANDA: Let those dishes go and come in front! (LAURA *appears with dish towel; gaily:*) Laura, come here and make a wish on the moon!

LAURA (*entering*): Moon—moon?

AMANDA: A little silver slipper of a moon. Look over your left shoulder, Laura, and make a wish! (LAURA *looks faintly puzzled as if called out of sleep.* AMANDA *seizes her shoulders and turns her at an angle by the door.*) No! Now, darling, *wish!*

LAURA: What shall I wish for, Mother?

AMANDA (*her voice trembling and her eyes suddenly filling with tears*): Happiness! Good Fortune!

(*The violin rises and the stage dims out.*)

Scene VI

(*Image: High school hero.*)

TOM: And so the following evening I brought Jim home to dinner. I had known Jim slightly in high school. In high school Jim was a hero. He had tremendous Irish good nature and vitality with the scrubbed and polished look of white chinaware. He seemed to move in a continual spotlight. He was a star in basketball, captain of the debating club, president of the senior class and the glee club and he sang the male lead in the annual light operas. He was always running or bounding, never just walking. He seemed always at the point of defeating the law of gravity. He was shooting with such velocity through his adolescence that you would logically expect him to arrive at nothing short of the White House by the time he was thirty. But Jim apparently ran into more interference after his graduation from Soldan. His speed had definitely slowed. Six years after he left high school he was holding a job that wasn't much better than mine.

(*Image: Clerk.*)

He was the only one at the warehouse with whom I was on friendly terms. I was valuable to him as someone who could remember his former glory, who had seen him win basketball games and the silver cup in debating. He knew of my secret practice of retiring to a cabinet of the washroom to work on poems when business was slack in the warehouse. He called me Shakespeare. And while the other boys in the warehouse regarded me with suspicious hostility, Jim took a humorous attitude toward me. Gradually his attitude affected the others, their hostility wore off and they also began to smile at me as people smile at an oddly fashioned dog who trots across their path at some distance.

I knew that Jim and Laura had known each other at Soldan, and I had heard Laura speak admiringly of his voice. I didn't know if Jim remembered her or not. In high school Laura had been as unobtrusive as Jim had been astonishing. If he did remember Laura, it was not as my sister, for when I asked him to dinner, he grinned and said, "You know, Shakespeare, I never thought of you as having folks!"

He was about to discover that I did. . . .

(*Light up stage.*)

(*Legend on screen: "The accent of a coming foot".*)

Friday evening. It is about five o'clock of a late spring evening which comes "scattering poems in the sky."

A delicate lemony light is in the Wingfield apartment.

AMANDA *has worked like a Turk in preparation for the gentleman caller. The results are astonishing. The new floor lamp with its rose-silk shade is in place, a colored paper lantern conceals the broken light fixture in the ceiling, new billowing white curtains are at the windows, chintz covers are on chairs and sofa, a pair of new sofa pillows make their initial appearance.*

Open boxes and tissue paper are scattered on the floor.

LAURA *stands in the middle with lifted arms while* AMANDA *crouches before her, adjusting the hem of the new dress, devout and ritualistic. The dress is colored and designed by memory. The arrangement of* LAURA*'s hair is changed; it is softer and more becoming. A fragile, unearthly prettiness has come out in* LAURA: *she is like a piece of translucent glass touched by light, given a momentary radiance, not actual, not lasting.*

AMANDA (*impatiently*): Why are you trembling?

LAURA: Mother, you've made me so nervous!

AMANDA: How have I made you nervous?

LAURA: By all this fuss! You make it seem so important!

AMANDA: I don't understand you, Laura. You couldn't be satisfied with just sitting home, and yet whenever I try to arrange something for you, you seem to resist it. (*She gets up.*) Now take a look at yourself. No, wait! Wait just a moment—I have an idea!

LAURA: What is it now?

(AMANDA *produces two powder puffs which she wraps in handkerchiefs and stuffs in* LAURA*'s bosom.*)

LAURA: Mother, what are you doing?

AMANDA: They call them "Gay Deceivers"!

LAURA: I won't wear them!

AMANDA: You will!

LAURA: Why should I?

AMANDA: Because, to be painfully honest, your chest is flat.

LAURA: You make it seem like we were setting a trap.

AMANDA: All pretty girls are a trap, a pretty trap, and men expect them to be. (*Legend: "A pretty trap."*) Now look at yourself, young lady. This is the prettiest you will ever be! I've got to fix myself now! You're going to be surprised by your mother's appearance! (*She crosses through portieres, humming gaily.*)

(LAURA *moves slowly to the long mirror and stares solemnly at herself.*

A wind blows the white curtains inward in a slow, graceful motion and with a faint, sorrowful sighing.)

AMANDA (*off stage*): It isn't dark enough yet. (*She turns slowly before the mirror with a troubled look.*)

(*Legend on screen: "This is my sister: celebrate her with strings!" Music.*)

AMANDA (*laughing, off*): I'm going to show you something. I'm going to make a spectacular appearance!

LAURA: What is it, mother?

AMANDA: Possess your soul in patience—you will see! Something I've resurrected from that old trunk! Styles haven't changed so terribly much after all. . . . (*She parts the portieres.*) Now just look at your mother! (*She wears a girlish frock of yellowed voile with a blue silk sash. She carries a bunch of jonquils—the legend of her youth is nearly revived; feverishly:*) This is the dress in which I led the cotillion. Won the cakewalk twice at Sunset Hill, wore one spring to the Governor's ball in Jackson! See how I sashayed around the ballroom, Laura? (*She raises her skirt and does a mincing step around the room.*) I wore it on Sundays for my gentlemen callers! I had it on the day I met your father—I had malaria fever all that spring. The change of climate from East Tennessee to the Delta—weakened resistance—I had a little temperature all the time—not enough to be serious just enough to make me restless and giddy! Invitations poured in—parties all over the Delta!—"Stay in bed," said Mother, "you have fever!"—but I just wouldn't—I took quinine but kept on going, going!—Evenings, dances!—Afternoons, long, long, rides! Picnics—lovely!—So lovely, that country in May.—All lacy with dogwood, literally flooded with jonquils!—That was the spring I had the craze for jonquils. Jonquils became an absolute obsession. Mother said, "Honey, there's no more room for jonquils." And still I kept bringing in more jonquils. Whenever, wherever I saw them, I'd say, "Stop! Stop! I see jonquils!" I made the young men help me gather the jonquils! It was a joke, Amanda and her jonquils! Finally there were no more vases to hold them, every available space was filled with jonquils. No vases to hold them? All right, I'll hold them myself! And then I—(*She stops in front of the picture. Music.*) met your father! Malaria fever and jonquils and then—this—boy. . . . (*She switches on the rose-colored lamp.*) I hope they get here before it starts to rain. (*She crosses upstage and places the jonquils in bowl on table.*) I gave your brother a little extra change so he and Mr. O'Connor could take the service car home.

LAURA (*with altered look*): What did you say his name was?

AMANDA: O'Connor.

LAURA: What is his first name?

AMANDA: I don't remember. Oh, yes, I do. It was—Jim!

(LAURA *sways slightly and catches hold of a chair.*)

(*Legend on screen: "Not Jim!"*)

LAURA (*faintly*): Not—Jim!

AMANDA: Yes, that was it, it was Jim! I've never known a Jim that wasn't nice!

(*Music: Ominous.*)

LAURA: Are you sure his name is Jim O'Connor?

AMANDA: Yes. Why?

LAURA: Is he the one that Tom used to know in high school?

AMANDA: He didn't say so. I think he just got to know him at the warehouse.

LAURA: There was a Jim O'Connor we both knew in high school—(*then, with effort:*) If that is the one that Tom is bringing to dinner—you'll have to excuse me, I won't come to the table.

AMANDA: What sort of nonsense is this?

LAURA: You asked me once if I'd ever liked a boy. Don't you remember I showed you this boy's picture?

AMANDA: You mean the boy you showed me in the year book?

LAURA: Yes, that boy.

AMANDA: Laura, Laura, were you in love with that boy?

LAURA: I don't know, Mother. All I know is I couldn't sit at the table if it was him!

AMANDA: It won't be him! It isn't the least bit likely. But whether it is or not, you will come to the table. You will not be excused.

LAURA: I'll have to be, Mother.

AMANDA: I don't intend to humor your silliness, Laura. I've had too much from you and your brother, both! So just sit down and compose yourself till they come. Tom has forgotten his key so you'll have to let them in, when they arrive.

LAURA (*panicky*): Oh, Mother—*you* answer the door!

AMANDA (*lightly*): I'll be in the kitchen—busy!

LAURA: Oh, Mother, please answer the door, don't make me do it!

AMANDA (*crossing into kitchenette*): I've got to fix the dressing for the salmon. Fuss, fuss—silliness!—over a gentleman caller!

(*Door swings shut.* LAURA *is left alone.*)

(*Legend: "Terror!"*)

(*She utters a low moan and turns off the lamp—sits stiffly on the edge of the sofa, knotting her fingers together.*)

(*Legend on screen: "The opening of a door!"*)

(TOM *and* JIM *appear on the fire-escape steps and climb to landing. Hearing their approach,* LAURA *rises with a panicky gesture. She retreats to the portieres.*

The doorbell. LAURA *catches her breath and touches her throat. Low drums.*)

AMANDA (*calling*): Laura, sweetheart! The door!

(LAURA *stares at it without moving.*)

JIM: I think we just beat the rain.

TOM: Uh-huh. (*He rings again, nervously.* JIM *whistles and fishes for a cigarette.*)

AMANDA (*very, very gaily*): Laura, that is your brother and Mr. O'Connor! Will you let them in, darling?

(LAURA *crosses toward kitchenette door.*)

LAURA (*breathlessly*): Mother—you go to the door!

(AMANDA *steps out of kitchenette and stares furiously* at LAURA. *She points imperiously at the door.*)

LAURA: Please, please!

AMANDA (*in a fierce whisper*): What is the matter with you, you silly thing?

LAURA (*desperately*): Please, you answer it, *please!*

AMANDA: I told you I wasn't going to humor you, Laura. Why have you chosen this moment to lose your mind?

LAURA: Please, please, please, you go!

AMANDA: You'll have to go to the door because I can't!

LAURA (*despairingly*): I can't either!

AMANDA: Why?

LAURA: I'm *sick!*

AMANDA: I'm sick, too—of your nonsense! Why can't you and your brother be normal people? Fantastic whims and behavior! (TOM *gives a long ring.*) Preposterous goings on! Can you give me one reason—(*calls out lyrically*) COMING! JUST ONE SECOND!—why should you be afraid to open a door? Now you answer it, Laura!

LAURA: Oh, oh, oh . . . (*She returns through the portieres. Darts to the victrola and winds it frantically and turns it on.*)

AMANDA: Laura Wingfield, you march right to that door!

LAURA: Yes—yes, Mother!

(*A faraway, scratchy rendition of "Dardanella" softens the air and gives her strength to move through it. She slips to the door and draws it cautiously open.* TOM *enters with the caller,* JIM O'CONNOR.)

TOM: Laura, this is Jim. Jim, this is my sister, Laura.

JIM (*stepping inside*): I didn't know that Shakespeare had a sister!

LAURA (*retreating stiff and trembling from the door*): How—how do you do?

JIM (*heartily extending his hand*): Okay!

(LAURA *touches it hesitantly with hers.*)

JIM: Your hand's *cold*, Laura!

LAURA: Yes, well—I've been playing the victrola. . . .

JIM: Must have been playing classical music on it! You ought to play a little hot swing music to warm you up!

LAURA: Excuse me—I haven't finished playing the victrola. . . .

(*She turns awkwardly and hurries into the front room. She pauses a second by the victrola. Then catches her breath and darts through the portieres like a frightened deer.*)

JIM (*grinning*): What was the matter?

TOM: Oh—with Laura? Laura is—terribly shy.

JIM: Shy, huh? It's unusual to meet a shy girl nowadays. I don't believe you ever mentioned you had a sister.

TOM: Well, now you know. I have one. Here is the *Post Dispatch.* You want a piece of it?

JIM: Uh-huh.

TOM: What piece? The comics?

JIM: Sports! (*glances at it*) Ole Dizzy Dean is on his bad behavior.

TOM (*disinterest*): Yeah? (*lights cigarette and crosses back to fire-escape door*)

JIM: Where are *you* going?

TOM: I'm going out on the terrace.

JIM (*goes after him*): You know, Shakespeare—I'm going to sell you a bill of goods!

TOM: What goods?

JIM: A course I'm taking.

TOM: Huh?

JIM: In public speaking! You and me, we're not the warehouse type.

TOM: Thanks—that's good news. But what has public speaking got to do with it?

JIM: It fits you for—executive positions!

TOM: Awww.

JIM: I tell you it's done a helluva lot for me.

(*Image: Executive at desk.*)

TOM: In what respect?

JIM: In every! Ask yourself what is the difference between you an' me and men in the office down front? Brains?—No!—Ability?—No! Then what? Just one little thing—

TOM: What is that one little thing?

JIM: Primarily it amounts to—social poise! Being able to square up to people and hold your own on any social level!

AMANDA (*off stage*): Tom?

TOM: Yes, Mother?

AMANDA: Is that you and Mr. O'Connor?

TOM: Yes, Mother.

AMANDA: Well, you just make yourselves comfortable in there.

TOM: Yes, Mother.

AMANDA: Ask Mr. O'Connor if he would like to wash his hands.

JIM: Aw—no—no—thank you—I took care of that at the warehouse. Tom—

TOM: Yes?

JIM: Mr. Mendoza was speaking to me about you.

TOM: Favorably?

JIM: What do you think?

TOM: Well—

JIM: You're going to be out of a job if you don't wake up.

TOM: I am waking up—

JIM: You show no signs.

TOM: The signs are interior.

(*Image on screen: The sailing vessel with Jolly Roger again.*)

TOM: I'm planning to change. (*He leans over the rail speaking with quiet exhilaration. The incandescent marquees and signs of the first-run movie houses light his face from across the alley. He looks like a voyager.*) I'm right at the point of committing myself to a future that doesn't include the warehouse and Mr. Mendoza or even a night-school course in public speaking.

JIM: What are you gassing about?

TOM: I'm tired of the movies.

JIM: Movies!

TOM: Yes, movies! Look at them—(*a wave toward the marvels of Grand Avenue*) All of those glamorous people—having adventures—hogging it all, gobbling the whole thing up! You know what happens? People go to the *movies* instead of *moving!* Hollywood characters are supposed to have all the adventures for everybody in America, while everybody in America sits in a dark room and watches them have them! Yes, until there's a war. That's when adventure becomes available to the masses! *Everyone's* dish, not only Gable's! Then the people in the dark room come out of the dark room to have some adventures themselves—Goody, goody!—It's our turn now, to go to the South Sea Island—to make a safari—to be exotic, far-off!—But I'm not patient. I don't want to wait till then. I'm tired of the *movies* and I am *about* to *move!*

JIM (*incredulously*): Move?

TOM: Yes.

JIM: When?

TOM: Soon!

JIM: Where? Where?

(*Theme three music seems to answer the question, while Tom thinks it over. He searches among his pockets.*)

TOM: I'm starting to boil inside. I know I seem dreamy, but inside—well, I'm boiling! Whenever I pick up a shoe, I shudder a little thinking how short life is and what I am doing!—Whatever that means. I know it doesn't mean shoes—except as something to wear on a traveler's feet! (*finds paper*) Look—

JIM: What?

TOM: I'm a member.

JIM (*reading*): The Union of Merchant Seamen.

TOM: I paid my dues this month, instead of the light bill.

JIM: You will regret it when they turn the lights off.

TOM: I won't be here.

JIM: How about your mother?

TOM: I'm like my father. The bastard son of a bastard! See how he grins? And he's been absent going on sixteen years!

JIM: You're just talking, you drip. How does your mother feel about it?

TOM: Shhh!—Here comes Mother! Mother is not acquainted with my plans!

AMANDA (*enters portieres*): Where are you all?

TOM: On the terrace, Mother.

(*They start inside. She advances to them.* TOM *is distinctly shocked at her appearance. Even* JIM *blinks a little. He is making his first contact with girlish Southern vivacity and in spite of the night-school course in public speaking is somewhat thrown off the beam by the unexpected outlay of social charm.*

Certain responses are attempted by JIM *but are swept aside by* AMANDA*'s gay laughter and chatter.* TOM *is embarrassed but after the first shock* JIM *reacts very warmly. Grins and chuckles, is altogether won over.*)

(*Image: Amanda as a girl.*)

AMANDA (*coyly smiling, shaking her girlish ringlets*): Well, well, well, so this is Mr. O'Connor. Introductions entirely unnecessary. I've heard so much about you from my boy. I finally said to him, Tom—good gracious!—why don't you bring this paragon to supper? I'd like to meet this nice young man at the warehouse!—Instead of just hearing him sing your praises so much! I don't know why my son is so stand-offish—that's not Southern behavior! Let's sit down and—I think we could stand a little more air in here! Tom, leave the door open. I felt a nice fresh breeze a moment ago. Where has it gone? Mmm, so warm already! And not quite summer, even. We're going to burn up when summer really gets started. However, we're having—we're having a very light supper. I think light things are better fo' this time of year. The same as light clothes are. Light clothes an' light food are what warm weather calls fo'. You know our blood gets so thick during th' winter—it takes a while fo' us to *adjust* ou'selves!—when the season changes . . . It's come so quick this year. I wasn't prepared. All of a sudden—heavens! Already summer!—I ran to the trunk an' pulled out this light dress—Terribly old! Historical almost! But feels so good—so good an' co-ol, y'know. . . .

TOM: Mother—

AMANDA: Yes, honey?

TOM: How about—supper?

AMANDA: Honey, you go ask Sister if supper is ready! You know that Sister is in full charge of supper! Tell her you hungry boys are waiting for it. (*to* JIM) Have you met Laura?

JIM: She—

AMANDA: Let you in? Oh, good, you've met already! It's rare for a girl as sweet an' pretty as Laura to be domestic! But Laura is, thank heavens, not only pretty but also very domestic. I'm not at all. I never was a bit. I never could make a thing but angel-food cake. Well, in the South we had so many servants. Gone, gone, gone. All vestige of gracious living! Gone completely! I wasn't prepared for what the future brought me. All of my gentlemen callers were sons of planters and so of course I assumed that I would be married to one and raise my family on a large piece of land with plenty of servants. But man proposes—and woman accepts the proposal!—To vary that old, old saying a little bit—I married no planter! I married a man who worked for the telephone company!—That gallantly smiling gentleman over there! (*points to the picture*) A telephone man who—fell in love with long-distance!—Now he travels and I don't even know where!—But what am I going on for about my—tribulations? Tell me yours—I hope you don't have any! Tom?

TOM (*returning*): Yes, Mother?

AMANDA: Is supper nearly ready?

TOM: It looks to me like supper is on the table.

AMANDA: Let me look—(*She rises prettily and looks through portieres.*) Oh, lovely!—But where is Sister?

TOM: Laura is not feeling well and she says that she thinks she'd better not come to the table.

AMANDA: What?—Nonsense!—Laura? Oh, Laura!

LAURA (*off stage, faintly*): Yes, Mother.

AMANDA: You really must come to the table. We won't be seated until you come to the table! Come in, Mr. O'Connor. You sit over there and I'll—Laura? Laura Wingfield! You're keeping us waiting, honey! We can't say grace until you come to the table!

(*The back door is pushed weakly open and* LAURA *comes in. She is obviously quite faint, her lips trembling, her eyes wide and staring. She moves unsteadily toward the table.*)

(*Legend: "Terror!"*)

(*Outside a summer storm is coming abruptly. The white curtains billow inward at the windows and there is a sorrowful murmur and deep blue dusk.*

LAURA *suddenly stumbles; she catches at a chair with a faint moan.*)

TOM: Laura!

AMANDA: Laura! (*There is a clap of thunder.*) (*Legend: "Ah!"*) (*despairingly:*) Why, Laura, you *are* sick, darling! Tom, help your sister into the living room, dear! Sit in the living room, Laura—rest on the sofa. Well! (*to the gentleman caller:*) Standing over the hot stove made her ill!—I told her that it was just too warm this evening, but—(TOM *comes back in.* LAURA *is on the sofa.*) Is Laura all right now?

TOM: Yes.

AMANDA: What *is* that? Rain? A nice cool rain has come up! (*She gives the gentleman caller a frightened look.*) I think we may—have grace—now . . . (TOM *looks at her stupidly.*) Tom, honey—you say grace!

TOM: Oh . . . "For these and all thy mercies—" (*They bow their heads,* AMANDA *stealing a nervous glance at* JIM. *In the living room* LAURA, *stretched on the sofa, clenches her hand to her lips, to hold back a shuddering sob.*) God's Holy Name be praised—

(*The scene dims out.*)

Scene VII

(*Legend: "A souvenir."*)

Half an hour later. Dinner is just being finished in the upstage area which is concealed by the drawn portieres.

As the curtain rises LAURA *is still huddled upon the sofa, her feet drawn under her, her head resting on a pale blue pillow, her eyes wide and mysteriously watchful. The new floor lamp with its shade of rose-colored silk gives a soft, becoming light to her face, bringing out the fragile, unearthly prettiness which usually escapes attention. There is a steady murmur of rain, but it is slackening and stops soon after the scene begins; the air outside becomes pale and luminous as the moon breaks out.*

A moment after the curtain rises, the lights in both rooms flicker and go out.

JIM: Hey, there, Mr. Light Bulb!

(AMANDA *laughs nervously.*)

(*Legend: "Suspension of a public service."*)

AMANDA: Where was Moses when the lights went out? Ha-ha. Do you know the answer to that one, Mr. O'Connor?

JIM: No, Ma'am, what's the answer?

AMANDA: In the dark! (JIM *laughs appreciably.*) Everybody sit still. I'll light the candles. Isn't it lucky we have them on the table? Where's a match? Which of you gentlemen can provide a match?

JIM: Here.

AMANDA: Thank you, sir.

JIM: Not at all, Ma'am!

AMANDA: I guess the fuse has burnt out. Mr. O'Connor, can you tell a burnt-out fuse? I know I can't and Tom is a total loss when it comes to mechanics. (*Sound: Getting up: voices recede a little to kitchenette.*) Oh, be careful you don't bump into something. We don't want our gentleman caller to break his neck. Now wouldn't that be a fine howdy-do?

JIM: Ha-ha! Where is the fuse-box?

AMANDA: Right here next to the stove. Can you see anything?

JIM: Just a minute.

AMANDA: Isn't electricity a mysterious thing? Wasn't it Benjamin Franklin who tied a key to a kite? We live in such a mysterious universe, don't we? Some people say that science clears up all mysteries for us. In my opinion it only creates more! Have you found it yet?

JIM: No, Ma'am. All these fuses look okay to me.

AMANDA: Tom!

TOM: Yes, Mother?

AMANDA: That light bill I gave you several days ago. The one I told you we got the notices about?

TOM: Oh.—Yeah.

(*Legend: "Ha!"*)

AMANDA: You didn't neglect to pay it by any chance?

TOM: Why, I—

AMANDA: Didn't! I might have known it!

JIM: Shakespeare probably wrote a poem on that light bill, Mrs. Wingfield.

AMANDA: I might have known better than to trust him with it! There's such a high price for negligence in this world!

JIM: Maybe the poem will win a ten-dollar prize.

AMANDA: We'll just have to spend the remainder of the evening in the nineteenth century, before Mr. Edison made the Mazda lamp!

JIM: Candlelight is my favorite kind of light.

AMANDA: That shows you're romantic! But that's no excuse for Tom. Well, we got through dinner. Very considerate of them to let us get through dinner before they plunged us into everlasting darkness, wasn't it, Mr, O'Connor?

JIM: Ha-ha!

AMANDA: Tom, as a penalty for your carelessness you can help me with the dishes.

JIM: Let me give you a hand.

AMANDA: Indeed you will not!

JIM: I ought to be good for something.

AMANDA: Good for something? (*Her tone is rhapsodic.*) *You?* Why, Mr. O'Connor, nobody, *nobody's* given me this much entertainment in years—as you have!

JIM: Aw, now, Mrs. Wingfield!

AMANDA: I'm not exaggerating, not one bit! But Sister is all by her lonesome. You go keep her company in the parlor! I'll give you this lovely old candelabrum that used to be on the altar at the church of the Heavenly Rest. It was melted a little out of shape when the church burnt down. Lightning struck it one spring. Gypsy Jones was holding a revival at the time and he intimated that the church was destroyed because the Episcopalians gave card parties.

JIM: Ha-ha.

AMANDA: And how about coaxing Sister to drink a little wine? I think it would be good for her! Can you carry both at once?

JIM: Sure. I'm Superman!

AMANDA: Now, Thomas, get into this apron!

(*The door of kitchenette swings closed on* AMANDA'*s gay laughter; the flickering light approaches the portieres.*

LAURA *sits up nervously as he enters. Her speech at first is low and breathless from the almost intolerable strain of being alone with a stranger.*)

(*The legend: "I don't suppose you remember me at all!"*)

(*In her first speeches in his scene, before* JIM'*s warmth overcomes her paralyzing shyness,* LAURA'*s voice is thin and breathless as though she has just run up a steep flight of stairs.*

JIM'S *attitude is gently humorous. In playing this scene it should be stressed that while the incident is apparently unimportant, it is to* LAURA *the climax of her secret life.*)

JIM: Hello, there, Laura.

LAURA (*faintly*): Hello. (*She clears her throat.*)

JIM: How are you feeling now? Better?

LAURA: Yes. Yes, thank you.

JIM: This is for you. A little dandelion wine. (*He extends it toward her with extravagant gallantry.*)

LAURA: Thank you.

JIM: Drink it—but don't get drunk! (*He laughs heartily.* LAURA *takes the glass uncertainly, laughs shyly.*) Where shall I set the candles?

LAURA: Oh—oh, anywhere . . .

JIM: How about here on the floor? Any objections?

LAURA: No.

JIM: I'll spread a newspaper under to catch the drippings. I like to sit on the floor. Mind if I do?

LAURA: Oh, no.

JIM: Give me a pillow?

LAURA: What?

JIM: A pillow!

LAURA: Oh . . . (*hands him one quickly*)

JIM: How about you? Don't you like to sit on the floor?

LAURA: Oh—yes.

JIM: Why don't you, then?

LAURA: I—will.

JIM: Take a pillow! (LAURA *does. Sits on the other side of the candelabrum.* JIM *crosses his legs and smiles engagingly at her.*) I can't hardly see you sitting way over there.

LAURA: I can—see you.

JIM: I know, but that's not fair, I'm in the limelight. (LAURA *moves her pillow closer.*) Good! Now I can see you! Comfortable?

LAURA: Yes.

JIM: So am I. Comfortable as a cow. Will you have some gum?

LAURA: No, thank you.

JIM: I think that I will indulge, with your permission. (*musingly unwraps it and holds it up*) Think of the fortune made by the guy that invented the first piece of chewing gum. Amazing, huh? The Wrigley Building is one of the sights of Chicago.—I saw it summer before last when I went up to the Century of Progress. Did you take in the Century of Progress?

LAURA: No, I didn't.

JIM: Well, it was quite a wonderful exposition. What impressed me most was the Hall of Science. Gives you an idea of what the future will be in America, even more wonderful than the present time is! (*pause; smiling at her:*) Your brother tells me you're shy. Is that right, Laura?

LAURA: I—don't know.

JIM: I judge you to be an old-fashioned type of girl. Well, I think that's a pretty good type to be. Hope you don't think I'm being too personal—do you?

LAURA (*hastily, out of embarrassment*): I believe I *will* take a piece of gum, if you—don't mind. (*clearing her throat*) Mr. O'Connor, have you—kept up with your singing?

JIM: Singing? Me?

LAURA: Yes, I remember what a beautiful voice you had.

JIM: When did you hear me sing?

(*Voice off stage in the pause.*)

VOICE: (*off stage*)

O blow, ye winds, heigh-ho,
A-roving I will go!
I'm off to my love
With a boxing glove—
Ten thousand miles away!

JIM: You say you've heard me sing?

LAURA: Oh, yes! Yes, very often . . . I—don't suppose you remember me—at all?

JIM (*smiling doubtfully*): You know I have an idea I've seen you before. I had that idea soon as you opened the door. It seemed almost like I was about to remember your name. But the name that I started to call you—wasn't a name! And so I stopped myself before I said it.

LAURA: Wasn't it—Blue Roses?

JIM (*springs up, grinning*): Blue Roses! My gosh, yes—Blue Roses! That's what I had on my tongue when you opened the door! Isn't it funny what tricks your memory plays? I didn't connect you with the high school somehow or other. But that's where it was; it was high school. I didn't even know you were Shakespeare's sister! Gosh, I'm sorry.

LAURA: I didn't expect you to. You—barely knew me!

JIM: But we did have a speaking acquaintance, huh?

LAURA: Yes, we—spoke to each other.

JIM: When did you recognize me?

LAURA: Oh, right away!

JIM: Soon as I came in the door?

LAURA: When I heard your name I thought it was probably you. I knew that Tom used to know you a little in high school. So when you came in the door—Well, then I was—sure.

JIM: Why didn't you *say* something, then?

LAURA (*breathlessly*): I didn't know what to say, I was—too surprised!

JIM: For goodness' sakes! You know, this sure is funny!

LAURA: Yes! Yes, isn't it, though . . .

JIM: Didn't we have a class in something together?

LAURA: Yes, we did.

JIM: What class was that?

LAURA: It was—singing—Chorus!

JIM: Aw!

LAURA: I sat across the aisle from you in the Aud.

JIM: Aw.

LAURA: Mondays, Wednesdays and Fridays.

JIM: Now I remember—you always came in late.

LAURA: Yes, it was so hard for me, getting upstairs. I had that brace on my leg—it clumped so loud!

JIM: I never heard any clumping.

LAURA (*wincing at the recollection*): To me it sounded like—thunder!

JIM: Well, well, well. I never even noticed.

LAURA: And everybody was seated before I came in. I had to walk in front of all those people. My seat was in the back row. I had to go clumping all the way up the aisle with everyone watching!

JIM: You shouldn't have been self-conscious.

LAURA: I know, but I was. It was always such a relief when the singing started.

JIM: Aw, yes. I've placed you now! I used to call you Blue Roses. How was it that I got started calling you that?

LAURA: I was out of school a little while with pleurosis. When I came back you asked me what was the matter. I said I had pleurosis—you thought I said Blue Roses. That's what you always called me after that!

JIM: I hope you didn't mind.

LAURA: Oh, no—I liked it. You see, I wasn't acquainted with many—people. . . .

JIM: As I remember you sort of stuck by yourself.

LAURA: I—I—never had much luck at—making friends.

JIM: I don't see why you wouldn't.

LAURA: Well, I—started out badly.

JIM: You mean being—

LAURA: Yes, it sort of—stood between me—

JIM: You shouldn't have let it!

LAURA: I know, but it did, and—

JIM: You were shy with people!

LAURA: I tried not to be but never could—

JIM: Overcome it?

LAURA: No, I—I never could!

JIM: I guess being shy is something you have to work out of kind of gradually.

LAURA (*sorrowfully*): Yes—I guess it—

JIM: Takes time!

LAURA: Yes—

JIM: People are not so dreadful when you know them. That's what you have to remember! And everybody has problems, not just you, but practically everybody has got some problems. You think of yourself as having the only problems, as being the only one who is disappointed. But just look around you and you will see lots of people as disappointed as you are. For instance, I hoped when I was going to high school that I would be further along at this time, six years later, than I am now—You remember that wonderful write-up I had in *The Torch?*

LAURA: Yes! (*She rises and crosses to table.*)

JIM: It said I was bound to succeed in anything I went into! (LAURA *returns with the annual.*) Holy Jeez! *The Torch!* (*He accepts it reverently. They smile across it with mutual wonder.* LAURA *crouches beside him and they begin to turn through it.* LAURA'*s shyness is dissolving in his warmth.*)

LAURA: Here you are in *Pirates of Penzance!*

JIM (*wistfully*): I sang the baritone lead in that operetta.

LAURA (*rapidly*): So—*beautifully!*

JIM (*protesting*): Aw—

LAURA: Yes, yes—beautifully—beautifully!

JIM: You heard me?

LAURA: All three times!

JIM: No!

LAURA: Yes!

JIM: All three performances?

LAURA (*looking down*): Yes.

JIM: Why?

LAURA: I—wanted to ask you to—autograph my program.

JIM: Why didn't you ask me to?

LAURA: You were always surrounded by your own friends so much that I never had a chance to.

JIM: You should have just—

LAURA: Well, I—thought you might think I was—

JIM: Thought I might think you was—what?

LAURA: Oh—

JIM (*with reflective relish*): I was beleaguered by females in those days.

LAURA: You were terribly popular!

JIM: Yeah—

LAURA: You had such a—friendly way—

JIM: I was spoiled in high school.

LAURA: Everybody—liked you!

JIM: Including you?

LAURA: I—yes, I—I did, too—(*She gently closes the book in her lap.*)

JIM: Well, well, well!—Give me that program, Laura. (*She hands it to him. He signs it with a flourish.*) There you are—better late than never!

LAURA: Oh, I—what a—surprise!

JIM: My signature isn't worth very much right now. But some day—maybe—it will increase in value! Being disappointed is one thing and being discouraged is something else. I am disappointed but I am not discouraged. I'm twenty-three years old. How old are you?

LAURA: I'll be twenty-four in June.

JIM: That's not old age!

LAURA: No, but—

JIM: You finished high school?

LAURA (*with difficulty*): I didn't go back.

JIM: You mean you dropped out?

LAURA: I made bad grades in my final examinations. (*She rises and replaces the book and the program; her voice strained:*) How is—Emily Meisenbach getting along?

JIM: Oh, that kraut-head!

LAURA: Why do you call her that?

JIM: That's what she was.

LAURA: You're not still—going with her?

JIM: I never see her.

LAURA: It said in the Personal Section that you were—engaged!

JIM: I know, but I wasn't impressed by that—propaganda!

LAURA: It wasn't—the truth?

JIM: Only in Emily's optimistic opinion!

LAURA: Oh—

(*Legend: "What have you done since high school?"*)

(JIM *lights a cigarette and leans indolently back on his elbows smiling at* LAURA *with a warmth and charm which lights her inwardly with altar candles. She remains by the table and turns in her hands a piece of glass to cover her tumult.*)

JIM (*after several reflective puffs on a cigarette*): What have you done since high school? (*She seems not to hear him.*) Huh? (LAURA *looks up.*) I said what have you done since high school, Laura?

LAURA: Nothing much.

JIM: You must have been doing something these six long years.

LAURA: Yes.

JIM: Well, then, such as what?

LAURA: I took a business course at business college—

JIM: How did that work out?

LAURA: Well, not very—well—I had to drop out, it gave me—indigestion—

(JIM *laughs gently.*)

JIM: What are you doing now?

LAURA: I don't do anything—much. Oh, please don't think I sit around doing nothing! My glass collection takes up a good deal of my time. Glass is something you have to take good care of.

JIM: What did you say—about glass?

LAURA: Collection I said—I have one—(*She clears her throat and turns away again, acutely shy.*)

JIM (*abruptly*): You know what I judge to be the trouble with you? Inferiority complex! Know what that is? That's what they call it when someone low-rates himself! I understand it because I had it, too. Although my case was not so aggravated as yours seems to be. I had it until I took up public speaking, developed my voice, and learned that I had an aptitude for science. Before that time I never thought of myself as being outstanding in any way whatsoever! Now I've never made a regular study of it, but I have a friend who says I can analyze people better than doctors that make a profession of it. I don't claim that to be necessarily true, but I can sure guess a person's psychology, Laura! (*takes out his gum*) Excuse me, Laura. I always take it out when the flavor is gone. I'll use this scrap of paper to wrap it in. I know how it is to get it stuck on a shoe. Yep—that's what I judge to be your principal trouble. A lack of confidence in yourself as a person. You don't have the proper amount of faith in yourself. I'm basing that fact on a number of your remarks and also on certain observations I've made. For instance that clumping you thought was so awful in high school. You say that you even dreaded to walk into class. You see what you did? You dropped out of school, you gave up an education because of a clump, which as far as I know was practically non-existent! A little physical defect is what you have. Hardly noticeable even! Magnified thousands of times by imagination! You know what my strong advice to you is? Think of yourself as *superior* in some way!

LAURA: In what way would I think?

JIM: Why, man alive, Laura! Just look about you a little. What do you see? A world full of common people! All of 'em born and all of 'em going to die! Which of them has one-tenth of your good points! Or mine! Or anyone else's, as far as that goes—Gosh! Everybody excels in some one thing. Some in many! (*unconsciously glances at himself in the mirror*) All you've got to do is discover in *what!* Take me, for instance. (*He adjusts his tie at the mirror.*) My interest happens to lie in electro-dynamics. I'm taking a course in radio engineering at night school, Laura, on top of a fairly responsible job at the warehouse. I'm taking that course and studying public speaking.

LAURA: Ohhhh.

JIM: Because I believe in the future of television! (*turning back to her*) I wish to be ready to go up right along with it. Therefore I'm planning to get in on the ground floor. In fact, I've already made the right connections and all that remains is for the industry itself to get under way! Full steam—(*His eyes are starry.*) *Knowledge*—Zzzzzp! *Money*—Zzzzzzp!—*Power!* That's the cycle democracy is built on! (*His attitude is convincingly dynamic.* LAURA *stares at him, even her shyness eclipsed in her absolute wonder. He suddenly grins.*) I guess you think I think a lot of myself!

LAURA: No—o-o-o, I—

JIM: Now how about you? Isn't there something you take more interest in than anything else?

LAURA: Well, I do—as I said—have my—glass collection—

(*A peal of girlish laughter from the kitchen.*)

JIM: I'm not right sure I know what you're talking about. What kind of glass is it?

LAURA: Little articles of it, they're ornaments mostly! Most of them are little animals made out of glass, the tiniest little animals in the world. Mother calls them a glass menagerie! Here's an example of one, if you'd like to see it! This one is one of the oldest. It's nearly thirteen. (*He stretches out his hand.*) (*Music: "The Glass Menagerie."*) Oh, be careful—if you breathe, it breaks!

JIM: I'd better not take it. I'm pretty clumsy with things.

LAURA: Go on, I trust you with him! (*places it in his palm*) There now—you're holding him gently! Hold him over the light, he loves the light! You see how the light shines through him?

JIM: It sure does shine!

LAURA: I shouldn't be partial, but he is my favorite one.

JIM: What kind of thing is this one supposed to be?

LAURA: Haven't you noticed the single horn on his forehead?

JIM: A unicorn, huh?

LAURA: Mmm-hmmm!

JIM: Unicorns, aren't they extinct in the modern world?

LAURA: I know!

JIM: Poor little fellow, he must feel sort of lonesome.

LAURA (*smiling*): Well, if he does he doesn't complain about it. He stays on a shelf with some horses that don't have horns and all of them seem to get along nicely together.

JIM: How do you know?

LAURA (*lightly*): I haven't heard any arguments among them!

JIM (*grinning*): No arguments, huh? Well, that's a pretty good sign! Where shall I set him?

LAURA: Put him on the table. They all like a change of scenery once in a while!

JIM (*stretching*): Well, well, well, well—Look how big my shadow is when I stretch!

LAURA: Oh, oh, yes—it stretches across the ceiling!

JIM: (*crossing to the door*): I think it's stopped raining. (*opens fire-escape door*) Where does the music come from?

LAURA: From the Paradise Dance Hall across the alley.

JIM: How about cutting the rug a little, Miss Wingfield?

AMANDA: Oh, I—

JIM: Or is your program filled up? Let me have a look at it. (*grasps imaginary card*) Why, every dance is taken! I'll just have to scratch some out. (*Waltz music: "La Golondrina"*) Ahhh, a waltz! (*He executes some sweeping turns by himself, then holds his arms toward* LAURA.)

LAURA (*breathlessly*): I—can't dance!

JIM: There you go, that inferiority stuff.

LAURA: I've never danced in my life!

JIM: Come on, try!

LAURA: Oh, but I'd step on you!

JIM: I'm not made out of glass.

LAURA: How—how—how do we start?

JIM: Just leave it to me. You hold your arms out a little.

LAURA: Like this?

JIM: A little bit higher. Right. Now don't tighten up, that's the main thing about it—relax.

LAURA (*laughing breathlessly*): It's hard not to.

JIM: Okay.

LAURA: I'm afraid you can't budge me.

JIM: What do you bet I can't? (*He swings her into motion.*)

LAURA: Goodness, yes, you can!

JIM: Let yourself go, now, Laura, just let yourself go.

LAURA: I'm—

JIM: Come on!

LAURA: Trying!

JIM: Not so stiff—Easy does it!

LAURA: I know but I'm—

JIM: Loosen th' backbone! There now, that's a lot better.

LAURA: Am I?

JIM: Lots, lots better! (*He moves her about the room in a clumsy waltz.*)

LAURA: Oh, my!

JIM: Ha-ha!

LAURA: Goodness, yes you can!

JIM: Ha-ha-ha! (*They suddenly bump into the table.* JIM *stops.*) What did we hit on?

LAURA: Table.

JIM: Did something fall off it? I think—

LAURA: Yes.

JIM: I hope that it wasn't the little glass horse with the horn!

LAURA: Yes.

JIM: Aw, aw, aw. Is it broken?

LAURA: Now it is just like all the other horses.

JIM: It's lost its—

LAURA: Horn! It doesn't matter. Maybe it's a blessing in disguise.

JIM: You'll never forgive me. I bet that that was your favorite piece of glass.

LAURA: I don't have favorites much. It's no tragedy, Freckles. Glass breaks so easily. No matter how careful you are. The traffic jars the shelves and things fall off them.

JIM: Still I'm awfully sorry that I was the cause.

LAURA (*smiling*). I'll just imagine he had an operation. The horn was removed to make him feel less—freakish! (*They both laugh.*) Now he will feel more at home with the other horses, the ones that don't have horns . . .

JIM: Ha-ha, that's very funny! (*suddenly serious:*) I'm glad to see that you have a sense of humor. You know—you're—well—very different! Surprisingly different from anyone else I know! (His *voice becomes soft and hesitant with a genuine feeling.*) Do you mind me telling you that? (LAURA *is abashed beyond speech.*) You make me feel sort of—I don't know how to put it! I'm usually pretty good at expressing things, but—This is something that I don't know how to say! (LAURA *touches her throat and clears it—turns the broken unicorn in her hands.*) (*even softer:*) Has anyone ever told you that you were pretty? (*Pause: Music*) (LAURA *looks up slowly, with wonder, and shakes her head.*) Well, you are! In a very different way from anyone else. And all the nicer because of the difference, too. (*His voice becomes low and husky.* LAURA *turns away, nearly faint with the novelty of her emotions.*) I wish that you were my sister. I'd teach you to have some confidence in yourself. The different people are not like other people, but being different is nothing to be ashamed of. Because other people are not such wonderful people. They're one hundred times one thousand. You're one times one! They walk all over the earth. You just stay here. They're common as—weeds, but—you—well, you're—*Blue Roses!*

(*Image on screen: Blue roses.*)

(*Music changes.*)

LAURA: But blue is wrong for—roses . . .

JIM: It's right for you—You're—pretty!

LAURA: In what respect am I pretty?

JIM: In all respects—believe me! Your eyes—your hair—are pretty! Your hands are pretty! (*He catches hold of her hand.*) You think I'm making this up because I'm invited to dinner and have to be nice. Oh, I could do that! I could put on an act for you, Laura, and say lots of things without being very sincere. But this time I am. I'm talking to you sincerely. I happened to notice you had this inferiority complex that keeps you from feeling comfortable with people. Somebody needs to build your confidence up and make you proud instead of shy and turning away and—blushing—Somebody ought to—Ought to—*kiss* you, Laura! (*His hand slips slowly up her arm to her shoulder.*) (*Music swells tumultuously.*) (*He suddenly turns her about and kisses her on the lips. When he releases her* LAURA *sinks on the sofa with a bright, dazed look.* JIM *backs away and fishes in his pocket for a cigarette.*) (*Legend on screen: "Souvenir"*) Stumble-john! (*He lights the cigarette, avoiding her look. There is a peal of girlish laughter from* AMANDA *in the kitchen.* LAURA *slowly raises and opens her hand. It still contains the little broken glass animal. She looks at it with a tender, bewildered expression.*) Stumble-john! I shouldn't have done that—That was way off the beam. You don't smoke, do you? (*She looks up, smiling, not hearing the question. He sits beside her a little gingerly. She looks at him speechlessly—waiting. He coughs decorously and moves a little farther aside as he considers the situation and senses her feelings, dimly, with perturbation; gently:*) Would you—care for a—mint? (*She doesn't seem to hear him but her look grows brighter even.*) Peppermint—Life Saver? My pocket's a regular drug store—wherever I go . . . (*He pops a mint in his mouth. Then gulps and decides to make a clean breast of it. He speaks slowly and gingerly.*) Laura, you know, if I had a sister like you, I'd do the same thing as Tom. I'd bring out fellows—introduce her to them. The right type of boys of a type to—appreciate her. Only—well—he made a mistake about me. Maybe I've got no call to be saying this. That may not have been the idea in having me over. But what if it was? There's nothing wrong about that. The only trouble is that in my case—I'm not in a situation to—do the right thing. I can't take down your number and say I'll phone. I can't call up next week and—ask for a date. I thought I had better explain the situation in case you misunderstood it and—hurt your feelings. . . . (*Pause. Slowly, very slowly,* LAURA'*s look changes, her eyes returning slowly from his to the ornament in her palm.*)

(AMANDA *utters another gay laugh in the kitchen.*)

LAURA (*faintly*): You—won't—call again?

JIM: No, Laura, I can't. (*He rises from the sofa.*) As I was just explaining, I've—got strings on me, Laura, I've—been going steady! I go out all the time with a girl named Betty. She's a home-girl like you, and Catholic, and Irish, and in a great many ways we—get along fine. I met her last summer on a moonlight boat trip up the river to Alton, on the *Majestic.* Well—right away from the start it was—love! (*Legend: Love!*) (LAURA *sways slightly forward and grips the arm of the sofa. He fails to notice, now enrapt in his own comfortable being.*) Being in love has made a new man of me! (*Leaning stiffly forward, clutching the arm of the sofa,* LAURA *struggles visibly with her storm. But* JIM *is oblivious; she is a long way off.*) The power of love is really pretty tremendous! Love is something that—changes the whole world, Laura! (*The storm abates a little and* LAURA *leans back. He notices her again.*) It happened that Betty's aunt took sick, she got a wire and had to go to Centralia. So Tom—when he asked me to dinner—I naturally just accepted the invitation, not knowing that you—that he—that I—(*He stops awkwardly.*) Huh—I'm a stumble-john! (*He flops back on the sofa. The holy candles in the altar of* LAURA'*s face have been snuffed out! There is a look of almost infinite desolation.* JIM *glances at her uneasily.*) I wish that you would— say something. (*She bites her lip which was trembling and then bravely smiles. She opens her hand again on the broken glass ornament. Then she gently takes his hand and raises it level with her own. She carefully places the unicorn in the palm of his hand, then pushes his fingers closed upon it.*) What are you—doing that for? You want me to have him?—Laura? (*She nods.*) What for?

LAURA: A—souvenir . . .

(*She rises unsteadily and crouches beside the victrola to wind it up.*)

(*Legend on screen: "Things have a way of turning out so badly"*)

(*Or image: "Gentleman caller waving goodbye!—gaily"*)

(*At this moment* AMANDA *rushes brightly back in the front room. She bears a pitcher of fruit punch in an old-fashioned cut-glass pitcher and a plate of macaroons. The plate has a gold border and poppies painted on it.*)

AMANDA: Well, well, well! Isn't the air delightful after the shower? I've made you children a little liquid refreshment. (*turns gaily to the gentleman caller*) Jim, do you know that song about lemonade?

"Lemonade, lemonade
Made in the shade and stirred with a spade—
Good enough for any old maid!"

JIM (*uneasily*): Ha-ha! No—I never heard it.

AMANDA: Why, Laura! You look so serious!

JIM: We were having a serious conversation.

AMANDA: Good! Now you're better acquainted!

JIM (*uncertainly*): Ha-ha! Yes.

AMANDA: You modern young people are much more serious-minded than my generation. I was so gay as a girl!

JIM: You haven't changed, Mrs. Wingfield.

AMANDA: Tonight I'm rejuvenated! The gaiety of the occasion, Mr. O'Connor! (*She tosses her head with a peal of laughter, spills lemonade.*) Oooo! I'm baptizing myself!

JIM: Here—let me—

AMANDA (*setting the pitcher down*): There now. I discovered we had some maraschino cherries. I dumped them in, juice and all!

JIM: You shouldn't have gone to that trouble, Mrs. Wingfield.

AMANDA: Trouble, trouble? Why it was loads of fun! Didn't you hear me cutting up in the kitchen? I bet your ears were burning! I told Tom how outdone with him I was for keeping you to himself so long a time! He should have brought you over much, much sooner! Well, now that you've found your way, I want you to be a very frequent caller! Not just occasional but all the time. Oh, we're going to have a lot of gay times together! I see them coming! Mmm, just breathe that air! So fresh, and the moon's so pretty! I'll skip back out—I know where my place is when young folks are having a—serious conversation!

JIM: Oh, don't go out, Mrs. Wingfield. The fact of the matter is I've got to be going.

AMANDA: Going, now? You're joking! Why, it's only the shank of the evening, Mr. O'Connor!

JIM: Well, you know how it is.

AMANDA: You mean you're a young workingman and have to keep working men's hours. We'll let you off early tonight. But only on the condition that next time you stay later. What's the best night for you? Isn't Saturday night the best night for you workingmen?

JIM: I have a couple of time-clocks to punch, Mrs. Wingfield. One at morning, another one at night!

AMANDA: My, but you *are* ambitious! You work at night, too?

JIM: No, Ma'am, not work but—Betty! (*He crosses deliberately to pick up his hat. The band at the Paradise Dance Hall goes into a tender waltz.*)

AMANDA: Betty? Betty? Who's—Betty! (*There is an ominous cracking sound in the sky.*)

JIM: Oh, just a girl. The girl I go steady with! (*He smiles charmingly. The sky falls.*)

(*Legend: "The sky falls"*)

AMANDA (*a long-drawn exhalation*): Ohhhh . . . Is it a serious romance, Mr. O'Connor?

JIM: We're going to be married the second Sunday in June.

AMANDA: Ohhhh—how nice! Tom didn't mention that you were engaged to be married.

JIM: The cat's not out of the bag at the warehouse yet. You know how they are. They call you Romeo and stuff like that. (*He stops at the oval mirror to put on his hat. He carefully shapes the brim and the crown to give a discreetly dashing effect.*) It's been a wonderful evening, Mrs. Wingfield. I guess this is what they mean by Southern hospitality.

AMANDA: It really wasn't anything at all.

JIM: I hope it don't seem like I'm rushing off. But I promised Betty I'd pick her up at the Wabash depot, an' by the time I get my jalopy down there her train'll be in. Some women are pretty upset if you keep 'em waiting.

AMANDA: Yes, I know—The tyranny of women! (*extends her hand*) Goodbye, Mr. O'Connor. I wish you luck—and happiness—and success! All three of them, and so does Laura!—Don't you, Laura?

LAURA: Yes!

JIM (*taking her hand*): Good-bye, Laura. I'm certainly going to treasure that souvenir. And don't you forget the good advice I gave you. (*raises his voice to a cheery shout*) So long, Shakespeare! Thanks again, ladies—Good night!

(*He grins and ducks jauntily out.*

Still bravely grimacing, AMANDA *closes the door on the gentleman caller. Then she turns back to the room with a puzzled expression. She and* LAURA *don't dare to face each other.* LAURA *crouches beside the victrola to wind it.*)

AMANDA (*faintly*): Things have a way of turning out so badly. I don't believe that I would play the victrola. Well, well—well—Our gentleman caller was engaged to be married! Tom!

TOM (*from back*): Yes, Mother?

AMANDA: Come in here a minute. I want to tell you something awfully funny.

TOM (*enters with a macaroon and a glass of the lemonade*): Has the gentleman caller gotten away already?

AMANDA: The gentleman caller has made an early departure. What a wonderful joke you played on us!

TOM: How do you mean?

AMANDA: You didn't mention that he was engaged to be married.

TOM: Jim? Engaged?

AMANDA: That's what he just informed us.

TOM: I'll be jiggered! I didn't know about that.

AMANDA: That seems very peculiar.

TOM: What's peculiar about it?

AMANDA: Didn't you call him your best friend down at the warehouse?

TOM: He is, but how did I know?

AMANDA: It seems extremely peculiar that you wouldn't know your best friend was going to be married!

TOM: The warehouse is where I work, not where I know things about people!

AMANDA: You don't know things anywhere! You live in a dream; you manufacture illusions! (*He crosses to door.*) Where are you going?

TOM: I'm going to the movies.

AMANDA: That's right, now that you've had us make such fools of ourselves. The effort, the preparations, all the expense! The new floor lamp, the rug, the clothes for Laura! All for what? To entertain some other girl's fiancé! Go to the movies, go! Don't think about us, a mother deserted, an unmarried sister who's crippled and has no job! Don't let anything interfere with your selfish pleasure! Just go, go, go—to the movies!

TOM: All right, I will! The more you shout about my selfishness to me the quicker I'll go, and I won't go to the movies!

AMANDA: Go, then! Then go to the moon—you selfish dreamer!

(TOM *smashes his glass on the floor. He plunges out on the fire-escape, slamming the door,* LAURA *screams—cut off by the door.*

Dance-hall music up. TOM *goes to the rail and grips it desperately, lifting his face in the chill white moonlight penetrating the narrow abyss of the alley.*)

(*Legend on screen: "And so good-bye . . ."*)

(TOM'S *closing speech is timed with the interior pantomime. The interior scene is played as though viewed through soundproof glass.* AMANDA *appears to be making a comforting speech to* LAURA *who is huddled upon the sofa. Now that we cannot hear the mother's speech, her silliness is gone and she has dignity and tragic beauty.* LAURA'*s dark hair hides her face until at the end of the speech she lifts it to smile at her mother.* AMANDA'*s gestures are slow and graceful, almost dancelike, as she comforts the daughter. At the end of her speech she glances a moment at the father's picture—then withdraws through the portieres. At close of* TOM'*s speech,* LAURA *blows out the candles, ending the play.*)

TOM: I didn't go to the moon, I went much further—for time is the longest distance between two places—Not long after that I was fired for writing a poem on the lid of a shoe-box. I left Saint Louis. I descended the steps of this fire-escape for a last time and followed, from then on, in my father's footsteps, attempting to find in motion what was lost in space—I traveled around a great deal. The cities swept about me like dead leaves, leaves that were brightly colored but torn away from the branches. I would have stopped, but I was pursued by something. It always came upon me unawares, taking me altogether by surprise. Perhaps it was a familiar bit of music. Perhaps it was only a piece of transparent glass—Perhaps I am walking along a street at night, in some strange city, before I have found companions. I pass the lighted window of a shop where perfume is sold. The window is filled with pieces of colored glass, tiny transparent bottles in delicate colors, like bits of a shattered rainbow. Then all at once my sister touches my shoulder. I turn around and look into her eyes . . . Oh, Laura, Laura, I tried to leave you behind me, but I am more faithful than I intended to be! I reach for a cigarette, I cross the street, I run into the movies or a bar, I buy a drink, I speak to the nearest stranger—anything that can blow your candles out! (LAURA *bends over the candles.*)—for nowadays the world is lit by lightning! Blow out your candles, Laura—and so good-bye. . . .

(*She blows the candles out.*)

(*The scene dissolves.*)

Death of a Salesman ARTHUR MILLER

Arthur Miller's (1915–2005) *Death of a Salesman* is a deceptively simple play. Its plot revolves around a day in the life of Willy Loman, a hard-working 63-year-old traveling salesman, whose ideas about professional success jar with the realities of his modest accomplishments. Audiences soon realize, however, that the play is enormously complex, structurally and philosophically.

Subtitled "Certain private conversations in two acts and a requiem," the play features a narrative that unwinds largely through Willy Loman's daydreams, private conversations revealing past hopes and betrayals, and dismal present circumstances.

Death of a Salesman, which premiered in 1949 in New York City, is for many the quintessential American play. It mirrors a sense of community and citizenship that most theatergoers—American or not—recognize as "American." Within a year of its premiere, this drama was playing in every major city in the United States. As early as 1951, *Death of a Salesman* was viewed by appreciative audiences all over the world. With the passing of Miller, also the author of *The Crucible* (1953), *Broken Glass* (1994), and many other plays, the American stage lost one of its most daring and socially committed voices, a playwright who, along with Eugene O'Neill and Tennessee Williams, first brought American drama to worldwide attention and acclaim.

CHARACTERS

Willy Loman
Linda
Biff
Happy
Bernard
The Woman
Charley
Uncle Ben
Howard Wagner
Jenny
Stanley
Miss Forsythe
Letta

The action takes place in Willy Loman*'s house and yard and in various places he visits in the New York and Boston of today.*

Throughout the play, in the stage directions, left and right mean stage left and stage right.

Act I

A melody is heard, played upon a flute. It is small and fine, telling of grass and trees and the horizon. The curtain rises.

Before us is the Salesman's house. We are aware of towering, angular shapes behind it, surrounding it on all sides. Only the blue light of the sky falls upon the house and forestage; the surrounding area shows an angry glow of orange. As more light appears, we see a solid vault of apartment houses around the small, fragile-seeming home. An air of the dream clings to the place, a dream rising out of reality. The kitchen at center seems actual enough, for there is a kitchen table with three chairs, and a refrigerator. But no other fixtures are seen. At the back of the kitchen there is a draped entrance, which leads to the living-room. To the right of the kitchen, on a level raised two feet, is a bedroom furnished only with a brass bedstead and a straight chair. On a shelf over the bed a silver athletic trophy stands. A window opens onto the apartment house at the side.

Behind the kitchen, on a level raised six and a half feet, is the boys' bedroom, at present barely visible. Two beds are dimly seen, and at the back of the room a dormer window. (This bedroom is above the unseen living-room.) At the left a stairway curves up to it from the kitchen.

The entire setting is wholly or, in some places, partially transparent. The roofline of the house is one-dimensional; under and over it we see the apartment buildings. Before the house lies an apron, curving beyond the forestage into the orchestra. This forward area serves as the back yard as well as the locale of all Willy's imaginings and of his city scenes. Whenever the action is in the present the actors observe the imaginary wall-lines, entering the house only through its door at the left. But in the scenes of the past these boundaries are broken, and characters enter or leave a room by stepping "through" a wall onto the forestage.

From the right, WILLY LOMAN, *the Salesman, enters, carrying two large sample cases. The flute plays on. He hears but is not aware of it. He is past sixty years of age, dressed quietly. Even as he crosses the stage to the doorway of the house, his exhaustion is apparent. He unlocks the door, comes into the kitchen, and thankfully lets his burden down, feeling the soreness of his palms. A word-sigh escapes his lips—it might be "Oh, boy, oh, boy." He closes the door, then carries his cases out into the living-room, through the draped kitchen doorway.*

LINDA, *his wife, has stirred in her bed at the right. She gets out and puts on a robe, listening. Most often jovial, she has developed an iron repression of her exceptions to* WILLY'S *behavior—she more than loves him, she admires him, as though his mercurial nature, his temper, his massive dreams and little cruelties, served her only as sharp reminders of the turbulent longings within him, longings which she shares but lacks the temperament to utter and follow to their end.*

LINDA (*hearing* WILLY *outside the bedroom, calls with some trepidation*): Willy!

WILLY: It's all right. I came back.

LINDA: Why? What happened? (*Slight pause.*) Did something happen, Willy?

WILLY: No, nothing happened.

LINDA: You didn't smash the car, did you?

WILLY (*with casual irritation*): I said nothing happened. Didn't you hear me?

LINDA: Don't you feel well?

WILLY: I'm tired to the death. (*The flute has faded away. He sits on the bed beside her, a little numb.*) I couldn't make it. I just couldn't make it, Linda.

LINDA (*very carefully, delicately*): Where were you all day? You look terrible.

WILLY: I got as far as a little above Yonkers. I stopped for a cup of coffee. Maybe it was the coffee.

LINDA: What?

WILLY (*after a pause*): I suddenly couldn't drive any more. The car kept going off onto the shoulder, y'know?

LINDA (*helpfully*): Oh. Maybe it was the steering again. I don't think Angelo knows the Studebaker.

WILLY: No, it's me, it's me. Suddenly I realize I'm goin' sixty miles an hour and I don't remember the last five minutes. I'm—I can't seem to—keep my mind to it.

LINDA: Maybe it's your glasses. You never went for your new glasses.

WILLY: No, I see everything. I came back ten miles an hour. It took me nearly four hours from Yonkers.

LINDA (*resigned*): Well, you'll just have to take a rest, Willy, you can't continue this way.

WILLY: I just got back from Florida.

LINDA: But you didn't rest your mind. Your mind is overactive, and the mind is what counts, dear.

WILLY: I'll start out in the morning. Maybe I'll feel better in the morning. (*She is taking off his shoes.*) These goddam arch supports are killing me.

LINDA: Take an aspirin. Should I get you an aspirin? It'll soothe you.

WILLY (*with wonder*): I was driving along, you understand? And I was fine. I was even observing the scenery. You can imagine, me looking at scenery, on the road every week of my life. But it's so beautiful up there, Linda, the trees are so thick, and the sun is warm. I opened the windshield and just let the warm air bathe over me. And then all of a sudden I'm goin' off the road! I'm tellin' ya, I absolutely forgot I was driving. If I'd've gone the other way over the white line I might've killed somebody. So I went on again—and five minutes later I'm dreamin' again, and I nearly— (*He presses two fingers against his eyes.*) I have such thoughts, I have such strange thoughts.

LINDA: Willy, dear. Talk to them again. There's no reason why you can't work in New York.

WILLY: They don't need me in New York. I'm the New England man. I'm vital in New England.

LINDA: But you're sixty years old. They can't expect you to keep traveling every week.

WILLY: I'll have to send a wire to Portland. I'm supposed to see Brown and Morrison tomorrow morning at ten o'clock to show the line. Goddammit, I could sell them! (*He starts putting on his jacket.*)

LINDA (*taking the jacket from him*): Why don't you go down to the place tomorrow and tell Howard you've simply got to work in New York? You're too accommodating, dear.

WILLY: If old man Wagner was alive I'd a been in charge of New York now! That man was a prince, he was a masterful man. But that boy of his, that Howard, he don't appreciate. When I went north the first time, the Wagner Company didn't know where New England was!

LINDA: Why don't you tell those things to Howard, dear?

WILLY (*encouraged*): I will, I definitely will. Is there any cheese?

LINDA: I'll make you a sandwich.

WILLY: No, go to sleep. I'll take some milk. I'll be up right away. The boys in?

LINDA: They're sleeping. Happy took Biff on a date tonight.

WILLY (*interested*): That so?

LINDA: It was so nice to see them shaving together, one behind the other, in the bathroom. And going out together. You notice? The whole house smells of shaving lotion.

WILLY: Figure it out. Work a lifetime to pay off a house. You finally own it, and there's nobody to live in it.

LINDA: Well, dear, life is a casting off. It's always that way.

WILLY: No, no, some people—some people accomplish something. Did Biff say anything after I went this morning?

LINDA: You shouldn't have criticized him, Willy, especially after he just got off the train. You mustn't lose your temper with him.

WILLY: When the hell did I lose my temper? I simply asked him if he was making any money. Is that a criticism?

LINDA: But, dear, how could he make any money?

WILLY (*worried and angered*): There's such an undercurrent in him. He became a moody man. Did he apologize when I left this morning?

LINDA: He was crestfallen, Willy. You know how he admires you. I think if he finds himself, then you'll both be happier and not fight any more.

WILLY: How can he find himself on a farm? Is that a life? A farmhand? In the beginning, when he was young, I thought, well, a young man, it's good for him to tramp around, take a lot of different jobs. But it's more than ten years now and he has yet to make thirty-five dollars a week!

LINDA: He's finding himself, Willy.

WILLY: Not finding yourself at the age of thirty-four is a disgrace!

LINDA: Shh!

WILLY: The trouble is he's lazy, goddammit!

LINDA: Willy, please!

WILLY: Biff is a lazy bum!

LINDA: They're sleeping. Get something to eat. Go on down.

WILLY: Why did he come home? I would like to know what brought him home.

LINDA: I don't know. I think he's still lost, Willy. I think he's very lost.

WILLY: Biff Loman is lost. In the greatest country in the world a young man with such—personal attractiveness, gets lost. And such a hard worker. There's one thing about Biff—he's not lazy.

LINDA: Never.

WILLY (*with pity and resolve*): I'll see him in the morning; I'll have a nice talk with him. I'll get him a job selling. He could be big in no time. My God! Remember how they used to follow him around in high school? When he smiled at one of them their faces lit up. When he walked down the street . . . (*He loses himself in reminiscences.*)

LINDA (*trying to bring him out of it*): Willy, dear, I got a new kind of American-type cheese today. It's whipped.

WILLY: Why do you get American when I like Swiss?

LINDA: I just thought you'd like a change—

WILLY: I don't want a change! I want Swiss cheese. Why am I always being contradicted?

LINDA (*with a covering laugh*): I thought it would be a surprise.

WILLY: Why don't you open a window in here, for God's sake?

LINDA (*with infinite patience*): They're all open, dear.

WILLY: The way they boxed us in here. Bricks and windows, windows and bricks.

LINDA: We should've bought the land next door.

WILLY: The street is lined with cars. There's not a breath of fresh air in the neighborhood. The grass don't grow any more, you can't raise a carrot in the back yard. They should've had a law against apartment houses. Remember those two beautiful elm trees out there? When I and Biff hung the swing between them?

LINDA: Yeah, like being a million miles from the city.

WILLY: They should've arrested the builder for cutting those down. They massacred the neighborhood. (*Lost*): More and more I think of those days, Linda. This time of year it was lilac and wisteria. And then the peonies would come out, and the daffodils. What fragrance in this room!

LINDA: Well, after all, people had to move somewhere.

WILLY: No, there's more people now.

LINDA: I don't think there's more people. I think—

WILLY: There'*s* more people! That's what's ruining this country! Population is getting out of control. The competition is maddening! Smell the stink from that apartment house! And another one on the other side . . . How can they whip cheese?

On WILLY'*s last line,* BIFF *and* HAPPY *raise themselves up in their beds, listening.*

LINDA: Go down, try it. And be quiet.

WILLY (*turning to* LINDA, *guiltily*): You're not worried about me, are you, sweetheart?

BIFF: What's the matter?

HAPPY: Listen!

LINDA: You've got too much on the ball to worry about.

WILLY: You're my foundation and my support, Linda.

LINDA: Just try to relax, dear. You make mountains out of molehills.

WILLY: I won't fight with him any more. If he wants to go back to Texas, let him go.

LINDA: He'll find his way.

WILLY: Sure. Certain men just don't get started till later in life. Like Thomas Edison, I think. Or B. F. Goodrich. One of them was deaf. (*He starts for the bedroom doorway.*) I'll put my money on Biff.

LINDA: And Willy—if it's warm Sunday we'll drive in the country. And we'll open the windshield, and take lunch.

WILLY: No, the windshields don't open on the new cars.

LINDA: But you opened it today.

WILLY: Me? I didn't. (*He stops.*) Now isn't that peculiar! Isn't that a remarkable— (*He breaks off in amazement and fright as the flute is beard distantly.*)

LINDA: What, darling?

WILLY: That is the most remarkable thing.

LINDA: What, dear?

WILLY: I was thinking of the Chevvy. (*Slight pause.*) Nineteen twenty-eight . . . when I had that red Chevvy—(*Breaks off.*) That funny? I coulda sworn I was driving that Chevvy today.

LINDA: Well, that's nothing. Something must've reminded you.

WILLY: Remarkable. Ts. Remember those days? The way Biff used to simonize that car? The dealer refused to believe there was eighty thousand miles on it. (*He shakes his head.*) Heh! (*To* LINDA): Close your eyes, I'll be right up. (*He walks out of the bedroom.*)

HAPPY (*to* BIFF): Jesus, maybe he smashed up the car again!

LINDA (*calling after* WILLY): Be careful on the stairs, dear! The cheese is on the middle shelf! (*She turns, goes over to the bed, takes his jacket, and goes out of the bedroom.*)

Light has risen on the boys' room. Unseen, WILLY *is heard talking to himself, "Eighty thousand miles," and a little laugh.* BIFF *gets out of bed, comes downstage a bit, and stands attentively.* BIFF *is two years older than his brother* HAPPY, *well built, but in these days bears a worn air and seems less self-assured. He has succeeded less, and his dreams are stronger and less acceptable than* HAPPY'*s.* HAPPY *is tall, powerfully made. Sexuality is like a visible color on him, or a scent that many women have discovered. He, like his brother, is lost, but in a different way, for he has never allowed himself to turn his face toward defeat and is thus more confused and hard-skinned, although seemingly more content.*

HAPPY (*getting out of bed*): He's going to get his license taken away if he keeps that up. I'm getting nervous about him, y'know, Biff?

BIFF: His eyes are going.

HAPPY: No, I've driven with him. He sees all right. He just doesn't keep his mind on it. I drove into the city with him last week. He stops at a green light and then it turns red and he goes. (*He laughs.*)

BIFF: Maybe he's color-blind.

HAPPY: Pop? Why he's got the finest eye for color in the business. You know that.

BIFF (*sitting down on his bed*): I'm going to sleep.

HAPPY: You're not still sour on Dad, are you, Biff?

BIFF: He's all right, I guess.

WILLY (*underneath them, in the living-room*): Yes, sir, eighty thousand miles—eighty-two thousand!

BIFF: You smoking?

HAPPY (*holding out a pack of cigarettes*): Want one?

BIFF (*taking a cigarette*): I can never sleep when I smell it.

WILLY: What a simonizing job, heh!

HAPPY (*with deep sentiment*): Funny, Biff, y'know? Us sleeping in here again? The old beds. (*He pats his bed affectionately.*) All the talk that went across those two beds, huh? Our whole lives.

BIFF: Yeah. Lotta dreams and plans.

HAPPY (*with a deep and masculine laugh*): About five hundred women would like to know what was said in this room.

They share a soft laugh.

BIFF: Remember that big Betsy something—what the hell was her name—over on Bushwick Avenue?

HAPPY (*combing his hair*): With the collie dog!

BIFF: That's the one. I got you in there, remember?

HAPPY: Yeah, that was my first time—I think. Boy, there was a pig! (*They laugh, almost crudely.*) You taught me everything I know about women. Don't forget that.

BIFF: I bet you forgot how bashful you used to be. Especially with girls.

HAPPY: Oh, I still am, Biff.

BIFF: Oh, go on.

HAPPY: I just control it, that's all. I think I got less bashful and you got more so. What happened, Biff? Where's the old humor, the old confidence? (*He shakes* BIFF'*s knee.* BIFF *gets up and moves restlessly about the room.*) What's the matter?

BIFF: Why does Dad mock me all the time?

HAPPY: He's not mocking you, he—

BIFF: Everything I say there's a twist of mockery on his face. I can't get near him.

HAPPY: He just wants you to make good, that's all. I wanted to talk to you about Dad for a long time, Biff. Something's—happening to him. He—talks to himself.

BIFF: I noticed that this morning. But he always mumbled.

HAPPY: But not so noticeable. It got so embarrassing I sent him to Florida. And you know something? Most of the time he's talking to you.

BIFF: What's he say about me?

HAPPY: I can't make it out.

BIFF: What's he say about me?

HAPPY: I think the fact that you're not settled, that you're still kind of up in the air . . .

BIFF: There's one or two other things depressing him, Happy.

HAPPY: What do you mean?

BIFF: Never mind. Just don't lay it all to me.

HAPPY: But I think if you just got started—I mean—is there any future for you out there?

BIFF: I tell ya, Hap, I don't know what the future is. I don't know—what I'm supposed to want.

HAPPY: What do you mean?

BIFF: Well, I spent six or seven years after high school trying to work myself up. Shipping clerk, salesman, business of one kind or another. And it's a measly manner of existence. To get on that subway on the hot mornings in summer. To devote your whole life to keeping stock, or making phone calls, or selling or buying. To suffer fifty weeks of the year for the sake of a two-week vacation, when all you really desire is to be outdoors, with your shirt off. And always to have to get ahead of the next fella. And still—that's how you build a future.

HAPPY: Well, you really enjoy it on a farm? Are you content out there?

BIFF (*with rising agitation*): Hap, I've had twenty or thirty different kinds of jobs since I left home before the war, and it always turns out the same. I just realized it lately. In Nebraska when I herded cattle, and the Dakotas, and Arizona, and now in Texas. It's why I came home now, I guess, because I realized it. This farm I work on, it's spring there now, see? And they've got about fifteen new colts. There's nothing more inspiring or—beautiful than the sight of a mare and a new colt. And it's cool there now, see? Texas is cool now, and it's spring. And whenever spring comes to where I am, I suddenly get the feeling, my God, I'm not gettin' anywhere! What the hell am I doing, playing around with horses twenty-eight dollars a week! I'm thirty-four years old, I oughta be makin' my future. That's when I come running home. And now, I get here, and I don't know what to do with myself. (*After a pause*): I've always made a point of not wasting my life, and everytime I come back here I know that all I've done is to waste my life.

HAPPY: You're a poet, you know that, Biff? You're a—you're an idealist!

BIFF: No, I'm mixed up very bad. Maybe I oughta get married. Maybe I oughta get stuck into something. Maybe that's my trouble. I'm like a boy. I'm not married, I'm not in business, I just—I'm like a boy. Are you content, Hap? You're a success, aren't you? Are you content?

HAPPY: Hell, no!

BIFF: Why? You're making money, aren't you?

HAPPY (*moving about with energy, expressiveness*): All I can do now is wait for the merchandise manager to die. And suppose I get to be merchandise manager? He's a good friend of mine, and he just built a terrific estate on Long Island. And he lived there about two months and sold it, and now he's building another one. He can't enjoy it once it's finished. And I know that's just what I would do. I don't know what the hell I'm workin' for. Sometimes I sit in my apartment—all alone. And I think of the rent I'm paying. And it's crazy. But then, it's what I always wanted. My own apartment, a car, and plenty of women. And still, goddammit, I'm lonely.

BIFF (*with enthusiasm*): Listen, why don't you come out West with me?

HAPPY: You and I, heh?

BIFF: Sure, maybe we could buy a ranch. Raise cattle, use our muscles. Men built like we are should be working out in the open.

HAPPY (*avidly*): The Loman Brothers, heh?

BIFF (*with vast affection*): Sure, we'd be known all over the counties!

HAPPY (*enthralled*): That's what I dream about, Biff. Sometimes I want to just rip my clothes off in the middle of the store and outbox that goddam merchandise manager. I mean I can outbox, outrun, and outlift anybody in that store, and I have to take orders from those common, petty sons-of-bitches till I can't stand it any more.

BIFF: I'm tellin' you, kid, if you were with me I'd be happy out there.

HAPPY (*enthused*): See, Biff, everybody around me is so false that I'm constantly lowering my ideals . . .

BIFF: Baby, together we'd stand up for one another, we'd have someone to trust.

HAPPY: If I were around you—

BIFF: Hap, the trouble is we weren't brought up to grub for money. I don't know how to do it.

HAPPY: Neither can I!

BIFF: Then let's go!

HAPPY: The only thing is—what can you make out there?

BIFF: But look at your friend. Builds an estate and then hasn't the peace of mind to live in it.

HAPPY: Yeah, but when he walks into the store the waves part in front of him. That's fifty-two thousand dollars a year coming through the revolving door, and I got more in my pinky finger than he's got in his head.

BIFF: Yeah, but you just said—

HAPPY: I gotta show some of those pompous, self-important executives over there that Hap Loman can make the grade. I want to walk into the store the way he walks in. Then I'll go with you, Biff. We'll be together yet, I swear. But take those two we had tonight. Now weren't they gorgeous creatures?

BIFF: Yeah, yeah, most gorgeous I've had in years.

HAPPY: I get that any time I want, Biff. Whenever I feel disgusted. The only trouble is, it gets like bowling or something. I just keep knockin' them over and it doesn't mean anything. You still run around a lot?

BIFF: Naa. I'd like to find a girl—steady, somebody with substance.

HAPPY: That's what I long for.

BIFF: Go on! You'd never come home.

HAPPY: I would! Somebody with character, with resistance! Like Mom, y'know? You're gonna call me a bastard when I tell you this. That girl Charlotte I was with tonight is engaged to be married in five weeks. (*He tries on his new hat.*)

BIFF: No kiddin'!

HAPPY: Sure, the guy's in line for the vice-presidency of the store. I don't know what gets into me, maybe I just have an overdeveloped sense of competition or something, but I went and ruined her, and furthermore I can't get rid of her. And he's the third executive I've done that to. Isn't that a crummy characteristic? And to top it all, I go to their weddings! (*Indignantly, but laughing*): Like I'm not supposed to take bribes. Manufacturers offer me a hundred-dollar bill now and then to throw an order their way, You know how honest I am, but it's like this girl, see. I hate myself for it. Because I don't want the girl, and, still I take it and—I love it!

BIFF: Let's go to sleep.

HAPPY: I guess we didn't settle anything, heh?

BIFF: I just got one idea that I think I'm going to try.

HAPPY: What's that?

BIFF: Remember Bill Oliver?

HAPPY: Sure, Oliver is very big now. You want to work for him again?

BIFF: No, but when I quit he said something to me. He put his arm on my shoulder, and he said, "Biff, if you ever need anything, come to me."

HAPPY: I remember that. That sounds good.

BIFF: I think I'll go to see him. If I could get ten thousand or even seven or eight thousand dollars I could buy a beautiful ranch.

HAPPY: I bet he'd back you. 'Cause he thought highly of you, Biff. I mean, they all do. You're well liked, Biff. That's why I say to come back here, and we both have the apartment. And I'm tellin' you, Biff, any babe you want . . .

BIFF: No, with a ranch I could do the work I like and still be something. I just wonder though. I wonder if Oliver still thinks I stole that carton of basketballs.

HAPPY: Oh, he probably forgot that long ago. It's almost ten years. You're too sensitive. Anyway, he didn't really fire you.

BIFF: Well, I think he was going to. I think that's why I quit. I was never sure whether he knew or not. I know he thought the world of me, though. I was the only one he'd let lock up the place.

WILLY (*below*): You gonna wash the engine, Biff?

HAPPY: Shh!

BIFF *looks at* HAPPY, *who is gazing down, listening.* WILLY *is mumbling in the parlor.*

HAPPY: You hear that?

They listen. WILLY *laughs warmly.*

BIFF (*growing angry*): Doesn't he know Mom can hear that?

WILLY: Don't get your sweater dirty, Biff!

A look of pain crosses BIFF'*s face.*

HAPPY: Isn't that terrible? Don't leave again, will you? You'll find a job here. You gotta stick around. I don't know what to do about him, it's getting embarrassing.

WILLY: What a simonizing job!

BIFF: Mom's hearing that!

WILLY: No kiddin', Biff, you got a date? Wonderful!

HAPPY: Go on to sleep. But talk to him in the morning, will you?

BIFF (*reluctantly getting into bed*): With her in the house. Brother!

HAPPY (*getting into bed*): I wish you'd have a good talk with him.

The light on their room begins to fade.

BIFF (*to himself in bed*): That selfish, stupid . . .
HAPPY: Sh . . . Sleep, Biff.

Their light is out. Well before they have finished speaking, WILLY'*s form is dimly seen below in the darkened kitchen. He opens the refrigerator, searches in there, and takes out a bottle of milk. The apartment houses are fading out, and the entire house and surroundings become covered with leaves. Music insinuates itself as the leaves appear.*

WILLY: Just wanna be careful with those girls, Biff, that's all. Don't make any promises. No promises of any kind. Because a girl, y'know, they always believe what you tell 'em, and you're very young, Biff, you're too young to be talking seriously to girls.

Light rises on the kitchen. WILLY, *talking, shuts the refrigerator door and comes downstage to the kitchen table. He pours milk into a glass. He is totally immersed in himself, smiling faintly.*

WILLY: Too young entirely, Biff. You want to watch your schooling first. Then when you're all set, there'll be plenty of girls for a boy like you. (*He smiles broadly at a kitchen chair.*) That so? The girls pay for you? (*He laughs.*) Boy, you must really be makin' a hit.

WILLY *is gradually addressing—physically—a point offstage, speaking through the wall of the kitchen, and his voice has been rising in volume to that of a normal conversation.*

WILLY: I been wondering why you polish the car so careful. Ha! Don't leave the hubcaps, boys. Get the chamois to the hubcaps. Happy, use newspaper on the windows, it's the easiest thing. Show him how to do it, Biff! You see, Happy? Pad it up, use it like a pad. That's it, that's it, good work. You're doin' all right, Hap. (*He pauses, then nods in approbation for a few seconds, then looks upward.*) Biff, first thing we gotta do when we get time is clip that big branch over the house. Afraid it's gonna fall in a storm and hit the roof. Tell you what. We get a rope and sling her around, and then we climb up there with a couple of saws and take her down. Soon as you finish the car, boys, I wanna see ya. I got a surprise for you, boys.
BIFF (*offstage*): Whatta ya got, Dad?
WILLY: No, you finish first. Never leave a job till you're finished—remember that. (*Looking toward the "big trees"*): Biff, up in Albany

I saw a beautiful hammock. I think I'll buy it next trip, and we'll hang it right between those two elms. Wouldn't that be something? Just swingin' there under those branches. Boy, that would be . . .

Young BIFF *and* Young HAPPY *appear from the direction* WILLY *was addressing.* HAPPY *carries rags and a pail of water.* BIFF, *wearing a sweater with a block "S," carries a football.*

BIFF (*pointing in the direction of the car offstage*): How's that, Pop, professional?

WILLY: Terrific. Terrific job, boys. Good work, Biff.

HAPPY: Where's the surprise, Pop?

WILLY: In the back seat of the car.

HAPPY: Boy! (*He runs off.*)

BIFF: What is it, Dad? Tell me, what'd you buy?

WILLY (*laughing, cuffs him*): Never mind, something I want you to have.

BIFF (*turns and starts off*): What is it, Hap?

HAPPY (*offstage*): It's a punching bag!

BIFF: Oh, Pop!

WILLY: It's got Gene Tunney's signature on it!

HAPPY *runs onstage with a punching bag.*

BIFF: Gee, how'd you know we wanted a punching bag?

WILLY: Well, it's the finest thing for the timing.

HAPPY (*lies down on his back and pedals with his feet*): I'm losing weight, you notice, Pop?

WILLY (*to* HAPPY): Jumping rope is good too.

BIFF: Did you see the new football I got?

WILLY (*examining the ball*): Where'd you get a new ball?

BIFF: The coach told me to practice my passing.

WILLY: That so? And he gave you the ball, heh?

BIFF: Well, I borrowed it from the locker room. (*He laughs confidentially.*)

WILLY (*laughing with him at the theft*): I want you to return that.

HAPPY: I told you he wouldn't like it!

BIFF (*angrily*): Well, I'm bringing it back!

WILLY (*stopping the incipient argument, to* HAPPY): Sure, he's gotta practice with a regulation ball, doesn't he? (*To* BIFF): Coach'll probably congratulate you on your initiative!

BIFF: Oh, he keeps congratulating my initiative all the time, Pop.

WILLY: That's because he likes you. If somebody else took that ball there'd be an uproar. So what's the report, boys, what's the report?

BIFF: Where'd you go this time, Dad? Gee, we were lonesome for you.

WILLY (*pleased, puts an arm around each boy and they come down to the apron*): Lonesome, heh?

BIFF: Missed you every minute.

WILLY: Don't say? Tell you a secret, boys. Don't breathe it to a soul. Someday I'll have my own business, and I'll never have to leave home any more.

HAPPY: Like Uncle Charley, heh?

WILLY: Bigger than Uncle Charley! Because Charley is not—liked. He's liked, but he's not—well liked.

BIFF: Where'd you go this time, Dad?

WILLY: Well, I got on the road, and I went north to Providence. Met the Mayor.

BIFF: The Mayor of Providence!

WILLY: He was sitting in the hotel lobby.

BIFF: What'd he say?

WILLY: He said, "Morning!" And I said, "You got a fine city here, Mayor." And then he had coffee with me. And then I went to Waterbury. Waterbury is a fine city. Big clock city, the famous Waterbury clock. Sold a nice bill there. And then Boston—Boston is the cradle of the Revolution. A fine city. And a couple of other towns in Mass., and on to Portland and Bangor and straight home!

BIFF: Gee, I'd love to go with you sometime, Dad.

WILLY: Soon as summer comes.

HAPPY: Promise?

WILLY: You and Hap and I, and I'll show you all the towns. America is full of beautiful towns and fine, upstanding people. And they know me, boys, they know me up and down New England. The finest people. And when I bring you fellas up, there'll be open sesame for all of us, 'cause one thing, boys: I have friends. I can park my car in any street in New England, and the cops protect it like their own. This summer, heh?

BIFF AND HAPPY (*together*): Yeah! You bet!

WILLY: We'll take our bathing suits.

HAPPY: We'll carry your bags, Pop!

WILLY: Oh, won't that be something! Me comin' into the Boston stores with you boys carryin' my bags. What a sensation!

BIFF *is prancing around, practicing passing the ball.*

WILLY: You nervous, Biff, about the game?

BIFF: Not if you're gonna be there.

WILLY: What do they say about you in school, now that they made you captain?

HAPPY: There's a crowd of girls behind him every time the classes change.

BIFF (*taking* WILLYS *hand*): This Saturday, Pop, this Saturday—just for you, I'm going to break through for a touchdown.

HAPPY: You're supposed to pass.

BIFF: I'm takin' one play for Pop. You watch me, Pop, and when I take off my helmet, that means I'm breakin' out. Then you watch me crash through that line!

WILLY (*kisses* BIFF): Oh, wait'll I tell this in Boston!

BERNARD *enters in knickers. He is younger than* BIFF, *earnest and loyal, a worried boy.*

BERNARD: Biff, where are you? You're supposed to study with me today.

WILLY: Hey, looka Bernard. What're you lookin' so anemic about, Bernard?

BERNARD: He's gotta study, Uncle Willy. He's got Regents next week.

HAPPY (*tauntingly, spinning* BERNARD *around*): Let's box, Bernard!

BERNARD: Biff! (*He gets away from* HAPPY.) Listen, Biff, I heard Mr. Birnbaum say that if you don't start studyin' math he's gonna flunk you, and you won't graduate. I heard him!

WILLY: You better study with him, Biff. Go ahead now.

BERNARD: I heard him!

BIFF: Oh, Pop, you didn't see my sneakers! (*He holds up a foot for* WILLY *to look at.*)

WILLY: Hey, that's a beautiful job of printing!

BERNARD (*wiping his glasses*): Just because he printed University of Virginia on his sneakers doesn't mean they've got to graduate him, Uncle Willy!

WILLY (*angrily*): What're you talking about? With scholarships to three universities they're gonna flunk him?

BERNARD: But I heard Mr. Birnbaum say—

WILLY: Don't be a pest, Bernard! (*To his boys*): What an anemic!

BERNARD: Okay, I'm waiting for you in my house, Biff.

BERNARD *goes off. The* Lomans *laugh.*

WILLY: Bernard is not well liked, is he?

BIFF: He's liked, but he's not well liked.

HAPPY: That's right, Pop.

WILLY: That's just what I mean. Bernard can get the best marks in school, y'understand, but when he gets out in the business world, y'understand, you are going to be five times ahead of him. That's why I thank Almighty God you're both built like Adonises. Because the man who makes an appearance in the business world, the man who creates personal interest, is the man who gets ahead. Be liked and you will never want. You take me, for instance. I never have to wait in line to see a buyer. "Willy Loman is here!" That's all they have to know, and I go right through.

BIFF: Did you knock them dead, Pop?

WILLY: Knocked 'em cold in Providence, slaughtered 'em in Boston.

HAPPY (*on his back, pedaling again*): I'm losing weight, you notice, Pop?

LINDA *enters, as of old, a ribbon in her hair, carrying a basket of washing.*

LINDA (*with youthful energy*): Hello, dear!

WILLY: Sweetheart!

LINDA: How'd the Chevvy run?

WILLY: Chevrolet, Linda, is the greatest car ever built. (*To the boys*): Since when do you let your mother carry wash up the stairs?

BIFF: Grab hold there, boy!

HAPPY: Where to, Mom?

LINDA: Hang them up on the line. And you better go down to your friends, Biff. The cellar is full of boys. They don't know what to do with themselves.

BIFF: Ah, when Pop comes home they can wait!

WILLY (*laughs appreciatively*): You better go down and tell them what to do, Biff.

BIFF: I think I'll have them sweep out the furnace room.

WILLY: Good work, Biff.

BIFF (*goes through wall-line of kitchen to doorway at back and calls down*): Fellas! Everybody sweep out the furnace room! I'll be right down!

VOICES: All right! Okay, Biff.

BIFF: George and Sam and Frank, come out back! We're hangin' up the wash! Come on, Hap, on the double! (*He and* HAPPY *carry out the basket.*)

LINDA: The way they obey him!

WILLY: Well, that's training, the training. I'm tellin' you, I was sellin' thousands and thousands, but I had to come home.

LINDA: Oh, the whole block'll be at that game. Did you sell anything?

WILLY: I did five hundred gross in Providence and seven hundred gross in Boston.

LINDA: No! Wait a minute, I've got a pencil. (*She pulls pencil and paper out of her apron pocket.*) That makes your commission . . . Two hundred—my God! Two hundred and twelve dollars!

WILLY: Well, I didn't figure it yet, but . . .

LINDA: How much did you do?

WILLY: Well, I—I did—about a hundred and eighty gross in Providence. Well, no—it came to—roughly two hundred gross on the whole trip.

LINDA (*without hesitation*): Two hundred gross. That's . . . (*She figures.*)

WILLY: The trouble was that three of the stores were half closed for inventory in Boston. Otherwise I woulda broke records.

LINDA: Well, it makes seventy dollars and some pennies. That's very good.

WILLY: What do we owe?

LINDA: Well, on the first there's sixteen dollars on the refrigerator—

WILLY: Why sixteen?

LINDA: Well, the fan belt broke, so it was a dollar eighty.

WILLY: But it's brand new.

LINDA: Well, the man said that's the way it is. Till they work themselves in, y'know.

They move through the wall-line into the kitchen.

WILLY: I hope we didn't get stuck on that machine.

LINDA: They got the biggest ads of any of them!

WILLY: I know, it's a fine machine. What else?

LINDA: Well, there's nine-sixty for the washing machine. And for the vacuum cleaner there's three and a half due on the fifteenth. Then the roof, you got twenty-one dollars remaining.

WILLY: It don't leak, does it?

LINDA: No, they did a wonderful job. Then you owe Frank for the carburetor.

WILLY: I'm not going to pay that man! That goddam Chevrolet, they ought to prohibit the manufacture of that car!

LINDA: Well, you owe him three and a half. And odds and ends, comes to around a hundred and twenty dollars by the fifteenth.

WILLY: A hundred and twenty dollars! My God, if business don't pick up I don't know what I'm gonna do!

LINDA: Well, next week you'll do better.

WILLY: Oh, I'll knock 'em dead next week. I'll go to Hartford. I'm very well liked in Hartford. You know, the trouble is, Linda, people don't seem to take to me.

They move onto the forestage.

LINDA: Oh, don't be foolish.

WILLY: I know it when I walk in. They seem to laugh at me.

LINDA: Why? Why would they laugh at you? Don't talk that way, Willy.

WILLY *moves to the edge of the stage.* LINDA *goes into the kitchen and starts to darn stockings.*

WILLY: I don't know the reason for it, but they just pass me by. I'm not noticed.

LINDA: But you're doing wonderful, dear. You're making seventy to a hundred dollars a week.

WILLY: But I gotta be at it ten, twelve hours a day. Other men—I don't know—they do it easier. I don't know why—I can't stop myself—I talk too much. A man oughta come in with a few words. One thing about Charley. He's a man of few words, and they respect him.

LINDA: You don't talk too much, you're just lively.

WILLY (*smiling*): Well, I figure, what the hell, life is short, a couple of jokes. (*To himself*): I joke too much! (*The smile goes.*)

LINDA: Why? You're—

WILLY: I'm fat. I'm very—foolish to look at, Linda. I didn't tell you, but Christmas time I happened to be calling on F.H. Stewarts, and a salesman I know, as I was going in to see the buyer I heard him say something about—walrus. And I—I cracked him right across the face. I won't take that. I simply will not take that. But they do laugh at me. I know that.

LINDA: Darling . . .

WILLY: I gotta overcome it. I know I gotta overcome it. I'm not dressing to advantage, maybe.

LINDA: Willy, darling, you're the handsomest man in the world—

WILLY: Oh, no, Linda.

LINDA: To me you are. (*Slight pause.*) The handsomest.

From the darkness is heard the laughter of a woman. WILLY *doesn't turn to it, but it continues through* LINDA'*s lines.*

LINDA: And the boys, Willy. Few men are idolized by their children the way you are.

Music is heard as behind a scrim, to the left of the house, THE WOMAN, *dimly seen, is dressing.*

WILLY (*with great feeling*): You're the best there is, Linda, you're a pal, you know that? On the road—on the road I want to grab you sometimes and just kiss the life outa you.

The laughter is loud now, and he moves into a brightening area at the left, where THE WOMAN *has come from behind the scrim and is standing, putting on her hat, looking into a "mirror" and laughing.*

WILLY: 'Cause I get so lonely—especially when business is bad and there's nobody to talk to. I get the feeling that I'll never sell anything again, that I won't make a living for you, or a business, a business for the boys. (*He talks through* THE WOMAN'*s subsiding laughter;* THE WOMAN *primps at the "mirror."*) There's so much I want to make for—

THE WOMAN: Me? You didn't make me, Willy. I picked you.

WILLY (*pleased*): You picked me?

THE WOMAN (*who is quite proper-looking,* WILLY'*s age*): I did. I've been sitting at that desk watching all the salesmen go by, day in, day out. But you've got such a sense of humor, and we do have such a good time together, don't we?

WILLY: Sure, sure. (*He takes her in his arms.*) Why do you have to go now?

THE WOMAN: It's two o'clock . . .

WILLY: No, come on in! (*He pulls her.*)

THE WOMAN: . . . my sisters'll be scandalized. When'll you be back?

WILLY: Oh, two weeks about. Will you come up again?

THE WOMAN: Sure thing. You do make me laugh. It's good for me. (*She squeezes his arm, kisses him.*) And I think you're a wonderful man.

WILLY: You picked me, heh?

THE WOMAN: Sure. Because you're so sweet. And such a kidder.

WILLY: Well, I'll see you next time I'm in Boston.

THE WOMAN: I'll put you right through to the buyers.

WILLY (*slapping her bottom*): Right. Well, bottoms up!

THE WOMAN (*slaps him gently and laughs*): You just kill me, Willy. (*He suddenly grabs her and kisses her roughly.*) You kill me. And thanks for the stockings. I love a lot of stockings. Well, good night.

WILLY: Good night. And keep your pores open!

THE WOMAN: Oh, Willy!

THE WOMAN *bursts out laughing, and* LINDA*'s laughter blends in.* THE WOMAN *disappears into the dark. Now the area at the kitchen table brightens.* LINDA *is sitting where she was at the kitchen table, but now is mending a pair of her silk stockings.*

LINDA: You are, Willy. The handsomest man. You've got no reason to feel that—

WILLY (*coming out of* THE WOMAN*'s dimming area and going over to* LINDA): I'll make it all up to you, Linda, I'll

LINDA: There's nothing to make up, dear. You're doing fine, better than—

WILLY (*noticing her mending*): What's that?

LINDA: Just mending my stockings. They're so expensive—

WILLY (*angrily, taking them from her*): I won't have you mending stockings in this house! Now throw them out!

LINDA *puts the stockings in her pocket.*

BERNARD (*entering on the run*): Where is he? If he doesn't study!

WILLY (*moving to the forestage, with great agitation*): You'll give him the answers!

BERNARD: I do, but I can't on a Regents! That's a state exam! They're liable to arrest me!

WILLY: Where is he? I'll whip him, I'll whip him!

LINDA: And he'd better give back that football, Willy, it's not nice.

WILLY: Biff! Where is he? Why is he taking everything?

LINDA: He's too rough with the girls, Willy. All the mothers are afraid of him!

WILLY: I'll whip him!

BERNARD: He's driving the car without a license!

THE WOMAN'*s laugh is heard.*

WILLY: Shut up!

LINDA: All the mothers—

WILLY: Shut up!

BERNARD (*backing quietly away and out*): Mr. Birnbaum says he's stuck up.

WILLY: Get outa here!

BERNARD: If he doesn't buckle down he'll flunk math! (*He goes off.*)

LINDA: He's right, Willy, you've gotta—

WILLY (*exploding at her*): There's nothing the matter with him! You want him to be a worm like Bernard? He's got spirit, personality . . .

As he speaks, LINDA, *almost in tears, exits into the living-room.* WILLY *is alone in the kitchen, wilting and staring. The leaves are gone. It is night again, and the apartment houses look down from behind.*

WILLY: Loaded with it. Loaded! What is he stealing? He's giving it back, isn't he? Why is he stealing? What did I tell him? I never in my life told him anything but decent things.

HAPPY *in pajamas has come down the stairs;* WILLY *suddenly becomes aware of* HAPPY'*s presence.*

HAPPY: Let's go now, come on.

WILLY (*sitting down at the kitchen table*): Huh! Why did she have to wax the floors herself? Everytime she waxes the floors she keels over. She knows that!

HAPPY: Shh! Take it easy. What brought you back tonight?

WILLY: I got an awful scare. Nearly hit a kid in Yonkers. God! Why didn't I go to Alaska with my brother Ben that time! Ben! That man was a genius, that man was success incarnate! What a mistake! He begged me to go.

HAPPY: Well, there's no use in—

WILLY: You guys! There was a man started with the clothes on his back and ended up with diamond mines!

HAPPY: Boy, someday I'd like to know how he did it.

WILLY: What's the mystery? The man knew what he wanted and went out and got it! Walked into a jungle, and comes out, the age of twenty-one, and he's rich! The world is an oyster, but you don't crack it open on a mattress!

HAPPY: Pop, I told you I'm gonna retire you for life.

WILLY: You'll retire me for life on seventy goddam dollars a week? And your women and your car and your apartment, and you'll retire me for life! Christ's sake, I couldn't get past Yonkers today! Where are you guys, where are you? The woods are burning! I can't drive a car!

CHARLEY *has appeared in the doorway. He is a large man, slow of speech, laconic, immovable. In all he says, despite what he says, there is pity, and, now, trepidation. He has a robe over pajamas, slippers on his feet. He enters the kitchen.*

CHARLEY: Everything all right?

HAPPY: Yeah, Charley, everything's . . .

WILLY: What's the matter?

CHARLEY: I heard some noise. I thought something happened. Can't we do something about the walls? You sneeze in here, and in my house hats blow off.

HAPPY: Let's go to bed, Dad. Come on.

CHARLEY *signals to* HAPPY *to go.*

WILLY: You go ahead, I'm not tired at the moment.

HAPPY (*to* WILLY): Take it easy, huh? (*He exits.*)

WILLY: What're you doin' up?

CHARLEY (*sitting down at the kitchen table opposite* WILLY): Couldn't sleep good. I had a heartburn.

WILLY: Well, you don't know how to eat.

CHARLEY: I eat with my mouth.

WILLY: No, you're ignorant. You gotta know about vitamins and things like that.

CHARLEY: Come on, let's shoot. Tire you out a little.

WILLY (*hesitantly*): All right. You got cards?

CHARLEY (*taking a deck from his pocket*): Yeah, I got them. Someplace. What is it with those vitamins?

WILLY (*dealing*): They build up your bones. Chemistry.

CHARLEY: Yeah, but there's no bones in a heartburn.

WILLY: What are you talkin' about? Do you know the first thing about it?

CHARLEY: Don't get insulted.

WILLY: Don't talk about something you don't know anything about.

They are playing. Pause.

CHARLEY: What're you doin' home?

WILLY: A little trouble with the car.

CHARLEY: Oh. (*Pause.*) I'd like to take a trip to California.

WILLY: Don't say.

CHARLEY: You want a job?

WILLY: I got a job, I told you that. (*After a slight pause*): What the hell are you offering me a job for?

CHARLEY: Don't get insulted.

WILLY: Don't insult me.

CHARLEY: I don't see no sense in it. You don't have to go on this way.

WILLY: I got a good job. (*Slight pause.*) What do you keep comin' in here for?

CHARLEY: You want me to go?

WILLY (*after a pause, withering*): I can't understand it. He's going back to Texas again. What the hell is that?

CHARLEY: Let him go.

WILLY: I got nothin' to give him, Charley, I'm clean, I'm clean.

CHARLEY: He won't starve. None a them starve. Forget about him.

WILLY: Then what have I got to remember?

CHARLEY: You take it too hard. To hell with it. When a deposit bottle is broken you don't get your nickel back.

WILLY: That's easy enough for you to say.

CHARLEY: That ain't easy for me to say.

WILLY: Did you see the ceiling I put up in the living-room?

CHARLEY: Yeah, that's a piece of work. To put up a ceiling is a mystery to me. How do you do it?

WILLY: What's the difference?

CHARLEY: Well, talk about it.

WILLY: You gonna put up a ceiling?

CHARLEY: How could I put up a ceiling?

WILLY: Then what the hell are you bothering me for?

CHARLEY: You're insulted again.

WILLY: A man who can't handle tools is not a man. You're disgusting.

CHARLEY: Don't call me disgusting, Willy.

UNCLE BEN, *carrying a valise and an umbrella, enters the forestage from around the right corner of the house. He is a stolid man, in his sixties, with a mustache and an authoritative air. He is utterly certain of his destiny, and there is an aura of far places about him. He enters exactly as* WILLY *speaks.*

WILLY: I'm getting awfully tired, Ben.

BEN'*s music is heard.* BEN *looks around at everything.*

CHARLEY: Good, keep playing; you'll sleep better. Did you call me Ben?

BEN *looks at his watch.*

WILLY: That's funny. For a second there you reminded me of my brother Ben.

BEN: I only have a few minutes. (*He strolls, inspecting the place.* WILLY *and* CHARLEY *continue playing.*)

CHARLEY: You never heard from him again, heh? Since that time?

WILLY: Didn't Linda tell you? Couple of weeks ago we got a letter from his wife in Africa. He died.

CHARLEY: That so.

BEN (*chuckling*): So this is Brooklyn, eh?

CHARLEY: Maybe you're in for some of his money.

WILLY: Naa, he had seven sons. There's just one opportunity I had with that man . . .

BEN: I must make a train, William. There are several properties I'm looking at in Alaska.

WILLY: Sure, sure! If I'd gone with him to Alaska that time, everything would've been totally different.

CHARLEY: Go on, you'd froze to death up there.

WILLY: What're you talking about?

BEN: Opportunity is tremendous in Alaska, William. Surprised you're not up there.

WILLY: Sure, tremendous.

CHARLEY: Heh?

WILLY: There was the only man I ever met who knew the answers.

CHARLEY: Who?

BEN: How are you all?

WILLY (*taking a pot, smiling*): Fine, fine.

CHARLEY: Pretty sharp tonight.

BEN: Is Mother living with you?

WILLY: No, she died a long time ago.

CHARLEY: Who?

BEN: That's too bad. Fine specimen of a lady, Mother.

WILLY (*to* Charley): Heh?

BEN: I'd hoped to see the old girl.

CHARLEY: Who died?

BEN: Heard anything from Father, have you?

WILLY (*unnerved*): What do you mean, who died?

CHARLEY (*taking a pot*): What're you talkin' about?

BEN (*looking at his watch*): William, it's half-past eight!

WILLY (*as though to dispel his confusion he angrily stops* CHARLEY'*s hand*): That's my build!

CHARLEY: I put the ace—

WILLY: If you don't know how to play the game I'm not gonna throw my money away on you!

CHARLEY (*rising*): It was my ace, for God's sake!

WILLY: I'm through, I'm through!

BEN: When did Mother die?

WILLY: Long ago. Since the beginning you never knew how to play cards.

CHARLEY (*picks up the cards and goes to the door*): All right! Next time I'll bring a deck with five aces.

WILLY: I don't play that kind of game!

CHARLEY (*turning to him*): You ought to be ashamed of yourself!

WILLY: Yeah?

CHARLEY: Yeah! (*He goes out.*)

WILLY (*slamming the door after him*): Ignoramus!

BEN (*as* WILLY *comes toward him through the wall-line of the kitchen*): So you're William.

WILLY (*shaking* BEN'*s hand*): Ben! I've been waiting for you so long! What's the answer? How did you do it?

BEN: Oh, there's a story in that.

LINDA *enters the forestage, as of old, carrying the wash basket.*

LINDA: Is this Ben?

BEN (*gallantly*): How do you do, my dear.

LINDA: Where've you been all these years? Willy's always wondered why you—

WILLY (*pulling* BEN *away from her impatiently*): Where is Dad? Didn't you follow him? How did you get started?

BEN: Well, I don't know how much you remember.

WILLY: Well, I was just a baby, of course, only three or four years old—

BEN: Three years and eleven months.

WILLY: What a memory, Ben!

BEN: I have many enterprises, William, and I have never kept books.

WILLY: I remember I was sitting under the wagon in—was it Nebraska?

BEN: It was South Dakota, and I gave you a bunch of wild flowers.

WILLY: I remember you walking away down some open road.

BEN (*laughing*): I was going to find Father in Alaska.

WILLY: Where is he?

BEN: At that age I had a very faulty view of geography, William. I discovered after a few days that I was heading due south, so instead of Alaska, I ended up in Africa.

LINDA: Africa!

WILLY: The Gold Coast!

BEN: Principally diamond mines.

LINDA: Diamond mines!

BEN: Yes, my dear. But I've only a few minutes—

WILLY: No! Boys! Boys! (*Young* BIFF *and* HAPPY *appear.*) Listen to this. This is your Uncle Ben, a great man! Tell my boys, Ben!

BEN: Why, boys, when I was seventeen I walked into the jungle, and when I was twenty-one I walked out. (*He laughs.*) And by God I was rich.

WILLY (*to the boys*): You see what I been talking about? The greatest things can happen!

BEN (*glancing at his watch*): I have an appointment in Ketchikan Tuesday week.

WILLY: No, Ben! Please tell about Dad. I want my boys to hear. I want them to know the kind of stock they spring from. All I remember is a man with a big beard, and I was in Mamma's lap, sitting around a fire, and some kind of high music.

BEN: His flute. He played the flute.

WILLY: Sure, the flute, that's right!

New music is heard, a high, rollicking tune.

BEN: Father was a very great and a very wild-hearted man. We would start in Boston, and he'd toss the whole family into the wagon, and then he'd drive the team right across the country; through Ohio, and Indiana, Michigan, Illinois, and all the Western states. And we'd stop in the towns and sell the flutes that he'd made on the way.

Great inventor, Father. With one gadget he made more in a week than a man like you could make in a lifetime.

WILLY: That's just the way I'm bringing them up, Ben—rugged, well liked, all-around.

BEN: Yeah? (*To* BIFF): Hit that, boy—hard as you can. (*He pounds his stomach.*)

BIFF: Oh, no, sir!

BEN (*taking boxing stance*): Come on, get to me! (*He laughs.*)

WILLY: Go to it, Biff! Go ahead, show him!

BIFF: Okay! (*He cocks his fists and starts in.*)

LINDA (*to* WILLY): Why must he fight, dear?

BEN (*sparring with* BIFF): Good boy! Good boy!

WILLY: How's that, Ben, heh?

HAPPY: Give him the left, Biff!

LINDA: Why are you fighting?

BEN: Good boy! (*Suddenly comes in, trips* BIFF, *and stands over him, the point of his umbrella poised over* BIFF*'s eye.*)

LINDA: Look out, Biff!

BIFF: Gee!

BEN (*patting* BIFF*'s knee*): Never fight fair with a stranger, boy. You'll never get out of the jungle that way. (*Taking* LINDA*'s hand and bowing*): It was an honor and a pleasure to meet you, Linda.

LINDA (*withdrawing her hand coldly, frightened*): Have a nice—trip.

BEN (*to* WILLY): And good luck with your—what do you do?

WILLY: Selling.

BEN: Yes. Well . . . (*He raises his hand in farewell to all.*)

WILLY: No, Ben, I don't want you to think . . . (*He takes* BEN*'s arm to show him.*) It's Brooklyn, I know, but we hunt too.

BEN: Really, now.

WILLY: Oh, sure, there's snakes and rabbits and—that's why I moved out here. Why, Biff can fell any one of these trees in no time! Boys! Go right over to where they're building the apartment house and get some sand. We're gonna rebuild the entire front stoop right now! Watch this, Ben!

HAPPY (*as he and* BIFF *run off*): I lost weight, Pop, you notice?

CHARLEY *enters in knickers, even before the boys are gone.*

CHARLEY: Listen, if they steal any more from that building the watchman'll put the cops on them!

LINDA (*to* WILLY): Don't let Biff . . .

BEN *laughs lustily.*

WILLY: You shoulda seen the lumber they brought home last week. At least a dozen six-by-tens worth all kinds a money.

CHARLEY: Listen, if that watchman—

WILLY: I gave them hell, understand. But I got a couple of fearless characters there.

CHARLEY: Willy, the jails are full of fearless characters.

BEN (*clapping* WILLY *on the back, with a laugh at* CHARLEY): And the stock exchange, friend!

WILLY (*joining in* BEN'*s laughter*): Where are the rest of your pants?

CHARLEY: My wife bought them.

WILLY: Now all you need is a golf club and you can go upstairs and go to sleep. (*To* BEN): Great athlete! Between him and his son BERNARD they can't hammer a nail!

BERNARD (*rushing in*): The watchman's chasing Biff!

WILLY (*angrily*): Shut up! He's not stealing anything!

LINDA (*alarmed, hurrying off left*): Where is he? Biff, dear! (*She exits.*)

WILLY (*moving toward the left, away from* BEN): There's nothing wrong. What's the matter with you?

BEN: Nervy boy. Good!

WILLY (*laughing*): Oh, nerves of iron, that Biff!

CHARLEY: Don't know what it is. My New England man comes back and he's bleedin', they murdered him up there.

WILLY: It's contacts, Charley, I got important contacts!

CHARLEY (*sarcastically*): Glad to hear it, Willy. Come in later, we'll shoot a little casino. I'll take some of your Portland money. (*He laughs at* WILLY *and exits.*)

WILLY (*turning to* BEN): Business is bad, it's murderous. But not for me, of course.

BEN: I'll stop by on my way back to Africa.

WILLY (*longingly*): Can't you stay a few days? You're just what I need, Ben, because I—I have a fine position here, but I—well, Dad left when I was such a baby and I never had a chance to talk to him and I still feel—kind of temporary about myself.

BEN: I'll be late for my train.

They are at opposite ends of the stage.

WILLY: Ben, my boys—can't we talk? They'd go into the jaws of hell for me, see, but I—

BEN: William, you're being first-rate with your boys. Outstanding, manly chaps!

WILLY (*hanging on to his words*): Oh, Ben, that's good to hear! Because sometimes I'm afraid that I'm not teaching them the right kind of—Ben, how should I teach them?

BEN (*giving great weight to each word, and with a certain vicious audacity*): William, when I walked into the jungle, I was seventeen. When I walked out I was twenty-one. And, by God, I was rich! (*He goes off into darkness around the right corner of the house.*)

WILLY: . . . was rich! That's just the spirit I want to imbue them with! To walk into a jungle! I was right! I was right! I was right!

BEN *is gone, but* WILLY *is still speaking to him as* LINDA, *in nightgown and robe, enters the kitchen, glances around for* WILLY, *then goes to the door of the house, looks out and sees him. Comes down to his left. He looks at her.*

LINDA: Willy, dear? Willy?

WILLY: I was right!

LINDA: Did you have some cheese? (*He can't answer.*) It's very late, darling. Come to bed, heh?

WILLY (*looking straight up*): Gotta break your neck to see a star in this yard.

LINDA: You coming in?

WILLY: Whatever happened to that diamond watch fob? Remember? When Ben came from Africa that time? Didn't he give me a watch fob with a diamond in it?

LINDA: You pawned it, dear. Twelve, thirteen years ago. For Biff's radio correspondence course.

WILLY: Gee, that was a beautiful thing. I'll take a Walk.

LINDA: But you're in your slippers.

WILLY (*starting to go around the house at the left*): I was right! I was! (*Half to* LINDA, *as he goes, shaking his head*): What a man! There was a man worth talking to. I was right!

LINDA (*calling after* WILLY): But in your slippers, Willy!

WILLY *is almost gone when* BIFF, *in his pajamas, comes down the stairs and enters the kitchen.*

BIFF: What is he doing out there?

LINDA: Sh!

BIFF: God Almighty, Mom, how long has he been doing this?

LINDA: Don't, he'll hear you.

BIFF: What the hell is the matter with him?

LINDA: It'll pass by morning.

BIFF: Shouldn't we do anything?

LINDA: Oh, my dear, you should do a lot of things, but there's nothing to do, so go to sleep.

HAPPY *comes down the stair and sits on the steps.*

HAPPY: I never heard him so loud, Mom.

LINDA: Well, come around more often; you'll hear him. (*She sits down at the table and mends the lining of* WILLY'*s jacket.*)

BIFF: Why didn't you ever write me about this, Mom?

LINDA: How would I write to you? For over three months you had no address.

BIFF: I was on the move. But you know I thought of you all the time. You know that, don't you, pal?

LINDA: I know, dear, I know. But he likes to have a letter. Just to know that there's still a possibility for better things.

BIFF: He's not like this all the time, is he?

LINDA: It's when you come home he's always the worst.

BIFF: When I come home?

LINDA: When you write you're coming, he's all smiles, and talks about the future, and—he's just wonderful. And then the closer you seem to come, the more shaky he gets, and then, by the time you get here, he's arguing, and he seems angry at you. I think it's just that maybe he can't bring himself to—to open up to you. Why are you so hateful to each other? Why is that?

BIFF (*evasively*): I'm not hateful, Mom.

LINDA: But you no sooner come in the door than you're fighting!

BIFF: I don't know why. I mean to change. I'm tryin', Mom, you understand?

LINDA: Are you home to stay now?

BIFF: I don't know. I want to look around, see what's doin'.

LINDA: Biff, you can't look around all your life, can you?

BIFF: I just can't take hold, Mom. I can't take hold of some kind of a life.

LINDA: Biff, a man is not a bird, to come and go with the springtime.

BIFF: Your hair . . . (*He touches her hair.*) Your hair got so gray.

LINDA: Oh, it's been gray since you were in high school. I just stopped dyeing it, that's all.

BIFF: Dye it again, will ya? I don't want my pal looking old. (*He smiles.*)

LINDA: You're such a boy! You think you can go away for a year and... You've got to get it into your head now that one day you'll knock on this door and there'll be strange people here—

BIFF: What are you talking about? You're not even sixty, Mom.

LINDA: But what about your father?

BIFF (*lamely*): Well, I meant him too.

HAPPY: He admires Pop.

LINDA: Biff, dear, if you don't have any feeling for him, then you can't have any feeling for me.

BIFF: Sure I can, Mom.

LINDA: No. You can't just come to see me, because I love him. (*With a threat, but only a threat, of tears*): He's the dearest man in the world to me, and I won't have anyone making him feel unwanted and low and blue. You've got to make up your mind now, darling, there's no leeway any more. Either he's your father and you pay him that respect, or else you're not to come here. I know he's not easy to get along with—nobody knows that better than me—but...

WILLY (*from the left, with a laugh*): Hey, hey, Biffo!

BIFF (*starting to go out after* Willy): What the hell is the matter with him? (HAPPY *stops him.*)

LINDA: Don't—don't go near him!

BIFF: Stop making excuses for him! He always, always wiped the floor with you. Never had an ounce of respect for you.

HAPPY: He's always had respect for—

BIFF: What the hell do you know about it?

HAPPY (*surlily*): Just don't call him crazy!

BIFF: He's got no character—Charley wouldn't do this. Not in his own house—spewing out that vomit from his mind.

HAPPY: Charley never had to cope with what he's got to.

BIFF: People are worse off than Willy Loman. Believe me, I've seen them!

LINDA: Then make Charley your father, Biff. You can't do that, can you? I don't say he's a great man. Willy Loman never made a lot of money. His name was never in the paper. He's not the finest character that ever lived. But he's a human being, and a terrible thing is happening to him. So attention must be paid. He's not to be allowed to fall into his grave like an old dog. Attention, attention must be finally paid to such a person. You called him crazy—

BIFF: I didn't mean—

LINDA: No, a lot of people think he's lost his—balance. But you don't have to be very smart to know what his trouble is. The man is exhausted.

HAPPY: Sure!

LINDA: A small man can be just as exhausted as a great man. He works for a company thirty-six years this March, opens up unheard-of territories to their trademark, and now in his old age they take his salary away.

HAPPY (*indignantly*): I didn't know that, Mom.

LINDA: You never asked, my dear! Now that you get your spending money someplace else you don't trouble your mind with him.

HAPPY: But I gave you money last—

LINDA: Christmas time, fifty dollars! To fix the hot water it cost ninety-seven fifty! For five weeks he's been on straight commission, like a beginner, an unknown!

BIFF: Those ungrateful bastards!

LINDA: Are they any worse than his sons? When he brought them business, when he was young, they were glad to see him. But now his old friends, the old buyers that loved him so and always found some order to hand him in a pinch—they're all dead, retired. He used to be able to make six, seven calls a day in Boston. Now he takes his valises out of the car and puts them back and takes them out again and he's exhausted. Instead of walking he talks now. He drives seven hundred miles, and when he gets there no one knows him any more, no one welcomes him. And what goes through a man's mind, driving seven hundred miles home without having earned a cent? Why shouldn't he talk to himself? Why? When he has to go to Charley and borrow fifty dollars a week and pretend to me that it's his pay? How long can that go on? How long? You see what I'm sitting here and waiting for? And you tell me he has no character? The man who never worked a day but for your benefit? When does he get the medal for that? Is this his reward—to turn around at the age of sixty-three and find his sons, who he loved better than his life, one a philandering bum—

HAPPY: Mom!

LINDA: That's all you are, my baby! (*To* BIFF): And you! What happened to the love you had for him? You were such pals! How you used to talk to him on the phone every night! How lonely he was till he could come home to you!

BIFF: All right, Mom. I'll live here in my room, and I'll get a job. I'll keep away from him, that's all.

LINDA: No, Biff. You can't stay here and fight all the time.

BIFF: He threw me out of this house, remember that.

LINDA: Why did he do that? I never knew why.

BIFF: Because I know he's a fake and he doesn't like anybody around who knows!

LINDA: Why a fake? In what way? What do you mean?

BIFF: Just don't lay it all at my feet. It's between me and him—that's all I have to say. I'll chip in from now on. He'll settle for half my pay check. He'll be all right. I'm going to bed. (*He starts for the stairs.*)

LINDA: He won't be all right.

BIFF (*turning on the stairs, furiously*): I hate this city and I'll stay here. Now what do you want?

LINDA: He's dying, Biff.

HAPPY *turns quickly to her, shocked.*

BIFF (*after a pause*): Why is he dying?

LINDA: He's been trying to kill himself.

BIFF (*with great horror*): How?

LINDA: I live from day to day.

BIFF: What're you talking about?

LINDA: Remember I wrote you that he smashed up the car again? In February?

BIFF: Well?

LINDA: The insurance inspector came. He said that they have evidence. That all these accidents in the last year—weren't—weren't—accidents.

HAPPY: How can they tell that? That's a lie.

LINDA: It seems there's a woman . . . (*She takes a breath as*)

BIFF (*sharply but contained*): What woman?

LINDA (*simultaneously*): . . . and this woman . . .

LINDA: What?

BIFF: Nothing. Go ahead.

LINDA: What did you say?

BIFF: Nothing. I just said what woman?

HAPPY: What about her?

LINDA: Well, it seems she was walking down the road and saw his car. She says that he wasn't driving fast at all, and that he didn't skid. She says he came to that little bridge, and then deliberately smashed into the railing, and it was only the shallowness of the water that saved him.

BIFF: Oh, no, he probably just fell asleep again.

LINDA: I don't think he fell asleep.

BIFF: Why not?

LINDA: Last month . . . (*With great difficulty*): Oh, boys, it's so hard to say a thing like this! He's just a big stupid man to you, but I tell you there's more good in him than in many other people. (*She chokes, wipes her eyes.*) I was looking for a fuse. The lights blew out, and I went down the cellar. And behind the fuse box—it happened to fall out—was a length of rubber pipe—just short.

HAPPY: No kidding?

LINDA: There's a little attachment on the end of it. I knew right away. And sure enough, on the bottom of the water heater there's a new little nipple on the gas pipe.

HAPPY (*angrily*): That—jerk.

BIFF: Did you have it taken off?

LINDA: I'm—I'm ashamed to. How can I mention it to him? Every day I go down and take away that little rubber pipe. But, when he comes home, I put it back where it was. How can I insult him that way? I don't know what to do. I live from day to day, boys. I tell you, I know every thought in his mind. It sounds so old-fashioned and silly, but I tell you he put his whole life into you and you've turned your backs on him. (*She is bent over in the chair, weeping, her face in her hands.*) Biff, I swear to God! Biff, his life is in your hands!

HAPPY (*to* BIFF): How do you like that damned fool!

BIFF (*kissing her*): All right, pal, all right. It's all settled now. I've been remiss. I know that, Mom. But now I'll stay, and I swear to you, I'll apply myself. (*Kneeling in front of her, in a fever of self-reproach*): It's just—you see, Mom, I don't fit in business. Not that I won't try. I'll try, and I'll make good.

HAPPY: Sure you will. The trouble with you in business was you never tried to please people.

BIFF: I know, I—

HAPPY: Like when you worked for Harrison's. Bob Harrison said you were tops, and then you go and do some damn fool thing like whistling whole songs in the elevator like a comedian.

BIFF (*against* HAPPY): So what? I like to whistle sometimes.

HAPPY: You don't raise a guy to a responsible job who whistles in the elevator!

LINDA: Well, don't argue about it now.

HAPPY: Like when you'd go off and swim in the middle of the day instead of taking the line around.

BIFF (*his resentment rising*): Well, don't you run off? You take off sometimes. don't you? On a nice summer day?

HAPPY: Yeah, but I cover myself!

LINDA: Boys!

HAPPY: If I'm going to take a fade the boss can call any number where I'm supposed to be and they'll swear to him that I just left. I'll tell you something that I hate to say, Biff, but in the business world some of them think you're crazy.

BIFF (*angered*): Screw the business world!

HAPPY: All right, screw it! Great, but cover yourself!

LINDA: Hap, Hap!

BIFF: I don't care what they think! They've laughed at Dad for years, and you know why? Because we don't belong in this nuthouse of a city! We should be mixing cement on some open plain, or—or carpenters. A carpenter is allowed to whistle!

WILLY *walks in from the entrance of the house, at left.*

WILLY: Even your grandfather was better than a carpenter. (*Pause. They watch him.*) You never grew up. Bernard does not whistle in the elevator, I assure you.

HAPPY (*as though to laugh* WILLY *out of it*): Yeah, but you do, Pop.

WILLY: I never in my life whistled in an elevator! And who in the business world thinks I'm crazy?

BIFF: I didn't mean it like that, Pop. Now don't make a whole thing out of it, will ya?

WILLY: Go back to the West! Be a carpenter, a cowboy, enjoy yourself!

LINDA: Willy, he was just saying—

WILLY: I heard what he said!

HAPPY (*trying to quiet* WILLY): Hey, Pop, come on now . . .

WILLY (*continuing over* HAPPY'*s line*): They laugh at me, heh? Go to Filene's, go to the Hub, go to Slattery's, Boston. Call out the name Willy Loman and see what happens! Big shot!

BIFF: All right, Pop.

WILLY: Big!

BIFF: All right!

WILLY: Why do you always insult me?

BIFF: I didn't say a word. (*To* LINDA): Did I say a word?

LINDA: He didn't say anything, Willy.

WILLY (*going to the doorway of the living-room*): All right, good night, good night.

LINDA: Willy, dear, he just decided . . .

WILLY (*to* BIFF): If you get tired hanging around tomorrow, paint the ceiling I put up in the living-room.

BIFF: I'm leaving early tomorrow.

HAPPY: He's going to see Bill Oliver, Pop.

WILLY (*interestedly*): Oliver? For what?

BIFF (*with reserve, but trying, trying*): He always said he'd stake me. I'd like to go into business, so maybe I can take him up on it.

LINDA: Isn't that wonderful?

WILLY: Don't interrupt. What's wonderful about it? There's fifty men in the City of New York who'd stake him. (*To* BIFF): Sporting goods?

BIFF: I guess so. I know something about it and—

WILLY: He knows something about it! You know sporting goods better than Spalding, for God's sake! How much is he giving you?

BIFF: I don't know, I didn't even see him yet, but—

WILLY: Then what're you talkin' about?

BIFF (*getting angry*): Well, all I said was I'm gonna see him, that's all!

WILLY (*turning away*): Ah, you're counting your chickens again.

BIFF (*starting left for the stairs*): Oh, Jesus, I'm going to sleep!

WILLY (*calling after him*): Don't curse in this house!

BIFF (*turning*): Since when did you get so clean?

HAPPY (*trying to stop them*): Wait a . . .

WILLY: Don't use that language to me! I won't have it!

HAPPY (*grabbing* BIFF *shouts*): Wait a minute! I got an idea. I got a feasible idea. Come here, Biff, let's talk this over now, let's talk some sense here. When I was down in Florida last time, I thought of a great idea to sell sporting goods. It just came back to me. You and I, Biff—we have a line, the Loman Line. We train a couple of weeks, and put on a couple of exhibitions, see?

WILLY: That's an idea!

HAPPY: Wait! We form two basketball teams, see? Two water-polo teams. We play each other. It's a million dollars' worth of publicity. Two brothers, see? The Loman Brothers. Displays in the Royal Palms—all the hotels. And banners over the ring and the basketball court: "Loman Brothers." Baby, we could sell sporting goods!

WILLY: That is a one-million-dollar idea!

LINDA: Marvelous!

BIFF: I'm in great shape as far as that's concerned.

HAPPY: And the beauty of it is, Biff, it wouldn't be like a business. We'd be out playin' ball again . . .

BIFF (*enthused*): Yeah, that's . . .

WILLY: Million-dollar . . .

HAPPY: And you wouldn't get fed up with it, Biff. It'd be the family again. There'd be the old honor, and comradeship, and if you wanted to go off for a swim or somethin'—well, you'd do it! Without some smart cooky gettin' up ahead of you!

WILLY: Lick the world! You guys together could absolutely lick the civilized world.

BIFF: I'll see Oliver tomorrow. Hap, if we could work that out . . .

LINDA: Maybe things are beginning to—

WILLY (*wildly enthused, to* LINDA): Stop interrupting! (*To* BIFF): But don't wear sport jacket and slacks when you see Oliver.

BIFF: No, I'll—

WILLY: A business suit, and talk as little as possible, and don't crack any jokes.

BIFF: He did like me. Always liked me.

LINDA: He loved you!

WILLY (*to* LINDA): Will you stop! (*To* BIFF): Walk in very serious. You are not applying for a boy's job. Money is to pass. Be quiet, fine, and serious. Everybody likes a kidder, but nobody lends him money.

HAPPY: I'll try to get some myself, Biff. I'm sure I can.

WILLY: I see great things for you kids, I think your troubles are over. But remember, start big and you'll end big. Ask for fifteen. How much you gonna ask for?

BIFF: Gee, I don't know—

WILLY: And don't say "Gee." "Gee" is a boy's word. A man walking in for fifteen thousand dollars does not say "Gee!"

BIFF: Ten, I think, would be top though.

WILLY: Don't be so modest. You always started too low. Walk in with a big laugh. Don't look worried. Start off with a couple of your good stories to lighten things up. It's not what you say, it's how you say it—because personality always wins the day.

LINDA: Oliver always thought the highest of him—

WILLY: Will you let me talk?

BIFF: Don't yell at her, Pop, will ya?

WILLY (*angrily*): I was talking, wasn't I?

BIFF: I don't like you yelling at her all the time, and I'm tellin' you, that's all.

WILLY: What're you, takin' over this house?

LINDA: Willy—

WILLY (*turning on her*): Don't take his side all the time, goddammit!

BIFF (*furiously*): Stop yelling at her!

WILLY (*suddenly pulling on his cheek, beaten down, guilt ridden*): Give my best to Bill Oliver—he may remember me. (*He exits through the living-room doorway.*)

LINDA (*her voice subdued*): What'd you have to start that for? (BIFF *turns away.*) You see how sweet he was as soon as you talked hopefully? (*She goes over to* BIFF.) Come up and say good night to him. Don't let him go to bed that way.

HAPPY: Come on, Biff, let's buck him up.

LINDA: Please, dear. Just say good night. It takes so little to make him happy. Come. (*She goes through the living-room doorway, calling upstairs from within the living-room*): Your pajamas are hanging in the bathroom, Willy!

HAPPY (*looking toward where* LINDA *went out*): What a woman! They broke the mold when they made her. You know that, Biff?

BIFF: He's off salary. My God, working on commission!

HAPPY: Well, let's face it: he's no hot-shot selling man. Except that sometimes, you have to admit, he's a sweet personality.

BIFF (*deciding*): Lend me ten bucks, will ya? I want to buy some new ties.

HAPPY: I'll take you to a place I know. Beautiful stuff. Wear one of my striped shirts tomorrow.

BIFF: She got gray. Mom got awful old. Gee, I'm gonna go in to Oliver tomorrow and knock him for a—

HAPPY: Come on up. Tell that to Dad. Let's give him a whirl. Come on.

BIFF (*steamed up*): You know, with ten thousand bucks, boy!

HAPPY (*as they go into the living-room*): That's the talk, Biff, that's the first time I've heard the old confidence out of you! (*From within the living-room, fading off*) You're gonna live with me, kid, and any babe you want, just say the word . . . (*The last lines are hardly heard. They are mounting the stairs to their parents' bedroom.*)

LINDA (*entering her bedroom and addressing* WILLY, *who is in the bathroom. She is straightening the bed for him*): Can you do anything about the shower? It drips.

WILLY (*from the bathroom*): All of a sudden everything falls to pieces! Goddam plumbing, oughta be sued, those people. I hardly finished putting it in and the thing . . . (*His words rumble off*).

LINDA: I'm just wondering if Oliver will remember him. You think he might?

WILLY (*coming out of the bathroom in his pajamas*): Remember him? What's the matter with you, you crazy? If he'd've stayed with Oliver he'd be on top by now! Wait'll Oliver gets a look at him. You don't know the average caliber any more. The average young man today—(*he is getting into bed*)—is got a caliber of zero. Greatest thing in the world for him was to bum around.

BIFF *and* HAPPY *enter the bedroom. Slight pause.*

WILLY (*stops short, looking at* BIFF): Glad to hear it, boy.

HAPPY: He wanted to say good night to you, sport.

WILLY (*to* BIFF): Yeah. Knock him dead, boy. What'd you want to tell me?

BIFF: Just take it easy, Pop. Good night. (*He turns to go.*)

WILLY (*unable to resist*): And if anything falls off the desk while you're talking to him—like a package or something—don't you pick it up. They have office boys for that.

LINDA: I'll make a big breakfast—

WILLY: Will you let me finish? (*To* BIFF): Tell him you were in the business in the West. Not farm work.

BIFF: All right, Dad.

LINDA: I think everything—

WILLY (*going right through her speech*): And don't undersell yourself. No less than fifteen thousand dollars.

BIFF (*unable to bear him*): Okay. Good night, Mom. (*He starts moving.*)

WILLY: Because you got a greatness in you, Biff, remember that. You got all kinds a greatness . . . (*He lies back, exhausted.* BIFF *walks out.*)

LINDA (*calling after* BIFF): Sleep well, darling!

HAPPY: I'm gonna get married, Mom. I wanted to tell you.

LINDA: Go to sleep, dear.

HAPPY (*going*): I just wanted to tell you.

WILLY: Keep up the good work. (HAPPY *exits.*) God . . . remember that Ebbets Field game? The championship of the city?

LINDA: Just rest. Should I sing to you?

WILLY: Yeah. Sing to me. (LINDA *hums a soft lullaby.*) When that team came out—he was the tallest, remember?

LINDA: Oh, yes. And in gold.

BIFF *enters the darkened kitchen, takes a cigarette, and leaves the house. He comes downstage into a golden pool of light. He smokes, staring at the night.*

WILLY: Like a young god. Hercules—something like that. And the sun, the sun all around him. Remember how he waved to me? Right up from the field, with the representatives of three colleges standing by? And the buyers I brought, and the cheers when he came out—Loman, Loman, Loman! God Almighty, he'll be great yet. A star like that, magnificent, can never really fade away!

The light on WILLY *is fading. The gas heater begins to glow through the kitchen wall, near the stairs, a blue flame beneath red coils.*

LINDA (*timidly*): Willy dear, what has he got against you?

WILLY: I'm so tired. Don't talk any more.

BIFF *slowly returns to the kitchen. He stops, stares toward the heater.*

LINDA: Will you ask Howard to let you work in New York?

WILLY: First thing in the morning. Everything'll be all right.

BIFF *reaches behind the heater and draws out a length of rubber tubing. He is horrified and turns his head toward* WILLY*'s room, still dimly lit, from which the strains of* LINDA*'s desperate but monotonous humming rise.*

WILLY (*staring through the window into the moonlight*): Gee, look at the moon moving between the buildings!

BIFF *wraps the tubing around his hand and quickly goes up the stairs.*

CURTAIN

Act II

Music is heard, gay and bright. The curtain rises as the music fades away. WILLY, *in shirt sleeves, is sitting at the kitchen table, sipping coffee, his hat in his lap.* LINDA *is filling his cup when she can.*

WILLY: Wonderful coffee. Meal in itself.

LINDA: Can I make you some eggs?

WILLY: No. Take a breath.

LINDA: You look so rested, dear.

WILLY: I slept like a dead one. First time in months. Imagine, sleeping till ten on a Tuesday morning. Boys left nice and early, heh?

LINDA: They were out of here by eight o'clock.

WILLY: Good work!

LINDA: It was so thrilling to see them leaving together. I can't get over the shaving lotion in this house!

WILLY (*smiling*): Mmm—

LINDA: Biff was very changed this morning. His whole attitude seemed to be hopeful. He couldn't wait to get downtown to see Oliver.

WILLY: He's heading for a change. There's no question, there simply are certain men that take longer to get—solidified. How did he dress?

LINDA: His blue suit. He's so handsome in that suit. He could be a—anything in that suit!

WILLY *gets up from the table.* LINDA *holds his jacket for him.*

WILLY: There's no question, no question at all. Gee, on the way home tonight I'd like to buy some seeds.

LINDA (*laughing*): That'd be wonderful. But not enough sun gets back there. Nothing'll grow any more.

WILLY: You wait, kid, before it's all over we're gonna get a little place out in the country, and I'll raise some vegetables, a couple of chickens . . .

LINDA: You'll do it yet, dear.

WILLY *walks out of his jacket.* LINDA *follows him.*

WILLY: And they'll get married, and come for a weekend. I'd build a little guest house. 'Cause I got so many fine tools. All I'd need would be a little lumber and some peace of mind.

LINDA (*joyfully*): I sewed the lining . . .

WILLY: I could build two guest houses, so they'd both come. Did he decide how much he's going to ask Oliver for?

LINDA (*getting him into the jacket*): He didn't mention it, but I imagine ten or fifteen thousand. You going to talk to Howard today?

WILLY: Yeah. I'll put it to him straight and simple. He'll just have to take me off the road.

LINDA: And Willy, don't forget to ask for a little advance, because we've got the insurance premium. It's the grace period now.

WILLY: That's a hundred . . . ?

LINDA: A hundred and eight, sixty-eight. Because we're a little short again.

WILLY: Why are we short?

LINDA: Well, you had the motor job on the car . . .

WILLY: That goddam Studebaker!

LINDA: And you got one more payment on the refrigerator . . .

WILLY: But it just broke again!

LINDA: Well, it's old, dear.

WILLY: I told you we should've bought a well-advertised machine. Charley bought a General Electric and it's twenty years old and it's still good, that son-of-a-bitch.

LINDA: But, Willy—

WILLY: Whoever heard of a Hastings refrigerator? Once in my life I would like to own something outright before it's broken! I'm always in a race with the junkyard! I just finished paying for the car and it's on its last legs. The refrigerator consumes belts like a goddam maniac. They time those things. They time them so when you finally paid for them, they're used up.

LINDA (*buttoning up his jacket as he unbuttons it*): All told, about two hundred dollars would carry us, dear. But that includes the last payment on the mortgage. After this payment, Willy, the house belongs to us.

WILLY: It's twenty-five years!

LINDA: Biff was nine years old when we bought it.

WILLY: Well, that's a great thing. To weather a twenty-five year mortgage is—

LINDA: It's an accomplishment.

WILLY: All the cement, the lumber, the reconstruction I put in this house! There ain't a crack to be found in it any more.

LINDA: Well, it served its purpose.

WILLY: What purpose? Some stranger'll come along, move in, and that's that. If only Biff would take this house, and raise a family . . . (*He starts to go.*) Good-by, I'm late.

LINDA (*suddenly remembering*): Oh, I forgot! You're supposed to meet them for dinner.

WILLY: Me?

LINDA: At Frank's Chop House on Forty-eighth near Sixth Avenue.

WILLY: Is that so! How about you?

LINDA: No, just the three of you. They're gonna blow you to a big meal!

WILLY: Don't say! Who thought of that?

LINDA: Biff came to me this morning, Willy, and he said, "Tell Dad, we want to blow him to a big meal." Be there six o'clock. You and your two boys are going to have dinner.

WILLY: Gee whiz! That's really somethin'. I'm gonna knock Howard for a loop, kid. I'll get an advance, and I'll come home with a New York job. Goddammit, now I'm gonna do it!

LINDA: Oh, that's the spirit, Willy!

WILLY: I will never get behind a wheel the rest of my life!

LINDA: It's changing, Willy, I can feel it changing!

WILLY: Beyond a question. G'by, I'm late. (*He starts to go again.*)

LINDA (*calling after him as she runs to the kitchen table for a handkerchief*): You got your glasses?

WILLY (*feels for them, then comes back in*): Yeah, yeah, got my glasses.

LINDA (*giving him the handkerchief*): And a handkerchief.

WILLY: Yeah, handkerchief.

LINDA: And your saccharine?

WILLY: Yeah, my saccharine.

LINDA: Be careful on the subway stairs.

She kisses him, and a silk stocking is seen hanging from her hand. WILLY *notices it.*

WILLY: Will you stop mending stockings? At least while I'm in the house. It gets me nervous. I can't tell you. Please.

LINDA *hides the stocking in her hand as she follows* WILLY *across the forestage in front of the house.*

LINDA: Remember, Frank's Chop House.

WILLY (*passing the apron*): Maybe beets would grow out there.

LINDA (*laughing*): But you tried so many times.

WILLY: Yeah. Well, don't work hard today. (*He disappears around the right corner of the house.*)

LINDA: Be careful!

As WILLY *vanishes,* LINDA *waves to him. Suddenly the phone rings. She runs across the stage and into the kitchen and lifts it.*

LINDA: Hello? Oh, Biff! I'm so glad you called, I just . . . Yes, sure, I just told him. Yes, he'll be there for dinner at six o'clock, I didn't forget. Listen, I was just dying to tell you. You know that little rubber pipe I told you about? That he connected to the gas heater? I finally decided to go down the cellar this morning and take it away and destroy it. But it's gone! Imagine? He took it away himself, it isn't there! (*She listens.*) When? Oh, then you took it. Oh—nothing, it's just that I'd hoped he'd taken it away himself. Oh, I'm not worried, darling, because this morning he left in such high spirits, it was like the old days! I'm not afraid any more. Did Mr. Oliver see you? . . . Well, you wait there then. And make a nice impression on him, darling. Just don't perspire too much before you see him. And have a nice time with Dad. He may have big news too! . . . That's right, a New York job. And be sweet to him tonight, dear. Be loving to him. Because he's only a little boat looking for a harbor. (*She is trembling with sorrow and joy.*) Oh, that's wonderful, Biff, you'll save his life. Thanks, darling. Just put your arm around him when he comes into the restaurant. Give him a smile. That's the boy . . . Good-by, dear . . . You got your comb? . . . That's fine. Good-by, Biff dear.

In the middle of her speech, HOWARD WAGNER, *thirty-six, wheels on a small typewriter table on which is a wire-recording machine and proceeds to plug it in. This is on the left forestage. Light slowly fades on* LINDA *as it rises on* HOWARD. HOWARD *is intent on threading the machine and only glances over his shoulder as* WILLY *appears.*

WILLY: Pst! Pst!

HOWARD: Hello, Willy, come in.

WILLY: Like to have a little talk with you, Howard.

HOWARD: Sorry to keep you waiting. I'll be with you in a minute.

WILLY: What's that, Howard?

HOWARD: Didn't you ever see one of these? Wire recorder.

WILLY: Oh. Can we talk a minute?

HOWARD: Records things. Just got delivery yesterday. Been driving me crazy, the most terrific machine I ever saw in my life. I was up all night with it.

WILLY: What do you do with it?

HOWARD: I bought it for dictation, but you can do anything with it. Listen to this. I had it home last night. Listen to what I picked up. The first one is my daughter. Get this. (*He flicks the switch and "Roll out the Barrel" is heard being whistled.*) Listen to that kid whistle.

WILLY: That is lifelike, isn't it?

HOWARD: Seven years old. Get that tone.

WILLY: Ts, ts. Like to ask a little favor if you . . .

The whistling breaks off, and the voice of HOWARD*'s daughter is heard.*

HIS DAUGHTER: "Now you, Daddy."

HOWARD: She's crazy for me! (*Again the same song is whistled.*) That's me! Ha! (*He winks.*)

WILLY: You're very good!

The whistling breaks off again. The machine runs silent for a moment.

HOWARD: Sh! Get this now, this is my son.

HIS SON: "The capital of Alabama is Montgomery; the capital of Arizona is Phoenix; the capital of Arkansas is Little Rock; the capital of California is Sacramento . . ." (*and on, and on.*)

HOWARD (*holding up five fingers*): Five years old, Willy!

WILLY: He'll make an announcer some day!

HIS SON (*continuing*): "The capital . . ."

HOWARD: Get that—alphabetical order! (*The machine breaks off suddenly.*)
Wait a minute. The maid kicked the plug out.

WILLY: It certainly is a—

HOWARD: Sh, for God's sake!

HIS SON: "It's nine o'clock, Bulova watch time. So I have to go to sleep."

WILLY: That really is—

HOWARD: Wait a minute! The next is my wife.

They wait.

HOWARD'S VOICE: "Go on, say something." (*Pause.*) "Well, you gonna talk?"

HIS WIFE: "I can't think of anything."

HOWARD'S VOICE: "Well, talk—it's turning."

HIS WIFE (*shyly, beaten*): "Hello." (*Silence.*) "Oh, Howard, I can't talk into this . . ."

HOWARD (*snapping the machine off*): That was my wife.

WILLY: That is a wonderful machine. Can we—

HOWARD: I tell you, Willy, I'm gonna take my camera, and my bandsaw, and all my hobbies, and out they go. This is the most fascinating relaxation I ever found.

WILLY: I think I'll get one myself.

HOWARD: Sure, they're only a hundred and a half. You can't do without it. Supposing you wanna hear Jack Benny, see? But you can't be at home at that hour. So you tell the maid to turn the radio on when Jack Benny comes on, and this automatically goes on with the radio . . .

WILLY: And when you come home you . . .

HOWARD: You can come home twelve o'clock, one o'clock, any time you like, and you get yourself a Coke and sit yourself down, throw the switch, and there's Jack Benny's program in the middle of the night!

WILLY: I'm definitely going to get one. Because lots of times I'm on the road, and I think to myself, what I must be missing on the radio!

HOWARD: Don't you have a radio in the car?

WILLY: Well, yeah, but who ever thinks of turning it on?

HOWARD: Say, aren't you supposed to be in Boston?

WILLY: That's what I want to talk to you about, Howard. You got a minute?

(*He draws a chair in from the wing.*)

HOWARD: What happened? What're you doing here?

WILLY: Well . . .

HOWARD: You didn't crack up again, did you?

WILLY: Oh, no. No . . .

HOWARD: Geez, you had me worried there for a minute. What's the trouble?

WILLY: Well, tell you the truth, Howard. I've come to the decision that I'd rather not travel any more.

HOWARD: Not travel! Well, what'll you do?

WILLY: Remember, Christmas time, when you had the party here? You said you'd try to think of some spot for me here in town.

HOWARD: With us?

WILLY: Well, sure.

HOWARD: Oh, yeah, yeah. I remember. Well, I couldn't think of anything for you, Willy.

WILLY: I tell ya, Howard. The kids are all grown up, y'know. I don't need much any more. If I could take home—well, sixty-five dollars a week, I could swing it.

HOWARD: Yeah, but Willy, see I—

WILLY: I tell ya why, Howard. Speaking frankly and between the two of us, y'know—I'm just a little tired.

HOWARD: Oh, I could understand that, Willy. But you're a road man, Willy, and we do a road business. We've only got a half-dozen salesmen on the floor here.

WILLY: God knows, Howard, I never asked a favor of any man. But I was with the firm when your father used to carry you in here in his arms.

HOWARD: I know that, Willy, but—

WILLY: Your father came to me the day you were born and asked me what I thought of the name of Howard, may he rest in peace.

HOWARD: I appreciate that, Willy, but there just is no spot here for you. If I had a spot I'd slam you right in, but I just don't have a single solitary spot.

He looks for his lighter. WILLY *has picked it up and gives it to him. Pause.*

WILLY (*with increasing anger*): Howard, all I need to set my table is fifty dollars a week.

HOWARD: But where am I going to put you, kid?

WILLY: Look, it isn't a question of whether I can sell merchandise, is it?

HOWARD: No, but it's a business, kid, and everybody's gotta pull his own weight.

WILLY (*desperately*): Just let me tell you a story, Howard—

HOWARD: 'Cause you gotta admit, business is business.

WILLY (*angrily*): Business is definitely business, but just listen for a minute. You don't understand this. When I was a boy—eighteen, nineteen—I was already on the road. And there was a question in my mind as to whether selling had a future for me. Because in those days I had a yearning to go to Alaska. See, there were three gold strikes in one month in Alaska, and I felt like going out. Just for the ride, you might say.

HOWARD (*barely interested*): Don't say.

WILLY: Oh, yeah, my father lived many years in Alaska. He was an adventurous man. We've got quite a little streak of self-reliance in our family. I thought I'd go out with my older brother and try to locate him, and maybe settle in the North with the old man. And I was almost decided to go, when I met a salesman in the Parker House. His name was Dave Singleman. And he was eighty-four years old, and he'd drummed merchandise in thirty-one states. And old Dave, he'd go up to his room, y'understand, put on his green velvet slippers—I'll never forget—and pick up his phone and call the buyers, and without ever leaving his room, at the age of eighty-four, he made his living. And when I saw that, I realized that selling was the greatest career a man could want. 'Cause what could be more satisfying than to be able to go, at the age of eighty-four, into twenty or thirty different cities, and pick up a phone, and be remembered and loved and helped by so many different people? Do you know? when he died—and by the way he died the death of a salesman, in his green velvet slippers in the smoker of the New York, New Haven and Hartford, going into Boston—when he died, hundreds of salesmen and buyers were at his funeral. Things were sad on a lotta trains for months after that. (*He stands up.* Howard *has not looked at him.*) In those days there was personality in it, Howard. There was respect, and comradeship, and gratitude in it. Today, it's all cut and dried, and there's no chance for bringing friendship to bear—or personality. You see what I mean? They don't know me any more.

HOWARD (*moving away, to the right*): That's just the thing, Willy.

WILLY: If I had forty dollars a week—that's all I'd need. Forty dollars, Howard.

HOWARD: Kid, I can't take blood from a stone, I—

WILLY (*desperation is on him now*): Howard, the year Al Smith was nominated, your father came to me and—

HOWARD (*starting to go off*): I've got to see some people, kid.

WILLY (*stopping him*): I'm talking about your father! There were promises made across this desk! You mustn't tell me you've got people to see—I put thirty-four years into this firm, Howard, and now I can't pay my insurance! You can't eat the orange and throw the peel away—a man is not a piece of fruit! (*After a pause*) Now pay attention. Your father—in 1928 I had a big year. I averaged a hundred and seventy dollars a week in commissions.

HOWARD (*impatiently*): Now, Willy, you never averaged—

WILLY (*banging his hand on the desk*): I averaged a hundred and seventy dollars a week in the year of 1928! And your father came to me—or rather, I was in the office here—it was right over this desk—and he put his hand on my shoulder—

HOWARD (*getting up*): You'll have to excuse me, Willy, I gotta see some people. Pull yourself together. (*Going out*) I'll be back in a little while.

On HOWARD'S *exit, the light on his chair grows very bright and strange.*

WILLY: Pull myself together! What the hell did I say to him? My God, I was yelling at him! How could I! (WILLY *breaks off, staring at the light, which occupies the chair, animating it. He approaches this chair, standing across the desk from it.*) Frank, Frank, don't you remember what you told me that time? How you put your hand on my shoulder, and Frank . . . (*He leans on the desk and as he speaks the dead man's name he accidentally switches on the recorder, and instantly*)

HOWARD'S SON: ". . . of New York is Albany. The capital of Ohio is Cincinnati, the capital of Rhode Island is . . ." (*The recitation continues.*)

WILLY (*leaping away with fright, shouting*): Ha! Howard! Howard! Howard!

HOWARD (*rushing in*): What happened?

WILLY (*pointing at the machine, which continues nasally, childishly, with the capital cities*): Shut it off! Shut it off!

HOWARD (*pulling the plug out*): Look, Willy . . .

WILLY (*pressing his hands to his eyes*): I gotta get myself some coffee. I'll get some coffee . . .

WILLY *starts to walk out.* HOWARD *stops him.*

HOWARD (*rolling up the cord*): Willy, look . . .

WILLY: I'll go to Boston.

HOWARD: Willy, you can't go to Boston for us.

WILLY: Why can't I go?

HOWARD: I don't want you to represent us. I've been meaning to tell you for a long time now.

WILLY: Howard, are you firing me?

HOWARD: I think you need a good long rest, Willy.

WILLY: Howard—

HOWARD: And when you feel better, come back, and we'll see if we can work something out.

WILLY: But I gotta earn money, Howard. I'm in no position to—

HOWARD: Where are your sons? Why don't your sons give you a hand?

WILLY: They're working on a very big deal.

HOWARD: This is no time for false pride, Willy. You go to your sons and you tell them that you're tired. You've got two great boys, haven't you?

WILLY: Oh, no question, no question, but in the meantime . . .

HOWARD: Then that's that, heh?

WILLY: All right, I'll go to Boston tomorrow.

HOWARD: No, no.

WILLY: I can't throw myself on my sons. I'm not a cripple!

HOWARD: Look, kid, I'm busy this morning.

WILLY (*grasping* HOWARD'*s arm*): Howard, you've got to let me go to Boston!

HOWARD (*hard, keeping himself under control*): I've got a line of people to see this morning. Sit down, take five minutes, and pull yourself together, and then go home, will ya? I need the office, Willy. (*He starts to go, turns, remembering the recorder, starts to push off the table holding the recorder.*) Oh, yeah. Whenever you can this week, stop by and drop off the samples. You'll feel better, Willy, and then come back and we'll talk. Pull yourself together, kid, there's people outside.

HOWARD *exits, pushing the table off left.* WILLY *stares into space, exhausted. Now the music is heard—*BEN'*s music—first distantly, then closer, closer. As* WILLY *speaks,* BEN *enters from the right. He carries valise and umbrella.*

WILLY: Oh, Ben, how did you do it? What is the answer? Did you wind up the Alaska deal already?

BEN: Doesn't take much time if you know what you're doing. Just a short business trip. Boarding ship in an hour. Wanted to say good-by.

WILLY: Ben, I've got to talk to you.

BEN (*glancing at his watch*): Haven't the time, William.

WILLY (*crossing the apron to* BEN): Ben, nothing's working out. I don't know what to do.

BEN: Now, look here, William. I've bought timberland in Alaska and I need a man to look after things for me.

WILLY: God, timberland! Me and my boys in those grand outdoors!

BEN: You've a new continent at your doorstep, William. Get out of these cities, they're full of talk and time payments and courts of law. Screw on your fists and you can fight for a fortune up there.

WILLY: Yes, yes! Linda, Linda!

LINDA *enters as of old, with the wash.*

LINDA: Oh, you're back?

BEN: I haven't much time.

WILLY: No, wait! Linda, he's got a proposition for me in Alaska.

LINDA: But he's got—(*To* BEN) He's got a beautiful job here.

WILLY: But in Alaska, kid, I could—

LINDA: You're doing well enough, Willy!

BEN (*to* Linda): Enough for what, my dear?

LINDA (*frightened of* BEN *and angry at him*): Don't say those things to him! Enough to be happy right here, right now. (*To* WILLY, *while* BEN *laughs*) Why must everybody conquer the world? You're well liked, and the boys love you, and someday—(*to* BEN)—why, old man Wagner told him just the other day that if he keeps it up he'll be a member of the firm, didn't he, Willy?

WILLY: Sure, sure. I am building something with this firm, Ben, and if a man is building something he must be on the right track, mustn't he?

BEN: What are you building? Lay your hand on it. Where is it?

WILLY (*hesitantly*): That's true, Linda, there's nothing.

LINDA: Why? (*To* BEN) There's a man eighty-four years old—

WILLY: That's right, Ben, that's right. When I look at that man I say, what is there to worry about?

BEN: Bah!

WILLY: It's true, Ben. All he has to do is go into any city, pick up the phone, and he's making his living and you know why?

BEN (*picking up his valise*): I've got to go.

WILLY (*holding* BEN *back*): Look at this boy!

BIFF, *in his high school sweater, enters carrying suitcase.* HAPPY *carries* BIFF*'s shoulder guards, gold helmet, and football pants.*

WILLY: Without a penny to his name, three great universities are begging for him, and from there the sky's the limit, because it's not what you do, Ben. It's who you know and the smile on your face! It's contacts, Ben, contacts! The whole wealth of Alaska passes over the lunch table at the Commodore Hotel, and that's the wonder, the wonder of this country, that a man can end with diamonds here on the basis of being liked! (*He turns to* BIFF. And that's why when you get out on that field today it's important. Because thousands of people will be rooting for you and loving you. (*To* BEN, *who has again begun to leave*) And Ben! when he walks into a business office his name will sound out like a bell and all the doors will open to him! I've seen it, Ben, I've seen it a thousand times! You can't feel it with your hand like timber, but it's there!

BEN: Good-by, William.

WILLY: Ben, am I right? Don't you think I'm right? I value your advice.

BEN: There's a new continent at your doorstep, William. You could walk out rich. Rich! (*He is gone.*)

WILLY: We'll do it here, Ben! You hear me? We're gonna do it here!

Young BERNARD *rushes in. The gay music of the Boys is heard.*

BERNARD: Oh, gee, I was afraid you left already!

WILLY: Why? What time is it?

BERNARD: It's half-past one!

WILLY: Well, come on, everybody! Ebbets Field[1] next stop! Where's the pennants? (*He rushes through the wall-line of the kitchen and out into the living-room.*)

LINDA (*to* BIFF): Did you pack fresh underwear?

HAPPY (*who has been limbering up*): I want to go!

BERNARD: Biff, I'm carrying your helmet, ain't I?

HAPPY: No, I'm carrying the helmet.

BERNARD: Oh, Biff, you promised me.

HAPPY: I'm carrying the helmet.

BERNARD: How am I going to get in the locker room?

LINDA: Let him carry the shoulder guards. (*She puts her coat and hat on in the kitchen.*)

---

1. **Ebbets Field:** Former historic professional ballpark in Brooklyn, New York. The old Brooklyn Dodgers football team also used Ebbets Field as its home stadium. Ebbets Field, demolished in 1960, is today considered one of the most classic, nostalgic, even mythical ball parks lost to the wrecking ball. Miller for a time himself lived very close to this ballpark.

BERNARD: Can I, Biff? 'Cause I told everybody I'm going to be in the locker room.
HAPPY: In Ebbets Field it's the clubhouse.
BERNARD: I meant the clubhouse. Biff!
HAPPY: Biff!
BIFF (*grandly, after a slight pause*): Let him carry the shoulder guards.
HAPPY (*as he gives* BERNARD *the shoulder guards*): Stay close to us now.

WILLY *rushes in with the pennants.*

WILLY (*handing them out*): Everybody wave when *Biff* comes out on the field. (HAPPY *and* BERNARD *run off.*) You set now, boy?

The music has died away.

BIFF: Ready to go, Pop. Every muscle is ready.
WILLY (*at the edge of the apron*): You realize what this means?
BIFF: That's right, Pop.
WILLY (*feeling* BIFF'*s muscles*): You're comin' home this afternoon captain of the All-Scholastic Championship Team of the City of New York.
BIFF: I got it, Pop. And remember, pal, when I take off my helmet, that touchdown is for you.
WILLY: Let's go! (*He is starting out, with his arm around* BIFF, *when* CHARLEY *enters, as of old, in knickers.*) I got no room for you, Charley.
CHARLEY: Room? For what?
WILLY: In the car.
CHARLEY: You goin' for a ride? I wanted to shoot some casino.
WILLY (*furiously*): Casino? (*Incredulously*) Don't you realize what today is?
LINDA: Oh, he knows, Willy. He's just kidding you.
WILLY: That's nothing to kid about!
CHARLEY: No, Linda, what's goin' on?
LINDA: He's playing in Ebbets Field.
CHARLEY: Baseball in this weather?
WILLY: Don't talk to him. Come on, come on! (*He is pushing them out.*)
CHARLEY: Wait a minute, didn't you hear the news?
WILLY: What?
CHARLEY: Don't you listen to the radio? Ebbets Field just blew up.

WILLY: You go to hell! (CHARLEY *laughs. Pushing them out*) Come on, come on! We're late.

CHARLEY (*as they go*): Knock a homer, Biff, knock a homer!

WILLY (*the last to leave, turning to* CHARLEY): I don't think that was funny, Charley. This is the greatest day of his life.

CHARLEY: Willy, when are you going to grow up?

WILLY: Yeah, heh? When this game is over, Charley, you'll be laughing out of the other side of your face. They'll be calling him another Red Grange. Twenty-five thousand a year.

CHARLEY (*kidding*): Is that so?

WILLY: Yeah, that's so.

CHARLEY: Well, then, I'm sorry, Willy. But tell me something.

WILLY: What?

CHARLEY: Who is Red Grange?

WILLY: Put up your hands. Goddam you, put up your hands!

CHARLEY, *chuckling, shakes his head and walks away, around the left corner of the stage.* WILLY *follows him. The music rises to a mocking frenzy.*

WILLY: Who the hell do you think you are, better than everybody else? You don't know everything, you big, ignorant, stupid . . . Put up your hands!

Light rises, on the right side of the forestage, on a small table in the reception room of CHARLEY'*s office. Traffic sounds are heard.* BERNARD, *now mature, sits whistling to himself. A pair of tennis rackets and an overnight bag are on the floor beside him.*

WILLY (*offstage*): What are you walking away for? Don't walk away! If you're going to say something say it to my face! I know you laugh at me behind my back. You'll laugh out of the other side of your goddam face after this game. Touchdown! Touchdown! Eighty thousand people! Touchdown! Right between the goal posts.

BERNARD *is a quiet, earnest, but self-assured young man.* WILLY'*s voice is coming from right upstage now.* BERNARD *lowers his feet off the table and listens.* JENNY, *his father's secretary, enters.*

JENNY (*distressed*): Say, Bernard, will you go out in the hall?

BERNARD: What is that noise? Who is it?

JENNY: Mr. Loman. He just got off the elevator.

BERNARD (*getting up*): Who's he arguing with?

JENNY: Nobody. There's nobody with him. I can't deal with him any more, and your father gets all upset everytime he comes. I've got a lot of typing to do, and your father's waiting to sign it. Will you see him?

WILLY (*entering*): Touchdown! Touch—(*He sees* JENNY.) Jenny, Jenny, good to see you. How're ya? Workin'? Or still honest?

JENNY: Fine. How've you been feeling?

WILLY: Not much any more, Jenny. Ha, ha! (*He is surprised to see the rackets.*)

BERNARD: Hello, Uncle Willy.

WILLY (*almost shocked*): Bernard! Well, look who's here! (*He comes quickly, guiltily, to* BERNARD *and warmly shakes his hand.*)

BERNARD: How are you? Good to see you.

WILLY: What are you doing here?

BERNARD: Oh, just stopped by to see Pop. Get off my feet till my train leaves. I'm going to Washington in a few minutes.

WILLY: Is he in?

BERNARD: Yes, he's in his office with the accountant. Sit down.

WILLY (*sitting down*): What're you going to do in Washington?

BERNARD: Oh, just a case I've got there, Willy.

WILLY: That so? (*Indicating the rackets*) You going to play tennis there?

BERNARD: I'm staying with a friend who's got a court.

WILLY: Don't say. His own tennis court. Must be fine people, I bet.

BERNARD: They are, very nice. Dad tells me Biff's in town.

WILLY (*with a big smile*): Yeah, Biff's in. Working on a very big deal, Bernard.

BERNARD: What's Biff doing?

WILLY: Well, he's been doing very big things in the West. But he decided to establish himself here. Very big. We're having dinner. Did I hear your wife had a boy?

BERNARD: That's right. Our second.

WILLY: Two boys! What do you know!

BERNARD: What kind of a deal has Biff got?

WILLY: Well, Bill Oliver—very big sporting-goods man—he wants Biff very badly. Called him in from the West. Long distance, carte blanche, special deliveries. Your friends have their own private tennis court?

BERNARD: You still with the old firm, Willy?

WILLY (*after a pause*): I'm—I'm overjoyed to see how you made the grade, Bernard, overjoyed. It's an encouraging thing to see a young man really—really—Looks very good for Biff—very—(*He breaks off, then*): Bernard—(*He is so fall of emotion, he breaks off again.*)

BERNARD: What is it, Willy?

WILLY (*small and alone*): What—what's the secret?

BERNARD: What secret?

WILLY: How—how did you? Why didn't he ever catch on?

BERNARD: I wouldn't know that, Willy.

WILLY (*confidentially, desperately*): You were his friend, his boyhood friend. There's something I don't understand about it. His life ended after that Ebbets Field game. From the age of seventeen nothing good ever happened to him.

BERNARD: He never trained himself for anything.

WILLY: But he did, he did. After high school he took so many correspondence courses. Radio mechanics; television; God Knows what, and never made the slightest mark.

BERNARD (*taking off his glasses*): Willy, do you want to talk candidly?

WILLY (*rising, faces* BERNARD): I regard you as a very brilliant man, Bernard. I value your advice.

BERNARD: Oh, the hell with the advice, Willy. I couldn't advise you. There's just one thing I've always wanted to ask you. When he was supposed to graduate, and the math teacher flunked him—

WILLY: Oh, that son-of-a-bitch ruined his life.

BERNARD: Yeah, but, Willy, all he had to do was go to summer school and make up that subject.

WILLY: That's right, that's right.

BERNARD: Did you tell him not to go to summer school?

WILLY: Me? I begged him to go. I ordered him to go!

BERNARD: Then why wouldn't he go?

WILLY: Why? Why! Bernard, that question has been trailing me like a ghost for the last fifteen years. He flunked the subject, and laid down and died like a hammer hit him!

BERNARD: Take it easy, kid.

WILLY: Let me talk to you—I got nobody to talk to. Bernard, Bernard, was it my fault? Y'see? It keeps going around in my mind, maybe I did something to him. I got nothing to give him.

BERNARD: Don't take it so hard.

WILLY: Why did he lay down? What is the story there? You were his friend!

BERNARD: Willy, I remember, it was June, and our grades came out. And he'd flunked math.

WILLY: That son-of-a-bitch!

BERNARD: No, it wasn't right then. Biff just got very angry, I remember, and he was ready to enroll in summer school.

WILLY (*surprised*): He was?

BERNARD: He wasn't beaten by it at all. But then, Willy, he disappeared from the block for almost a month. And I got the idea that he'd gone up to New England to see you. Did he have a talk with you then?

WILLY *stares in silence.*

BERNARD: Willy?

WILLY (*with a strong edge of resentment in his voice*): Yeah, he came to Boston. What about it?

BERNARD: Well, just that when he came back—I'll never forget this, it always mystifies me. Because I'd thought so well of Biff, even though he'd always taken advantage of me. I loved him, Willy, y'know? And he came back after that month and took his sneakers—remember those sneakers with "University of Virginia" printed on them? He was so proud of those, wore them every day. And he took them down in the cellar, and burned them up in the furnace. We had a fist fight. It lasted at least half an hour. Just the two of us, punching each other down in the cellar, and crying right through it. I've often thought of how strange it was that I knew he'd given up his life. What happened in Boston, Willy?

WILLY *looks at him as at an intruder.*

BERNARD: I just bring it up because you asked me.

WILLY (*angrily*): Nothing. What do you mean, "What happened?" What's that got to do with anything?

BERNARD: Well, don't get sore.

WILLY: What are you trying to do, blame it on me? If a boy lays down is that my fault?

BERNARD: Now, Willy, don't get—

WILLY: Well, don't—don't talk to me that way! What does that mean, "What happened?"

CHARLEY *enters. He is in his vest, and he carries a bottle of bourbon.*

CHARLEY: Hey, you're going to miss that train. (*He waves the bottle.*)

BERNARD: Yeah, I'm going. (*He takes the bottle.*) Thanks, Pop. (*He picks up his rackets and bag.*) Good-by, Willy, and don't worry about it. You know, "If at first you don't succeed . . ."

WILLY: Yes, I believe in that.

BERNARD: But sometimes, Willy, it's better for a man just to walk away.

WILLY: Walk away?

BERNARD: That's right.

WILLY: But if you can't walk away?

BERNARD (*after a slight pause*): I guess that's when it's tough. (*Extending his hand*) Good-by, Willy.

WILLY (*shaking* BERNARD'*s hand*): Good-by, boy.

CHARLEY (*an arm on* BERNARD'*s shoulder*): How do you like this kid? Gonna argue a case in front of the Supreme Court.

BERNARD (*protesting*): Pop!

WILLY (*genuinely shocked, pained, and happy*): No! The Supreme Court!

BERNARD: I gotta run. 'By, Dad!

CHARLEY: Knock 'em dead, Bernard!

BERNARD *goes off*

WILLY (*as* CHARLEY *takes out his wallet*): The Supreme Court! And he didn't even mention it!

CHARLEY (*counting out money on the desk*): He don't have to—he's gonna do it.

WILLY: And you never told him what to do, did you? You never took any interest in him.

CHARLEY: My salvation is that I never took any interest in anything. There's some money—fifty dollars. I got an accountant inside.

WILLY: Charley, look . . . (*With difficulty*) I got my insurance to pay. If you can manage it—I need a hundred and ten dollars.

CHARLEY *doesn't reply for a moment; merely stops moving.*

WILLY: I'd draw it from my bank but Linda would know, and I . . .

CHARLEY: Sit down, Willy.

WILLY (*moving toward the chair*): I'm keeping an account of everything, remember. I'll pay every penny back. (*He sits.*)

CHARLEY: Now listen to me, Willy.

WILLY: I want you to know I appreciate . . .

CHARLEY (*sitting down on the table*): Willy, what're you doin'? What the hell is goin' on in your head?

WILLY: Why? I'm simply . . .

CHARLEY: I offered you a job. You can make fifty dollars a week. And I won't send you on the road.

WILLY: I've got a job.

CHARLEY: Without pay? What kind of a job is a job without pay? (*He rises.*) Now, look, kid, enough is enough. I'm no genius but I know when I'm being insulted.

WILLY: Insulted!

CHARLEY: Why don't you want to work for me?

WILLY: What's the matter with you? I've got a job.

CHARLEY: Then what're you walkin' in here every week for?

WILLY (*getting up*): Well, if you don't want me to walk in here—

CHARLEY: I am offering you a job.

WILLY: I don't want your goddam job!

CHARLEY: When the hell are you going to grow up?

WILLY (*furiously*): You big ignoramus, if you say that to me again I'll rap you one! I don't care how big you are! (*He's ready to fight.*)

Pause.

CHARLEY (*kindly, going to him*): How much do you need, Willy?

WILLY: Charley, I'm strapped. I'm strapped. I don't know what to do. I was just fired.

CHARLEY: Howard fired you?

WILLY: That snotnose. Imagine that? I named him. I named him Howard.

CHARLEY: Willy, when're you gonna realize that them things don't mean anything? You named him Howard, but you can't sell that. The only thing you got in this world is what you can sell. And the funny thing is that you're a salesman, and you don't know that.

WILLY: I've always tried to think otherwise, I guess. I always felt that if a man was impressive, and well liked, that nothing—

CHARLEY: Why must everybody like you? Who liked J. P. Morgan.[2] Was he impressive? In a Turkish bath he'd look like a butcher. But with

---

2. **J. P. Morgan:** The iconic multimillionaire whose fortunes were earned through his extensive railroad, steel, and banking investments

his pockets on he was very well liked. Now listen, Willy, I know you don't like me, and nobody can say I'm in love with you, but I'll give you a job because—just for the hell of it, put it that way. Now what do you say?

WILLY: I—I just can't work for you, Charley.

CHARLEY: What're you, jealous of me?

WILLY: I can't work for you, that's all, don't ask me why.

CHARLEY (*angered, takes out more bills*): You been jealous of me all your life, you damned fool! Here, pay your insurance. (*He puts the money in* WILLY*'s hand.*)

WILLY: I'm keeping strict accounts.

CHARLEY: I've got some work to do. Take care of yourself. And pay your insurance.

WILLY (*moving to the right*): Funny, y'know? After all the highways, and the trains, and the appointments, and the years, you end up worth more dead than alive.

CHARLEY: Willy, nobody's worth nothin' dead. (*After a slight pause*): Did you hear what I said?

WILLY *stands still, dreaming.*

CHARLEY: Willy!

WILLY: Apologize to Bernard for me when you see him. I didn't mean to argue with him. He's a fine boy. They're all fine boys, and they'll end up big—all of them. Someday they'll all play tennis together. Wish me luck, Charley. He saw Bill Oliver today.

CHARLEY: Good luck.

WILLY (*on the verge of tears*): Charley, you're the only friend I got. Isn't that a remarkable thing? (*He goes out.*)

CHARLEY: Jesus!

CHARLEY *stares after him a moment and follows. All light blacks out. Suddenly raucous music is heard, and a red glow rises behind the screen at right.* STANLEY, *a young waiter, appears, carrying a table, followed by* HAPPY, *who is carrying two chairs.*

STANLEY (*putting the table down*): That's all right, Mr. Loman, I can handle it myself. (*He turns and takes the chairs from* HAPPY *and places them at the table.*)

HAPPY (*glancing around*): Oh, this is better.

STANLEY: Sure, in the front there you're in the middle of all kinds a noise. Whenever you got a party, Mr. Loman, you just tell me and

I'll put you back here. Y'know, there's a lotta people they don't like it private, because when they go out they like to see a lotta action around them because they're sick and tired to stay in the house by theirself. But I know you, you ain't from Hackensack. You know what I mean?

HAPPY (*sitting down*): So how's it coming, Stanley?

STANLEY: Ah, it's a dog's life. I only wish during the war they'd a took me in the Army. I coulda been dead by now.

HAPPY: My brother's back, Stanley.

STANLEY: Oh, he come back, heh? From the Far West.

HAPPY: Yeah, big cattle man, my brother, so treat him right. And my father's coming too.

STANLEY: Oh, your father too!

HAPPY: You got a couple of nice lobsters?

STANLEY: Hundred per cent, big.

HAPPY: I want them with the claws.

STANLEY: Don't worry, I don't give you no mice. (HAPPY *laughs.*) How about some wine? It'll put a head on the meal.

HAPPY: No. You remember, Stanley, that recipe I brought you from overseas? With the champagne in it?

STANLEY: Oh, yeah, sure. I still got it tacked up yet in the kitchen. But that'll have to cost a buck apiece anyways.

HAPPY: That's all right.

STANLEY: What'd you, hit a number or somethin'?

HAPPY: No, it's a little celebration. My brother is—I think he pulled off a big deal today. I think we're going into business together.

STANLEY: Great! That's the best for you. Because a family business, you know what I mean?—that's the best.

HAPPY: That's what I think.

STANLEY: 'Cause what's the difference? Somebody steals? It's in the family. Know what I mean? (*Sotto voce.*)[3] Like this bartender here. The boss is goin' crazy what kinda leak he's got in the cash register. You put it in but it don't come out.

HAPPY (*raising his head*): Sh!

STANLEY: What?

HAPPY: You notice I wasn't lookin' right or left, was I?

STANLEY: No.

---

3. **sotto voce:** Italian for "In a soft voice"

HAPPY: And my eyes are closed.

STANLEY: So what's the—?

HAPPY: Strudel's comin'.

STANLEY (*catching on, looks around*): Ah, no, there's no—

He breaks off as a furred, lavishly dressed girl enters and sits at the next table. Both follow her with their eyes.

STANLEY: Geez, how'd ya know?

HAPPY: I got radar or something. (*Staring directly at her profile*) Oooooooo . . . Stanley.

STANLEY: I think that's for you, Mr. Loman.

HAPPY: Look at that mouth. Oh, God. And the binoculars.

STANLEY: Geez, you got a life, Mr. Loman.

HAPPY: Wait on her.

STANLEY (*going to the girl's table*): Would you like a menu, ma'am?

GIRL: I'm expecting someone, but I'd like a—

HAPPY: Why don't you bring her—excuse me, miss, do you mind? I sell champagne, and I'd like you to try my brand. Bring her a champagne, Stanley.

GIRL: That's awfully nice of you.

HAPPY: Don't mention it. It's all company money. (*He laughs.*)

GIRL: That's a charming product to be selling, isn't it?

HAPPY: Oh, gets to be like everything else. Selling is selling, y' know.

GIRL: I suppose.

HAPPY: You don't happen to sell, do you?

GIRL: No, I don't sell.

HAPPY: Would you object to a compliment from a stranger? You ought to be on a magazine cover.

GIRL (*looking at him a little archly*): I have been.

STANLEY *comes in with a glass of champagne.*

HAPPY: What'd I say before, Stanley? You see? She's a cover girl.

STANLEY: Oh, I could see, I could see.

HAPPY (*to the* GIRL): What magazine?

GIRL: Oh, a lot of them. (*She takes the drink.*) Thank you.

HAPPY: You know what they say in France, don't you? "Champagne is the drink of the complexion"—Hya, Biff!

BIFF *has entered and sits with* HAPPY.

BIFF: Hello, kid. Sorry I'm late.

HAPPY: I just got here. Uh, Miss—?

GIRL: Forsythe.

HAPPY: Miss Forsythe, this is my brother.

BIFF: Is Dad here?

HAPPY: His name is Biff. You might've heard of him. Great football player.

GIRL: Really? What team?

HAPPY: Are you familiar with football?

GIRL: No, I'm afraid I'm not.

HAPPY: Biff is quarterback with the New York Giants.

GIRL: Well, that is nice, isn't it? (*She drinks.*)

HAPPY: Good health.

GIRL: I'm happy to meet you.

HAPPY: That's my name. Hap. It's really Harold, but at West Point they called me Happy.

GIRL (*now really impressed*): Oh, I see. How do you do? (*She turns her profile.*)

BIFF: Isn't Dad coming?

HAPPY: You want her?

BIFF: Oh, I could never make that.

HAPPY: I remember the time that idea would never come into your head. Where's the old confidence, Biff?

BIFF: I just saw Oliver—

HAPPY: Wait a minute. I've got to see that old confidence again. Do you want her? She's on call.

BIFF: Oh, no. (*He turns to look at the* GIRL.)

HAPPY: I'm telling you. Watch this. (*Turning to the* GIRL) Honey? (*She turns to him.*) Are you busy?

GIRL: Well, I am . . . but I could make a phone call.

HAPPY: Do that, will you, honey? And see if you can get a friend. We'll be here for a while. Biff is one of the greatest football players in the country.

GIRL (*standing up*): Well, I'm certainly happy to meet you.

HAPPY: Come back soon.

GIRL: I'll try.

HAPPY: Don't try, honey, try hard.

The GIRL *exits.* STANLEY *follows, shaking his head in bewildered admiration.*

HAPPY: Isn't that a shame now? A beautiful girl like that? That's why I can't get married. There's not a good woman in a thousand. New York is loaded with them, kid!

BIFF: Hap, look—

HAPPY: I told you she was on call!

BIFF (*strangely unnerved*): Cut it out, will ya? I want to say something to you.

HAPPY: Did you see Oliver?

BIFF: I saw him all right. Now look, I want to tell Dad a couple of things and I want you to help me.

HAPPY: What? Is he going to back you?

BIFF: Are you crazy? You're out of your goddam head, you know that?

HAPPY: Why? What happened?

BIFF (*breathlessly*): I did a terrible thing today, Hap. It's been the strangest day I ever went through. I'm all numb, I swear.

HAPPY: You mean he wouldn't see you?

BIFF: Well, I waited six hours for him, see? All day. Kept sending my name in. Even tried to date his secretary so she'd get me to him, but no soap.

HAPPY: Because you're not showin' the old confidence, Biff. He remembered you, didn't he?

BIFF (*stopping* HAPPY *with a gesture*): Finally, about five o'clock, he comes out. Didn't remember who I was or anything. I felt like such an idiot, Hap.

HAPPY: Did you tell him my Florida idea?

BIFF: He walked away. I saw him for one minute. I got so mad I could've torn the walls down! How the hell did I ever get the idea I was a salesman there? I even believed myself that I'd been a salesman for him! And then he gave me one look and—I realized what a ridiculous lie my whole life has been! We've been talking in a dream for fifteen years. I was a shipping clerk.

HAPPY: What'd you do?

BIFF (*with great tension and wonder*): Well, he left, see. And the secretary went out. I was all alone in the waiting-room. I don't know what came over me, Hap. The next thing I know I'm in his office—paneled walls, everything. I can't explain it. I—Hap, I took his fountain pen.

HAPPY: Geez, did he catch you?

BIFF: I ran out. I ran down all eleven flights. I ran and ran and ran.

HAPPY: That was an awful dumb—what'd you do that for?

BIFF (*agonized*): I don't know, I just—wanted to take something, I don't know. You gotta help me, Hap, I'm gonna tell Pop.

HAPPY: You crazy? What for?

BIFF: Hap, he's got to understand that I'm not the man somebody lends that kind of money to. He thinks I've been spiting him all these years and it's eating him up.

HAPPY: That's just it. You tell him something nice.

BIFF: I can't.

HAPPY: Say you got a lunch date with Oliver tomorrow.

BIFF: So what do I do tomorrow?

HAPPY: You leave the house tomorrow and come back at night and say Oliver is thinking it over. And he thinks it over for a couple of weeks, and gradually it fades away and nobody's the worse.

BIFF: But it'll go on forever!

HAPPY: Dad is never so happy as when he's looking forward to something!

WILLY *enters.*

HAPPY: Hello, scout!

WILLY: Gee, I haven't been here in years!

STANLEY *has followed* WILLY *in and sets a chair for him.* STANLEY *starts off but* HAPPY *stops him.*

HAPPY: Stanley!

STANLEY *stands by, waiting for an order.*

HAPPY (*going to* WILLY *with guilt, as to an invalid*): Sit down, Pop. You want a drink?

WILLY: Sure, I don't mind.

BIFF: Let's get a load on.

WILLY: You look worried.

BIFF: N-no. (*To* STANLEY): Scotch all around. Make it doubles.

STANLEY: Doubles, right. (*He goes.*)

WILLY: You had a couple already, didn't you?

BIFF: Just a couple, yeah.

WILLY: Well, what happened, boy? (*Nodding affirmatively, with a smile*) Everything go all right?

BIFF (*takes a breath, then reaches out and grasps* WILLY'*s hand*): Pal . . . (*He is smiling bravely, and* WILLY *is smiling too*) I had an experience today.

HAPPY: Terrific, Pop.

WILLY: That so? What happened?

BIFF (*high, slightly alcoholic, above the earth*): I'm going to tell you everything: from first to last. It's been a strange day. (*Silence. He looks around, composes himself as best he can, but his breath keeps breaking the rhythm of his voice.*) I had to wait quite a while for him, and—

WILLY: Oliver?

BIFF: Yeah, Oliver. All day, as a matter of cold fact. And a lot of—instances—facts, Pop, facts about my life came back to me. Who was it, Pop? Who ever said I was a salesman with Oliver?

WILLY: Well, you were.

BIFF: No, Dad, I was a shipping clerk.

WILLY: But you were practically—

BIFF (*with determination*): Dad, I don't know who said it first, but I was never a salesman for Bill Oliver.

WILLY: What're you talking about?

BIFF: Let's hold on to the facts tonight, Pop. We're not going to get anywhere bullin' around. I was a shipping clerk.

WILLY (*angrily*): All right, now listen to me—

BIFF: Why don't you let me finish?

WILLY: I'm not interested in stories about the past or any crap of that kind because the woods are burning, boys, you understand? There's a big blaze going on all around. I was fired today.

BIFF (*shocked*): How could you be?

WILLY: I was fired, and I'm looking for a little good news to tell your mother, because the woman has waited and the woman has suffered. The gist of it is that I haven't got a story left in my head, Biff. So don't give me a lecture about facts and aspects. I am not interested. Now what've you got to say to me?

STANLEY *enters with three drinks. They wait until he leaves.*

WILLY: Did you see Oliver?

BIFF: Jesus, Dad!

WILLY: You mean you didn't go up there?

HAPPY: Sure he went up there.

BIFF: I did. I—saw him. How could they fire you?

WILLY (*on the edge of his chair*): What kind of a welcome did he give you?

BIFF: He won't even let you work on commission?

WILLY: I'm out! (*Driving*): So tell me, he gave you a warm welcome?

HAPPY: Sure, Pop, sure!

BIFF (*driven*): Well, it was kind of—

WILLY: I was wondering if he'd remember you. (*To* HAPPY) Imagine, man doesn't see him for ten, twelve years and gives him that kind of a welcome!

HAPPY: Damn right!

BIFF (*trying to return to the offensive*): Pop, look—

WILLY: You know why he remembered you, don't you? Because you impressed him in those days.

BIFF: Let's talk quietly and get this down to the facts, huh?

WILLY (*as though* BIFF *had been interrupting*): Well, what happened? It's great news, Biff. Did he take you into his office or'd you talk in the waiting-room?

BIFF: Well, he came in, see, and—

WILLY (*with a big smile*): What'd he say? Betcha he threw his arm around you.

BIFF: Well, he kinda—

WILLY: He's a fine man. (*To* HAPPY) Very hard man to see, y'know.

HAPPY (*agreeing*): Oh, I know.

WILLY (*to* BIFF): Is that where you had the drinks?

BIFF: Yeah, he gave me a couple of—no, no!

HAPPY (*cutting in*): He told him my Florida idea.

WILLY: Don't interrupt. (*To* BIFF) How'd he react to the Florida idea?

BIFF: Dad, will you give me a minute to explain?

WILLY: I've been waiting for you to explain since I sat down here! What happened? He took you into his office and what?

BIFF: Well—I talked. And—and he listened, see.

WILLY: Famous for the way he listens, y'know. What was his answer?

BIFF: His answer was— (*He breaks off, suddenly angry.*) Dad, you're not letting me tell you what I want to tell you!

WILLY (*accusing, angered*): You didn't see him, did you?

BIFF: I did see him!

WILLY: What'd you insult him or something? You insulted him, didn't you?

BIFF: Listen, will you let me out of it, will you just let me out of it!

HAPPY: What the hell!

WILLY: Tell me what happened!

BIFF (*to* HAPPY): I can't talk to him!

A single trumpet note jars the ear. The light of green leaves stains the house, which holds the air of night and a dream. YOUNG BERNARD *enters and knocks on the door of the house.*

YOUNG BERNARD (*frantically*): Mrs. Loman, Mrs. Loman!

HAPPY: Tell him what happened!

BIFF (to HAPPY): Shut up and leave me alone!

WILLY: No, no! You had to go and flunk math!

BIFF: What math? What're you talking about?

YOUNG BERNARD: Mrs. Loman, Mrs. Loman!

LINDA *appears in the house, as of old.*

WILLY (*wildly*): Math, math, math!

BIFF: Take it easy, Pop!

YOUNG BERNARD: Mrs. Loman!

WILLY (*furiously*): If you hadn't flunked you'd've been set by now!

BIFF: Now, look, I'm gonna tell you what happened, and you're going to listen to me.

YOUNG BERNARD: Mrs. Loman!

BIFF: I waited six hours—

HAPPY: What the hell are you saying?

BIFF: I kept sending in my name but he wouldn't see me. So finally he . . . (*He continues unheard as light fades low on the restaurant.*)

YOUNG BERNARD: Biff flunked math!

LINDA: No!

YOUNG BERNARD: Birnbaum flunked him! They won't graduate him!

LINDA: But they have to. He's gotta go to the university. Where is he? Biff! Biff!

YOUNG BERNARD: No, he left. He went to Grand Central.

LINDA: Grand—You mean he went to Boston!

YOUNG BERNARD: Is Uncle Willy in Boston?

LINDA: Oh, maybe Willy can talk to the teacher. Oh, the poor, poor boy!

Light on house area snaps out.

BIFF (*at the table, now audible, holding up a gold fountain pen*): . . . so I'm washed up with Oliver, you understand? Are you listening to me?

WILLY (*at a loss*): Yeah, sure. If you hadn't flunked—

BIFF: Flunked what? What're you talking about?

WILLY: Don't blame everything on me! I didn't flunk math—you did! What pen?

HAPPY: That was awful dumb, Biff, a pen Like that is worth—

WILLY (*seeing the pen for the first time*): You took Oliver's pen?

BIFF (*weakening*): Dad, I just explained it to you.

WILLY: You stole Bill Oliver's fountain pen!

BIFF: I didn't exactly steal it! That's just what I've been explaining to you!

HAPPY: He had it in his hand and just then Oliver walked in, so he got nervous and stuck it in his pocket!

WILLY: My God, Biff!

BIFF: I never intended to do it, Dad!

OPERATOR'S VOICE: Standish Arms, good evening!

WILLY (*shouting*): I'm not in my room!

BIFF (*frightened*): Dad, what's the matter? (*He and* HAPPY *stand up.*)

OPERATOR: Ringing Mr. Loman for you!

WILLY: I'm not there, stop it!

BIFF (*horrified, gets down on one knee before* WILLY): Dad, I'll make good, I'll make good. (WILLY *tries to get to his feet.* BIFF *holds him down.*) Sit down now.

WILLY: No, you're no good, you're no good for anything.

BIFF: I am, Dad, I'll find something else, you understand? Now don't worry about anything. (*He holds up* WILLY*'s face*) Talk to me, dad.

OPERATOR: Mr. Loman does not answer. Shall I page him?

WILLY (*attempting to stand, as though to rush and silence the* OPERATOR): No, no, no!

HAPPY: He'll strike something, Pop.

WILLY: No, no . . .

BIFF (*desperately, standing over* WILLY): Pop, listen! Listen to me! I'm telling you something good. Oliver talked to his partner about the Florida idea. You listening? He—he talked to his partner, and he came to me . . . I'm going to be all right, you hear? Dad, listen to me, he said it was just a question of the amount!

WILLY: Then you . . . got it?

HAPPY: He's gonna be terrific, Pop!

WILLY (*trying to stand*): Then you got it, haven't you? You got it! You got it!

BIFF (*agonized, holds* WILLY *down*): No, no. Look, Pop. I'm supposed to have lunch with them tomorrow. I'm just telling you this so you'll know that I can still make an impression, Pop. And I'll make good somewhere, but I can't go tomorrow, see?

WILLY: Why not? You simply—

BIFF: But the pen, Pop!

WILLY: You give it to him and tell him it was an oversight!

HAPPY: Sure, have lunch tomorrow!

BIFF: I can't say that—

WILLY: You were doing a crossword puzzle and accidentally used his pen!

BIFF: Listen, kid, I took those balls years ago, now I walk in with his fountain pen? That clinches it, don't you see? I can't face him like that! I'll try elsewhere.

PAGE'S VOICE: Paging Mr. Loman!

WILLY: Don't you want to be anything?

BIFF: Pop, how can I go back?

WILLY: You don't want to be anything, is that what's behind it?

BIFF (*now angry at* WILLY *for not crediting his sympathy*): Don't take it that way! You think it was easy walking into that office after what I'd done to him? A team of horses couldn't have dragged me back to Bill Oliver!

WILLY: Then why'd you go?

BIFF: Why did I go? Why did I go! Look at you! Look at what's become of you!

Off left, THE WOMAN *laughs.*

WILLY: Biff, you're going to go to that lunch tomorrow, or—

BIFF: I can't go. I've got no appointment!

HAPPY: Biff, for . . . !

WILLY: Are you spiting me?

BIFF: Don't take it that way! Goddammit!

WILLY (*strikes* BIFF *and falters away from the table*): You rotten little louse! Are you spiting me?

THE WOMAN: Someone's at the door, Willy!

BIFF: I'm no good, can't you see what I am?

HAPPY (*separating them*): Hey, you're in a restaurant! Now cut it out, both of you! (*The girls enter.*) Hello, girls, sit down.

THE WOMAN *laughs, off left.*

MISS FORSYTHE: I guess we might as well. This is Letta.

THE WOMAN: Willy, are you going to wake up?

BIFF (*ignoring* WILLY): How're ya, miss, sit down. What do you drink?

MISS FORSYTHE: Letta might not be able to stay long.

LETTA: I gotta get up very early tomorrow. I got jury duty. I'm so excited! Were you fellows ever on a jury?

BIFF: No, but I been in front of them! (*The girls laugh.*) This is my father.

LETTA: Isn't he cute? Sit down with us, Pop.

HAPPY: Sit him down, Biff!

BIFF (*going to him*): Come on, slugger, drink us under the table. To hell with it! Come on, sit down, pal.

On BIFF'*s last insistence,* WILLY *is about to sit.*

THE WOMAN (*now urgently*): Willy, are you going to answer the door!

THE WOMAN'*s call pulls* WILLY *back. He starts right, befuddled.*

BIFF: Hey, where are you going?

WILLY: Open the door.

BIFF: The door?

WILLY: The washroom . . . the door . . . where's the door?

HAPPY (*leading* WILLY *to the left*): Just go straight down.

WILLY *moves left.*

THE WOMAN: Willy, Willy, are you going to get up, get up, get up, get up?

WILLY *exits left.*

LETTA: I think it's sweet you bring your daddy along.

MISS FORSYTHE: Oh, he isn't really your father!

BIFF (*at left, turning to her resentfully*): Miss Forsythe, you've just seen a prince walk by. A fine, troubled prince. A hardworking, unappreciated prince. A pal, you understand? A good companion. Always for his boys.

LETTA: That's so sweet.

HAPPY: Well, girls, what's the program? We're wasting time. Come on, Biff. Gather round. Where would you like to go?

BIFF: Why don't you do something for him?

HAPPY: Me!

BIFF: Don't you give a damn for him, Hap?

HAPPY: What're you talking about? I'm the one who—

BIFF: I sense it, you don't give a good goddam about him. (*He takes the rolled-up hose from his pocket and puts it on the table in front of* HAPPY.) Look what I found in the cellar, for Christ's sake. How can you bear to let it go on?

HAPPY: Me? Who goes away? Who runs off and—

BIFF: Yeah, but he doesn't mean anything to you. You could help him—I can't! Don't you understand what I'm talking about? He's going to kill himself, don't you know that?

HAPPY: Don't I know it! Me!

BIFF: Hap, help him! Jesus . . . help him . . . Help me, help me, I can't bear to look at his face! (*Ready to weep, he hurries out, up right.*)

HAPPY (*starting after him*): Where are you going?

MISS FORSYTHE: What's he so mad about?

HAPPY: Come on, girls, we'll catch up with him.

MISS FORSYTHE (*as* HAPPY *pushes her out*): Say, I don't like that temper of his!

HAPPY: He's just a little overstrung, he'll be all right!

WILLY (*off left, as* THE WOMAN *laughs*): Don't answer! Don't answer!

LETTA: Don't you want to tell your father—

HAPPY: No, that's not my father. He's just a guy. Come on, we'll catch Biff, and, honey, we're going to paint this town! Stanley, where's the check! Hey, Stanley!

They exit. STANLEY *looks toward left.*

STANLEY (*calling to* HAPPY *indignantly*): Mr. Loman! Mr. Loman!

STANLEY *picks up a chair and follows them off. Knocking is heard off left.* THE WOMAN *enters, laughing.* WILLY *follows her. She is in a black slip; he is buttoning his shirt. Raw, sensuous music accompanies their speech.*

WILLY: Will you stop laughing? Will you stop?

THE WOMAN: Aren't you going to answer the door? He'll wake the whole hotel.

WILLY: I'm not expecting anybody.

THE WOMAN: Whyn't you have another drink, honey, and stop being so damn self-centered?

WILLY: I'm so lonely.

THE WOMAN: You know you ruined me, Willy? From now on, whenever you come to the office, I'll see that you go right through to the buyers. No waiting at my desk any more, Willy. You ruined me.

WILLY: That's nice of you to say that.

THE WOMAN: Gee, you are self-centered! Why so sad? You are the saddest, self-centeredest soul I ever did see-saw. (*She laughs. He kisses her.*) Come on inside, drummer boy. It's silly to be dressing in the middle of the night. (*As knocking is heard*) Aren't you going to answer the door?

WILLY: They're knocking on the wrong door.

THE WOMAN: But I felt the knocking. And he heard us talking in here. Maybe the hotel's on fire!

WILLY (*his terror rising*): It's a mistake.

THE WOMAN: Then tell him to go away!

WILLY: There's nobody there.

THE WOMAN: It's getting on my nerves, Willy. There's somebody standing out there and it's getting on my nerves!

WILLY (*pushing her away from him*): All right, stay in the bathroom here, and don't come out. I think there's a law in Massachusetts about it, so don't come out. It may be that new room clerk. He looked very mean. So don't come out. It's a mistake, there's no fire.

The knocking is heard again. He takes a few steps away from her, and she vanishes into the wing. The light follows him, and now he is facing YOUNG BIFF, *who carries a suitcase.* BIFF *steps toward him. The music is gone.*

BIFF: Why didn't you answer?

WILLY: Biff! What are you doing in Boston?

BIFF: Why didn't you answer? I've been knocking for five minutes, I called you on the phone—

WILLY: I just heard you. I was in the bathroom and had the door shut. Did anything happen home?

BIFF: Dad—I let you down.

WILLY: What do you mean?

BIFF: Dad . . .

WILLY: Biffo, what's this about? (*Putting his arm around* BIFF) Come on, let's go downstairs and get you a malted.

BIFF: Dad, I flunked math.

WILLY: Not for the term?

BIFF: The term. I haven't got enough credits to graduate.

WILLY: You mean to say Bernard wouldn't give you the answers?

BIFF: He did, he tried, but I only got a sixty-one.

WILLY: And they wouldn't give you four points?

BIFF: Birnbaum refused absolutely. I begged him, Pop, but he won't give me those points. You gotta talk to him before they close the school. Because if he saw the kind of man you are, and you just talked to him in your way, I'm sure he'd come through for me. The class came right before practice, see, and I didn't go enough. Would you talk to him? He'd like you, Pop. You know the way you could talk.

WILLY: You're on. We'll drive right back.

BIFF: Oh, Dad, good work! I'm sure he'll change it for you!

WILLY: Go downstairs and tell the clerk I'm checkin' out. Go right down.

BIFF: Yes, sir! See, the reason he hates me, Pop—one day he was late for class so I got up at the blackboard and imitated him. I crossed my eyes and talked with a lithp.

WILLY (*laughing*): You did? The kids like it?

BIFF: They nearly died laughing!

WILLY: Yeah? What'd you do?

BIFF: The thquare root of thixthy twee is . . . (WILLY *bursts out laughing;* BIFF *joins him.*) And in the middle of it he walked in!

WILLY *laughs and* THE WOMAN *joins in offstage.*

WILLY (*without hesitation*): Hurry downstairs and—

BIFF: Somebody in there?

WILLY: No, that was next door.

THE WOMAN *laughs offstage.*

BIFF: Somebody got in your bathroom!

WILLY: No, it's the next room, there's a party—

THE WOMAN (*enters, laughing. She lisps this*): Can I come in? There's something in the bathtub, Willy, and it's moving!

WILLY *looks at* BIFF, *who is staring open-mouthed and horrified at* THE WOMAN.

WILLY: Ah—you better go back to your room. They must be finished painting by now. They're painting her room so I let her take a shower here. Go back, go back . . . (*He pushes her.*)

THE WOMAN (*resisting*): But I've got to get dressed, Willy, I can't—

WILLY: Get out of here! Go back, go back . . . (*Suddenly striving for the ordinary*) This is Miss Francis, Biff, she's a buyer. They're painting her room. Go back, Miss Francis, go back . . .

THE WOMAN: But my clothes, I can't go out naked in the hall!

WILLY (*pushing her offstage*): Get outa here! Go back, go back!

BIFF *slowly sits down on his suitcase as the argument continues offstage.*

THE WOMAN: Where's my stockings? You promised me stockings, Willy!

WILLY: I have no stockings here!

THE WOMAN: You had two boxes of size nine sheers for me, and I want them!

WILLY: Here, for God's sake, will you get outa here!

THE WOMAN (*enters holding a box of stockings*): I just hope there's nobody in the hall. That's all I hope. (*To* BIFF) Are you football or baseball?

BIFF: Football.

THE WOMAN (*angry, humiliated*): That's me too. G'night. (*She snatches her clothes from* WILLY, *and walks out.*)

WILLY (*after a pause*): Well, better get going. I want to get to the school first thing in the morning. Get my suits out of the closet. I'll get my valise. (BIFF *doesn't move.*) What's the matter? (BIFF *remains motionless, tears falling.*) She's a buyer. Buys for J. H. Simmons. She lives down the hall—they're painting. You don't imagine—(*He breaks off. After a pause*) Now listen, pal, she's just a buyer. She sees merchandise in her room and they have to keep it looking just so . . . (*Pause. Assuming command*) All right, get my suits. (BIFF *doesn't move.*) Now stop crying and do as I say. I gave you an order. Biff, I gave you an order! Is that what you do when I give you an order? How dare you cry! (*Putting his arm around* BIFF) Now look, Biff, when you grow up you'll understand about these things. You mustn't—you mustn't overemphasize a thing like this. I'll see Birnbaum first thing in the morning.

BIFF: Never mind.

WILLY (*getting down beside* BIFF): Never mind! He's going to give you those points. I'll see to it.

BIFF: He wouldn't listen to you.

WILLY: He certainly will listen to me. You need those points for the U. of Virginia.

BIFF: I'm not going there.

WILLY: Heh? If I can't get him to change that mark you'll make it up in summer school. You've got all summer to—

BIFF: (*his weeping breaking from him*): Dad . . .

WILLY (*infected by it*): Oh, my boy . . .

BIFF: Dad . . .

WILLY: She's nothing to me, Biff. I was lonely, I was terribly lonely.

BIFF: You—you gave her Mama's stockings! (*His tears break through and he rises to go.*)

WILLY (*grabbing for* BIFF): I gave you an order!

BIFF: Don't touch me, you—liar!

WILLY: Apologize for that!

BIFF: You fake! You phony little fake! You fake! (*Overcome, he turns quickly and weeping fully goes out with his suitcase.* WILLY *is left on the floor on his knees.*)

WILLY: I gave you an order! Biff, come back here or I'll beat you! Come back here! I'll whip you!

STANLEY *comes quickly in from the right and stands in front* of WILLY.

WILLY (*shouts at* STANLEY): I gave you an order . . .

STANLEY: Hey, let's pick it up, pick it up, Mr. Loman. (*He helps* WILLY *to his feet.*) Your boys left with the chippies. They said they'll see you home.

A second waiter watches some distance away.

WILLY: But we were supposed to have dinner together.

Music is heard, WILLY'*s theme.*

STANLEY: Can you make it?

WILLY: I'll—sure, I can make it. (*Suddenly concerned about his clothes*): Do I—I look all right?

STANLEY: Sure, you look all right. (*He flicks a speck off* WILLY'*s lapel.*)

WILLY: Here—here's a dollar.

STANLEY: Oh, your son paid me. It's all right.

WILLY (*putting it in* STANLEY'*s hand*): No, take it. You're a good boy.

STANLEY: Oh, no, you don't have to . . .

WILLY: Here—here's some more, I don't need it any more. (*After a slight pause*) Tell me—is there a seed store in the neighborhood?

STANLEY: Seeds? You mean like to plant?

As WILLY *turns,* STANLEY *slips the money back into his jacket pocket.*

WILLY: Yes. Carrots, peas . . .

STANLEY: Well, there's hardware stores on Sixth Avenue, but it may be too late now.

WILLY (*anxiously*): Oh, I'd better hurry. I've got to get some seeds. (*He starts off to the right.*) I've got to get some seeds, right away. Nothing's planted. I don't have a thing in the ground.

WILLY *hurries out as the light goes down.* STANLEY *moves over to the right after him, watches him off. The other waiter has been staring at* WILLY.

STANLEY (*to the waiter*): Well, whatta you looking at?

The waiter picks up the chairs and moves off right. STANLEY *takes the table and follows him. The light fades on this area. There is a long pause, the sound of the flute coming over. The light gradually rises on the kitchen, which is empty.* HAPPY *appears at the door of the house, followed by* BIFF. HAPPY *is carrying a large bunch of long-stemmed roses. He enters the kitchen, looks around for* LINDA. *Not seeing her, he turns to* BIFF, *who is just outside the house door, and makes a gesture with his hands, indicating "Not here, I guess." He looks into the living-room and freezes. Inside,* LINDA, *unseen, is seated,* WILLY'*s coat on her lap. She rises ominously and quietly and moves toward* HAPPY, *who backs up into the kitchen, afraid.*

HAPPY: Hey, what're you doing up? (LINDA *says nothing but moves toward him implacably.*) Where's Pop? (*He keeps backing to the right, and now* LINDA *is in full view in the doorway to the living-room.*) Is he sleeping?

LINDA: Where were you?

HAPPY (*trying to laugh it off*): We met two girls, Mom, very fine types. Here, we brought you some flowers. (*Offering them to her*) Put them in your room, Ma.

She knocks them to the floor at BIFF'*s feet. He has now come inside and closed the door behind him. She stares at* BIFF, *silent.*

HAPPY: Now what'd you do that for? Mom, I want you to have some flowers—

LINDA (*cutting* HAPPY *off, violently to* BIFF): Don't you care whether he lives or dies?

HAPPY (*going to the stairs*): Come upstairs, Biff.

BIFF (*with a flare of disgust, to* HAPPY): Go away from me! (*To* LINDA) What do you mean, lives or dies? Nobody's dying around here, pal.

LINDA: Get out of my sight! Get out of here!

BIFF: I wanna see the boss.

LINDA: You're not going near him!

BIFF: Where is he? (*He moves into the living-room and* LINDA *follows.*)

LINDA (*shouting after* BIFF): You invite him for dinner. He looks forward to it all day—(BIFF *appears in his parents' bedroom, looks around, and exits*)—and then you desert him there. There's no stranger you'd do that to!

HAPPY: Why? He had a swell time with us. Listen, when I—(LINDA *comes back into the kitchen*)—desert him I hope I don't outlive the day!

LINDA: Get out of here!

HAPPY: Now look, Mom . . .

LINDA: Did you have to go to women tonight? You and your lousy rotten whores!

BIFF *re-enters the kitchen.*

HAPPY: Mom, all we did was follow Biff around trying to cheer him up! (*To* BIFF): Boy, what a night you gave me!

LINDA: Get out of here, both of you, and don't come back! I don't want you tormenting him any more. Go on now, get your things together! (*To* BIFF): You can sleep in his apartment. (*She starts to pick up the flowers and stops herself.*) Pick up this stuff, I'm not your maid any more. Pick it up, you bum, you!

HAPPY *turns his back to her in refusal.* BIFF *slowly moves over and gets down on his knees, picking up the flowers.*

LINDA: You're a pair of animals! Not one, not another living soul would have had the cruelty to walk out on that man in a restaurant!

HAPPY (*not looking at her*): Is that what he said?

LINDA: He didn't have to say anything. He was so humiliated he nearly limped when he came in.

HAPPY: But, Mom, he had a great time with us—

BIFF (*cutting him off violently*): Shut up!

Without another word, HAPPY *goes upstairs.*

LINDA: You! You didn't even go in to see if he was all right!

BIFF (*still on the floor in front of* LINDA, *the flowers in his hand; with self-loathing*) No. Didn't. Didn't do a damned thing. How do you like that, heh? Left him babbling in a toilet.

LINDA: You louse. You . . .

BIFF: Now you hit it on the nose! (*He gets up throws the flowers in the wastebasket.*) The scum of the earth, and you're looking at him!

LINDA: Get out of here!

BIFF: I gotta talk to the boss, Mom. Where is he?

LINDA: You're not going near him. Get out of this house!

BIFF (*with absolute assurance, determination*): No. We're gonna have an abrupt conversation, him and me.

LINDA: You're not talking to him!

Hammering is heard from outside the house, off right. BIFF *turns toward the noise.*

LINDA (*suddenly pleading*): Will you please leave him alone?

BIFF: What's he doing out there?

LINDA: He's planting the garden!

BIFF (*quietly*): Now? Oh, my God!

BIFF *moves outside,* LINDA *following. The light dies down on them and comes up on the center of the apron as* WILLY *walks into it. He is carrying a flashlight, a hoe, and a handful of seed packets. He raps the top of the hoe sharply to fix it firmly, and then moves to the left, measuring off the distance with his foot. He holds the flashlight to look at the seed packets, reading off the instructions. He is in the blue of night.*

WILLY: Carrots . . . quarter-inch apart. Rows . . . one-foot rows. (*He measures it off.*) One foot. (*He puts down a package and measures off.*) Beets. (*He puts down another package and measures again.*) Lettuce. (*He reads the package, puts it down.*) One foot—(*He breaks off as* BEN *appears at the right and moves slowly down to him.*) What a proposition, ts, ts. Terrific, terrific. 'Cause she's suffered, Ben, the woman has suffered. You understand me? A man can't go out the way he came in, Ben, a man has to, to add up to something. You can't, you can't—(BEN *moves toward him as though to interrupt.*) You gotta consider, now. Don't answer so quick. Remember, it's a guaranteed twenty-thousand-dollar proposition. Now look, Ben, I want you to go through the ins and outs of this thing with me. I've got nobody to talk to, Ben, and the woman has suffered, you hear me?

BEN (*standing still, considering*): What's the proposition?

WILLY: It's twenty thousand dollars on the barrelhead. Guaranteed, gilt-edged, you understand?

BEN: You don't want to make a fool of yourself. They might not honor the policy.

WILLY: How can they dare refuse? Didn't I work like a coolie to meet every premium on the nose? And now they don't pay off? Impossible!

BEN: It's called a cowardly thing, William.

WILLY: Why? Does it take more guts to stand here the rest of my life ringing up a zero?

BEN (*yielding*): That's a point, William. (*He moves, thinking, turns.*) And twenty thousand—that *is* something one can feel with the hand, it is there.

WILLY (*now assured, with rising power*): Oh, Ben, that's the whole beauty of it! I see it like a diamond, shining in the dark, hard and rough, that I can pick up and touch in my hand. Not like—like an appointment! This would not be another damned-fool appointment, Ben, and it changes all the aspects. Because he thinks I'm nothing, see, and so he spites me. But the funeral—(*Straightening up*) Ben, that funeral will be massive! They'll come from Maine, Massachusetts, Vermont, New Hampshire! All the old-timers with the strange license plates—that boy will be thunder-struck, Ben, because he never realized—I am known! Rhode Island, New York, New Jersey—I am known, Ben, and he'll see it with his eyes once and for all. He'll see what I am, Ben! He's in for a shock, that boy!

BEN (*coming down to the edge of the garden*): He'll call you a coward.

WILLY (*suddenly fearful*): No, that would be terrible.

BEN: Yes. And a damned fool.

WILLY: No, no, he mustn't, I won't have that! (*He is broken and desperate.*)

BEN: He'll hate you, William.

The gay music of the Boys is heard.

WILLY: Oh, Ben, how do we get back to all the great times? Used to be so full of light, and comradeship, the sleigh-riding in winter, and the ruddiness on his cheeks. And always some kind of good news coming up, always something nice coming up ahead. And never even let me carry the valises in the house, and simonizing, simonizing that little red car! Why, why can't I give him something and not have him hate me?

BEN: Let me think about it. (*He glances at his watch.*) I still have a little time. Remarkable proposition, but you've got to be sure you're not making a fool of yourself.

BEN *drifts off upstage and goes out of sight.* BIFF *comes down from the left.*

WILLY (*suddenly conscious of* BIFF, *turns and looks up at him, then begins picking up the packages of seeds in confusion*): Where the hell is that seed? (*Indignantly*) You can't see nothing out here! They boxed in the whole goddam neighborhood!

BIFF: There are people all around here. Don't you realize that?

WILLY: I'm busy. Don't bother me.

BIFF (*taking the hoe from* WILLY): I'm saying good-by to you, Pop. (WILLY *looks at him, silent, unable to move.*) I'm not coming back any more.

WILLY: You're not going to see Oliver tomorrow?

BIFF: I've got no appointment, Dad.

WILLY: He put his arm around you, and you've got no appointment?

BIFF: Pop, get this now, will you? Everytime I've left it's been a fight that sent me out of here. Today I realized something about myself and I tried to explain it to you and I—I think I'm just not smart enough to make any sense out of it for you. To hell with whose fault it is or anything like that. (*He takes* WILLY'*s arm.*) Let's just wrap it up, heh? Come on in, we'll tell Mom. (*He gently tries to pull* WILLY *to left.*)

WILLY (*frozen, immobile, with guilt in his voice*): No, I don't want to see her.

BIFF: Come on! (*He pulls again, and* WILLY *tries to pull away.*)

WILLY (*highly nervous*): No, no, I don't want to see her.

BIFF (*tries to look into* WILLY'*s face, as if to find the answer there*): Why don't you want to see her?

WILLY (*more harshly now*): Don't bother me, will you?

BIFF: What do you mean, you don't want to see her? You don't want them calling you yellow, do you? This isn't your fault; it's me, I'm a bum. Now come inside! (WILLY *strains to get away.*) Did you hear what I said to you?

WILLY *pulls away and quickly goes by himself into the house.* BIFF *follows.*

LINDA (to WILLY): Did you plant, dear?

BIFF (*at the door, to* LINDA): All right, we had it out. I'm going and I'm not writing any more.

LINDA (*going to* WILLY *in the kitchen*): I think that's the best way, dear. 'Cause there's no use drawing it out, you'll just never get along.

WILLY *doesn't respond.*

BIFF: People ask where I am and what I'm doing, you don't know, and you don't care. That way it'll be off your mind and you can start brightening up again. All right? That clears it, doesn't it? (WILLY *is silent, and* BIFF *goes to him.*) You gonna wish me luck, scout? (*He extends his hand*) What do you say?

LINDA: Shake his hand, Willy.

WILLY (*turning to her, seething with hurt*): There's no necessity to mention the pen at all, y'know.

BIFF (*gently*): I've got no appointment, Dad.

WILLY (*erupting fiercely*): He put his arm around . . . ?

BIFF: Dad, you're never going to see what I am, so what's the use of arguing? If I strike oil I'll send you a check. Meantime forget I'm alive.

WILLY (*to* LINDA): Spite, see?

BIFF: Shake hands, Dad.

WILLY: Not my hand.

BIFF: I was hoping not to go this way.

WILLY: Well, this is the way you're going. Good-by.

BIFF *looks at him a moment, then turns sharply and goes to the stairs.*

WILLY (*stops him with*): May you rot in hell if you leave this house!

BIFF (*turning*): Exactly what is it that you want from me?

WILLY: I want you to know, on the train, in the mountains, in the valleys, wherever you go, that you cut down your life for spite!

BIFF: No, no.

WILLY: Spite, spite, is the word for your undoing! And when you're down and out, remember what did it. When you're rotting somewhere beside the railroad tracks, remember, and don't you dare blame it on me!

BIFF: I'm not blaming it on you!

WILLY: I won't take the rap for this, you hear?

HAPPY *comes down the stairs and stands on the bottom step, watching.*

BIFF: That's just what I'm telling you!

WILLY (*sinking into a chair at the table, with full accusation*): You're trying to put a knife in me—don't think I don't know what you're doing!

BIFF: All right, phony! Then let's lay it on the line. (*He whips the rubber tube out of his pocket and puts it on the table.*)

HAPPY: You crazy—

LINDA: Biff! (*She moves to grab the hose, but* BIFF *holds it down with his hand.*)

BIFF: Leave it there! Don't move it!

WILLY (*not looking at it*): What is that?

BIFF: You know goddam well what that is.

WILLY (*caged, wanting to escape*): I never saw that.

BIFF: You saw it. The mice didn't bring it into the cellar! What is this supposed to do, make a hero out of you? This supposed to make me sorry for you?

WILLY: Never heard of it.

BIFF: There'll be no pity for you, you hear it? No pity!

WILLY (*to* LINDA): You hear the spite!

BIFF: No, you're going to hear the truth—what you are and what I am!

LINDA: Stop it!

WILLY: Spite!

HAPPY (*coming down toward* BIFF): You cut it now!

BIFF (*to* HAPPY): The man don't know who we are! The man is gonna know! (*To* WILLY) We never told the truth for ten minutes in this house!

HAPPY: We always told the truth!

BIFF (*turning on him*): You big blow, are you the assistant buyer? You're one of the two assistants to the assistant, aren't you?

HAPPY: Well, I'm practically—

BIFF: You're practically full of it! We all are! And I'm through with it. (*To* WILLY): Now hear this, Willy, this is me.

WILLY: I know you!

BIFF: You know why I had no address for three months? I stole a suit in Kansas City and I was in jail. (*To* LINDA, *who is sobbing*) Stop crying. I'm through with it.

LINDA *turns away from them, her hands covering her face.*

WILLY: I suppose that's my fault!

BIFF: I stole myself out of every good job since high school!

WILLY: And whose fault is that?

BIFF: And I never got anywhere because you blew me so full of hot air I could never stand taking orders from anybody! That's whose fault it is!

WILLY: I hear that!

LINDA: Don't, Biff!

BIFF: It's goddam time you heard that! I had to be boss big shot in two weeks, and I'm through with it!

WILLY: Then hang yourself! For spite, hang yourself!

BIFF: No! Nobody's hanging himself, Willy! I ran down eleven flights with a pen in my hand today. And suddenly I stopped, you hear me? And in the middle of that office building, do you hear this? I stopped in the middle of that building and I saw—the sky. I saw the things that I love in this world. The work and the food and time to sit and smoke. And I looked at the pen and said to myself, what the hell am I grabbing this for? Why am I trying to become what I don't want to be? What am I doing in an office, making a contemptuous, begging fool of myself, when all I want is out there, waiting for me the minute I say I know who I am! Why can't I say that, Willy? (*He tries to make* WILLY *face him, but* WILLY *pulls away and moves to the left.*)

WILLY (*with hatred, threateningly*): The door of your life is wide open!

BIFF: Pop! I'm a dime a dozen, and so are you!

WILLY (*turning on him now in an uncontrolled outburst*): I am not a dime a dozen! I am Willy Loman, and you are Biff Loman!

BIFF *starts for* WILLY, *but is blocked by* HAPPY. *In his fury,* BIFF *seems on the verge of attacking his father.*

BIFF: I am not a leader of men, Willy, and neither are you. You were never anything but a hard-working drummer who landed in the ash can like all the rest of them! I'm one dollar an hour, Willy! I tried seven states and couldn't raise it. A buck an hour! Do you gather my meaning? I'm not bringing home any prizes any more, and you're going to stop waiting for me to bring them home!

WILLY (*directly to* BIFF): You vengeful, spiteful mut!

BIFF *breaks from* HAPPY. WILLY, *in fright, starts up the stairs.* BIFF *grabs him.*

BIFF (*at the peak of his fury*): Pop, I'm nothing! I'm nothing, Pop. Can't you understand that? There's no spite in it any more. I'm just what I am, that's all.

BIFF'*s fury has spent itself, and be breaks down, sobbing, holding on to* WILLY, *who dumbly fumbles for* BIFF'*s face.*

WILLY (*astonished*): What're you doing? What're you doing? (*To* LINDA): Why is he crying?

BIFF (*crying, broken*): Will you let me go, for Christ's sake? Will you take that phony dream and burn it before something happens? (*Struggling to contain himself, he pulls away and moves to the stairs.*) I'll go in the morning. Put him—put him to bed. (*Exhausted,* BIFF *moves up the stairs to his room.*)

WILLY (*after a long pause, astonished, elevated*): Isn't that—isn't that remarkable? Biff—he likes me!

LINDA: He loves you, Willy!

HAPPY (*deeply moved*): Always did, Pop.

WILLY: Oh, Biff! (*Staring wildly*): He cried! Cried to me. (*He is choking with his love, and now cries out his promise*) That boy—that boy is going to be magnificent!

BEN *appears in the light just outside the kitchen.*

BEN: Yes, outstanding, with twenty thousand behind him.

LINDA (*sensing the racing of his mind, fearfully, carefully*): Now come to bed, Willy. It's all settled now.

WILLY (*finding it difficult not to rush out of the house*): Yes, we'll sleep. Come on. Go to sleep, Hap.

BEN: And it does take a great kind of a man to crack the jungle.

In accents of dread, BEN'*s idyllic music starts up.*

HAPPY (*his arm around* LINDA): I'm getting married, Pop, don't forget it. I'm changing everything. I'm gonna run that department before the year is up. You'll see, Mom. (*He kisses her.*)

BEN: The jungle is dark but full of diamonds, Willy.

WILLY *turns, moves listening to* BEN.

LINDA: Be good. You're both good boys, just act that way, that's all.

HAPPY: 'Night, Pop. (*He goes upstairs.*)

LINDA (*to* WILLY): Come, dear.

BEN (*with greater force*): One must go in to fetch a diamond out.

WILLY (*to* LINDA, *as he moves slowly along the edge of the kitchen, toward the door*): I just want to get settled down, Linda. Let me sit alone for a little.

LINDA (*almost uttering her fear*): I want you upstairs.

WILLY (*taking her in his arms*): In a few minutes, Linda. I couldn't sleep right now. Go on, you look awful tired. (*He kisses her.*)

BEN: Not like an appointment at all. A diamond is rough and hard to the touch.

WILLY: Go on now. I'll be right up.

LINDA: I think this is the only way, Willy.

WILLY: Sure, it's the best thing.

BEN: Best thing!

WILLY: The only way. Everything is gonna be—go on, kid, get to bed. You look so tired.

LINDA: Come right up.

WILLY: Two minutes.

LINDA *goes into the living-room, then reappears in her bedroom.* WILLY *moves just outside the kitchen door.*

WILLY: Loves me. (*Wonderingly*) Always loved me. Isn't that a remarkable thing? Ben, he'll worship me for it!

BEN (*with promise*): It's dark there, but full of diamonds.

WILLY: Can you imagine that magnificence with twenty thousand dollars in his pocket?

LINDA (*calling from her room*): Willy! Come up!

WILLY (*calling into the kitchen*): Yes! Yes. Coming! It's very smart, you realize that, don't you, sweetheart! Even Ben sees it. I gotta go, baby. 'By! 'By! (*Going over to* BEN, *almost dancing*) Imagine? When the mail comes he'll be ahead of Bernard again!

BEN: A perfect proposition all around.

WILLY: Did you see how he cried to me? Oh, if I could kiss him, Ben!

BEN: Time, William, time!

WILLY: Oh, Ben, I always knew one way or another we were gonna make it, Biff and I!

BEN (*looking at his watch*): The boat. We'll be late. (*He moves slowly off into the darkness.*)

WILLY (*elegiacally, turning to the house*): Now when you kick off, boy, I want a seventy-yard boot, and get right down the field under the ball, and when you hit, hit low and hit hard, because it's important, boy. (*He swings around and faces the audience.*) There's all kinds of important people in the stands, and the first thing you know . . . (*Suddenly realizing he is alone*) Ben! Ben, where do I . . . ? (*He makes a sudden movement of search.*) Ben, how do I . . . ?

LINDA (*calling*): Willy, you coming up?

WILLY (*uttering a gasp of fear, whirling about as if to quiet her*): Sh! (*He turns around as if to find his way; sounds, faces, voices, seem to be swarming in upon him and he flicks at them, crying*), Sh! Sh! (*Suddenly music, faint and high, stops him. It rises in intensity, almost to an unbearable scream. He goes up and down on his toes, and rushes off around the house.*) Shhh!

LINDA: Willy?

There is no answer. LINDA *waits.* BIFF *gets up off his bed. He is still in his clothes.* HAPPY *sits up.* BIFF *stands listening.*

LINDA (*with real fear*): Willy, answer me! Willy!

There is the sound of a car starting and moving away at full speed.

LINDA: No!

HAPPY (*rushing down the stairs*): Pop!

As the car speeds off, the music crashes down in a frenzy of sound, which becomes the soft pulsation of a single cello string. BIFF *slowly returns to his bedroom. He and* HAPPY *gravely don their jackets.* LINDA *slowly walks out of her room. The music has developed into a dead march. The leaves of day are appearing over everything.* CHARLEY *and* BERNARD, *somberly dressed, appear and knock on the kitchen door.* BIFF *and* HAPPY *slowly descend the stairs to the kitchen as* CHARLEY *and* BERNARD *enter. All stop a moment when* LINDA, *in clothes of mourning, bearing a little bunch of roses, comes through the draped doorway into the kitchen. She goes to* CHARLEY *and takes his arm. Now all move toward the audience, through the wall-line of the kitchen. At the limit of the apron,* LINDA *lays down the flowers, kneels, and sits back on her beels. All stare down at the grave.*

Requiem

CHARLEY: It's getting dark, Linda.

LINDA *doesn't react. She stares at the grave.*

BIFF: How about it, Mom? Better get some rest, heh? They'll be closing the gate soon.

LINDA *makes no move. Pause.*

HAPPY (*deeply angered*): He had no right to do that. There was no necessity for it. We would've helped him.

CHARLEY (*grunting*): Hmmm.

BIFF: Come along, Mom.

LINDA: Why didn't anybody come?

CHARLEY: It was a very nice funeral.

LINDA: But where are all the people he knew? Maybe they blame him.

CHARLEY: Naa. It's a rough world, Linda. They wouldn't blame him.

LINDA: I can't understand it. At this time especially. First time in thirty-five years we were just about free and clear. He only needed a little salary. He was even finished with the dentist.

CHARLEY: No man only needs a little salary.

LINDA: I can't understand it.

BIFF: There were a lot of nice days. When he'd come home from a trip; or on Sundays, making the stoop; finishing the cellar; putting on the new porch; when he built the extra bathroom; and put up the garage. You know something, Charley, there's more of him in that front stoop than in all the sales he ever made.

CHARLEY: Yeah. He was a happy man with a batch of cement.

LINDA: He was so wonderful with his hands.

BIFF: He had the wrong dreams. All, all wrong.

HAPPY (*almost ready to fight* BIFF): Don't say that!

BIFF: He never knew who he was.

CHARLEY (*stopping* HAPPY'*s movement and reply. To* BIFF): Nobody dast blame this man. You don't understand: Willy was a salesman. And for a salesman, there is no rock bottom to the life. He don't put a bolt to a nut, he don't tell you the law or give you medicine. He's a man way out there in the blue, riding on a smile and a shoeshine. And when they start not smiling back—that's an earthquake. And then you get yourself a couple of spots on your hat, and you're finished. Nobody dast blame this man. A salesman is got to dream, boy. It comes with the territory.

BIFF: Charley, the man didn't know who he was.

HAPPY (*infuriated*): Don't say that!

BIFF: Why don't you come with me, Happy?

HAPPY: I'm not licked that easily. I'm staying right in this city, and I'm gonna beat this racket! (*He looks at* BIFF, *his chin set.*) The Loman Brothers!

BIFF: I know who I am, kid.

HAPPY: All right, boy. I'm gonna show you and everybody else that Willy Loman did not die in vain. He had a good dream. It's the only dream you can have—to come out number-one man. He fought it out here, and this is where I'm gonna win it for him.

BIFF (*with a hopeless glance at* HAPPY, *bends toward his mother*): Let's go, Mom.

LINDA: I'll be with you in a minute. Go on, Charley. (*He hesitates.*) I want to, just for a minute. I never had a chance to say good-by.

CHARLEY *moves away, followed by* HAPPY. BIFF *remains a slight distance up and left of* LINDA. *She sits there, summoning herself. The flute begins, not far away, playing behind her speech.*

LINDA: Forgive me, dear. I can't cry. I don't know what it is, but I can't cry. I don't understand it. Why did you ever do that? Help me, Willy, I can't cry. It seems to me that you're just on another trip. I keep expecting you. Willy, dear, I can't cry. Why did you do it? I search and search and I search, and I can't understand it, Willy. I made the last payment on the house today. Today, dear. And there'll be nobody home. (*A sob rises in her throat.*) We're free and clear. (*Sobbing more fully, released*) We're free. (BIFF *comes slowly toward her.*) We're free . . . We're free . . .

BIFF *lifts her to her feet and moves out up right with her in his arms.* LINDA *sobs quietly.* BERNARD *and* CHARLEY *come together and follow them, followed by* HAPPY. *Only the music of the flute is left on the darkening stage as over the house the hard towers of the apartment buildings rise into sharp focus, and*

THE CURTAIN FALLS

Edward Albee (born in 1928) created a fable of anxiety and identity in *The Zoo Story.* First staged in Berlin, Germany, in 1959, the play embodies many of the qualities that have since come to characterize Albee's oeuvre. The paradoxical mixture of love and hate, the cleverly abrasive dialogues, the religious and political textures, the necessity of ritualized confrontation, and the tragic force of abandonment and death all coalesce in Albee's first play. The play elevates its two seemingly indeterminate figures, Peter and Jerry, to tragic proportions.

Throughout this compact and intense drama, Jerry reflects that "sometimes a person has to go a very long distance out of his way to come back a short distance correctly," a reflection that culminates in a fatal chance meeting with Peter in New York City's Central Park. The play revolves around the clash of two men—and their very different worlds—whose values and attitudes seem as separate as the men representing them. In the play's shocking ending, Jerry not only gains the purpose and atonement for which he has been searching, but he also shatters Peter's predictable world and shocks him into self-awareness.

In 2004, Albee staged *Peter and Jerry,* a full-length play that combined *The Zoo Story* with a prequel, *Homelife,* that focuses on Peter and his wife, Ann, the morning of Peter's fateful confrontation with Jerry hours later. Today *The Zoo Story,* along with Albee's longer plays *Who's Afraid of Virginia Woolf?* and *A Delicate Balance,* are regarded as classics of the modern American stage. With the passing of Arthur Miller in 2005 Albee is now viewed by many as the elder statesman of the American stage.

THE PLAYERS

PETER: *A man in his early forties, neither fat nor gaunt, neither handsome nor homely. He wears tweeds, smokes a pipe, carries horn-rimmed glasses. Although he is moving into middle age, his dress and his manner would suggest a man younger.*

JERRY: *A man in his late thirties, not poorly dressed, but carelessly. What was once a trim and lightly muscled body has begun to go to fat; and while he is no longer handsome, it is evident that he once was. His fall from physical grace should not suggest debauchery; he has, to come closest to it, a great weariness.*

THE SCENE: *It is Central Park; a Sunday afternoon in summer; the present. There are two park benches, one toward either side of the stage; they both face the audience. Behind them: foliage, trees, sky. At the beginning, Peter is seated on one of the benches.*

STAGE DIRECTIONS: *As the curtain rises,* PETER *is seated on the bench stage-right. He is reading a book. He stops reading, cleans his glasses, goes back to reading.* JERRY *enters.*

JERRY: I've been to the zoo. (PETER *doesn't notice*) I said, I've been to the zoo. MISTER, I'VE BEEN TO THE ZOO!

PETER: Hm? . . . What? . . . I'm sorry, were you talking to me?

JERRY: I went to the zoo, and then I walked until I came here. Have I been walking north?

PETER (*Puzzled*): North? Why . . . I . . . I think so. Let me see.

JERRY: (*Pointing past the audience*) Is that Fifth Avenue?

PETER: Why yes; yes, it is.

JERRY: And what is that cross street there; that one, to the right?

PETER: That? Oh, that's Seventy-fourth Street.

JERRY: And the zoo is around Sixty-fifth Street; so, I've been walking north.

PETER: (*Anxious to get back to his reading*) Yes; it would seem so.

JERRY: Good old north.

PETER: (*Lightly, by reflex*) Ha, ha.

JERRY: (*After a slight pause*) But not due north.

PETER: I . . . well, no, not due north; but, we . . . call it north. It's northerly.

JERRY: (*Watches as* PETER, *anxious to dismiss him, prepares his pipe*) Well, boy; *you're* not going to get lung cancer, are you?

PETER: (*Looks up, a little annoyed, then smiles*) No, sir. Not from this.

JERRY: No, sir. What you'll probably get is cancer of the mouth, and then you'll have to wear one of those things Freud wore after they took one whole side of his jaw away. What do they call those things?

PETER (*Uncomfortable*): A prosthesis?

JERRY: The very thing! A prosthesis. You're an educated man, aren't you? Are you a doctor?

PETER: Oh, no; no. I read about it somewhere; *Time* magazine, I think. (*He turns to his book*)

JERRY: Well, *Time* magazine isn't for blockheads.

PETER: No, I suppose not.

JERRY: (*After a pause*) Boy, I'm glad that's Fifth Avenue there.

PETER (*Vaguely*): Yes.

JERRY: I don't like the west side of the park much.

PETER: Oh? (*Then, slightly wary, but interested*) Why?

JERRY: (*Offhand*) I don't know.

PETER: Oh. (*He returns to his book*)

JERRY: (*He stands for a few seconds, looking at* PETER, *who finally looks up again, puzzled*) Do you mind if we talk?

PETER: (*Obviously minding*) Why . . . no, no.

JERRY: Yes you do; you do.

PETER: (*Puts his book down, his pipe out and away, smiling*) No, really; I don't mind.

JERRY: Yes you do.

PETER: (*Finally decided*) No; I don't mind at all, really.

JERRY: It's . . . it's a nice day.

PETER: (*Stares unnecessarily at the sky*) Yes. Yes, it is; lovely.

JERRY: I've been to the zoo.

PETER: Yes, I think you said so . . . didn't you?

JERRY: You'll read about it in the papers tomorrow, if you don't see it on your TV tonight. You have TV, haven't you?

PETER: Why yes, we have two; one for the children.

JERRY: You're married!

PETER: (*With pleased emphasis*) Why, certainly.

JERRY: It isn't a law, for God's sake.

PETER: No . . . no, of course not.

JERRY: And you have a wife.

PETER: (*Bewildered by the seeming lack of communication*) Yes!

JERRY: And you have children.

PETER: Yes; two.

JERRY: Boys?

PETER: No, girls . . . both girls.

JERRY: But you wanted boys.

PETER: Well . . . naturally, every man wants a son, but . . .

JERRY: (*Lightly mocking*) But that's the way the cookie crumbles?

PETER (*Annoyed*): I wasn't going to say that.

JERRY: And you're not going to have any more kids, are you?

PETER: (*A bit distantly*) No. No more. (*Then back, and irksome*) Why did you say that? How would you know about that?

JERRY: The way you cross your legs, perhaps; something in the voice. Or maybe I'm just guessing. Is it your wife?

PETER: (*Furious*) That's none of your business! (*A silence*) Do you understand? (JERRY *nods,* PETER *is quiet now*) Well, you're right. We'll have no more children.

JERRY: (*Softly*) That *is* the way the cookie crumbles.

PETER: (*Forgiving*) Yes . . . I guess so.

JERRY: Well, now; what else?

PETER: What were you saying about the zoo . . . that I'd read about it, or see . . . ?

JERRY: I'll tell you about it, soon. Do you mind if I ask you questions?

PETER: Oh, not really.

JERRY: I'll tell you why I do it; I don't talk to many people—except to say like: give me a beer, or where's the john, or what time does the feature go on, or keep your hands to yourself, buddy. You know—things like that.

PETER: I must say I don't . . .

JERRY: But every once in a while I like to talk to somebody, really *talk;* like to get to know somebody, know all about him.

PETER: (*Lightly laughing, still a little uncomfortable*) And am I the guinea pig for today?

JERRY: On a sun-drenched Sunday afternoon like this? Who better than a nice married man with two daughters and . . . ah . . . a dog? (PETER *shakes his head*) No? Two dogs. (PETER *shakes his head again*) Hm. No dogs? (PETER *shakes his head, sadly*) Oh, that's a shame. But you look like an animal man. CATS? (PETER *nods his head, ruefully*) Cats! But, that can't be your idea. No, sir. Your wife and daughters? (PETER *nods his head*) Is there anything else I should know?

PETER: (*He has to clear his throat*) There are . . . there are two parakeets. One . . . uh . . . one for each of my daughters.

JERRY: Birds.

PETER: My daughters keep them in a cage in their bedroom.

JERRY: Do they carry disease? The birds.

PETER: I don't believe so.

JERRY: That's too bad. If they did you could set them loose in the house and the cats could eat them and die, maybe. (PETER *looks blank for a moment, then laughs*) And what else? What do you do to support your enormous household?

PETER: I . . . uh . . . I have an executive position with a . . . a small publishing house. We . . . uh . . . we publish textbooks.

JERRY: That sounds nice; very nice. What do you make?

PETER: (*Still cheerful*) Now look here!

JERRY: Oh, come on.

PETER: Well, I make around eighteen thousand a year, but I don't carry more than forty dollars at any one time . . . in case you're a . . . a holdup man . . . ha, ha, ha.

JERRY: (*Ignoring the above*) Where do you live? (PETER *is reluctant*) Oh, look; I'm not going to rob you, and I'm not going to kidnap your parakeets, your cats, or your daughters.

PETER: (*Too loud*) I live between Lexington and Third Avenue, on Seventy-fourth Street.

JERRY: That wasn't so hard, was it?

PETER: I didn't mean to seem . . . ah . . . it's that you don't really carry on a conversation; you just ask questions, and I'm . . . I'm normally. . . . uh . . . reticent. Why do you just stand there?

JERRY: I'll start walking around in a little while, and eventually I'll sit down. (*Recalling*) Wait until you see the expression on his face.

PETER: What? Whose face? Look here; is this something about the zoo?

JERRY: (*Distantly*) The what?

PETER: The zoo; the zoo. Something about the zoo.

JERRY: The zoo?

PETER: You've mentioned it several times.

JERRY: (*Still distant, but returning abruptly*) The zoo? Oh, yes; the zoo. I was there before I came here. I told you that. Say, what's the dividing line between upper-middle-middle-class and lower-upper-middle-class?

PETER: My dear fellow, I . . .

JERRY: Don't my dear fellow me.

PETER: (*Unhappily*) Was I patronizing? I believe I was; I'm sorry. But, you see, your question about the classes bewildered me.

JERRY: And when you're bewildered you become patronizing?

PETER: I . . . I don't express myself too well, sometimes. (*He attempts a joke on himself*) I'm in publishing, not writing.

JERRY: (*Amused, but not at the humor*) So be it. The truth *is: I* was being patronizing.

PETER: Oh, now; you needn't say that.

(It is at this point that JERRY *may begin to move about the stage with slowly increasing determination and authority, but pacing himself, so that the long speech about the dog comes at the high point of the arc)*

JERRY: All right. Who are your favorite writers? Baudelaire and J.P. Marquand?

PETER: (*Wary*) Well, I like a great many writers; I have a considerable . . . catholicity of taste, if I may say so. Those two men are fine, each in his way. (*Warming up*) Baudelaire, of course . . . uh . . . is by far the finer of the two, but Marquand has a place . . . in our . . . uh . . . national . . .

JERRY: Skip it.

PETER: I . . . sorry.

JERRY: Do you know what I did before I went to the zoo today? I walked all the way up Fifth Avenue from Washington Square; all the way.

PETER: Oh; you live in the Village! (*This seems to enlighten* PETER)

JERRY: No, I don't. I took the subway down to the Village so I could walk all the way up Fifth Avenue to the zoo. It's one of those things a person has to do; sometimes a person has to go a very long distance out of his way to come back a short distance correctly.

PETER: (*Almost pouting*) Oh, I thought you lived in the Village.

JERRY: What were you trying to do? Make sense out of things? Bring order? The old pigeonhole bit? Well, that's easy; I'll tell you. I live in a four-story brownstone roominghouse on the upper West Side between Columbus Avenue and Central Park West. I live on the top floor; rear; west. It's a laughably small room, and one of my walls is made of beaverboard; this beaverboard separates my room from another laughably small room, so I assume that the two rooms were once one room, a small room, but not necessarily laughable. The room beyond my beaverboard wall is occupied by a colored queen who always keeps his door open; well, not always, but *always* when he's plucking his eyebrows, which he does with Buddhist concentration. This colored queen has rotten teeth, which is rare, and he has a Japanese kimono, which is also pretty rare; and he wears this kimono to and from the john in the hall, which is pretty frequent. I mean, he goes to the john a lot. He never bothers me, and he never brings anyone up to his room. All he does is pluck his eyebrows, wear his kimono and go to the john. Now, the two front rooms on my floor are a little larger, I guess; but they're pretty small, too. There's a Puerto Rican family in one of them, a husband, a wife, and some kids; I don't know how many. These people entertain a lot. And in the other front room, there's somebody living there, but I don't know who it is. I've never seen who it is. Never. Never ever.

PETER: (*Embarrassed*) Why . . . why do you live there?

JERRY: (*From a distance again*) I don't know.

PETER: It doesn't sound like a very nice place . . . where you live.

JERRY: Well, no; it isn't an apartment in the East Seventies. But, then again, I don't have one wife, two daughters, two cats and two parakeets. What I do have, I have toilet articles, a few clothes, a hot plate that I'm not supposed to have, a can opener, one that works with a key, you know; a knife, two forks, and two spoons, one small, one large; three plates, a cup, a saucer, a drinking glass, two picture frames, both empty, eight or nine books, a pack of pornographic playing cards, regular deck, an old Western Union typewriter that prints nothing but capital letters, and a small strongbox without a lock which has in it . . . what? Rocks! Some rocks . . . sea-rounded rocks I picked up on the beach when I was a kid. Under which . . . weighed down . . . are some letters . . . please letters . . . please why don't you do this, and please when will you do that letters. And when letters, too. When will you write? When will you come? When? These letters are from more recent years.

PETER: (*Stares glumly at his shoes, then*) About those two empty picture frames . . . ?

JERRY: I don't see why they need any explanation at all. Isn't it clear? I don't have pictures of anyone to put in them.

PETER: Your parents . . . perhaps . . . a girl friend . . .

JERRY: You're a very sweet man, and you're possessed of a truly enviable innocence. But good old Mom and good old Pop are dead . . . you know? . . . I'm broken up about it, too . . . I mean really. BUT. That particular vaudeville act is playing the cloud circuit now, so I don't see how I can look at them, all neat and framed. Besides, or, rather, to be pointed about it, good old Mom walked out on good old Pop when I was ten and a half years old; she embarked on an adulterous turn of our southern states . . . a journey of a year's duration . . . and her most constant companion . . . among others, among many others . . . was a Mr. Barleycorn. At least, that's what good old Pop told me after he went down . . . came back . . . brought her body north. We'd received the news between Christmas and New Year's, you see, that good old Mom had parted with the ghost in some dump in Alabama. And, without the ghost . . . she was less welcome. I mean, what was she? A stiff . . . a northern stiff. At any rate, good old Pop celebrated the New Year for an even two weeks and then slapped into the front of a somewhat moving city omnibus, which sort of cleaned things out family-wise. Well no; then there was Mom's sister, who was given neither to sin nor the consolations of the bottle. I moved in on her, and my memory of her is slight excepting I remember still that she did all things dourly: sleeping, eating, working, praying. She dropped dead on the stairs to her apartment, my apartment then, too, on the afternoon of my high school graduation. A terribly middle-European joke, if you ask me.

PETER: Oh, my; oh, my.

JERRY: Oh, your what? But that was a long time ago, and I have no feeling about any of it that I care to admit to myself. Perhaps you can see, though, why good old Mom and good old Pop are frameless. What's your name? Your first name?

PETER: I'm Peter.

JERRY: I'd forgotten to ask you. I'm Jerry.

PETER: (*With a slight, nervous laugh*) Hello, Jerry.

JERRY: (*Nods his hello*) And let's see now; what's the point of having a girl's picture, especially in two frames? I have two picture frames, you remember. I never see the pretty little ladies more than once, and most of them wouldn't be caught in the same room with a camera. It's odd, and I wonder if it's sad.

PETER: The girls?

JERRY: No. I wonder if it's sad that I never see the little ladies more than once. I've never been able to have sex with, or, how is it put? . . . make love to anybody more than once. Once; that's it. . . . Oh, wait; for a week and a half, when I was fifteen . . . and I hang my head in shame that puberty was late . . . I was a h-o-m-o-s-e-x-u-a-l. I mean, I was queer . . . (*Very fast*) . . . queer, queer, queer . . . with bells ringing, banners snapping in the wind. And for those eleven days, I met at least twice a day with the park superintendent's son . . . a Greek boy, whose birthday was the same as mine, except he was a year older. I think I was very much in love . . . maybe just with sex. But that was the jazz of a very special hotel, wasn't it? And now; oh, do I love the little ladies; really, I love them. For about an hour.

PETER: Well, it seems perfectly simple to me. . . .

JERRY: (*Angry*) Look! Are you going to tell me to get married and have parakeets?

PETER: (*Angry himself*) Forget the parakeets! And stay single if you want to. It's no business of mine. I didn't start this conversation in the . . .

JERRY: All right, all right. I'm sorry. All right? You're not angry?

PETER: (*Laughing*) No, I'm not angry.

JERRY: (*Relieved*) Good. (*Now back to his previous tone*) Interesting that you asked me about the picture frames. I would have thought that you would have asked me about the pornographic playing cards.

PETER: (*With a knowing smile*) Oh, I've seen those cards.

JERRY: That's not the point. (*Laughs*) I suppose when you were a kid you and your pals passed them around, or you had a pack of your own.

PETER: Well, I guess a lot of us did.

JERRY: And you threw them away just before you got married.

PETER: Oh, now; look here. I didn't *need* anything like that when I got older.

JERRY: No?

PETER: (*Embarrassed*) I'd rather not talk about these things.

JERRY: So? Don't. Besides, I wasn't trying to plumb your post-adolescent sexual life and hard times; what I wanted to get at is the value difference between pornographic playing cards when you're a kid, and pornographic playing cards when you're older. It's that when you're a kid you use the cards as a substitute for a real experience, and when you're older you use real experience as a substitute for the fantasy. But I imagine you'd rather hear about what happened at the zoo.

PETER: (*Enthusiastic*) Oh, yes; the zoo. (*Then, awkward*) That is . . . if you. . . .

JERRY: Let me tell you about why I went . . . well, let me tell you some things. I've told you about the fourth floor of the roominghouse where I live. I think the rooms are better as you go down, floor by floor. I guess they are; I don't know. I don't know any of the people on the third and second floors. Oh, wait! I do know that there's a lady living on the third floor, in the front. I know because she cries all the time. Whenever I go out or come back in, whenever I pass her door, I always hear her crying, muffled, but . . . very determined. Very determined indeed. But the one I'm getting to, and all about the dog, is the landlady. I don't like to use words that are too harsh in describing people. I don't like to. But the landlady is a fat, ugly, mean, stupid, unwashed, misanthropic, cheap, drunken bag of garbage. And you may have noticed that I very seldom use profanity, so I can't describe her as well as I might.

PETER: You describe her . . . vividly.

JERRY: Well, thanks. Anyway, she has a dog, and I will tell you about the dog, and she and her dog are the gatekeepers of my dwelling. The woman is bad enough; she leans around in the entrance hall, spying to see that I don't bring in things or people, and when she's had her mid-afternoon pint of lemon-flavored gin she always stops me in the hall, and grabs ahold of my coat or my arm, and she presses her disgusting body up against me to keep me in a corner so she can talk to me. The smell of her body and her breath . . . you can't imagine it . . . and somewhere, somewhere in the back of that pea-sized brain of hers, an organ developed just enough to let her eat, drink, and emit, she has some foul parody of sexual desire. And I, Peter, I am the object of her sweaty lust.

PETER: That's disgusting. That's . . . horrible.

JERRY: But I have found a way to keep her off. When she talks to me, when she presses herself to my body and mumbles about her room and how I should come there, I merely say: but, Love; wasn't yesterday enough for you, and the day before? Then she puzzles, she makes slits of her tiny eyes, she sways a little, and then, Peter . . . and it is at this moment that I think I might be doing some good in that tormented house . . . a simple-minded smile begins to form on her unthinkable face, and she giggles and groans as she thinks about yesterday and the day before; as she believes and relives what never happened. Then, she motions to that black monster of a dog she has, and she goes back to her room. And I am safe until our next meeting.

PETER: It's so . . . unthinkable. I find it hard to believe that people such as that really *are.*

JERRY: (*Lightly mocking*) It's for reading about, isn't it?

PETER: (*Seriously*) Yes.

JERRY: And fact is better left to fiction. You're right, Peter. Well, what I have been meaning to tell you about is the dog; I shall, now.

PETER: (*Nervously*) Oh, yes; the dog.

JERRY: Don't go. You're not thinking of going, are you?

PETER: Well . . . no, I don't think so.

JERRY: (*As if to a child*) Because after I tell you about the dog, do you know what then? Then . . . then I'll tell you about what happened at the zoo.

PETER: (*Laughing faintly*) You're . . . you're full of stories, aren't you?

JERRY: You don't *have* to listen. Nobody is holding you here; remember that. Keep that in your mind.

PETER: (*Irritably*) I know that.

JERRY: You do? Good. (*The following long speech, it seems to me, should be done with a great deal of action, to achieve a hypnotic effect on* PETER, *and on the audience, too. Some specific actions have been suggested, but the director and the actor playing* JERRY *might best work it out for themselves)* ALL RIGHT *(As if reading from a huge billboard)* THE STORY OF JERRY AND THE DOG! *(Natural again)* What I am going to tell you has something to do with how sometimes it's necessary to go a long distance out of the way in order to come back a short distance correctly; or, maybe I only think that it has something to do with that. But, it's why I went to the zoo today, and why I walked north . . . northerly, rather . . . until I came here. All right. The dog, I think I told you, is a black monster of a beast: an oversized head, tiny, tiny ears, and eyes . . . bloodshot, infected, maybe; and a body you can see the ribs through the skin. The dog is black, all black; all black except for the bloodshot eyes, and . . . yes . . . and an open sore on its . . . *right* forepaw; that is red, too. And, oh yes; the poor monster, and I do believe it's an old dog . . . it's certainly a misused one . . . almost always has an erection . . . of sorts. That's red, too. And . . . what else? . . . oh, yes; there's a gray-yellow-white color, too, when he bares his fangs. Like this: Grrrrrrr! Which is what he did when he saw me for the first time . . . the day I moved in. I worried about that animal the very first minute I met him. Now, animals don't take to me like Saint Francis[1] had birds hanging off him all the time. What I mean is: animals are indifferent to me . . . like people *(He smiles slightly)* . . . most of the time. But this dog wasn't indifferent. From the very beginning he'd snarl and then go for me, to get one of my legs. Not like he was rabid, you know; he was sort of a stumbly dog, but he wasn't half-assed, either. It was a good, stumbly run; but I always got away. He got a piece of my trouser leg, look, you can see right here, where it's mended; he got that the second day I lived there; but, I kicked free and got upstairs fast, so that was that. *(Puzzles)* I still don't know to this day how the other roomers manage it, but you know what I *think:* I think it had to do only with me. Cozy. So. Anyway, this went on for over a week, whenever I came in; but never when I went out. That's funny. Or, it *was* funny. I could pack up and live in the street for all the dog cared. Well, I thought about it up in

1. **Saint Francis:** an allusion to Saint Francis of Assisi, born in 1182, the beloved patron saint of animals

my room one day, one of the times after I'd bolted upstairs, and I made up my mind. I decided: First, I'll kill the dog with kindness, and if that doesn't work . . . I'll just kill him. (PETER *winces*) Don't react, Peter; just listen. So, the next day I went out and bought a bag of hamburgers, medium rare, no catsup, no onion; and on the way home I threw away all the rolls and kept just the meat.

(*Action for the following, perhaps*)

When I got back to the roominghouse the dog was waiting for me. I half opened the door that led into the entrance hall, and there he was; waiting for me. It figured. I went in, very cautiously, and I had the hamburgers, you remember; I opened the bag, and I set the meat down about twelve feet from where the dog was snarling at me. Like so! He snarled; stopped snarling; sniffed; moved slowly; then faster; then faster toward the meat. Well, when he got to it he stopped, and he looked at me. I smiled; but tentatively, you understand. He turned his face back to the hamburgers, smelled, sniffed some more, and then . . . RRRAAAAGGGGGHHHH, like that . . . he tore into them. It was as if he had never eaten anything in his life before, except like garbage. Which might very well have been the truth. I don't think the landlady ever eats anything but garbage. But. He ate all the hamburgers, almost all at once, making sounds in his throat like a woman. *Then,* when he'd finished the meat, the hamburger, and tried to eat the paper, too, he sat down and smiled. I think he smiled; I know cats do. It was a very gratifying few moments. Then, BAM, he snarled and made for me again. He didn't get me this time, either. So, I got upstairs, and I lay down on my bed and started to think about the dog again. To be truthful, I was offended, and I was damn mad, too. It was six perfectly good hamburgers with not enough pork in them to make it disgusting. I was offended. But, after a while, I decided to try it for a few more days. If you think about it, this dog had what amounted to an antipathy toward me; really. And, I wondered if I mightn't overcome this antipathy. So, I tried it for five more days, but it was always the same: snarl, sniff; move; faster; stare; gobble; RAAGGGHHH; smile; snarl; BAM. Well, now; by this time Columbus Avenue was strewn with hamburger rolls and I was less offended than disgusted. So, I decided to kill the dog.

(PETER *raises a hand in protest*)

Oh, don't be so alarmed, Peter; I didn't succeed. The day I tried to kill the dog I bought only one hamburger and what I thought was a murderous portion of rat poison. When I bought the hamburger I asked the man not to bother with the roll, all I wanted was the meat. I expected some reaction from him, like: we don't sell no hamburgers without rolls; or, wha' d'ya wanna do, eat it out'a ya han's? But no; he smiled benignly, wrapped up the hamburger in waxed paper, and said: A bite for ya pussy-cat? I wanted to say: No, not really; it's part of a plan to poison a dog I know. But, you can't say "a dog I know" without sounding funny; so I said, a little too loud, I'm afraid, and too formally: YES, A BITE FOR MY PUSSY-CAT. People looked up. It always happens when I try to simplify things; people look up. But that's neither hither nor thither. So. On my way back to the roominghouse, I kneaded the hamburger and the rat poison together between my hands, at that point feeling as much sadness as disgust. I opened the door to the entrance hall, and there the monster was, waiting to take the offering and then jump me. Poor bastard; he never learned that the moment he took to smile before he went for me gave me time enough to get out of range. BUT, there he was; malevolence with an erection, waiting. I put the poison patty down, moved toward the stairs and watched. The poor animal gobbled the food down as usual, smiled, which made me almost sick, and then, BAM. But, I sprinted up the stairs, as usual, and the dog didn't get me, as usual. AND IT CAME TO PASS THAT THE BEAST WAS DEATHLY ILL. I knew this because he no longer attended me, and because the landlady sobered up. She stopped me in the hall the same evening of the attempted murder and confided the information that God had struck her puppy-dog a surely fatal blow. She had forgotten her bewildered lust, and her eyes were wide open for the first time. They looked like the dog's eyes. She sniveled and implored me to pray for the animal. I wanted to say to her: Madam, I have myself to pray for, the colored queen, the Puerto Rican family, the person in the front room whom I've never seen, the woman who cries deliberately behind her closed door, and the rest of the people in all roominghouses, everywhere; besides, Madam, I don't understand how to pray. But . . . to simplify things . . . I told her I would pray. She looked up. She said that I was a liar, and that I probably wanted the dog to die. I told her, and there was so much truth here, that I didn't want the dog to die. I didn't, and not just because I'd poisoned him. I'm afraid that I must tell you I wanted the dog to live so that I could see what our new relationship might come to.

(PETER *indicates his increasing displeasure and slowly growing antagonism*)

Please understand, Peter; that sort of thing is important. You must believe me; it *is* important. We have to know the effect of our actions. (*Another deep sigh*) Well, anyway; the dog recovered. I have no idea why, unless he was a descendant of the puppy that guarded the gates of hell or some such resort. I'm not up on my mythology. (*He pronounces the word myth-o*-logy) Are you?

(PETER *sets to thinking, but* JERRY *goes on*)

At any rate, and you've missed the eight-thousand-dollar question, Peter; at any rate, the dog recovered his health and the landlady recovered her thirst, in no way altered by the bow-wow's deliverance. When I came home from a movie that was playing on Forty-second Street, a movie I'd seen, or one that was very much like one or several I'd seen, after the landlady told me puppykins was better, I was so hoping for the dog to be waiting for me. I was . . . well, how would you put it . . . enticed? . . . fascinated? . . . no, I don't think so . . . heart-shatteringly anxious, that's it; I was heart-shatteringly anxious to confront my friend again.

(PETER *reacts scoffingly*)

Yes, Peter; friend. That's the only word for it. I was heart-shatteringly et cetera to confront my doggy friend again. I came in the door and advanced, unafraid, to the center of the entrance hall. The beast was there . . . looking at me. And, you know, he looked better for his scrape with the nevermind. I stopped; I looked at him; he looked at me. I think . . . I think we stayed a long time that way . . . still, stone-statue . . . just looking at one another. I looked more into his face than he looked into mine. I mean, I can concentrate longer at looking into a dog's face than a dog can concentrate at looking into mine, or into anybody else's face, for that matter. But during that twenty seconds or two hours that we looked into each other's face, we made contact. Now, here is what I had wanted to happen: I loved the dog now, and I wanted him to love me. I had tried to love, and I had tried to kill, and both had been unsuccessful by themselves. I hoped . . . and I don't really know why I expected the dog to understand anything, much less my motivations . . . I hoped that the dog would understand.

(PETER *seems to .be hypnotized*)

It's just . . . it's just that . . . (JERRY *is abnormally tense, now*) . . . it's just that if you can't deal with people, you have to make a start somewhere. WITH ANIMALS! (*Much faster now, and like a conspirator*) Don't you see? A person has to have some way of dealing with SOMETHING. If not with people . . . if not with people . . . SOMETHING. With a bed, with a cockroach, with a mirror . . . no, that's too hard, that's one of the last steps. With a cockroach, with a . . . with a . . . with a carpet, a roll of toilet paper . . . no, not that, either . . . that's a mirror, too; always check bleeding. You see how hard it is to find things? With a street corner, and too many lights, all colors reflecting on the oily-wet streets . . . with a wisp of smoke, a wisp . . . of smoke . . . with . . . with pornographic playing cards, with a strongbox . . . WITHOUT A LOCK . . . with love, with vomiting, with crying, with fury because the pretty little ladies aren't pretty little ladies, with making money with your body which is an act of love and I could prove it, with howling because you're alive; with God. How about that? WITH GOD WHO IS A COLORED QUEEN WHO WEARS A KIMONO AND PLUCKS HIS EYEBROWS, WHO IS A WOMAN WHO CRIES WITH DETERMINATION BEHIND HER CLOSED DOOR . . . with God who, I'm told, turned his back on the whole thing some time ago . . . with . . . some day, with people. (JERRY *sighs the next word heavily*) People. With an idea; a concept. And where better, where ever better in this humiliating excuse for a jail, where better to communicate one single, simple-minded idea than in an entrance hall? Where? It would be A START! Where better to make a beginning . . . to understand and just possibly be understood . . . a beginning of an understanding, than with . . .

(*Here* JERRY *seems to fall into almost grotesque fatigue*)

. . . than with A DOG. Just that; a dog.

(*Here there is a silence that might be prolonged for a moment or so; then* JERRY *wearily finishes his story*)

A dog. It seemed like a perfectly sensible idea. Man is a dog's best friend, remember. So: the dog and I looked at each other. I longer than the dog. And what I saw then has been the same ever since. Whenever the dog and I see each other we both stop where we are. We regard each other with a mixture of sadness and suspicion, and then we feign indifference. We walk past each other safely; we have an understanding. It's very sad, but you'll have to admit that it is an understanding. We had made many attempts at contact, and we had failed. The dog has returned to garbage, and I to solitary but free passage. I have not returned. I mean to say, I have *gained* solitary free passage, if that much further loss can be said to be gain. I have learned that neither kindness nor cruelty by themselves, independent of each other, creates any effect beyond themselves; and I have learned that the two combined, together, at the same time, are the teaching emotion. And what is gained is loss. And what has been the result: the dog and I have attained a compromise; more of a bargain, really. We neither love nor hurt because we do not try to reach each other. And, *was* trying to feed the dog an act of love? And, perhaps, was the dog's attempt to bite me *not* an act of love? If we can so misunderstand, well then, why have we invented the word love in the first place?

(*There is silence.* JERRY *moves to* PETER*'s bench and sits down beside him. This is the first time* JERRY *has sat down during the play*)

The Story of Jerry and the Dog: the end.

(PETER *is silent*)

Well, Peter? (JERRY *is suddenly cheerful*) Well, Peter? Do you think I could sell that story to the *Reader's Digest* and make a couple of hundred bucks for *The Most Unforgettable Character I've Ever Met?* Huh?

(JERRY *is animated, but* PETER *is disturbed*)

Oh, come on now, Peter; tell me what you think.

PETER: (*Numb*) I . . . I don't understand what . . . I don't think I . . . (*Now, almost tearfully*) Why did you tell me all of this?

JERRY: Why not?

PETER: I DON'T UNDERSTAND!

JERRY: (*Furious, but whispering*) That's a lie.

PETER: No. No, it's not.

JERRY: (*Quietly*) I tried to explain it to you as I went along. I went slowly; it all has to do with . . .

PETER: I DON'T WANT TO HEAR ANY MORE. I don't understand you, or your landlady, or her dog. . . .

JERRY: *Her* dog! I thought it was my . . . No. No, you're right. It *is* her dog. (*Looks at* PETER *intently, shaking his head*) I don't know what I was thinking about; of course you don't understand. (*In a monotone, wearily*) I don't live in your block; I'm not married to two parakeets, or whatever your setup is. I am a *permanent transient*, and my home is the sickening roominghouses on the West Side of New York City, which is the greatest city in the world. Amen.

PETER: I'm . . . I'm sorry; I didn't mean to . . .

JERRY: Forget it. I suppose you don't quite know what to make of me, eh?

PETER: (*A joke*) We get all kinds in publishing. (*Chuckles*)

JERRY: You're a funny man. (*He forces a laugh*) You know that? You're a very . . . a richly comic person.

PETER: (*Modestly, but amused*) Oh, now, not really. (*Still chuckling*)

JERRY: Peter, do I annoy you, or confuse you?

PETER: (*Lightly*) Well, I must confess that this wasn't the kind of afternoon I'd anticipated.

JERRY: You mean, I'm not the gentleman you were expecting.

PETER: I wasn't expecting anybody.

JERRY: No, I don't imagine you were. But I'm here, and I'm not leaving.

PETER: (*Consulting his watch*) Well, you may not be, but I must be getting home soon.

JERRY: Oh, come on; stay a while longer.

PETER: I really should get home; you see . . .

JERRY: (*Tickles* PETER'*s ribs with his fingers*) Oh, come on.

PETER: (*He is very ticklish; as* JERRY *continues to tickle him his voice becomes falsetto*)

No, I . . . OHHHHH! Don't do that. Stop, Stop. Ohhh, no, no.

JERRY: Oh, come on.

PETER: (*As* JERRY *tickles*) Oh, hee, hee, hee. I must go. I . . . hee, hee, hee. After all, stop, stop, hee, hee, hee, after all, the parakeets will be getting dinner ready soon. Hee, hee. And the cats are setting the table. Stop, stop, and, and . . . (PETER *is beside himself now*) . . . and we're having . . . hee, hee . . . uh . . . ho, ho, ho.

(JERRY *stops tickling* PETER, *but the combination of the tickling and his own mad whimsy has* PETER *laughing almost hysterically. As his laughter continues, then subsides,* JERRY *watches him, with a curious fixed smile*)

JERRY: Peter?

PETER: Oh, ha, ha, ha, ha, ha. What? What?

JERRY: Listen, now.

PETER: Oh, ho, ho. What . . . what is it, Jerry? Oh, my.

JERRY: (*Mysteriously*) Peter, do you want to know what happened at the zoo?

PETER: Ah, ha, ha. The what? Oh, yes; the zoo. Oh, ho, ho. Well, I had my own zoo there for a moment with . . . hee, hee, the parakeets getting dinner ready, and the . . . ha, ha, whatever it was, the . . .

JERRY: (*Calmly*) Yes, that was very funny, Peter. I wouldn't have expected it. But do you want to hear about what happened at the zoo, or not?

PETER: Yes. Yes, by all means; tell me what happened at the zoo. Oh, my. I don't know what happened to me.

JERRY: Now I'll let you in on what happened at the zoo; but first, I should tell you why I went to the zoo. I went to the zoo to find out more about the way people exist with animals, and the way animals exist with each other, and with people too. It probably wasn't a fair test, what with everyone separated by bars from everyone else, the animals for the most part from each other, and always the people from the animals. But, if it's a zoo, that's the way it is. (*He pokes* PETER *on the arm*) Move over.

PETER: (*Friendly*) I'm sorry, haven't you enough room? (*He shifts a little*)

JERRY: (*Smiling slightly*) Well, all the animals are there, and all the people are there, and it's Sunday and all the children are there. (*He pokes* PETER *again*) Move over.

PETER: (*Patiently, still friendly*) All right. (*He moves some more, and* JERRY *has all the room he might need*)

JERRY: And it's a hot day, so all the stench is there, too, and all the balloon sellers, and all the ice cream sellers, and all the seals are barking, and all the birds are screaming. (*Pokes* PETER *harder*) Move over!

PETER: (*Beginning to be annoyed*) Look here, you have more than enough room! (*But he moves more, and is now fairly cramped at one end of the bench*)

JERRY: And I am there, and it's feeding time at the lions' house, and the lion keeper comes into the lion cage, one of the lion cages, to feed one of the lions. (*Punches* PETER *on the arm, hard*) MOVE OVER!

PETER: (*Very annoyed*) I can't move over any more, and stop hitting me. What's the matter with you?

JERRY: Do you want to hear the story? (*Punches* PETER*'s arm again*)

PETER: (*Flabbergasted*) I'm not so sure! I certainly don't want to be punched in the arm.

JERRY: (*Punches* PETER*'s arm again*) Like that?

PETER: Stop it! What's the matter with you?

JERRY: I'm crazy, you bastard.

PETER: That isn't funny.

JERRY: Listen to me, Peter. I want this bench. You go sit on the bench over there, and if you're good I'll tell you the rest of the story.

PETER: (*Flustered*) But . . . whatever for? What *is* the matter with you? Besides, I see no reason why I should give up this bench. I sit on this bench almost every Sunday afternoon, in good weather. It's secluded here; there's never anyone sitting here, so I have it all to myself.

JERRY: (*Softly*) Get off this bench, Peter; I want it.

PETER: (*Almost whining*) No.

JERRY: I said I want this bench, and I'm going to have it. Now get over there.

PETER: People can't have everything they want. You should know that; it's a rule; people can have some of the things they want, but they can't have everything.

JERRY: (*Laughs*) Imbecile! You're slow-witted!

PETER: Stop that!

JERRY: You're a vegetable! Go lie down on the ground.

PETER: (*Intense*) Now *you* listen to me. I've put up with you all afternoon.

JERRY: Not really.

PETER: LONG ENOUGH. I've put up with you long enough. I've listened to you because you seemed . . . well, because I thought you wanted to talk to somebody.

JERRY: You put things well; economically, and, yet . . . oh, what is the word I want to put justice to your . . . JESUS, you make me sick . . . get off here and give me my bench.

PETER: MY BENCH!

JERRY: (*Pushes* PETER *almost, but not quite, off the bench*) Get out of my sight.

PETER: (*Regaining his position*) God da . . . mn you. That's enough! I've had enough of you. I will not give up this bench; you can't have it, and that's that. Now, go away.

(JERRY *snorts but does not move*)

Go away, I said.

(JERRY *does not move*)

Get away from here. If you don't move on . . . you're a bum . . . that's what you are. . . . If you don't move on, I'll get a policeman here and make you go.

(JERRY *laughs, stays*)

I warn you, I'll call a policeman.

JERRY: (*Softly*) You won't find a policeman around here; they're all over on the west side of the park chasing fairies down from trees or out of the bushes. That's all they do. That's their function. So scream your head off; it won't do you any good.

PETER: POLICE! I warn you, I'll have you arrested. POLICE! (*Pause*) I said POLICE! (*Pause*) I feel ridiculous.

JERRY: You look ridiculous: a grown man screaming for the police on a bright Sunday afternoon in the park with nobody harming you. If a policeman *did* fill his quota and come sludging over this way he'd probably take you in as a nut.

PETER: (*With disgust and impotence*) Great God, I just came here to read, and now you want me to give up the bench. You're mad.

JERRY: Hey, I got news for you, as they say. I'm on your precious bench, and you're never going to have it for yourself again.

PETER: (*Furious*) Look, you; get off my bench. I don't care if it makes any sense or not. I want this bench to myself; I want you OFF IT!

JERRY: (*Mocking*) Aw . . . look who's mad.

PETER: GET OUT!

JERRY: No.

PETER: I WARN YOU!

JERRY: Do you know how ridiculous you look *now?*

PETER: (*His fury and self-consciousness have possessed him*) It doesn't matter. (*He is almost crying*) GET AWAY FROM MY BENCH!

JERRY: Why? You have everything in the world you want; you've told me about your home, and your family, and *your own* little zoo. You have everything, and now you want this bench. Are these the things men fight for? Tell me, Peter, is this bench, this iron and this wood, is this your honor? Is this the thing in the world you'd fight for? Can you think of anything more absurd?

PETER: Absurd? Look, I'm not going to talk to you about honor, or even try to explain it to you. Besides, it isn't a question of honor; but even if it were, you wouldn't understand.

JERRY: (*Contemptuously*) You don't even know what you're saying, do you? This is probably the first time in your life you've had anything more trying to face than changing your cats' toilet box. Stupid! Don't you have any idea, not even the slightest, what other people *need?*

PETER: Oh, boy, listen to you; well, you don't need this bench. That's for sure.

JERRY: Yes; yes, I do.

PETER: (*Quivering*) I've come here for years; I have hours of great pleasure, great satisfaction, right here. And that's important to a man. I'm a responsible person, and I'm a GROWNUP. This is my bench, and you have no right to take it away from me.

JERRY: Fight for it, then. Defend yourself; defend your bench.

PETER: You've *pushed* me to it. Get up and fight.

JERRY: Like a man?

PETER: (*Still angry*) Yes, like a man, if you insist on mocking me even further.

JERRY: I'll have to give you credit for one thing: you *are* a vegetable, and a slightly nearsighted one, I think . . .

PETER: THAT'S ENOUGH. . . .

JERRY: . . . but, you know, as they say on TV all the time—you know—and I mean this, Peter, you have a certain dignity; it surprises me. . . .

PETER: STOP!

JERRY: (*Rises lazily*) Very well, Peter, we'll battle for the bench, but we're not evenly matched. (*He takes out and clicks open an ugly-looking knife*)

PETER: (*Suddenly awakening to the reality of the situation*)You *are* mad! You're stark raving mad! YOU'RE GOING TO KILL ME! (*But before* PETER *has time to think what to do,* JERRY *tosses the knife at* PETER'*s feet*)

JERRY: There you go. Pick it up. You have the knife and we'll be more evenly matched.

PETER: (*Horrified*) No!

JERRY: (*Rushes over to* PETER, *grabs him by the collar;* PETER *rises; their faces almost touch*) Now you pick up that knife and you fight with me. You fight for your self-respect; you fight for that goddamned bench.

PETER: (*Struggling*) No! Let . . . let go of me! He . . . Help!

JERRY: (*Slaps* PETER *on each "fight"*) You fight, you miserable bastard; fight for that bench; fight for your parakeets; fight for your cats, fight for your two daughters; fight for your wife; fight for your manhood, you pathetic little vegetable. (*Spits in* PETER'*s face*) You couldn't even get your wife with a male child.

PETER: (*Breaks away, enraged*) It's a matter of genetics, not manhood, you . . . you monster. (*He darts down, picks up the knife and backs off a little; he is breathing heavily*) I'll give you one last chance; get out of here and leave me alone! (*He holds the knife with a firm arm, but far in front of him, not to attack, but to defend*)

JERRY: (*Sighs heavily*) So be it! (*With a rush he charges* PETER *and impales himself on the knife. Tableau: For just a moment, complete silence,* JERRY *impaled on the knife at the end of* PETER'*s still firm arm. Then* PETER *screams, pulls away, leaving the knife in* JERRY. JERRY *is motionless, on point. Then he, too, screams, and it must be the sound of an infuriated and fatally wounded animal. With the knife in him, he stumbles back to the bench that* PETER *had vacated. He crumbles there, sitting, facing* PETER, *his eyes wide in agony, his mouth open*)

PETER: (*Whispering*) Oh my God, oh my God, oh my God. . . . (*He repeats these words many times, very rapidly*)

JERRY: (JERRY *is dying; but now his expression seems to change. His features relax, and while his voice varies, sometimes wrenched with pain, for the most part he seems removed from his dying. He smiles*) Thank you, Peter. I mean that, now; thank you very much. (PETER'*s mouth drops open. He cannot move; he is transfixed*)

Oh, Peter, I was so afraid I'd drive you away. (*He laughs as best he can*) You don't know how afraid I was you'd go away and leave me. And now I'll tell you what happened at the zoo. I think . . . I think this is what happened at the zoo . . . I think. I think that while I was at the zoo I decided that I would walk north . . . northerly, rather . . . until I found you . . . or somebody . . . and I decided that I would talk to you . . . I would tell you things . . . and things that I would tell you would . . . Well, here we are. You see? Here we *are*. But . . . I don't know . . . could I have planned all this? No . . . no, I couldn't have. But I think I did. And now I've told you what you wanted to know, haven't I? And now you know all about what happened at the zoo. And now you know what you'll see in your TV, and the face I told you about . . . you remember . . . the face I told you about . . . my face, the face you see right now. Peter . . . Peter? . . . Peter . . . thank you. I came unto you (*He laughs, so faintly*) and you have comforted me. Dear Peter.

PETER: (*Almost fainting*) Oh my God!

JERRY: You'd better go now. Somebody might come by, and you don't want to be here when anyone comes.

PETER: (*Does not move, but begins to weep*) Oh my God, oh my God.

JERRY: (*Most faintly, now; he is very near death*) You won't be coming back here any more, Peter; you've been dispossessed. You've lost your bench, but you've defended your honor. And Peter, I'll tell you something now; you're not really a vegetable; it's all right, you're an animal. You're an animal, too. But you'd better hurry now, Peter. Hurry, you'd better go . . . see?

(JERRY *takes a handkerchief and with great effort and pain wipes the knife handle clean of fingerprints*)

Hurry away, Peter.

(PETER *begins to stagger away*)

Wait . . . wait, Peter. Take your book . . . book. Right here . . . beside me . . . on your bench . . . my bench, rather. Come . . . take your book.

(PETER *starts for the book, but retreats*)

Hurry . . . Peter.

(PETER *rushes to the bench, grabs the book, retreats*)

Very good, Peter . . . very good. Now . . . hurry away.

(PETER *hesitates for a moment, then flees, stageleft*)

Hurry away . . . (*His eyes are closed now*) Hurry away, your parakeets are making the dinner . . . the cats . . . are setting the table . . .

PETER: (*Off stage*) (*A pitiful howl*) OH MY GOD!

JERRY: (*His eyes still closed, he shakes his head and speaks; a combination of scornful mimicry and supplication*) Oh . . . my . . . God. (*He is dead*)

CURTAIN

In *Glengarry Glen Ross* (1983), David Mamet (born in 1947) dramatizes the high-pressure real estate sales profession as seen through the plight of a group of small-time salesmen. Greed and deception lie at the center of the play, with the characters resorting to any means necessary to rise to the top of the "board" (a chart depicting who is in the running to win the ultimate prize: a Cadillac).

As in *American Buffalo* (1975), Mamet's earlier breakthrough play, *Glengarry Glen Ross* relies on the myth of the American Dream as its ideological backdrop. The title refers to worthless real estate in the Florida swamps, not to land in the Scottish highlands, as one might expect—an indication of the extent of irony in this drama. In this play, the pursuit of money under the guise of free enterprise becomes an excuse to deceive and steal. Characters follow the unfettered pursuit of The Deal throughout. The play, which Harold Pinter encouraged Mamet to stage, earned Mamet a Pulitzer Prize. The play's language demonstrates Mamet's skill as a master of writing dialogue.

Mamet was one of a host of younger writers, including Adrienne Kennedy, Sam Shepard, John Guare, and Marsha Norman, who reinvigorated the American stage in the 1970s and 1980s. A successful Hollywood writer as well, whose films include *House of Games, The Spanish Prisoner,* and many others, Mamet today is considered one of the best contemporary American playwrights.

THE CHARACTERS

WILLIAMSON, BAYLEN, ROMA, LINGK
Men in their early forties.
LEVENE, MOSS, AARONOW
Men in their fifties.

THE SCENE: *The three scenes of Act One take place in a Chinese restaurant. Act Two takes place in a real estate office.*

ALWAYS BE CLOSING. (*Practical Sales Maxim*)

Act One

Scene One

A booth at a Chinese restaurant, WILLIAMSON *and* LEVENE *are seated at the booth.*

LEVENE: John . . . John . . . John. Okay. John. John. Look: (*Pause.*) The Glengarry Highland's leads, you're sending Roma out. Fine. He's a good man. We know what he is. He's fine. All I'm saying, you look at the *board*, he's throwing . . . wait, wait, wait, he's throwing them *away*, he's throwing the leads away. All that I'm saying, that you're wasting leads. I don't want to tell you your *job*. All that I'm saying, things get *set*, I know they do, you get a certain *mindset*. . . . A guy gets a reputation. We know how this . . . all I'm saying, put a *closer* on the job. There's more than one man for the . . . Put a . . . wait a second, put a *proven man out* . . . and you watch, now *wait* a second—and you watch your *dollar* volumes . . . . You start closing them for *fifty* 'stead *of twenty-five* . . . you put a *closer* on the . . .

WILLIAMSON: Shelly, you blew the last. . .

LEVENE: No. John. No. Let's wait, let's back up here, I did . . . will you please? Wait a second. Please. I didn't "blow" them. No. I didn't "blow" them. No. One kicked *out*, one I closed . . .

WILLIAMSON: . . . you didn't close . . .

LEVENE: . . . I, if you'd *listen* to me. Please. I *closed* the cocksucker. His *ex*, John, his *ex*, *I* didn't know he was married . . . he, the *judge* invalidated the . . .

WILLIAMSON: Shelly . . .

LEVENE: . . . and what is that, John? What? Bad *luck*. That's all it is. I pray in your *life* you will never find it runs in streaks. That's what it does, that's all it's doing. Streaks. I pray it misses you. That's all I want to say.

WILLIAMSON (*Pause*): What about the other two?

LEVENE: What two?

WILLIAMSON: Four. You had four leads. One kicked out, one the *judge*, you say . . .

LEVENE: . . . you want to see the court records? John? Eh? You want to go down . . .

WILLIAMSON: . . . no . . .

LEVENE: . . . do you want to go down*town* . . . ?

WILLIAMSON: . . . no . . .

LEVENE: . . . then . . .

WILLIAMSON: . . . I only . . .

LEVENE: . . . then what is this "you *say*" shit, what is that? (*Pause.*) What is that . . . ?

WILLIAMSON: All that I'm saying . . .

LEVENE: What is this "you *say*"? A deal kicks out . . . I got to *eat. Shit,* Williamson, *shit.* You . . . Moss . . . Roma . . . look at the *sheets* . . . look at the *sheets.* Nineteen *eighty,* eighty-*one* . . . eighty-*two* . . . six months of eighty-two . . . who's there? Who's up there?

WILLIAMSON: Roma.

LEVENE: Under him?

WILLIAMSON: Moss.

LEVENE: Bullshit. John. Bull*shit.* April, September 1981. It's *me.* It isn't *fucking* Moss. Due respect, he's an *order* taker, John. He *talks,* he talks a good game, look at the *board,* and it's *me,* John, it's me . . .

WILLIAMSON: Not lately it isn't.

LEVENE: Lately kiss my ass lately. That isn't how you build an org . . . talk, talk to Murray. Talk to Mitch. When we were on Peterson, who paid for his fucking *car*? You talk to him. The *Seville* . . . ? He came in, "You bought that for me Shelly." Out of *what*? Cold *calling. Nothing.* Sixty-*five,* when we were there, with Glen *Ross* Farms? You call 'em downtown. What was that? *Luck*? That was "luck"? *Bull*shit, John. You're burning my ass, I can't get a fucking *lead* . . . you think that was luck. My stats for those years? Bull*shit* . . . over that period of time . . . ? Bull*shit.* It wasn't luck. It was *skill.* You want to throw that away, John . . . ? You want to throw that away?

WILLIAMSON: It isn't me . . .

LEVENE: . . . it isn't you . . . ? Who *is* it? Who is this I'm talking to? I need the *leads* . . .

WILLIAMSON: . . . after the thirtieth . . .

LEVENE: Bull*shit* the thirtieth, I don't get on the board the thirtieth, they're going to can my ass. I need the leads. I need them now. Or I'm gone, and you're going to miss me, John, I swear to you.

WILLIAMSON: Murray . . .

LEVENE: . . . you *talk* to Murray . . .

WILLIAMSON: I have. And my job is to marshal those leads . . .

LEVENE: Marshal the leads . . . marshal the leads? What the fuck, what bus did *you* get off of, we're here to fucking *sell. Fuck* marshaling the leads. What the fuck talk is that? What the fuck talk is that? Where did you learn that? In school? (*Pause.*) That's "talk," my friend, that's "talk." Our job is to *sell.* I'm the *man* to sell. I'm getting garbage. (*Pause.*) You're giving it to me, and what I'm saying is it's *fucked.*

WILLIAMSON: You're saying that I'm fucked.

LEVENE: Yes. (*Pause.*) I am. I'm sorry to antagonize you.

WILLIAMSON: Let me . . .

LEVENE: . . . and I'm going to get bounced and you're . . .

WILLIAMSON: . . . let me . . . are you listening to me . . . ?

LEVENE: Yes.

WILLIAMSON: Let me tell you something, Shelly. I do what I'm hired to do. I'm . . . wait a second. I'm *hired* to watch the leads. I'm given . . . hold on, I'm given a *policy. My* job is to *do that.* What I'm *told.* That's it. You, wait a second, *anybody* falls below a certain mark I'm not *permitted* to give them the premium leads.

LEVENE: Then how do they come up above that mark? With *dreck* . . . ? That's *nonsense.* Explain this to me. 'Cause it's a waste, and it's a stupid waste. I want to tell you something . . .

WILLIAMSON: You know what those leads cost?

LEVENE: The premium leads. Yes. I know what they cost. John. Because I, *I* generated the dollar revenue sufficient to *buy* them. Nineteen senny-*nine*, you know what I made? Senny-*nine*? Ninety-six thousand dollars. John? For *Murray* . . . For *Mitch* . . . look at the sheets . . .

WILLIAMSON: Murray said . . .

LEVENE: *Fuck* him. *Fuck* Murray. John? You know? You tell him I said so. What does *he* fucking know? He's going to have a "sales" contest . . . you know what our sales contest used to be? *Money.* A *fortune.* Money lying on the ground. Murray? When was the last time *he* went out on a sit? Sales contest? It's *laughable.* It's cold out there now, John. It's tight. Money is *tight.* This ain't sixty-five. It ain't. It just ain't. See? See? Now, I'm a good *man*—but I need a . . .

WILLIAMSON: Murray said . . .

LEVENE: John. John . . .

WILLIAMSON: Will you please wait a second. Shelly. Please. Murray told me: the hot leads . . .

LEVENE: . . . ah, *fuck* this . . .

WILLIAMSON: The . . . Shelly? (*Pause.*) The hot leads are assigned according to the board. During the contest. *Period.* Anyone who beats fifty per . . .

LEVENE: That's fucked. That's fucked. You don't look at the fucking *percentage.* You look at the *gross.*

WILLIAMSON: Either way. You're out.

LEVENE: I'm out.

WILLIAMSON: Yes.

LEVENE: I'll tell you why I'm out. I'm *out*, you're giving me toilet paper. John. I've *seen* those leads. I saw them when I was at Homestead, we pitched those cocksuckers. Rio Rancho nineteen sixty-*nine* they wouldn't buy. They couldn't buy a fucking *toaster*. They're *broke*, John. They're cold. They're deadbeats, you can't judge on that. Even so. Even so. Alright. Fine. Fine. Even so. I go in, FOUR FUCKING LEADS they got their money in a *sock*. They're fucking *Polacks*, John. Four leads. I close two. *Two*. Fifty per . . .

WILLIAMSON: . . . they kicked out.

LEVENE: They *all* kick out. You run in *streaks*, pal. *Streaks*. I'm . . . I'm . . . don't look at the *board*, look at *me*. Shelly Levene. *Anyone*. *Ask* them on Western. Ask Getz at Homestead. Go ask Jerry Graff. You know who I am . . . I NEED A SHOT. I got to get on the fucking board. Ask them. *Ask* them. Ask them who ever picked up a check I was flush. Moss, Jerry Graff, Mitch himself . . . Those guys *lived* on the business I brought in. They *lived* on it . . . and so did Murray, John. You were here you'd of benefited from it too. And now I'm saying this. Do I want charity? Do I want *pity*? I want *sits*. I want leads don't come right out of a *phone book*. Give me a lead hotter than that, I'll go in and close it. Give me a chance. That's all I want. I'm going to *get* up on that fucking board and all I want is a chance. It's a *streak* and I'm going to turn it around. (*Pause*.) I need your help. (*Pause*.)

WILLIAMSON: I can't do it, Shelly. (*Pause*.)

LEVENE: Why?

WILLIAMSON: The leads are assigned randomly . . .

LEVENE: *Bullshit*, *bullshit*, you assign them . . . . What are you *telling* me?

WILLIAMSON: . . . apart from the top men on the contest board.

LEVENE: Then put me on the board.

WILLIAMSON: You start closing again, you'll *be* on the board.

LEVENE: I can't close these leads, John. No one can. It's a joke. John, look, just give me a hot lead. Just give me two of the premium leads. As a "test," alright? As a "test" and I promise you . . .

WILLIAMSON: I can't do it, Shel. (*Pause*.)

LEVENE: I'll give you ten percent. (*Pause*.)

WILLIAMSON: Of what?

LEVENE: Of my end what I close.

WILLIAMSON: And what if you don't close.

LEVENE: I *will* close.

WILLIAMSON: What if you *don't* close . . . ?

LEVENE: I *will* close.

WILLIAMSON: What if you *don't*? Then I'm *fucked.* You see . . . ? Then it's *my* job. That's what I'm *telling* you.

LEVENE: I *will* close. John, John, ten percent. I can get hot. You *know* that . . .

WILLIAMSON: Not lately you can't . . .

LEVENE: Fuck that. That's defeatist. Fuck that. Fuck it. . . . Get on my side. *Go* with me. Let's *do* something. You want to run this office, *run* it.

WILLIAMSON: Twenty percent. (*Pause.*)

LEVENE: Alright.

WILLIAMSON: And fifty bucks a lead.

LEVENE: John. (*Pause.*) Listen. I want to talk to you. Permit me to do this a second. I'm older than you. A man acquires a reputation. On the street. What he does when he's *up*, what he does otherwise. . . . I said "ten," you said "no." You said "twenty." I said "fine," I'm not going to fuck with you, how can I beat that, you tell me? . . . Okay. Okay. We'll . . . Okay. Fine. We'll . . . Alright, twenty percent, and fifty bucks a lead. That's fine. For now. That's fine. A month or two we'll talk. A month from now. Next month. After the thirtieth. (*Pause.*) We'll talk.

WILLIAMSON: What are we going to say?

LEVENE: No. You're right. That's for later. We'll talk in a month. What have you got? I want two sits. Tonight.

WILLIAMSON: I'm not sure I have two.

LEVENE: I saw the board. You've got *four* . . .

WILLIAMSON (*Snaps*): I've got *Roma.* Then I've got Moss . . .

LEVENE: *Bullshit.* They ain't been in the office yet. Give 'em some stiff. We have a deal or not? Eh? Two sits. The Des Plaines. Both of 'em, six and ten, you can do it . . . six and ten . . . eight and eleven, I don't give a shit, you set 'em up? Alright? The two sits in Des Plaines.

WILLIAMSON: Alright.

LEVENE: Good. Now we're talking. (*Pause.*)

WILLIAMSON: A hundred bucks. (*Pause.*)

LEVENE: Now? (*Pause.*) *Now?*

WILLIAMSON: Now. (*Pause.*) *Yes . . . When?*

LEVENE: Ah, *shit*, John. (*Pause.*)

WILLIAMSON: I wish I could.

LEVENE: You fucking asshole. (*Pause.*) I haven't got it. (*Pause.*) I haven't got it, John. (*Pause.*) I'll pay you tomorrow. (*Pause.*) I'm coming in here with the sales, I'll pay you *tomorrow.* (*Pause.*) I haven't *got* it, when I pay, the *gas*... I get back the hotel, I'll bring it in tomorrow.

WILLIAMSON: Can't do it.

LEVENE: I'll give you thirty on them now, I'll bring the rest tomorrow. I've got it at the hotel. (*Pause.*) John? (*Pause.*) We do that, for chrissake?

WILLIAMSON: No.

LEVENE: I'm asking you. As a favor to me? (*Pause.*) John. (*Long pause.*) John: my *daughter*...

WILLIAMSON: I can't do it, Shelly.

LEVENE: Well, I want to tell you something, fella, wasn't long I could pick up the phone, call *Murray* and I'd have your job. You know that? Not too *long* ago. For what? For *nothing.* "Mur, this new kid burns my ass." "Shelly, he's out." You're gone before I'm back from lunch. I bought him a trip to Bermuda once...

WILLIAMSON: I have to go... (*Gets up.*)

LEVENE: Wait. Alright. Fine. (*Starts going in pocket for money.*) The one. Give me the lead. Give me the one lead. The best one you have.

WILLIAMSON: I can't split them. (*Pause.*)

LEVENE: Why?

WILLIAMSON: Because I say so.

LEVENE (*Pause*): Is that it? Is that it? You want to do business that way...?

WILLIAMSON *gets up, leaves money on the table.*

LEVENE: You want to do business that way...? Alright. Alright. Alright. Alright. What is there on the other list...?

WILLIAMSON: You want something off the B list?

LEVENE: *Yeah.* Yeah.

WILLIAMSON: Is that what you're saying?

LEVENE: That's what I'm saying. Yeah. (*Pause.*) I'd like something off the other list. Which, very least, that I'm entitled to. If I'm still *working* here, which for the moment I guess that I am. (*Pause.*) What? I'm sorry I spoke harshly to you.

WILLIAMSON: That's alright.

LEVENE: The deal still stands, our other thing.

WILLIAMSON *shrugs. Starts out of the booth.*

LEVENE: Good. Mmm. I, you know, I left my wallet back at the hotel.

Scene Two

A booth at the restaurant. MOSS *and* AARONOW *seated. After the meal.*

MOSS: Polacks and deadbeats.

AARONOW: . . . Polacks . . .

MOSS: Deadbeats *all.*

AARONOW: . . . they hold on to their money . . .

MOSS: All of 'em. They, *hey*: it happens to us all.

AARONOW: Where am I going to work?

MOSS: You have to cheer up, George, you aren't out yet.

AARONOW: I'm not?

MOSS: You missed a fucking sale. Big deal. A deadbeat Polack. Big deal. How you going to sell 'em in the *first* place . . . ? Your mistake, you shoun'a took the lead.

AARONOW: I had to.

MOSS: You had to, yeah. Why?

AARONOW: To get on the . . .

MOSS: To get on the board. Yeah. How you goan'a get on the board sell'n a Polack? And I'll tell you, I'll tell you what *else.* You listening? I'll tell you what else: don't ever try to sell an Indian.

AARONOW: I'd never try to sell an Indian.

MOSS: You get those names come up, you ever get 'em, "Patel"?

AARONOW: Mmm . . .

MOSS: You ever get 'em?

AARONOW: Well, I think I had one once.

MOSS: You did?

AARONOW: I . . . I don't know.

MOSS: You had one you'd know it. *Patel.* They keep coming up. I don't know. They like to talk to salesmen. (*Pause.*) They're *lonely*, something. (*Pause.*) They like to feel *superior*, I don't know. Never bought a fucking thing. You're sitting down "The Rio Rancho *this*, the blah blah blah," "The Mountain View—" "Oh yes. My brother told me that. . . ." They got a grapevine. Fuckin' Indians, George. Not my cup of tea. Speaking of which I want to tell you something: (*Pause*) I never got a cup of tea with them. You see them in the restaurants.

A supercilious race. What is this *look* on their face all the time? I don't know. (*Pause.*) I don't know. Their broads all look like they just got fucked with a dead *cat, I* don't know. (*Pause.*) I don't know. I don't like it. Christ . . .

AARONOW: What?

MOSS: The whole fuckin' thing . . . The pressure's just too great. You're ab . . . you're absolu . . . they're too important. All of them. You go in the door. I . . . "I got to *close* this fucker, or I don't eat lunch," "or I don't win the *Cadillac.* . . ." We fuckin' work too hard. You work too hard. We all, I remember when we were at Platt . . . huh? Glen Ross Farms . . . *didn't* we sell a bunch of that . . . ?

AARONOW: They came in and they, you know . . .

MOSS: Well, they fucked it up.

AARONOW: They did.

MOSS: They killed the goose.

AARONOW: They did.

MOSS: And now . . .

AARONOW: We're stuck with *this* . . .

MOSS: We're stuck with *this* fucking shit . . .

AARONOW: . . . *this* shit . . .

MOSS: It's too . . .

AARONOW: It is.

MOSS: Eh?

AARONOW: It's too . . .

MOSS: You get a bad month, all of a . . .

AARONOW: You're on this . . .

MOSS: All of, they got you on this "board . . ."

AARONOW: I, I . . . I . . .

MOSS: Some *contest* board . . .

AARONOW: I . . .

MOSS: It's not right.

AARONOW: It's not.

MOSS: No. (*Pause.*)

AARONOW: And it's not right to the *customers.*

MOSS: I know it's not. I'll tell you, you got, you know, you got . . . what did I learn as a kid on Western? Don't sell a guy one car. Sell him *five* cars over fifteen years.

AARONOW: That's right?

MOSS: Eh . . . ?

AARONOW: That's right?

MOSS: Goddamn right, that's right. Guys come on: "Oh, the blah blah blah, *I* know what I'll do: I'll go in and rob everyone blind and go to Argentina cause nobody ever *thought* of this before."

AARONOW: . . . that's right . . .

MOSS: Eh?

AARONOW: No. That's absolutely right.

MOSS: And so they kill the goose. I, I, I'll . . . and a fuckin' *man*, worked all his *life* has got to . . .

AARONOW: . . . that's right . . .

MOSS: . . . cower in his boots . . .

AARONOW (*simultaneously with "boots"*): Shoes, boots, yes . . .

MOSS: For some fuckin' "Sell ten thousand and you win the steak knives . . ."

AARONOW: For some *sales* pro . . .

MOSS: . . . sales promotion, "You *lose*, then we fire your . . ." No. It's *medieval* . . . it's wrong. "Or we're going to fire your ass." It's wrong.

AARONOW: Yes.

MOSS: Yes, it is. And you know who's responsible?

AARONOW: Who?

MOSS: You know who it is. It's Mitch. And Murray. 'Cause it doesn't have to be this way.

AARONOW: No.

MOSS: Look at Jerry Graff. He's *clean*, he's doing business for *himself*, he's got his, that *list* of his with the *nurses* . . . see? You see? That's *thinking*. Why take ten percent? A ten percent comm . . . why are we giving the rest away? What are we giving ninety per . . . for *nothing*. For some jerk sit in the office tell you "Get out there and close." "Go win the Cadillac." Graff. He goes out and *buys*. He pays top dollar for the . . . you see?

AARONOW: Yes.

MOSS: That's *thinking*. Now, he's got the leads, he goes in business for *himself*. He' s . . . that's what I . . . that's *thinking*! "Who? Who's got a steady *job*, a couple bucks nobody's touched, who?"

AARONOW: Nurses.

MOSS: So Graff buys a fucking list of nurses, one grand—if he paid two I'll eat my hat—four, five thousand nurses, and he' s going *wild* . . .

AARONOW: He is?

MOSS: He's doing *very* well.

AARONOW: I heard that they were running cold.

MOSS: The nurses?

AARONOW: Yes.

MOSS: You hear a *lot* of things. . . . He's doing very well. He's doing *very* well.

AARONOW: With River Oaks?

MOSS: River Oaks, Brook Farms. *All* of that shit. Somebody told me, you know what he's clearing *himself*? Fourteen, fifteen grand a *week.*

AARONOW: Himself?

MOSS: That's what I'm *saying.* Why? The *leads.* He's got the good leads . . . what are we, we're sitting in the shit here. Why? We have to go to *them* to *get* them. Huh. Ninety percent our sale, we're *paying* to the *office* for the *leads.*

AARONOW: The leads, the overhead, the telephones, there's *lots* of things.

MOSS: What do you need? A *telephone,* some broad to say "Good morning," nothing . . . nothing . . .

AARONOW: No, it's not that simple, Dave . . .

MOSS: *Yes.* It *is.* It *is* simple, and you know what the hard part is?

AARONOW: What?

MOSS: Starting up.

AARONOW: What hard part?

MOSS: Of doing the thing. The dif . . . the difference. Between me and Jerry Graff. Going to business for yourself. The hard part is . . . you know what it is?

AARONOW: What?

MOSS: Just the *act.*

AARONOW: What act?

MOSS: To say "I'm going on my own." 'Cause what you do, George, let me tell you what you do: you find yourself in *thrall* to someone else. And we *enslave* ourselves. To *please.* To win some fucking *toaster* . . . to . . . to . . . and the guy who got there first made *up* those . . .

AARONOW: That's right . . .

MOSS: He made *up* those rules, and we're working for *him.*

AARONOW: That's the truth . . .

MOSS: That's the *God's* truth. And it gets me depressed. I *swear* that it does. At MY AGE. To see a goddamn: "Somebody wins the Cadillac this month. P.S. Two guys get fucked."

AARONOW: *Huh.*

MOSS: You don't *ax* your sales force.

AARONOW: No.

MOSS: You . . .

AARONOW: You . . .

MOSS: You *build* it!

AARONOW: That's what I . . .

MOSS: You fucking *build* it! Men come . . .

AARONOW: Men come *work* for you . . .

MOSS: . . . you're absolutely right.

AARONOW: They . . .

MOSS: They have . . .

AARONOW: When they . . .

MOSS: Look look look look, when they *build* your business, then you can't fucking turn around, *enslave* them, treat them like *children*, fuck them up the ass, leave them to fend for themselves . . . no. (*Pause.*) No. (*Pause.*) You're absolutely right, and I want to tell you something.

AARONOW: What?

MOSS: I want to tell you what somebody should do.

AARONOW: What?

MOSS: Someone should stand up and strike *back.*

AARONOW: What do you mean?

MOSS: *Somebody* . . .

AARONOW: Yes . . . ?

MOSS: Should do something to *them.*

AARONOW: What?

MOSS: Something. To pay them back. (*Pause.*) Someone, someone should hurt them. Murray and Mitch.

AARONOW: Someone should hurt them.

MOSS: Yes.

AARONOW (*Pause.*): How?

MOSS: How? Do something to hurt them. Where they live.

AARONOW: What? (*Pause.*)

MOSS: Someone should rob the office.

AARONOW: Huh.

MOSS: That's what I'm *saying.* We were, if we were that kind of guys, to knock it off, and *trash* the joint, it looks like robbery, and *take* the fuckin' leads out of the files. . . go to Jerry Graff. (*Long pause.*)

AARONOW: What could somebody get for them?

MOSS: What could we *get* for them? I don't know. Buck a *throw* . . . buck-a-half a throw . . . I don't know. . . . Hey, who knows what they're worth, what do they *pay* for them? All told . . . must be, I'd . . . three bucks a throw . . . *I* don't know.

AARONOW: How many leads have we got?

MOSS: The *Glengarry* . . . the premium leads . . . ? I'd say we got five thousand. Five. Five thousand leads.

AARONOW: And you're saying a fella could take and sell these leads to Jerry Graff.

MOSS: Yes.

AARONOW: How do you know he'd buy them?

MOSS: Graff? Because I worked for him.

AARONOW: You haven't talked to him.

MOSS: No. What do you mean? Have I talked to him about *this*? (*Pause.*)

AARONOW: Yes. I mean are you actually *talking* about this, or are we just . . .

MOSS: No, we're just . . .

AARONOW: We're just "*talking*" about it.

MOSS: We're just *speaking* about it. (*Pause.*) As an *idea.*

AARONOW: As an idea.

MOSS: Yes.

AARONOW: We're not actually *talking* about it.

MOSS: No.

AARONOW: Talking about it as a . . .

MOSS: *No.*

AARONOW: As a *robbery.*

MOSS: As a "robbery"?! No.

AARONOW: *Well.* Well . . .

MOSS: *Hey.* (*Pause.*)

AARONOW: So all this, um, you didn't, actually, you didn't actually go talk to Graff.

MOSS: Not actually, no. (*Pause.*)

AARONOW: You didn't?

MOSS: No. Not actually.

AARONOW: Did you?

MOSS: What did I say?

AARONOW: What did you say?

MOSS: Yes. (*Pause.*) I said, "Not actually." The fuck *you* care, George? We're just *talking* . . .

AARONOW: We are?

MOSS: Yes. (*Pause.*)

AARONOW: Because, because, you know, it's a *crime.*

MOSS: That's right. It's a crime. It is a crime. It's also very safe.

AARONOW: You're actually *talking* about this?

MOSS: That's right. (*Pause.*)

AARONOW: You're going to steal the leads?

MOSS: Have I said that? (*Pause.*)

AARONOW: Are you? (*Pause.*)

MOSS: Did I say that?

AARONOW: Did you talk to Graff?

MOSS: Is that what I said?

AARONOW: What did he say?

MOSS: What did he say? He'd *buy* them. (*Pause.*)

AARONOW: You're going to steal the leads and sell the leads to him? (*Pause.*)

MOSS: Yes.

AARONOW: What will he pay?

MOSS: A buck a shot.

AARONOW: For five thousand?

MOSS: However they are, that's the deal. A buck a throw. Five thousand dollars. Split it half and half.

AARONOW: You're saying "me."

MOSS: Yes. (*Pause.*) Twenty-five hundred apiece. One night's work, and the job with Graff. Working the premium leads. (*Pause.*)

AARONOW: A job with Graff.

MOSS: Is that what I said?

AARONOW: He'd give me a job.

MOSS: He would take you on. Yes. (*Pause.*)

AARONOW: Is that the truth?

MOSS: Yes. It is, George. (*Pause.*) Yes. It's a big decision. (*Pause.*) And its a big reward. (*Pause.*) It's a big reward. For one night's work. (*Pause.*) But it's got to be tonight.

AARONOW: What?

MOSS: What? What? The *leads.*

AARONOW: You have to steal the leads tonight?

MOSS: That's *right,* the guys are moving them downtown. After the thirtieth. Murray and Mitch. After the contest.

AARONOW: You're, you're saying so you have to go in there tonight and . . .

MOSS: *You* . . .

AARONOW: I'm sorry?

MOSS: *You.* (*Pause.*)

AARONOW: Me?

MOSS: *You* have to go in. (*Pause.*) *You* have to get the leads. (*Pause.*)

AARONOW: I do?

MOSS: Yes.

AARONOW: I . . .

MOSS: It's not something for nothing, George, I took you in on this, you have to go. That's your thing. I've made the deal with Graff. I can't go. I can't go in, I've spoken on this too much. I've got a big mouth. (*Pause.*) "The fucking leads" et cetera, blah blah blah ". . . the fucking tight ass company . . ."

AARONOW: They'll know when you go over to Graff . . .

MOSS: What will they know? That I stole the leads? I *didn't* steal the leads, I'm going to the *movies* tonight with a friend, and then I'm going to the Como Inn. Why did I go to Graff? I got a better deal. *Period.* Let 'em prove something. They can't prove anything that's not the case. (*Pause.*)

AARONOW: *Dave.*

MOSS: Yes.

AARONOW: You want me to break into the office tonight and steal the leads?

MOSS: Yes. (*Pause.*)

AARONOW: No.

MOSS: Oh, yes, George.

AARONOW: What does that mean?

MOSS: Listen to this. I have an alibi, I'm going to the Como Inn, why? Why? The place gets robbed, they're going to come looking for *me.* Why? Because I probably did it. Are you going to turn me in? (*Pause.*) George? Are you going to turn me in?

AARONOW: What if you don't get caught?

MOSS: They come to you, you going to turn me in?

AARONOW: Why would they come to me?

MOSS: They're going to come to *everyone.*

AARONOW: Why would I *do* it?

MOSS: You wouldn't, George, that's why I'm talking to you. Answer me. They come to you. You going to turn me in?

AARONOW: No.

MOSS: Are you sure?

AARONOW: Yes. I'm sure.

MOSS: Then listen to this: I have to get those leads tonight. That's something I have to do. If I'm not at the *movies* . . . if I'm not eating over at the inn . . . If you don't do this, then *I* have to come in here . . .

AARONOW: . . . you don't have to come in . . .

MOSS: . . . and *rob* the place . . .

AARONOW: . . . I thought that we were only talking . . .

MOSS: . . . they *take* me, then. They're going to ask me who were my accomplices.

AARONOW: *Me*?

MOSS: Absolutely.

AARONOW: That's ridiculous.

MOSS: Well, to the law, you're an accessory. Before the fact.

AARONOW: I didn't ask to be.

MOSS: Then tough luck, George, because you are.

AARONOW: Why? *Why*, because you only *told* me about it?

MOSS: That's right.

AARONOW: Why are you doing this to me, Dave. Why are you talking this way to me? I don't understand. Why are you doing this at *all* . . . ?

MOSS: That's none of your fucking business . . .

AARONOW: Well, well, well, *talk* to me, we sat down to eat *dinner*, and here I'm a *criminal* . . .

MOSS: You *went* for it.

AARONOW: In the abstract . . .

MOSS: So I'm making it concrete.

AARONOW: Why?

MOSS: Why? Why *you* going to give me five grand?

AARONOW: Do you need five grand?

MOSS: Is that what I just said?

AARONOW: You need money? Is that the . . .

MOSS: Hey, hey, let's just keep it simple, what I need is not the . . . what do *you* need . . . ?

AARONOW: What is the five grand? (*Pause.*) What is the, you said that we were going to *split* five . . .

MOSS: I lied. (*Pause.*) Alright? My end is *my* business. Your end's twenty-five. In or out. You tell me, you're out you take the consequences.

AARONOW: I do?

MOSS: Yes. (*Pause.*)

AARONOW: And why is that?

MOSS: Because you listened.

Scene Three

The restaurant. ROMA *is seated alone at the booth.* LINGK *is at the booth next to him.* ROMA *is talking to him.*

ROMA: . . . all train compartments smell vaguely of shit. It gets so you don't mind it. That's the worst thing that I can confess. You know how long it took me to get there? A long time. When you *die* you're going to regret the things you don't do. You think you're *queer* . . . ? I'm going to tell you something: we're *all* queer. You think that you're a *thief*? So *what*? You get befuddled by a middle-class morality . . . ? *Get shut* of it. Shut it out. You cheated on your wife . . . ? You *did* it, *live* with it. (*Pause.*) You fuck little girls, so *be* it. There's an absolute morality? May *be*. And *then* what? If you *think* there is, then *be* that thing. Bad people go to hell? I don't *think* so. If you think that, act that way. A hell exists on earth? Yes. I won't live in it. That's *me*. You ever take a dump made you feel you'd just slept for twelve hours . . . ?

LINGK: Did I . . . ?

ROMA: Yes.

LINGK: I don't know.

ROMA: Or a *piss* . . . ? A great meal fades in reflection. Everything else gains. You know why? 'Cause it's only food. This shit we eat, it keeps us going. But it's only food. The great fucks that you may have had. What do you remember about them?

LINGK: What do I . . . ?

ROMA: Yes.

LINGK: Mmmm . . .

ROMA: I don't know. For *me*, I'm saying, what it is, it's probably not the orgasm. Some broads, forearms on your neck, something her *eyes* did. There was a *sound* she made . . . or, me, lying, in the, I'll tell you: me lying in bed; the next day she brought me café au lait. She gives me a cigarette, my balls feel like concrete. Eh? What I'm saying, what is our life? (*Pause.*) It's looking forward or it's looking back. And that's our life. That's *it*. Where is the *moment*? (*Pause.*) And what is it that we're afraid of? Loss. What else? (*Pause.*) The *bank* closes. We get *sick*, my wife died on a plane, the stock market collapsed . . . the house burnt down . . . what of these happen . . . ? None of 'em. We worry anyway. What does this mean? I'm not *secure*. How can I be secure? (*Pause.*) Through amassing wealth beyond all measure? No. And what's beyond all measure? That's a sickness. That's a trap. There is no measure. Only greed. How can we act? The right way, we would say, to deal with this: "There is a one-in-a-million chance that so and so will happen. . . . *Fuck* it, it won't happen to *me*. . . ." No. We know that's not the right way I think. (*Pause.*) We say the *correct* way to deal with this is "There is a one-in-so-and-so chance this will happen . . . God *protect* me. I am powerless, let it not happen to me. . . ." But no to *that*. I say. There's something else. What is it? "If it happens, AS IT MAY for that is not within our powers, I will *deal* with it, just as I do *today* with what draws my concern today." I say *this* is how we must act. I do those things which seem correct to me *today*. I trust myself. And if security concerns me, I do that which *today* I think will make me secure. And every day I *do* that, when that day *arrives* that I need a reserve, (a) odds are that I have it, and (b) the *true* reserve that I have is the strength that I have of *acting each day* without fear. (*Pause.*) According to the dictates of my mind. (*Pause.*) Stocks, bonds, objects of art, real estate. Now: what are they? (*Pause.*) An opportunity. To what? To make money? Perhaps. To *lose* money? Perhaps. To "indulge" and to "learn" about ourselves? Perhaps. *So fucking what*? What *isn't*? They're an *opportunity*. That's all. They're an *event*. A guy comes up to you, you make a call, you send in a brochure, it doesn't matter, "There're these *properties* I'd like for you to see." What does it mean? What you *want* it to mean. (*Pause.*) Money? (*Pause.*) If that's what it signifies to you. Security? (*Pause.*) Comfort? (*Pause.*) All it is is THINGS THAT HAPPEN TO YOU. (*Pause.*) That's all it is. How are they different? (*Pause.*) Some poor newly married guy gets run down by a cab. Some *busboy* wins the lottery. (*Pause.*) All it is, it's a carnival. What's special . . . what *draws* us? (*Pause.*) We're all different. (*Pause.*) We're not the same. (*Pause.*) We are not the same. (*Pause.*) Hmmm. (*Pause. Sighs.*) It's been a long day. (*Pause.*) What are you drinking?

LINGK: Gimlet.

ROMA: Well, let's have a couple more. My name is Richard Roma, what's yours?

LINGK: Lingk. James Lingk.

ROMA: James. I'm glad to meet you. (*They shake hands.*) I'm glad to meet you, James. (*Pause.*) I want to show you something. (*Pause.*) It might mean *nothing* to you . . . and it might not. I don't know. I don't know anymore. (*Pause. He takes out a small map and spreads it on a table.*) What is that? Florida. Glengarry Highlands. Florida.

"Florida. *Bullshit*" And maybe that's true; and that's what *I* said: but look *here*: what is this? This is a piece of land. Listen to what I'm going to tell you now:

Act Two

The real estate office. Ransacked. A broken plateglass window boarded up, glass all over the floor. AARONOW *and* WILLIAMSON *standing around, smoking.*

Pause.

AARONOW: People used to say that there are numbers of such magnitude that multiplying them by two made no difference. (*Pause.*)

WILLIAMSON: Who used to say that?

AARONOW: In school. (*Pause.*)

BAYLEN, *a detective, comes out of the inner office.*

BAYLEN: Alright . . . ?

ROMA *enters from the street.*

ROMA: *Williamson . . . Williamson,* they stole the *contracts . . .* ?

BAYLEN: Excuse me, sir . . .

ROMA: Did they get my contracts?

WILLIAMSON: They got . . .

BAYLEN: Excuse me, fella.

ROMA: . . . did they . . .

BAYLEN: Would you excuse us, please . . . ?

ROMA: Don't *fuck* with me, fella. I'm talking about a fuckin' Cadillac car that you owe me . . .

WILLIAMSON: They didn't get your contract. I filed it before I left.

ROMA: They didn't get my contracts?

WILLIAMSON: They—excuse me . . . (*He goes back into inner room with the* Detective.)

ROMA: Oh, *fuck. Fuck.* (*He starts kicking the desk.*) FUCK FUCK FUCK! WILLIAMSON!!! WILLIAMSON!!! (*Goes to the door* WILLIAMSON *went into, tries the door; it's locked.*) OPEN THE FUCKING . . . WILLIAMSON . . .

BAYLEN (*coming out*): Who are you?

WILLIAMSON *comes out.*

WILLIAMSON: They didn't get the contracts.

ROMA: Did they . . .

WILLIAMSON: They got, listen to me . . .

ROMA: Th . . .

WILLIAMSON: Listen to me: They got *some* of them.

ROMA: Some of them . . .

BAYLEN: Who told you . . . ?

ROMA: Who told me wh . . . ? You've got a fuckin', you've . . . a . . . who is this . . . ? You've got a board-up on the window. . . . *Moss* told me.

BAYLEN (*Looking back toward the inner office.*): *Moss* . . . Who told him?

ROMA: How the fuck do *I* know? (*To* WILLIAMSON:) *What . . . talk* to me.

WILLIAMSON: They took *some* of the con . . .

ROMA: . . . some of the contracts . . . Lingk. James Lingk. I closed . . .

WILLIAMSON: You closed him yesterday.

ROMA: *Yes.*

WILLIAMSON: It went down. I filed it.

ROMA: You did?

WILLIAMSON: Yes.

ROMA: Then I'm over the fucking top and you owe me a Cadillac.

WILLIAMSON: I . . .

ROMA: And I don't want any fucking shit and I don't give a shit, Lingk puts me over the top, you filed it, that's fine, any other shit kicks out *you* go back. You . . . *you* reclose it, 'cause I *closed* it and you . . . you owe me the car.

BAYLEN: Would you excuse us, please.

AARONOW: I, um, and may . . . maybe they're in . . . they're in . . . you should, John, if we're ins . . .

WILLIAMSON: I'm sure that we're insured, George . . . (*Going back inside.*)

ROMA: Fuck insured. You owe me a car.

BAYLEN (*Stepping back into the inner room*): Please don't leave. I'm going to talk to you. What's your name?

ROMA: Are you talking to me? (*Pause.*)

BAYLEN: Yes. (*Pause.*)

ROMA: My name is Richard Roma.

BAYLEN *goes back into the inner room.*

AARONOW: I, you know, they should be insured.

ROMA: What do *you* care . . . ?

AARONOW: Then, you know, they wouldn't be so ups . . .

ROMA: Yeah. That's swell. Yes. You're right. (*Pause.*) How are you?

AARONOW: I'm fine. You mean the *board*? You mean the *board* . . . ?

ROMA: I don't . . . yes. Okay, the board.

AARONOW: I'm, I'm, I'm, I'm fucked on the board. *You*. You see how . . . I . . . (*Pause.*) I can't . . . my mind must be in other places. 'Cause I can't do any . . .

ROMA: *What*? You can't do any *what*? (*Pause.*)

AARONOW: I can't close 'em.

ROMA: Well, they're old. I saw the shit that they were giving you.

AARONOW: Yes.

ROMA: Huh?

AARONOW: Yes. They are old.

ROMA: They're ancient.

AARONOW: Clear . . .

ROMA: Clear Meadows. That shits dead. (*Pause.*)

AARONOW: It *is* dead.

ROMA: It's a waste of time.

AARONOW: Yes. (*Long pause.*) I'm no fucking good.

ROMA: That's . . .

AARONOW: Everything I . . . *you* know . . .

ROMA: That's not . . . Fuck that shit, George. You're a, *hey*, you had a bad month. You're a good man, George.

AARONOW: I am?

ROMA: You hit a bad streak. We've all . . . look at this: fifteen units Mountain View, the flicking things get stole.

AARONOW: He said he filed . . .

ROMA: He filed half of them, he filed the *big* one. All the little ones, I have, I have to go back and . . . ah, *fuck*, I got to go out like a fucking schmuck hat in my hand and reclose the . . . (*Pause.*) I mean, talk about a bad streak. That would sap *anyone's* self confi . . . I got to go out and reclose all my . . . Where's the phones?

AARONOW: They stole . . .

ROMA: They stole the . . .

AARONOW: What. What kind of outfit are we running where . . . where anyone . . .

ROMA (*To himself*): They stole the phones.

AARONOW: Where criminals can come in here . . . they take the . . .

ROMA: They stole the phones. They stole the leads. They're . . . *Christ.* (*Pause.*) What am I going to do this month? Oh, *shit* . . . (*Starts for the door.*)

AARONOW: You think they're going to catch . . . where are you going?

ROMA: Down the street.

WILLIAMSON (*Sticking his head out of the door*): Where are you going?

ROMA: To the restaura . . . what do you fucking . . . ?

WILLIAMSON: Aren't you going out today?

ROMA: With what? (*Pause.*) With what, John, they took the leads . . .

WILLIAMSON: I have the stuff from last year's . . .

ROMA: Oh. Oh. Oh, your "nostalgia" file, that's fine. No. Swell. 'Cause I don't have to . . .

WILLIAMSON: . . . you want to go out today . . . ?

ROMA: 'Cause I don't have to *eat* this month. No. Okay. *Give* 'em to me . . . (*To himself:*) Fucking Mitch and Murray going to shit a br . . . what am I going to *do* all . . .

WILLIAMSON *starts back into the office. He is accosted by* AARONOW.

AARONOW: Were the leads . . .

ROMA: . . . what am I going to *do* all month . . . ?

AARONOW: Were the leads insured?

WILLIAMSON: I don't know, George, why?

AARONOW: 'Cause, you know, 'cause they weren't, I know that Mitch and Murray uh . . . (*Pause.*)

WILLIAMSON: What?

AARONOW: That they're going to be upset.

WILLIAMSON: That's right. (*Going back into his office. Pause. To* ROMA:) You want to go out today . . . ?

Pause. WILLIAMSON *returns to his office.*

AARONOW: He said we're all going to have to go talk to the guy.

ROMA: What?

AARONOW: He said we . . .

ROMA: To the cop?

AARONOW: Yeah.

ROMA: Yeah. That's swell. *Another* waste of time.

AARONOW: A waste of time? Why?

ROMA: *Why?* 'Cause they aren't going to find the guy.

AARONOW: The cops?

ROMA: Yes. The cops. No.

AARONOW: They aren't?
ROMA: No.
AARONOW: Why don't you think so?
ROMA: Why? Because they're *stupid.* "Where were you last night . . ."
AARONOW: Where were you?
ROMA: Where was *I*?
AARONOW: Yes.
ROMA: I was at home, where were *you*?
AARONOW: At home.
ROMA: *See* . . . ? Were you the guy who broke in?
AARONOW: Was I?
ROMA: Yes.
AARONOW: No.
ROMA: Then don't sweat it, George, you know why?
AARONOW: No.
ROMA: You have nothing to hide.
AARONOW (*Pause*): When I talk to the police, I get nervous.
ROMA: Yeah. You know who doesn't?
AARONOW: No, who?
ROMA: Thieves.
AARONOW: Why?
ROMA: They're inured to it.
AARONOW: You think so?
ROMA: Yes. (*Pause.*)
AARONOW: But what should I *tell* them?
ROMA: The truth, George. Always tell the truth. Its the easiest thing to remember.

WILLIAMSON *comes out of the office with leads.* ROMA *takes one, reads it.*

ROMA: *Patel*? Ravidam *Patel*? How am I going to make a living on these deadbeat *wogs*? Where did you get this, from the *morgue*?
WILLIAMSON: If you don't want it, give it back.
ROMA: I don't "want" it, if you catch my drift.
WILLIAMSON: I'm giving you *three* leads. You . . .
ROMA: What's the fucking point in *any* case . . . ? What's the *point.* I got to argue with *you*, I got to knock heads with the *cops*, I'm busting my *balls*, sell you *dirt* to fucking *deadbeats* money in the *mattress*, I come back you can't even manage to keep the contracts safe, I have to go back and close them *again.* . . . What the fuck am I wasting my time, fuck this shit. I'm going out and reclose last week's . . .

WILLIAMSON: The word from Murray is: leave them alone. If we need a new signature he'll go out himself, he'll be the *president*, just come *in*, from out of *town* . . .

ROMA: Okay, okay, okay, gimme this shit. Fine. (*Takes the leads.*)

WILLIAMSON: Now, I'm giving you three . . .

ROMA: Three? I count *two.*

WILLIAMSON: Three.

ROMA: Patel? Fuck *you.* Fuckin' *Shiva* handed him a million dollars, told him "sign the deal," he wouldn't sign. And Vishnu, too. Into the bargain. Fuck *that*, John. You know your business, I know mine. Your business is being an *asshole*, and I find out whose fucking *cousin* you are, I'm going to go to him and figure out a way to have your *ass* . . . fuck you— I'll wait for the new leads.

SHELLY LEVENE *enters.*

LEVENE: Get the *chalk*. Get the *chalk* . . . get the *chalk*! I closed 'em! I *closed* the cocksucker. Get the chalk and put me on the *board.* I'm going to Hawaii! Put me on the Cadillac board, Williamson! Pick up the fuckin' chalk. Eight units. Mountain View . . .

ROMA: You sold eight Mountain View?

LEVENE: You bet your ass. Who wants to go to lunch? Who wants to go to lunch? I'm buying. (*Slaps contract down on Williamson's desk.*) Eighty-two fucking grand. And twelve grand in commission. John. (*Pause.*) On fucking deadbeat magazine subscription leads.

WILLIAMSON: Who?

LEVENE (*Pointing to contract*): *Read* it. Bruce and Harriett Nyborg. (*Looking around.*) What happened here?

AARONOW: Fuck. I had them on River Glen.

LEVENE *looks around.*

LEVENE: What happened?

WILLIAMSON: Somebody broke in.

ROMA: Eight units?

LEVENE: That's right.

ROMA: *Shelly* . . . !

LEVENE: Hey, big fucking deal. Broke a bad streak . . .

AARONOW: Shelly, the Machine, Levene.

LEVENE: You . . .

AARONOW: That's great.

LEVENE: Thank you, George.

BAYLEN *sticks his head out of the room; calls in, "Aaronow."* AARONOW *goes into the side room.*

LEVENE: Williamson, get on the phone, call Mitch . . .

ROMA: They took the phones . . .

LEVENE: They . . .

BAYLEN: *Aaronow . . .*

ROMA: They took the typewriters, they took the leads, they took the *cash*, they took the *contracts . . .*

LEVENE: Wh ... wh ... Wha . . . ?

AARONOW: We had a robbery. (*Goes into the inner room.*)

LEVENE: (*Pause.*) When?

ROMA: Last night, this morning. (*Pause.*)

LEVENE: They took the leads?

ROMA: Mmm.

MOSS *comes out of the interrogation.*

MOSS: Fuckin' asshole.

ROMA: What, they beat you with a rubber bat?

MOSS: Cop couldn't find his dick two hands and a map. Anyone talks to this guy's an *asshole . . .*

ROMA: You going to turn State's?

MOSS: Fuck you, Ricky. I ain't going out today. I'm going home. I'm going home because nothing's *accomplished* here. . . . Anyone *talks* to this guy is . . .

ROMA: Guess what the Machine did?

MOSS: Fuck the Machine.

ROMA: Mountain View. Eight units.

MOSS: Fuckin' cop's got no right talk to me that way. I didn't rob the place . . .

ROMA: You hear what I said?

MOSS: Yeah. He closed a deal.

ROMA: Eight units. Mountain View.

MOSS (*To* LEVENE): You did that?

LEVENE: Yeah. (*Pause.*)

MOSS: Fuck you.

ROMA: Guess who?

MOSS: When . . .

LEVENE: Just now.

ROMA: Guess who?

MOSS: You just this morning . . .

ROMA: Harriett and blah blah Nyborg.

MOSS: You did that?

LEVENE: Eighty-two thousand dollars. (*Pause.*)

MOSS: Those fuckin' *deadbeats* . . .

LEVENE: My ass. I told 'em. (*To* ROMA:) Listen to this: I said . . .

MOSS: Hey, I don't want to hear your fucking war stories . . .

ROMA: Fuck *you*, Dave . . .

LEVENE: "You have to believe in *yourself* . . . you"—look—"alright . . . ?"

MOSS (*To* WILLIAMSON): Give me some leads. I'm going out . . . I'm getting out of . . .

LEVENE: ". . . you have to believe in *yourself* . . ."

MOSS: Na, fuck the leads, I'm going home.

LEVENE: "Bruce, Harriett . . . Fuck *me*, believe in your*self* . . ."

ROMA: We haven't got a lead . . .

MOSS: Why not?

ROMA: They took 'em . . .

MOSS: Hey, they're fuckin' garbage any case. . . . This whole goddamn . . .

LEVENE: ". . . You look around, you say, 'This one has so-and-so, and I have nothing . . .'"

MOSS: *Shit.*

LEVENE: "'*Why*? Why don't I get the opportunities . . . ?'"

MOSS: And did they steal the contracts . . . ?

ROMA: Fuck *you* care . . . ?

LEVENE: "I want to tell you something, Harriett . . ."

MOSS: . . . the fuck is *that* supposed to mean . . . ?

LEVENE: Will you shut up, I'm telling you this . . .

AARONOW *sticks his head out.*

AARONOW: Can we get some coffee . . . ?

MOSS: How ya doing? (*Pause.*)

AARONOW: Fine.

MOSS: Uh-huh.

AARONOW: If anyone's going, I could use some coffee.

LEVENE: "You *do* get the . . ." (*To* ROMA:) Huh? Huh?

MOSS: *Fuck* is that supposed to mean?

LEVENE: "You *do* get the opportunity. . . . You *get* them. As *I* do, as *anyone* does . . ."

MOSS: Ricky? . . . That I don't care they stole the contracts? (*Pause.*)

LEVENE: I got 'em in the kitchen. I'm eating her crumb cake.

MOSS: What does that mean?

ROMA: It *means*, Dave, you haven't closed a good one in a month, none of my business, you want to push me to answer you. (*Pause.*) And so you haven't got a contract to get stolen or so forth.

MOSS: You have a mean streak in you, Ricky, you know that . . . ?

LEVENE: Rick. Let me tell you. Wait, we're in the . . .

MOSS: Shut the fuck up. (*Pause.*) Ricky. You have a mean streak in you. . . . (*To* LEVENE:) And what the fuck are *you* babbling about . . . ? (*To* ROMA:) Bring that shit up. Of my volume. You were on a bad one and I brought it up to *you* you'd harbor it. (*Pause.*) You'd harbor it a long long while. And you'd be right.

ROMA: Who said "Fuck the Machine"?

MOSS: *"Fuck the Machine"? "Fuck the Machine"?* What is this. *Courtesy* class . . . ? You're *fucked*, Rick—are you fucking *nuts*? You're hot, so you think you're the *ruler* of this place . . . ?! You want to . . .

LEVENE: Dave . . .

MOSS: . . . Shut up. Decide who should be dealt with how? Is that the thing? I come into the fuckin' office today, I get humiliated by some jagoff cop. I get accused of . . . I get this *shit* thrown in my face by you, you genuine shit, because you're top name on the board . . .

ROMA: Is that what I did? Dave? I humiliated you? My *God* . . . I'm *sorry* . . .

MOSS: Sittin' on top of the *world*, sittin' on top of the *world*, everything's fucking *peach*fuzz . . .

ROMA: Oh, and I don't get a moment to spare for a bust-out *humanitarian* down on his luck lately. Fuck *you*, Dave, you know you got a big *mouth*, and *you* make a close the whole *place* stinks with your *farts* for a week. "How much you just ingested," what a big *man* you are, "Hey, let me buy you a pack of gum. I'll show you how to *chew* it." Your *pal* closes, all that comes out of your mouth is *bile*, how fucked *up* you are . . .

MOSS: *Who's* my pal . . . ? And what are you, Ricky, huh, what are you, Bishop *Sheean*? Who the fuck are *you*, Mr. Slick . . . ? What are you, friend to the *workingman*? Big deal. Fuck *you*, you got the memory a fuckin' *fly*. I never liked you.

ROMA: What is this, your farewell speech?

MOSS: I'm going home.

ROMA: Your farewell to the troops?

MOSS: I'm not going home. I'm going to Wis*con*sin.

ROMA: Have a good trip.

MOSS (*Simultaneously with "trip"*): And fuck *you.* Fuck the *lot* of you. Fuck you *all.*

MOSS *exits. Pause.*

ROMA (*To* LEVENE): You were saying? (*Pause.*) Come on. Come on, you got them in the kitchen, you got the stats spread out, you're in your shirtsleeves, you can *smell* it. Huh? Snap out of it, you're eating her *crumb* cake. (*Pause.*)

LEVENE: I'm eating her *crumb* cake . . .

ROMA: How was it . . . ?

LEVENE: From the store.

ROMA: Fuck *her* . . .

LEVENE: "What we have to do is *admit* to ourself that we see that opportunity . . . and *take* it. (*Pause.*) And thats it." And we *sit* there. (*Pause.*) I got the pen out . . .

ROMA: "Always be closing . . ."

LEVENE: That's what I'm *saying.* The *old* ways The *old* ways . . . convert the motherfucker . . . *sell* him . . . *sell* him . . . *make him sign the check.* (*Pause.*) *The* . . . Bruce, Harriett . . . the kitchen, blah: they got their money in *government* bonds. . . . I say *fuck* it, we're going to go the whole route. I plat it out eight units. Eighty-two grand. I tell them. "This is now. This is that *thing* that you've been dreaming of, you're going to find that suitcase on the train, the guy comes in the door, the bag that's full of money. This is it, *Harriett* . . ."

ROMA (*Reflectively*): Harriett . . .

LEVENE: *Bruce* . . . "I don't want to fuck *around* with you. I don't want to go *round* this, and *pussyfoot* around the thing, you have to look back on this. I do, too. I came here to do good for you and me. For *both* of us. Why take an interim position? *The only arrangement I'll accept* is full investment. Period. The whole eight units. I know that you're saying 'be safe,' I know what you're saying. I know if I left you to yourselves, you'd say 'come back tomorrow,' and when I walked out that door, you'd make a cup of *coffee* . . . you'd sit *down* . . . and you'd think 'let's be safe . . . 'and not to disappoint me you'd go *one* unit or maybe two, because you'd become scared because you'd met possi-*bil*ity. But this won't do, and that's not the subject. . . ." Listen to this, I actually said this. "That's not the subject of our *evening* together." Now I handed them the pen. I held it in my hand. I turned the contract, eight units eighty-two grand. "Now I want you to sign." (*Pause.*) I sat there. Five minutes. Then, I sat there, Ricky, *twenty two minutes* by the kitchen *clock.* (*Pause.*) Twenty-two minutes by the kitchen clock. Not a *word,* not a *motion.* What am I thinking? "My arm's getting tired?" *No.* I *did* it. I *did* it. Like in the *old* days, Ricky. Like I was taught . . . Like, like, like I *used* to do . . . I did it.

ROMA: Like you taught me . . .

LEVENE: Bullshit, you're . . . No. That's raw . . . well, if I *did,* then I'm *glad* I did. I, *well.* I locked on them. All on them, nothing on me. All my thoughts are on them. I'm holding the last thought that I spoke: "Now is the time." (*Pause.*) They signed, Ricky. It was *great.* It was fucking great. It was like they wilted all at once. No *gesture* . . . nothing. Like together. They, I swear to God, they both kind *of imperceptibly slumped.* And he reaches and takes the pen and signs, he passes it to her, she signs. It was so fucking solemn. I just let it sit. I nod like this. I nod again. I grasp his hands. I shake his hands. I grasp *her* hands. I nod at her like this. "Bruce . . . Harriett . . ." I'm beaming at them. I'm nodding like this. I point back in the living room, back to the sideboard. (*Pause.*) *I didn't fucking know there was a sideboard there!!* He goes back, he brings us a drink. Little shot glasses. A pattern in 'em. And we toast. In silence. (*Pause.*)

ROMA: That was a great sale, Shelly. (*Pause.*)

LEVENE: Ah, fuck. Leads! Leads! Williamson! (WILLIAMSON *sticks his head out of the office.*) Send me *out!* Send me *out!*

WILLIAMSON: The leads are coming.

LEVENE: *Get* 'em to me!

WILLIAMSON: I talked to Murray and Mitch an hour ago. They're coming in, you understand they're a bit *upset* over this morning's . . .

LEVENE: Did you tell 'em my sale?

WILLIAMSON: How could I tell 'em your sale? Eh? I don't have a tel . . . I'll tell 'em your sale when they bring in the leads. Alright? Shelly. Alright? We had a little . . . You closed a deal. You made a good sale. Fine.

LEVENE: It's better than a good sale. It's a . . .

WILLIAMSON: Look: I have a lot of things on my mind, they're coming in, alright, they're very upset, I'm trying to make some *sense* . . .

LEVENE: All that I'm *telling* you: that one thing you can tell them it's a remarkable sale.

WILLIAMSON: The only thing remarkable is who you made it to.

LEVENE: What does *that* fucking mean?

WILLIAMSON: That if the sale sticks, it will be a miracle.

LEVENE: Why should the sale not stick? Hey, *fuck* you. That's what I'm saying. You have no idea of your job. A man's his job and you're *fucked* at yours. You hear what I'm saying to you? Your "end of month board . . ." You can't run an office. I don't care. You don't know what it *is*, you don't have the *sense*, you don't have the *balls*. You ever been on a sit? *Ever*? Has this cocksucker ever been . . . you ever sit down with a cust. . .

WILLIAMSON: I were you, I'd calm down, Shelly.

LEVENE: *Would* you? *Would* you . . . ? Or you're gonna *what*, fire me?

WILLIAMSON: It's not impossible.

LEVENE: On an eighty-thousand dollar *day*? And it ain't even *noon*.

ROMA: You closed 'em today?

LEVENE: Yes. I did. This *morning*. (*To* WILLIAMSON:) What I'm *saying* to you: things can *change*. You *see*? This is where you fuck *up*, because this is something you don't *know*. You can't look down the *road*. And see what's *coming*. Might be someone *else*, John. It might be someone *new*, eh? Someone *new*. And you can't look *back*. 'Cause you don't know *history*. You ask them. When we were at Rio Rancho, who was top man? A month . . . ? Two months . . . ? Eight months in twelve for three years in a row. You know what that means? You know what that means? Is that *luck*? Is that some, some, some purloined leads? That's *skill*. That's *talent*, that's, that's . . .

ROMA: . . . *yes* . . .

LEVENE: . . . and you don't *remember*. 'Cause you weren't *around*. That's cold *calling*. Walk up to the door. I don't even know their *name*. I'm selling something they don't even *want*. You talk about soft sell . . . before we had a name for it . . . before we called it anything, we did it.

ROMA: That's right, Shel.

LEVENE: And, and, and, I *did* it. And I put a kid through *school*. She . . . and . . . Cold *calling*, fella. Door to door. But you don't know. You don't know. You never heard of a *streak*. You never heard of "marshaling your sales force. . . ." What are you, you're a *secretary*, John. Fuck *you*. That's my message to you. Fuck you and kiss my ass. You don't like it, I'll go talk to Jerry Graff. Period. Fuck you. Put me on the board. And I want three worthwhile leads today and I don't want any bullshit about them and I want 'em close together 'cause I'm going to hit them all today. That's all I have to say to you.

ROMA: He's right, Williamson.

WILLIAMSON *goes into a side office. Pause.*

LEVENE: It's not right. I'm sorry, and I'll tell you who's to blame is Mitch and Murray.

ROMA *sees something outside the window.*

ROMA (*Sotto*): Oh, Christ.

LEVENE: The hell with him. We'll go to lunch, the leads won't be up for . . .

ROMA: You're a client. I just sold you five waterfront Glengarry Farms. I rub my head, throw me the cue "Kenilworth."

LEVENE: What is it?

ROMA: Kenilw . . .

LINGK *enters the office.*

ROMA (*To* LEVENE): *I* own the property, my *mother* owns the property, I put her *into* it. I'm going to show you on the plats. You look when you get home A–3 through A–14 and 26 through 30. You take your time and if you still feel.

LEVENE: No, Mr. Roma. I don't need the time, I've made a lot of *investments* in the last. . .

LINGK: I've got to talk to you.

ROMA (*Looking up*): Jim! What are you doing here? Jim Lingk, D. Ray Morton . . .

LEVENE: Glad to meet you.

ROMA: I just put Jim into Black Creek . . . are you acquainted with . . .

LEVENE: No . . . Black *Creek.* Yes. In *Florida*?

ROMA: Yes.

LEVENE: I wanted to *speak* with you about . . .

ROMA: Well, we'll do that this weekend.

LEVENE: My *wife* told me to look into . . .

ROMA: *Beautiful.* Beautiful rolling land. I was telling Jim and Jinny, Ray, I want to tell you something. (*To* LEVENE:) You, Ray, you eat in a lot of restaurants. I know you do. . . . (*To* LINGK:) Mr. Morton's with American Express . . . he's . . . (*To* LEVENE:) I can tell Jim what you do . . . ?

LEVENE: Sure.

ROMA: Ray is director of all European sales and services for American Ex . . . (*To* LEVENE:) But I'm saying you haven't had a *meal* until you've tasted . . . I was at the Lingks' last . . . as a matter of fact, what was that service feature you were talking about . . . ?

LEVENE: Which . . .

ROMA: "Home Cooking" . . . what did you call it, you said it . . . it was a tag phrase that you had . . .

LEVENE: Uh . . .

ROMA: Home . . .

LEVENE: Home cooking . . .

ROMA: The monthly interview . . . ?

LEVENE: Oh! For the *magazine* . . .

ROMA: Yes. Is this something that I can talk ab . . .

LEVENE: Well, it isn't coming *out* until the February iss . . . *sure.* Sure, go ahead, Ricky.

ROMA: You're sure?

LEVENE (*nods*): Go ahead.

ROMA: Well, Ray was eating at one of his company's men's home in France . . . the man's French, isn't he?

LEVENE: No, his *wife* is.

ROMA: Ah. Ah, his wife is. Ray: what *time* do you have . . . ?

LEVENE: Twelve-fifteen.

ROMA: Oh! My God . . . I've got to get you on the *plane!*

LEVENE: Didn't I say I was taking the two o' . . .

ROMA: No. You said the one. That's why you said we couldn't talk till Kenilworth.

LEVENE: Oh, my God, you're right! I'm on the one. . . . (*Getting up.*) Well, let's *scoot* . . .

LINGK: I've got to talk to you . . .

ROMA: I've got to get Ray to O'Hare . . . (*To* LEVENE:) Come on, let's hustle . . . . (*Over his shoulder*:) John! Call American Express in *Pittsburgh* for Mr. Morton, will you, tell them he's on the one o'clock. (*To* LINGK:) I'll see you. . . . Christ, I'm sorry you came all the way in. . . . I'm running Ray over to O'Hare . . . . You wait here, I'll . . . no. (*To* LEVENE:) I'm meeting your man at the bank . . . . (*To* LINGK:) I wish you'd phoned. . . . I'll tell you, wait: are you and Jinny going to be home tonight? (*Rubs forehead.*)

LINGK: I . . .

LEVENE: Rick.

ROMA: What?

LEVENE: *Kenilworth* . . . ?

ROMA: I'm sorry . . . ?

LEVENE: *Kenilworth.*

ROMA: Oh, God . . . Oh, God . . . (ROMA *takes* LINGK *aside, sotto*) Jim, excuse me. . . . Ray, I told you, who he is is *the* senior vice-president American Express. His family owns 32 per. . . . Over the past years I've sold him . . . I can't tell you the dollar amount, but *quite* a lot of land. I promised five *weeks* ago that I'd go to the wife's birthday party in Kenilworth tonight. (*Sighs.*) I *have* to go. You understand. They treat me like a member of the family, so I have to go. It's funny, you know, you get a picture of the Corporation-Type Company Man, all business . . . this man, *no.* We'll go out to his home sometime. Let's see. (*He checks his datebook.*) Tomorrow. No. Tomorrow, I'm in L. A. . . . *Monday* . . . I'll take you to lunch, where would you like to go?

LINGK: My wife . . . (Roma *rubs his head.*)

LEVENE (*Standing in the door*): Rick . . . ?

ROMA: I'm sorry, Jim. I can't talk now. I'll call you tonight . . . I'm sorry. I'm coming, Ray. (*Starts for the door.*)

LINGK: My wife said I have to cancel the deal.

ROMA: Its a common reaction, Jim. I'll tell you what it is, and I know that that's why you married her. One of the reasons is *prudence.* It's a sizable investment. One thinks *twice* . . . it's also something *women* have. It's just a reaction to the size of the investment. *Monday,* if you'd invite me for dinner again . . . (*To* LEVENE:) This woman can *cook* . . .

LEVENE (*Simultaneously*): I'm sure she can . . .

ROMA (*To* LINGK): We're going to talk. I'm going to *tell* you something. Because (*Sotto:*) there's something about your acreage I want you to know. I can't talk about it now. I really shouldn't. And, in fact, by *law,* I . . . (*Shrugs, resigned.*) The man next to you, he bought his lot at *forty-two,* he phoned to say that he'd *already* had an offer . . . (ROMA *rubs his head.*)

LEVENE: Rick . . . ?

ROMA: I'm coming, Ray . . . what a day! I'll call you this evening, Jim. I'm sorry you had to come in . . . Monday, lunch.

LINGK: My wife . . .

LEVENE: Rick, we really have to go.

LINGK: My wife . . .

ROMA: Monday.

LINGK: She called the consumer . . . the attorney, I don't know. The attorney gen . . . they said we have three days . . .

ROMA: *Who* did she call?

LINGK: I don't know, the attorney gen . . . the . . . some consumer office, umm . . .

ROMA: Why did she do *that,* Jim?

LINGK: I don't know. (*Pause.*) They said we have three days. (*Pause.*) They said we have three days.

ROMA: Three days.

LINGK: To . . . you know. (*Pause.*)

ROMA: No, I don't know. *Tell* me.

LINGK: To change our minds.

ROMA: Of *course* you have three days. (*Pause.*)

LINGK: So we can't talk *Monday.* (*Pause.*)

ROMA: Jim, Jim, you saw my book . . . I *can't, you* saw my book . . .

LINGK: But we have to *before* Monday. To get our money ba . . .

ROMA: Three *business* days. They mean three *business* days.

LINGK: Wednesday, Thursday, Friday.

ROMA: I don't understand.

LINGK: That's what they are. Three business . . . if I wait till Monday, my time limit runs out.

ROMA: You don't count Saturday.

LINGK: I'm not.

ROMA: No, I'm saying you don't include Saturday . . . in your three days. It's not a *business* day.

LINGK: But I'm not *counting* it. (*Pause.*) Wednesday. Thursday. Friday. So it would have elapsed.

ROMA: What would have elapsed?

LINGK: If we wait till Mon . . .

ROMA: When did you write the check?

LINGK: Yest. . .

ROMA: What was yesterday?

LINGK: Tuesday.

ROMA: And when was that check cashed?

LINGK: I don't know.

ROMA: What was the *earliest* it could have been cashed? (*Pause.*)

LINGK: I don't know.

ROMA: *Today.* (*Pause.*) *Today.* Which, in any case, it was not, as there were a couple of points on the agreement I wanted to go over with you in any case.

LINGK: The check wasn't cashed?

ROMA: I just called downtown, and it's on their desk.

LEVENE: Rick . . .

ROMA: One moment, I'll be right with you. (*To* LINGK:) In fact, a . . . *one* point, which I spoke to you of which (*Looks around.*) I can't talk to you about here.

Detective *puts his head out of the doorway.*

BAYLEN: Levene!!!

LINGK: I, I . . .

ROMA: Listen to me, the *statute*, it's for your protection. I have no complaints with that, in fact, I was a member of the board when we *drafted* it, so quite the *opposite.* It *says* that you can change your mind three working days from the time the deal is closed.

BAYLEN: Levene!

ROMA: Which, wait a second, which is not until the check is cashed.

BAYLEN: Levene!!

AARONOW *comes out of the* Detective's *office.*

AARONOW: I'm *through,* with *this* fucking meshugaas. No one should talk to a man that way. How are you *talking* to me that . . . ?

BAYLEN: Levene! (WILLIAMSON *puts his head out of the office.*)

AARONOW: . . . how can you *talk* to me that . . . that . . .

LEVENE (*To* ROMA): Rick, I'm going to flag a cab.

AARONOW: *I* didn't rob . . .

WILLIAMSON *sees* LEVENE.

WILLIAMSON: Shelly: get in the office.

AARONOW: *I* didn't . . . why should *I* . . . "Where were you last . . ." Is anybody listening to me . . . ? Where's Moss . . . ? Where . . . ?

BAYLEN: Levene? (*To* WILLIAMSON:) Is this Lev . . . (BAYLEN *accosts* LINGK.)

LEVENE (*Taking* BAYLEN *into the office*): Ah. Ah. Perhaps I can advise you on that. . . . (*To* ROMA *and* LINGK, as *he exits:*) *Excuse* us, will you . . . ?

AARONOW (*Simultaneous with* LEVENE'S *speech above*). . . . Come in here . . . I *work* here, I don't come in here to be *mistreated* . . .

WILLIAMSON: Go to *lunch,* will you . . .

AARONOW: I want to *work* today, that's why I came . . .

WILLIAMSON: The leads come in, I'll let . . .

AARONOW: . . . that's why I came in. I thought I . . .

WILLIAMSON: Just go to lunch.

AARONOW: I don't *want* to go to lunch.

WILLIAMSON: Go to lunch, George.

AARONOW: Where does he get off to talk that way to a working man? It's not . . .

WILLIAMSON (*Buttonholes him*): Will you take it outside, we have people trying to do *business* here . . .

AARONOW: That's what, that's what, that's what *I* was trying to do. (*Pause.*) That's why I came *in* . . . I meet *gestapo* tac . . .

WILLIAMSON (*Going back into his office*): Excuse me . . .

AARONOW: I meet *gestapo* tactics . . . I meet *gestapo* tactics. . . . That's not right. . . . No man has the right to . . . "Call an attorney," that means you're guilt . . . you're under sus . . . "Co . . .," he says, "cooperate" or we'll go downtown. *That's* not . . . as long as I've . . .

WILLIAMSON (*Bursting out of his office*): Will you get out of here. Will you get *out* of here. Will you. I'm trying to run an *office* here. Will you go to lunch? Go to lunch. Will you go to lunch? (*Retreats into office.*)

ROMA (*To* AARONOW): Will you excuse . . .

AARONOW: Where did Moss . . . ? I . . .

ROMA: Will you excuse us please?

AARONOW: Uh, uh, did he go to the restaurant?

(*Pause.*) I . . . I . . . (*Exits.*)

ROMA: I'm *very* sorry, Jimmy. I apologize to you.

LINGK: It's not me, it's my wife.

ROMA (*Pause*): What is?

LINGK: I told you.

ROMA: Tell me again.

LINGK: What's going on here?

ROMA: Tell me again. Your wife.

LINGK: I told you.

ROMA: You tell me again.

LINGK: She wants her money back.

ROMA: We're going to speak to her.

LINGK: No. She told me "right now."

ROMA: We'll speak to her, Jim . . .

LINGK: She won't listen.

Detective *sticks his head out.*

BAYLEN: *Roma.*

LINGK: She told me if not, I have to call the State's attorney.

ROMA: No, no. That's just something she "said." We don't have to do that.

LINGK: She told me I *have* to.

ROMA: No, Jim.

LINGK: I *do.* If I don't get my *money* back . . .

WILLIAMSON *points out* ROMA *to* BAYLEN.

BAYLEN: Roma! (*To* ROMA:) I'm talking to you . . .

ROMA: I've . . . look. (*Generally*:) Will someone get this guy off my back.

BAYLEN: You have a problem?

ROMA: Yes, I have a problem. Yes, I *do*, my fr . . . It's not me that ripped the joint off, I'm doing *business.* I'll be with you in a *while.* You got it . . . ? (*Looks back.* LINGK *is heading for the door.*) Where are you going?

LINGK: I'm . . .

ROMA: Where are you going . . . ? This is *me.* . . . This is Ricky, Jim. Jim, anything you *want,* you *want* it, you *have* it. You understand? This is *me.* Something *upset* you. Sit down, now sit down. You tell me what it is. (*Pause.*) Am I going to help you fix it? You're goddamned right I am. Sit down. Tell you something . . . ? *Sometimes* we need someone from *outside.* It's . . . no, sit down. . . . Now *talk* to me.

LINGK: I can't negotiate.

ROMA: What does that mean?

LINGK: That . . .

ROMA: . . . what, what, *say* it. Say it to me . . .

LINGK: I . . .

ROMA: What . . . ?

LINGK: I . . .

ROMA: What . . . ? Say the words.

LINGK: I don't have the *power.* (*Pause.*) I said it.

ROMA: What power?

LINGK: The power to negotiate.

ROMA: To negotiate what? (*Pause.*) To negotiate what?

LINGK: *This.*

ROMA: What, "this"? (*Pause.*)

LINGK: The deal.

ROMA: The "deal," *forget* the deal. *Forget* the deal, you've got something on your mind, Jim, what is it?

LINGK (*rising*): I can't talk to you, *you* met my wife, I . . . (*Pause.*)

ROMA: What? (*Pause.*) What? (*Pause.*) What, Jim: I tell you what, let's get out of here . . . let's go get a drink.

LINGK: She told me not to talk to you.

ROMA: Let's . . . no one's going to know, let's go around the *corner* and we'll get a drink.

LINGK: She told me I had to get back the check or call the State's att . . .

ROMA: *Forget* the deal, Jimmy. (*Pause.*) *Forget* the deal . . . you know me. The deal's *dead.* Am I talking about the *deal*? That's *over.* Please. Let's talk about *you.* Come on. (*Pause.* ROMA *rises and starts walking toward the front door.*) Come on. (*Pause.*) Come on, Jim. (*Pause.*) I want to tell you something. Your life is your own. You have a contract with your wife. You have certain things you do *jointly,* you have a *bond* there . . . and there are *other* things. Those things are yours. You needn't feel *ashamed,* you needn't feel that you're being *untrue* . . . or that she would abandon you if she knew. This is your life. (*Pause.*) *Yes.* Now I want to *talk* to you because you're obviously upset and that *concerns* me. Now let's go. Right now.

LINGK *gets up and they start for the door.*

BAYLEN (*Sticks his head out of the door*): Roma . . .

LINGK: . . . and . . . and . . . (*Pause.*)

ROMA: What?

LINGK: And the check is . . .

ROMA: What did I *tell* you? (*Pause.*) What did I say about the three days . . . ?

BAYLEN: Roma, would you, I'd like to get some lunch . . .

ROMA: I'm talking with Mr. Lingk. If you please, I'll be back in. (*Checks watch.*) I'll be back in a while. . . . I told you, check with Mr. Williamson.

BAYLEN: The people downtown said . . .

ROMA: You call them again. Mr. Williamson . . . !

WILLIAMSON: Yes.

ROMA: Mr. Lingk and I are going to . . .

WILLIAMSON: Yes. Please. Please. (*To* LINGK:) The police (*Shrugs.*) can be . . .

LINGK: What are the police doing?

ROMA: It's nothing.

LINGK: What are the *police* doing here . . . ?

WILLIAMSON: We had a slight burglary last night.

ROMA: It was nothing . . . I was assuring Mr. Lingk . . .

WILLIAMSON: Mr. Lingk. James Lingk. Your contract went out. Nothing to . . .

ROMA: John . . .

WILLIAMSON: Your contract went out to the bank.

LINGK: You cashed the check?

WILLIAMSON: We . . .

ROMA: . . . Mr. Williamson . . .

WILLIAMSON: Your check was cashed yesterday afternoon. And we're completely insured, as you know, in *any* case. (*Pause.*)

LINGK (*To* ROMA): You cashed the check?

ROMA: Not to my knowledge, no . . .

WILLIAMSON: I'm sure we can . . .

LINGK: Oh, Christ . . . (*Starts out the door.*) Don't follow me. . . . Oh, Christ. (*Pause. To* ROMA:) I know I've let you down. I'm sorry. For . . . Forgive . . . for . . . I don't know anymore. (*Pause.*) Forgive me. (LINGK *exits. Pause.*)

ROMA (*To* WILLIAMSON): You stupid fucking cunt. *You,* Williamson ... I'm talking to *you,* shithead.... You just cost me *six thousand dollars.* (*Pause.*) Six thousand dollars. And one Cadillac. That's right. What are you going to do about it? What are you going to do about it, asshole. You fucking *shit.* Where did you learn your *trade.* You stupid fucking *cunt.* You *idiot.* Whoever told you you could work with *men*?

BAYLEN: Could I ...

ROMA: I'm going to have your *job,* shithead. I'm going *downtown* and talk to Mitch and Murray, and I'm going to Lemkin. I don't care *whose* nephew you are, who you know, whose dick you're sucking on. You're going *out,* I swear to you, you're going ...

BAYLEN: Hey, fella, let's get this done ...

ROMA: Anyone in this office lives on their *wits....* (*To* BAYLEN:) I'm going to be with you in a second. (*To* WILLIAMSON:) What you're hired for is to *help* us — does that seem clear to you? To *help* us. *Not* to fuck us up ... to help *men* who are going *out* there to try to earn a *living.* You *fairy.* You company man ... I'll tell you something else. I hope you knocked the joint off, I can tell our friend here something might help him catch you. (*Starts into the room.*) You want to learn the first rule you'd know if you ever spent a day in your life ... you never open your mouth till you know what the shot is. (*Pause.*) You fucking *child* ... (ROMA *goes to the inner room.*)

LEVENE: You *are* a shithead, Williamson ... (*Pause.*)

WILLIAMSON: Mmm.

LEVENE: You can't think on your feet you should keep your mouth closed. (*Pause.*) You hear me? I'm *talking* to you. Do you hear me ... ?

WILLIAMSON: Yes. (*Pause.*) I hear you.

LEVENE: You can't learn that in an office. Eh? He's right. You have to learn it on the streets. You can't *buy* that. You have to *live* it.

WILLIAMSON: Mmm.

LEVENE: *Yes.* Mmm. *Yes. Precisely. Precisely.* 'Cause your partner *depends* on it. (*Pause.*) I'm *talking* to you, I'm trying to tell you something.

WILLIAMSON: You are?

LEVENE: Yes, I am.

WILLIAMSON: What are you trying to tell me?

LEVENE: What Roma's trying to tell you. What I told you yesterday. Why you don't belong in this business.

WILLIAMSON: Why I don't ...

LEVENE: You listen to me, someday you might say, "Hey ..." No, fuck that, you just listen what I'm going to say: your partner *depends* on you. Your partner ... a man who's your "partner" *depends* on you . . . you have to go *with* him and *for* him . . . or you're shit, you're *shit*, you can't exist alone . . .

WILLIAMSON (*Brushing past him*): Excuse me . . .

LEVENE: . . . excuse you, *nothing*, you be as cold as you want, but you just fucked a good man out of six thousand dollars and his goddamn bonus 'cause you didn't know the *shot*, if you can do that and you aren't man enough that it gets you, then I don't know what, if you can't take *some thing* from that . . . (*Blocking his way.*) you're *scum*, you're fucking white-bread. You be as cold as you want. A *child* would know it, he's right. (*Pause.*) You're going to make something up, be sure it will *help* or keep your mouth closed. (*Pause.*)

WILLIAMSON: Mmm. (LEVENE *lifts up his arm.*)

LEVENE: Now I'm done with you. (*Pause.*)

WILLIAMSON: How do you know I made it up?

LEVENE (*Pause*): What?

WILLIAMSON: How do you know I made it up?

LEVENE: What are you talking about?

WILLIAMSON: You said, "You don't make something up unless it's sure to help." (*Pause.*) How did you know that I made it up?

LEVENE: What are you talking about?

WILLIAMSON: I told the customer that his contracts had gone to the bank.

LEVENE: Well, hadn't it?

WILLIAMSON: No. (*Pause.*) It hadn't.

LEVENE: Don't *fuck* with me, John, don't *fuck* with me . . . what are you saying?

WILLIAMSON: Well, I'm saying this, Shel: usually I take the contracts to the bank. Last night I didn't. How did you know that? One night in a year I left a contract on my desk. Nobody knew that but *you*. Now how did you know that? (*Pause.*) You want to talk to me, you want to talk to someone *else* . . . because this is *my* job. This is my job on the line, and you are going to *talk* to me. Now how did you know that contract was on my desk?

LEVENE: You're so full of shit.

WILLIAMSON: You robbed the office.

LEVENE (*Laughs*): Sure! I robbed the office. Sure.

WILLIAMSON: What'd you do with the leads? (*Pause. Points to the* Detective's *room.*) You want to go in there? I tell him what I know, he's going to dig up *something*. . . . You got an alibi last night? You better have one. What did you do with the leads? If you tell me what you did with the leads, we can talk.

LEVENE: I don't know what you are saying.

WILLIAMSON: If you tell me where the leads are, I won't turn you in. If you *don't*, I am going to tell the cop you stole them, Mitch and Murray will see that you go to jail. Believe me they will. Now, what did you do with the leads? I'm walking in that door—you have five seconds to tell me: or you are going to jail.

LEVENE: I . . .

WILLIAMSON: I don't care. You understand? *Where are the leads?* (*Pause.*) Alright. (WILLIAMSON *goes to open the office door.*)

LEVENE: I sold them to Jerry Graff.

WILLIAMSON: How much did you get for them? (*Pause.*) How much did you get for them?

LEVENE: Five thousand. I kept half.

WILLIAMSON: Who kept the other half? (*Pause.*)

LEVENE: Do I have to tell you? (*Pause.* WILLIAMSON *starts to open the door.*) Moss.

WILLIAMSON: *That* was easy, *wasn't* it? (*Pause.*)

LEVENE: It was his idea.

WILLIAMSON: *Was* it?

LEVENE: I . . . I'm sure he got more than the five, actually.

WILLIAMSON: Uh-huh?

LEVENE: He told me my share was twenty-five.

WILLIAMSON: Mmm.

LEVENE: Okay: I . . . look: I'm going to make it worth your while. I am. I turned this thing around. I closed the *old* stuff, I can do it again. *I'm* the one's going to close 'em. *I* am! *I* am! 'Cause I turned this thing a . . . I can do *that*, I can do *anyth* . . . last night. I'm going to tell you, I was ready to Do the Dutch. Moss gets me, "Do this, we'll get well. . . ." Why not. Big fuckin' deal. I'm halfway hoping to get caught. To put me out of my . . . (*Pause.*) But it *taught* me something. What it taught me, that you've got to get *out* there. Big deal. So I wasn't cut out to be a thief. I was cut out to be a salesman. And now I'm back, and I got my *balls* back . . . and, you know, John, you have the *advantage* on me now. Whatever it takes to make it right, we'll make it right. We're going to make it right.

WILLIAMSON: I want to tell you something, Shelly. You have a big mouth. (*Pause.*)

LEVENE: What?

WILLIAMSON: You've got a big mouth, and now I'm going to show you an even bigger one. (*Starts toward the* Detective's *door.*)

LEVENE: Where are you going, John? . . . you can't do that, you don't want to do that . . . hold, hold on . . . hold on . . . wait . . . wait . . . wait . . . (*Pulls money out of his pockets.*) Wait . . . uh, look . . . (*Starts splitting money.*) Look, twelve, twenty, two, twen . . . twenty-five hundred, it's . . . take it. (*Pause.*) Take it all. . . . (*Pause.*) Take it!

WILLIAMSON: No, I don't think so, Shel.

LEVENE: I . . .

WILLIAMSON: No, I think I don't want your money. I think you fucked up my office. And I think you're going away.

LEVENE: I . . . what? Are you, are you, that's why . . . ? Are you nuts? I'm . . . I'm going to *close* for you, I'm going to . . . (*Thrusting money at him.*) Here, here, I'm going to *make* this office . . . I'm going to be back there Number One. . . . Hey, hey, hey! This is only the beginning. . . . List . . . list . . . listen. Listen. Just one moment. List . . . here's what . . . here's what we're going to do. Twenty percent. I'm going to give you twenty percent of my sales. . . . (*Pause.*) Twenty percent. (*Pause.*) For as long as I am with the firm. (*Pause.*) Fifty percent. (*Pause.*) You're going to be my partner. (*Pause.*) Fifty percent. Of all my sales.

WILLIAMSON: What sales?

LEVENE: What sales . . . ? I just *closed* eighty-two *grand.* . . . Are you fuckin' . . . I'm *back* . . . I'm *back*, this is only the beginning.

WILLIAMSON: Only the beginning . . .

LEVENE: Abso . . .

WILLIAMSON: Where have you been, Shelly? Bruce and Harriett Nyborg. Do you want to see the *memos* . . . ? They're nuts . . . they used to call in every week. When I was with Webb. And we were selling Arizona . . . they're nuts . . . did you see how they were *living*? How can you delude yours . . .

LEVENE: I've got the check . . .

WILLIAMSON: Forget it. Frame it. It's worthless. (*Pause.*)

LEVENE: The check's no good?

WILLIAMSON: You stick around I'll pull the memo for you. (*Starts for the door.*) I'm busy now . . .

LEVENE: Their check's no good? They're nuts . . . ?

WILLIAMSON: Call up the bank. *I* called them.

LEVENE: You did?

WILLIAMSON: I called them when we had the lead . . . four months ago. (*Pause.*) The people are insane. They just like talking to salesmen. (WILLIAMSON *starts for door.*)

LEVENE: Don't.

WILLIAMSON: I'm sorry.

LEVENE: *Why?*

WILLIAMSON: Because I don't like you.

LEVENE: John: John: . . . my *daughter* . . .

WILLIAMSON: Fuck you. (ROMA *comes out of the* Detective's *door.* WILLIAMSON *goes in.*)

ROMA (*To* BAYLEN): Asshole . . . (*To* LEVENE:) Guy couldn't find his fuckin' couch the *living room* . . . Ah, Christ . . . what a day, what a day . . . I haven't even had a cup of *coffee* . . . . Jagoff John opens his mouth he blows my Cadillac. . . . (*Sighs.*) I swear . . . it's not a world of men . . . it's not a world of men, Machine . . . it's a world of clock watchers, bureaucrats, officeholders . . . what it is, it's a fucked-up world . . . there's no adventure *to* it. (*Pause.*) Dying breed. Yes it is. (*Pause.*) We are the members of a dying breed. That's . . . that's. . . that's why we have to stick together. Shel: I want to talk to you. I've wanted to talk to you for some time. For a long time, actually. I said, "The Machine, there's a man I would work with. There's a man . . ." You know? I never said a thing. I should have, don't know why I didn't. And that shit you were slinging on my guy today was *so* good . . . it . . . it was, and, excuse me, 'cause it isn't even my place to say it. It was admirable . . . it was the old stuff. Hey, I've been on a hot streak, so *what*? There's things that I could learn from you. You eat today?

LEVENE: Me.

ROMA: Yeah.

LEVENE: Mm.

ROMA: Well, you want to swing by the Chinks, watch me eat, we'll talk?

LEVENE: I think I'd better stay here for a while.

BAYLEN *sticks his head out of the room:*

BAYLEN: Mr. *Levene* . . . ?

ROMA: You're done, come down and let's . . .

BAYLEN: Would you come in here, please?

ROMA: And let's put this together. Okay? Shel? Say okay. (*Pause.*)

LEVENE (*Softly, to himself*): Huh.

BAYLEN: Mr. Levene, I think we have to talk.

ROMA: I'm going to the Chinks. You're done, come down, we're going to smoke a cigarette.

LEVENE: I . . .

BAYLEN (*Comes over*): . . . Get in the room.

ROMA: Hey, hey, hey, *easy* friend, That's the "Machine." That is Shelly "The Machine" Lev . . .

BAYLEN: Get in the goddamn room. (BAYLEN *starts manhandling* SHELLY *into the room.*)

LEVENE: Ricky, I . . .

ROMA: Okay, okay, I'll be at the resta . . .

LEVENE: Ricky . . .

BAYLEN: "Ricky" can't help you, pal.

LEVENE: . . . I only want to . . .

BAYLEN: Yeah. What do you want? You want to *what*? (*He pushes* LEVENE *into the room, closes the door behind him. Pause.*)

ROMA: Williamson: listen to me: when the *leads* come in . . . listen to me: when the *leads* come in I want my top two off the list. For *me.* My usual two. Anything you give *Levene* . . .

WILLIAMSON: . . . I wouldn't worry about it.

ROMA: Well I'm *going* to worry about it, and so are you, so shut up and *listen.* (*Pause.*) I GET HIS ACTION. My stuff is *mine*, whatever *he* gets for himself, I'm talking half. You put me in with him.

AARONOW *enters.*

AARONOW: Did they . . . ?

ROMA: You understand?

AARONOW: Did they catch . . . ?

ROMA: Do you understand? My stuff is mine, his stuff is ours. I'm taking half of his commissions—now, *you* work it out.

WILLIAMSON: Mmm.

AARONOW: Did they find the guy who broke into the office yet?

ROMA: No. *I* don't know. (*Pause.*)

AARONOW: Did the leads come in yet?

ROMA: No.

AARONOW (*Settling into a desk chair*): Oh, God, I hate this job.

ROMA (*Simultaneous with "job," exiting the office*): I'll be at the restaurant.

The Dumb Waiter HAROLD PINTER

Winner of the 2005 Nobel Prize for Literature, England's Harold Pinter (born in 1930) has been writing plays for more than fifty years. Many consider Pinter to be one of the leading playwrights of the Theater of the Absurd, a movement that came to prominence during the mid-twentieth century. The Theater of the Absurd is a movement that calls into question the very nature of human existence. An absurdist play presents a world bereft of both logical action and moral values, and even such dramatic conventions as language, plot, and narrative themselves are called into question.

In this Pinter play, Ben and Gus, the only two characters in the play, are hired killers waiting to murder—someone. Set in a basement, *The Dumb Waiter* is full of suspense and mystery. We know little if anything about Ben and Gus, their backgrounds or their motivations. Who are they waiting for? Who will they murder? Why? The dialogue is filled with what is now known as the famous "Pinter pause," a silence and hesitancy that adds much to the play's tensions.

With such plays as *The Birthday Party* (1958), *The Homecoming* (1965), *The Hothouse* (1980), and, more recently, *Ashes to Ashes* (1996), and *War* (2003), Pinter continues to shape and energize the contemporary British stage.

CHARACTERS

BEN
GUS

SCENE: *A basement room. Two beds, flat against the back wall. A serving hatch, closed, between the beds. A door to the kitchen and lavatory, left. A door to a passage, right. Ben is lying on a bed, left, reading a paper. Gus is sitting on a bed, right, tying his shoelaces, with difficulty. Both are dressed in shirts, trousers, and braces.*

Silence.

Gus ties his laces, rises, yawns, and begins to walk slowly to the door, left. He stops, looks down, and shakes his foot.

Ben lowers his paper and watches him. Gus kneels and unties his shoelace and slowly takes off the shoe. He looks inside it and brings out a flattened matchbox. He shakes it and examines it. Their eyes meet. Ben rattles his paper and reads. Gus puts the matchbox in his pocket and bends down to put on his shoe. He ties his lace, with difficulty. Ben lowers his paper and watches him. Gus walks to the door, left, stops, and shakes the other foot. He kneels, unties his shoelace, and slowly takes off the shoe. He looks inside it and brings out a flattened cigarette packet. He shakes it and examines it. Their eyes meet. Ben rattles his paper and reads. Gus puts the packet in his pocket, bends down, puts on his shoe, and ties the lace.

He wanders off, left.

Ben slams the paper down on the bed and glares after him. He picks up the paper and lies on his back, reading.

Silence.

A lavatory chain is pulled twice, off left, but the lavatory does not flush.

Silence.

Gus reenters, left, and halts at the door, scratching his head.

Ben slams down the paper.

BEN: Kaw!

(*He picks up the paper.*)

What about this? Listen to this!

(*He refers to the paper.*)

A man of eighty-seven wanted to cross the road. But there was a lot of traffic, see? He couldn't see how he was going to squeeze through. So he crawled under a lorry.[1]

GUS: He what?

BEN: He crawled under a lorry. A stationary lorry.

GUS: No?

BEN: The lorry started and ran over him.

GUS: Go on!

BEN: That's what it says here.

GUS: Get away.

BEN: It's enough to make you want to puke, isn't it?

GUS: Who advised him to do a thing like that?

BEN: A man of eighty-seven crawling under a lorry!

GUS: It's unbelievable.

BEN: It's down here in black and white.

GUS: Incredible.

(*Silence.*)

(GUS *shakes his head and exits.* BEN *lies back and reads.*)

(*The lavatory chain is pulled once off left, but the lavatory does not flush.*)

(BEN *whistles at an item in the paper.*)

(GUS *reenters.*)

I want to ask you something.

BEN: What are you doing out there?

GUS: Well, I was just —

[1]**lorry:** British term for a truck

BEN: What about the tea?

GUS: I'm just going to make it.

BEN: Well, go on, make it.

GUS: Yes, I will. (*He sits in a chair. Ruminatively.*) He's laid on some very nice crockery this time, I'll say that. It's sort of striped. There's a white stripe.

(BEN *reads.*)

It's very nice. I'll say that.

(BEN *turns the page.*)

You know, sort of round the cup. Round the rim. All the rest of it's black, you see. Then the saucer's black, except for right in the middle, where the cup goes, where it's white.

(BEN *reads.*)

Then the plates are the same, you see. Only they've got a black stripe—the plates—right across the middle. Yes, I'm quite taken with the crockery.

BEN (*still reading*): What do you want plates for? You're not going to eat.

GUS: I've brought a few biscuits.

BEN: Well, you'd better eat them quick.

GUS: I always bring a few biscuits. Or a pie. You know I can't drink tea without anything to eat.

BEN: Well, make the tea then, will you? Time's getting on.

(GUS *brings out the flattened cigarette packet and examines it.*)

GUS: You got any cigarettes? I think I've run out.

(*He throws the packet high up and leans forward to catch it.*)

I hope it won't be a long job, this one.

(*Aiming carefully, he flips the packet under his bed.*)

Oh, I wanted to ask you something.

BEN (*slamming his paper down*): Kaw!

GUS: What's that?

BEN: A child of eight killed a cat!

GUS: Get away.

BEN: It's a fact. What about that, eh? A child of eight killing a cat!

GUS: How did he do it?

BEN: It was a girl.
GUS: How did she do it?
BEN: She—

(*He picks up the paper and studies it.*)

It doesn't say.
GUS: Why not?
BEN: Wait a minute. It just says—Her brother, aged eleven, viewed the incident from the toolshed.
GUS: Go on!
BEN: That's bloody ridiculous.

(*Pause.*)

GUS: I bet he did it.
BEN: Who?
GUS: The brother.
BEN: I think you're right.

(*Pause.*)

(*Slamming down the paper.*) What about that, eh? A kid of eleven killing a cat and blaming it on his little sister of eight! It's enough to—

(*He breaks off in disgust and seizes the paper.* GUS *rises.*)

GUS: What time is he getting in touch?

(BEN *reads.*)

What time is he getting in touch?
BEN: What's the matter with you? It could be any time. Any time.
GUS (*moves to the foot of Ben's bed*): Well, I was going to ask you something.
BEN: What?
GUS: Have you noticed the time that tank takes to fill?
BEN: What tank?
GUS: In the lavatory.
BEN: No. Does it?
GUS: Terrible.
BEN: Well, what about it?
GUS: What do you think's the matter with it?
BEN: Nothing.
GUS: Nothing?
BEN: It's got a deficient ballcock, that's all.

GUS: A deficient what?

BEN: Ballcock.

GUS: No? Really?

BEN: That's what I should say.

GUS: Go on! That didn't occur to me.

(GUS *wanders to his bed and presses the mattress.*)

I didn't have a very restful sleep today, did you? It's not much of a bed. I could have done with another blanket too. (*He catches sight of a picture on the wall.*) Hello, what's this? (*Peering at it.*) "The First Eleven."[2] Cricketers. You seen this, Ben?

BEN (*reading*): What?

GUS: The first eleven.

BEN: What?

GUS: There's a photo here of the first eleven.

BEN: What first eleven?

GUS (*studying the photo*): It doesn't say.

BEN: What about that tea?

GUS: They all look a bit old to me.

(GUS *wanders downstage, looks out front, then all about the room.*)

I wouldn't like to live in this dump. I wouldn't mind if you had a window, you could see what it looked like outside.

BEN: What do you want a window for?

GUS: Well, I like to have a bit of a view, Ben. It whiles away the time.

(*He walks about the room.*)

I mean, you come into a place when it's still dark, you come into a room you've never seen before, you sleep all day, you do your job, and then you go away in the night again.

(*Pause.*)

I like to get a look at the scenery. You never get the chance in this job.

BEN: You get your holidays, don't you?

GUS: Only a fortnight.

[2]**The First Eleven:** an Aboriginal Australian cricket team who toured England in 1868

BEN (*lowering the paper*): You kill me. Anyone would think you're working every day. How often do we do a job? Once a week? What are you complaining about?

GUS: Yes, but we've got to be on tap though, haven't we? You can't move out of the house in case a call comes.

BEN: You know what your trouble is?

GUS: What?

BEN: You haven't got any interests.

GUS: I've got interests.

BEN: What? Tell me one of your interests.

(*Pause.*)

GUS: I've got interests.

BEN: Look at me. What have I got?

GUS: I don't know. What?

BEN: I've got my woodwork. I've got my model boats. Have you ever seen me idle? I'm never idle. I know how to occupy my time, to its best advantage. Then when a call comes, I'm ready.

GUS: Don't you ever get a bit fed up?

BEN: Fed up? What with?

(*Silence.*)

(BEN *reads.* GUS *feels in the pocket of his jacket, which hangs on the bed.*)

GUS: You got any cigarettes? I've run out.

(*The lavatory flushes off left.*)

There she goes.

(GUS *sits on his bed.*)

No, I mean, I say the crockery's good. It is. It's very nice. But that's about all I can say for this place. It's worse than the last one. Remember that last place we were in? Last time, where was it? At least there was a wireless there. No, honest. He doesn't seem to bother much about our comfort these days.

BEN: When are you going to stop jabbering?

GUS: You'd get rheumatism in a place like this, if you stay long.

BEN: We're not staying long. Make the tea, will you? We'll be on the job in a minute.

(GUS *picks up a small bag by his bed and brings out a packet of tea. He examines it and looks up.*)

GUS: Eh, I've been meaning to ask you.

BEN: What the hell is it now?

GUS: Why did you stop the car this morning, in the middle of that road?

BEN (*lowering the paper*): I thought you were asleep.

GUS: I was, but I woke up when you stopped. You did stop, didn't you?

(*Pause.*)

In the middle of that road. It was still dark, don't you remember? I looked out. It was all misty. I thought perhaps you wanted to kip,[3] but you were sitting up dead straight, like you were waiting for something.

BEN: I wasn't waiting for anything.

GUS: I must have fallen asleep again. What was all that about then? Why did you stop?

BEN (*picking up the paper*): We were too early.

GUS: Early? (*He rises.*) What do you mean? We got the call, didn't we, saying we were to start right away. We did. We shoved out on the dot. So how could we be too early?

BEN (*quietly*): Who took the call, me or you?

GUS: You.

BEN: We were too early.

GUS: Too early for what?

(*Pause.*)

You mean someone had to get out before we got in?

(*He examines the bedclothes.*)

I thought these sheets didn't look too bright. I thought they ponged[4] a bit. I was too tired to notice when I got in this morning. Eh, that's taking a bit of a liberty, isn't it? I don't want to share my bed sheets. I told you things were going down the drain. I mean, we've always had clean sheets laid on up till now. I've noticed it.

BEN: How do you know those sheets weren't clean?

GUS: What do you mean?

BEN: How do you know they weren't clean? You've spent the whole day in them, haven't you?

---

[3]**kip:** British term for a nap [4]**ponged:** British term for smelled

GUS: What, you mean it might be my pong? (*He sniffs sheets.*) Yes. (*He sits slowly on bed.*) It could be my pong, I suppose. It's difficult to tell. I don't really know what I pong like, that's the trouble.

BEN (*referring to the paper*): Kaw!

GUS: Eh, Ben.

BEN: Kaw!

GUS: Ben.

BEN: What?

GUS: What town are we in? I've forgotten.

BEN: I've told you. Birmingham.

GUS: Go on!

(*He looks with interest about the room.*)

That's in the Midlands. The second biggest city in Great Britain. I'd never have guessed.

(*He snaps his fingers.*)

Eh, it's Friday today, isn't it? It'll be Saturday tomorrow.

BEN: What about it?

GUS (*excited*): We could go and watch the Villa.[5]

BEN: They're playing away.

GUS: No, are they? Caarr! What a pity.

BEN: Anyway, there's no time. We've got to get straight back.

GUS: Well, we have done in the past, haven't we? Stayed over and watched a game, haven't we? For a bit of relaxation.

BEN: Things have tightened up, mate. They've tightened up.

(GUS *chuckles to himself.*)

GUS: I saw the Villa get beat in a cup tie once. Who was it against now? White shirts. It was one-all at halftime. I'll never forget it. Their opponents won by a penalty. Talk about drama. Yes, it was a disputed penalty. Disputed. They got beat two-one, anyway, because of it. You were there yourself.

BEN: Not me.

GUS: Yes, you were there. Don't you remember that disputed penalty?

BEN: No.

---

[5]**Villa:** a reference to a soccer team

GUS: He went down just inside the area. Then they said he was just acting. I didn't think the other bloke touched him myself. But the referee had the ball on the spot.

BEN: Didn't touch him! What are you talking about? He laid him out flat!

GUS: Not the Villa. The Villa don't play that sort of game.

BEN: Get out of it.

(*Pause.*)

GUS: Eh, that must have been here, in Birmingham.

BEN: What must?

GUS: The Villa. That must have been here.

BEN: They were playing away.

GUS: Because you know who the other team was? It was the Spurs. It was Tottenham Hotspur.

BEN: Well, what about it?

GUS: We've never done a job in Tottenham.

BEN: How do you know?

GUS: I'd remember Tottenham.

(BEN *turns on his bed to look at him.*)

BEN: Don't make me laugh, will you?

(BEN *turns back and reads.* GUS *yawns and speaks through his yawn.*)

GUS: When's he going to get in touch?

(*Pause.*)

Yes, I'd like to see another football match. I've always been an ardent football fan. Here, what about coming to see the Spurs tomorrow?

BEN (*tonelessly*): They're playing away.

GUS: Who are?

BEN: The Spurs.

GUS: Then they might be playing here.

BEN: Don't be silly.

GUS: If they're playing away they might be playing here. They might be playing the Villa.

BEN (*tonelessly*): But the Villa are playing away.

(*Pause. An envelope slides under the door, right.* GUS *sees it. He stands, looking at it.*)

GUS: Ben.

BEN: Away. They're all playing away.
GUS: Ben, look here.
BEN: What?
GUS: Look.

(BEN *turns his head and sees the envelope. He stands.*)

BEN: What's that?
GUS: I don't know.
BEN: Where did it come from?
GUS: Under the door.
BEN: Well, what is it?
GUS: I don't know.

(*They stare at it.*)

BEN: Pick it up.
GUS: What do you mean?
BEN: Pick it up!

(GUS *slowly moves toward it, bends, and picks it up.*)

What is it?
GUS: An envelope.
BEN: Is there anything on it?
GUS: No.
BEN: Is it sealed?
GUS: Yes.
BEN: Open it.
GUS: What?
BEN: Open it!

(GUS *opens it and looks inside.*)

What's in it?

(GUS *empties twelve matches into his hand.*)

GUS: Matches.
BEN: Matches?
GUS: Yes.
BEN: Show it to me.

(GUS *passes the envelope.* BEN *examines it.*)

Nothing on it. Not a word.
GUS: That's funny, isn't it?

BEN: It came under the door?

GUS: Must have done.

BEN: Well, go on.

GUS: Go on where?

BEN: Open the door and see if you can catch anyone outside.

GUS: Who, me?

BEN: Go on!

(GUS *stares at him; puts the matches in his pocket, goes to his bed, and brings a revolver from under the pillow. He goes to the door, opens it, looks out, and shuts it.*)

GUS: No one.

(*He replaces the revolver.*)

BEN: What did you see?

GUS: Nothing.

BEN: They must have been pretty quick.

(GUS *takes the matches from pocket and looks at them.*)

GUS: Well, they'll come in handy.

BEN: Yes.

GUS: Won't they?

BEN: Yes, you're always running out, aren't you?

GUS: All the time.

BEN: Well, they'll come in handy then.

GUS: Yes.

BEN: Won't they?

GUS: Yes, I could do with them. I could do with them too.

BEN: You could, eh?

GUS: Yes.

BEN: Why?

GUS: We haven't got any.

BEN: Well, you've got some now, haven't you?

GUS: I can light the kettle now.

BEN: Yes, you're always cadging[6] matches. How many have you got there?

GUS: About a dozen.

BEN: Well, don't lose them. Red too. You don't even need a box.

(GUS *probes his ear with a match.*)

[6]**cadging:** British term for begging

(*Slapping his hand.*) Don't waste them! Go on, go and light it.

GUS: Eh?

BEN: Go and light it.

GUS: Light what?

BEN: The kettle.

GUS: You mean the gas.

BEN: Who does?

GUS: You do.

BEN (*his eyes narrowing*): What do you mean, I mean the gas?

GUS: Well, that's what you mean, don't you? The gas.

BEN (*powerfully*): If I say go and light the kettle I mean go and light the kettle.

GUS: How can you light a kettle?

BEN: It's a figure of speech! Light the kettle. It's a figure of speech!

GUS: I've never heard it.

BEN: Light the kettle! It's common usage!

GUS: I think you've got it wrong.

BEN (*menacing*): What do you mean?

GUS: They say put on the kettle.

BEN (*taut*): Who says?

(*They stare at each other, breathing hard.*)

(*Deliberately.*) I have never in all my life heard anyone say put on the kettle.

GUS: I bet my mother used to say it.

BEN: Your mother? When did you last see your mother?

GUS: I don't know, about—

BEN: Well, what are you talking about your mother for?

(*They stare.*)

Gus, I'm not trying to be unreasonable. I'm just trying to point out something to you.

GUS: Yes, but—

BEN: Who's the senior partner here, me or you?

GUS: You.

BEN: I'm only looking after your interests, Gus. You've got to learn, mate.

GUS: Yes, but I've never heard—

BEN (*vehemently*): Nobody says light the gas! What does the gas light?

GUS: What does the gas—?

BEN (*grabbing him with two hands by the throat, at arm's length*): THE KETTLE, YOU FOOL!

(GUS *takes the hands from his throat.*)

GUS: All right, all right.

(*Pause.*)

BEN: Well, what are you waiting for?
GUS: I want to see if they light.
BEN: What?
GUS: The matches.

(*He takes out the flattened box and tries to strike.*)

No.

(*He throws the box under the bed.*)
(BEN *stares at him.*)
(GUS *raises his foot.*)

Shall I try it on here?

(BEN *stares.* GUS *strikes a match on his shoe. It lights.*)

Here we are.
BEN (*wearily*): Put on the bloody kettle, for Christ's sake.

(BEN *goes to his bed, but, realizing what he has said, stops and half turns. They look at each other.* GUS *slowly exits, left.* BEN *slams his paper down on the bed and sits on it, head in hands.*)

GUS (*entering*): It's going.
BEN: What?
GUS: The stove.

(GUS *goes to his bed and sits.*)

I wonder who it'll be tonight.

(*Silence.*)

Eh, I've been wanting to ask you something.
BEN (*putting his legs on the bed*): Oh, for Christ's sake.
GUS: No. I was going to ask you something.

(*He rises and sits on* BEN's *bed.*)

BEN: What are you sitting on my bed for?

(GUS *sits.*)

What's the matter with you? You're always asking me questions. What's the matter with you?

GUS: Nothing.

BEN: You never used to ask me so many damn questions. What's come over you?

GUS: No, I was just wondering.

BEN: Stop wondering. You've got a job to do. Why don't you just do it and shut up?

GUS: That's what I was wondering about.

BEN: What?

GUS The job.

BEN: What job?

GUS (*tentatively*): I thought perhaps you might know something.

(BEN *looks at him.*)

I thought perhaps you—I mean—have you got any idea—who it's going to be tonight?

BEN: Who what's going to be?

(*They look at each other.*)

GUS (*at length*): Who it's going to be.

(*Silence.*)

BEN: Are you feeling all right?

GUS: Sure.

BEN: Go and make the tea.

GUS: Yes, sure.

(GUS *exits, left,* BEN *looks after him. He then takes his revolver from under the pillow and checks it for ammunition.* GUS *reenters.*)

The gas has gone out.

BEN: Well, what about it?

GUS: There's a meter.

BEN: I haven't got any money.

GUS: Nor have I.

BEN: You'll have to wait.

GUS: What for?

BEN: For Wilson.

GUS: He might not come. He might just send a message. He doesn't always come.

BEN: Well, you'll have to do without it, won't you?

GUS: Blimey.

BEN: You'll have a cup of tea afterwards. What's the matter with you?

GUS: I like to have one before.

(BEN *holds the revolver up to the light and polishes it.*)

BEN: You'd better get ready anyway.

GUS: Well, I don't know, that's a bit much, you know, for my money.

(*He picks up a packet of tea from the bed and throws it into the bag.*)

I hope he's got a shilling, anyway, if he comes. He's entitled to have. After all, it's his place, he could have seen there was enough gas for a cup of tea.

BEN: What do you mean, it's his place?

GUS: Well, isn't it?

BEN: He's probably only rented it. It doesn't have to be his place.

GUS: I know it's his place. I bet the whole house is. He's not even laying on any gas now either.

(GUS *sits on his bed.*)

It's his place all right. Look at all the other places. You go to this address, there's a key there, there's a teapot, there's never a soul in sight—(*He pauses.*) Eh, nobody ever hears a thing, have you ever thought of that? We never get any complaints, do we, too much noise or anything like that? You never see a soul, do you?—except the bloke who comes. You ever noticed that? I wonder if the walls are soundproof. (*He touches the wall above his bed.*) Can't tell. All you do is wait, eh? Half the time he doesn't even bother to put in an appearance, Wilson.

BEN: Why should he? He's a busy man.

GUS (*thoughtfully*): I find him hard to talk to, Wilson. Do you know that, Ben?

BEN: Scrub round it, will you?

(*Pause.*)

GUS: There are a number of things I want to ask him. But I can never get round to it, when I see him.

(*Pause.*)

I've been thinking about the last one.

BEN: What last one?

GUS: That girl.

(BEN *grabs the paper, which he reads.*)

(*Rising, looking down at Ben.*) How many times have you read that paper?

(BEN *slams the paper down and rises.*)

BEN (*angrily*): What do you mean?

GUS: I was just wondering how many times you'd—

BEN: What are you doing, criticizing me?

GUS: No, I was just—

BEN: You'll get a swipe round your earhole if you don't watch your step.

GUS: Now look here, Ben—

BEN: I'm not looking anywhere! (*He addresses the room.*) How many times have I—! A bloody liberty!

GUS: I didn't mean that.

BEN: You just get on with it, mate. Get on with it, that's all.

(BEN *gets back on the bed.*)

GUS: I was just thinking about that girl, that's all.

(GUS *sits on his bed.*)

She wasn't much to look at, I know, but still. It was a mess though, wasn't it? What a mess. Honest, I can't remember a mess like that one. They don't seem to hold together like men, women. A looser texture, like. Didn't she spread, eh? She didn't half spread. Kaw! But I've been meaning to ask you.

(BEN *sits up and clenches his eyes.*)

Who clears up after we've gone? I'm curious about that. Who does the clearing up? Maybe they don't clear up. Maybe they just leave them there, eh? What do you think? How many jobs have we done? Blimey, I can't count them. What if they never clear anything up after we've gone.

BEN (*pityingly*): You mutt. Do you think we're the only branch of this organization? Have a bit of common. They got departments for everything.

GUS: What cleaners and all?

BEN: You birk.[7]

GUS: No, it was that girl made me start to think—

(*There is a loud clatter and racket in the bulge of wall between the beds, of something descending. They grab their revolvers, jump up, and face the wall. The noise comes to a stop. Silence. They look at each other.* BEN *gestures sharply toward the wall.* GUS *approaches the wall slowly. He bangs it with his revolver. It is hollow.* BEN *moves to the head of his bed, his revolver cocked.* GUS *puts his revolver on his bed and pats along the bottom of the center panel. He finds a rim. He lifts the panel. Disclosed is a serving hatch, a "dumb waiter." A wide box is held by pulleys.* GUS *peers into the box. He brings out a piece of paper.*)

BEN: What is it?

GUS: You have a look at it.

BEN: Read it.

GUS (*reading*): Two braised steak and chips. Two sago puddings. Two teas without sugar.

BEN: Let me see that. (*He takes the paper.*)

GUS (*to himself*): Two teas without sugar.

BEN: Mmnn.

GUS: What do you think of that?

BEN: Well—

(*The box goes up.* BEN *levels his revolver.*)

GUS: Give us a chance? They're in a hurry, aren't they?

(BEN *rereads the note.* GUS *looks over his shoulder.*)

That's a bit—that's a bit funny, isn't it?

BEN (*quickly*): No. It's not funny. It probably used to be a café here, that's all. Upstairs. These places change hands very quickly.

GUS: A café?

BEN: Yes.

GUS: What, you mean this was the kitchen, down here?

BEN: Yes, they change hands overnight, these places. Go into liquidation. The people who run it, you know, they don't find it a going concern, they move out.

GUS: You mean the people who ran this place didn't find it a going concern and moved out?

---

[7]**birk:** British term for a fool

BEN: Sure.

GUS: WELL, WHO'S GOT IT NOW?

(*Silence.*)

BEN: What do you mean, who's got it now?

GUS: Who's got it now? If they moved out, who moved in?

BEN: Well, that all depends—

(*The box descends with a clatter and bang.* BEN *levels his revolver.* GUS *goes to the box and brings out a piece of paper.*)

GUS (*reading*): Soup of the day. Liver and onions. Jam tart.

(*A pause.* GUS *looks at* BEN. BEN *takes the note and reads it. He walks slowly to the hatch.* GUS *follows.* BEN *looks into the hatch but not up it.* GUS *puts his hand on* BEN's *shoulder.* BEN *throws it off.* GUS *puts his finger to his mouth. He leans on the hatch and swiftly looks up it.* BEN *flings him away in alarm.* BEN *looks at the note. He throws his revolver on the bed and speaks with decision.*)

BEN: We'd better send something up.

GUS: Eh?

BEN: We'd better send something up.

GUS: Oh! Yes. Yes. Maybe you're right.

(*They are both relieved at the decision.*)

BEN (*purposefully*): Quick! What have you got in that bag?

GUS: Not much.

(GUS *goes to the hatch and shouts up it.*)

Wait a minute!

BEN: Don't do that!

(GUS *examines the contents of the bag and brings them out, one by one.*)

GUS: Biscuits. A bar of chocolate. Half a pint of milk.

BEN: That all?

GUS: Packet of tea.

BEN: Good.

GUS: We can't send the tea. That's all the tea we've got.

BEN: Well, there's no gas. You can't do anything with it, can you?

GUS: Maybe they can send us down a bob.[8]

---

[8]**bob:** a shilling (British currency)

BEN: What else is there?
GUS: (*reaching into bag*): One Eccles cake.
BEN: One Eccles cake?
GUS: Yes.
BEN: You never told me you had an Eccles cake.
GUS: Didn't I?
BEN: Why only one? Didn't you bring one for me?
GUS: I didn't think you'd be keen.
BEN: Well, you can't send up one Eccles cake, anyway.
GUS: Why not?
BEN: Fetch one of those plates.
GUS: All right.

(GUS *goes toward the door, left, and stops.*)

Do you mean I can keep the Eccles cake then?
BEN: Keep it?
GUS: Well, they don't know we've got it, do they?
BEN: That's not the point.
GUS: Can't I keep it?
BEN: No, you can't. Get the plate.

(GUS *exits, left.* BEN *looks in the bag. He brings out a packet of crisps.*[9] *Enter* GUS *with a plate.*)

(*Accusingly, holding up the crisps.*) Where did these come from?
GUS: What?
BEN: Where did these crisps come from?
GUS: Where did you find them?
BEN (*hitting him on the shoulder*): You're playing a dirty game, my lad!
GUS: I only eat those with beer!
BEN: Well, where were you going to get the beer?
GUS: I was saving them till I did.
BEN: I'll remember this. Put everything on the plate.

(*They pile everything on to the plate. The box goes up without the plate.*)

Wait a minute!

(*They stand.*)

---

[9]**crisps:** British term for potato chips

GUS: It's gone up.
BEN: It's all your stupid fault, playing about!
GUS: What do we do now?
BEN: We'll have to wait till it comes down.

(BEN *puts the plate on the bed, puts on his shoulder holster, and starts to put on his tie.*)

You'd better get ready.

(Gus *goes to his bed, puts on his tie, and starts to fix his holster.*)

GUS: Hey, Ben.
BEN: What?
GUS: What's going on here?

(*Pause.*)

BEN: What do you mean?
GUS: How can this be a café?
BEN: It used to be a café.
GUS: Have you seen the gas stove?
BEN: What about it?
GUS: It's only got three rings.
BEN: So what?
GUS: Well, you couldn't cook much on three rings, not for a busy place like this.
BEN (*irritably*): That's why the service is slow!

(BEN *puts on his waistcoat.*)

GUS: Yes, but what happens when we're not here? What do they do then? All these menus coming down and nothing going up. It might have been going on like this for years.

(BEN *brushes his jacket.*)

What happens when we go?

(BEN *puts on his jacket.*)

They can't do much business.

(*The box descends. They turn about.* GUS *goes to the hatch and brings out a note.*)

GUS (*reading*): Macaroni Pastitsio. Ormitha Macarounada.

BEN: What was that?

GUS: Macaroni Pastitsio. Ormitha Macarounada.

BEN: Greek dishes.

GUS: No.

BEN: That's right.

GUS: That's pretty high class.

BEN: Quick before it goes up.

(GUS *puts the plate in the box.*)

GUS (*calling up the hatch*): Three McVitie and Price! One Lyons Red Label! One Smith's Crisps! One Eccles cake! One Fruit and Nut!

BEN: Cadbury's.

GUS (*up the hatch*): Cadbury's!

BEN (*handing the milk*): One bottle of milk.

GUS (*up the hatch*): One bottle of milk! Half a pint! (*He looks at the label.*) Express Dairy! (*He puts the bottle in the box.*)

(*The box goes up.*)

Just did it.

BEN: You shouldn't shout like that.

GUS: Why not?

BEN: It isn't done.

(BEN *goes to his bed.*)

Well, that should be all right, anyway, for the time being.

GUS: You think so, eh?

BEN: Get dressed, will you? It'll be any minute now.

(GUS *puts on his waistcoat.* BEN *lies down and looks up at the ceiling.*)

GUS: This is some place. No tea and no biscuits.

BEN: Eating makes you lazy, mate. You're getting lazy, you know that? You don't want to get slack on your job.

GUS: Who me?

BEN: Slack, mate, slack.

GUS: Who me? Slack?

BEN: Have you checked your gun? You haven't even checked your gun. It looks disgraceful, anyway. Why don't you ever polish it?

(GUS *rubs his revolver on the sheet.* BEN *takes out a pocket mirror and straightens his tie.*)

GUS: I wonder where the cook is. They must have had a few, to cope with that. Maybe they had a few more gas stoves. Eh! Maybe there's another kitchen along the passage.

BEN: Of course there is! Do you know what it takes to make an Ormitha Macarounada?

GUS: No, what?

BEN: An Ormitha—! Buck your ideas up, will you?

GUS: Takes a few cooks, eh?

(GUS *puts his revolver in its holster.*)

The sooner we're out of this place the better.

(*He puts on his jacket.*)

Why doesn't he get in touch? I feel like I've been here years. (*He takes his revolver out of its holster to check the ammunition.*) We've never let him down though, have we? We've never let him down. I was thinking only the other day, Ben. We're reliable, aren't we?

(*He puts his revolver back in its holster.*)

Still, I'll be glad when it's over tonight.

(*He brushes his jacket.*)

I hope the bloke's not going to get excited tonight, or anything. I'm feeling a bit off. I've got a splitting headache.

(*Silence.*)

(*The box descends.* BEN *jumps up.*)

(GUS *collects the note.*)

(*Reading.*) One Bamboo Shoots, Water Chestnuts and Chicken. One Char Siu and Beansprouts.

BEN: Beansprouts?

GUS: Yes.

BEN: Blimey.

GUS: I wouldn't know where to begin.

(*He looks back at the box. The packet of tea is inside it. He picks it up.*)

They've sent back the tea.

BEN (*anxious*): What'd they do that for?

GUS: Maybe it isn't tea-time.

(*The box goes up. Silence.*)

BEN (*throwing the tea on the bed, and speaking urgently*): Look here. We'd better tell them.

GUS: Tell them what?

BEN: That we can't do it, we haven't got it.

GUS: All right then.

BEN: Lend us your pencil. We'll write a note.

(GUS, *turning for a pencil, suddenly discovers the speaking tube, which hangs on the right wall of the hatch facing his bed.*)

GUS: What's this?

BEN: What?

GUS: This.

BEN (*examining it*): This? It's a speaking tube.

GUS: How long has that been there?

BEN: Just the job. We should have used it before, instead of shouting up there.

GUS: Funny I never noticed it before.

BEN: Well, come on.

GUS: What do you do?

BEN: See that? That's a whistle.

GUS: What, this?

BEN: Yes, take it out. Pull it out.

(GUS *does so.*)

That's it.

GUS: What do we do now?

BEN: Blow into it.

GUS: Blow?

BEN: It whistles up there if you blow. Then they know you want to speak. Blow.

(GUS *blows. Silence.*)

GUS (*tube at mouth*): I can't hear a thing.

BEN: Now you speak! Speak into it!

(GUS *looks at* BEN, *then speaks into the tube.*)

GUS: The larder's bare!

BEN: Give me that!

(*He grabs the tube and puts it to his mouth.*)

(*Speaking with great deference.*) Good evening. I'm sorry to—bother you, but we just thought we'd better let you know that we haven't got anything left. We sent up all we had. There's no more food down here.

(*He brings the tube slowly to his ear.*)

What?

(*To mouth.*)

What?

(*To ear. He listens. To mouth.*)

No, all we had we sent up.

(*To ear. He listens. To mouth.*)

Oh, I'm very sorry to hear that.

(*To ear. He listens. To* GUS.)

The Eccles cake was stale.

(*He listens. To* GUS.)

The chocolate was melted.

(*He listens. To* GUS.)

The milk was sour.

GUS: What about the crisps?

BEN (*listening*): The biscuits were moldy.

(*He glares at* GUS. *Tube to mouth.*)

Well, we're very sorry about that.

(*Tube to ear.*)

What?

(*To mouth.*)

What?

(*To ear.*)

Yes. Yes.

(*To mouth.*)

Yes certainly. Certainly. Right away.

(*To ear. The voice has ceased. He hangs up the tube.*)

(*Excitedly.*) Did you hear that?

GUS: What?

BEN: You know what he said? Light the kettle! Not put on the kettle! Not light the gas! But light the kettle!

GUS: How can we light the kettle?

BEN: What do you mean?

GUS: There's no gas.

BEN (*clapping hand to head*): Now what do we do?

GUS: What did he want us to light the kettle for?

BEN: For tea. He wanted a cup of tea.

GUS: *He* wanted a cup of tea! What about me? I've been wanting a cup of tea all night!

BEN (*despairingly*): What do we do now?

GUS: What are we supposed to drink?

(BEN *sits on his bed, staring.*)

What about us?

(BEN *sits.*)

I'm thirsty too. I'm starving. And he wants a cup of tea. That beats the band, that does.

(BEN *lets his head sink on to his chest.*)

I could do with a bit of sustenance myself. What about you? You look as if you could do with something too.

(GUS *sits on his bed.*)

We send him up all we've got and he's not satisfied. No, honest, it's enough to make the cat laugh. Why did you send him up all that stuff? (*Thoughtfully.*) Why did I send it up?

(*Pause.*)

Who knows what he's got upstairs? He's probably got a salad bowl. They must have something up there. They won't get much from down here. You notice they didn't ask for any salads? They've probably got a salad bowl up there. Cold meat, radishes, cucumbers. Watercress. Roll mops.[10]

(*Pause.*)

Hardboiled eggs.

(*Pause.*)

The lot. They've probably got a crate of beer too. Probably eating my crisps with a pint of beer now. Didn't have anything to say about those crisps, did he? They do all right, don't worry about that. You don't think they're just going to sit there and wait for stuff to come up from down here, do you? That'll get them nowhere.

(*Pause.*)

They do all right.

(*Pause.*)

And he wants a cup of tea.

(*Pause.*)

That's past a joke, in my opinion.

(*He looks over at* BEN, *rises, and goes to him.*)

What's the matter with you? You don't look too bright. I feel like an Alka-Seltzer myself.

(BEN *sits up.*)

BEN (*in a low voice*): Time's getting on.
GUS: I know. I don't like doing a job on an empty stomach.
BEN (*wearily*): Be quiet a minute. Let me give you your instructions.
GUS: What for? We always do it the same way, don't we?
BEN: Let me give you your instructions.

(GUS *sighs and sits next to* BEN *on the bed. The instructions are stated and repeated automatically.*)

When we get the call, you go over and stand behind the door.
GUS: Stand behind the door.
BEN: If there's a knock on the door you don't answer it.

---

[10]**roll mops:** herring with pickles

GUS: If there's a knock on the door I don't answer it.
BEN: But there won't be a knock on the door.
GUS: So I won't answer it.
BEN: When the bloke comes in—
GUS: When the bloke comes in—
BEN: Shut the door behind him.
GUS: Shut the door behind him.
BEN: Without divulging your presence.
GUS: Without divulging my presence.
BEN: He'll see me and come towards me.
GUS: He'll see you and come towards you.
BEN: He won't see you.
GUS (*absently*): Eh?
BEN: He won't see you.
GUS: He won't see me.
BEN: But he'll see me.
GUS: He'll see you.
BEN: He won't know you're there.
GUS: He won't know you're there.
BEN: He won't know *you're* there.
GUS: He won't know I'm there.
BEN: I take out my gun.
GUS: You take out your gun.
BEN: He stops in his tracks.
GUS: He stops in his tracks.
BEN: If he turns round—
GUS: If he turns round—
BEN: You're there.
GUS: I'm here.

(BEN *frowns and presses his forehead.*)

You've missed something out.
BEN: I know. What?
GUS: I haven't taken my gun out, according to you.
BEN: You take your gun out—
GUS: After I've closed the door.
BEN: After you've closed the door.
GUS: You've never missed that out before, you know that?
BEN: When he sees you behind him—

GUS: Me behind him—
BEN: And me in front of him—
GUS: And you in front of him—
BEN: He'll feel uncertain—
GUS: Uneasy.
BEN: He won't know what to do.
GUS: So what will he do?
BEN: He'll look at me and he'll look at you.
GUS: We won't say a word.
BEN: We'll look at him.
GUS: He won't say a word.
BEN: He'll look at us.
GUS: And we'll look at him.
BEN: Nobody says a word.

(*Pause.*)

GUS: What do we do if it's a girl?
BEN: We do the same.
GUS: Exactly the same?
BEN: Exactly.

(*Pause.*)

GUS: We don't do anything different?
BEN: We do exactly the same.
GUS: Oh.

(GUS *rises and shivers.*)

Excuse me.

(*He exits through the door on the left.* BEN *remains sitting on the bed, still.*)

(*The lavatory chain is pulled once off left, but the lavatory does not flush.*)

(*Silence.*)

(GUS *reenters and stops inside the door, deep in thought. He looks at* BEN, *then walks slowly across to his own bed. He is troubled. He stands, thinking. He turns and looks at* BEN. *He moves a few paces toward him.*)

(*Slowly in a low, tense voice.*) Why did he send us matches if he knew there was no gas?

(*Silence.*)

(BEN *stares in front of him.* GUS *crosses to the left side of* BEN, *to the foot of his bed, to get to his other ear.*)

Ben. Why did he send us matches if he knew there was no gas?

(BEN *looks up.*)

Why did he do that?

BEN: Who?

GUS: Who sent us those matches?

BEN: What are you talking about?

(GUS *stares down at him.*)

GUS (*thickly*): Who is it upstairs?

BEN (*nervously*): What's one thing to do with another?

GUS: Who is it, though?

BEN: What's one thing to do with another?

(BEN *fumbles for his paper on the bed.*)

GUS: I asked you a question.

BEN: Enough!

GUS (*with growing agitation*): I asked you before. Who moved in? I asked you. You said the people who had it before moved out. Well, who moved in?

BEN (*hunched*): Shut up.

GUS: I told you, didn't I?

BEN (*standing*): Shut up!

GUS (*feverishly*): I told you before who owned this place, didn't I? I told you.

(BEN *hits him viciously on the shoulder.*)

I told you who ran this place, didn't I?

(BEN *hits him viciously on the shoulder.*)

(*Violently.*) Well, what's he playing all these games for? That's what I want to know. What's he doing it for?

BEN: What games?

GUS (*passionately, advancing*): What's he doing it for? We've been through our tests, haven't we? We got right through our tests, years ago, didn't we? We took them together, don't you remember, didn't we? We've proved ourselves before now, haven't we? We've always done our job. What's he doing all this for? What's the idea? What's he playing these games for?

(*The box in the shaft comes down behind them. The noise is this time accompanied by a shrill whistle, as it falls.* GUS *rushes to the hatch and seizes the note.*)

(*Reading.*) Scampi!

(*He crumples the note, picks up the tube, takes out the whistle, blows, and speaks.*)

WE'VE GOT NOTHING LEFT! NOTHING! DO YOU UNDERSTAND?

(BEN *seizes the tube and flings* GUS *away. He follows* GUS *and slaps him hard, back-handed, across the chest.*)

BEN: Stop it! You maniac!
GUS: But you heard!
BEN (*savagely*): That's enough! I'm warning you!

(*Silence.*)

(BEN *hangs the tube. He goes to his bed and lies down. He picks up his paper and reads.*)

(*Silence.*)
(*The box goes up.*)
(*They turn quickly, their eyes meet.* BEN *turns to his paper.*)
(*Slowly* GUS *goes back to his bed, and sits.*)
(*Silence.*)
(*The hatch falls back into place.*)
(*They turn quickly, their eyes meet.* BEN *turns back to his paper.*)
(*Silence.*)
(BEN *throws his paper down.*)

BEN: Kaw!

(*He picks up the paper and looks at it.*)

Listen to this!

(*Pause.*)

What about that, eh?

(*Pause.*)

Kaw!

(*Pause.*)

Have you ever heard such a thing?

GUS (*dully*): Go on!

BEN: It's true.

GUS: Get away.

BEN: It's down here in black and white.

GUS (*very low*): Is that a fact?

BEN: Can you imagine it.

GUS: It's unbelievable.

BEN: It's enough to make you want to puke, isn't it?

GUS (*almost inaudible*): Incredible.

(BEN *shakes his head. He puts the paper down and rises. He fixes the revolver in his holster.*)

(GUS *stands up. He goes toward the door on the left.*)

BEN: Where are you going?

GUS: I'm going to have a glass of water.

(*He exits.* BEN *brushes dust off his clothes and shoes. The whistle in the speaking tube blows. He goes to it, takes the whistle out, and puts the tube to his ear. He listens. He puts it to his mouth.*)

BEN: Yes.

(*To ear. He listens. To mouth.*)

Straight away. Right.

(*To ear. He listens. To mouth.*)

Sure we're ready.

(*To ear. He listens. To mouth.*)

Understood. Repeat. He has arrived and will be coming in straight away. The normal method to be employed. Understood.

(*To ear. He listens. To mouth.*)

Sure we're ready.

(*To ear. He listens. To mouth.*)

Right.

(*He hangs the tube up.*)

Gus!

(*He takes out a comb and combs his hair, adjusts his jacket to diminish the bulge of the revolver. The lavatory flushes off left.* BEN *goes quickly to the door, left.*)

Gus!

(*The door right opens sharply.* BEN *turns, his revolver leveled at the door.*)

(GUS *stumbles in.*)

(*He is stripped of his jacket, waistcoat, tie, holster, and revolver.*)

(*He stops, body stooping, his arms at his sides.*)

(*He raises his head and looks at* BEN.)

(*A long silence.*)

(*They stare at each other.*)

Dialogue and Rebuttal (A Play in Two Parts)

GAO XINGJIAN

Translated by Gilbert C. F. Fong

Gao Xingjian (born in 1940), who won the Nobel Prize for literature in 2000, is the first Chinese writer to be so honored. He writes plays that demonstrate both his Eastern background and his awareness of Western literature traditions, especially absurdist theater. Although he claims his plays are not like that of absurdists Samuel Beckett, Harold Pinter, or Luigi Pirandello, Xingjian's *Dialogue and Rebuttal* clearly shows something of the absurdist tradition, a tradition in which traditional notions of logic, reason, and human experience do not follow expected patterns.

The characters in *Dialogue and Rebuttal*, which was first staged in Vienna, Austria, in 1992, are named simply Man, Girl, and Monk. Their conversations seem scattered and nonsensical. The audience is keenly aware of the theatricality of the play, as the Monk, who does not speak much, performs gymnastics and balances eggs on a stick. When the first act ends with the murders of the Man and the Woman, and Act 2, the "second half," stages dialogues and rebuttals from the dead, Xingjian invites the audience to question the nature of reality itself.

Gao Xingjian, a painter and novelist as well as a playwright, left China and settled in France in 1988. Now a French citizen, he continues to write experimental work. Although his work seems deeply political, he sees its power more in its aesthetic appeal and in its focus on the predicament of the individual.

Time and location uncertain.

An empty stage, some clothing, several objects.

CHARACTERS

A Young Girl
A Middle-Aged Man
A Monk
Two Heads: One Male, One Female

First Half

(*The stage is white* [*if possible*], *on which one sees* A YOUNG GIRL *and* A MIDDLE-AGED MAN. *A black overcoat and a travelling tote bag have been thrown to one side; on the other side towards the back, there lies a bathrobe, which has been tossed down in a heap. At front stage on the right, a wooden fish*[1] *has been placed on the floor.*)

GIRL: Finished?
MAN: Finished.
GIRL: How was it?
MAN: Quite good. (*Pause.*) How about you?
GIRL: Not bad. (*Pause.*) Quite good, I should say.

(MAN *tries to say something but stops.*)

GIRL: So . . .
MAN: What?
GIRL: Nothing much.
MAN: Nothing much what?

(GIRL *smiles slightly.*)

MAN: What are you smiling at?
GIRL: Nothing.
MAN: Why are you still smiling?
GIRL: I'm not smiling.

(*Helpless,* MAN *stares at her.*
GIRL *avoids his stare and looks away.*)

MAN: Is it over?
GIRL: Isn't it better this way?
MAN: Are you always like this?
GIRL: What?
MAN: With men . . .
GIRL: Of course, you're not the first one.

(MAN *is taken aback, then laughs out loud.*)

GIRL: You're all the same.
MAN (*Happily.*): Do you mean we—
GIRL: I mean you, you men!
MAN (*Corrects her.*): Men and women!

(*Both laugh.* GIRL *stops laughing abruptly.* MAN *also stops.*)

MAN: What's wrong?
GIRL: Nothing.

[1]**wooden fish:** a percussion instrument made out of hollow wood

MAN: I'm sorry.
GIRL (*Coldly.*): There's nothing to be sorry about.

(MAN *walks away and puts on bathrobe.*)

GIRL: If we had known . . .
MAN: Speak for yourself.
GIRL: Hypocrite!
MAN: But I love you—

(*Immediately* GIRL *starts to laugh out loud.* MAN *also laughs heartily.* MONK *enters slowly from the right side of the stage. He is bald, wearing a* kasaya, *a Buddhist robe, and a pair of straw sandals. With his eyes lowered and his palms clasped, he is chanting "Amitabha Buddha!"*
MAN *and* GIRL *stop laughing.*
MONK *walks to a corner at right stage, turns around until his back is facing the audience, sits down with his legs crossed and starts to beat the wooden fish.*
MAN *and* GIRL *restrain themselves. They both look down, listening carefully to the continuous beating of the wooden fish.*)

GIRL (*Softly.*): She doesn't understand why, why she followed such a man, but she followed him anyway, following him to . . .

MAN (*Softly.*): She understands everything, she knew it very well, it's all very simple and clear, both had the need . . .

GIRL (*Softly.*): No, she only wanted to know if it could happen . . . She knew it was possible but not entirely unavoidable . . .

MAN (*Softly.*): Things are bound to happen anytime, anywhere in the world, when something happens, you'll just have to go along with it and have some fun.

GIRL (*Softly.*): He may look eager and willing, but she knows very well that he's faking it, if she'd only arched her back and held him off, the whole thing wouldn't have happened.

MAN (*Softly.*): One minute early or one minute late, it's all the same. Why put on an act? You and I are no different, that's the way it is.

GIRL (*Softly.*): Of course she'd been expecting it, she knew right from the beginning how it would end, but she never thought it would be so sudden, so hasty, and the end would come so fast.

(MONK *beats the wooden fish twice.*)

GIRL: Forget it! There's nothing worth celebrating.
MAN: I didn't say anything.
GIRL: Better keep it that way.

(MAN *droops his head.*
MONK *starts to beat lightly on the wooden fish, chanting softly and continually: "Amitabha Buddha."*)

GIRL: How come you're not saying anything?
MAN: What's there to say?
GIRL: Anything you want.
MAN: You talk, I'll listen.
GIRL: Tell me about yourself.
MAN: I'm a man.
GIRL: You don't have to tell me that.
MAN: What shall I tell you then?
GIRL: Don't you know how to talk with people?
MAN: I'm afraid you won't like it.
GIRL: The problem is you've got to have something to talk about.
MAN: Except love—
GIRL: Don't talk to me about love!
MAN: Tell me, what else is there to talk about with a woman?

(GIRL *stands up to get her overcoat.*)

MAN: Where are you going?
GIRL: It's none of your business.
MAN: I can ask, can't I?
GIRL: But you really don't want to know.
MAN: Why not? I do want to know.
GIRL: You only want a woman's body, you don't understand women, not even a tiny bit.
MAN: I don't understand myself either.
GIRL: Well said. You're such a pig!
MAN: And you?
GIRL: You think I'm that low-down?
MAN: That's not what I meant.
GIRL: Your attitude, it's disgusting!
MAN: To tell you the truth, I also disgust myself.
GIRL: What a wonderful confession! (*Turns and puts on her overcoat.*)
MAN (*Snatches away her overcoat.*): Don't go!
GIRL: What more do you want?
MAN: Don't go! You've got to listen to me.
GIRL: You don't have the right to stop me. (*Struggles free.*) I've got to agree first!

MAN (*Apprehensive.*): Now that you're here, well, of course I invited you, and I'm very glad—

GIRL: You—you're an out-and-out bastard!

(MAN *laughs.*)

GIRL: What are you laughing at?

MAN: Myself, I'm laughing at myself. What is it to you?

GIRL: Fine then, let me go.

MAN (*Blocking her.*): I love you, really I do!

GIRL: Stop acting. (*Pushes him away.*)

(MONK *picks up wooden fish and beats on it while chanting "Amitabha Buddha." He exits left stage as* GIRL *watches.*)

MAN: I don't understand, it's really hard to figure you out. Tell me, what are you going to do? What is it that you want?

GIRL (*Nonchalantly.*): Don't ask me, I don't know. I only, only wanted to know . . .

MAN: You already know everything there is to know.

GIRL: What do I know?

MAN: That I'm a man. Other men, aren't they the same?

GIRL: Don't talk to me about men!

MAN: Then what shall we talk about?

GIRL: Something interesting, cheerful, something which makes people happy. How stupid can you get?

MAN: Really?

GIRL: You only think you're smart.

MAN: And you're a smart Girl.

GIRL: Not necessarily. Otherwise I wouldn't have come here with you.

MAN: In fact I prefer stupid women.

GIRL: Because they're submissive, gullible, and easy to manipulate, is that it?

MAN: No, I'm only talking about myself, that way I can be more relaxed.

(*Monotonous beating on the wooden fish.* MONK *has not yet entered.*)

MAN: You want to drink something?

GIRL: No, I guess I'd better be going.

MAN: It's raining outside.

GIRL (*Listening.*): I don't think so.

MAN: If I say it's raining, it's got to be raining.

GIRL: Who do you think you are, God?

MAN: I can hear it raining. I know all the sounds in and outside this place, the wind, the rain, the water heater, and the leaking toilet, every single one of them. I've owned this place for years.

GIRL: Leave me out of your ownership, I belong to me, and me only.

MAN: Is that very important?

GIRL: I don't know, maybe. Anyway, I still haven't found the right person to belong to.

MAN: Obviously I'm not that person.

GIRL: At last you've said something intelligent.

MAN: Thanks for the compliment.

GIRL: Intelligent men are a rare breed nowadays.

MAN: Most women are also stupid dingbats. Of course you're an exception.

GIRL: Do you really think so?

MAN: I never lie, don't you believe me?

GIRL: Do you say the same thing to every woman you're with?

MAN: You know why I said it to you? It's only because you like to hear people say that about you.

GIRL: You're—really—very bad.

(MAN *laughs, and* GIRL *laughs with him.*)

MAN: Are you sure you don't want anything to drink?

GIRL: Only if you promise not to mix anything in it. Nothing's worse than that.

MAN: That's to say you must have done it yourself. I'm sure you must've had tons of strange things happening to you before.

GIRL: I mean when somebody puts something in your drink and you don't realize it even after you've drunk the darn thing.

MAN: You mean just now, at the bar? If anybody put anything in it, it was definitely not me.

GIRL: I meant it happened once, in India.

MAN: But this certainly isn't India.

GIRL: I'm saying I went on a trip to India once.

MAN: With your friend, one of your many boyfriends, if I'm not mistaken?

GIRL: You might as well save that little bit of intelligence you have for something else. Of course I wasn't alone. Travelling alone can bore you to tears.

MAN: But if I were going on a trip, I'd never coax my female companion into doing drugs.

GIRL: It doesn't take any coaxing, does it? We're not kids any more.

MAN: Of course taking drugs is only human. Tell me, what do you use as a regular?

GIRL: I'm telling you I don't have the habit!

MAN: But how come you said when you were in India—

GIRL: I was in this small village close to the Tibetan border. The sky was real blue, I've never seen such a blue sky before. The clouds were real close, and as I watched them dissipating strand by strand in mid-air, I got dizzy, I couldn't climb up any more. My head was aching, my ears were ringing, as if some guy was ringing a bell like crazy next to my ears . . . He wanted to take some shots of the glaciers, you know, my friend was into photography, so I took the car and went back alone to a town where there was a small inn. There was this Indian man standing by the door and he asked me if I wanted any marijuana. He spoke some English, and he led me to his house to get some.

MAN: And you went with him just like that?

GIRL: Yes, I did, so what?

MAN: So what? It's the same as your coming here with me, isn't it?

GIRL: You sell marijuana too?

MAN: If you really want some.

GIRL: You don't know how to listen, do you?

MAN: Go on!

GIRL: I don't want to tell you any more.

(MONK *enters, one hand holding an alms bowl, the other carrying a small bell. As he chants "Amitabha Buddha" in a low voice, he sprinkles some water into the bowl with his middle finger and rings the bell softly.*)

MAN: Did he force you to take any drugs?

GIRL: No.

MAN: Did he make love to you?

GIRL: He was very gentle and very polite.

(MAN *wants to say something but stops.*)

GIRL: There were these two women in his house, the younger one must have been his daughter, and they both bowed to me. He asked me to sit down and told the women to bring some wine, it was kind of sweet. The women stood on the side waiting on us, they only watched and smiled at me. I drank two cups in one go, and then they brought in some dried fruit and some sticky rice cakes.

(GIRL *listens attentively to the ringing of the bell.*)

MAN: Go on, go on.

GIRL: I didn't know why but somehow I felt sleepy. I think for a whole week I was just lying down, not wanting to move.

MAN: Did you go back to the inn?

GIRL: No, I was in his room, on his bed—

MAN: Naked?

GIRL: Is that important?

MAN: When you're telling a story, you've got to give details.

GIRL: Anyway, my body didn't seem to belong to me, my hands and feet were too heavy to move, and my mind was totally blank . . . But I was still conscious . . .

MAN: Weren't you scared?

GIRL: The two women would come in every now and then, whenever he was not there they would come to give me something to eat or drink. I wanted to speak and scream, but they didn't say anything except to touch and stroke me all the time. Then without knowing it I fell asleep again until he came back and woke me up . . .

MAN: Did he rape you?

GIRL: No, I think . . . I don't know . . . Maybe I accepted it, I also, enjoyed . . . Maybe I wanted it too, there was no way out. Do you find this exciting?

MAN: Not really, I mean, he ruined you.

GIRL: Didn't you?

MAN: It's not the same, under the circumstances, he could have abused you until you died and no one would know anything about it.

GIRL: He was very gentle from beginning to end, he didn't force me at all, I gave him all he wanted without holding anything back . . . You know, I gave him everything I had until I became a total void . . . Except that after one week, I realized later that it'd been a whole week, it was either daytime or at night when I found myself completely paralysed, I didn't even want to move a finger, the room had only one oil lamp and it smelled real bad.

MAN: Maybe it was burning tallow, or animal fat, a kind of beef oil.

GIRL: Have you been there as well?

MAN: I read about it in some travel book on Tibet. Didn't you say the place was right next to Tibet?

GIRL: Uh-huh . . .

(*The bell stops ringing.*)

MAN: Go on, why have you stopped talking?

GIRL: What else should I talk about?

MAN: Talk about the smell.

GIRL: As I was saying, that was when I woke up for the first time, afterwards I didn't smell it any more, I only felt I was warm all over, I thought, I must have had that smell on me as well. Afterwards I washed again and again but I just couldn't get rid of . . .

MAN: That greasy muttony smell?

GIRL: No, the smell of his body.

MAN: Stop it! I've had enough.

(MONK *has finished sprinkling and bends down as if to splash water onto the ground. He exits, holding up his sleeves with his hands.*)

GIRL (*Collects her thoughts and turns to look at him.*): Why?

MAN: There's no why.

GIRL: You don't like what I said?

MAN: I'm listening.

GIRL: What do you want to listen to?

MAN: It's up to you, whatever you want to say.

GIRL: You want me to say that I'm horny all the time?

MAN: You said it, not me.

GIRL: Don't you want every woman to be horny?

MAN: Women, they're actually like that.

GIRL: That's only in a man's imagination.

MAN: Believe me, men are no different.

GIRL: Then what's there to be curious about?

MAN: It's just the sex that's different.

GIRL: How about between one woman and another, are they the same to you?

MAN: Can't you change the subject?

GIRL: Shall we talk about the smell then?

MAN: To hell with the smell!

GIRL: You're really no fun!

MAN: What? Fine, fine, let's talk about the smell then.

GIRL: I don't want to talk about it any more.

(MONK *enters tumbling in the air. He has taken off his* kasaya *and is dressed in a casual jacket and pants. He holds his breath and stands motionlessly kungfu style.*)

MAN (*Looks towards* MONK *and speaks softly.*): You can never understand what really goes on in a woman's mind. (*Loudly.*) An interesting story, very interesting. (*Turns to look at* GIRL.) How come he didn't kill you?

GIRL: Why?

MAN: There's no why.

GIRL: All you men want to do is to possess, possess, and possess until everything's all busted and gone! (*Sighs.*) Men are so selfish, they only think of themselves.

MAN: Men this, men that, why do you have to keep babbling on about men?

GIRL: Aren't you one of them?

MAN: If anything, I'm still a person, a real, tangible, living human being.

GIRL: But you haven't been treating me like one. Let me tell you, I'm not just some plaything for venting your sexual desires. And one woman is different from another—

MAN: When we first started, we were talking in general terms, now it's different—

GIRL: How different?

MAN: Now it's you and me, and not men and women in the general sense. We're face to face with each other, we can see each other, and we've had some contact, I don't just mean physical contact, we're bound to have some feelings, some understanding of each other, because we're two living human beings.

GIRL: Wait a minute. You mean when you made love to me just now, you were treating me like your so-called women in the general sense, in other words, just a plaything.

MAN: Don't talk like that, because you and I were in the same boat, weren't we? We were like two people possessed—

GIRL: Let me finish. You didn't even ask me my name, as soon as we entered the door, you . . .

MAN: Don't forget, you didn't exactly refuse me.

GIRL: That's true, but . . .

MAN: I see, my sincerest apologies.

(MONK *successfully completes a handstand. Then he tries to take away one hand to attempt a one-hand handstand, but at once he loses his balance and hurriedly lands his feet on the ground.*)

MAN (*Softly.*): What's wrong?

GIRL (*At a loss.*): Nothing.

(*Silence.* MONK *again attempts a one-hand handstand.*)

MAN (*Takes a look at her tote bag.*): Tell me, what happened afterwards? How about that friend of yours?

GIRL: We split up a long time ago.

MAN: So now you're on your own and you're wandering all over the globe?

GIRL: I've been looking for a companion, but none lasted.

MAN: Yes, nowadays it's the in thing to do, like fashion, which tends to change from one year to another, or from one season to the next.

GIRL (*Looks around.*): You don't look like you're living alone, eh?

MAN: Of course I've had, how should I put it, a wife? What's the matter? You don't like that word?

GIRL: I can't stand being tied down.

MAN: Well, I guess we're no different from each other there.

(*Both laugh heartily.* MONK, *who is doing a handstand, again takes away one hand and fails once more. He hurriedly lands his feet on the ground.*)

MAN (*Very carefully.*): May I ask your name?

GIRL: Is that important? Try to remember it well and make sure that you don't get it wrong.

MAN: Why? Somebody did?

GIRL: I hope you're not as bad.

(*Both laugh somewhat bitterly.*
Monk kneads his hands and attempts a handstand for the third time.)

GIRL: Maria or Anna, which one do you prefer?

MAN: The question is which one is your real name?

GIRL: If I told you it's Maria, then would I surely be Maria?

MAN: That's a real problem. But if I called you Anna, you'd still be you and not someone called Anna, therefore, you really shouldn't worry too much about it.

GIRL (*Dryly.*): I don't want to be a stand-in for somebody else!

MAN: Of course. A name is just a code, what's important is not the sign itself but the actual person behind that sign. You can call me whatever you like, even if it's some name you're familiar with, or some name that accidentally slips from your tongue, anything, I don't think I'd mind.

GIRL: I don't want to waste any more time on this subject. I don't want to know your name either, it's useless to me. And don't bother making up a fake name and then forget about it in short order. When it's over, it's over.

MAN: But we've just begun, how could it be over so soon? Now that you've agreed that a name isn't important and that it's a real burden, let's get to the important part: between you and me . . .

GIRL: Between a man and a woman? How interesting!

MAN: The whole thing would become more pure, and the relationship more sincere and more real, don't you think?

(MONK *completes a handstand and takes away one hand, but he fails again just when it looks as if he is going to succeed. He exits dejected.*)

GIRL: You really can't get it.

MAN (*Quite interested.*): Get what?

GIRL: Impossible, it's impossible. I mean, a woman's heart.

MAN: If I guessed right, you're talking about love, aren't you? That of course is a very delicate subject.

GIRL: I'm talking about emotion, which you can't possibly understand.

MAN: Try me, you never know.

GIRL: How?

MAN: Between you and me—

GIRL: We've tried that before.

MAN: Try again. If it doesn't work, we'll just try again.

GIRL (*On guard.*): No, you can never have it, you can never have anything!

MAN: Just now I was too rushed, really.

GIRL (*Smiles coldly.*): You're always in a rush.

MAN (*Somewhat repentant.*): Can I make it up to you in any way?

GIRL: Don't think that because you've had a lot of women . . . You don't know women, you'll never be loved, it's in your destiny.

(GIRL *turns around.* MONK *enters carrying a wooden stick. He looks around for something.*)

MAN (*Sarcastically.*): What's love? Try to explain it to me.

GIRL: It can't be explained.

MAN: There's no harm in trying.

GIRL: There are things you can explain, and there are things you can't. Don't you know that?

MAN: Of course I do, but I still want to know about love.

GIRL: What a fool!

MAN: Then go find yourself someone who isn't.

GIRL: Aren't we discussing something? And the topic is love?

MAN: We just made love, do we have to discuss it too?

GIRL: Isn't it true that you like to discuss all kinds of things?

MAN: Well, go find someone that you can discuss with and discuss them all you want!

GIRL: Why are you so hotheaded?

(MONK *finally finds a spot and tries very carefully to stand the stick up on the floor. But once he removes his hand, the stick falls and he at once grabs it and holds on to it. He turns to find another spot.*

(MAN *looks at* MONK *and can't help feeling a bit depressed.*)

GIRL: Answer me, are you or are you not a philosopher?

MAN: Philosophy can go to hell.

GIRL: You're such an overgrown kid. (*Embraces his head.*) Be careful, I'm beginning to like you.

MAN: Isn't that nice?

GIRL: It's very dangerous.

MAN (*Gets away from her.*): Why?

GIRL: Dangerous for you and for me.

MAN: As far as I'm concerned, if you want to stay then stay, you won't be in my way. I've got everything here, a bathroom, a kitchen, a bedroom, and a bed, of course, there's only one bed, but there's everything that a woman needs.

GIRL: Do you have shampoo, make-up, and a nightgown too?

MAN: Yes, if you need them, except underwear, you know, everyone is a different size. Make yourself at home, as a matter of fact, I won't mind if you treat this place like your own home—

GIRL: As long as none of your girlfriends is coming?

MAN: At least none is coming right now. You can stay as long as you like, it's free. When you want to eat something, just go to the fridge and help yourself, and don't bother to pay me.

GIRL: I can't stay with a man all the time.

MAN: There's no need to. Anyway, if you want to go, it'll be very simple.

GIRL: And very cheap.

MAN: I'm doing this out of good will, you can stay if you don't have anywhere else to go, that is, if you really want to stay.

GIRL: Thanks, I don't live off men, so you don't have to worry about that.

MAN: I'm not worrying. I can even give you a key, just leave it behind when you go.

GIRL: Do you entertain women like this all the time?

MAN: Not all the time, only sometimes, it's the same with any other single man, there's nothing unusual about it.

GIRL: What's unusual is—Is there anything that's unusual about you?

MAN: Well, I do have a strange habit. I can't stand people shaving their armpits in front of me. Don't get me wrong, I'm not against hair or anything. We're born with it, and it's natural and it can be very exciting. And of course, I have no objection to a woman dressing herself up.

GIRL: For me, I can't stand anyone snoring beside me.

MAN: Fortunately I'm not that old yet, well, at least I haven't noticed it, and no women have left me because of it.

GIRL: Why did they leave you then?

MAN: It's very simple, either I couldn't stand them or they couldn't stand me.

GIRL: May I ask why couldn't they stand you?

MAN: I like eating raw garlic.

GIRL: It shouldn't be much of a problem, as long as you brush your teeth afterwards.

MAN: Another thing is probably that I don't have patience, and I just can't stand neurotic behaviour.

GIRL: Well, there's no woman who isn't neurotic.

MAN: And you too?

GIRL: It depends on the person and the time. (*Silence.*) What else shall we talk about?

MAN (*Scrutinizing her.*): Are you still at school? I'm just asking. What I mean is, you're so young.

GIRL: You want to see my diploma or something? Are you planning to hire me?

MAN: Come to think of it, I might. But how shall I put it, I can't afford to pay you.

GIRL: I don't want to be a maid to wait on people, I don't do cleaning, and I hate washing dishes.

MAN: I don't entertain at home much, unless it's some young girl like you. What I mean to say is, sometimes I do need to use the desk at night. If you're still at school and you've got homework to do, there could be a slight problem.

GIRL: Do you write? Are you a writer?

MAN (*Hurriedly.*): No, we're living in an age of women writers, every woman likes to write something. All men's books have already been written. And when men write about women it's just not as realistic as women writing about themselves.

GIRL: Do you read only books written by women?

MAN: Not necessarily. I've read some. As for women writing about men . . . How shall I put it? . . .

GIRL: Too exciting? Or too neurotic?

MAN: Too sissyish. I don't mean to criticize, let's leave criticism to the critics, it's their job. What I mean is, women don't understand men, just as men don't understand women.

GIRL: If I were to write about men—

MAN: They'd all be bastards?

GIRL: Not necessarily.

MAN: Even worse than bastards?

GIRL: They don't even qualify, they'd just be cowards.

MAN (*Hesitantly.*): Actually, it'd be quite interesting if you were to write like that. Have you written anything yet?

GIRL: I want to write, but I know I'll never be a writer.

MAN: Whoever writes is a writer, you don't need a diploma to be one. It's as simple as that.

GIRL: But who's going to support me? I've got to pay my rent first, you know.

MAN: Of course, you can't live on writing. Nowadays writing has become a luxury and an extravagant habit.

GIRL: You seem to like literature, don't you? Do you prefer poetry or fiction?

MAN: Why just poetry or fiction? Only women read those nowadays. Oh, I beg your pardon, what I mean is—

GIRL: Why apologize? (*Teasing him.*) I'm no poet and I can't write fiction, I'm not any of those, I'm just a woman.

MAN: Thank God for that. These days men are always busy earning money and making deals. On weekends? Well, they either have business engagements or they can't wait to go away with their girlfriends. Only women can afford to have the leisure and the time to read.

GIRL: Not all women read, they're also busy living. We only live once, don't you think?

MAN: I know. Nowadays, anyone who writes a book has to read it himself.

GIRL: You don't look like a businessman. Tell me, do you write books just for yourself to read?

MAN: I don't have the luxury. Once in a while, I'll take a look at the books other people have written.

GIRL: May I ask what kind of books do you read?

MAN: Books on politics.

GIRL: Wow! Are you a politician? Are you involved in politics in any way?

MAN: Thank God no, I think it's better to leave the politicians alone.

GIRL: Then why do you still read about politics then?

MAN: I only read political memoirs.

GIRL: Then you must be studying history, right?

MAN: Not exactly studying. I only want to see how the politicians can lie with a straight face, cheat on one another, swindle, and play with public opinion as if it were a card game. And you know, they'll only let out a little bit of truth in their memoirs after they've been kicked out. And like you said, we only live once, right? So don't let them take you for a ride.

GIRL: Please don't talk to me about politics. All men like politics, 'cause they want to show people they have the talent and the intelligence to run the ship of the state.

MAN: Relax, it's more interesting to talk about women when you're with a woman.

GIRL: You've got to know how, otherwise you'll just make a real pest of yourself.

MAN: Of course, flirting is an art, or the art of living even. It's a lot more interesting than playing cards. Cards are dead and people are living creatures, and they're all different from one another, don't you think?

GIRL: Are you done yet?

MAN: Yes.

(MONK *finally manages to stand the stick up.* MAN *and* GIRL *both look at him.*)

GIRL: What else shall we talk about?

MAN: We'll keep on talking about women of course.

GIRL: Generally, or shall we pick a specific one?

MAN: Why don't you talk about yourself? I want to get to know you, but please don't mention that India thing again.

GIRL: You wouldn't believe me if I did.

MAN: Have you been feeding me lies?

GIRL: Haven't you lied before? Haven't you ever cheated on your wife? Don't lie to me!

MAN: Of course I did, I never said I was a saint.

GIRL: Exactly. You know why women cheat? It's only because they've learned the tricks from men first.

MAN: You mean people cheat on you all the time?

GIRL: Cheating is a form of self-defence.

MAN: Does that include cheating on oneself?

GIRL: Everyone cheats, otherwise it'd be impossible to live.

MAN: You seem to be living quite painfully, don't you?

GIRL: Everyone's in pain. You don't look like you're too happy yourself.

MAN: Can't you change the way you talk?

GIRL: How? How should I change it? C'mon, tell me.

MAN: You're always so defensive, it's so hard to talk to you.

GIRL: The same here. It's really tiring talking to you.

MAN: You're like that too. Now I've got a headache.

GIRL (*Somewhat sympathetic.*): Come on, let's change to a lighter subject, something that'll cheer us up.

(*Having completed his previous stunt,* MONK *rubs his hands and starts to become enthusiastic again. He takes out an egg from inside his robe and tries to stand the egg on the tip of the stick.*)

MAN: What else shall we talk about? Something in praise of women or what? But everything that has to be said has been said already, there's really nothing new left to say any more. Perhaps I should say that you're young and beautiful? That you're charming and attractive? Or that you're sexy? By the way, these are not empty words, and they're not meant to flatter you or to make you feel good, they're all true.

GIRL: My dear, you seem to be more lovely when you're not using your brain. For once can't you just honestly talk about yourself? Tell me, how do you spend your time?

MAN: You mean right now?

GIRL: Yes, at this very moment—

MAN: Make love, if someone's willing.

GIRL: What if there's nobody around? Then what would you do?

MAN: I dream, when I'm doing nothing I always dream. Dreams are more real than reality itself, they're closer to the self. Don't you think so? (*Lights a candle.*)

GIRL: Me too, I dream almost every day. Tell me about your dreams.

MAN: One day, I dreamt that I was sinking into the ground, my whole body was trapped deep inside, there were two extremely high walls on either side of me, or should I say huge crags, no matter how hard I tried I just couldn't climb over them and get out . . . What are you laughing at?

GIRL: You made it all up, you're only thinking about women.

MAN: You can't really tell what happens in your dream, can you? If you're dreaming things happen in no particular order and you're confused, when you wake up and try to talk about it, you'd simply lay it on and fabricate, or you'd deceive yourself, and later when you tell your dream to somebody, you'd add on your own fantasies for self-gratification. In a dream, you're only living in your feelings at the time, that's all. (*Looks at* MONK.) There's no plot, just narration.

(*The egg falls from the tip of the stick onto the ground.* MONK *takes another egg from inside his robe and tries patiently to stand it on the tip of the stick again.* GIRL *smiles surreptitiously.*)

MAN: It's just wishful thinking trying to tell a dream.

GIRL: You're an idiot.

MAN: That's right. You're you only when you're dreaming.

GIRL (*Steps back to inspect him.*): Are you saying that at this very moment you aren't real?

MAN: Who cares if I'm real or not? You're only concerned with how you feel, right? Only feelings can be real.

GIRL: Now you're beginning to scare me.

MAN: You weren't scared when that Indian guy raped you, and you're telling me that you're scared now? (*Walking closer to her.*)

GIRL: Don't even try, I'm going.

MAN: You're not going anywhere.

GIRL: Don't try to intimidate me.

MAN: Just playing. You get scared easily when we play for real.

GIRL: Because it's not fun.

MAN: Well then, why don't you tell me how we should play?

GIRL: It's got to be more relaxing, more cheerful. But you just keep annoying people.

MAN: All right. Whatever you say, I'm game. Tell me, how do you want to play? (*Puts down the candlestick.*)

(*Again the egg falls and rolls on the ground.* MONK *takes out a third egg from inside his robe. He rubs it in his palms and then places it on the tip of the stick.*)

GIRL: Fine. Take off your clothes for me, take them all off! That's what you want, right?

(MONK *turns his head as if to take a glance at them.*)

GIRL: I can't stand your bathrobe, don't you think it's ugly? It makes me sick!

(MONK *turns back his head to continue with his task.*
MAN *takes off his bathrobe and throws it on the ground.*)

MAN: Okay, now it's your turn.

GIRL: Can't you put it more gently?

MAN: How?

GIRL: Do I have to teach you that too?

MAN: When you're stark naked you're more natural, and more beautiful.

GIRL (*Sighs.*): Your trouble is you're lonely, so lonely that you're dying for someone to give you a little tender loving care.

(*When* MONK *takes his hand away, the egg falls rolling onto the ground as before.* GIRL *takes off her blouse.* MONK *keeps looking at the egg, not knowing what to do.*)

MAN (*At once getting excited.*): You're a real knockout!

GIRL: You only found out just now? It sure took you long enough. You really don't know how to appreciate what you've got, or how to cherish it.

MAN: It's still not too late. Come over here . . . No, go stand over there!

GIRL: Where?

MAN: On the opposite side. Look at me, and put your hands down.

(GIRL *drops her hands and laughs, facing him.*
MONK *sighs and again takes out an egg from inside his robe.*)

MAN: Spread your arms like a bird in flight. You're a bird, a living and breathing big bird. Spread your arms for me!

GIRL: What if I don't?

(MONK *is persisting, still trying to place the egg on the tip of the stick.*)

MAN: When I say spread, spread. Don't you like birds?

GIRL: You're a bird, not me.

MAN: Spread your arms!

GIRL: No.

(MAN *and* GIRL *are locked in a stalemate.*
Frustrated, MONK *cracks the egg on the tip of the stick, and the egg shell finally stands on the stick.*)

GIRL (*Begging.*): Say something nice to me.

MAN: I want you . . . Close your eyes.

(GIRL *reluctantly spreads her arms and closes her eyes.*
MONK *rubs his hands and exits satisfied.*)

MAN (*Man quietly circles to the back of Girl.*): On your knees now. (*Takes a knife from inside his bathrobe.*)

GIRL: No, you're disgusting. (*Reluctant, half kneeling and half sitting down.*)

MAN: Put your hands on the floor. We're playing a game, are we not? (*He hides the knife behind him and pulls her hands down on the floor and holds them there with his other hand.*)

GIRL (*Frees herself from his hand.*): No, I'm not a dog! You're really sick. (*Gets up.*)

MAN: Are we playing or not? You wanted it, and you started it first—

GIRL: That's enough. Can't you just use your imagination?

MAN (*Coaxing her.*): All right, then you'll be a fish, now try to imagine you're a fish, a bouncy and jumping mermaid fish dragged out of the water and landed on dry land, okay?

GIRL: To hell with you. I'm not your plaything, go play with yourself.

MAN: But you started it first. After you've got people interested, you turn around and say you don't want to play any more. It just isn't fair.

GIRL: You make me sick! You understand?

MAN: Has it ever crossed your mind that you make people sick also? Everybody's sick of everybody! Everyone is sickening!

GIRL: You're just a log! A rotten log, rotten to the core!

(MAN *and* GIRL *face each other in silence. Suddenly* GIRL *laughs out loud.* MAN *is dejected. He quietly puts the knife back inside his bathrobe.*)

GIRL: Dance for me!

MAN (*Confounded.*): What?

GIRL: Are you playing or not?

MAN: Forget it, let's knock it off. I'm not interested any more.

GIRL: But now I am. You forced me to play when I wasn't interested, didn't you? (*Pleading with him.*) Please, dance for me, just one dance, okay?

MAN: I don't know how to.

GIRL: Then what do you know? Or do you only know how to think?

MAN: Don't talk to me about thinking or not thinking.

GIRL: Then go and stand over there, you do know how, don't you? Please, please do me a favour, go and stand over there.

MAN: Where?

GIRL: There, stand there like Michelangelo's David, but act like you're thinking.

MAN (*Goes to the other side reluctantly.*): You act like one of those woman executives. Do you enjoy ordering men around?

GIRL: It'd be nice if I could. Listen, David represents man at his best, I'm making it easy for you.

MAN: You're an unqualified witch!

GIRL: That's it! Raise your hands for me, just like a Michelangelo.

MAN: Michelangelo was gay.

(GIRL *laughs heartily.* MAN *reluctantly raises his hands and laughs.*)

GIRL: I like being gay. Nobody asked you to become impotent!

MAN: Gosh, what a she-devil!

GIRL: I'm going to hurt you, hurt you real bad! Run, I say run!

(*Continuous beating of the cymbal.* MONK *still has not entered.*)

MAN: How?

GIRL: Run in a circle around me!

MAN: Do you want everyone to run around you?

GIRL: Aren't you the same? You won't be happy until you turn every woman into your slave. (*Very excited.*) Raise your hand now like you're throwing a javelin.

MAN (*Screaming.*): I'm not a model!

GIRL: Why is it that only women can be models? Now try it and see what it's like! Didn't you say this is the age of women? Who told you to lose your sense of imagination? Run! I say run!

MAN (*Running and shouting.*): If a woman became God, the world would turn into a pandemonium, much more horrible than it is now. I don't know, maybe it'd be better, but it'd more likely be much worse, like some chick's tantrum!

GIRL: So what if for once we were God Almighty? (*Blocks his way.*) Blindfold yourself!

MAN: Stop fooling around, I beg you. Okay?

GIRL: Oh, so you can fool around but I can't, is that what you're saying? If we're going to fool around, let's fool around together, you and I, until we both can't take it any more!

(GIRL *takes the chance to strip* MAN *of his clothes. He kisses her, taking advantage of the situation. She wraps the clothes around his head, covering his eyes.*
MONK *enters beating a gong.*
GIRL *hurriedly takes out a pair of pantyhose from her handbag, ties it around* MAN'S *clothes and pushes him away.*)

GIRL: Over here.

MAN: I'm going to get you! You little devil you!

(MAN *chases after* GIRL. *Both of them run in circles.*)

MAN: You pigfeet—you dirty little rat—where are you?

GIRL: Here I am . . . (*Quietly picks up the overcoat.*)

MAN: You won't get away this time! (*Jumps on* GIRL.)

(*Just as he is about to catch her, she sticks out a leg and he trips and misses her.* MONK *is stunned and exits.*)

MAN (*Yanks off her pantyhose and throws it on the ground.*): What the hell are you doing?

GIRL (*Giggling.*): Isn't this what you want? Isn't it?

MAN (*Irritated.*): You must be out of your mind. Are you crazy or something?

GIRL: You're crazy, you're sick, not me! All you want is sex, sex, sex and getting yourself turned on. It's your sexual fantasy, not mine.

MAN (*Grabs her at once.*): Now let's see if you can go on bullshitting!

GIRL (*Pushes him away.*): Get away from me! You want fantasies, right? Go fantasize yourself! (*Picks up the handbag.*)

MAN (*Knocks her to the ground.*): Don't even think of running away! You'll never make it! (*Fishes out the knife from inside his bathrobe.*) I'll kill you first!

GIRL (*Startled. She moves back and tries to block him with her handbag.*): What? Are you crazy or something? Stay away from me!

MAN (*Forces his way towards her and grabs her handbag.*): Slut! Whore! You want to run? Go ahead and try!—(*Kisses her by force.*)

GIRL (*Seizes a pencil case, wallet, underwear, notebook, book, make-up, a set of keys, and other unimaginable sundry items from her handbag and throws them at* MAN *one after another.*): No, don't! Don't—!

MAN: Stop—it! (*Grabs her.*) I'm going to make a whore out of you yet!

GIRL: I'm no—

MAN: I don't care if you aren't, you still have to pretend once—

GIRL: No! Get away from me! Let—me—go—! Let me go! Let go! I—don't—(*Becomes hysterical and strikes him again and again.*)

MAN (*Letting go of her, stunned.*): I was just fooling around. Didn't you start it first? You started the whole thing, didn't you?

(MAN *puts down the knife and walks away perplexed.*
MONK *enters, beating the wooden fish in his hand. He chants loudly:*

"A . . . mi . . . tabha! Great mercy, great pity, Amitabha! Sympathy . . . goodness! Virtuous men, virtuous women, purify your hearts! And in your highest voices, recite the Five Wisdoms Sutra![2] Since the time of the ancients, such a doctrine, this doctrine of thoughtlessness, has been upheld in sudden enlightenment, and in gradual enlightenment. The body is without form, the essence without entity."

GIRL *covers her face with her hands and crouches down slowly. She starts to sob. When* MAN *hears her sobbing, he shakes his head and frowns, finally turns around and returns to her side. He stretches out his hand and bends down to stroke her head and neck.*)

GIRL: Don't touch me, I have no feelings . . . (*Starts to wail loudly.*) No feelings! No feelings! No feelings . . .

(MAN *jumps on* GIRL. *She falls onto the ground and wails and cries continuously.* MONK *walks slowly to front stage and sits down, his legs crossed. He beats the wooden fish and chants the sutra:*

"Monks of the Buddha, nuns of the Buddha, and man disciples, woman disciples, and the wise men in all directions, they all subscribe to the Law. The Law is neither long nor short, one moment is ten thousand years. No being is not being, all directions are before your eyes. The extremely big is the same as small, all boundaries forgotten; the extremely small is the same as big, all limits

[2]**Five Wisdoms Sutra:** a Buddhist text outlining various kinds of wisdom

disappeared. Presence is absence, absence is presence. Anything that is not so, it is not worth keeping. One is all, all is one. If this could be so, how could any worry remain unresolved?")

MAN: This world, it's all gone crazy,

GIRL (*Mumbling.*): Just because of loneliness,

MAN (*Whispering.*): Just because of boredom,

GIRL: Just because of thirst and hunger,

MAN: Just because of desires,

GIRL: It's unbearable,

MAN: Just because it's unbearable,

GIRL: Just because it's unbearable to be a woman,

MAN: Just because to be a man is unbearable,

GIRL: Just because not only being a woman but also being human,

MAN: A living human being, a body of flesh and blood,

GIRL: It's only to have feelings,

MAN: It's only to resist death,

GIRL: Just because of the fear of death,

MAN: Just because the yearning for life,

GIRL: It's only to experience the fear of death,

MAN: It's only to prove the existence of the self,

GIRL: It's only for the reason of just because—

MAN: Just because of the reason of it's only for—

GIRL: It's only because just because . . .

MAN: No therefore there is no purpose.

(MONK *starts to turn the beads of his Buddhist rosary, reciting the sutra in silence. The sound of the wooden fish becomes increasingly lighter, and* MONK *closes his eyes in meditation. Sound of wooden fish fades completely.*)

GIRL: A sound, sharp and piercing . . .

MAN: A greenish grey sun, gyrating in the dark . . .

GIRL: Dead at knife-point, dead in space . . .

MAN: Motorcars howling ferociously—

GIRL: And the fingers are very cruel!

MAN: Zooming past, zooming, zooming and gone . . .

GIRL: Void and empty, all over the body . . .

MAN: A swollen leather bag . . .

GIRL: Flowing from the inside of the body to the outside . . .

MAN: Window panes shaking furiously forever . . .

GIRL: Up and down and all over, no more existence, no more weight, all shapes have vanished—

MAN: Only hear something breathing—

GIRL: Water's dripping, where is it?

MAN (*Listening.*): No sound.

GIRL: Still dripping, and still dripping . . .

MAN: Any more troubles?

GIRL: Not turned off properly . . . How come it can't be turned off completely?

MAN: Turn off what completely?

GIRL: The tap, the tap in the bathroom.

MAN: Let it drip.

GIRL: Go turn it off, I beg you.

MAN (*Sits up and observes her.*): The doors, the windows, and all the taps have been shut off properly!

GIRL: But I'm still uneasy . . .

MAN: You're hypersensitive.

GIRL: I'm always frightened, always afraid . . .

MAN: What's there to be afraid of?

GIRL: Afraid of death, afraid of dark houses, I've been afraid of staying in a room by myself since I was young, even when I was sleeping, I had got to turn on the light. First I was afraid of growing up, then I was afraid of men, and afraid of becoming a woman, a real woman, of course I'm not afraid of that any more, but I'm still afraid, afraid that someone might just suddenly kill me, just like that, with no particular reason . . .

MAN (*Becoming alert.*): What are you talking about? Who wants to kill you?

GIRL: I don't know, but I'm afraid, there's always a certain fear, always afraid that . . . When I was eighteen I was afraid of being twenty, when I was twenty I was afraid of being over twenty, and after twenty I felt that death was getting closer day by day.

MAN (*Relieved.*): According to what you said, it's the same with everybody. But you're still young.

GIRL: When I'm alone at night I'm always jumpy. I'm afraid of weekends, afraid of spending the days by myself. I'm afraid of mornings, afraid that someday crinkles might appear at the corner of my eyes, I'm afraid, afraid that someday I'll suddenly grow old.

MAN: Tell me, how old are you really?

GIRL: I'm close to twenty six, I'm not young any more.

MAN: What is twenty six? I was still a kid when I was twenty six. I didn't even know how to fart properly, let alone knowing women.

GIRL: But that's you, to a woman, once she reaches thirty it spells death, and that's the truth!

MAN: According to you, I should have been dead a long time ago, shouldn't I?

GIRL: For a man, life begins at thirty, but for a woman, the best time of her life is over and done with already.

MAN: There's no need to worry. You're still in your prime, still fresh as a daisy—

GIRL: Really? Am I still fresh?

MAN: When did you first do it? Your first time?

GIRL: Let me think, sixteen, no, at that time I was . . . only fourteen.

MAN: Did you do it with a classmate? Or with a dirty old man?

GIRL: No, my teacher, a physical education teacher.

MAN: The bastard!

GIRL: He told me that I had a good figure, that I had long legs and I was agile, so he would give me special lessons. He invited me to his place and gave me some candies, I was very fond of candies then. He told me to take off my clothes. You see, there wasn't anybody else at his place. Then he told me to demonstrate some movements for him to look at and he would correct me. First he held my waist to help me press my legs down, then . . . he . . . raped me.

MAN (*Letting go of her.*): You only thought he did?

GIRL: At the time I felt . . . I also wanted to know something about my body . . .

MAN: And since then you've been going all out to use yourself up, to consume it all. (*Sits up.*)

GIRL: Aren't you also using yourself up? And you think that's love, don't you? Go pull a fast one on some wide-eyed teenybopper!

MAN: You're always flirting, has it ever occurred to you that you've got some kind of psychological problem?

GIRL: Problem? Everyone has a problem, including you, me, everyone. Have you seen how men stare at women? The look in your eyes, the way you whisper, the way you behave, and the way you leer at women's clothing, aren't they all meant to encourage women, so that they'll make themselves sexy for men? The bras, panties, necklaces, jewellery, and perfume, by the way, men also use perfume, only the brand names are different, aren't they all designed by men and for men's excitement? Women themselves don't need these things at all. Movies, television, fashion, advertisements, pop songs, bars and nightclubs, is there anything that's not meant to turn people on? You men all want to turn women into playthings, and you, you're not much better.

MAN: I knew it, I knew it. You're a feminist!

GIRL: You don't know anything. I'm no believer in feminism or any other ism. I'm a living human being, I only want to live life to the fullest as a woman.

MAN: Wonderful! So why are you still complaining?

GIRL: I'm not complaining, I'm only saying that I'm afraid, afraid that all these will disappear . . .

MAN: That's why you're trying desperately to seize every moment?

GIRL: Aren't you doing the same thing? Whenever you see an opportunity, you never let it go.

MAN (*Stands up.*): Everybody is sick, the whole world is sick.

(GIRL *tenderly caresses* MAN'*s leg, her face leaning close to him.*
MONK *lifts his head and beats softly on the wooden fish.*)

MAN (*Looks at* MONK *and talks to himself.*): We'll all be used up before we die.

(MONK *holds up the wooden fish and beats on it. The sounds become louder.* MONK *exits.*)

GIRL: Don't leave me.

MAN (*Stroking her head.*): I'm right by your side, am I not?

GIRL: I don't have anybody to rely on, you wouldn't understand even if I told you.

MAN: You and I are in the same boat, the world is a desert.

GIRL: I'm afraid that tomorrow . . .

MAN: Tomorrow, tomorrow, it's still early . . .

GIRL: No one's coming?

MAN: Tomorrow, no one.

GIRL: Do I have your word for it?

MAN: You're a silly girl.

GIRL: A silly woman.

MAN: And a silly child.

GIRL: Do you deserve to have a child?

(MAN *is silent. He just holds her head and looks at it closely.*)

GIRL: You must be thinking of something. Don't look at me like that! (*Pushes him away.*)

MAN: What's wrong with that?

GIRL: You know exactly what's wrong.

MAN (*Letting her go.*): I don't understand you, I just don't understand what goes on in your mind.

GIRL: Is that important?

MAN (*Somewhat troubled.*): I can't decide whether or not I should love you.

GIRL: It's the same here.

MAN: You mean you love me?

GIRL: Don't take it too seriously. (*Sincerely.*) At least, I like you.

MAN: You've set my mind at ease. I like you too, really.

GIRL: Since when?

MAN: In the pub, when I caught sight of you right away. Remember that corner with the light hanging on the wall? You were sitting there, your face towards the entrance.

GIRL (*Smiling.*): And you came over to me just like that, without even asking, right?

MAN: The light was shining on your neck ... in the shadow, I couldn't quite see your eyes.

GIRL: It's not nice to look at other people's eyes.

MAN: Tell me, what should I look at then?

GIRL: Anyway, you shouldn't look without asking, it's very rude.

MAN: I was only looking at a shadow, that soft shadow in between your breasts. And then the old black guy on the stage was singing some jazz song, it was so melancholy. When I sat down in the chair opposite you, you didn't say anything, did you?

GIRL: For a girl you didn't know, you really shouldn't have looked at her that way.

MAN: But you didn't exactly refuse me at the time. You didn't have a date, you were only waiting, waiting for that someone, until he sat down opposite you, weren't you?

GIRL: Remember, you just said something very pleasing to the ear.

MAN: Good, then I'll keep my mouth shut.

GIRL: You know, . . . today is my birthday.

MAN: Why didn't you tell me earlier? Let's celebrate!

GIRL: We did already. (*Silence. Then softly.*) Just now.

MAN: That was your birthday celebration?

GIRL: Yes, my twenty-sixth birthday. I was born at midnight, what time is it?

MAN: I know now, you just wanted to prove that you're still young, still attractive to men.

GIRL: There's no need to prove anything. All women at my age are still attractive. I just wanted . . .

MAN: What?

GIRL: To wait for a miracle.

(GIRL *does not say anything,* MAN *walks away.*)

MAN: I didn't know. At first I thought . . .

GIRL: I'm exactly what you thought I was, don't you see? (*Pulls up her dress.*)

MAN (*Begging.*): Fine, fine. Stop flirting, please . . .

GIRL: Who's flirting? Tell me, how much were you prepared to pay me?

MAN: Really, you devil you!

GIRL: No, not a devil, but a cock-teasing goddess! Your idol, your whore. (*Opens her arms to him.*)

MAN: Don't abuse yourself.

GIRL: You did already. Stop acting like you're a gentleman.

MAN: All right then. You want a cheque or something? A ring? Or a necklace?

GIRL: Things that've been thrown away by other women, right?

MAN: Then how much? Give it to me straight, don't give me the run-around!

GIRL: I want you to make up for my birthday, I want you to spend the night with me before I turn into a totally incurable slut. You think I'm still sexy, don't you?

MAN: Wait, wait, calm down. Listen, you're still young, you can start all over again, there's no need to destroy yourself like that.

GIRL (*Laughs loudly.*): You're more honest when you're not preaching. Hypocrite, an out-and-out hypocrite!

MAN: What is it that you really want? Tell me!

GIRL (*Looking at the knife on the floor.*): I want your head.

MAN: That'd be kind of hard. Have you had too much to drink? Are you on drugs or something?

GIRL: This isn't India.

MAN: Will you stop making up stories? You just can't quit playing your game, can you?

GIRL: Isn't making love like playing a game? Either you're playing with me or I'm playing with you. What are you going to say to that?

MAN: I really should have killed you!

GIRL: I know. You're only wishing, you wouldn't dare. I've already seen through you ever since I first caught sight of you. You know, the look in your eyes actually gave you away. I'm telling you, you're a piece of crap.

MAN (*Becoming very angry.*): Why did you come here then? You stinking whore!

GIRL (*Calmly.*): I just wanted to prove something.

MAN: That you also put yourself up for sale?

GIRL: All women do, there's no need to prove that.

MAN (*Puzzled.*): Then what were you trying to prove?

GIRL (*Pauses. Laughs.*): . . . Do you want to play one last game with me?

MAN: What more is there to play?

GIRL: Play with death, a game of death.

MAN: That's not a bad idea. How do we play?

GIRL: Let's borrow your head for the time being.

MAN: Do you really want my head?

GIRL (*Giggles.*): I said borrow.

MAN (*Thinks for a moment. Goes over to her and lowers his head.*): All right, take it.

(GIRL *circles to* MAN's *back. Suddenly she seizes the knife and raises it up high. Immediately the lights on the stage darken. Two loud and clear drum beats.* MAN *falls down.*

MONK *enters, bareback and with a piece of red cloth tied around his waist. He is holding an axe in one hand and a wooden stick in the other, his head lowered.*

GIRL *picks up the black overcoat and quietly covers* MAN's *body with it.* MONK *bends down to look for a spot. He finally finds it at the other corner of the stage. He supports the wooden stick with one hand and softly bangs on it with the axe.*

MAN *walks to the back of* GIRL. *He is wrapped in the black overcoat with its collar pulled up. His face is cold and grey.*)

GIRL (*Without turning her head.*): You . . . you're not dead yet?

MAN (*In a low voice.*): An eye for an eye? It's only fair. (*Raises the knife.*)

(MONK *succeeds in making the wooden stick stand up. He raises the axe with both hands and hammers it down. The stick is nailed onto the floor.* MONK *is stupefied. In the dark, both* MAN *and* GIRL *fall down quietly at the same time.*

MONK *picks up an egg from the floor and exits.*)

Second Half

(*The stage has been cleaned and tidied up. It is empty except for two heads under the beaming light, one male and the other female.*
MAN *and* GIRL *are lying down and resting in the dark.*
Sound of a tinkling bell.)

GIRL: The place is so quiet . . . as if it would break once you touched it . . .

MAN: What?

GIRL: Listen, how can it be so quiet, like there's absolutely nothing here, nothing has happened . . .

MAN: What's happening?

GIRL: Hush! Don't say a word—

(GIRL *gets to her feet and listens. The ringing disappears.*)

GIRL: Someone's coming!

MAN: No one would come at this hour.

GIRL: Listen! Listen carefully—

MAN (*Lifts his head.*): You're too sensitive. (*Lies down again.*)

(*Crystal clear sound of bell ringing as if it's unreal.*)

GIRL: Someone's at the door!

MAN: It's impossible.

GIRL: There's a knock on the door, I heard it. Someone's right there at the door.

MAN: Yeah, you heard it, so? Nobody can possibly come in here.

GIRL: Didn't you give someone the key?

MAN: That was a long time ago . . .

GIRL: How long ago?

MAN: I can't remember. It must have been years ago.

GIRL: Why didn't you ask for the key back?

MAN: I didn't bother. Anyway, it was ancient history, why mention it now?

GIRL: But if that someone suddenly remembered?

MAN: Who are you talking about? Who remembered?

GIRL: The one you gave the key to.

MAN: Remembered what?

GIRL: Remembered you. That person can come here any time, right?

MAN: Apart from you, is there anyone else who'd be thinking of me right now?

GIRL: You're so screwy.

MAN (*Sits up and looks at her.*): Don't worry, no one's going to come any more. There's only you and me. Besides, we're dead already. Who'd think of visiting the dead? Don't be daft.

GIRL: Listen, listen, it's right above us. (*Looks up.*)

MAN (*Listening.*): I don't hear anything. Besides, the place is so big, even if there were dead bodies rotting in here our neighbours wouldn't know anything about it, and they won't come knocking at the door unless the corridor smells.

GIRL: But we're both dead already, aren't we?

(MAN *and* GIRL *lower their heads, silently gathering their thoughts.*)

MAN: It looks like it. (*Looking at the two heads.*) Only you and me, nobody else knows. Besides, you can't tell, I can't tell, and it's impossible, absolutely impossible for anybody to tell the outside world!

GIRL: Are we going to be locked up here forever?

MAN: It wouldn't be too bad if this were a desert island, isolated from the rest of the world and without any sign of human habitation. But there's no blue sky to look at, and no beautiful sea to behold. If only we could hear the sound of surging waves from the sea . . .

GIRL: And you can't tell if it's day or night.

MAN: There's no sound, there's no movement, we're left in oblivion and stuck in a forgotten corner, no, an enclosed black box. It's not a coffin, it's not anything. We don't even know the time, is there time any more? Ah, time is no more than a notion, if you think there's time, then there's time. And death, it isn't such a horrible thing, is it?

GIRL: What's so scary is that you can't die quickly, this fear . . .

MAN: Nonsense! What's there to be scared of any more? You and I are already dead.

GIRL: I don't know, am I . . . ?

MAN: Are you what? Now you want to change your mind?

GIRL: I don't know, I don't know anything, is death better than living? I really can't say, everything is so confusing, so elusive . . . Please, please don't ask me any more questions.

MAN (*Delightedly, like a child.*): You and I can't go back any more! Whether you like it or not, ha ha, we are stuck together forever like a man and his shadow. You and I, we're each other's shadow.

GIRL: Why are you still gloating now that you've turned into a shadow, a slave at the feet of a woman? I don't get you.

MAN: It doesn't matter, you and I are in the same boat, nobody can leave anybody. It makes no difference if you're my shadow or if I'm your shadow.

GIRL: You said it, not me.

MAN: So? The bottom line is ... I love you.

GIRL: Me too.

MAN: We can't afford not to, we're inseparable now! Inseparable forever ...

GIRL (*Moved.*): Stay by me, like a good kid. (*Wants to kiss him.*)

MAN (*Moves away.*): I'm tired. I don't have the urge.

GIRL: It's better this way. Stay by me, as long as I can hear your voice.

MAN: What more shall we talk about?

GIRL: You decide, anything's fine with me. Just say something, for instance, something you're thinking of.

MAN: I ... can't think.

GIRL: How about your sarcasm, your mockery, and your ridicule? You enjoy doing these things, don't you?

MAN: I've said everything I can say ... I really can't think of anything else ... what else can I say?

GIRL: Maybe you could fantasize. Let's talk about your fantasies about women.

MAN: I've become impotent.

GIRL (*Startled.*): That's no fun, what has become of that little bit of intelligence you had?

MAN: I'm really very drowsy ...

GIRL: Don't close your eyes. Look at me and say something!

MAN: Leave me alone, I'm totally exhausted ...

GIRL: How miserable ... How can you be so boring ...

MAN: Who? Who's boring?

GIRL: I mean it's really boring when a person dies. (*Looks at* GIRL*'s head.*)

(GIRL *crawls in front of the head and stares at it.*)

MAN: What are you doing?

GIRL: Nothing.

MAN (*Sits up.*): Just like a nightmare. (*Also looks at Man's head.*) This is ... is this my head? Do you believe in resurrection?

GIRL: What?

MAN: Transmigration.

GIRL: What did you say?

MAN: Nothing.

(*The two sit quietly back to back.*)

GIRL (*Persistently.*): She asks, what did you say?
MAN (*Wearily.*): You say, you didn't say anything.
GIRL: She says she clearly heard you say something.
MAN (*Without looking at her.*): You ask what did she hear you say?
GIRL: She says would she ask you if she knew?
MAN: You say that means you didn't say anything.
GIRL: Then she says, Oh. (*Turns to face the audience:*)

(GIRL *sits up straight, then she covers her face with her hands, her head lowered.* MAN *looks at woman's head.*)

MAN: Then you see a contemptuous face. You say even if you wanted to say something, you wouldn't be saying it to her, and you say even if you actually said something, it wouldn't have anything to do with her, you're only talking about yourself. And the you that you're referring to only means you, which is no more than your self, you mean you, that self of yourself, keep on troubling you.
GIRL: She says she's afraid of silence, she can't stand people not talking when they're face to face with each other, she finds that suffocating. She's much more afraid of silence than of death, death is more bearable than not talking to each other like this.
MAN: You say you, you're only talking to yourself.
GIRL: She says she, she's only left with her memories.
MAN: You say you, the only way you can get a little bit of comfort is by talking to yourself.
GIRL: She says she, the only way she can invoke a little bit of fantasy is through her memories.
MAN: You say you, you can feel somewhat relaxed only when you're talking to yourself.
GIRL: She says she, she can see herself clearly only when she's fantasizing.
MAN: You say it's not that you don't want to get away from your self, but you're always talking to yourself, in that way the self will never go away and it'll never stop haunting you.
GIRL: She says only when she indulges herself in fantasies can she empty herself of her worries, be carefree and recall her past feelings. Even though they may have been scary feelings, they still manage to touch her heart.

(MAN *stands up slowly and walks in front of* MAN'*s head.*)

MAN: You have to get rid of the baggage in your mind completely, let bygones be bygones, get away from it all, and get it off your back forever.

GIRL: She's falling asleep . . . It's best to sleep deeply and never wake up, but she just can't sleep well, she's suffering from anxieties all the time . . .

MAN (*Circles around the head and inspects it.*): You've got to find a way to get out of here!

GIRL: Dreams, one after another, intermittent and disjointed, there's no beginning, there's no end . . .

MAN (*Lifts his head.*): It doesn't matter where you're going, when you've got to go, you've got to go!

GIRL: Her head is swooning and she's unsteady on her feet, she has no idea where she is . . .

MAN: You're groping around, you're trying hard to find a way out, you're afraid that you might bump into something . . .

GIRL: A wall, it is collapsing in silence, right in front of her eyes . . .

MAN: Finally you manage to find a door, it must be a door, it is tightly shut . . .

GIRL: That high wall, the one which has been standing erect in front of her, suddenly collapses just like that, without a sound, nobody has touched it . . .

MAN: You must open the door, even if it's only a little crack, as long as you can . . . squeeze through it sideways . . .

GIRL: She actually sees a patch of sky, misty and grey . . . just like fog . . .

MAN: You carefully walk into a dark and shady long corridor . . . it's curved and bent . . . there's no end . . .

GIRL: A big patch of misty grey sky, it's dark and light at the same time, like it's neither morning nor evening . . .

MAN (*Lowers his head.*): Strange, where did this top hat come from? You don't know, should you or shouldn't you pick it up?

GIRL: Then she clearly hears a squeaking sound.

MAN: But you're afraid it might be a trap—(*Lifts his head.*)

GIRL: She knows that a knife is cutting—

MAN: You lift it up—(*Bends down to pick up the top hat.*)

GIRL: Cutting open a naked body—

MAN: Oh, a nest of ants! (*Immediately retreats.*)

GIRL: She sees it now, there's a crowd surrounding a woman, they're cutting open her stomach to dig out her internal organs.

MAN (*Inspecting the top hat in his hand.*): It looks like your own hat, you haven't worn it for a long time, how could you have forgotten about it?

GIRL: They're butchering her, the're dissecting and discussing at the same time. There's also a woman mixed in among them, can't tell how old she is.

MAN (*Puts on the hat.*): It actually fits. Only your own hat would fit this well.

GIRL: She lifts her head and looks around. A pair of hollow eye sockets! She takes to her feet at once!

MAN (*Pulls down the brim of the hat.*): You can't go without a hat, a man without a hat is like a man without clothes.

GIRL (*She bends down until her head touches the ground.*): Something's flowing down her thigh, she knows it may be blood, she feels awfully embarrassed.

MAN (*Somewhat comforted, he raises his voice slightly.*): You walk down the pitch-dark corridor, at the same time you're groping for a way, you know what you should avoid, as if you've passed through the same corridor once, twice, and even three times before.

GIRL: She's actually not afraid of bleeding, just that she's afraid of the sight of blood. Once when she was a small girl she went fishing with the grownups, she saw them toss a big fish onto the shore, they'd just caught that fish, it was all shiny and glittering, and then they started to cut it open right there on a piece of rock, their fingers became sticky with blood, and the fish was still struggling and jerking up and down. She felt rather sorry for that fish, it hadn't died and yet it couldn't live any longer.

MAN (*Wobbles backward rather purposely.*): You know it very well, there is no end, but still you have to keep on going, turning wherever there's a turn. There's no end, you can't stop because you have to go on, even though you know nothing will ever come of it.

GIRL: She really wants to cry, but she can't, she has no more tears. She knows her heart is hardened and dried, a barren stretch of desolation, just like those naked hills behind the old house she lived in when she was a child. She only went there once, she was alone, after that she didn't dare to go any more, the naked branches in the bushes were shaking, shaking with the wailing wind among those hills.

MAN (*Finally he cannot stand steadily.*): You don't know where you should go, should you stop, or perhaps should you turn and go back?

GIRL (*Gets up, at a loss.*): She doesn't know how it happened, but somehow she's in this railway station, it's all deserted and empty, there're no signs on the platform. She wants to know where the next train is going, but she can't find anyone to ask. She feels a bit scared, from here to there in this mammoth platform, she can only hear the hollow tapping of her own footsteps.

(MAN *walks behind her, staring at her back.*
She walks away at once and then suddenly stops.
He takes two steps forward and follows her.)

GIRL (*Closes her eyes and holds her breath.*): She knows there's someone behind her, she can feel that he's staring at her, her back is cold, she is waiting for that someone to raise the knife, she has no strength to lift her feet— (*Panting.*)

(MAN *extends his hands towards her, and she runs away as if she is possessed.*
MAN *drops his hands.*)

GIRL (*Running and panting for breath.*): She says she's terrified, but then she's not really terrified, she knows she's only terrified of her memories of terror.

(MAN *droops his head.*)

GIRL: Nobody can save her except herself, but she feels too weak even to think of saving herself. (*Dejected.*)

(MAN *stares at his feet.*
GIRL *looks at him at a distance.*)

GIRL: At last she sees someone in front of her, a man she's long been waiting for, a man who can perhaps save her! She really wants to see his face clearly, but it's just a blur, she can't quite make it out no matter how hard she tries. (*Walks around him and looks at him closely.*) My God, it's only a shadow!

(*Disappointed, she retreats step by step, head down.*)

MAN (*Slowly lifts his head and marches forward.*): Shit. (*Crouches down to tie the shoelace on his right shoe, gets up, and starts to put forward his right foot.*) Shit! (*Crouches down to tie the shoelace on his left shoe, gets up, and starts to put forward his left foot.*) Shit! (*Crouches down to tie right shoelace again, gets up, and puts forward his right foot.*) Fucking shi—(*Turns to look at left foot, takes back right foot, crouches down to tie left shoelace again, gets up, and starts to lift right foot.*) Mother fucking shit! (*Lifts his right foot in the air to tie shoelace. Then with his right foot touching the ground, he raises the tip of his left foot.*) Mother fucking sh—(*Frustrated, he takes off both shoes, throws them away and sits on the ground trying to figure out what to do next.*)

GIRL (*Looks at herself all over.*): She has no idea, is she also a shadow herself? (*Looks at the shadow under her feet and turns around again and again on the same spot.*) Is the shadow herself? (*Becoming dizzy.*) Or is she no more than the shadow of this shadow? (*Closes her eyes.*) Who is the real she?

(MONK *enters dancing. He is holding a horsetail whisk to dust himself. He picks up an imaginary leaf from his shoulder and blows on it, making a whistling sound. Then he closes his eyes and chants: "Good men and women, good knowledge, purify your nature, purify your heart, Amitabha Buddha!"* MONK *exits. Afterwards* MAN *and* GIRL*'s behaviour becomes increasingly abnormal and strange.*)

MAN (*Talking to himself.*): Behind that door, perhaps there is nothing.

GIRL (*Asking herself.*): No memories?

MAN (*Ruminating.*): That door, behind that door, perhaps there is really nothing, do you believe that?

GIRL: No fantasies?

MAN: That's right, there's nothing behind that door, you thought there was something, but there's nothing.

GIRL: And no dreams either?

MAN (*To audience.*): That door, behind that door, there's nothing.

GIRL: She can't remember anything.

MAN (*To himself.*): There's absolutely nothing behind that door. (*Giggles.*)

GIRL (*To audience.*): What happened?

MAN (*Softly, his back facing* GIRL.): That door, behind that door, there is nothing.

GIRL (*Softly.*): And no memories.

MAN: Absolutely, absolutely.

GIRL: And no fantasies.

MAN: Absolutely, absolutely. (*Nods his head.*)

GIRL: And no dreams either.

MAN: Absolutely, absolutely! (*Becoming contemptuous, his head to one side.*)

GIRL (*More softly.*): Can't say.

MAN (*Very softly.*): Why?
GIRL (*With certainty.*): Can't say.
MAN: Why can't you say it?
GIRL (*Almost whispering.*): Can't say!

(MAN *is speechless.*
MONK *enters. Sound of running water.*
MONK *hastens forward, kneels on one knee, bends down and clasps his hands as if to cup the water. He dips his little finger in the water to wash his ears. After cleaning both ears, he rises and listens respectfully. His mouth opens slowly and reveals a Buddha-like smile. He exits quietly.*)

GIRL: She can't believe that she actually said it, she said something that can't be said, but she said it, clearly this can't be said but why did she have to say it? It ought not to be said it can't be said but she said it regardless, it's her misfortune, it's her disaster, it's her sin.

MAN (*Gets up, looks around and speaks loudly.*): And no door! (*Facing audience.*) The door? Where's the door? The door? The door? The door . . . (*Lowers his head.*) If you think you see it then you see it, if you think there's something then there's something, but what if you think there isn't? The door? Of course it's not there. (*Laughs to himself.*) That door of yours—no doubt it's something out of nothing, you're just being nosy, you just want to find a way out. What if you can't find a way out? Isn't that just as good? (*Laughs loudly.*)

GIRL (*On her knees, murmuring.*): Her sin, well, if she feels guilty then she's guilty. She's afraid of this and afraid of that, afraid of this, afraid of that, afraid, afraid, afraid, but she's not afraid of her, not afraid of herself. But what happens if she's also afraid of herself? Then wouldn't she be not afraid?

MAN: A way out, a way out, since there's no way out, why go and look for it? You only want to prove you're not trapped, or look at it another way, you're looking just to prove that you're trapped? What if you were to stop looking? Then you're not trapped, and you aren't not trapped? Either you're trapped or you're not trapped, either you're not trapped or you aren't not trapped, isn't it all your own doing?

GIRL: If she feels she's not guilty, what's there to be afraid of? She's afraid because she feels she's guilty, she feels guilty because she's afraid. And if she's not afraid then she no longer—(*Pauses.*) That's even more horrifying than Silent Extinction . . .

MAN: If you weren't you, there wouldn't be the need to prove anything, would it? But if you weren't you, then who are you?

GIRL: A silkworm, which gets enmeshed in its own cocoon.

MAN: Do you care who you are? Why can't you put down this you of yours?

GIRL: Left with only the remnants of a broken wish?

MAN: You keep on babbling only to show that you are you, that you're not like other people.

GIRL: A wisp of silk at large.

MAN: You are you because you're still talking, that's all there is to it.

GIRL: Wind.

MAN: Actually you don't know what you're talking about, you talk only because you want to. (*Shakes his head.*)

GIRL: Hollow.

MAN: You can't understand the meaning of your own words, you're just the slave of language, but you can't stop yourself from talking endlessly—(*Shakes his head.*)

GIRL: Tin soldier.

MAN: You can't free yourself from language's entanglement, just like a spider—(*Shakes his head.*) No, you're not a spider, but you're still a spider. (*Shakes his head.*)

GIRL: Candle.

MAN: You're not free to move, being trapped in the web of language of your own making— (*Shakes his head.*)

GIRL: Sa, send, da, la, wood—

MAN: Drunk city, mourning, stone statue—(*Listening to himself attentively.*) Why mourn a stone statue? Is the whole city drunk, or is everyone drunk all over the city? Or is someone or something mourning the idol with drunkenness? Stones are heartless, do humans have a heart? Is the city drunk? Does the stone know?

GIRL: Trap, jump, show, mouth, cut—

MAN: Hut—sin—grief—chime—bell. (*Tilting his head to think.*) Who's actually grieving for who? Is this the hut owner's death or the instruments' pain? Do the instruments know their suffering? If they don't, how can they mourn? Where is the mourner? How does one know? This one, that one, what are they mourning? What is there to mourn? It's all utter nonsense!

(MONK *enters sweeping the floor. He is holding a big broom, his back to the audience. He stops when he comes to front stage and sees the two heads.*

The lights on stage gradually darken, except for the light shining on the heads, which becomes brighter. MONK *turns to observe* MAN *and* GIRL.
MAN *and* GIRL*'s movements become very slow.*)

GIRL (*Murmuring.*): Win—ter . . .
MAN (*Observing her.*): Aha!
GIRL: Makes . . .
MAN: What?
GIRL: Tea—pot . . .
MAN (*Sarcastically.*): Winter makes teapot?
GIRL: Teapot . . .
MAN: Teapot what?
GIRL: Makes . . .
MAN: Makes what?
GIRL: Winter . . .
MAN: Teapot makes winter?
GIRL: Makes . . .
MAN: And then—?
GIRL: Teapot . . .
MAN: And then makes teapot?
GIRL: It is . . .
MAN: It is what? Speak!
GIRL: It is not . . .
MAN: It is it is not?
GIRL: Is . . .
MAN: Is it is it not—is it winter makes teapot or teapot makes winter? (*Getting angry.*) Or is it it is not winter makes teapot or teapot makes winter? Or it is it is not is it not winter makes teapot or is it it is teapot makes winter? Or is it winter makes teapot makes winter? Or it is it is not is it winter makes teapot and then makes winter? Speak, speak, speak, go on!

(MONK *ignores them, sweeping more earnestly.*
MAN *and* GIRL *move and speak faster with the quickening rhythm of the broom. Their bodies become more contorted, like two strange crawling reptiles.*)

GIRL: Crack . . .
MAN: What crack?
GIRL: A crack . . .
MAN: What kind of a crack?
GIRL: A crack line . . .
MAN: What crack line?

GIRL: A crack . . .
MAN: What's this crack like?
GIRL: A crack . . .
MAN: Why a crack?
GIRL: A crack . . .
MAN: Where's this crack?
GIRL: A crack ...
MAN: Why is it called a crack?
GIRL: A crack ...
MAN: A crack and a crack!
GIRL: A crack ...
MAN: Why is there just a crack?
GIRL: A crack ...
MAN: A crack is a crack!
GIRL: A crack ...
MAN: Okay, fine, a crack, so? What about it?
GIRL: A crack ...
MAN: To hell with the crack!
GIRL: A crack ...
MAN: Only one crack?
GIRL: A crack ...
MAN: Another crack?
GIRL: A crack ...
MAN (*Exploding.*): A cr—a—ck—?
GIRL: A crack ...
MAN (*Laughs bitterly.*): A crack.
GIRL: A crack ...
MAN (*Talking to himself.*): A crack ...
GIRL: A crack ...
MAN (*Murmuring.*): A crack ...
MAN & GIRL (*Almost simultaneously.*): A crack—

(MONK *coughs and throws the broom on the ground at the same time. He halts.* MAN *and* GIRL *are stunned by the noise, staring at* MONK. MONK *turns to face the audience. He inhales deeply and slowly and then exhales as slowly. All lights go out.* MONK *turns to open a curtain, revealing a greyish blue sky.* MONK *stands motionless and looks outside the door, his back to the audience. Gradually the wind starts to blow.*)

THE END

How I Learned to Drive PAULA VOGEL

Paula Vogel (born 1951) won, among several other notable awards, the Pulitzer Prize for *How I Learned to Drive* in 1997. It is a challenging play for audiences, both in terms of its subject matter and its characters.

On one level, this is a drama about a sexual relationship (though unconsummated), sexual exploitation, and pedophilia. It concerns Peck, a man in his forties, who sexually takes advantage of a young girl/woman, Li'l Bit. On another level, however, the playwright insists that this is not a play "about" pedophilia and that she "didn't have it in my mind at all" when writing the play. Peck, paradoxically, emerges not merely as a deeply troubled and troubling man, but also as a caring individual who teaches Li'l Bit certain life lessons her parents should have taught her. Peck literally teaches her to drive (a car), but, figuratively and more importantly, he teaches her how to drive her life—about control, power, and self-confidence. The driving metaphor also works on a sexual level, obviously—and Peck has clearly crossed the road's white line, but it leads to a larger lesson of Li'l Bit taking responsibility for her own life.

Vogel's other plays include *Desdemona* (1979), *The Baltimore Waltz* (1992), and *The Long Christmas Ride Home* (2004), among many others. She also teaches playwriting at Brown University.

CHARACTERS

LI'L BIT, *A woman who ages forty-something to eleven years old. (See Notes on the New York Production.)*

PECK, *Attractive man in his forties. Despite a few problems, he should be played by an actor one might cast in the role of Atticus in* To Kill a Mockingbird.

THE GREEK CHORUS, *If possible, these three members should be able to sing three-part harmony.*

MALE GREEK CHORUS, *Plays Grandfather, Waiter, High School Boys. Thirties–forties. (See Notes on the New York Production.)*

FEMALE GREEK CHORUS, *Plays Mother, Aunt Mary, High School Girls. Thirty–fifty. (See Notes on the New York Production.)*

TEENAGE GREEK CHORUS, *Plays Grandmother, high school girls and the voice of eleven-year-old Li'l Bit. Note on the casting of this actor: I would strongly recommend casting a young woman who is "of legal age," that is, twenty-one to twenty-five years old, who can look as close to eleven as possible. The contrast with the other cast members will help. If the actor is too young, the audience may feel uncomfortable. (See Notes on the New York Production.)*

PRODUCTION NOTES

I urge directors to use the GREEK CHORUS *in staging as environment and, well, part of the family—with the exception of the* TEENAGE GREEK CHORUS *member who, after the last time she appears onstage, should perhaps disappear.*

As For Music: Please have fun. I wrote sections of the play listening to music like Roy Orbison's "Dream Baby" and The Mamas and the Papa's "Dedicated to the One I Love." The vaudeville sections go well to the Tijuana Brass or any music that sounds like a *Laugh-In* soundtrack. Other sixties music is rife with pedophilish (?) reference: the "You're Sixteen" genre hits; The Beach Boys' "Little Surfer Girl"; Gary Puckett and the Union Gap's "This Girl Is a Woman Now"; "Come Back When You Grow Up," etc.

And whenever possible, please feel free to punctuate the action with traffic signs: "No Passing," "Slow Children," "Dangerous Curves," "One Way," and the visual signs for children, deer crossings, hills, school buses, etc. (See Notes on the New York Production.)

This script uses the notion of slides and projections, which were not used in the New York production of the play.

On Titles: Throughout the script there are bold-faced titles. In production these should be spoken in a neutral voice (the type of voice that driver education films employ). In the New York Production these titles were assigned to various members of the Greek Chorus and were done live.

NOTES ON THE NEW YORK PRODUCTION

The role of LI'L BIT *was originally written as a character who is forty-something. When we cast Mary-Louise Parker in the role of* LI'L BIT, *we cast the* GREEK CHORUS *members with younger actors as the* FEMALE GREEK *and the* MALE GREEK, *and cast the* TEENAGE GREEK *with an older (that is, mid-twenties) actor as well. There is a great deal of flexibility in age. Directors should change the age in the last monologue for* LI'L BIT *("And before you know it, I'll be thirty-five. . . .") to reflect the actor's age who is playing* LI'L BIT.

As the house lights dim, a Voice announces:

Safety First—You and Driver Education

Then the sound of a key turning the ignition of a car. LI'L BIT *steps into a spotlight on the stage; "well-endowed," she is a softer-looking woman in the present time than she was at seventeen.*

LI'L BIT: Sometimes to tell a secret, you first have to teach a lesson. We're going to start our lesson tonight on an early, warm summer evening.

In a parking lot overlooking the Beltsville Agricultural Farms in suburban Maryland.

Less than a mile away, the crumbling concrete of U.S. One wends its way past one-room revival churches, the porno drive-in, and boarded-up motels with For Sale signs tumbling down.

Like I said, it's a warm summer evening.

Here on the land the Department of Agriculture owns, the smell of sleeping farm animal is thick on the air. The smells of clover and hay mix in with the smells of the leather dashboard. You can still imagine how Maryland used to be, before the malls took over. This countryside was once dotted with farmhouses—from their porches you could have witnessed the Civil War raging in the front fields.

Oh yes. There's a moon over Maryland tonight, that spills into the car where I sit beside a man old enough to be—did I mention how still the night is? Damp soil and tranquil air. It's the kind of night that makes a middle-aged man with a mortgage feel like a country boy again.

It's 1969. And I am very old, very cynical of the world, and I know it all. In short, I am seventeen years old, parking off a dark lane with a married man on an early summer night.

(*Lights up on two chairs facing front—or a Buick Riviera, if you will. Waiting patiently, with a smile on his face,* PECK *sits sniffing the night air.* LI'L BIT *climbs in beside him, seventeen years old and tense. Throughout the following, the two sit facing directly front. They do not touch. Their bodies remain passive. Only their facial expressions emote.*)

PECK: Ummm. I love the smell of your hair.

LI'L BIT: Uh-huh.

PECK: Oh, Lord. Ummmm. (*Beat*) A man could die happy like this.

LI'L BIT: Well, *don't.*

PECK: What shampoo is this?

LI'L BIT: Herbal Essence.

PECK: Herbal Essence. I'm gonna buy me some. Herbal Essence. And when I'm alone in the house, I'm going to get into the bathtub and uncap the bottle and—

LI'L BIT: Be good.

PECK: What?

LI'L BIT: Stop being . . . bad.

PECK: What did you think I was going to say? What do you think I'm going to do with the shampoo?

LI'L BIT: I don't want to know. I don't want to hear it.

PECK: I'm going to wash my hair. That's all.

LI'L BIT: Oh.

PECK: What did you think I was going to do?

LI'L BIT: Nothing. . . . I don't know. Something . . . nasty.

PECK: With shampoo? Lord, gal—your mind!

LI'L BIT: And whose fault is it?

PECK: Not mine. I've got the mind of a boy scout.

LI'L BIT: Right. A horny boy scout.

PECK: Boy scouts are always horny. What do you think the first Merit Badge is for?

LI'L BIT: There. You're going to be nasty again.

PECK: Oh, no. I'm good. Very good.

LI'L BIT: It's getting late.

PECK: Don't change the subject. I was talking about how good I am. (*Beat*) Are you ever gonna let me show you how good I am?

LI'L BIT: Don't go over the line now.

PECK: I won't. I'm not gonna do anything you don't want me to do.

LI'L BIT: That's right.

PECK: And I've been good all week.

LI'L BIT: You have?

PECK: Yes. All week. Not a single drink.

LI'L BIT: Good boy.

PECK: Do I get a reward? For not drinking?

LI'L BIT: A small one. It's getting late.

PECK: Just let me undo you. I'll do you back up.

LI'L BIT: All right. But be quick about it. (PECK *pantomimes undoing* LI'L BIT'*s brassiere with one hand*) You know, that's amazing. The way you can undo the hooks through my blouse with one hand.

PECK: Years of practice.

LI'L BIT: You would make an incredible brain surgeon with that dexterity.

PECK: I'll bet Clyde—what's the name of the boy taking you to the prom?

LI'L BIT: Claude Souders.

PECK: Claude Souders. I'll bet it takes him two hands, lights on, and you helping him on to get to first base.

LI'L BIT: Maybe.

(*Beat.*)

PECK: Can I . . . kiss them? Please?

LI'L BIT: I don't know.

PECK: Don't make a grown man beg.

LI'L BIT: Just one kiss.

PECK: I'm going to lift your blouse.

LI'L BIT: It's a little cold.

(PECK *laughs gently.*)

PECK: That's not why you're shivering. (*They sit, perfectly still, for a long moment of silence.* PECK *makes gentle, concentric circles with his thumbs in the air in front of him*) How does that feel?

(LI'L BIT *closes her eyes, carefully keeps her voice calm:*)

LI'L BIT: It's . . . okay.

(*Sacred music, organ music or a boy's choir swells beneath the following.*)

PECK: I tell you, you can keep all the cathedrals of Europe. Just give me a second with these—these celestial orbs—

(PECK *bows his head as if praying. But he is kissing her nipple,* LI'L BIT, *eyes still closed, rears back her head on the leather Buick car seat.*)

LI'L BIT: Uncle Peck—we've got to go. I've got graduation rehearsal at school tomorrow morning. And you should get on home to Aunt Mary—

PECK: All right. Li'l Bit.

LI'L BIT: *Don't* call me that no more. (*Calmer*) Any more. I'm a big girl now, Uncle Peck. As you know.

(LI'L BIT *pantomimes refastening her bra behind her back.*)

PECK: That you are. Going on eighteen. Kittens will turn into cats. (*Sighs*) I live all week long for these few minutes with you—you know that?

LI'L BIT: I'll drive.

(*A Voice cuts in with:*)

Idling in the Neutral Gear

(*Sound of car revving cuts off the sacred music;* LI'L BIT, *now an adult, rises out of the car and comes to us.*)

LI'L BIT: In most families, relatives get names like "Junior," or "Brother," or "Bubba." In my family, if we call someone "Big Papa," it's not because he's tall. In my family, folks tend to get nicknamed for their genitalia. Uncle Peck, for example. My mama's adage was "the titless wonder," and my cousin Bobby got branded for life as "B.B."

(*In unison with* GREEK CHORUS:)

LI'L BIT: For blue balls. GREEK CHORUS: For blue balls.

FEMALE GREEK CHORUS (*As* MOTHER): And of course, we were so excited to have a baby girl that when the nurse brought you in and said, "It's a girl! It's a baby girl!" I just had to see for myself. So we whipped your diapers down and parted your chubby little legs—and right between your legs there was—

(PECK *has come over during the above and chimes along:*)

PECK: Just a little bit. GREEK CHORUS: Just a little bit.

FEMALE GREEK CHORUS (*As* MOTHER): And when you were born, you were so tiny that you fit in Uncle Peck's outstretched hand.

(PECK *stretches his hand out.*)

PECK: Now that's a fact. I held you, one day old, right in this hand.

(*A traffic signal is projected of a bicycle in a circle with a diagonal red slash.*)

LI'L BIT: Even with my family background, I was sixteen or so before I realized that pedophilia did not mean people who loved to bicycle. . . .

(*A Voice intrudes:*)

Driving in First Gear

LI'L BIT: 1969. A typical family dinner.

FEMALE GREEK CHORUS (*As* MOTHER): Look, Grandma. Li'l Bit's getting to be as big in the bust as you are.

LI'L BIT: Mother! Could we please change the subject?

TEENAGE GREEK CHORUS (*As* GRANDMOTHER): Well, I hope you are buying her some decent bras. I never had a decent bra, growing up in the Depression, and now my shoulders are just crippled—crippled from the weight hanging on my shoulders—the dents from my bra straps are big enough to put your finger in.—Here, let me show you—

(*As* GRANDMOTHER *starts to open her blouse:*)

LI'L BIT: Grandma! Please don't undress at the dinner table.

PECK: I thought the entertainment came after the dinner.

LI'L BIT (*To the audience*): This is how it always starts. My grandfather, Big Papa, will chime in next with—

MALE GREEK CHORUS (*As* GRANDFATHER): Yup. If Li'l Bit gets any bigger, we're gonna haveta buy her a wheelbarrow to carry in front of her—

LI'L BIT: Damn it—

PECK: How about those Redskins on Sunday, Big Papa?

LI'L BIT (*To the audience*): The only sport Big Papa followed was chasing Grandma around the house—

MALE GREEK CHORUS (*As* GRANDFATHER): Or we could write to Kate Smith. Ask her for somma her used brassieres she don't want anymore—she could maybe give to Li'l Bit here—

LI'L BIT: I can't stand it. I can't.

PECK: Now, honey, that's just their way—

FEMALE GREEK CHORUS (*As* MOTHER): I tell you, Grandma, Li'l Bit's at that age. She's so sensitive, you can't say boo—

LI'L BIT: I'd like some privacy, that's all. Okay? Some goddamn privacy—

PECK: Well, at least she didn't use the savior's name—

LI'L BIT (*To the audience*): And Big Papa wouldn't let a dead dog lie. No sirree.

MALE GREEK CHORUS (*As* GRANDFATHER): Well, she'd better stop being so sensitive. 'Cause five minutes before Li'l Bit turns the corner, her tits turn first—

LI'L BIT (*Starting to rise from the table*): That's it. That's it.

PECK: Li'l Bit, you can't let him get to you. Then he wins.

LI'L BIT: I hate him. Hate him.

PECK: That's fine. But hate him and eat a good dinner at the same time.

(LI'L BIT *calms down and sits with perfect dignity.*)

LI'L BIT: The gumbo is really good, Grandma.

MALE GREEK CHORUS (*As* GRANDFATHER): A'course, Li'l Bit's got a big surprise coming for her when she goes to that fancy college this fall—

PECK: Big Papa—let it go.

MALE GREEK CHORUS (*As* GRANDFATHER): What does she need a college degree for? She's got all the credentials she'll need on her chest.

LI'L BIT: Maybe I want to learn things. Read. Rise above my cracker[1] background—

PECK: Whoa, now, Li'l Bit—

MALE GREEK CHORUS (*As* GRANDFATHER): What kind of things do you want to read?

LI'L BIT: There's a whole semester course, for example, on Shakespeare—

(GREEK CHORUS, *as* GRANDFATHER, *laughs until he weeps.*)

MALE GREEK CHORUS (*As* GRANDFATHER): Shakespeare. That's a good one. Shakespeare is really going to help you in life.

PECK: I think it's wonderful. And on scholarship!

MALE GREEK CHORUS (*As* GRANDFATHER): How is Shakespeare going to help her lie on her back in the dark?

(LI'L BIT *is on her feet.*)

LI'L BIT: You're getting old, Big Papa. You are going to die—very very soon. Maybe even tonight. And when you get to heaven, God's going to be a beautiful black woman in a long white robe. She's gonna look at your chart and say: Uh-oh. Fornication. Dog-ugly mean with blood relatives. Oh. Uh-oh. Voted for George Wallace. Well, one last chance: If you can name the play, all will be forgiven. And then she'll quote: "The quality of mercy is not strained." Your answer? Oh, too bad—*Merchant of Venice:* Act IV, Scene iii. And then she'll send your ass to fry in hell with all the other crackers. Excuse me, please.

(*To the audience*) And as I left the house, I would always hear Big Papa say:

MALE GREEK CHORUS (*As* GRANDFATHER): Lucy, your daughter's got a mouth on her. Well, no sense in wasting good gumbo. Pass me her plate, Mama.

LI'L BIT: And Aunt Mary would come up to Uncle Peck:

FEMALE GREEK CHORUS (*As* AUNT MARY): Peck, go after her, will you? You're the only one she'll listen to when she gets like this.

---

[1]**cracker:** an unflattering word referring to a poor white person from the South

PECK: She just needs to cool off.

FEMALE GREEK CHORUS (*As* AUNT MARY): Please, honey—Grandma's been on her feet cooking all day.

PECK: All right.

LI'L BIT: And as he left the room, Aunt Mary would say:

FEMALE GREEK CHORUS (*As* AUNT MARY): Peck's so good with them when they get to be this age.

(LI'L BIT *has stormed to another part of the stage, her back turned, weeping with a teenage fury.* PECK, *cautiously, as if stalking a deer, comes to her. She turns away even more. He waits a bit.*)

PECK: I don't suppose you're talking to family. (*No response*) Does it help that I'm in-law?

LI'L BIT: Don't you dare make fun of this.

PECK: I'm not. There's nothing funny about this. (*Beat*) Although I'll bet when Big Papa is about to meet his maker, he'll remember *The Merchant of Venice.*

LI'L BIT: I've got to get away from here.

PECK: You're going away. Soon. Here, take this.

(PECK *hands her his folded handkerchief.* LI'L BIT *uses it, noisily. Hands it back. Without her seeing, he reverently puts it back.*)

LI'L BIT: I hate this family.

PECK: Your grandfather's ignorant. And you're right—he's going to die soon. But he's family. Family is . . . family.

LI'L BIT: Grown-ups are always saying that. Family.

PECK: Well, when you get a little older, you'll see what we're saying.

LI'L BIT: Uh-huh. So family is another acquired taste, like French kissing?

PECK: Come again?

LI'L BIT: You know, at first it really grosses you out, but in time you grow to like it?

PECK: Girl, you are . . . a handful.

LI'L BIT: Uncle Peck—you have the keys to your car?

PECK: Where do you want to go?

LI'L BIT: Just up the road.

PECK: I'll come with you.

LI'L BIT: No—please? I just need to . . . to drive for a little bit. Alone.

(PECK *tosses her the keys.*)

PECK: When can I see you alone again?

LI'L BIT: Tonight.

(LI'L BIT *crosses to center stage where the lights dim around her. A Voice directs:*)

Shifting Forward from First to Second Gear

LI'L BIT: There were a lot of rumors about why I got kicked out of that fancy school in 1970. Some say I got caught with a man in my room. Some say as a kid on scholarship I fooled around with a rich man's daughter.

(LI'L BIT *smiles innocently at the audience*) I'm not talking.

But the real truth was I had a constant companion in my dorm room—who was less than discreet. Canadian V.O. A fifth a day.

1970. A Nixon recession. I slept on the floors of friends who were out of work themselves. Took factory work when I could find it. A string of dead-end jobs that didn't last very long.

What I did, most nights, was cruise the Beltway and the back roads of Maryland, where there was still country, past the battlefields and farmhouses. Racing in a 1965 Mustang—and as long as I had gasoline for my car and whiskey for me, the nights would pass. Fully tanked, I would speed past the churches and the trees and the bend, thinking just one notch of the steering wheel would be all it would take, and yet some . . . reflex took over. My hands on the wheel in the nine and three o' clock position—I never so much as got a ticket. He taught me well.

(*A Voice announces:*)

You and the Reverse Gear

LI'L BIT: Back up. 1968. On the Eastern Shore. A celebration dinner.

(LI'L BIT *joins* PECK *at a table in a restaurant.*)

PECK: Feeling better, missy?

LI'L BIT: The bathroom's really amazing here, Uncle Peck! They have these little soaps—instead of borax or something—and they're in the shape of shells.

PECK: I'll have to take a trip to the gentlemen's room just to see.

LI'L BIT: How did you know about this place?

PECK: This inn is famous on the Eastern shore—it's been open since the seventeenth century. And I know how you like history . . .

(LI'L BIT *is shy and pleased.*)

LI'L BIT: It's great.

PECK: And you've just done your first, legal, long-distance drive. You must be hungry.

LI'L BIT: I'm starved.

PECK: I would suggest a dozen oysters to start, and the crab imperial . . . (LI'L BIT *is genuinely agog*) You might be interested to know the town history. When the British sailed up this very river in the dead of night—see outside where I'm pointing?—they were going to bombard the heck out of this town. But the town fathers were ready for them. They crept up all the trees with lanterns so that the British would think they saw the town lights and they aimed their cannons too high. And that's why the inn is still here for business today.

LI'L BIT: That's a great story.

PECK (*Casually*): Would you like to start with a cocktail?

LI'L BIT: You're not . . . you're not going to start drinking, are you, Uncle Peck?

PECK: Not me. I told you, as long as you're with me, I'll never drink. I asked you if you'd like a cocktail before dinner. It's nice to have a little something with the oysters.

LI'L BIT: But . . . I'm not . . . legal. We could get arrested. Uncle Peck, they'll never believe I'm twenty-one!

PECK: So? Today we celebrate your driver's license—on the first try. This establishment reminds me a lot of places back home.

LI'L BIT: What does that mean?

PECK: In South Carolina, like here on the Eastern Shore, they're . . . (*Searches for the right euphemism*) . . . "European." No so puritanical. And very understanding if gentlemen wish to escort very attractive young ladies who might want a before-dinner cocktail. If you want one, I'll order one.

LI'L BIT: Well—sure. Just . . . one.

(*The* FEMALE GREEK CHORUS *appears in a spot.*)

FEMALE GREEK CHORUS (*As* MOTHER): A Mother's Guide to Social Drinking: A lady never gets sloppy—she may, however, get tipsy and a little gay.

Never drink on an empty stomach. Avail yourself of the bread basket and generous portions of butter. Slather the butter on your bread.

Sip your drink, slowly, let the beverage linger in your mouth—interspersed with interesting, fascinating conversation. Sip, never . . . slurp or gulp. Your glass should always be three-quarters full when his glass is empty.

Stay away from ladies' drinks: drinks like pink ladies, slow gin fizzes, daiquiris, gold Cadillacs, Long Island iced teas, margaritas, piña coladas, mai tais, planters punch, white Russians, black Russians, red Russians, melon balls, blue balls, hummingbirds, hemorrhages and hurricanes. In short, avoid anything with sugar, or anything with an umbrella. Get your vitamin C from fruit. Don't order anything with Voodoo or Vixen in the title or sexual positions in the name like Dead Man Screw or the Missionary. (*She sort of titters*)

Believe me, they are lethal. . . . I think you were conceived after one of those.

Drink, instead, like a man: straight up or on the rocks, with plenty of water in between.

Oh, yes. And never mix your drinks. Stay with one all night long, like the man you came in with: bourbon, gin, or tequila till dawn, damn the torpedoes, full speed ahead!

(*As the* FEMALE GREEK CHORUS *retreats, the* MALE GREEK CHORUS *approaches the table as a* WAITER.)

MALE GREEK CHORUS (*As* WAITER): I hope you all are having a pleasant evening. Is there something I can bring you, sir, before you order?

(LI'L BIT *waits in anxious fear. Carefully,* UNCLE PECK *says with command:*)

PECK: I'll have a plain iced tea. The lady would like a drink, I believe.

(*The* MALE GREEK CHORUS *does a double take; there is a moment when* UNCLE PECK *and he are in silent communication.*)

MALE GREEK CHORUS (*As* WAITER): Very good. What would the . . . lady like?

LI'L BIT (*A bit flushed*): Is there . . . is there any sugar in a martini?

PECK: None that I know of.

LI'L BIT: That's what I'd like then—a dry martini. And could we maybe have some bread?

PECK: A drink fit for a woman of the world.—Please bring the lady a dry martini, be generous with the olives, straight up.

(*The* MALE GREEK CHORUS *anticipates a large tip.*)

MALE GREEK CHORUS (*As* WAITER): Right away. Very good sir.

(*The* MALE GREEK CHORUS *returns with an empty martini glass which he puts in front of* LI'L BIT.)

PECK: Your glass is empty. Another martini, madam?

LI'L BIT: Yes, thank you. (PECK *signals the* MALE GREEK CHORUS, *who nods*). So why did you leave South Carolina, Uncle Peck?

PECK: I was stationed in D.C. after the war, and decided to stay. Go North, Young Man, someone might have said.

LI'L BIT: What did you do in the service anyway?

PECK (*Suddenly taciturn*): I . . . I did just this and that. Nothing heroic or spectacular.

LI'L BIT: But did you see fighting? Or go to Europe?

PECK: I served in the Pacific Theater. It's really nothing interesting to talk about.

LI'L BIT: It is to me. (*The* WAITER *has brought another empty glass*) Oh, goody. I love the color of the swizzle sticks. What were we talking about?

PECK: Swizzle sticks.

LI'L BIT: Do you ever think of going back?

PECK: To the Marines?

LI'L BIT: No—to South Carolina.

PECK: Well, we do go back. To visit.

LI'L BIT: No, I mean to live.

PECK: Not very likely. I think it's better if my mother doesn't have a daily reminder of her disappointment.

LI'L BIT: Are these floorboards slanted?

PECK: Yes, the floor is very slanted. I think this is the original floor.

LI'L BIT: Oh, good.

(*The* FEMALE GREEK CHORUS *as* MOTHER *enters swaying a little, a little past tipsy.*)

FEMALE GREEK CHORUS (*As* MOTHER): Don't leave your drink unattended when you visit the ladies' room. There is such a thing as white slavery; the modus operandi is to spike an unsuspecting young girl's drink with a "mickey" when she's left the room to powder her nose.

But if you feel you have had more than your sufficiency in liquor, do go to the ladies' room—often. Pop your head out of doors for a refreshing breath of the night air. If you must, wet your face and head with tap water. Don't be afraid to dunk your head if necessary. A wet woman is still less conspicuous than a drunk woman.

(*The* FEMALE GREEK CHORUS *stumbles a little; conspiratorially*) When in the course of human events it becomes necessary, go to a corner stall and insert the index and middle finger down the throat almost to the epiglottis. Divulge your stomach before rejoining your beau waiting for you at your table.

Oh, no. Don't be shy or embarrassed. In the very best of establishments, there's always one or two debutantes crouched in the corner stalls, their beaded purses tossed willy-nilly, sounding like cats in heat, heaving up the contents of their stomachs.

(*The* FEMALE GREEK CHORUS *begins to wander off*) I wonder what it is they do in the men's rooms . . .

LI'L BIT: So why is your mother disappointed in you, Uncle Peck?

PECK: Every mother in Horry County has Great Expectations.

LI'L BIT: Could I have another mar-ti-ni, please?

PECK: I think this is your last one.

(PECK *signals the* WAITER. *The* WAITER *looks at* LI'L BIT *and shakes his head no.* PECK *raises an eyebrow, raises his finger to indicate one more, and then rubs his fingers together. It looks like a secret code. The* WAITER *sighs, shakes his head sadly, and brings over another empty martini glass. He glares at* PECK.)

LI'L BIT: The name of the county where you grew up is "Horry?" (LI'L BIT, *plastered, begins to laugh. Then she stops*) I think your mother should be proud of you.

(PECK *signals for the check.*)

PECK: Well, missy, she wanted me to do—to *be* everything my father was not. She wanted me to amount to something.

LI'L BIT: But you have! You've amounted a lot. . . .

PECK: I'm just a very ordinary man.

(*The* WAITER *has brought the check and waits.* PECK *draws out a large bill and hands it to the* WAITER. LI'L BIT *is in the soppy stage.*)

LI'L BIT: I'll bet your mother loves you, Uncle Peck.

(PECK *freezes a bit. To* MALE GREEK CHORUS *as* WAITER:)

PECK: Thank you. The service was exceptional. Please keep the change.

MALE GREEK CHORUS (*As* WAITER, *in a tone that could freeze*): Thank you, sir. Will you be needing any help?

PECK: I think we can manage, thank you.

(*Just then, the* FEMALE GREEK CHORUS *as* MOTHER *lurches on stage; the* MALE GREEK CHORUS *as* WAITER *escorts her off as she delivers:*)

FEMALE GREEK CHORUS (*As* MOTHER): Thanks to judicious planning and several trips to the ladies' loo, your mother once out-drank an entire regiment of British officers on a good-will visit to Washington! Every last man of them! Milquetoasts! How'd they ever kick Hitler's cahones, huh? No match for an American lady—I could drink every man in here under the table.

(*She delivers one last crucial hint before she is gently "bounced"*) As a last resort, when going out for an evening on the town, be sure to wear a skin-tight girdle—so tight that only a surgical knife or acetylene torch can get it off you—so that if you do pass out in the arms of your escort, he'll end up with rubber burns on his fingers before he can steal your virtue—

(*A Voice punctures the interlude with:*)

Vehicle Failure

Even with careful maintenance and preventive operation of your automobile, it is all too common for us to experience an unexpected breakdown. If you are driving at any speed when a breakdown occurs, you must slow down and guide the automobile to the side of the road.

(PECK *is slowly propping up* LI'L BIT *as they work their way to his car in the parking lot of the inn.*)

PECK: How are you doing, missy?

LI'L BIT: It's so far to the car, Uncle Peck. Like the lanterns in the trees the British fired on . . .

(LI'L BIT *stumbles.* PECK *swoops her up in his arms.*)

PECK: Okay. I think we're going to take a more direct route.

(LI'L BIT *closes her eyes*) Dizzy? (*She nods her head*) Don't look at the ground. Almost there—do you feel sick to your stomach? (LI'L BIT *nods. They reach the "car."* PECK *gently deposits her on the front seat*)

Just settle here a little while until things stop spinning. (LI'L BIT *opens her eyes*)

LI'L BIT: What are we doing?

PECK: We're just going to sit here until your tummy settles down.

LI'L BIT: It's such nice upholst'ry—

PECK: Think you can go for a ride, now?

LI'L BIT: Where are you taking me?

PECK: Home.

LI'L BIT: You're not taking me—upstairs? There's no room at the inn? (LI'L BIT *giggles*)

PECK: Do you want to go upstairs? (LI'L BIT *doesn't answer*) Or home?

LI'L BIT: This isn't right, Uncle Peck.

PECK: What isn't right?

LI'L BIT: What we're doing. It's wrong. It's very wrong.

PECK: What are we doing? (LI'L BIT *does not answer*) We're just going out to dinner.

LI'L BIT: You know. It's not nice to Aunt Mary.

PECK: You let me be the judge of what's nice and not nice to my wife.

(*Beat.*)

LI'L BIT: Now you're mad.

PECK: I'm not mad. It's just that I thought you . . . understood me, Li'l Bit. I think you're the only one who does.

LI'L BIT: Someone will get hurt.

PECK: Have I forced you to do anything?

(*There is a long pause as* LI'L BIT *tries to get sober enough to think this through.*)

LI'L BIT: . . . I guess not.

PECK: We are just enjoying each other's company. I've told you, nothing is going to happen between us until you want it to. Do you know that?

LI'L BIT: Yes.

PECK: Nothing is going to happen until you want it to. (*A second more, with* PECK *staring ahead at the river while seated at the wheel of his car. Then, softly:*) Do you want something to happen?

(PECK *reaches over and strokes her face, very gently,* LI'L BIT *softens, reaches for him, and buries her head in his neck. Then she kisses him. Then she moves away, dizzy again.*)

LI'L BIT: . . . I don't know.

(PECK *smiles; this has been good news for him—it hasn't been a "no."*)

PECK: Then I'll wait. I'm a very patient man. I've been waiting for a long time. I don't mind waiting.

LI'L BIT: Someone is going to get hurt.

PECK: No one is going to get hurt, (LI'L BIT *closes her eyes*) Are you feeling sick?

LI'L BIT: Sleepy.

(*Carefully,* PECK *props* LI'L BIT *up on the seat.*)

PECK: Stay here a second.

LI'L BIT: Where're you going?

PECK: I'm getting something from the back seat.

LI'L BIT (*Scared: too loud*): What? What are you going to do?

(PECK *reappears in the front seat with a lap rug.*)

PECK: Shhh. (PECK *covers* LI'L BIT. *She calms down*) There. Think you can sleep?

(LI'L BIT *nods. She slides over to rest on his shoulder. With a look of happiness,* PECK *turns the ignition key. Beat.* PECK *leaves* LI'L BIT *sleeping in the car and strolls down to the audience. Wagner's Flying Dutchman comes up faintly.*

A Voice interjects:)

Idling in the Neutral Gear

TEENAGE GREEK CHORUS: Uncle Peck Teaches Cousin Bobby How to Fish.

PECK: I get back once or twice a year—supposedly to visit Mama and the family, but the real truth is to fish. I miss this the most of all. There's a smell in the Low country—where the swamp and fresh inlet join the saltwater—a scent of sand and cypress, that I haven't found anywhere yet.

I don't say this very often up North because it will just play into the stereotype everyone has, but I will tell you: I didn't wear shoes in the summertime until I was sixteen. It's unnatural down here to pen up your feet in leather. Go ahead—take 'em off. Let yourself breathe—it really will make you feel better.

We're going to aim for some pompano today—and I have to tell you, they're a very shy, mercurial fish. Takes patience, and psychology. You have to believe it doesn't matter if you catch one or not.

Sky's pretty spectacular—there's some beer in the cooler next to the crab salad I packed, so help yourself if you get hungry. Are you hungry? Thirsty? Holler if you are.

Okay. You don't want to lean over the bridge like that—pompano feed in shallow water, and you don't want to get too close—they're frisky and shy little things—wait, check your line. Yep, something's been munching while we were talking.

Okay, look: We take the sand flea and you take the hook like this—right through his little sand flea rump. Sand fleas should always keep their backs to the wall. Okay. Cast it in, like I showed you. That's great! I can taste that pompano now, sautéed with some pecans and butter, and a little bourbon—now—let it lie on the bottom—now, reel, jerk, reel, jerk—

Look—look at your line. There's something calling, all right. Okay, tip the rod up—not too sharp—hook it—all right, now easy, reel and then rest—let it play. And reel—play it out, that's right—really good! I can't believe it! It's a pompano.—Good work! Way to go! You are an official fisherman now. Pompano are hard to catch. We are going to have a delicious little—

What? Well, I don't know how much pain a fish feels—you can't think of that. Oh, no, don't cry, come on now, it's just a fish—the other guys are going to see you.—No, no, you're just real sensitive, and I think that's wonderful at your age— look, do you want me to cut it free? You do?

Okay, hand me those pliers—look—I'm cutting the hook—okay? And we're just going to drop it in—no I'm not mad. It's just for fun, okay? There—it's going to swim back to its lady friend and tell her what a terrible day it had and she's going to stroke him with her fins until he feels better, and then they'll do something alone together that will make them both feel good and sleepy. . . .

(PECK *bends down, very earnest*) I don't want you to feel ashamed about crying. I'm not going to tell anyone, okay? I can keep secrets. You know, men cry all the time. They just don't tell anybody, and they don't let anybody catch them. There's nothing you could do that would make me feel ashamed of you. Do you know that? Okay. (PECK *straightens up, smiles*)

Do you want to pack up and call it a day? I tell you what—I think I can still remember—there's a really neat tree house where I used to stay for days. I think it's still here—it was the last time I looked. But it's a secret place—you can't tell anybody we've gone there—least of all your mom or your sisters.—This is something special just between you and me. Sound good? We'll climb up there and have a beer and some crab salad—okay, B.B.? Bobby? Robert . . .

(LI'L BIT *sits at a kitchen table with the two* FEMALE GREEK CHORUS *members.*)

LI'L BIT (*To the audience*): Three women, three generations, sit at the kitchen table. On Men, Sex, and Women: Part I:

FEMALE GREEK CHORUS (*As* MOTHER): Men only want one thing.

LI'L BIT (*Wide-eyed*): But what? What is it they want?

FEMALE GREEK CHORUS (*As* MOTHER): And once they have it, they lose all interest. So Don't Give It to Them.

TEENAGE GREEK CHORUS (*As* GRANDMOTHER): I never had the luxury of the rhythm method. Your grandfather is just a big bull. A big bull. Every morning, every evening.

FEMALE GREEK CHORUS (*As* MOTHER, *whispers to* LI'L BIT): And he used to come home for lunch every day.

LI'L BIT: My god, Grandma!

TEENAGE GREEK CHORUS (*As* GRANDMOTHER): Your grandfather only cares that I do two things: have the table set and the bed turned down.

FEMALE GREEK CHORUS (*As* MOTHER): And in all that time, Mother, you never have experienced—?

LI'L BIT (*To the audience*): No, my grandmother believed in all the sacraments of the church, to the day she died. She believed in Santa Claus and the Easter Bunny until she was fifteen. But she didn't believe in—

TEENAGE GREEK CHORUS (*As* GRANDMOTHER): Orgasm! That's just something you and Mary have made up! I don't believe you.

FEMALE GREEK CHORUS (*As* MOTHER): Mother, it happens to women all the time—

TEENAGE GREEK CHORUS (*As* GRANDMOTHER): Oh, now you're going to tell me about the G force!

LI'L BIT: No, Grandma, I think that's astronauts—

FEMALE GREEK CHORUS (*As* MOTHER): Well, Mama, after all, you were a child bride when Big Papa came and got you—you were a married woman and you still believed in Santa Claus.

TEENAGE GREEK CHORUS (*As* GRANDMOTHER): It was legal, what Daddy and I did! I was fourteen and in those days, fourteen was a grown-up woman—

(BIG PAPA *shuffles in the kitchen for a cookie.*)

MALE GREEK CHORUS (*As* GRANDFATHER): Oh, now we're off on Grandma and the Rape of the Sa-bean Women!

TEENAGE GREEK CHORUS (*As* GRANDMOTHER): Well, you were the one in such a big hurry—

MALE GREEK CHORUS (*As* GRANDFATHER *to* LI'L BIT): I picked your grandmother out of that herd of sisters just like a lion chooses the gazelle—the plump, slow, flaky gazelle dawdling at the edge of the herd—your sisters were too smart and too fast and too scrawny—

LI'L BIT (*To the audience*): The family story is that when Big Papa came for Grandma, my Aunt Lily was waiting for him with a broom—and she beat him over the head all the way down the stairs as he was carrying out Grandma's hope chest—

MALE GREEK CHORUS (*As* GRANDFATHER): —and they were mean. 'Specially Lily.

FEMALE GREEK CHORUS (*As* MOTHER): Well, you were robbing the baby of the family!

TEENAGE GREEK CHORUS (*As* GRANDMOTHER): I still keep a broom handy in the kitchen! And I know how to use it! So get your hand out of the cookie jar and don't you spoil your appetite for dinner—out of the kitchen!

(MALE GREEK CHORUS *as* GRANDFATHER *leaves chuckling with a cookie.*)

FEMALE GREEK CHORUS (*As* MOTHER): Just one thing a married woman needs to know how to use—the rolling pin or the broom. I prefer a heavy, cast-iron fry pan—they're great on a man's head, no matter how thick the skull is.

TEENAGE GREEK CHORUS (*As* GRANDMOTHER): Yes, sir, your father is ruled by only two bosses! Mr. Gut and Mr. Peter! And sometimes, first thing in the morning, Mr. Sphincter Muscle!

FEMALE GREEK CHORUS (*As* MOTHER): It's true. Men are like children. Just like little boys.

TEENAGE GREEK CHORUS (*As* GRANDMOTHER): Men are bulls! Big bulls!

(THE GREEK CHORUS *is getting aroused.*)

FEMALE GREEK CHORUS (*As* MOTHER): They'd still be crouched on their haunches over a fire in a cave if we hadn't cleaned them up!

TEENAGE GREEK CHORUS (*As* GRANDMOTHER, *flushed*): Coming in smelling of sweat—

FEMALE GREEK CHORUS (*As* MOTHER): Looking at those naughty pictures like boys in a dime store with a dollar in their pockets!

TEENAGE GREEK CHORUS (*As* GRANDMOTHER; *raucous*): No matter to them what they smell like! They've got to have it, right then, on the spot, right there! Nasty!—

FEMALE GREEK CHORUS (*As* MOTHER): Vulgar!

TEENAGE GREEK CHORUS (*As* GRANDMOTHER): Primitive!—

FEMALE GREEK CHORUS (*As* MOTHER): —Hot!—

LI'L BIT: And just about then, Big Papa would shuffle in with—

MALE GREEK CHORUS (*As* GRANDFATHER): What are you all cackling about in here?

TEENAGE GREEK CHORUS (*As* GRANDMOTHER): Stay out of the kitchen! This is just for girls!

(*As* GRANDFATHER *leaves:*)

MALE GREEK CHORUS (*As* GRANDFATHER): Lucy, you'd better not be filling Mama's head with sex! Every time you and Mary come over and start in about sex, when I ask a simple question like, "What time is dinner going to be ready?" Mama snaps my head off!

TEENAGE GREEK CHORUS (*As* GRANDMOTHER): Dinner will be ready when I'm good and ready! Stay out of this kitchen!

(LI'L BIT *steps out.*
A Voice directs:)

When Making a Left Turn, You Must Downshift While Going Forward

LI'L BIT: 1979. A long bus trip to Upstate New York. I settled in to read, when a young man sat beside me.

MALE GREEK CHORUS (*As* YOUNG MAN; *voice cracking*): "What are you reading?"

LI'L BIT: He asked. His voice broke into that miserable equivalent of vocal acne, not quite falsetto and not tenor, either. I glanced a side view. He was appealing in an odd way, huge ears at a defiant angle springing forward at ninety degrees. He must have been shaving, because his face, with a peach sheen, was speckled with nicks and styptic. "I have a class tomorrow," I told him.

MALE GREEK CHORUS (*As* YOUNG MAN): "You're taking a class?"

LI'L BIT: "I'm teaching a class." He concentrated on lowering his voice.

MALE GREEK CHORUS (*As* YOUNG MAN): "I'm a senior. Walt Whitman High."

LI'L BIT: The light was fading outside, so perhaps he was—with a very high voice. I felt his "interest" quicken. Five steps ahead of the hopes in his head, I slowed down, waited, pretended surprise, acted at listening, all the while knowing we would get off the bus, he would just then seem to think to ask me to dinner, he would chivalrously insist on walking me home, he would continue to converse in the street until I would casually invite him up to my room—and—I was only into the second moment of conversation and I could see the whole evening before me.

And dramaturgically speaking, after the faltering and slightly comical "first act," there was the very briefest of intermissions, and an extremely capable and forceful and sustained second act. And after the second act climax and a gentle denouement—before the post-play discussion—I lay on my back in the dark and I thought about you, Uncle Peck. Oh. Oh—this is the allure. Being older. Being the first. Being the translator, the teacher, the epicure, the already jaded. This is how the giver gets taken.

(LI'L BIT *changes her tone*) On Men, Sex, and Women: Part II:

(LI'L BIT *steps back into the scenes as a fifteen-year-old, gawky and quiet, as the gazelle at the edge of the herd.*)

TEENAGE GREEK CHORUS (*As* GRANDMOTHER; *to* LI'L BIT): You're being mighty quiet, missy. Cat Got Your Tongue?

LI'L BIT: I'm just listening. Just thinking.

TEENAGE GREEK CHORUS (*As* GRANDMOTHER): Oh, yes, Little Miss Radar Ears? Soaking it all in? Little Miss Sponge? Penny for your thoughts?

(LI'L BIT *hesitates to ask but she really wants to know.*)

LI'L BIT: Does it—when you do it—you know, theoretically when I do it and I haven't done it before—I mean—does it hurt?

FEMALE GREEK CHORUS (*As* MOTHER): Does what hurt, honey?

LI'L BIT: When a . . . when a girl does it for the first time—with a man—does it hurt?

TEENAGE GREEK CHORUS (*As* GRANDMOTHER; *horrified*): That's what you're thinking about?

FEMALE GREEK CHORUS (*As* MOTHER; *calm*): Well, just a little bit. Like a pinch. And there's a little blood.

TEENAGE GREEK CHORUS (*As* GRANDMOTHER): Don't tell her that! She's too young to be thinking those things!

FEMALE GREEK CHORUS (*As* MOTHER): Well, if she doesn't find out from me, where is she going to find out? In the street?

TEENAGE GREEK CHORUS (*As* GRANDMOTHER): Tell her it hurts! It's agony! You think you're going to die! Especially if you do it before marriage!

FEMALE GREEK CHORUS (*As* MOTHER): Mama! I'm going to tell her the truth! Unlike you, you left me and Mary completely in the dark with fairy tales and told us to go to the priest! What does an eighty-year-old priest know about love-making with girls!

LI'L BIT (*Getting upset*): It's not fair!

FEMALE GREEK CHORUS (*As* MOTHER): Now, see, she's getting upset—you're scaring her.

TEENAGE GREEK CHORUS (*As* GRANDMOTHER): Good! Let her be good and scared! It hurts! You bleed like a stuck pig! And you lay there and say, "Why, O Lord, have you forsaken me?!"

LI'L BIT: It's not fair! Why does everything have to hurt for girls? Why is there always blood?

FEMALE GREEK CHORUS (*As* MOTHER): It's not a lot of blood—and it feels wonderful after the pain subsides . . .

TEENAGE GREEK CHORUS (*As* GRANDMOTHER): You're encouraging her to just go out and find out with the first drugstore joe who buys her a milk shake!

FEMALE GREEK CHORUS (*As* MOTHER): Don't be scared. It won't hurt you—if the man you go to bed with really loves you. It's important that he loves you.

TEENAGE GREEK CHORUS (*As* GRANDMOTHER): Why don't you just go out and rent a motel room for her, Lucy?

FEMALE GREEK CHORUS (*As* MOTHER): I believe in telling my daughter the truth! We have a very close relationship! I want her to be able to ask me anything—I'm not scaring her with stories about Eve's sin and snakes crawling on their bellies for eternity and women bearing children in mortal pain—

TEENAGE GREEK CHORUS (*As* GRANDMOTHER): If she stops and thinks before she takes her knickers off, maybe someone in this family will finish high school!

(LI'L BIT *knows what is about to happen and starts to retreat from the scene at this point.*)

FEMALE GREEK CHORUS (*As* MOTHER): Mother! If you and Daddy had helped me—I wouldn't have had to marry that—that no-good-son-of-a—

TEENAGE GREEK CHORUS (*As* GRANDMOTHER): He was good enough for you on a full moon! I hold you responsible!

FEMALE GREEK CHORUS (*As* MOTHER): You could have helped me! You could have told me something about the facts of life!

TEENAGE GREEK CHORUS (*As* GRANDMOTHER): I told you what my mother told me! A girl with her skirt up can outrun a man with his pants down!

(*The* MALE GREEK CHORUS *enters the fray;* LI'L BIT *edges further downstage.*)

FEMALE GREEK CHORUS (*As* MOTHER): And when I turned to you for a little help, all I got afterwards was—

MALE GREEK CHORUS (*As* GRANDFATHER): You Made Your Bed; Now Lie On It!

(*The* GREEK CHORUS *freezes, mouths open, argumentatively.*)

LI'L BIT (*To the audience*): Oh, please! I still can't bear to listen to it, after all these years—

(*The* MALE GREEK CHORUS *"unfreezes," but out of his open mouth as if to his surprise, comes a base refrain from a Motown song.*)

MALE GREEK CHORUS: "Do-Bee-Do-Wha!"

(*The* FEMALE GREEK CHORUS *member is also surprised; but she, too, unfreezes.*)

FEMALE GREEK CHORUS: "Shoo-doo-be-doo-be-doo; shoo-doo-be-doo-be-doo."

(*The* MALE *and* FEMALE GREEK CHORUS *members continue with their harmony, until the* TEENAGER *member of the* CHORUS *starts in with Motown lyrics such as "Dedicated to the One I Love," or "In the Still of the Night," or "Hold Me"—any Sam Cooke will do. The three modulate down into three-part harmony, softly, until they are submerged by the actual recording playing over the radio in the car in which* UNCLE PECK *sits in the driver's seat, waiting.* LI'L BIT *sits in the passenger's seat.*)

LI'L BIT: Ahh. That's better.

(UNCLE PECK *reaches over and turns the volume down; to* LI'L BIT:)

PECK: How can you hear yourself think?

(LI'L BIT *does not answer.*
A Voice insinuates itself in the pause:)

Before You Drive

Always check under your car for obstructions—broken bottles, fallen tree branches, and the bodies of small children. Each year hundreds of children are crushed beneath the wheels of unwary drivers in their own driveways. Children depend on you to watch them.

(*Pause.*
The Voice continues:)

You and the Reverse Gear

(*In the following section, it would be nice to have slides of erotic photographs of women and cars: women posed over the hood; women draped along the sideboards; women with water hoses spraying the car; and the actress playing* LI'L BIT *with a Bel Air or any 1950s car one can find for the finale.*)

LI'L BIT: 1967. In a parking lot of the Beltsville Agriculture Farms. The Initiation into a Boy's First Love.

PECK (*With a soft look on his face*): Of course, my favorite car will always be the '56 Bel Air Sports Coupe. Chevy sold more '55s, but the '56!—a V-8 with Corvette option, 225 horsepower; went from zero to sixty miles per hour in 8.9 seconds.

LI'L BIT (*To the audience*): Long after a mother's tits, but before a woman's breasts:

PECK: Super-Turbo-Fire! What a Power Pack—mechanical lifters, twin four-barrel carbs, lightweight valves, dual exhausts—

LI'L BIT (*To the audience*): After the milk but before the beer.

PECK: A specific intake manifold, higher-lift camshaft, and the tightest squeeze Chevy had ever made—

LI'L BIT (*To the audience*): Long after he's squeezed down the birth canal but before he's pushed his way back in: The boy falls in love with the thing that bears his weight with speed.

PECK: I want you to know your automobile inside and out.—Are you there? Li'l Bit?

(*Slides end here.*)

LI'L BIT: —What?

PECK: You're drifting. I need you to concentrate.

LI'L BIT: Sorry.

PECK: Okay. Get into the driver's seat. (LI'L BIT *does*) Okay. Now. Show me what you're going to do before you start the car.

(LI'L BIT *sits, with her hands in her lap. She starts to giggle.*)

PECK: Now, come on. What's the first thing you're going to adjust?

LI'L BIT: My bra strap?—

PECK: Li'l Bit. What's the most important thing to have control of on the inside of the car?

LI'L BIT: That's easy. The radio. I tune the radio from Mama's old fart tunes to—

(LI'L BIT *turns the radio up so we can hear a 1960s tune. With surprising firmness,* PECK *commands:*)

PECK: Radio off. Right now. (LI'L BIT *turns the radio off*) When you are driving your car, with your license, you can fiddle with the stations all you want. But when you are driving with a learner's permit in my car, I want all your attention to be on the road.

LI'L BIT: Yes, sir.

PECK: Okay. Now the seat—forward and up. (LI'L BIT *pushes it forward*) Do you want a cushion?

LI'L BIT: No—I'm good.

PECK: You should be able to reach all the switches and controls. Your feet should be able to push the accelerator, brake and clutch all the way down. Can you do that?

LI'L BIT: Yes.

PECK: Okay, the side mirrors. You want to be able to see just a bit of the right side of the car in the right mirror—can you?

LI'L BIT: Turn it out more.

PECK: Okay. How's that?

LI'L BIT: A little more. . . . Okay, that's good.

PECK: Now the left—again, you want to be able to see behind you—but the left lane—adjust it until you feel comfortable. (LI'L BIT *does so*) Next. I want you to check the rearview mirror. Angle it so you have a clear vision of the back. (LI'L BIT *does so*) Okay. Lock your door. Make sure all the doors are locked.

LI'L BIT (*Making a joke of it*): But then I'm locked in with you.

PECK: Don't fool.

LI'L BIT: All right. We're locked in.

PECK: We'll deal with the air vents and defroster later. I'm teaching you on a manual—once you learn manual, you can drive anything. I want you to be able to drive any car, any machine. Manual gives you control. In ice, if your brakes fail, if you need more power—okay? It's a little harder at first, but them it becomes like breathing.

Now. Put your hands on the wheel. I never want to see you driving with one hand. Always two hands. (LI'L BIT *hesitates*) What? What is it now?

LI'L BIT: If I put my hands on the wheel—how do I defend myself?

PECK (*Softly*): Now listen. Listen up close. We're not going to fool around with this. This is serious business. I will never touch you when you are driving a car. Understand?

LI'L BIT: Okay.

PECK: Hands on the nine o'clock and three o'clock position gives you maximum control and turn.

(PECK *goes silent for a while.* LI'L BIT *waits for more instruction*)

Okay. Just relax and listen to me, Li'l Bit, okay? I want you to lift your hands for a second and look at them. (LI'L BIT *feels a bit silly, but does it*)

Those are your two hands. When you are driving, you life is in your own two hands. Understand? (LI'L BIT *nods*)

I don't have any sons. You're the nearest to a son I'll ever have—and I want to give you something. Something that really matters to me.

There's something about driving—when you're in control of the car, just you and the machine and the road—that nobody can take from you. A power. I feel more myself in my car than anywhere else. And that's what I want to give to you.

There's a lot of assholes out there. Crazy men, arrogant idiots, drunks, angry kids, geezers who are blind—and you have to be ready for them. I want to teach you to drive like a man.

LI'L BIT: What does that mean?

PECK: Men are taught to drive with confidence—with aggression. The road belongs to them. They drive defensively—always looking out for the other guy. Women tend to be polite—to hesitate. And that can be fatal.

You're going to learn to think what the other guy is going to do before he does it. If there's an accident, and ten cars pile up, and people get killed, you're the one who's gonna steer through it, put your foot on the gas if you have to, and be the only one to walk away. I don't know how long you or I are going to live, but we're for damned sure not going to die in a car.

So if you're going to drive with me, I want you to take this very seriously.

LI'L BIT: I will, Uncle Peck. I want you to teach me to drive.

PECK: Good. You're going to pass your test on the first try. Perfect score. Before the next four weeks are over, you're going to know this baby inside and out. Treat her with respect.

LI'L BIT: Why is it a "she"?

PECK: Good question. It doesn't have to be a "she"—but when you close your eyes and think of someone who responds to your touch—someone who performs just for you and gives you what you ask for—I guess I always see a "she." You can call her what you like.

LI'L BIT (*To the audience*): I closed my eyes—and decided not to change the gender.

(*A Voice:*)

Defensive driving involves defending yourself from hazardous and sudden changes in your automotive environment. By thinking ahead, the defensive driver can adjust to weather, road conditions and road kill. Good defensive driving involves mental and physical preparation. Are you prepared?

(*Another Voice chimes in:*)

You and the Reverse Gear

LI'L BIT: 1966. The Anthropology of the Female Body in Ninth Grade—Or A Walk Down Mammary Lane.

(*Throughout the following, there is occasional rhythmic beeping, like a transmitter signaling.* LI'L BIT *is aware of it, but can't figure out where it is coming from. No one else seems to hear it.*)

MALE GREEK CHORUS: In the hallway of Francis Scott Key Middle School.

(*A bell rings; the* GREEK CHORUS *is changing classes and meets in the hall, conspiratorially.*)

TEENAGE GREEK CHORUS: She's coming!

(LI'L BIT *enters the scene; the* MALE GREEK CHORUS *member has a sudden, violent sneezing and lethal allergy attack.*)

FEMALE GREEK CHORUS: Jerome? Jerome? Are you all right?

MALE GREEK CHORUS: I—don't—know. I can't breathe—get Li'l Bit—

TEENAGE GREEK CHORUS: He needs oxygen!—

FEMALE GREEK CHORUS: Can you help us here?

LI'L BIT: What's wrong? Do you want me to get the school nurse—

(*The* MALE GREEK CHORUS *member wheezes, grabs his throat and sniffs at* LI'L BIT*'s chest, which is beeping away.*)

MALE GREEK CHORUS: No—it's okay—I only get this way when I'm around an allergy trigger—

LI'L BIT: Golly. What are you allergic to?

MALE GREEK CHORUS (*With a sudden grab of her breast*): Foam rubber.

(*The* GREEK CHORUS *members break up with hilarity;* JEROME *leaps away from* LI'L BIT*'s kicking rage with agility; as he retreats:*)

LI'L BIT: Jerome! Creep! Cretin! Cro-Magnon!

TEENAGE GREEK CHORUS: Rage is not attractive in a girl.

FEMALE GREEK CHORUS: Really. Get a Sense of Humor.

(*A voice echoes:*)

Good Defensive Driving Involves Mental and Physical Preparation. Were You Prepared?

FEMALE GREEK CHORUS: Gym Class: In the showers.

(*The sudden sound of water; the* FEMALE GREEK CHORUS *members and* LI'L BIT, *while fully clothed, drape towels across their fronts, miming nudity. They stand, hesitate, at an imaginary shower's edge.*)

LI'L BIT: Water looks hot.

FEMALE GREEK CHORUS: Yesss. . . .

(FEMALE GREEK CHORUS *members are not going to make the first move. One dips a tentative toe under the water, clutching the towel around her.*)

LI'L BIT: Well, I guess we'd better shower and get out of here.

FEMALE GREEK CHORUS: Yep. You go ahead. I'm still cooling off.

LI'L BIT: Okay. —Sally? Are you gonna shower?

TEENAGE GREEK CHORUS: After you—

(LI'L BIT *takes a deep breath for courage, drops the towel and plunges in: The two* FEMALE GREEK CHORUS *members look at* LI'L BIT *in the all together, laugh, gasp and high-five each other.*)

TEENAGE GREEK CHORUS: Oh my god! Can you believe—

FEMALE GREEK CHORUS: Told you it's not foam rubber! I win! Jerome owes me fifty cents.

(*A Voice editorializes:*)

Were You Prepared?

(LI'L BIT *tries to cover up; she is exposed, as suddenly 1960s Motown fills the room and we segue into:*)

FEMALE GREEK CHORUS: The Sock Hop.

(LI'L BIT *stands against the wall with her female classmates.* TEENAGE GREEK CHORUS *is mesmerized by the music and just sways alone, lip-synching the lyrics.*)

LI'L BIT: I don't know. Maybe it's just me—but—do you ever feel like you're just a walking Mary Jane joke?

FEMALE GREEK CHORUS: I don't know what you mean.

LI'L BIT: You haven't heard the Mary Jane jokes? (FEMALE GREEK CHORUS *member shakes her head no*) Okay. "Little Mary Jane is walking through the woods, when all of a sudden this man who was hiding behind a tree jumps out, rips open Mary Jane's blouse, and plunges his hands on her breasts. And Little Mary Jane just laughed and laughed because she knew her money was in her shoes."

(LI'L BIT *laughs; the* FEMALE GREEK CHROUS *does not.*)

FEMALE GREEK CHORUS: You're weird.

(*In another space, in a strange light,* UNCLE PECK *stands and stares at* LI'L BIT*'s body. He is setting up a tripod, but he just stands, appreciative, watching her.*)

LI'L BIT: Well, don't you ever feel . . . self-conscious? Like you're being looked at all the time?

FEMALE GREEK CHORUS: That's not a problem for me.—Oh—look—Greg's coming over to ask you to dance.

(TEENAGE GREEK CHORUS *becomes attentive, flustered.* MALE GREEK CHORUS *member, as* GREG, *bends slightly as a very short young man, whose head is at* LI'L BIT*'s chest level. Ardent, sincere and socially inept,* GREG *will become a successful gynecologist.*)

TEENAGE GREEK CHORUS (*Softly*): Hi, Greg.

(GREG *does not hear. He is intent on only one thing.*)

MALE GREEK CHORUS (*As* GREG, to LI'L BIT): Good Evening. Would you care to dance?

LI'L BIT (*Gently*): Thank you very much, Greg—but I'm going to sit this one out.

MALE GREEK CHORUS (*As* GREG): Oh. Okay. I'll try my luck later.

(*He disappears.*)

TEENAGE GREEK CHORUS: Oohhh.

(LI'L BIT *relaxes. Then she tenses, aware of* PECK*'s gaze.*)

FEMALE GREEK CHORUS: Take pity on him. Someone should.

LI'L BIT: But he's too short.

TEENAGE GREEK CHORUS: He can't help it.

LI'L BIT: But his head comes up to (LI'L BIT *gestures*) here. And I think he asks me on the fast dances so he can watch me—you know—jiggle.

FEMALE GREEK CHORUS: I wish I had your problems.

(*The tune changes;* GREG *is across the room in a flash.*)

MALE GREEK CHORUS (*As* GREG): Evening again. May I ask you for the honor of a spin on the floor?

LI'L BIT: I'm . . . very complimented, Greg. But I . . . I just don't do fast dances.

MALE GREEK CHORUS (*As* GREG): Oh. No problem. That's okay.

(*He disappears.* TEENAGE GREEK CHORUS *watches him go.*)

TEENAGE GREEK CHORUS: That is just so—*sad.*

(LI'L BIT *becomes aware of* PECK *waiting.*)

FEMALE GREEK CHORUS: You know, you should take it as a compliment that the guys want to watch you jiggle. They're guys. That's what they're supposed to do.

LI'L BIT: I guess you're right. But sometimes I feel like these alien life forces, these two mounds of flesh have grafted themselves onto my chest, and they're using me until they can "propagate" and take over the world and they'll just keep growing, with a mind of their own until I collapse under their weight and they suck all the nourishment out of my body and I finally just waste away while they get bigger and bigger and—(LI'L BIT*'s classmates are just staring at her in disbelief*)

FEMALE GREEK CHORUS: You are the strangest girl I have ever met.

(LI'L BIT*'s trying to joke but feels on the verge of tears.*)

LI'L BIT: Or maybe someone's implanted radio transmitters in my chest at a frequency I can't hear, that girls can't detect, but they're sending out these signals to men who get mesmerized, like sirens, calling them to dash themselves on these "rocks"—

(*Just then, the music segues into a slow dance, perhaps a Beach Boys tune like "Little Surfer," but over the music there's a rhythmic, hypnotic beeping transmitted, which both* GREG *and* PECK *hear.* LI'L BIT *hears it too, and in horror she stares at her chest. She, too, is almost hypnotized. In a trance,* GREG *responds to the signals and is called to her side—actually, her front. Like a zombie, he stands in front of her, his eyes planted on her two orbs.*)

MALE GREEK CHORUS (*As* GREG): This one's a slow dance. I hope your dance card isn't . . . filled?

(LI'L BIT *is aware of* PECK; *but the signals are calling her to him. The signals are no longer transmitters, but an electromagnetic force, pulling* LI'L BIT *to his side, where he again waits for her to join him. She must get away from the dance floor.*)

LI'L BIT: Greg—you really are a nice boy. But I don't like to dance.

MALE GREEK CHORUS (*As* GREG): That's okay. We don't have to move or anything. I could just hold you and we could just sway a little—

LI'L BIT: —No! I'm sorry—but I think I have to leave; I hear someone calling me—

(LI'L BIT *starts across the dance floor, leaving* GREG *behind. The beeping stops. The lights change, although the music does not. As* LI'L BIT *talks to the audience, she continues to change and prepare for the coming session. She should be wearing a tight tank top or a sheer blouse and very tight pants. To the audience:*)

In every man's home some small room, some zone in his house, is set aside. It might be the attic, or the study, or a den. And there's an invisible sign as if from the old treehouse: Girls Keep Out.

Here, away from female eyes, lace doilies and crochet, he keeps his manly toys: the Vargas pinups, the tackle. A scent of tobacco and WD-40. (*She inhales deeply*) A dash of his Bay Rum. Ahh . . . (LI'L BIT *savors it for just a moment more*)

Here he keeps his secrets; a violin or saxophone, drum set or darkroom, and the stacks of *Playboy.* (*In a whisper*) Here, in my aunt's home, it was the basement. Uncle Peck's turf.

(*A Voice commands:*)

You and the Reverse Gear

LI'L BIT: 1965. The Photo Shoot.

(LI'L BIT *steps into the scene as a nervous but curious thirteen-year-old. Music, from the previous scene, continues to play, changing into something like Roy Orbison later—something seductive with a beat.* PECK *fiddles, all business, with his camera. As in the driving lesson, he is all competency and concentration.* LI'L BIT *stands awkwardly. He looks through the Leica camera on the tripod, adjusts the back lighting, etc.*)

PECK: Are you cold? The lights should heat up some in a few minutes—

LI'L BIT: Aunt Mary is?

PECK: At the National Theatre matinee. With your mother. We have time.

LI'L BIT: But—what if—

PECK: And so what if they return? I told them you and I were going to be working with my camera. They won't come down. (LI'L BIT *is quiet, apprehensive*)—Look, are you sure you want to do this?

LI'L BIT: I said I'd do it. But—

PECK: I know. You've drawn the line.

LI'L BIT (*Reassured*): That's right. No frontal nudity.

PECK: Good heavens, girl, where did you pick that up?

LI'L BIT (*Defensive*): I *read.*

(PECK *tries not to laugh.*)

PECK: And I read *Playboy* for the interviews. Okay. Let's try some different music.

(PECK *goes to an expensive reel-to-reel and forwards. Something like "Sweet Dreams" begins to play.*)

LI'L BIT: I didn't know you listened to this.

PECK: I'm not dead, you know. I try to keep up. Do you like this song? (LI'L BIT *nods with pleasure*) Good. Now listen—at professional photo shoots, they always play music for the models. Okay? I want you to just enjoy the music. Listen to it with your body, and just—respond.

LI'L BIT: Respond to the music with my . . . body?

PECK: Right. Almost like dancing. Here—let's get you on the stool, first. (PECK *comes over and helps her up*)

LI'L BIT: But nothing showing—

(PECK *firmly, with his large capable hands, brushes back her hair, angles her face.* LI'L BIT *turns to him like a plant to the sun.*)

PECK: Nothing showing. Just a peek.
(*He holds her by the shoulders, looking at her critically. Then he unbuttons her blouse to the midpoint, and runs his hands over the flesh of her exposed sternum, arranging the fabric, just touching her. Deliberately, calmly. Asexually.* LI'L BIT *quiets, sits perfectly still, and closes her eyes*)
Okay?

LI'L BIT: Yes.

(PECK *goes back to his camera.*)

PECK: I'm going to keep talking to you. Listen without responding to what I'm saying; you want to *listen* to the music. Sway, move just your torso or your head—I've got to check the light meter.

LI'L BIT: But—you'll be watching.

PECK: No—I'm not here—just my voice. Pretend you're in your room all alone on a Friday night with your mirror—and the music feels good—just move for me, Li'l Bit—

(LI'L BIT *closes her eyes. At first self-conscious; then she gets more into the music and begins to sway. We hear the camera start to whir. Throughout the shoot, there can be a slide montage of actual shots of the actor playing* LI'L BIT*—interspersed with other models à la Playboy, Calvin Klein and Victoriana/Lewis Carroll's Alice Liddell*)

That's it. That looks great. Okay. Just keep doing that. Lift your head up a bit more, good, good, just keep moving, that a girl—you're a beautiful young woman. Do you know that? (LI'L BIT *looks up, blushes.* PECK *shoots the camera. The audience should see this shot on the screen*)

LI'L BIT: No. I don't know that.

PECK: Listen to the music. (LI'L BIT *closes her eyes again*) Well you are. For a thirteen-year-old, you have a body a twenty-year-old woman would die for.

LI'L BIT: The boys in school don't think so.

PECK: The boys in school are little Neanderthals in short pants. You're ten years ahead of them in maturity; it's gonna take a while for them to catch up.

(PECK *clicks another shot; we see a faint smile on* LI'L BIT *on the screen*)

Girls turn into women long before boys turn into men.

LI'L BIT: Why is that?

PECK: I don't know, Li'l Bit. But it's a blessing for men.

(LI'L BIT *turns silent*) Keep moving. Try arching your back on the stool, hands behind you, and throw your head back. (*The slide shows a* Playboy *model in this pose*) Oohh, great. That one was great. Turn head away, same position. (*Whir*) Beautiful.

(LI'L BIT *looks at him a bit defiantly.*)

LI'L BIT: I think Aunt Mary is beautiful.

(PECK *stands still.*)

PECK: My wife is a very beautiful woman. Her beauty doesn't cancel yours out. (*More casually; he returns to the camera*) All the women in your family are beautiful. In fact, I think all women are. You're not listening to the music. (PECK *shoots some more film in silence*) All right, turn your head to the left. Good. Now take the back of your right hand and put it on your right cheek—your elbow angled up—now slowly, slowly, stroke your cheek, draw back your hair with the back of your hand. (*Another classic* Playboy *or* Vargas) Good. One hand above and behind your head; stretch your body; smile. (*Another pose*)

Li'l Bit. I want you to think of something that makes you laugh—

LI'L BIT: I can't think of anything.

PECK: Okay. Think of Big Papa chasing Grandma around the living room. (LI'L BIT *lifts her head and laughs. Click. We should see this shot*) Good. Both hands behind your head. Great! Hold that. (*From behind his camera*) You're doing great work. If we keep this up, in five years we'll have a really professional portfolio.

(LI'L BIT *stops.*)

LI'L BIT: What do you mean in five years?

PECK: You can't submit work to *Playboy* until you're eighteen.—

(PECK *continues to shoot; he knows he's made a mistake.*)

LI'L BIT: Wait a minute. You're joking aren't you, Uncle Peck?

PECK: Heck, no. You can't get into *Playboy* unless you're the very best. And you are the very best.

LI'L BIT: I would never do that!

(PECK *stops shooting. He turns off the music.*)

PECK: Why? There's nothing wrong with *Playboy*—it's a very classy maga—

LI'L BIT (*More upset*): But I thought you said I should go to college!

PECK: Wait—Li'l Bit—it's nothing like that. Very respectable women model for *Playboy*—actresses with major careers—women in college—there's an Ivy League issue every—

LI'L BIT: I'm never doing anything like that! You'd show other people these—other *men*—these—what I'm doing.—Why would you do that?! Any *boy* around here could just pick up, just go to The Stop & Go and *buy*— Why would you ever want to—to share—

PECK: Whoa, whoa. Just stop a second and listen to me. Li'l Bit. Listen. There's nothing wrong in what we're doing. I'm very proud of you. I think you have a wonderful body and an even more wonderful mind. And of course I want other people to *appreciate* it. It's not anything shameful.

LI'L BIT (*Hurt*): But this is something—that I'm only doing for you. This is something—that you said was just between us.

PECK: It is. And if that's how you feel, five years from now, it will remain that way. Okay? I know you're not going to do anything you don't feel like doing.

(*He walks back to the camera*) Do you want me to stop now? I've got just a few more shots on this roll—

LI'L BIT: I don't want anyone seeing this.

PECK: I swear to you. No one will. I'll treasure this—that you're doing this only for me.

(LI'L BIT *still shaken, sits on the stool. She closes her eyes*) Li'l Bit? Open your eyes and look at me. (LI'L BIT *shakes her head no*) Come on. Just open your eyes, honey.

LI'L BIT: If I look at you—if I look at the camera: You're gonna know what I'm thinking. You'll see right through me—

PECK: No, I won't. I want you to look at me. All right, then. I just want you to listen. Li'l Bit. (*She waits*) I love you. (LI'L BIT *opens her eyes; she is startled.* PECK *captures the shot. On the screen we see right through her.* PECK *says softly*) Do you know that? (LI'L BIT *nods her head yes*) I have loved you every day since the day you were born.

LI'L BIT: Yes.

(LI'L BIT *and* PECK *just look at each other. Beat. Beneath the shot of herself on the screen,* LI'L BIT, *still looking at her uncle, begins to unbutton her blouse.*

A neutral Voice cuts off the above scene with:)

Implied Consent

As an individual operating a motor vehicle in the state of Maryland, you must abide by "Implied Consent." If you do not consent to take the blood alcohol content test, there may be severe penalties: a suspension of license, a fine, community service and a possible jail sentence.

(*The Voice shifts tone:*)

Idling in Neutral Gear

MALE GREEK CHORUS (*Announcing*): Aunt Mary on behalf of her husband.

(FEMALE GREEK CHORUS *checks her appearance, and with dignity comes to the front of the stage and sits down to talk to the audience.*)

FEMALE GREEK CHORUS (*As* AUNT MARY): My husband was such a good man—is. Is such a good man. Every night, he does the dishes. The second he comes home, he's taking out the garbage, or doing the yard work, lifting the heavy things I can't. Everyone in the neighborhood borrows Peck—it's true—women with husbands of their own, men who just don't have Peck's abilities—there's always a knock on our door for a jump start on cold mornings, when anyone else needs a ride, or help shoveling the sidewalk—I look out, and there Peck is, without a coat, pitching in.

I know I'm lucky. The man works from dawn to dusk. And the overtime he does every year—my poor sister. She sits every Christmas when I come to dinner with a new stole, or diamonds, or with the tickets to Bermuda.

I know he has troubles. And we don't talk about them. I wonder, sometimes, what happened to him during the war. The men who fought World War II didn't have "rap sessions" to talk about their feelings. Men in his generation were expected to be quiet about it and get on with their lives. And sometimes I can feel him just fighting the trouble—whatever has burrowed deeper than the scar tissue—and we don't talk about it. I know he's having a bad spell because he comes looking for me in the house, and just hangs around me until it passes. And I keep my banter light—I discuss a new recipe, or sales, or gossip—because I think domesticity can be a balm for men when they're lost. We sit in the house and listen to the peace of the clock ticking in his well-ordered living room, until it passes.

(*Sharply*) I'm not a fool. I know what's going on. I wish you could feel how hard Peck fights against it—he's swimming against the tide, and what he needs is to see me on the shore, believing in him, knowing he won't go under, he won't give up—

And I want to say this about my niece. She's a sly one, that one is. She knows exactly what she's doing; she's twisted Peck around her little finger and thinks it's all a big secret. Yet another one who's borrowing my husband until it doesn't suit her anymore.

Well. I'm counting the days until she goes away to school. And she manipulates someone else. And then he'll come back again, and sit in the kitchen while I bake, or beside me on the sofa when I sew in the evenings. I'm a very patient woman. But I'd like my husband back.

I am counting the days.

(*A Voice repeats:*)

You and the Reverse Gear

MALE GREEK CHORUS: Li'l Bit's Thirteenth Christmas. Uncle Peck Does the Dishes. Christmas 1964.

(PECK *stands in a dress shirt and tie, nice pants, with an apron. He is washing dishes. He's in a mood we haven't seen. Quiet, brooding.* LI'L BIT *watches him a moment before seeking him out.*)

LI'L BIT: Uncle Peck? (*He does not answer. He continues to work on the pots*) I didn't know where you'd gone to. (*He nods. She takes this as a sign to come in*) Don't you want to sit with us for a while?

PECK: No. I'd rather do the dishes.

(*Pause.* LI'L BIT *watches him.*)

LI'L BIT: You're the only man I know who does dishes. (PECK *says nothing*) I think it's really nice.

PECK: My wife has been on her feet all day. So's your grandmother and your mother.

LI'L BIT: I know. (*Beat*) Do you want some help?

PECK: No. (*He softens a bit towards her*) You can help by just talking to me.

LI'L BIT: Big Papa never does the dishes. I think it's nice.

PECK: I think men should be nice to women. Women are always working for us. There's nothing particularly manly in wolfing down food and then sitting around in a stupor while the women clean up.

LI'L BIT: That looks like a really neat camera that Aunt Mary got you.

PECK: It is. It's a very nice one.

(*Pause, as* PECK *works on the dishes and some demon that* LI'L BIT *intuits.*)

LI'L BIT: Did Big Papa hurt your feelings?

PECK (*Tired*): What? Oh, no—it doesn't hurt me. Family is family. I'd rather have him picking on me than—I don't pay him any mind, Li'l Bit.

LI'L BIT: Are you angry with us?

PECK: No, Li'l Bit. I'm not angry.

(*Another pause.*)

LI'L BIT: We missed you at Thanksgiving. . . . I did. I missed you.

PECK: Well, there were . . . "things" going on. I didn't want to spoil anyone's Thanksgiving.

LI'L BIT: Uncle Peck? (*Very carefully*) Please don't drink anymore tonight.

PECK: I'm not . . . overdoing it.

LI'L BIT: I know. (*Beat*) Why do you drink so much?

(PECK *stops and thinks, carefully.*)

PECK: Well, Li'l Bit—let me explain it this way. There are some people who have a . . . a "fire" in the belly. I think they go to work on Wall Street or they run for office. And then there are people who have a "fire" inside their heads—and they become writers or scientists or historians. (*He smiles a little at her*) You. You've got a "fire" in the head. And then there are people like me.

LI'L BIT: Where do you have . . . a fire?

PECK: I have a fire in my heart. And sometimes the drinking helps.

LI'L BIT: There's got to be other things that can help.

PECK: I suppose there are.

LI'L BIT. Does it help—to talk to me?

PECK: Yes. I does. (*Quietly*) I don't get to see you very much.

LI'L BIT: I know. (LI'L BIT *thinks*) You could talk to me more.

PECK: Oh?

LI'L BIT: I could make a deal with you, Uncle Peck.

PECK: I'm listening.

LI'L BIT: We could meet and talk—once a week. You could just store up whatever's bothering you during the week—and then we could talk.

PECK: Would you like that?

LI'L BIT: As long as you don't drink. I'd meet you somewhere for lunch or for a walk—on the weekends—as long as you stop drinking. And we could talk about whatever you want.

PECK: You would do that for me?

LI'L BIT: I don't think I'd want Mom to know. Or Aunt Mary. I wouldn't want them to think—

PECK: No. It would just be us talking.

LI'L BIT: I'll tell Mom I'm going to a girlfriend's. To study. Mom doesn't get home until six, so you can call me after school and tell me where to meet you.

PECK: You get home at four?

LI'L BIT: We can meet once a week. But only in public. You've got to let me—draw the line. And once it's drawn, you mustn't cross it.

PECK: Understood.

LI'L BIT: Would that help?

(PECK *is very moved.*)

PECK: Yes. Very much.

LI'L BIT: I'm going to join the others in the living room now. (LI'L BIT *turns to go*)

PECK: Merry Christmas, Li'l Bit.

(LI'L BIT *bestows a very warm smile on him.*)

LI'L BIT: Merry Christmas, Uncle Peck.

(*A Voice dictates:*)

Shifting Forward from Second to Third Gear

(*The* MALE *and* FEMALE GREEK CHORUS *members come forward.*)

MALE GREEK CHORUS: 1969. Days and Gifts: A Countdown:

FEMALE GREEK CHORUS: A note. "September 3, 1969. Li'l Bit: You've only been away two days and it feels like months. Hope your dorm room is cozy. I'm sending you this tape cassette—it's a new model—so you'll have some music in your room. Also that music you're reading about for class—*Carmina Burana.* Hope you enjoy. Only ninety days to go!—Peck."

MALE GREEK CHORUS: September 22. A bouquet of roses. A note: "Miss you like crazy. Sixty-nine days . . ."

TEENAGE GREEK CHORUS: September 25. A box of chocolates. A card: "Don't worry about the weight gain. You still look great. Got a post office box—write to me there. Sixty-six days.—Love, your candy man."

MALE GREEK CHORUS: October 16. A note: "Am trying to get through the Jane Austen you're reading—*Emma*—here's a book in return: *Liaisons Dangereuses.* Hope you're saving time for me." Scrawled in the margin the number: "47."

FEMALE GREEK CHORUS: November 16. "Sixteen days to go!—Hope you like the perfume.—Having a hard time reaching you on the dorm phone. You must be in the library a lot. Won't you think about me getting you your own phone so we can talk?"

TEENAGE GREEK CHORUS: November 18. "Li'l Bit—got a package and returned it to the P.O. Box. Have you changed dorms? Call me at work or write to the P.O. Am still on the wagon. Waiting to see you. Only two weeks more!"

MALE GREEK CHORUS: November 23. A letter: "Li'l Bit. So disappointed you couldn't come home for the turkey. Sending you some money for a nice dinner out—nine days and counting!"

GREEK CHORUS (*In unison*): November 25th. A letter:

LI'L BIT: "Dear Uncle Peck: I am sending this to you at work. Don't come up next weekend for my birthday. I will not be here—"

(*A Voice directs:*)

Shifting Forward from Third to Fourth Gear

MALE GREEK CHORUS: December 10, 1969. A hotel room. Philadelphia. There is no moon tonight.

(PECK *sits on the side of the bed while* LI'L BIT *paces. He can't believe she's in his room, but there's a desperate edge to his happiness.* LI'L BIT *is furious, edgy. There is a bottle of champagne in an ice bucket in a very nice hotel room.*)

PECK: Why don't you sit?

LI'L BIT: I don't want to.—What's the champagne for?

PECK: I thought we might toast your birthday—

LI'L BIT—I am so pissed off at you, Uncle Peck.

PECK: Why?

LI'L BIT: I mean, are you crazy?

PECK: What did I do?

LI'L BIT: You scared the holy crap out of me—sending me that stuff in the mail—

PECK—They were gifts! I just wanted to give you some little perks your first semester—

LI'L BIT—Well, what the hell were those numbers all about! Forty-four days to go—only two more weeks.—And then just numbers—69—68—67—like some serial killer!

PECK: Li'l Bit! Whoa! This is me you're talking to—I was just trying to pick up your spirits, trying to celebrate your birthday.

LI'L BIT: My *eighteenth* birthday. I'm not a child, Uncle Peck. You were counting down to my eighteenth birthday.

PECK: So?

LI'L BIT: So? So statutory rape is not in effect when a young woman turns eighteen. And you and I both know it.

(PECK *is walking on ice.*)

PECK: I think you misunderstand.

LI'L BIT: I think I understand all too well. I know what you want to do five steps ahead of you doing it: Defensive Driving 101.

PECK: Then why did you suggest we meet here instead of the restaurant?

LI'L BIT: I don't want to have this conversation in public.

PECK: Fine. Fine. We have a lot to talk about.

LI'L BIT: Yeah. We do.

(LI'L BIT *doesn't want to do what she has to do*) Could I . . . have some of that champagne?

PECK: Of course, madam! (PECK *makes a big show of it*) Let me do the honors. I wasn't sure which you might prefer—Tattingers or Veuve Clicquot—so I thought we'd start out with an old standard—Pierrier Jouet. (*The bottle is popped*)

Quick—Li'l Bit—your glass! (UNCLE PECK *fills* LI'L BIT'*s glass. He puts the bottle back in the ice and goes for a can of ginger ale*) Let me get some of this ginger ale—my bubbly—and toast you.

(*He turns and sees that* LI'L BIT *has not waited for him.*)

LI'L BIT: Oh—sorry, Uncle Peck. Let me have another. (PECK *fills her glass and reaches for his ginger ale; she stops him*) Uncle Peck—maybe you should join me in the champagne.

PECK: You want me to—drink?

LI'L BIT: It's not polite to let a lady drink alone.

PECK: Well, missy, if you insist. . . . (PECK *hesitates*)—Just one. It's been a while. (PECK *fills another flute for himself*) There. I'd like to propose a toast to you and your birthday! (PECK *sips it tentatively*) I'm not used to this anymore.

LI'L BIT: You don't have anywhere to go tonight, do you?

(PECK *hopes this is a good sign.*)

PECK: I'm all yours.—God, it's good to see you! I've gotten so used to . . . to . . . talking to you in my head. I'm used to seeing you every week—there's so much—I don't quite know where to begin. How's school, Li'l Bit?

LI'L BIT: I—it's hard. Uncle Peck. Harder than I thought it would be. I'm in the middle of exams and papers and—I don't know.

PECK: You'll pull through. You always do.

LI'L BIT: Maybe. I . . . might be flunking out.

PECK: You always think the worst, Li'l Bit, but when the going gets tough—(LI'L BIT *shrugs and pours herself another glass*)—Hey, honey, go easy on that stuff, okay?

LI'L BIT: Is it very expensive?

PECK: Only the best for you. But the cost doesn't matter—champagne should be "sipped." (LI'L BIT *is quiet*) Look—if you're in trouble in school—you can always come back home for a while.

LI'L BIT: No—(LI'L BIT *tries not to be so harsh*)—Thanks, Uncle Peck, but I'll figure some way out of this.

PECK: You're supposed to get in scrapes, your first year away from home.

LI'L BIT: Right. How's Aunt Mary?

PECK: She's fine. (*Pause*) Well—how about the new car?

LI'L BIT: It's real nice. What is it, again?

PECK: It's a Cadillac El Dorado.

LI'L BIT: Oh. Well, I'm real happy for you, Uncle Peck.

PECK: I got it for you.

LI'L BIT: What?

PECK: I always wanted to get a Cadillac—but I thought, Peck, wait until Li'l Bit's old enough—and thought maybe you'd like to drive it, too.

LI'L BIT (*Confused*): Why would I want to drive your car?

PECK: Just because it's the best—I want you to have the best.

(*They are running out of "gas"; small talk.*)

LI'L BIT: Listen, Uncle Peck, I don't know how to begin this, but—

PECK: I have been thinking of how to say this in my head, over and over—

PECK: Sorry.

LI'L BIT: You first.

PECK: Well, your going away—has just made me realize how much I miss you. Talking to you and being alone with you. I've really come to depend on you, Li'l Bit. And it's been so hard to get in touch with you lately—the distance and—and you're never in when I call—I guess you've been living in the library—

LI'L BIT: No—the problem is, I haven't been in the library—

PECK: Well, it doesn't matter—I hope you've been missing me as much.

LI'L BIT: Uncle Peck—I've been thinking a lot about this—and I came here tonight to tell you that—I'm not doing very well. I'm getting very confused—I can't concentrate on my work—and now that I'm away—I've been going over and over it in my mind—and I don't want us to "see" each other anymore. Other than with the rest of the family.

PECK (*Quiet*): Are you seeing other men?

LI'L BIT (*Getting agitated*): I—no, that's not the reason—I—well, yes, I am seeing other—listen, it's not really anybody's business!

PECK: Are you in love with anyone else?

LI'L BIT: That's not what this is about.

PECK: Li'l Bit—you're scared. Your mother and your grandparents have filled your head with all kinds of nonsense about men—I hear them working on you all the time—and you're scared. It won't hurt you—if the man you go to bed with really loves you. (LI'L BIT *is scared. She starts to tremble*) And I have loved you since the day I held you in my hand. And I think everyone's just gotten you frightened to death about something that is just like breathing—

LI'L BIT: Oh, my god—(*She takes a breath*) I can't see you anymore, Uncle Peck.

(PECK *downs the rest of his champagne.*)

PECK: Li'l Bit. Listen. Listen. Open your eyes and look at me. Come on. Just open your eyes, honey. (LI'L BIT, *eyes squeezed shut, refuses*) All right then. I just want you to listen. Li'l Bit—I'm going to ask you this just once. Of your own free will. Just lie down on the bed with me—our clothes on—just lie down with me, a man and a woman . . . and let's . . . hold one another. Nothing else. Before you say anything else. I want the chance to . . . hold you. Because sometimes the body knows things that the mind isn't listening to . . . and after I've held you, then I want you to tell me what you feel.

LI'L BIT: You'll just . . . hold me?

PECK: Yes. And then you can tell me what you're feeling.

(LI'L BIT—*half wanting to run, half wanting to get it over with, half wanting to be held by him:*)

LI'L BIT: Yes. All right. Just hold. Nothing else.

(PECK *lies down on the bed and holds his arms out to her.* LI'L BIT *lies beside him, putting her head on his chest. He looks as if he's trying to soak her into his pores by osmosis. He strokes her hair, and she lies very still. The* MALE GREEK CHORUS *member and the* FEMALE GREEK CHORUS *member as* AUNT MARY *come into the room.*)

MALE GREEK CHORUS: Recipe for a Southern Boy:

FEMALE GREEK CHORUS (*As* AUNT MARY): A drawl of molasses in the way he speaks.

MALE GREEK CHORUS: A gumbo of red and brown mixed in the cream of his skin.

(*While* PECK *lies, his eyes closed,* LI'L BIT *rises in the bed and responds to her aunt.*)

LI'L BIT: Warm brown eyes—

FEMALE GREEK CHORUS (*As* AUNT MARY): Bedroom eyes—

MALE GREEK CHORUS: A dash of Southern Baptist Fire and Brimstone—

LI'L BIT: A curl of Elvis on his forehead—

FEMALE GREEK CHORUS (*As* AUNT MARY): A splash of Bay Rum—

MALE GREEK CHORUS: A closely shaven beard that he razors just for you—

FEMALE GREEK CHORUS (*As* AUNT MARY): Large hands—rough hands—

LI'L BIT: Warm hands—

MALE GREEK CHORUS: The steel of the military in his walk—

LI'L BIT: The slouch of the fishing skiff in his walk—

MALE GREEK CHORUS: Neatly pressed khakis—

FEMALE GREEK CHORUS (*As* AUNT MARY): And under the wide leather of his belt—

LI'L BIT: Sweat of cypress and sand—

MALE GREEK CHORUS: Neatly pressed khakis—

LI'L BIT: His heart beating Dixie—

FEMALE GREEK CHORUS (*As* AUNT MARY): The whisper of the zipper—you could reach out with your hand and—

LI'L BIT: His mouth—

FEMALE GREEK CHORUS (*As* AUNT MARY): You could just reach out and—

LI'L BIT: Hold him in your hand—

FEMALE GREEK CHORUS (*As* AUNT MARY): And his mouth—

(LI'L BIT *rises above her uncle and looks at his mouth; she starts to lower herself to kiss him—and wrenches herself free. She gets up from the bed.*)

LI'L BIT: I've got to get back.

PECK: Wait—Li'l Bit. Did you . . . feel nothing?

LI'L BIT (*Lying*): No. Nothing.

PECK: Do you—do you think of me?

(*The* GREEK CHORUS *whispers:*)

FEMALE GREEK CHORUS: Khakis—
MALE GREEK CHORUS: Bay Rum—
FEMALE GREEK CHORUS: The whisper of the—
LI'L BIT: No.

(PECK, *in a rush, trembling, gets something out of his pocket.*)

PECK: I'm forty-five. That's not old for a man. And I haven't been able to do anything else but think of you. I can't concentrate on my work—Li'l Bit. You've got to—I want you to think about what I am about to ask you.
LI'L BIT: I'm listening.

(PECK *opens a small ring box.*)

PECK: I want you to be my wife.
LI'L BIT: This isn't happening.
PECK: I'll tell Mary I want a divorce. We're not blood-related. It would be legal—
LI'L BIT: What have you been thinking! You are married to my aunt, Uncle Peck. She's my family. You have—you have gone way over the line. Family is family.

(*Quickly,* LI'L BIT *flies through the room, gets her coat*) I'm leaving. Now. I am not seeing you. Again.

(PECK *lies down on the bed for a moment, trying to absorb the terrible news. For a moment, he almost curls into a fetal position*)

I'm not coming home for Christmas. You should go home to Aunt Mary. Go home now, Uncle Peck.

(PECK *gets control, and sits, rigid*)

Uncle Peck?—I'm sorry but I have to go.

(*Pause*)

Are you all right?

(*With a discipline that comes from being told that boys don't cry,* PECK *stands upright.*)

PECK: I'm fine. I just think—I need a real drink.

(*The* MALE GREEK CHORUS *has become a bartender. At a small counter, he is lining up shots for* PECK. *As* LI'L BIT *narrates, we see* PECK *sitting, carefully and calmly downing shot glasses.*)

LI'L BIT (*To the audience*): I never saw him again. I stayed away from Christmas and Thanksgiving for years after.

It took my uncle seven years to drink himself to death. First he lost his job, then his wife, and finally his driver's license. He retreated to his house, and had his bottles delivered.

(PECK *stands, and puts his hands in front of him—almost like Superman flying*)

One night he tried to go downstairs to the basement—and he flew down the steep basement stairs. My aunt came by weekly to put food on the porch, and she noticed the mail and the papers stacked up, uncollected.

They found him at the bottom of the stairs. Just steps away from his dark room.

Now that I'm old enough, there are some questions I would have liked to have asked him. Who did it to you, Uncle Peck? How old were you? Were you eleven?

(PECK *moves to the driver's seat of his car and waits*)

Sometimes I think of my uncle as a kind of Flying Dutchman. In the opera, the Dutchman is doomed to wander the sea; but every seven years he can come ashore, and if he finds a maiden who will love him of her own free will—he will be released.

And I see Uncle Peck in my mind, in his Chevy '56, a spirit driving up and down the back roads of Carolina—looking for a young girl who, of her own free will, will love him. Release him.

(*A Voice states:*)

You and the Reverse Gear

LI'L BIT: The summer of 1962. On Men, Sex, and Women: Part III:

(LI'L BIT *steps, as an eleven year old, into:*)

FEMALE GREEK CHORUS (*As* MOTHER): It is out of the question. End of Discussion.

LI'L BIT: But why?

FEMALE GREEK CHORUS (*As* MOTHER): Li'l Bit—we are not discussing this. I said no.

LI'L BIT: But I could spend an extra week at the beach! You're not telling me why!

FEMALE GREEK CHORUS (*As* MOTHER): Your uncle pays entirely too much attention to you.

LI'L BIT: He listens to me when I talk. And—and he talks to me. He teaches me about things. Mama—he knows an awful lot.

FEMALE GREEK CHORUS (*As* MOTHER): He's a small town hick who's learned how to mix drinks from Hugh Hefner.

LI'L BIT: Who's Hugh Hefner?

(*Beat.*)

FEMALE GREEK CHORUS (*As* MOTHER): I am not letting an eleven-year-old girl spend seven hours alone in the car with a man. . . . I don't like the way your uncle looks at you.

LI'L BIT: For god's sake, mother! Just because you've gone through a bad time with my father—you think every man is evil!

FEMALE GREEK CHORUS (*As* MOTHER): Oh no, Li'l Bit—not all men. . . . We . . . we just haven't been very lucky with the men in our family.

LI'L BIT: Just because you lost your husband—I still deserve a chance at having a father! Someone! A man who will look out for me! Don't I get a chance?

FEMALE GREEK CHORUS (*As* MOTHER): I will feel terrible if something happens.

LI'L BIT: Mother! It's in your head! Nothing will happen! I can take care of myself. And I can certainly handle Uncle Peck.

FEMALE GREEK CHORUS (*As* MOTHER): All right. But I'm warning you—if anything happens, I hold you responsible.

(LI'L BIT *moves out of this scene and toward the car.*)

LI'L BIT: 1962 On the Back Roads of Carolina: The First Driving Lesson.

(*The* TEENAGE GREEK CHORUS *member stands apart on stage. She will speak all of* LI'L BIT's *lines.* LI'L BIT *sits beside* PECK *in the front seat. She looks at him closely, remembering.*)

PECK: Li'l Bit? Are you getting tired?

TEENAGE GREEK CHORUS: A little.

PECK: It's a long drive. But we're making really good time. We can take the back road from here and see . . . a little scenery. Say—I've got an idea—(PECK *checks his rearview mirror*)

TEENAGE GREEK CHORUS: Are we stopping, Uncle Peck.

PECK: There's no traffic here. Do you want to drive?

TEENAGE GREEK CHORUS: I can't drive.

PECK: It's easy. I'll show you how. I started driving when I was your age. Don't you want to?—

TEENAGE GREEK CHORUS: But it's against the law at my age!

PECK: And that's why you can't tell anyone I'm letting you do this—

TEENAGE GREEK CHORUS: But—I can't reach the pedals.

PECK: You can sit in my lap and steer. I'll push the pedals for you. Did your father ever let you drive his car?

TEENAGE GREEK CHORUS: No way.

PECK: Want to try?

TEENAGE GREEK CHORUS: Okay. (LI'L BIT *moves into* PECK*'s lap. She leans against him, closing her eyes*)

PECK: You're just a little thing, aren't you? Okay—now think of the wheel as a big clock—I want you to put your right hand on the clock where three o'clock would be; and your left hand on the nine—

(LI'L BIT *puts one hand to* PECK*'s face, to stroke him. Then, she takes the wheel.*)

TEENAGE GREEK CHORUS: Am I doing this right?

PECK: That's right. Now, whatever you do, don't let go of the wheel. You tell me whether to go faster or slower—

TEENAGE GREEK CHORUS: Not so fast, Uncle Peck!

PECK: Li'l Bit—I need you to watch the road—

*(*PECK *puts his hands on* LI'L BIT*'s breasts. She relaxes against him, silent, accepting his touch.)*

TEENAGE GREEK CHORUS: Uncle Peck—what are you doing?

PECK: Keep driving. (*He slips his hand under her blouse*)

TEENAGE GREEK CHORUS: Uncle Peck—please don't do this—

PECK: Just a moment longer . . . (PECK *tenses against* LI'L BIT)

TEENAGE GREEK CHORUS (*Trying not to cry*): This isn't happening.

(PECK *tenses more, sharply. He buries his face in* LI'L BIT*'s neck, and moans softly. The* TEENAGE GREEK CHORUS *exits, and* LI'L BIT *steps out of the car.* PECK, *too, disappears.*

A Voice reflects:)

Driving in Today's World

LI'L BIT: That day was the last day I lived in my body. I retreated above the neck, and I've lived inside the "fire" in my head ever since.

And now that seems like a long, long time ago. When we were both very young.

And before you know it, I'll be thirty-five. That's getting up there for a woman. And I find myself believing in things that a younger self vowed never to believe in. Things like family and forgiveness.

I know I'm lucky. Although I still have never known what it feels like to jog or dance. Anything like that . . . "jiggles." I do like to watch people on the dance floor, or out on the running paths, just jiggling away. And I say—good for them. (LI'L BIT *moves to the car with pleasure*)

The nearest sensation I feel—of flight in the body—I guess I feel when I'm driving. On a day like today. It's five A.M. The radio says it's going to be clear and crisp. I've got five hundred miles of highway ahead of me—and some back roads too. I filled the tank last night, and had the oil checked. Checked the tires, too. You've got to treat her . . . with respect.

First thing I do is: Check under the car. To see if any two-year-olds or household cats have crawled beneath, and strategically placed their skulls behind my back tires. (LI'L BIT *crouches*)

Nope. Then I get in the car. (LI'L BIT *does so*)

I lock the doors. And turn the key. Then I adjust the most important control on the dashboard—the radio—(LI'L BIT *turns the radio on: We hear all of the* GREEK CHORUS *overlapping, and static:*)

FEMALE GREEK CHORUS (*Overlapping*): "You were so tiny you fit in his hand—"

MALE GREEK CHORUS (*Overlapping*): "How is Shakespeare gonna help her lie on her back in the—"

TEENAGE GREEK CHORUS (*Overlapping*): —"Am I doing it right?"

(LI'L BIT *fine-tunes the radio station. A song like "Dedicated to the One I Love" or Orbison's "Sweet Dreams" comes on, and cuts off the* GREEK CHORUS.)

LI'L BIT: Ahh . . . (*Beat*) I adjust my seat. Fasten my seat belt. Then I check the right side mirror—check the left side. (*She does*) Finally I adjust the rearview mirror. (*As* LI'L BIT *adjusts the rearview mirror, a faint light strikes the spirit of* UNCLE PECK, *who is sitting in the back seat of the car. She sees him in the mirror. She smiles at him, and he nods at her. They are happy to be going for a long drive together.* LI'L BIT *slips the car into first gear; to the audience:*) And then—I floor it. (*Sound of a car taking off. Blackout*)

END OF PLAY

Topdog/Underdog SUZAN-LORI PARKS

While Suzan-Lori Parks (born 1964) had been writing plays for more than a decade, it was *Topdog/Underdog* (2001) that caught the attention of the theater-going public at large. With its inventive language and unique perspective on American history, *Topdog/Underdog* won the Pulitzer Prize in 2002.

The play involves the lives of two brothers whose now-absent father named them Lincoln and Booth. The play indeed re-enacts, in its own postmodern terms, the assassination of Abraham Lincoln by John Wilkes Booth. Both brothers engage with each other throughout the play, alternating the control relationship of topdog and underdog. Playing Three-Card Monte, a card game, while revisiting their own personal histories, these brothers at the same time are participating in a fratricidal end game.

While in college, Parks studied with James Baldwin, who encouraged her writing. Her other plays include *Imperceptible Mutabilities in the Third Kingdom* (1989), *The Death of the Last Black Man in the Entire World* (1990), *Devotees in the Garden of Love* (1992), *The America Play* (1994), *Venus* (1996), *In the Blood* (1999), and *Fucking A* (2003). They take on such issues as the re-thinking of history and the importance of writing down a racial history and memory that has long been erased or distorted. Today Parks is considered one of the freshest voices of the contemporary American stage.

THE PLAYERS

LINCOLN, *the topdog*
BOOTH (aka 3-Card), *the underdog*

AUTHOR'S NOTES: FROM THE "ELEMENTS OF STYLE"

I'm continuing the use of my slightly unconventional theatrical elements. Here's a road map.

- (*Rest*)
  Take a little time, a pause, a breather, make a transition.

- A Spell
  An elongated and heightened (Rest). *Denoted by repetition of figures' names with no dialogue. Has sort of an architectural look:*

LINCOLN
BOOTH
LINCOLN
BOOTH

This is a place where the figures experience their pure true simple state. While no action or stage business is necessary, directors should fill this moment as they best see fit.

- [*Brackets in the text indicate optional cuts for production.*]
- (*Parentheses around dialogue indicate softly spoken passages (asides; sotto voce)*).

I am God in nature; I am a weed by the wall. (Ralph Waldo Emerson
From "Circles", *Essays: First Series* (1841))

Scene I

Thursday evening. A seedily furnished rooming house room. A bed, a reclining chair, a small wooden chair, some other stuff but not much else. Booth, a black man in his early 30s, practices his 3-card monte scam on the classic setup: 3 playing cards and the cardboard playing board atop 2 mismatched milk crates. His moves and accompanying patter are, for the most part, studied and awkward.

BOOTH: Watch me close watch me close now: who-see-thuh-red-card-who-see-thuh-red-card? I-see-thuh-red-card. Thuh-red-card-is-thuh-winner. Pick-thuh-red-card-you-pick-uh-winner. Pick-uh-black-card-you-pick-uh-loser. Theres-thuh-loser, yeah, theres-thuh-black-card, theres-thuh-other-loser-and-theres-thuh-red-card, thuh-winner.

(*Rest*)

Watch me close watch me close now: 3-Card-throws-thuh-cards-lightning-fast. 3-Card-thats-me-and-Ima-last. Watch-me-throw-cause-here-I-go. One-good-pickll-get-you-in, 2-good-picks-and-you-gone-win. See-thuh-red-card-see-thuh-red-card-who-see-thuh-red-card?

(*Rest*)

Dont touch my cards, man, just point to thuh one you want. You-pick-that-card-you-pick-a-loser, yeah, that-cards-a-loser. You-pick-that-card-thats-thuh-other-loser. You-pick-that-card-you-pick-a-winner. Follow that card. You gotta chase that card. You-pick-thuh-dark-deuce-thats-a-loser-other-dark-deuces-thuh-other-loser, red-deuce, thuh-deuce-of-heartsll-win-it-all. Follow thuh red card.

(*Rest*)

Ima show you thuh cards: 2 black cards but only one heart. Now watch me now. Who-sees-thuh-red-card-who-knows-where-its-at? Go on, man, point to thuh card. Put yr money down cause you aint no clown. No? Ah you had thuh card, but you didnt have thuh heart.

(*Rest*)

You wanna bet? 500 dollars? Shoot. You musta been watching 3-Card real close. Ok. Lay the cash in my hand cause 3-Cards thuh man. Thank you, mister. This card you say?

(*Rest*)

Wrong! Sucker! Fool! Asshole! Bastard! I bet yr daddy heard how stupid you was and drank himself to death just cause he didnt wanna have nothing to do witchu! I bet yr mama seen you when you comed out and she walked away from you with thuh afterbirth still hanging from out twixt her legs, sucker! Ha Ha Ha! And 3-Card, once again, wins all thuh money!!

(*Rest*)

What? Cops looking my way? Fold up thuh game, and walk away. Sneak outa sight. Set up on another corner.

(*Rest*)

Yeah.

(*Rest*)

Having won the imaginary loot and dodged the imaginary cops, BOOTH *sets up his equipment and starts practicing his scam all over again.* LINCOLN *comes in quietly. He is a black man in his later 30s. He is dressed in an antique frock coat and wears a top hat and fake beard, that is, he is dressed to look like Abraham Lincoln. He surreptitiously walks into the room to stand right behind* BOOTH, *who, engrossed in his cards, does not notice* LINCOLN *right away.*

BOOTH: Watch me close watch me close now; who-see-thuh-red-card-who-see-thuh-red-card? I-see-thuh-red-card. Thuh-red-card-is-thuh-winner. Pick-thuh-red-card-you-pick-uh-winner. Pick-uh-black-card-you-pick-uh-loser.Theres-thuh-loser-yeah-theres-thuh-black-card, theres-thuh-other-loser-and-theres-thuh-red-card, thuh-winner. Don’t touch my cards, man, don’t—

(*Rest*)

Dont do that shit. Dont do that shit. Dont do that shit!

BOOTH, *sensing someone behind him, whirls around, pulling a gun from his pants. While the presence of* LINCOLN *doesnt surprise him, the* LINCOLN *costume does.*

BOOTH: And woah, man dont *ever* be doing that shit! Who thuh fuck you think you is coming in my shit all spooked out and shit. You pull that one more time I'll shoot you!

LINCOLN: I only had a minute to make the bus.

BOOTH: Bullshit.

LINCOLN: Not completely. I mean, its either bull or shit, but not a complete lie so it aint bullshit, right?

(*Rest*)

Put yr gun away.

BOOTH: Take off the damn hat at least.

LINCOLN *takes off the stovepipe hat.* BOOTH *puts his gun away.*

LINCOLN: Its cold out there. This thing kept my head warm.

BOOTH: I dont like you wearing that bullshit, that shit that bull that disguise that getup that motherdisfuckinguise anywhere in the vicinity of my humble abode.

LINCOLN *takes off the beard.*

LINCOLN: Better?

BOOTH: Take off the damn coat too. Damn, man. Bad enough you got to wear that shit all day you come up in here wearing it. What my women gonna say?

LINCOLN: What women?

BOOTH: I got a date with Grace tomorrow. Shes in love with me again but she dont know it yet. Aint no man can love her the way I can. She sees you in that getup its gonna reflect bad on me. She coulda seen you coming down the street. Shit. Could be standing outside right now taking her ring off and throwing it on the sidewalk.

BOOTH *takes a peek out the window.*

BOOTH: I got her this ring today. Diamond. Well, diamond-esque, but it looks just as good as the real thing. Asked her what size she wore. She say 7 so I go boost a size 6 and a half, right? Show it to her and she loves it and I shove it on her finger and its a tight fit right, so she cant just take it off on a whim, like she did the last one I gave her. Smooth, right?

BOOTH *takes another peek out the window.*

LINCOLN: She out there?

BOOTH: Nope. Coast is clear.

LINCOLN: You boosted a ring?

BOOTH: Yeah. I thought about spending my inheritance on it but— take off that damn coat, man, you make me nervous standing there looking like a spook, and that damn face paint, take it off. You should take all of it off at work and leave it there.

LINCOLN: I dont bring it home someone might steal it.

BOOTH: At least *take it off* there, then.

LINCOLN: Yeah.

(*Rest*)

LINCOLN *takes off the frock coat and applies cold cream, removing the whiteface.*

LINCOLN: I was riding the bus. Really I only had a minute to make my bus and I was sitting in the arcade thinking, should I change into my street clothes or should I make the bus? Nobody was in there today anyway. Middle of week middle of winter. Not like on weekends. Weekends the place is packed. So Im riding the bus home. And this kid asked me for my autograph. I pretended I didnt hear him at first. I'd had a long day. But he kept asking. Theyd just done Lincoln in history class and he knew all about him, he'd been to the arcade but, I dunno, for some reason he was tripping cause there was Honest Abe right beside him on the bus. I wanted to tell him to go fuck hisself. But then I got a look at him. A little rich kid. Born on easy street, you know the type. So I waited until I could tell he really wanted it, the autograph, and I told him he could have it for 10 bucks. I was gonna say 5, cause of the Lincoln connection but something in me made me ask for 10.

BOOTH: But he didnt have a 10. All he had was a penny. So you took the penny.

LINCOLN: All he had was a *20*. So I took the 20 and told him to meet me on the bus tomorrow and Honest Abe would give him the change.

BOOTH: Shit.

LINCOLN: Shit is right.

(*Rest*)

BOOTH: Whatd you do with thuh 20?

LINCOLN: Bought drinks at Luckys. A round for everybody. They got a kick out of the getup.

BOOTH: You shoulda called me down.

LINCOLN: Next time, bro.

(*Rest*)

You making bookshelves? With the milk crates, you making bookshelves?

BOOTH: Yeah, big bro, Im making bookshelves.

LINCOLN: Whats the cardboard part for?

BOOTH: Versatility.

LINCOLN: Oh.

BOOTH: I was thinking we dont got no bookshelves we dont got no dining room table so Im making a sorta modular unit you put the books in the bottom and the table top on top. We can eat and store our books. We could put the photo album in there.

BOOTH *gets the raggedy family photo album and puts it in the milk crate.*

BOOTH: Youd sit there, I'd sit on the edge of the bed. Gathered around the dinner table. Like old times.

LINCOLN: We just gotta get some books but thats great, Booth, thats real great.

BOOTH: Dont be calling me Booth no more, K?

LINCOLN: You changing yr name?

BOOTH: Maybe.

LINCOLN:

BOOTH:

LINCOLN: What to?

BOOTH: Im not ready to reveal it yet.

LINCOLN: You already decided on something?

BOOTH: Maybe.

LINCOLN: You gonna call yrself something african? That be cool. Only pick something thats easy to spell and pronounce, man, cause you know, some of them african names, I mean, ok, Im down with the power to the people thing, but, no ones gonna hire you if they cant say yr name. And some of them fellas who got they african names, no one can say they names and they cant say they names neither. I mean, you dont want yr new handle to obstruct yr employment possibilities.

BOOTH:

LINCOLN:

BOOTH: You bring dinner?

LINCOLN: "Shango" would be a good name. The name of the thunder god. If you aint decided already Im just throwing it in the pot. I brought chinese.

BOOTH: Lets try the table out.
LINCOLN: Cool.

They both sit at the new table. The food is far away near the door.

LINCOLN:
BOOTH:
LINCOLN: I buy it you set it up. Thats the deal. Thats the deal, right?
BOOTH: You like this place?
LINCOLN: Ssallright.
BOOTH: But a little cramped sometimes, right?
LINCOLN: You dont hear me complain. Although that recliner sometimes Booth, man—no Booth, right—man, Im too old to be sleeping in that chair.
BOOTH: Its my place. You dont got a place. Cookie, she threw you out. And you cant seem to get another woman. Yr lucky I let you stay.
LINCOLN: Every Friday you say *mi casa es su casa.*
BOOTH: Every Friday you come home with yr paycheck. Today is Thursday and I tell you brother, its a long way from Friday to Friday. All kinds of things can happen. All kinds of bad feelings can surface and erupt while yr little brother waits for you to bring in yr share.
(*Rest*)
I got my Thursday head on, Link. Go get the food.

LINCOLN *doesnt budge.*

LINCOLN: You dont got no running water in here, man.
BOOTH: So?
LINCOLN: You dont got no toilet you dont got no sink.
BOOTH: Bathrooms down the hall.
LINCOLN: You living in thuh Third World, fool! Hey, I'll get thuh food.

LINCOLN *goes to get the food. He sees a stray card on the floor and examines it without touching it. He brings the food over, putting it nicely on the table.*

LINCOLN: You been playing cards?
BOOTH: Yeah.
LINCOLN: Solitaire?
BOOTH: Thats right. Im getting pretty good at it.
LINCOLN: Thats soup and thats sauce. I got you the meat and I got me the skrimps.
BOOTH: I wanted the skrimps.

LINCOLN: You said you wanted the meat. This morning when I left you said you wanted the meat.

(*Rest*)

Here man, take the skrimps. No sweat.

They eat. Chinese food from styrofoam containers, cans of soda, fortune cookies. LINCOLN *eats slowly and carefully,* BOOTH *eats ravenously.*

LINCOLN: Yr getting good at solitaire?

BOOTH: Yeah. How about we play a hand after eating?

LINCOLN: Solitaire?

BOOTH: Poker or rummy or something.

LINCOLN: You know I dont touch thuh cards, man.

BOOTH: Just for fun.

LINCOLN: I dont touch thuh cards.

BOOTH: How about for money?

LINCOLN: You dont got no money. All the money you got I bring in here.

BOOTH: I got my inheritance.

LINCOLN: Thats like saying you dont got no money cause you aint never gonna do nothing with it so its like you dont got it.

BOOTH: At least I still got mines. You blew yrs.

LINCOLN:

BOOTH:

LINCOLN: You like the skrimps?

BOOTH: Ssallright.

LINCOLN: Whats yr fortune?

BOOTH: "Waste not want not." Whats yrs?

LINCOLN: "Your luck will change!"

BOOTH *finishes eating. He turns his back to* LINCOLN *and fiddles around with the cards, keeping them on the bed, just out of* LINCOLNS *sight. He mutters the 3-card patter under his breath. His moves are still clumsy. Every once and a while he darts a look over at* LINCOLN *who does his best to ignore* BOOTH.

BOOTH: ((((Watch me close watch me close now: who-see-thuh-red-card-who-see-thuh-red-card? I-see-thuh-red-card. Thuh-red-card-is-thuh-winner. Pick-thuh-red-card-you-pick-uh-winner. Pick-uh-black-card-and-you-pick-uh-loser. Theres-thuh-loser, yeah, theres-thuh-black-card, theres-thuh-other-loser-and-theres-thuh-red-card, thuh-winner! Cop C, Stick, Cop C! Go on—))))

LINCOLN: ((Shit.))

BOOTH: (((((((One-good-pickll-get-you-in, 2-good-picks-and-you-gone-win. Dont touch my cards, man, just point to thuh one you want. You-pick-that-card-you-pick-uh-loser, yeah, that-cards-uh-loser. You-pick-that-card-thats-thuh-other-loser. You-pick-that-card-you-pick-uh-winner. Follow-that-card. You-gatta-chase-that-card!)))))))

LINCOLN: You wanna hustle 3-card monte, you gotta do it right, you gotta break it down. Practice it in smaller bits. Yr trying to do the whole thing at once thats why you keep fucking it up.

BOOTH: Show me.

LINCOLN: No. Im just saying you wanna do it you gotta do it right and if you gonna do it right you gotta work on it in smaller bits, thatsall.

BOOTH: You and me could team up and do it together. We'd clean up, Link.

LINCOLN: I'll clean up—bro.

LINCOLN *cleans up. As he clears the food,* BOOTH *goes back to using the "table" for its original purpose.*

BOOTH: My new names 3-Card. 3-Card, got it? You wanted to know it so now you know it. 3-card monte by 3-Card. Call me 3-Card from here on out.

LINCOLN: 3-Card. Shit.

BOOTH: Im getting everybody to call me 3-Card. Grace likes 3-Card better than Booth. She says 3-Cards got something to it. Anybody not calling me 3-Card gets a bullet.

LINCOLN: Yr too much, man.

BOOTH: Im making a point.

LINCOLN: Point made, 3-Card. Point made.

LINCOLN *picks up his guitar. Plays at it.*

BOOTH: Oh, come on, man, we could make money you and me. Throwing down the cards. 3-Card and Link: look out! We could clean up you and me. You would throw the cards and I'd be yr Stickman. The one in the crowd who looks like just an innocent passerby, who looks like just another player, like just another customer, but who gots intimate connections with you, the Dealer, the one throwing the cards, the main man. I'd be the one who brings in the crowd, I'd be the one who makes them want to put they money down, you do yr moves and I do mines. You turn yr head and I turn the card—

LINCOLN: It aint as easy as all that. Theres—

BOOTH: We could be a team, man. Rake in the money! Sure thered be some cats out there with fast eyes, some brothers and sisters who would watch real close and pick the right card, and so thered be some days when we would lose money, but most of the days we would come out on top! Pockets bulging, plenty of cash! And the ladies would be thrilling! You could afford to get laid! Grace would be all over me again.

LINCOLN: I thought you said she was all over you.

BOOTH: She is she is. Im seeing her tomorrow but today we gotta solidify the shit twixt you and me. Big brother Link and little brother Booth—

LINCOLN: 3-Card.

BOOTH: Yeah. Scheming and dreaming. No one throws the cards like you, Link. And with yr moves and my magic, and we get Grace and a girl for you to round out the posse. We'd be golden, bro! Am I right?

LINCOLN:

LINCOLN:

BOOTH: Am I right?

LINCOLN: I dont touch thuh cards, 3-Card. I dont touch thuh cards no more.

LINCOLN:

BOOTH:

LINCOLN:

BOOTH:

BOOTH: You know what Mom told me when she was packing to leave? You was at school motherfucker you was at school. You got up that morning and sat down in yr regular place and read the cereal box while Dad read the sports section and Mom brought you yr dick toast and then you got on the damn school bus cause you didnt have the sense to do nothing else you was so into yr own shit that you didnt have the sense to feel nothing else going on. I had the sense to go back cause I was feeling something going on man, I was feeling something changing. So I—

LINCOLN: Cut school that day like you did almost every day—

BOOTH: She was putting her stuff in bags. She had all them nice suitcases but she was putting her stuff in bags.

(*Rest*)

Packing up her shit. She told me to look out for you. I told her I was the little brother and the big brother should look out after the little brother. She just said it again. That I should look out for you. Yeah. So who gonna look out for me. Not like you care. Here I am interested in an economic opportunity, willing to work hard, willing to take risks and all you can say you shiteating motherfucking pathetic limpdick uncle tom, all you can tell me is how you dont do no more what I be wanting to do. Here I am trying to earn a living and you standing in my way. YOU STANDING IN MY WAY, LINK!

LINCOLN: Im sorry.

BOOTH: Yeah, you sorry all right.

LINCOLN: I cant be hustling no more, bro.

BOOTH: What you do all day aint no hustle?

LINCOLN: Its honest work.

BOOTH: Dressing up like some crackerass white man, some dead president and letting people shoot at you sounds like a hustle to me.

LINCOLN: People know the real deal. When people know the real deal it aint a hustle.

BOOTH: We do the card game people will know the real deal. Sometimes we will win sometimes they will win. They fast they win, we faster we win.

LINCOLN: I aint going back to that, bro. I aint going back.

BOOTH: You play Honest Abe. You aint going back but you going all the way back. Back to way back then when folks was slaves and shit.

LINCOLN: Dont push me.

BOOTH:

LINCOLN:

BOOTH: You gonna have to leave.

LINCOLN: I'll be gone tomorrow.

BOOTH: Good. Cause this was only supposed to be a temporary arrangement.

LINCOLN: I will be gone tomorrow.

BOOTH: Good.

BOOTH *sits on his bed.* LINCOLN, *sitting in his easy chair with his guitar, plays and sings.*

LINCOLN: My dear mother left me, my fathers gone away
My dear mother left me and my fathers gone away
I dont got no money, I dont got no place to stay.

My best girl, she threw me out into the street

My favorite horse, they ground him into meat
Im feeling cold from my head down to my feet.

My luck was bad but now it turned to worse
My luck was bad but now it turned to worse
Dont call me up a doctor, just call me up a hearse.

BOOTH: You just made that up?
LINCOLN: I had it in my head for a few days.
BOOTH: Sounds good.
LINCOLN: Thanks.
(*Rest*)
Daddy told me once why we got the names we do.
BOOTH: Yeah?
LINCOLN: Yeah.
(*Rest*)
He was drunk when he told me, or maybe I was drunk when he told me. Anyway he told me, may not be true, but he told me. Why he named us both. Lincoln and Booth.
BOOTH: How come. How come, man?
LINCOLN: It was his idea of a joke.

Both men relax back as the lights fade.

Scene II

Friday evening. The very next day. BOOTH *comes in looking like he is bundled up against the cold. He makes sure his brother isnt home, then stands in the middle of the room. From his big coat sleeves he pulls out one new shoe then another, from another sleeve come two more shoes. He then slithers out a belt from each sleeve. He removes his coat. Underneath he wears a very nice new suit. He removes the jacket and pants revealing another new suit underneath. The suits still have the price tags on them. He takes two neckties from his pockets and two folded shirts from the back of his pants. He pulls a magazine from the front of his pants. Hes clearly had a busy day of shoplifting. He lays one suit out on* LINCOLNS *easy chair. The other he lays out on his own bed. He goes out into the hall returning with a folding screen which he sets up between the bed and the recliner creating 2 separate spaces. He takes out a bottle of whiskey and two glasses, setting them on the two stacked milk crates. He hears footsteps and sits down in the small wooden chair reading the magazine.* LINCOLN, *dressed in street clothes, comes in.*

LINCOLN: Taaaaadaaaaaaaa!

BOOTH: Lordamighty, Pa, I smells money!
LINCOLN: Sho nuff, Ma. Poppas brung home thuh bacon.
BOOTH: Bringitherebringitherebringithere.

With a series of very elaborate moves LINCOLN *brings the money over to* BOOTH.

BOOTH: Put it in my hands, Pa!
LINCOLN: I want ya tuh smells it first, Ma!
BOOTH: Put it neath my nose then, Pa!
LINCOLN: Take yrself a good long whiff of them greenbacks.
BOOTH: Oh lordamighty Ima faint, Pa! Get me muh med-sin!

LINCOLN *quickly pours two large glasses of whiskey.*

LINCOLN: Dont die on me, Ma!
BOOTH: Im fading fast, Pa!
LINCOLN: Thinka thuh children, Ma! Thinka thuh farm!
BOOTH: 1-2-3.

Both men gulp down their drinks simultaneously.

LINCOLN AND BOOTH: AAAAAAAAAAAAAAAAAAAAAH!

Lots of laughing and slapping on the backs.

LINCOLN: Budget it out man budget it out.
BOOTH: You in a hurry?
LINCOLN: Yeah. I wanna see how much we got for the week.
BOOTH: You rush in here and dont even look around. Could be a fucking. A-bomb in the middle of the floor you wouldnt notice. Yr wife, Cookie—
LINCOLN: X-wife—
BOOTH: —could be in my bed you wouldnt notice—
LINCOLN: She was once—
BOOTH: Look the fuck around please.

LINCOLN *looks around and sees the new suit on his chair.*

LINCOLN: Wow.
BOOTH: Its yrs.
LINCOLN: Shit.
BOOTH: Got myself one too.
LINCOLN: Boosted?
BOOTH: Yeah, I boosted em. Theys stole from a big-ass department store. That store takes in more money in one day than we will in our whole life. I stole and I stole generously. I got one for me and I

got one for you. Shoes belts shirts ties socks in the shoes and everything. Got that screen too.

LINCOLN: You all right, man.

BOOTH: Just cause I aint good as you at cards dont mean I cant do nothing.

LINCOLN: Lets try em on.

They stand in their separate sleeping spaces, BOOTH *near his bed,* LINCOLN *near his recliner, and try on their new clothes.*

BOOTH: Ima wear mine tonight, Gracell see me in this and *she* gonna ask me tuh marry *her.*

(*Rest*)

I got you the blue and I got me the brown. I walked in there and walked out and they didnt as much as bat an eye. Thats how smooth lil bro be, Link.

LINCOLN: You did good. You did real good, 3-Card.

BOOTH: All in a days work.

LINCOLN: They say the clothes make the man. All day long I wear that getup. But that dont make me who I am. Old black coat not even real old just fake old. Its got worn spots on the elbows, little raggedy places thatll break through into holes before the winters out. Shiny strips around the cuffs and the collar. Dust from the cap guns on the left shoulder where they shoot him, where they shoot me I should say but I never feel like they shooting me. The fella who had the gig before I had it wore the same coat. When I got the job they had the getup hanging there waiting for me. Said thuh fella before me just took it off one day and never came back.

(*Rest*)

Remember how Dads clothes used to hang in the closet?

BOOTH: Until you took em outside and burned em.

(*Rest*)

He had some nice stuff. What he didnt spend on booze he spent on women. What he didnt spend on them two he spent on clothes. He had some nice stuff. I would look at his stuff and calculate thuh how long it would take till I was big enough to fit it. Then you went and burned it all up.

LINCOLN: I got tired of looking at em without him in em.

(*Rest*)

They said thuh fella before me—he took off the getup one day, hung it up real nice, and never came back. And as they offered me thuh job, saying of course I would have to wear a little makeup and accept less than what they would offer a—another guy—

BOOTH: Go on, say it. "White." Theyd pay you less than theyd pay a white guy.

LINCOLN: I said to myself thats exactly what I would do: wear it out and then leave it hanging there and not come back. But until then, I would make a living at it. But it dont make me. Worn suit coat, not even worn by the fool that Im supposed to be playing, but making fools out of all those folks who come crowding in for they chance to play at something great. Fake beard. Top hat. Dont make me into no Lincoln. I was Lincoln on my own before any of that.

The men finish dressing. They style and profile.

BOOTH: Sharp, huh?

LINCOLN: Very sharp.

BOOTH: You look sharp too, man. You look like the real you. Most of the time you walking around all bedraggled and shit. You look good. Like you used to look back in thuh day when you had Cookie in love with you and all the women in the world was eating out of yr hand.

LINCOLN: This is real nice, man. I dont know where Im gonna wear it but its real nice.

BOOTH: Just wear it around. Itll make you feel good and when you feel good yll meet someone nice. Me I aint interested in meeting no one nice, I mean, I only got eyes for Grace. You think she'll go for me in this?

LINCOLN: I think thuh tie you gave me'll go better with what you got on.

BOOTH: Yeah?

LINCOLN: Grace likes bright colors dont she? My ties bright, yrs is too subdued.

BOOTH: Yeah. Gimmie yr tie.

LINCOLN: You gonna take back a gift?

BOOTH: I stole the damn thing didnt I? Gimmie yrs! I'll give you mines.

They switch neckties. BOOTH *is pleased.* LINCOLN *is* more *pleased.*

LINCOLN: Do thuh budget.

BOOTH: Right. Ok lets see: we got 314 dollars. We put 100 aside for the rent. 100 a week times 4 weeks makes the rent and—

LINCOLN AND BOOTH: we dont want thuh rent spent.

BOOTH: That leaves 214. We put aside 30 for the electric leaving 184. We put aside 50 for thuh phone leaving 134.

LINCOLN: We dont got a phone.

BOOTH: We pay our bill theyll turn it back on.

LINCOLN: We dont need no phone.

BOOTH: How you gonna get a woman if you dont got a phone? Women these days are more cautious, more whaddacallit, more circumspect. You go into a club looking like a fast daddy, you get a filly to give you her numerophono and gone is the days when she just gives you her number and dont ask for yrs.

LINCOLN: Like a woman is gonna call me.

BOOTH: She dont wanna call you she just doing a preliminary survey of the property. Shit, Link, you dont know nothin no more.

(*Rest*)

She gives you her number and she asks for yrs. You give her yr number. The phone number of yr home. Thereby telling her 3 things: 1) you got a home, that is, you aint no smooth talking smooth dressing *homeless* joe; 2) that you is in possession of a telephone and a working telephone number which is to say that you got thuh cash and thuh wherewithal to acquire for yr self the worlds most revolutionary communication apparatus and you together enough to pay yr bills!

LINCOLN: Whats 3?

BOOTH: You give her yr number you telling her that its cool to call if she should so please, that is, that you aint got no wife or wife approximation on the premises.

(*Rest*)

50 for the phone leaving 134. We put aside 40 for "med-sin."

LINCOLN: The price went up. 2 bucks more a bottle.

BOOTH: We'll put aside 50, then. That covers the bills. We got 84 left. 40 for meals together during the week leaving 44.30 for me 14 for you. I got a woman I gotta impress tonight.

LINCOLN: You didnt take out for the phone last week.

BOOTH: Last week I was depressed. This week things is looking up. For both of us.

LINCOLN: Theyre talking about cutbacks at the arcade. I only been there 8 months, so—

BOOTH: Dont sweat it man, we'll find something else.

LINCOLN: Not nothing like this. I like the job. This is sit down, you know, easy work. I just gotta sit there all day. Folks come in kill phony Honest Abe with the phony pistol. I can sit there and let my mind travel.

BOOTH: Think of women.

LINCOLN: Sometimes./

(*Rest*)

All around the whole arcade is buzzing and popping. Thuh whirring of thuh duckshoot, baseballs smacking the back wall when someone misses the stack of cans, some woman getting happy cause her fella just won the ring toss. The Boss playing the barker talking up the fake freaks. The smell of the ocean and cotton candy and rat shit. And in thuh middle of all that, I can just sit and let my head go quiet. Make up songs, make plans. Forget.

(*Rest*)

You should come down again.

BOOTH: Once was plenty, but thanks.

(*Rest*)

Yr Best Customer, he come in today?

LINCOLN: Oh, yeah, he was there.

BOOTH: He shoot you?

LINCOLN: He shot Honest Abe, yeah.

BOOTH: He talk to you?

LINCOLN: In a whisper. Shoots on the left whispers on the right.

BOOTH: Whatd he say this time?

LINCOLN: "Does thuh show stop when no ones watching or does thuh show go on?"

BOOTH: Hes getting deep.

LINCOLN: Yeah.

BOOTH: Whatd he say, that one time? "Yr only yrself—"

LINCOLN: "—when no ones watching," yeah.

BOOTH: Thats deep shit.

(*Rest*)

Hes a brother, right?

LINCOLN: I think so.

BOOTH: He know yr a brother?

LINCOLN: I dunno. Yesterday he had a good one. He shoots me, Im playing dead, and he leans in close then goes: "God aint nothing but a parasite."

BOOTH: Hes one *deep* black brother.

LINCOLN: Yeah. He makes the day interesting.

BOOTH:

(*Rest*)

Thats a fucked-up job you got.

LINCOLN: Its a living.

BOOTH: But you aint living.

LINCOLN: Im alive aint I?

(*Rest*)

One day I was throwing the cards. Next day Lonny died. Somebody shot him. I knew I was next, so I quit. I saved my life.

(*Rest*)

The arcade gig is the first lucky break Ive ever had. And Ive actually grown to like the work. And now theyre talking about cutting me.

BOOTH: You was lucky with thuh cards.

LINCOLN: Lucky? Aint nothing lucky about cards. Cards aint luck. Cards is work. Cards is skill. Aint never nothing lucky about cards.

(*Rest*)

I dont wanna lose my job.

BOOTH: Then you gotta jazz up yr act. Elaborate yr moves, you know. You was always too stiff with it. You cant just sit there! Maybe, when they shoot you, you know, leap up flail yr arms then fall down and wiggle around and shit so they gotta shoot you more than once. Blam Blam Blam! Blam!

LINCOLN: Help me practice. I'll sit here like I do at work and you be like one of the tourists.

BOOTH: No thanks.

LINCOLN: My paychecks on the line, man.

BOOTH: I got a date. Practice on yr own.

(*Rest*)

I got a rendezvous with Grace. Shit she so sweet she makes my teeth hurt.

(*Rest*)

Link, uh, howbout slipping me an extra 5 spot. Its the biggest night of my life.

LINCOLN:

BOOTH:

LINCOLN *gives* BOOTH *a 5er.*

BOOTH: Thanks.

LINCOLN: No sweat.

BOOTH: Howabout I run through it with you when I get back. Put on yr getup and practice till then.

LINCOLN: Sure.

BOOTH *leaves.* LINCOLN *stands there alone. He takes off his shoes, giving them a shine. He takes off his socks and his fancy suit, hanging it neatly over the little wooden chair. He takes his getup out of his shopping bag. He puts it on, slowly, like an actor preparing for a great role: frock coat, pants, beard, top hat, necktie. He leaves his feet bare. The top hat has an elastic band which he positions securely underneath his chin. He picks up the white pancake makeup but decides against it. He sits. He pretends to get shot, flings himself on the floor and thrashes around. He gets up, considers giving the new moves another try, but instead pours himself a big glass of whiskey and sits there drinking.*

Scene III

Much later that same Friday evening. The recliner is reclined to its maximum horizontal position and LINCOLN *lies there asleep. He wakes with a start. He is horrific, bleary eyed and hungover, in his full* LINCOLN *regalia. He takes a deep breath, realizes where he is and reclines again, going back to sleep.* BOOTH *comes in full of swagger. He slams the door trying to wake his brother who is dead to the world. He opens the door and slams it again. This time* LINCOLN *wakes up, as hungover and horrid as before.* BOOTH *swaggers about, his moves are exaggerated, rooster-like. He walks round and round* LINCOLN *making sure his brother sees him.*

LINCOLN: You hurt yrself?

BOOTH: I had me "an evening to remember."

LINCOLN: You look like you hurt yrself.

BOOTH: Grace Grace Grace. *Grace.* She wants me back. She wants me back so bad she wiped her hand over the past where we wasnt together just so she could say we aint never been apart. She wiped her hand over our breakup. She wiped her hand over her childhood, her teenage years, her first boyfriend, just so she could say that she been mine since the dawn of time.

LINCOLN: Thats great, man.

BOOTH: And all the shit I put her through: she wiped it clean. And the women I saw while I was seeing her—

LINCOLN: Wiped clean too?

BOOTH: Mister Clean, Mister, Mister Clean!

LINCOLN: Whered you take her?

BOOTH: We was over at her place. I brought thuh food. Stopped at the best place I could find and stuffed my coat with only the best. We had candlelight, we had music we had—

LINCOLN: She let you do it?

BOOTH: Course she let me do it.

LINCOLN: She let you do it without a rubber?

BOOTH: Yeah.

LINCOLN: Bullshit.

BOOTH: I put my foot down—and she *melted.* And she was—huh— she was something else. I dont wanna get you jealous, though.

LINCOLN: Go head, I dont mind.

BOOTH:

(*Rest*)

Well, you know what she looks like.

LINCOLN: She walks on by and the emergency room fills up cause all the guys get whiplash from lookin at her.

BOOTH: Thats right thats right. Well—she comes to the door wearing nothing but her little nightie, eats up the food I'd brought like there was no tomorrow and then goes and eats on me.

(*Rest*)

LINCOLN: Go on.

BOOTH: I dont wanna make you feel bad, man.

LINCOLN: Ssallright. Go on.

BOOTH:

(*Rest*)

Well, uh, you know what shes like. Wild. Goodlooking. So sweet my teeth hurt.

LINCOLN: Sexmachine.

BOOTH: Yeah.

LINCOLN: Hotsy-Totsy.

BOOTH: Yeah.

LINCOLN: Amazing Grace.

BOOTH: Amazing Grace! Yeah. Thats right. She let me do her how I wanted. And no rubber.

(*Rest*)

LINCOLN: Go on.

BOOTH: You dont wanna hear the mushy shit.

LINCOLN: Sure I do.

BOOTH: You hate mushy shit. You always hated thuh mushy shit.

LINCOLN: Ive changed. Go head. You had "an evening to remember," remember? I was just here alone sitting here. Drinking. Go head. Tell Link thuh stink.

(*Rest*)

Howd ya do her?

BOOTH: Dogstyle.

LINCOLN: Amazing Grace.

BOOTH: In front of a mirror.

LINCOLN: So you could see her. Her face her breasts her back her ass. Graces got a great ass.

BOOTH: Its all right.

LINCOLN: Amazing Grace!

BOOTH *goes into his bed area and takes off his suit, tossing the clothes on the floor.*

BOOTH: She said next time Ima have to use a rubber. She let me have my way this time but she said that next time I'd have to put my boots on.

LINCOLN: Im sure you can talk her out of it.

BOOTH: Yeah.

(*Rest*)

What kind of rubbers you use, I mean, when you was with Cookie.

LINCOLN: We didnt use rubbers. We was married, man.

BOOTH: Right. But you had other women on the side. What kind you use when you was with them?

LINCOLN: Magnums.

BOOTH: Thats thuh kind I picked up. For next time. Grace was real strict about it.

While BOOTH *sits on his bed fiddling with his box of condoms,* LINCOLN *sits in his chair and resumes drinking.*

LINCOLN: Im sure you can talk her out of it. You put yr foot down and she'll melt.

BOOTH: She was real strict. Sides I wouldnt wanna be taking advantage of her or nothing. Putting my foot down and her melting all over thuh place.

LINCOLN: Magnums then.

(*Rest*)

Theyre for "the larger man."

BOOTH: Right. Right.

LINCOLN *keeps drinking as* BOOTH, *sitting in the privacy of his bedroom, fiddles with the condoms, perhaps trying to put one on.*

LINCOLN: Thats right.

BOOTH: Graces real different from them fly-by-night gals I was making do with. Shes in school. Making something of herself. Studying cosmetology. You should see what she can do with a womans hair and nails.

LINCOLN: Too bad you aint a woman.

BOOTH: What?

LINCOLN: You could get yrs done for free, I mean.

BOOTH: Yeah. She got this way of sitting. Of talking. Everything she does is. Shes just so hot.

(*Rest*)

We was together 2 years. Then we broke up. I had my little employment difficulty and she needed time to think.

LINCOLN: And shes through thinking now.

BOOTH: Thats right.

LINCOLN:

BOOTH:

LINCOLN: Whatcha doing back there?

BOOTH: Resting. That girl wore me out.

LINCOLN: You want some med-sin?

BOOTH: No thanks.

LINCOLN: Come practice my moves with me, then.

BOOTH: Lets hit it tomorrow, K?

LINCOLN: I been waiting. I got all dressed up and you said if I waited up—come on, man, they gonna replace me with a wax dummy.

BOOTH: No shit.

LINCOLN: Thats what theyre talking about. Probably just talk, but—come on, man, I even lent you 5 bucks.

BOOTH: Im tired.

LINCOLN: You didnt get shit tonight.

BOOTH: You jealous, man. You just jail-us.

LINCOLN: You laying over there yr balls blue as my boosted suit. Laying over there waiting for me to go back to sleep or black out so I wont hear you rustling thuh pages of yr fuck book.

BOOTH: Fuck you, man.

LINCOLN: I was over there looking for something the other week and theres like 100 fuck books under yr bed and theyre matted together like a bad fro, bro, cause you spunked in the pages and didnt wipe them off.

BOOTH: Im hot. I need constant sexual release. If I wasnt taking care of myself by myself I would be out there running around on thuh town which costs cash that I dont have so I would be doing worse: I'd be out there doing who knows what, shooting people and shit. Out of a need for unresolved sexual release. I'm a hot man. I aint apologizing for it. When I dont got a woman, I gotta make do. Not like you, Link. When you dont got a woman you just sit there. Letting yr shit fester. Yr dick, if it aint falled off yet, is hanging there between yr legs, little whiteface shriveled-up blank-shooting grub worm. As goes thuh man so goes thuh mans dick. Thats what I say. Least my shits intact.

(*Rest*)

You a limp dick jealous whiteface motherfucker whose wife dumped him cause he couldnt get if up and she told me so. Came crawling to me cause she needed a man.

(*Rest*)

I gave it to Grace good tonight. So goodnight.

LINCOLN:

(*Rest*)

Goodnight.

LINCOLN:

BOOTH:

LINCOLN:

BOOTH:

LINCOLN:

BOOTH:

LINCOLN *sitting in his chair.* BOOTH *lying in bed. Time passes.*
BOOTH *peeks out to see if* LINCOLN *is asleep.* LINCOLN *is watching for him.*

LINCOLN: You can hustle 3-card monte without me you know.

BOOTH: Im planning to.

LINCOLN: I could contact my old crew. You could work with them. Lonny aint around no more but theres the rest of them. Theyre good.

BOOTH: I can get my own crew. I dont need yr crew. Buncha has-beens. I can get my own crew.

LINCOLN: My crews experienced. We usedta pull down a thousand a day. Thats 7 G a week. That was years ago. They probably do twice, 3 times that now.

BOOTH: I got my own connections, thank you.

LINCOLN: Theyd take you on in a heartbeat. With my say. My say still counts with them. They know you from before, when you tried to hang with us but—wernt ready yet. They know you from then, but I'd talk you up. I'd say yr my bro, which they know, and I'd say youd been working the west coast. Little towns. Mexican border. Taking tourists. I'd tell them you got moves like I dreamed of having. Meanwhile youd be working out yr shit right here, right in this room, getting good and getting better every day so when I did do the reintroductions youd have some marketable skills. Youd be passable.

BOOTH: I'd be more than passable, I'd be the be all end all.

LINCOLN: Youd be the be all end all. And youd have my say. If yr interested.

BOOTH: Could do.

LINCOLN: Youd have to get a piece. They all pack pistols, bro.

BOOTH: I *got* a piece.

LINCOLN: Youd have to be packing something more substantial than that pop gun, 3-Card. These hustlers is upper echelon hustlers they pack upper echelon heat, not no Saturday night shit, now.

BOOTH: Whata you know of heat? You aint hung with those guys for 6, 7 years. You swore off em. Threw yr heat in thuh river and you "Dont touch thuh cards." I know more about heat than you know about heat.

LINCOLN: Im around guns every day. At the arcade. Theyve all been reworked so they only fire caps but I see guns every day. Lots of guns.

BOOTH: What kinds?

LINCOLN: You been there, you seen them. Shiny deadly metal each with their own deadly personality.

BOOTH: Maybe I *could* visit you over there. I'd boost one of them guns and rework it to make it shoot for real again. What kind you think would best suit my personality?

LINCOLN: You aint stealing nothing from the arcade.

BOOTH: I go in there and steal if I want to go in there and steal I go in there and steal.

LINCOLN: It aint worth it. They dont shoot nothing but blanks.

BOOTH: Yeah, like you. Shooting blanks.

(*Rest*)

(*Rest*)

You ever wonder if someones gonna come in there with a real gun? A real gun with real slugs? Someone with uh axe tuh grind or something?

LINCOLN: No.

BOOTH: Someone who hates you come in there and guns you down and gets gone before anybody finds out.

LINCOLN: I dont got no enemies.

BOOTH: Yr X.

LINCOLN: Cookie dont hate me.

BOOTH: Yr Best Customer? Some miscellaneous stranger?

LINCOLN: I cant be worrying about the actions of miscellaneous strangers.

BOOTH: But there they come day in day out for a chance to shoot Honest Abe.

(*Rest*)

Who are they mostly?

LINCOLN: I dont really look.

BOOTH: You must see something.

LINCOLN: Im supposed to be staring straight ahead. Watching a play, like Abe was.

BOOTH: All day goes by and you never ever take a sneak peek at who be pulling the trigger.

Pulled in by his own curiosity, BOOTH *has come out of his bed area to stand on the dividing line between the two spaces.*

LINCOLN: Its pretty dark. To keep thuh illusion of thuh whole thing.

(*Rest*)

But on thuh wall opposite where I sit theres a little electrical box, like a fuse box. Silver metal. Its got uh dent in it like somebody hit it with they fist. Big old dent so everything reflected in it gets reflected upside down. Like yr looking in uh spoon. And thats where I can see em. The assassins.

(*Rest*)

Not behind me yet but I can hear him coming. Coming in with his gun in hand, thuh gun he already picked out up front when he paid his fare. Coming on in. But not behind me yet. His dress shoes making too much noise on the carpet, the carpets too thin, Boss should get a new one but hes cheap. Not behind me yet. Not behind me yet. Cheap lightbulb just above my head.

(*Rest*)

And there he is. Standing behind me. Standing in position. Standing upside down. Theres some feet shapes on the floor so he knows just where he oughta stand. So he wont miss. Thuh gun is always cold. Winter or summer thuh gun is always cold. And when the gun touches me he can feel that Im warm and he knows Im alive. And if Im alive then he can shoot me dead. And for a minute, with him hanging back there behind me, its real. Me looking at him upside down and him looking at me looking like LINCOLN. Then he shoots.

(*Rest*)

I slump down and close my eyes. And he goes out thuh other way. More come in. Uh whole day full. Bunches of kids, little good for nothings, in they school uniforms. Businessmen smelling like two for one martinis. Tourists in they theme park t-shirts trying to catch it on film. Housewives with they mouths closed tight, shooting more than once.

(*Rest*)

They all get so into it. I do my best for them. And now they talking bout replacing me with uh wax dummy. Itll cut costs.

BOOTH: You just gotta show yr boss that you can do things a wax dummy cant do. You too dry with it. You gotta add spicy shit.

LINCOLN: Like what.

BOOTH: Like when they shoot you, I dunno, scream or something.

LINCOLN: Scream?

BOOTH *plays the killer without using his gun.*

BOOTH: Try it. I'll be the killer. Bang!

LINCOLN: Aaaah!

BOOTH: Thats good.

LINCOLN: A wax dummy can scream. They can put a voicebox in it and make it like its screaming.

BOOTH: You can curse. Try it. Bang!

LINCOLN: Motherfucking cocksucker!

BOOTH: Thats good, man.

LINCOLN: They aint going for that, though.

BOOTH: You practice rolling and wiggling on the floor?

LINCOLN: A little.

BOOTH: Lemmie see. Bang!

LINCOLN *slumps down, falls on the floor and silently wiggles around.*

BOOTH: You look more like a worm on the sidewalk. Move yr arms. Good. Now scream or something.

LINCOLN: Aaaah! Aaaaah! Aaaah!

BOOTH: A little tougher than that, you sound like yr fucking.

LINCOLN: Aaaaaah!

BOOTH: Hold yr head or something, where I shotcha. Good. And look at me! I am the assassin! *I am Booth!!* Come on man this is life and death! Go all out!

LINCOLN *goes all out.*

BOOTH: Cool, man thats cool. Thats enough.

LINCOLN: Whatdoyathink?

BOOTH: I dunno, man. Something about it. I dunno. It was looking too real or something.

LINCOLN: They dont want it looking too real. I'd scare the customers. Then I'd be out for sure. Yr trying to get me fired.

BOOTH: Im trying to help. Cross my heart.

LINCOLN: People are funny about they Lincoln shit. Its historical. People like they historical shit in a certain way. They like it to unfold the way they folded it up. Neatly like a book. Not raggedy and bloody and screaming. You trying to get me fired.

(*Rest*)

I am uh brother playing Lincoln. Its uh stretch for anyones imagination. And it aint easy for me neither. Every day I put on that shit, I leave my own shit at the door and I put on that shit and I go out there and I make it work. I make it look easy but its hard. That shit is hard. But it works. Cause I work it. And you trying to get me fired.

(*Rest*)

I swore off them cards. Took nowhere jobs. Drank. Then Cookie threw me out. What thuh fuck was I gonna do? I seen that "Help Wanted" sign and I went up in there and I looked good in the getup and agreed to the whiteface and they really dug it that me and Honest Abe got the same name.

(*Rest*)

Its a sit down job. With benefits. I dont wanna get fired. They wont give me a good reference if I get fired.

BOOTH: Iffen you was tuh get fired, then, well—then you and me could—hustle the cards together. We'd have to support ourselves somehow.

(*Rest*)

Just show me how to do the hook part of the card hustle, man. The part where the Dealer looks away but somehow he sees—

LINCOLN: I couldnt remember if I wanted to.

BOOTH: Sure you could.

LINCOLN: No.

(*Rest*)

Night, man.

BOOTH: Yeah.

LINCOLN *stretches out in his recliner.* BOOTH *stands over him waiting for him to get up, to change his mind. But* LINCOLN *is fast asleep.* BOOTH *covers him with a blanket then goes to his bed, turning off the lights as he goes. He quietly rummages underneath his bed for a girlie magazine which, as the lights fade, he reads with great interest.*

Scene IV

Saturday. Just before dawn. LINCOLN *gets up. Looks around.* BOOTH *is fast asleep, dead to the world.*

LINCOLN: No fucking running water.

He stumbles around the room looking for something which he finally finds: a plastic cup, which he uses as a urinal. He finishes peeing and finds an out of the way place to stow the cup. He claws at his LINCOLN *getup, removing it and tearing it in the process. He strips down to his t-shirt and shorts.*

LINCOLN: Hate falling asleep in this damn shit. Shit. Ripped the beard. I can just hear em tomorrow. Busiest day of the week. They looking me over to make sure Im presentable. They got a slew of guys working but Im the only one they look over every day. "Yr beards ripped, pal. Sure, we'll getcha new one but its gonna be coming outa yr pay." Shit. I should quit right then and there. I'd yank off the beard, throw it on the ground and stomp it, then go strangle the fucking boss. Thatd be good. My hands around his neck and his bug eyes bugging out. You been ripping me off since I took this job and now Im gonna have to take it outa yr pay, motherfucker. Shit.

(*Rest*)

Sit down job. With benefits.

(*Rest*)

Hustling. Shit, I was good. I was great. Hell I was the be all end all. I was throwing cards like throwing cards was made for me. Made for me and me alone. I was the best anyone ever seen. Coast to coast. Everybody said so. And I never lost. Not once. Not one time. Not never. Thats how much them cards was mines. I was the be all end all. I was that good.

(*Rest*)

Then you woke up one day and you didnt have the taste for it no more. Like something in you knew—. Like something in you knew it was time to quit. Quit while you was still ahead. Something in you was telling you—. But hells no. Not Link thuh stink. So I went out there and threw one more time. What thuh fuck. And Lonny died.

(*Rest*)

Got yrself a good job. And when the arcade lets you go yll get another good job. I dont gotta spend my whole life hustling. Theres more to Link than that. More to me than some cheap hustle. More to life than cheating some idiot out of his paycheck or his life savings.

(*Rest*)

Like that joker and his wife from out of town. Always wanted to see the big city. I said you could see the bigger end of the big city with a little more cash. And if they was fast enough, faster than me, and here I slowed down my moves I slowed em way down and my Lonny, my right hand, my Stickman, spanish guy who looked white and could draw a customer in like nothing else, Lonny could draw a fly from fresh shit, he could draw Adam outa Eve just with that look he had, Lonny always got folks playing.

(*Rest*)

Somebody shot him. They dont know who. Nobody knows nobody cares.

(*Rest*)

We took that man and his wife for hundreds. No, thousands. We took them for everything they had and everything they ever wanted to have. We took a father for the money he was gonna get his kids new bike with and he cried in the street while we vanished. We took a mothers welfare check, she pulled a knife on us and we ran. She threw it but her aim werent shit. People shopping. Greedy. Thinking they could take me and they got took instead.

(*Rest*)

Swore off thuh cards. Something inside me telling me—.
But I was good.

LINCOLN:

LINCOLN:

He sees a packet of cards. He studies them like an alcoholic would study a drink. Then he reaches for them, delicately picking them up and choosing 3 cards.

LINCOLN: Still got my moves. Still got my touch. Still got my chops. Thuh feel of it. And I aint hurting no one, God. Link is just here hustling hisself.

(*Rest*)

Lets see whatcha got.

He stands over the monte setup. Then he bends over it placing the cards down and moving them around. Slowly at first, aimlessly, as if hes just making little ripples in water. But then the game draws him in. Unlike BOOTH, LINCOLNS *patter and moves are deft, dangerous, electric.*

LINCOLN: (((Lean in close and watch me now: who see thuh black card who see thuh black card I see thuh black card black cards thuh winner pick thuh black card thats thuh winner pick thuh red card thats thuh loser pick thuh other red card thats thuh other loser pick thuh black card you pick thuh winner. Watch me as I throw thuh cards. Here we go.)))

(*Rest*)

(((Who see thuh black card who see thuh black card? You pick thuh red card you pick a loser you pick that red card you pick a loser you pick thuh black card thuh deuce of spades you pick a winner who sees thuh deuce of spades thuh one who sees it never fades watch me now as I throw thuh cards. Red losers black winner follow thuh deuce of spades chase thuh black deuce. Dark deuce will get you thuh win.)))

Even though LINCOLN *speaks softly,* BOOTH *wakes and, unbeknownst to* LINCOLN, *listens intently.*

(*Rest*)

LINCOLN: ((10 will get you 20, 20 will get you 40.))

(*Rest*)

((Ima show you thuh cards: 2 red cards but only one spade. Dark winner in thuh center and thuh red losers on thuh sides. Pick uh red card you got a loser pick thuh other red card you got a loser pick thuh black card you got a winner. One good pickll get you in, 2 good picks and you gone win. Watch me come on watch me now.))

(*Rest*)

((Who sees thuh winner who knows where its at? You do? You sure? Go on then, put yr money where yr mouth is. Put yr money down you aint no clown. No? Ah, you had thuh card but you didnt have thuh heart.))

(*Rest*)

((Watch me now as I throw thuh cards watch me real close. Ok, man, you know which card is the deuce of spades? Was you watching Links lightning fast express? Was you watching Link cause he the best? So you sure, huh? Point it out first, then place yr bet and Linkll show you yr winner.))

(*Rest*)

((500 dollars? You thuh man of thuh hour you thuh man with thuh power. You musta been watching Link real close. You must be thuh man who know thuh most. Ok. Lay the cash in my hand cause Link the man. Thank you, mister. This card you say?))

(*Rest*)

((Wrong! Ha!))

(*Rest*)

((Thats thuh show. We gotta go.))

LINCOLN *puts the cards down. He moves away from the monte setup. He sits on the edge of his easy chair, but he can't take his eyes off the cards.*

Intermission

Scene V

Several days have passed. Its now Wednesday night. BOOTH *is sitting in his brand-new suit. The monte setup is nowhere in sight. In its place is a table with two nice chairs. The table is covered with a lovely tablecloth and there are nice plates, silverware, champagne glasses and candles. All the makings of a very romantic dinner for two. The whole apartment in fact takes its cue from the table. Its been cleaned up considerably. New curtains on the windows, a doily-like object on the recliner.* BOOTH *sits at the table darting his eyes around, making sure everything is looking good.*

BOOTH: Shit.

He notices some of his girlie magazines visible from underneath his bed. He goes over and nudges them out of sight. He sits back down. He notices that theyre still visible. He goes over and nudges them some more, kicking at them finally. Then he takes the spread from his bed and pulls it down, hiding them. He sits back down. He gets up. Checks the champagne on much melted ice. Checks the food.

BOOTH: Foods getting cold, Grace!! Dont worry man, she'll get here, she'll get here.

He sits back down. He goes over to the bed. Checks it for springiness. Smoothes down the bedspread. Double-checks 2 matching silk dressing gowns, very expensive, marked "His" and "Hers." Lays the dressing gowns across the bed again. He sits back down. He cant help but notice the visibility of the girlie magazines again. He goes to the bed, kicks them fiercely, then on his hands and knees shoves them. Then he begins to get under the bed to push them, but he remembers his nice clothing and takes off his jacket. After a beat he removes his pants and, in this half-dressed way, he crawls under the bed to give those telltale magazines a good and final shove. LINCOLN *comes in. At first* BOOTH, *still stripped down to his underwear, thinks its his date. When he realizes its his brother, he does his best to keep* LINCOLN *from entering the apartment.* LINCOLN *wears his frock coat and carries the rest of his getup in a plastic bag.*

LINCOLN: You in the middle of it?

BOOTH: What the hell you doing here?

LINCOLN: If yr in thuh middle of it I can go. Or I can just be real quiet and just—sing a song in my head or something.

BOOTH: The casas off limits to you tonight.

LINCOLN: You know when we lived in that 2-room place with the cement backyard and the frontyard with nothing but trash in it, Mom and Pops would do it in the middle of the night and I would always hear them but I would sing in my head, cause, I dunno, I couldnt bear to listen.

BOOTH: You gotta get out of here.

LINCOLN: I would make up all kinds of songs. Oh, sorry, yr all up in it. No sweat, bro. No sweat. Hey, Grace, howyadoing?!

BOOTH: She aint here yet, man. Shes running late. And its a good thing too cause I aint all dressed yet. Yr gonna spend thuh night with friends?

LINCOLN: Yeah.

BOOTH *waits for* LINCOLN *to leave.* LINCOLN *stands his ground.*

LINCOLN: I lost my job.

BOOTH: Hunh.

LINCOLN: I come in there right on time like I do every day and that motherfucker gives me some song and dance about cutbacks and too many folks complaining.

BOOTH: Hunh.

LINCOLN: Showd me thuh wax dummy—hes buying it right out of a catalog.

(*Rest*)

I walked out still wearing my getup.

(*Rest*)

I could go back in tomorrow. I could tell him I'll take another pay cut. Thatll get him to take me back.

BOOTH: Link. Yr free. Dont go crawling back. Yr free at last! Now you can do anything you want. Yr not tied down by that job. You can—you can do something else. Something that pays better maybe.

LINCOLN: You mean Hustle.

BOOTH: Maybe. Hey, Graces on her way. You gotta go.

LINCOLN *flops into his chair.* BOOTH *is waiting for him to move.* LINCOLN *doesnt budge.*

LINCOLN: I'll stay until she gets here. I'll act nice. I wont embarrass you.

BOOTH: You gotta go.

LINCOLN: What time she coming?

BOOTH: Shes late. She could be here any second.

LINCOLN: I'll meet her. I met her years ago. I'll meet her again

(*Rest*)

How late is she?

BOOTH: She was supposed to be here at 8.

LINCOLN: Its after 2 a.m. Shes—shes late.

(*Rest*)

Maybe when she comes you could put the blanket over me and I'll just pretend like Im not here.

(*Rest*)

I'll wait. And when she comes I'll go. I need to sit down. I been walking around all day.

BOOTH:

LINCOLN:

BOOTH *goes to his bed and dresses hurriedly.*

BOOTH: Pretty nice, right? The china thuh silver thuh crystal.

LINCOLN: Its great.

(*Rest*)

Boosted?

BOOTH: Yeah.

LINCOLN: Thought you went and spent yr inheritance for a minute, you had me going I was thinking shit, Booth—3-Card—that 3-Cards gone and spent his inheritance and the gal is—late.

BOOTH: Its boosted. Every bit of it.

(*Rest*)

Fuck this waiting bullshit.

LINCOLN: She'll be here in a minute. Dont sweat it.

BOOTH: Right.

BOOTH *comes to the table. Sits. Relaxes as best he can.*

BOOTH: How come I got a hand for boosting and I dont got a hand for throwing cards? Its sorta the same thing—you gotta be quick—and slick. Maybe yll show me yr moves sometime.

LINCOLN:

BOOTH:

LINCOLN:

BOOTH:

LINCOLN: Look out the window. When you see Grace coming, I'll go.

BOOTH: Cool. Cause youd jinx it, youd really jinx it. Maybe you being here has jinxed it already. Naw. Shes just a little late. You aint jinxed nothing.

BOOTH *sits by the window, glancing out, watching for his date.* LINCOLN *sits in his recliner. He finds the whiskey bottle, sips from it. He then rummages around, finding the raggedy photo album. He looks through it.*

LINCOLN: There we are at that house. Remember when we moved in?

BOOTH: No.

LINCOLN: You were 2 or 3.

BOOTH: I was 5.

LINCOLN: I was 8. We all thought it was the best fucking house in the world.

BOOTH: Cement backyard and a frontyard full of trash, yeah, dont be going down memory lane man, yll jinx thuh vibe I got going in here. Gracell be walking in here and wrinkling up her nose cause you done jinxed up thuh joint with yr raggedy recollections.

LINCOLN: We had some great times in that house, bro. Selling lemonade on thuh corner, thuh treehouse out back, summers spent lying in thuh grass and looking at thuh stars.

BOOTH: We never did none of that shit.

LINCOLN: But we had us some good times. That row of nails I got you to line up behind Dads car so when he backed out the driveway to work—

BOOTH: He came back that night, only time I ever seen his face go red, 4 flat tires and yelling bout how thuh white man done sabotaged him again.

LINCOLN: And neither of us flinched. Neither of us let on that itd been us.

BOOTH: It was at dinner, right? What were we eating?

LINCOLN: Food.

BOOTH: We was eating pork chops, mashed potatoes and peas. I remember cause I had to look at them peas real hard to keep from letting on. And I would glance over at you, not really glancing not actually turning my head, but I was looking at you out thuh corner of my eye. I was sure he was gonna find us out and then he woulda whipped us good. But I kept glancing at you and you was cool, man. Like nothing was going on. You was coooooool.

(*Rest*)

What time is it?

LINCOLN: After 3.

(*Rest*)

You should call her. Something mighta happened.

BOOTH: No man, Im cool. She'll be here in a minute. Patience is a virtue. She'll be here.

LINCOLN: You look sad.

BOOTH: Nope. Im just, you know, Im just—

LINCOLN: Cool.

BOOTH: Yeah. Cool.

BOOTH *comes over, takes the bottle of whiskey and pours himself a big glassful. He returns to the window looking out and drinking.*

BOOTH: They give you a severance package, at thuh job?

LINCOLN: A weeks pay.

BOOTH: Great.

LINCOLN: I blew it. Spent it all.

BOOTH: On what?

LINCOLN: —.Just spent it.

(*Rest*)

It felt good, spending it. Felt really good. Like back in thuh day when I was really making money. Throwing thuh cards all day and strutting and rutting all night. Didnt have to take no shit from no fool, didnt have to worry about getting fired in favor of some damn wax dummy. I was thuh shit and they was my fools.

(*Rest*)

Back in thuh day.

(*Rest*)

(*Rest*)

Why you think they left us, man?

BOOTH: Mom and Pops? I dont think about it too much.

LINCOLN: I dont think they liked us.

BOOTH: Naw. That aint it.

LINCOLN: I think there was something out there that they liked more than they liked us and for years they was struggling against moving towards that more liked something. Each of them had a special something that they was struggling against. Moms had hers. Pops had his. And they was struggling. We moved out of that nasty apartment into a house. A whole house. It wernt perfect but it was a house and theyd bought it and they brought us there and everything we owned, figuring we could be a family in that house and them things, them two separate things each of them was struggling against, would just leave them be. Them things would see thuh house and be impressed and just leave them be. Would see thuh job Pops had and how he shined his shoes every night before he went to bed, shining them shoes whether they needed it or not, and thuh thing he was struggling against would see all that and just let him be, and thuh thing Moms was struggling against, it would see the food on the table every night and listen to her voice when she'd read to us sometimes, the clean clothes, the buttons sewed on all right and it would just let her be. Just let us all be, just regular people living in a house. That wernt too much to ask.

BOOTH: Least we was grown when they split.

LINCOLN: 16 and 13 aint grown.

BOOTH: 16s grown. Almost. And I was ok cause you were there.

(*Rest*)

Shit man, it aint like they both one day both, together packed all they shit up and left us so they could have fun in thuh sun on some tropical island and you and me would have to grub in thuh dirt forever. They didnt leave together. That makes it different. She left. 2 years go by. Then he left. Like neither of them couldnt handle it no more. She split then he split. Like thuh whole family mortgage bills going to work thing was just too much. And I dont blame them. You dont see me holding down a steady job. Cause its bullshit and I know it. I seen how it cracked them up and I aint going there.

(*Rest*)

It aint right me trying to make myself into a one woman man just because she wants me like that. One woman rubber-wearing motherfucker. Shit. Not me. She gonna walk in here looking all hot and shit trying to see how much she can get me to sweat, how much she can get me to give her before she gives me mines. Shit.

LINCOLN:

BOOTH:

LINCOLN: Moms told me I shouldnt never get married.

BOOTH: She told me thuh same thing.

LINCOLN: They gave us each 500 bucks then they cut out.

BOOTH: Thats what Im gonna do. Give my kids 500 bucks then cut out. Thats thuh way to do it.

LINCOLN: You dont got no kids.

BOOTH: Im gonna have kids then Im gonna cut out.

LINCOLN: Leaving each of yr offspring 500 bucks as yr splitting.

BOOTH: Yeah.

(*Rest*)

Just goes to show Mom and Pops had some agreement between them.

LINCOLN: How so.

BOOTH: Theyd stopped talking to eachother. Theyd stopped *screwing* eachother. But they had an agreement. Somewhere in there when it looked like all they had was hate they sat down and did thuh "split" budget.

(*Rest*)

When Moms splits she gives me 5 hundred-dollar bills rolled up and tied up tight in one of her nylon stockings. She tells me to put it in a safe place, to spend it only in case of an emergency, and not to tell nobody I got it, not even you. 2 years later Pops splits and before he goes—

LINCOLN: He slips me 10 fifties in a clean handkerchief: "Hide this somewheres good, dont go blowing it, dont tell no one you got it, especially that Booth."

BOOTH: Theyd been scheming together all along. They left separately but they was in agreement. Maybe they arrived at the same place at the same time, maybe they renewed they wedding vows, maybe they got another family.

LINCOLN: Maybe they got 2 new kids. 2 boys. Different than us, though. Better.

BOOTH: Maybe.

Their glasses are empty. The whiskey bottle is empty too. BOOTH *takes the champagne bottle from the ice tub. He pops the cork and pours drinks for his brother and himself.*

BOOTH: I didnt mind them leaving cause you was there. Thats why Im hooked on us working together. If we could work together it would be like old times. They split and we got that room downtown. You was done with school and I stopped going. And we had to run around doing odd jobs just to keep the lights on and the heat going and thuh child protection bitch off our backs. It was you and me against thuh world, Link. It could be like that again.

LINCOLN:

BOOTH:

LINCOLN:

BOOTH:

LINCOLN: Throwing thuh cards aint as easy as it looks.

BOOTH: I aint stupid.

LINCOLN: When you hung with us back then, you was just on thuh sidelines. Thuh perspective from thuh sidelines is thuh perspective of a customer. There was all kinds of things you didnt know nothing about.

BOOTH: Lonny would entice folks into thuh game as they walked by. Thuh 2 folks on either side of ya looked like they was playing but they was only pretending tuh play. Just tuh generate excitement. You was moving thuh cards as fast as you could hoping that yr hands would be faster than yr customers eyes. Sometimes you won sometimes you lost what else is there to know?

LINCOLN: Thuh customer is actually called the "Mark." You know why?

BOOTH: Cause hes thuh one you got yr eye on. You mark him with yr eye.

LINCOLN:

LINCOLN:

BOOTH: Im right, right?

LINCOLN: Lemmie show you a few moves. If you pick up these yll have a chance.

BOOTH: Yr playing.

LINCOLN: Get thuh cards and set it up.

BOOTH: No shit.

LINCOLN: Set it up set it up.

In a flash, BOOTH *clears away the romantic table setting by gathering it all up in the tablecloth and tossing it aside. As he does so he reveals the "table" underneath: the 2 stacked monte milk crates and the cardboard playing surface.* LINCOLN *lays out the cards. The brothers are ready.* LINCOLN *begins to teach* BOOTH *in earnest.*

LINCOLN: Thuh deuce of spades is thuh card tuh watch.

BOOTH: I work with thuh deuce of hearts. But spades is cool.

LINCOLN: Theres thuh Dealer, thuh Stickman, thuh Sides, thuh Lookout and thuh Mark. I'll be thuh Dealer.

BOOTH: I'll be thuh Lookout. Lemmie be thuh Lookout, right? I'll keep an eye for thuh cops. I got my piece on me.

LINCOLN: You got it on you right now?

BOOTH: I always carry it.

LINCOLN: Even on a date? In yr own home?

BOOTH: You never know, man.

(*Rest*)

So Im thuh Lookout.

LINCOLN: Gimmie yr piece.

BOOTH *gives* LINCOLN *his gun.* LINCOLN *moves the little wooden chair to face right in front of the setup. He then puts the gun on the chair.*

LINCOLN: We dont need nobody standing on the corner watching for cops cause there aint none.

BOOTH: I'll be thuh Stickman, then.

LINCOLN: Stickman knows the game inside out. You aint there yet. But you will be. You wanna learn good, be my Sideman. Playing along with the Dealer, moving the Mark to lay his money down. You wanna learn, right?

BOOTH: I'll be thuh Side.

LINCOLN: Good.

(*Rest*)

First thing you learn is what is. Next thing you learn is what aint. You dont know what is you dont know what aint, you dont know shit.

BOOTH: Right.

LINCOLN:

BOOTH:

BOOTH: Whatchu looking at?

LINCOLN: Im sizing you up.

BOOTH: Oh yeah?!

LINCOLN: Dealer always sizes up thuh crowd.

BOOTH: Im yr Side, Link, Im on yr team, you dont go sizing up yr own team. You save looks like that for yr Mark.

LINCOLN: Dealer always sizes up thuh crowd. Everybody out there is part of the crowd. His crew is part of the crowd, he himself is part of the crowd. Dealer always sizes up thuh crowd.

LINCOLN *looks* BOOTH *over some more then looks around at an imaginary crowd.*

BOOTH: Then what then what?

LINCOLN: Dealer dont wanna play.

BOOTH: Bullshit man! Come on you promised!

LINCOLN: Thats thuh Dealers attitude. He *acts* like he dont wanna play. He holds back and thuh crowd, with their eagerness to see his skill and their willingness to take a chance, and their greediness to win his cash, the larceny in their hearts, all goad him on and push him to throw his cards, although of course the Dealer has been wanting to throw his cards all along. Only he dont never show it.

BOOTH: Thats some sneaky shit, Link.

LINCOLN: It sets thuh mood. You wanna have them in yr hand before you deal a hand, K?

BOOTH: Cool. —K.

LINCOLN: Right.

LINCOLN:

BOOTH:

BOOTH: You sizing me up again?

LINCOLN: Theres 2 parts to throwing thuh cards. Both parts are fairly complicated. Thuh moves and thuh grooves, thuh talk and thuh walk, thuh patter and thuh pitter pat, thuh flap and thuh rap: what yr doing with yr mouth and what yr doing with yr hands.

BOOTH: I got thuh words down pretty good.

LINCOLN: You need to work on both.

BOOTH: K.

LINCOLN: A goodlooking walk and a dynamite talk captivates their entire attention. The Mark focuses with 2 organs primarily: his eyes and his ears. Leave one out you lose yr shirt. Captivate both, yr golden.

BOOTH: So them times I seen you lose, them times I seen thuh Mark best you, that was a time when yr hands werent fast enough or yr patter werent right.

LINCOLN: You could say that.

BOOTH: So, there was plenty of times—

LINCOLN *moves the cards around.*

LINCOLN: You see what Im doing? Dont look at my hands, man, look at my eyes. Know what is and know what aint.

BOOTH: What is?

LINCOLN: My eyes.

BOOTH: What aint?

LINCOLN: My hands. Look at my eyes not my hands. And you standing there thinking how thuh fuck I gonna learn how tuh throw thuh cards if I be looking in his eyes? Look into my eyes and get yr focus. Dont think about learning how tuh throw thuh cards. Dont think about nothing. Just look into my eyes. Focus.

BOOTH: Theyre red.

LINCOLN: Look into my eyes.

BOOTH: You been crying?

LINCOLN: Just look into my eyes, fool. Now. Look down at thuh cards. I been moving and moving and moving them around. Ready?

BOOTH: Yeah.

LINCOLN: Ok, Sideman, thuh Marks got his eye on you. Yr gonna show him its easy.

BOOTH: K.

LINCOLN: Pick out thuh deuce of spades. Dont pick it up just point to it.

BOOTH: This one, right?

LINCOLN: Dont ask thuh Dealer if yr right, man, point to yr card with confidence.

BOOTH *points.*

BOOTH: That one.
(*Rest*)
Flip it over, man.

LINCOLN *flips over the card. It is in fact the deuce of spades.* BOOTH *struts around gloating like a rooster.* LINCOLN *is mildly crestfallen.*

BOOTH: Am I right or am I right?! Make room for 3-Card! Here comes thuh champ!

LINCOLN: Cool. Stay focused. Now we gonna add the second element. Listen.

LINCOLN *moves the cards and speaks in a low hypnotic voice.*

LINCOLN: Lean in close and watch me now: who see thuh black card who see thuh black card I see thuh black card black cards thuh winner pick thuh black card thats thuh winner pick thuh red card thats thuh loser pick thuh other red card thats thuh other loser pick thuh black card you pick thuh winner. Watch me as I throw thuh cards. Here we go.

(*Rest*)

Who see thuh black card who see thuh black card? You pick thuh red card you pick a loser you pick that red card you pick a loser you pick thuh black card thuh deuce of spades you pick a winner who sees thuh deuce of spades thuh one who sees it never fades watch me now as I throw thuh cards. Red losers black winner follow thuh deuce of spades chase thuh black deuce. Dark deuce will get you thuh win. One good pickll get you in 2 good picks you gone win. 10 will get you 20, 20 will get you 40.

(*Rest*)

Ima show you thuh cards: 2 red cards but only one spade. Dark winner in thuh center and thuh red losers on thuh sides. Pick uh red card you got a loser pick thuh other red card you got a loser pick thuh black card you got a winner. Watch me watch me watch me now.

(*Rest*)

Ok, 3-Card, you know which cards thuh deuce of spades?

BOOTH: Yeah.

LINCOLN: You sure? Yeah? You sure you sure or you just think you sure? Oh you sure you sure huh? Was you watching Links lightning fast express? Was you watching Link cause he the best? So you sure, huh? Point it out. Now, place yr bet and Linkll turn over yr card.

BOOTH: What should I bet?

LINCOLN: Dont bet nothing man, we just playing. Slap me 5 and point out thuh deuce.

BOOTH *slaps* LINCOLN *5, then points out a card which* LINCOLN *flips over. It is in fact again the deuce of spades.*

BOOTH: Yeah, baby! 3-Card got thuh moves! You didnt know lil bro had thuh stuff, huh? Think again, Link, think again.

LINCOLN: You wanna learn or you wanna run yr mouth?

BOOTH: Thought you had fast hands. Wassup? What happened tuh "Links Lightning Fast Express"? Turned into uh local train looks like tuh me.

LINCOLN: Thats yr whole motherfucking problem. Yr so busy running yr mouth you aint never gonna learn nothing! You think you something but you aint shit.

BOOTH: I aint shit, I am *The* Shit. Shit. Wheres thuh dark deuce? Right there! Yes, baby!

LINCOLN: Ok, 3-Card. Cool. Lets switch. Take thuh cards and show me whatcha got. Go on. Dont touch thuh cards too heavy just—its a light touch. Like yr touching Graces skin. Or, whatever, man, just a light touch. Like uh whisper.

BOOTH: Like uh whisper.

BOOTH *moves the cards around, in an awkward imitation of his brother.*

LINCOLN: Good.

BOOTH: Yeah. All right. Look into my eyes.

BOOTHS *speech is loud and his movements are jerky. He is doing worse than when he threw the cards at the top of the play.*

BOOTH: Watch-me-close-watch-me-close-now: who see thuh-dark-card-who-see-thuh-dark-card? I-see-thuh-dark-card. Here-it-is. Thuh-dark-card-is-thuh-winner. Pick-thuh-dark-card-and-you-pick-uh-winner. Pick-uh-red-card-and-you-pick-uh-loser. Theres-thuh-loser-yeah-theres-thuh-red-card, theres-thuh-other-loser-and-theres-thuh-black-card, thuh-winner. Watch-me-close-watch-me-close-now: 3-Card-throws-thuh-cards-lightning-fast. 3-Card-thats-me-and-Ima-last. Watch-me-throw-cause-here-I-go. See thuh black card? Yeah? Who see I see you see thuh black card?

LINCOLN: Hahahahhahahahahahahah!

LINCOLN *doubles over laughing.* BOOTH *puts on his coat and pockets his gun.*

BOOTH: What?

LINCOLN: Nothing, man, nothing.

BOOTH: *What?!*

LINCOLN: Yr just, yr just a little wild with it. You talk like that on thuh street cards or no cards and theyll lock you up, man. Shit. Reminds me of that time when you hung with us and we let you try being thuh Stick cause you wanted to so bad. Thuh hustle was so simple.

Remember? I told you that when I put my hand in my left pocket you was to get thuh Mark tuh pick thuh card on that side. You got to thinking something like Links left means my left some dyslexic shit and turned thuh wrong card. There was 800 bucks on the line and you fucked it up.

(*Rest*)

But it was cool, little bro, cause we made the money back.
It worked out cool.

(*Rest*)

So, yeah, I said a light touch, little bro. Throw thuh cards light. Like uh whisper.

BOOTH: Like Graces skin.

LINCOLN: Like Graces skin.

BOOTH: What time is it?

LINCOLN *holds up his watch.* BOOTH *takes a look.*

BOOTH: Bitch. *Bitch!* She said she was gonna show up around 8. 8-a-fucking-clock.

LINCOLN: Maybe she meant 8 *a.m.*

BOOTH: Yeah. She gonna come all up in my place talking bout how she *love* me. How she cant stop *thinking* bout me. Nother mans shit up in her nother mans thing in her nother mans dick on her breath.

LINCOLN: Maybe something happened to her.

BOOTH: Something happened to her all right. She trying to make a chump outa me. I aint her chump. I aint nobodys chump.

LINCOLN: Sit. I'll go to the payphone on the corner. I'll—

BOOTH: Thuh world puts its foot in yr face and you dont move. You tell thuh world tuh keep on stepping. But Im my own man, Link. I aint you.

BOOTH *goes out, slamming the door behind him.*

LINCOLN: You got that right.

After a moment LINCOLN *picks up the cards. He moves them around fast, faster, faster.*

Scene VI

Thursday night. The room looks empty, as if neither brother is home. LINCOLN *comes in. Hes fairly drunk. He strides in, leaving the door slightly ajar.*

LINCOLN: Taaadaaaa!

(*Rest*)
(*Rest*)

Taadaa, motherfucker. Taadaa!

(*Rest*)

Booth—uh, 3-Card—you here? Nope. Good. Just as well. Ha Ha *Ha Ha Ha*!

He pulls an enormous wad of money from his pocket. He counts it, slowly and luxuriously, arranging and smoothing the bills and sounding the amounts under his breath. He neatly rolls up the money, secures it with a rubber band and puts it back in his pocket. He relaxes in his chair. Then he takes the money out again, counting it all over again, but this time quickly, with the touch of an expert hustler.

LINCOLN: You didnt go back, Link, you got back, you got it back you got yr shit back in thuh saddle, man, you got back in business. Walking in Luckys and you seen how they was looking at you? Lucky starts pouring for you when you walk in. And the women. You see how they was looking at you? Bought drinks for everybody. Bought drinks for Lucky. Bought drinks for Luckys damn dog. Shit. And thuh women be hanging on me and purring. And I be feeling that old call of thuh wild calling. I got more phone numbers in my pockets between thuh time I walked out that door and thuh time I walked back in than I got in my whole life. Cause my shit is *back*. And back better than It was when it left too. Shoot. Who thuh man? Link. Thats right. Purrrrring all up on me and letting me touch them and promise them shit. 3 of them sweethearts in thuh restroom on my dick all at once and I was *there* my shit was there. And Cookie just went out of my mind which is cool which is very cool. 3 of them. Fighting over it. Shit Cause they knew I'd been throwing thuh cards. Theyd seen me on thuh corner with thuh old crew or if they aint seed me with they own eyes theyd heard word. Links thuh stink! Theyd heard word and they seed uh sad face on some poor sucker or a tear in thuh eye of some stupid fucking tourist and they figured it was me whod just took thuh suckers last dime, it was me who had all thuh suckers loot. They knew. They knew.

BOOTH *appears in the room. He was standing behind the screen, unseen all this time. He goes to the door, soundlessly, just stands there.*

LINCOLN: And they was all in Luckys. Shit. And they was waiting for me to come in from my last throw. Cant take too many fools in one day, its bad luck, Link, so they was all waiting in there for me to come in thuh door and let thuh liquor start flowing and thuh music start going and let thuh boys who dont have thuh balls to get nothing but a regular job and uh weekly paycheck, let them crowd around and get in somehow on thuh excitement, and make way for thuh ladies, so they can run they hands on my clothes and feel thuh magic and imagine thuh man, with plenty to go around, living and breathing underneath.

(*Rest*)

They all thought I was down and out! They all thought I was some NoCount HasBeen LostCause motherfucker. But I got my shit back. Thats right. They stepped on me and kept right on stepping. Not no more. Who thuh man?! Goddamnit, who thuh—

BOOTH *closes the door.*

LINCOLN:

BOOTH:

(*Rest*)

LINCOLN: Another evening to remember, huh?

BOOTH:

(*Rest*)

Uh—yeah, man, yeah. Thats right, thats right.

LINCOLN: Had me a memorable evening myself.

BOOTH: I got news.

(*Rest*)

What you been up to?

LINCOLN: Yr news first.

BOOTH: Its good.

LINCOLN: Yeah?

BOOTH: Yeah.

LINCOLN: Go head then.

BOOTH:

(*Rest*)

Grace got down on her knees. Down on her knees, man.
Asked *me* tuh marry *her*.

LINCOLN: Shit.

BOOTH: Amazing Grace!

LINCOLN: Lucky you, man.

BOOTH: And guess where she was, I mean, while I was here waiting for her. She was over at her house watching tv. I'd told her come over Thursday and I got it all wrong and was thinking I said Wednesday and here I was sitting waiting my ass off and all she was doing was over at her house just watching tv.

LINCOLN: Howboutthat.

BOOTH: She wants to get married right away. Shes tired of waiting. Feels her clock ticking and shit. Wants to have my baby. But dont look so glum man, we gonna have a boy and we gonna name it after you.

LINCOLN: Thats great, man. Thats really great.

BOOTH:

LINCOLN:

BOOTH: Whats yr news?

LINCOLN:

(*Rest*)

Nothing.

BOOTH: Mines good news, huh?

LINCOLN: Yeah. Real good news, bro.

BOOTH: Bad news is—well, shes real set on us living together. And she always did like this place.

(*Rest*)

Yr gonna have to leave. Sorry.

LINCOLN: No sweat.

BOOTH: This was only a temporary situation anyhow.

LINCOLN: No sweat man. You got a new life opening up for you, no sweat. Graces moving in today? I can leave right now.

BOOTH: I dont mean to put you out.

LINCOLN: No sweat. I'll just pack up.

LINCOLN *rummages around finding a suitcase and begins to pack his things.*

BOOTH: Just like that, huh? "No sweat"?! Yesterday you lost yr damn job. You dont got no cash. You dont got no friends, no nothing, but you clearing out just like that and its "no sweat"?!

LINCOLN: Youve been real generous and you and Grace need me gone and its time I found my own place.

BOOTH: No sweat.

LINCOLN: No sweat.

(*Rest*)

K. I'll spill it. I got another job, so getting my own place aint gonna be so bad.

BOOTH: You got a new job! Doing what?

LINCOLN: Security guard.

BOOTH:

(*Rest*)

Security guard. Howaboutthat.

LINCOLN *continues packing the few things he has. He picks up a whiskey bottle.*

BOOTH: Go head, take thuh med-sin, bro. You gonna need it more than me. I got, you know, I got my love to keep me warm and shit.

LINCOLN: You gonna have to get some kind of work, or are you gonna let Grace support you?

BOOTH: I got plans.

LINCOLN: She might want you now but she wont want you for long if you dont get some kind of job. Shes a smart chick. And she cares about you. But she aint gonna let you treat her like some pack mule while shes out working her ass off and yr laying up in here scheming and dreaming to cover up thuh fact that you dont got no skills.

BOOTH: Grace is very cool with who I am and where Im at, thank you.

LINCOLN: It was just some advice. But, hey, yr doing great just like yr doing.

LINCOLN:

BOOTH:

LINCOLN:

BOOTH:

BOOTH: When Pops left he didnt take nothing with him. I always thought that was fucked-up.

LINCOLN: He was a drunk. Everything he did was always half regular and half fucked-up.

BOOTH: Whyd he leave his clothes though? Even drunks gotta wear clothes.

LINCOLN: Whyd he leave his clothes whyd he leave us? He was uh drunk, bro. He—whatever, right? I mean, you aint gonna figure it out by thinking about it. Just call it one of thuh great unsolved mysteries of existence.

BOOTH: Moms had a man on thuh side.

LINCOLN: Yeah? Pops had side shit going on too. More than one. He would take me with him when he went to visit them. Yeah.

(*Rest*)

Sometimes he'd let me meet the ladies. They was all very nice. Very polite. Most of them real pretty. Sometimes he'd let me watch. Most of thuh time I was just outside on thuh porch or in thuh lobby or in thuh car waiting for him but sometimes he'd let me watch.

BOOTH: What was it like?

LINCOLN: Nothing. It wasnt like nothing. He made it seem like it was this big deal this great thing he was letting me witness but it wasnt like nothing.

(*Rest*)

One of his ladies liked me, so I would do her after he'd done her. On thuh sly though. He'd be laying there, spent and sleeping and snoring and her and me would be sneaking it.

BOOTH: Shit.

LINCOLN: It was alright.

BOOTH:

LINCOLN:

LINCOLN *takes his crumpled Abe Lincoln getup from the closet. Isnt sure what to do with it.*

BOOTH: Im gonna miss you coming home in that getup. I dont even got a picture of you in it for the album.

LINCOLN:

(*Rest*)

Hell, I'll put it on. Get thuh camera get thuh camera.

BOOTH: Yeah?

LINCOLN: What thuh fuck, right?

BOOTH: Yeah, what thuh fuck.

BOOTH *scrambles around the apartment and finds the camera.* LINCOLN *quickly puts on the getup, including 2 thin smears of white pancake makeup, more like war paint than whiteface.*

LINCOLN: They didnt fire me cause I wasnt no good. They fired me cause they was cutting back. Me getting dismissed didnt have no reflection on my performance. And I was a damn good Honest Abe considering.

BOOTH: Yeah. You look great man, really great. Fix yr hat. Get in thuh light. Smile.

LINCOLN: Lincoln didnt never smile.

BOOTH: Sure he smiled.

LINCOLN: No he didnt, man, you seen thuh pictures of him. In all his pictures he was real serious.

BOOTH: You got a new job, yr having a good day, right?

LINCOLN: Yeah.

BOOTH: So smile.

LINCOLN: Snapshots gonna look pretty stupid with me—

BOOTH *takes a picture.*

BOOTH: Thisll look great in thuh album.

LINCOLN: Lets take one together, you and me.

BOOTH: No thanks. Save the film for the wedding.

LINCOLN: This wasnt a bad job. I just outgrew it. I could put in a word for you down there, maybe when business picks up again theyd hire you.

BOOTH: No thanks. That shit aint for me. I aint into pretending Im someone else all day.

LINCOLN: I was just sitting there in thuh getup. I wasnt pretending nothing.

BOOTH: What was going on in yr head?

LINCOLN: I would make up songs and shit.

BOOTH: And think about women.

LINCOLN: Sometimes.

BOOTH: Cookie.

LINCOLN: Sometimes.

BOOTH: And how she came over here one night looking for you.

LINCOLN: I was at Luckys.

BOOTH: She didnt know that.

LINCOLN: I was drinking.

BOOTH: All she knew was you couldnt get it up. You couldnt get it up with her so in her head you was tired of her and had gone out to screw somebody new and this time maybe werent never coming back.

(*Rest*)

She had me pour her a drink or 2. I didnt want to. She wanted to get back at you by having some fun of her own and when I told her to go out and have it, she said she wanted to have her fun right here. With me.

(*Rest*)

[And then, just like that, she changed her mind.

(*Rest*)

But she'd hooked me. That bad part of me that I fight down everyday. You beat yrs down and it stays there dead but mine keeps coming up for another round. And she hooked the bad part of me. And the bad part of me opened my mouth and started promising her things. Promising her things I knew she wanted and you couldnt give her. And the bad part of me took her clothing off and carried her into thuh bed and had her, Link, yr Cookie. It wasnt just thuh bad part of me it was all of me, man,] I had her. Yr damn wife. Right in that bed.

LINCOLN: I used to think about her all thuh time but I dont think about her no more.

BOOTH: I told her if she dumped you I'd marry her but I changed my mind.

LINCOLN: I dont think about her no more.

BOOTH: You dont go back.

LINCOLN: Nope.

BOOTH: Cause you cant. No matter what you do you cant get back to being who you was. Best you can do is just pretend to be yr old self.

LINCOLN: Yr outa yr mind.

BOOTH: Least Im still me!

LINCOLN: Least I work. You never did like to work. You better come up with some kinda way to bring home the bacon or Gracell drop you like a hot rock.

BOOTH: I got plans!

LINCOLN: Yeah, you gonna throw thuh cards, right?

BOOTH: Thats right!

LINCOLN: You a double left-handed motherfucker who dont stand a chance in all get out out there throwing no cards.

BOOTH: You scared.

LINCOLN: Im gone.

LINCOLN *goes to leave.*

BOOTH: Fuck that!

LINCOLN: Yr standing in my way.

BOOTH: You scared I got yr shit.

LINCOLN: The only part of my shit you got is the part of my shit you think you got and that aint shit.

BOOTH: Did I pick right them last times? Yes. Oh, I got yr shit.

LINCOLN: Set up the cards.

BOOTH: Thought you was gone.

LINCOLN: Set it up.

BOOTH: I got yr shit and Ima go out there and be thuh man and you aint gonna be nothin.

LINCOLN: Set it up!

BOOTH *hurriedly sets up the milk crates and cardboard top.* LINCOLN *throws the cards.*

LINCOLN: Lean in close and watch me now: who see thuh black card who see thuh black card I see thuh black card black cards thuh winner pick thuh black card thats thuh winner pick thuh red card thats thuh loser pick thuh other red card thats thuh other loser pick thuh black card you pick thuh winner. Who see thuh black card who see thuh black card? You pick thuh red card you pick a loser you pick that red card you pick a loser you pick thuh black card thuh deuce of spades you pick a winner who sees thuh deuce of spades thuh one who sees it never fades watch me now as I throw thuh cards. Red losers black winner follow thuh deuce of spades chase thuh black deuce. Dark deuce will get you thuh win. 10 will get you 20, 20 will get you 40. One good pickll get you in 2 good picks and you gone win.

(*Rest*)

Ok, man, wheres thuh black deuce?

BOOTH *points to a card.* LINCOLN *flips it over. It is the deuce of spades.*

BOOTH: Who thuh man?!

LINCOLN *turns over the other 2 cards, looking at them confusedly.*

LINCOLN: Hhhhh.

BOOTH: Who thuh man, Link?! Huh? Who thuh man, Link?!?!

LINCOLN: You thuh man, man.

BOOTH: I got yr shit down.

LINCOLN: Right.

BOOTH: "Right"? All you saying is "right"?

(*Rest*)

You was out on the street throwing. Just today. Werent you? You wasnt gonna tell me.

LINCOLN: Tell you what?

BOOTH: That you was out throwing.

LINCOLN: I was gonna tell you, sure. Cant go and leave my little bro out thuh loop, can I? Didnt say nothing cause I thought you heard. Did all right today but Im still rusty, I guess. But hey—yr getting good.

BOOTH: But I'll get out there on thuh street and still fuck up, wont I?

LINCOLN: You seem pretty good, bro.

BOOTH: You gotta do it for real, man.

LINCOLN: I am doing it for real. And yr getting good.

BOOTH: I dunno. It didnt feel real. Kinda felt—well it didnt feel real.

LINCOLN: We're missing the essential elements. The crowd, the street, thuh traffic sounds, all that.

BOOTH: We missing something else too, thuh thing thatll really make it real.

LINCOLN: Whassat, bro?

BOOTH: Thuh cash. Its just bullshit without thuh money. Put some money down on thuh table then itd be real, then youd do it for real, then I'd win it for real.

(*Rest*)

And dont be looking all glum like that. I know you got money. A whole pocketful. Put it down.

LINCOLN:

BOOTH:

BOOTH: You scared of losing it to thuh man, chump? Put it down, less you think thuh kid who got two left hands is gonna give you uh left hook. Put it down, bro, put it down.

LINCOLN *takes the roll of bills from his pocket and places it on the table.*

BOOTH: How much you got there?

LINCOLN: 500 bucks.

BOOTH: Cool.

(*Rest*)

Ready?

LINCOLN: Does it feel real?

BOOTH: Yeah. Clean slate. Take it from the top. "One good pickll get you in 2 good picks and you gone win."

(*Rest*)

Go head.

LINCOLN: Watch me now:

BOOTH: Woah, man, woah.

(*Rest*)

You think Ima chump.

LINCOLN: No I dont.

BOOTH: You aint going full out.

LINCOLN: I was just getting started.

BOOTH: But when you got good and started you wasnt gonna go full out. You wasnt gonna go all out. You was gonna do thuh pussy shit, not thuh real shit.

LINCOLN: I put my money down. Money makes it real.

BOOTH: But not if I dont put no money down tuh match it.

LINCOLN: You dont got no money.

BOOTH: I got money!

LINCOLN: You aint worked in years. You dont got shit.

BOOTH: I got money.

LINCOLN: Whatcha been doing, skimming off my weekly paycheck and squirreling it away?

BOOTH: I got money.

(*Rest*)

They stand there sizing each other up. BOOTH *breaks away, going over to his hiding place from which he gets an old nylon stocking with money in the toe, a knot holding the money secure.*

LINCOLN:

BOOTH:

BOOTH: You know she was putting her stuff in plastic bags? She was just putting her stuff in plastic bags not putting but shoving. She was shoving her stuff in plastic bags and I was standing in thuh doorway watching her and she was so busy shoving thuh shit she didnt see me. "I aint made of money," thats what he always saying. The guy she had on the side. I would catch them together sometimes. Thuh first time I cut school I got tired of hanging out so I goes home—figured I could tell Mom I was sick and cover my ass. Come in thuh house real slow cause Im sick and moving slow and quiet. He had her bent over. They both had all they clothes on like they was about to do something like go out dancing cause they was dressed to thuh 9s but at thuh last minute his pants had fallen down and her dress had flown up and theyd ended up doing something else.

(*Rest*)

They didnt see me come in, they didnt see me watching them, they didnt see me going out. That was uh Thursday. Something told me tuh cut school thuh next Thursday and sure enough—. He was her Thursday man. Every Thursday. Yeah. And Thursday nights she was always all cleaned up and fresh and smelling nice. Serving up dinner. And Pops would grab her cause she was all bright and she would look at me, like she didnt know that I knew but she was asking me not to tell nohow. She was asking me to—oh who knows.

(*Rest*)

She was talking with him one day, her sideman, her Thursday dude, her backdoor man, she needed some money for something, thered been some kind of problem some kind of mistake had been made some kind of mistake that needed cleaning up and she was asking Mr. Thursday for some money to take care of it. "I aint made of money," he says. He was putting his foot down. And then there she was 2 months later not showing yet, maybe she'd got rid of it maybe she hadnt maybe she'd stuffed it along with all her other things in them plastic bags while he waited outside in thuh car with thuh motor running. She musta known I was gonna walk in on her this time cause she had my payoff—my *inheritance*—she had it all ready for me. 500 dollars in a nylon stocking. Huh.

He places the stuffed nylon stocking on the table across from LINCOLNS *money roll.*

BOOTH: Now its real.

LINCOLN: Dont put that down.

BOOTH: Throw thuh cards.

LINCOLN: I dont want to play.

BOOTH: Throw thuh fucking cards, man!!

LINCOLN:

(*Rest*)

2 red cards but only one black. Pick thuh black you pick thuh winner. All thuh cards are face down you point out thuh cards and then you move them around. Now watch me now, now watch me real close. Put thuh winning deuce down in the center put thuh loser reds on either side then you just move thuh cards around. Move them slow or move them fast, Links thuh king he gonna last.

(*Rest*)

Wheres thuh deuce of spades?

BOOTH *chooses a card and chooses correctly*

BOOTH: HA!

LINCOLN: One good pickll get you in 2 good picks and you gone win.

BOOTH: I know man I know.

LINCOLN: Im just doing thuh talk.

BOOTH: Throw thuh fucking cards!

LINCOLN *throws the cards.*

LINCOLN: Lean in close and watch me now: who see thuh black card who see thuh black card I see thuh black card black cards thuh winner pick thuh black card thats thuh winner pick thuh red card thats thuh loser pick thuh other red card thats thuh other loser pick thuh black card you pick thuh winner. Watch me as I throw thuh cards. Here we go.

(*Rest*)

Ima show you thuh cards: 2 red cards but only one spade. Dark winner in thuh center and thuh red losers on thuh sides. Pick uh red card you got a loser pick thuh other red card you got a loser pick thuh black card you got a winner. Watch me watch me watch me now.

(*Rest*)

Who see thuh black card who see thuh black card? You pick thuh red card you pick a loser you pick that red card you pick a loser you pick thuh black card thuh deuce of spades you pick a winner who sees thuh deuce of spades thuh one who sees it never fades watch me now as I throw thuh cards. Red losers black winner follow thuh deuce of spades chase thuh black deuce. Dark deuce will get you thuh win.

(*Rest*)

Ok, 3-Card, you know which cards thuh deuce of spades? This is for real now, man. You pick wrong Im in yr wad and I keep mines.

BOOTH: I pick right I got yr shit.

LINCOLN: Yeah.

BOOTH: Plus I beat you for real.

LINCOLN: Yeah.

(*Rest*)

You think we're really brothers?

BOOTH: Huh?

LINCOLN: I know we *brothers*, but is we really brothers, you know, blood brothers or not, you and me, whatduhyathink?

BOOTH: I think we're brothers.

BOOTH:

LINCOLN:

BOOTH:

LINCOLN:

BOOTH:

LINCOLN:

LINCOLN: Go head man, wheres thuh deuce?

In a flash BOOTH *points out a card.*

LINCOLN: You sure?

BOOTH: Im sure!

LINCOLN: Yeah? Dont touch thuh cards, now.

BOOTH: Im sure.

The 2 brothers lock eyes. LINCOLN *turns over the card that* BOOTH *selected and* BOOTH, *in a desperate break of concentration, glances down to see that he has chosen the wrong card.*

LINCOLN: Deuce of hearts, bro. Im sorry. Thuh deuce of spades was this one.

(*Rest*)

I guess all this is mines.

He slides the money toward himself.

LINCOLN: You were almost right. Better luck next time.

(*Rest*)

Aint yr fault if yr eyes aint fast. And you cant help it if you got 2 left hands, right? Throwing cards aint thuh whole world. You got other shit going for you. You got Grace.

BOOTH: Right.

LINCOLN: Whassamatter?

BOOTH: Mm.

LINCOLN: Whatsup?

BOOTH: Nothing.

LINCOLN:

(*Rest*)

It takes a certain kind of understanding to be able to play this game.

(*Rest*)

I still got thuh moves, dont I?

BOOTH: Yeah you still got thuh moves.

LINCOLN *cant help himself. He chuckles.*

LINCOLN: I aint laughing at you, bro, Im just laughing. Shit there is so much to this game. This game is—there is just so much to it.

LINCOLN, *still chuckling, flops down in the easy chair. He takes up the nylon stocking and fiddles with the knot.*

LINCOLN: Woah, she sure did tie this up tight, didnt she?

BOOTH: Yeah. I aint opened it since she gived it to me.

LINCOLN: Yr kidding. 500 and you aint never opened it? Shit. Sure is tied tight. She said heres 500 bucks and you didnt undo thuh knot to get a look at the cash? You aint needed to take a peek in all these years? Shit. I woulda opened it right away. Just a little peek.

BOOTH: I been saving it.

(*Rest*)

Oh, dont open it, man.

LINCOLN: How come?

BOOTH: You won it man, you dont gotta go opening it.

LINCOLN: We gotta see whats in it.

BOOTH: We *know* whats in it. Dont open it.

LINCOLN: You are a chump, bro. There could be millions in here! There could be nothing! I'll open it.

BOOTH: Dont.

LINCOLN:

BOOTH:

(*Rest*)

LINCOLN: Shit this knot aint coming out. I could cut it, but that would spoil the whole effect, wouldnt it? Shit. Sorry. I aint laughing at you Im just laughing. Theres so much about those cards. You think you can learn them just by watching and just by playing but there is more to them cards than that. And—. Tell me something, Mr. 3-Card, she handed you this stocking and she said there was money in it and then she split and you say you didnt open it. Howd you know she was for real?

BOOTH: She was for real.

LINCOLN: How you know? She coulda been jiving you, bro. Jiving you that there really *was* money in this thing. Jiving you big time. Its like thuh cards. And ooooh you certainly was persistent. But you was in such a hurry to learn thuh last move that you didnt bother learning thuh first one. That was yr mistake. Cause its thuh first move that separates thuh Player from thuh Played. And thuh first move is to know that there aint no winning. It may look like you got a chance but the only time you pick right is when thuh man lets you. And when its thuh real deal, when its thuh real fucking deal, bro, and thuh moneys on thuh line, thats when thuh man wont want you picking right. He will want you picking wrong so he will make you pick wrong. Wrong wrong wrong. Ooooh, you thought you was finally happening, didnt you? You thought yr ship had come in or some shit, huh? Thought you was uh Player. But I played you, bro.

BOOTH: Fuck you. Fuck you FUCK YOU *FUCK YOU*!!

LINCOLN: Whatever, man. Damn this knot is tough. Ima cut it.

LINCOLN *reaches in his boot, pulling out a knife. He chuckles all the while.*

LINCOLN: Im not laughing at you, bro, Im just laughing.

BOOTH *chuckles with him.* LINCOLN *holds the knife high, ready to cut the stocking.*

LINCOLN: Turn yr head. You may not wanna look.

BOOTH *turns away slightly. They both continue laughing.* LINCOLN *brings the knife down to cut the stocking.*

BOOTH: I popped her.

LINCOLN: Huh?

BOOTH: Grace. I popped her. Grace.

(*Rest*)

Who thuh fuck she think she is doing me like she done? Telling me I dont got nothing going on. I showed her what I got going on. Popped her good. Twice. 3 times. Whatever.

(*Rest*)

She aint dead.

(*Rest*)

She werent wearing my ring I gived her. Said it was too small. Fuck that. Said it hurt her. Fuck that. Said she was into bigger things. *Fuck* that. Shes alive not to worry, she aint going out that easy, shes alive shes shes—.

LINCOLN: Dead. Shes—

BOOTH: Dead.

LINCOLN: Ima give you back yr stocking, man. Here, bro—

BOOTH: Only so long I can stand that little brother shit. Can only take it so long. Im telling you—

LINCOLN: Take it back, man—

BOOTH: That little bro shit had to go—

LINCOLN: Cool—

BOOTH: Like Booth went—

LINCOLN: Here, 3-Card—

BOOTH: That Booth shit is over. 3-Cards thuh man now—

LINCOLN: Ima give you yr stocking back, 3-Card—

BOOTH: Who thuh man now, huh? Who thuh man now?! Think you can fuck with me, motherfucker think again motherfucker think again! Think you can take me like Im just some chump some two lefthanded pussy dickbreath chump who you can take and then go laugh at. Aint laughing at me you was just laughing bunch uh bullshit and you know it.

LINCOLN: Here. Take it.

BOOTH: I aint gonna be needing it. Go on. You won it you open it.

LINCOLN: No thanks.

BOOTH: Open it open it open it open it. *OPEN IT!!!!*

(*Rest*)

Open it up, bro.

LINCOLN:

BOOTH:

LINCOLN *brings the knife down to cut the stocking. In a flash,* BOOTH *grabs* LINCOLN *from behind. He pulls his gun and thrusts it into the left side of* LINCOLNS *neck. They stop there poised.*

LINCOLN: Dont.

BOOTH *shoots* LINCOLN. LINCOLN *slumps forward, falling out of his chair and onto the floor. He lies there dead.* BOOTH *paces back and forth, like a panther in a cage, holding his gun.*

BOOTH: Think you can take my shit? My shit. That shit was mines. I kept it. Saved it. All this while. Through thick and through thin. Through fucking thick and through fucking thin, motherfucker. And you just gonna come up in here and mock my shit and call me two lefthanded talking bout how she coulda been jiving me then go steal from me? My *inheritance.* You stole my *inheritance,* man. That aint right. That aint right and you know it. You had yr own. And you blew it. You *blew* it, motherfucker! I saved mines and you blew yrs. Thinking you all that and blew yr shit. And I *saved* mines.

(*Rest*)

You aint gonna be needing yr fucking money-roll no more, dead motherfucker, so I will pocket it thank you.

(*Rest*)

Watch me close watch me close now: Ima go out there and make a name for myself that dont have nothing to do with you. And 3-Cards gonna be in everybodys head and in everybodys mouth like Link was.

(*Rest*)

Ima take back my inheritance too. It was mines anyhow. Even when you stole it from me it was still mines cause she gave it to me. She didnt give it to you. And I been saving it all this while.

He bends to pick up the money-filled stocking. Then he just crumples. As he sits beside LINCOLNS *body, the money-stocking falls away.* BOOTH *holds* LINCOLNS *body, hugging him close. He sobs.*

BOOTH: *AAAAAAAAAAAAAAAAAAAAH!*

END OF PLAY

APPENDIXES

GLOSSARY OF DRAMATIC TERMS

Act. A major division in the action of a play. The act is also textually unique to drama. While some earlier plays were divided into four or five acts by the playwrights, today one-, two-, and three-act plays are preferred by most dramatists.

Action. What drives the play; the key events that animate the plot.

Agon. The Greek word for *contest.* In Greek tragedy the *agon* was often a formal debate in which the **chorus** divided and took the sides of the major characters and their respective arguments.

Allegory. A literary work that is coherent on at least two levels simultaneously: a literal level consisting of recognizable characters and events and an allegorical level in which the literal characters and events represent moral, political, religious, or other ideas and meanings.

Alternative theater. Any theater—most often political or experimental that sets itself up in opposition to the **conventions** of the mainstream theater of its time. In the United States this mainstream theater is often associated with Broadway.

Anagnorisis. Greek word for a character's discovery or recognition of someone or something previously unknown. *Anagnorisis* often triggers a reversal of fortune (see **peripeteia**).

Antagonist. A character or force in conflict with the **protagonist.** The antagonist is often another character but may also be an intangible force such as nature or society. The dramatic conflict can also take the form of a struggle with the protagonist's own character.

Anticlimax. See **plot.**

Antihero. A character playing a hero's part but lacking the grandeur typically associated with a **hero.** Such a character may be comic or may exist to force the audience to reconsider its notions of heroism.

Antimasque. See **masque.**

Antistrophe. The second of the three parts of the verse ode sung by the **chorus** in Greek drama. While singing the **strophe** the chorus moves in a dance rhythm from right to left, and during the antistrophe it moves from left to right back to its original position. The third part, the **epode,** was sung standing still.

Aside. A short speech made by a character to the audience which, by **convention**, the other characters on stage cannot hear.

Avant-garde. Literally, the "advance guard"; the term usually refers to the most innovative, experimental, or unorthodox artists in a given historical period. The term is invoked mainly to describe selected plays from the late nineteenth through the twentieth century.

Black comedy. See **comedy.**

Blank verse. An unrhymed verse form often used in writing drama. Blank verse is composed of ten-syllable lines accented on the second, fourth, sixth, eighth, and tenth syllables (**iambic pentameter**).

Bombast. A loud, pompous speech whose inflated diction is disproportionate to the subject matter it expresses.

Bourgeois drama. Drama that treats middle-class subject matter or characters rather than the lives of the rich and powerful.

Bunraku. Japanese puppet theater, developed in the 1600s and 1700s, in which the puppeteers work in full view of the audience, and work with four-foot-tall puppets.

Catastrophe. See **plot.**

Catharsis. The feeling of intense emotional purgation or release that, according to Aristotle, an audience should feel after watching a tragedy.

Character. Any person appearing in a drama or narrative.

Characterization. The process by which writer and actor make a character distinct and believable to an audience. One of the six **elements** of drama identified by Aristotle.

- **Stock character.** A stereotypical character type whose behavior, qualities, or beliefs conform to familiar dramatic **conventions,** such as the clever servant or the braggart soldier. (Also called *type character.*)

Choragos. An influential citizen chosen to pay for the training and costuming of the **chorus** in Greek drama competitions. He probably also paid for the musicians and met other financial production demands not paid for by the state. ***Choragos*** also refers to the leader of the chorus.

Chorus. A masked group that sang and danced in Greek tragedy. The chorus usually chanted in unison, offering advice and commentary on the action but rarely participating. See also **strophe, antistrophe,** and **epode.**

City Dionysia (also called Great or Greater Dionysia). The most important of the four Athenian festivals in honor of Dionysus. This spring festival sponsored the first tragedy competitions; comedy was associated with the winter festival, the Lenaea.

Climax. See **plot.**

Comedy. A type of drama intended to interest and amuse rather than to concern the audience deeply. Although characters experience various discomfitures, the audience feels confident that they will overcome their ill fortune and find happiness at the end.

- **Black comedy.** A type of comedy in which the traditional material of tragedy (that is, suffering or even death) is staged to provoke (sometimes satiric) laughter.
- **Comedy of humors.** Form of comedy developed by Ben Jonson in the seventeenth century in which characters' actions are determined by the preponderance in their systems of one of the four bodily fluids or humors—blood, phlegm, choler (yellow bile), and melancholy (black bile). Characters' dispositions are exaggerated and stereotyped; common types are the melancholic and the belligerent bully.
- **Comedy of manners.** Realistic, often satiric comedy concerned with the manners and conventions of high society. Usually refers to the Restoration comedies of late seventeenth-century England, which feature witty dialogue or **repartee.**
- **Drawing room comedy.** A type of comedy of manners concerned with life in polite society. The action generally takes place in a drawing room.
- **Farce.** A short dramatic work that depends on exaggerated, improbable situations, incongruities, coarse wit, and horseplay for its comic effect.
- **High comedy.** Comedy that appeals to the intellect, often focusing on the pretensions, foolishness, and incongruity of human action. Comedy of manners with its witty dialogue is a type of high comedy.
- **Low comedy.** Comedy that lacks the intellectual appeal of **high comedy,** depending instead on jokes for its comedic impact.
- **New Comedy.** Emerging between the fourth and third centuries BC in ancient Greece, New Comedy replaced the farcical **Old Comedy.** New Comedy, usually associated with Meander, is witty and intellectually engaging; it is often thought of as the first high comedy.
- **Old Comedy.** Greek comedy of the fifth century that uses stock characters and bawdy farce to attack satirically social, religious, and political institutions. Old Comedy is usually associated with Aristophanes.
- **Sentimental comedy.** Comedy populated by stereotypical virtuous **protagonists** and villainous antagonists that resolves the domestic trials of middle-class people in a happy ending.

- **Slapstick. Low comedy** that involves little plot or character development but lots of physical horseplay and/or practical jokes.

Comic relief. The use of funny characters, speeches, or scenes in an otherwise serious or tragic drama.

Commedia dell'arte. Italian **low comedy** dating from around the mid-sixteenth century in which professional actors playing stock characters improvised dialogue to fit a given scenario.

Complication. See **plot.**

Confidant. A character, major or minor, to whom another character confides secrets so that the audience can "overhear" the transaction and be apprised of unseen events.

Conflict. See **plot.**

Convention. Any feature of a literary work that has become standardized over time, such as the **aside** or the **stock character.**

Cosmic irony. See **irony.**

Cycle. A group of medieval **mystery plays** written in the vernacular (in English rather than Latin) for performance outside the church. Cycles, each of which treated biblical stories from creation through the last judgment, are named after the town in which they were produced

Decorum. A quality that exists when the style of a work is appropriate to the speaker, the occasion, and the subject matter. Kings should speak in a "high style" and clowns in a "low style," according to many Renaissance authors.

Denouement. See **plot.**

Deus ex machina. Latin for "a god out of a machine." In Greek drama, a mechanical device that could lower "gods" onto the stage to solve the seemingly unsolvable problems of mortal characters. Also used to describe a playwright's use of a forced or improbable solution to plot complications—for example, the discovery of a lost will or inheritance that will pay off the evil landlord.

Dialogue. Spoken interchange or conversation between two or more characters. Also see **soliloquy.**

Diction. One of the six elements of drama identified by Aristotle, diction involves how the actors deliver the language of the play.

Dionysus. Greek nature god of wine, mystic revelry, and irrational impulse. Greek tragedy, many historians feel, came from dramatized ritual choral celebrations in his honor.

Domestic tragedy. See **tragedy.**

Double plot. See **plot.**

Drama. A play written in prose or verse that tells a story through **dialogue** and actions performed by actors impersonating the characters of the story. The primary difference between drama and **theater** is that drama refers to the written text of the play and theater refers to that play in live performance.

Dramatic illusion. The illusion of reality created by drama and accepted by the audience for the duration of the play.

Dramatic irony. See **irony.**

Drawing room comedy. See **comedy.**

Elements of drama. The six essential features identified by Aristotle in the *Poetics* as keys to successful drama. They are **plot, characterization, theme, diction, melody,** and **spectacle.**

Empathy. The sense of feeling *with* a character. This is different from sympathy, which is feeling *for* a character.

Epic Theater. A type of theater first associated with German director Erwin Piscator (1893–1966). Bertolt Brecht (1898–1956) used the term to distinguish his own theater from the "dramatic" theater that created the illusion of reality and invited the audience to identify and empathize with the characters. Brecht criticized the dramatic theater for encouraging the audience to believe that social conditions were "natural" and therefore unchangeable. According to Brecht, the theater should show human beings as dependent on certain political and economic factors and at the same time as capable of altering them. Epic theater calls attention to itself as theater, bringing the stage lights in front of the curtain and interrupting the linear flow of the action to help the audience analyze the action and characters onstage.

Epilogue. A final speech added to the end of a play.

Episode. In Greek drama, the scenes of dialogue that occur between the choral odes. Today, it is any small unit of drama that has its own completeness and internal unity.

Epode. The third of three parts of the verse ode sung by the **chorus** in a Greek drama. The epode follows the **strophe** and **antistrophe.**

Exodos. The concluding scene of a Greek drama, which includes the exit of all characters and the **chorus.**

Exposition. See **plot.**

Expressionism. Early twentieth-century literary movement that posited that art should represent powerful emotional states and moods. Expressionists abandon **realism** and **verisimilitude,** producing distorted, nightmarish images of the individual unconscious. Sometimes music and lighting effects highlight the inner drama experienced by the play's important characters.

Falling action. See **plot.**

Farce. See **comedy.**

Foil. A character who, through difference or similarity, brings out a particular aspect of another character.

Foreshadowing. Ominous warnings of impending events that produce an air of suspense and tension within a play.

Fourth wall. The theatrical convention, dating from the nineteenth century, whereby the audience seems to be looking and listening through an invisible fourth wall, usually into a room in a private residence. The fourth wall is primarily associated with realism and domestic dramas.

Genre. A basic type of a play or other work of literature. While the most basic genres are comedy and tragedy, many others are recognized, including **tragicomedy,** romance, melodrama, and so on.

Hamartia. An error or wrong act through which the fortunes of the **protagonist** are reversed in a tragedy.

Hero, heroine. Sometimes used to refer to the protagonist, the term more properly applies only to a great figure from legend or history or to a character who performs in a remarkably honorable and selfless manner. In the twentieth century, Arthur Miller (and many others) believe that a "common" person, such as Willy Loman in *Death of a Salesman,* can also be properly viewed as a modern-day hero of sorts. (See also **antihero.**)

High comedy. See **comedy.**

History play. A drama set in a time other than that in which it was written. The term usually refers to late Elizabethan drama, such as Shakespeare's Henry plays, that draws its plots from English historical materials.

Hubris. Overweening pride or ambition. In ancient Greek tragedy *hubris* often causes the **protagonist**'s fall from grace.

Irony. The use of words to suggest a meaning that is the opposite of the literal meaning. Irony is present in a literary work that gives expression to contradictory attitudes or impulses to entertain ambiguity or maintain detachment.

- **Cosmic irony.** Irony present when destiny or the gods seem to be in favor of the **protagonist** but are actually engineering his or her downfall. (Same as *irony of fate.*)
- **Dramatic irony.** Irony present when the outcome of an event or situation is the opposite of what a character expects.
- **Tragic irony.** Irony that exists when a character's lack of complete knowledge or understanding (which the audience possesses) results in his or her fall or has tragic consequences for loved ones.

Kabuki. Form of Japanese popular theater originating in the early seventeenth century. Kabuki tends to encompass both comic and serious elements in elaborate and conventional performances that sometimes lasted from ten to twelve hours; it includes live acting, narration, music, and singing.

Koryphaios. The leader of the **chorus** in Greek drama.

Kyogen. Form of Japanese popular theater, characterized by brief, humorous performances, which are often enacted during the intermission of a Noh play.

Liturgical drama. Short dramatized sections of the medieval church service. Some scholars believe that these playlets evolved into the vernacular **mystery plays,** which were performed outside the church by lay people.

Low comedy. See **comedy.**

Mask. A covering used to disguise or ornament the face; used by actors in Greek drama and revived in the later ***commedia dell'arte*** and court **masque** to heighten dramatic effect.

Masque (also **mask**). A short but ornately staged court drama, often filled with myth and allegory, mainly acted and danced by masked courtiers. Popular in England during the late sixteenth and early seventeenth centuries, masques were often commissioned to honor a particular person or event.

- **Antimasque.** A parody of the court **masque** developed by Ben Jonson featuring broad humor, grotesque characters, and ludicrous actions.

Melodrama. A suspenseful play filled with situations that appeal excessively to the audience's emotions. Justice triumphs in a happy ending: the good characters (completely virtuous) are rewarded and the bad characters (thoroughly villainous) are punished.

Melody. One of the six elements of drama identified by Aristotle. Since the Greek chorus communicated through song and dance, melody was an important part of even the most serious play, though it is now largely confined to musical comedy.

Mime. Brief, bawdy form of comedy, developed in ancient Rome.

Mimesis. The Greek word for imitation. Aristotle used the term to define the role of art as an "imitation of nature."

Miracle play. A type of medieval sacred drama that depicts the lives of saints, focusing especially on the miracles performed by saints. The term is often used interchangeably with **mystery play.**

Morality play. Didactic late medieval drama (flourishing in England ca. 1400–1550) that uses **allegory** to dramatize some aspects of the Christian moral life. Abstract qualities or entities such as Virtue, Vice, Good Deeds, Knowledge, and Death are cast as characters who discuss with the **protagonist** issues related to salvation and the afterlife.

Mystery play. A sacred medieval play dramatizing biblical events such as the creation, the fall of Adam and Eve, and Christ's birth and resurrection. The genre probably evolved from **liturgical drama;** mystery plays were often incorporated into larger **cycles** of plays.

Naturalism. A major literary movement that greatly influenced drama during the later part of the nineteenth century and at least the first half of the twentieth century. A naturalistic world view suggests that a play may be a scientifically accurate reflection of life. The naturalistic writer believes that each person is a product of heredity and a malevolent environment driven by internal and external forces beyond his or her control. At its core, Naturalism suggests that we live in a grimly deterministic world in which the individual is reduced to an insignificant speck in the universe over which he or she has little or no control. Biology, fate, chance, random acts of nature, and so on conspire to overwhelm, oftentimes, the hero of the play.

New Comedy. See **comedy.**

Noh. Japanese classical theater dating from the fourteenth century; the plays are highly poetic dramas given extremely formal production onstage. Noh drama was admired by Yeats and by other modern playwrights and writers.

Ode. A dignified Greek three-part song sung by the **chorus** in Greek drama. The parts are the **strophe,** the **antistrophe,** and the **epode.**

Old Comedy. See **comedy.**

One act. A short play that is complete in one act.

Orchestra. A circular stage; Greek chorus performed there.

Pantomime. Silent acting using facial expression, body movement, and gesture to convey the plot and the characters' feelings, which developed in ancient Rome.

Parodos. The often stately entrance song of the **chorus** in Greek drama. The term also refers to the aisles (plural, *paradoi*) on either side of the orchestra by which the chorus entered the Greek theater.

Pastoral drama. A dramatic form glorifying shepherds and rural life in an idealized natural setting; usually implies a negative comparison to city life.

Pathos. The quality of evoking pity.

Peking Opera. Elaborate form of Chinese theater involving an onstage orchestra, ornate costumes, music, and dance.

Peripeteia. A reversal of fortune, for better or worse, for the **protagonist.** Used especially to describe the main character's fall in Greek tragedy.

Play. A literary genre whose plot is usually presented dramatically by actors portraying characters before an audience.

Play-within-the-play. A brief secondary drama presented to or by the characters of a play that reflects or comments on the larger work.

Plot. The events of a play or narrative. The sequence and relative importance a **dramatist** assigns to these events.

- **Anticlimax.** An unexpectedly trivial or significant conclusion to a series of significant events; an unsatisfying resolution that often occurs in place of a conventional **climax.**
- **Catastrophe.** The outcome or conclusion of a play; usually applied specifically to tragedy. (**Denouement** is a parallel term applied to both comedy and tragedy.)
- **Climax.** The turning point in a drama's action, preceded by the **rising action** and followed by the **falling action.** Also known as crisis.
- **Complication.** The part of the plot preceding the **climax** that establishes the entanglements to be untangled in the **denouement.** Part of the **rising action.**
- **Conflict.** The struggle between the **protagonist** and the **antagonist** that propels the **rising action** of the plot and is resolved in the **denouement.**
- **Denouement.** The "unknotting" of the plot's **complication;** the resolution of a drama's action. See **catastrophe.**
- **Double plot.** A dramatic structure in which two related plots function simultaneously.
- **Exposition.** The presentation of essential information, especially about events that have occurred prior to the first scene of a play. The exposition appears early in the play and initiates the **rising action.**
- **Falling action.** The events of the plot following the **climax** and ending in the **catastrophe** or resolution.
- **Rising action.** The events of the plot leading up to the **climax.**
- **Subplot.** A secondary plot intertwined with the main plot, often reflecting or commenting on the main plot.
- **Underplot.** Same as **subplot.**

Problem play. A drama that argues a point or presents a problem—usually an important social problem.

Prologos. In Greek drama, an introductory scene for actor or actors that precedes the entrance of the **chorus.** This **convention,** invented by Euripides, has evolved into the modern dramatic introductory monologue or **prologue.**

Prologue. A preface or introduction preceding the play.

Protagonist. The main character in a drama. This character is usually the most interesting and sympathetic and is the person involved in the **conflict** driving the **plot.**

Protasis. Classical term for the introductory act or **exposition** of a drama.

Realism. The literary movement and philosophy that holds that art should accurately reproduce an image of life. Avoids the use of dramatic *conventions* such as asides and soliloquies to depict ordinary people in ordinary situations. Much of American drama evolved from an exceedingly realistic tradition, though many playwrights would alter and challenge such a tradition.

Repartee. Clever and pointed verbal exchanges.

Resolution. A satisfying outcome that effectively ends the conflict of a play.

Revenge tragedy. See **tragedy.**

Riposte. A quick or sharp reply; similar to **repartee.**

Rising action. See **plot.**

Sanskrit drama. Epic plays from ancient India, which explored a variety of human emotions and moods, and always ended on a positive note.

Satire. A work that makes fun of a social institution or human foible, often in an intellectually sophisticated way, to persuade the audience to share the author's views. Moliere's *The Misanthrope* contains social satire.

Satyr play. A comic play performed after the tragic trilogy in Greek tragedy competitions. The satyr play provided **comic relief** and was usually a farcical, boisterous treatment of mythological material.

Scene. Division of an **act** in a drama. By traditional definition a scene has no major shift in place or time frame, and it is performed by a static group of actors onstage (if an actor enters or exits, the group is altered and the scene, technically, should change). The term also refers to the physical surroundings or locale in which a play's action is set.

Setting. All details of time, location, and environment relating to a play.

Slapstick. See **comedy.**

Soliloquy. A speech in which an actor, usually alone onstage, utters his or her thoughts aloud, revealing his or her most personal, inner feelings.

Spectacle. In Aristotle's terms, the costumes and scenery in a drama the elements that appeal to the eye.

Stage directions. Written instructions in the script telling actors how to move on the stage or how to deliver a particular line. To facilitate reading of scripts and distinguish them from dialogue, stage directions are typically placed in parentheses and written in italics. In modern plays, some of the stage directions (sometimes referred to as the "didascalia") function as a kind of omniscient narrator or, in selected plays, as incredibly brief "short stories" that reveal important details about the overall theme of the play and about the spiritual condition of the key characters.

Staging. Choices made either by the playwright or performing group's director and crew regarding the overall appearance of the stage, props, lighting, music, and costumes.

Stichomythia. Dialogue in which two speakers engage in a verbal duel in alternating lines.

Stock character. See **characterization.**

Strophe. The first of three parts of an **ode** sung by the Greek **chorus.** While singing the strophe the chorus moves in a dance-like pattern from right to left. See also **antistrophe** and **epode.**

Structure. The organization of a play into plot elements, and into scenes and acts.

Subplot. See **plot.**

Subtext. A level of meaning implicit or underlying the surface meaning of a text.

Suspense. The sense of tension aroused by an audience's uncertainty about the resolution of dramatic conflicts.

Suspension of disbelief. An audience's willingness to accept the world of the drama as reality during the course of a play.

Symbolism. A literary device in which an object, event, or action is used to suggest a meaning beyond its literal meaning.

Theater. A term used to refer to drama in live performance. See also **drama.**

Theater of the Absurd. Modern plays that present the human condition as meaningless, absurd, and illogical. Language is sometimes devalued and traditional notions of plot and character subverted. Albert Camus, the French existentialist writer and philosopher, called the "absurd" a feeling that the individual is divorced from Nature and his or her society.

Theme. The central idea(s) explored by a play or literary work. One of the six elements of drama identified by Aristotle.

Thespian. Of or related to theater, from the early Greek playwright and actor Thespis.

Total theater. A concept of the theater as an experience synthesizing all the expressive arts including music, dance, lighting, and so on.

Tragedy. Serious drama in which a **protagonist,** traditionally of noble position, suffers a series of unhappy events culminating in a **catastrophe** such as death or spiritual breakdown.

- **Domestic tragedy.** A serious play usually focusing on the family and depicting the fall of a middle-class **protagonist** rather than of a powerful or noble hero. Also called bourgeois tragedy.
- **Revenge tragedy.** Sensational tragedy popularized during the Elizabethan age that is notable for bloody plots involving such elements as murder, ghosts, insanity, and crimes of lust.

Tragic irony. See **irony.**

Tragicomedy. A play that combines elements of tragedy and comedy; Chekhov's *The Cherry Orchard* is an example. Tragicomedies often include a serious plot in which the expected tragic **catastrophe** is replaced by a happy ending.

Underplot. See **plot.**

Unity. The sense that the events of a play and the actions of the characters follow one another naturally to form one complete action. Unity is present when characters' behavior seems motivated and the work is perceived to be a connected artistic whole.

Verisimilitude. The degree to which a dramatic representation approximates an appearance of reality.

Well-made play. Drama that relies for effect on the suspense generated by its logical, cleverly constructed plot rather than on characterization. Plots often involve a withheld secret, a battle of wits between hero and villain, and a resolution in which the secret is revealed and the protagonist saved.

SELECTED AUDIO AND VIDEO RESOURCES

EDWARD ALBEE

Edward Albee. 52 minutes, color. VHS, DVD.

SUSAN GLASPELL

***A Jury of Her Peers* (based on the short story version of *Trifles*).** 30 minutes, color, 1980. VHS. Directed by Sally Heckel. Distributed by Home Vision Entertainment.

HENRIK IBSEN

A Doll's House. 180 minutes, 1993. 3 audiocassettes. Read by Flo Gibson. Distributed by Audio Book Contractors.

A Doll's House. 98 minutes, color, 1973. VHS, 16-mm film. With Jane Fonda, Edward Fox, and Trevor Howard. Screenplay by Christopher Hampton. Distributed by Prism Entertainment.

DAVID MAMET

Glengarry Glen Ross. 100 minutes, 1992. VHS, DVD. With Jack Lemmon, Al Pacino, and Kevin Spacey. Directed by James Foley. Distributed by Artisan Entertainment.

ARTHUR MILLER

Death of a Salesman. 135 minutes, color, 1985. Beta, VHS, DVD. With Dustin Hoffman, John Malkovich, Charles Durning, and Stephen Lang. Directed by Volker Schlondorff. Distributed by Facets Multimedia and Warner Home Video.

Death of a Salesman. 2 audiocassettes. Performed by Lee J. Cobb and Mildred Dunnock. Distributed by Caedmon/Harper Audio.

***Private Conversations on the Set of* Death of a Salesman.** 82 minutes, color, 1985. Beta, VHS. With Arthur Miller, Dustin Hoffman, Volker Schlondorff, and John Malkovich. Distributed by Video Learning Library.

HAROLD PINTER

The Dumb Waiter. 108 minutes, color, 1987. VHS and DVD. With John Travolta and Tom Conti. Directed by Robert Altman. Studio: Prism.

WILLIAM SHAKESPEARE

Hamlet. 153 minutes, b/w, 1948. VHS, beta, laser disc, DVD. With Laurence Olivier, Basil Sydney, Felix Aylmer, Jean Simmons, Stanley Holloway, Peter Cushing, and Christopher Lee. Voice of John Gielgud. Directed by Olivier. Distributed by Paramount Home Video.

Hamlet. 135 minutes, color, 1990. VHS, DVD. With Mel Gibson, Glenn Close, Alan Bates, Paul Scofield, Ian Holm, and Helena

Hamlet. 242 minutes, color, 1996. Laser, DDS, VHS. With Kenneth Branagh, Kate Winslet, Julie Christie, and Charlton Heston. Directed by Kenneth Branagh. Distributed by Columbia Tristar Home Video.

Hamlet. 112 minutes, color, 2000. VHS, DVD. Starring Ethan Hawke, Kyle MacLachlan, Sam Shepard, Bill Murray, Diane Verona, Liev Schreiber, and Julia Stiles. Directed by Michael Almereyda. Distributed by Miramax Home Entertainment.

SOPHOCLES

Antigonê. 120 minutes, 1987. VHS, 3/4" U-matic cassette, DVD. With Juliet Stevenson, John Shrapnel, and John Gielgud. Staged version. Distributed by Films for the Humanities and Sciences.

Antigonê. 58 minutes, color, 1994. VHS. With Seymour Simon. Distributed by RMI Media Productions.

TENNESSEE WILLIAMS

The Glass Menagerie. 134 minutes, color, 1987. Beta, VHS. With Joanne Woodward, Karen Allen, John Malkovich, and James Naughton. Directed by Paul Newman. See local retailer.

The Glass Menagerie. 2 audiocassettes. Performed by Montgomery Clift and Julie Harris. Distributed by Caedmon/Harper Audio.

GAO XINGJIANG

Gao Xingjiang, *Nobel Lecture.* 37 minutes, color, in Chinese, with English subtitles, 2000. Available online via the Nobel Prize Web site at <nobel.se/literature/ laureates/ 2000/gao-lecture.html>.

SELECTED BIBLIOGRAPHY

Edward Albee

Bigsby, C. W. E. *Albee.* Edinburgh: Oliver & Boyd, 1969.

———, ed. *Edward Albee: A Collection of Critical Essays,* Englewood Cliffs, NJ: Prentice-Hall, 1975.

Bottoms, Stephen J., ed. *The Cambridge Companion to Edward Albee,* Cambridge: Cambridge University Press, 2005.

Bloom, Harold, ed. *Edward Albee* (Modern Critical Views). New York: Chelsea House, 2000.

Gussow, Mel. *Edward Albee: A Singular Journey: A Biography.* New York: Simon & Schuster, 1999.

Hayman, Ronald. *Edward Albee.* London: Heinemann, 1971.

Horn, Barbara Lee. *Edward Albee: A Research and Production Sourcebook* Westport: Praeger, 2003.

Kolin, Philip C., ed. *Conversations with Edward Albee.* Jackson, MS: University Press of Mississippi, 1988.

Kolin, Philip C., and J. Madison Davis, eds. *Critical Essays on Edward Albee.* Boston: G. K. Hall, 1986.

Mann, Bruce J., ed. *Edward Albee: A Casebook.* New York: Routledge, 2003.

McCarthy, Gerry. *Edward Albee.* New York: St. Martin's Press, 1987.

Paolucci, Anne. *From Tension to Tonic: The Plays of Edward Albee.* Carbondale, IL: Southern Illinois University Press, 1972.

Roudané, Matthew. *Understanding Edward Albee.* Columbia: University of South Carolina Press, 1987.

———. *Who's Afraid of Virginia Woolf?: Necessary Fictions, Terrifying Realities.* New York: Twayne, 1990.

Wasserman, Julian N., et al., eds. *Edward Albee: An Interview and Essays.* Houston: University of St. Thomas, 1983.

Susan Glaspell

Ben-Zvi, Linda. "'Murder, She Wrote': The Genesis of Susan Glaspell's *Trifles.*" *Theatre Journal* 44.2 (1992): 141–62.

———, ed. *Susan Glaspell: Essays on Her Theater and Fiction.* Ann Arbor: University of Michigan Press, 1995.

———. *Susan Glaspell: Her Life and Times,* Oxford: Oxford University Press, 2005.

Makowsky, Veronica. *Susan Glaspell's Century of American Women: A Critical Interpretation of Her Work.* New York: Oxford University Press, 1993.

Noe, Marcia. "Region as Metaphor in the Plays of Susan Glaspell." *Western Illinois Regional Studies* 4.1 (1981): 77–85.

———. "Reconfiguring the Subject/Recuperating Realism: Susan Glaspell's Unseen Woman." *American Drama* 4.2 (1995): 36–54.

Ozieblo, Barbara. "Rebellion and Rejection: The Plays of Susan Glaspell." *Modern American Drama: The Female Canon.* Ed. June Schlueter. Rutherford: Fairleigh Dickinson University Press, 1990.

———. "Susan Glaspell." *American Drama.* Ed. Clive Bloom. New York: St. Martin's, 1995. 6–20.

———. *Susan Glaspell: A Critical Biography.* Chapel Hill: University of North Carolina Press, 2000.

Papke, Mary B. *Susan Glaspell: A Research and Production Sourcebook.* Westport: Greenwood, 1993.

Henrik Ibsen

Ackerman, Gretchen P. *Ibsen and the English Stage,* 1889–1903. New York: Garland, 1987.

Chamberlain, John S. *Ibsen: The Open Vision.* London: Athlone, 1982.

Egan, Michael, ed. *Ibsen: The Critical Heritage.* London: Routledge, 1972.

Ferguson, Robert. *Henrik Ibsen: A New Biography.* London: R. Cohen, 1996.

Fjelde, Rolf, ed. *Ibsen: A Collection of Critical Essays.* Englewood Cliffs: Prentice, 1965.

Gaskell, Ronald. *Drama and Reality: The European Theatre since Ibsen.* London: Routledge, 1972.

Goldman, Michael. *Ibsen: The Dramaturgy of Fear.* New York: Columbia University Press, 1999.

Lebowitz, Naomi. *Ibsen and the Great World.* Baton Rouge: Louisiana University Press, 1990.

Marker, Frederick J. *Ibsen's Lively Art: A Performance Study of the Major Plays.* New York: Cambridge University Press, 1989.

McFarlane, James, ed. *Discussions of Henrik Ibsen.* Boston: Heath, 1962.

———, ed. *The Cambridge Companion to Ibsen.* Cambridge: Cambridge University Press, 1994.

Meyer, Michael. *Henrik Ibsen: A Biography.* 3 vols. Garden City: Doubleday, 1971.

Noreng, Harald, et al., eds. *Contemporary Approaches to Ibsen.* Oslo: Universitetsforlaget, 1977.

Northam, John. *Ibsen: A Critical Study.* Cambridge: Cambridge University Press, 1973.

Shaw, Bernard. *The Quintessence of Ibsenism.* New York: Hill, 1957.

Shepherd-Barr, Kirsten. *Ibsen and Early Modernist Theatre, 1890–1900.* Westport: Greenwood, 1997.

Theoharis, Constantine. *Ibsen Drama: Right Action and Tragic Joy.* New York: St. Martin's, 1996.

Thomas, David. *Henrik Ibsen.* New York: Grove, 1984.

David Mamet

Bigsby, Christopher, ed. *The Cambridge Companion to David Mamet.* Cambridge: Cambridge University Press, 2004.

Dean, Anne. *David Mamet: Language as Dramatic Action.* Rutherford: Fairleigh Dickinson University Press, 1990.

Kane, Leslie, ed. *David Mamet: A Casebook.* New York: Garland, 1992.

———, ed. *David Mamet's* Glengarry Glen Ross: *Text and Performance.* New York: Garland, 1996.

———, ed. *David Mamet in Conversation.* Ann Arbor: University of Michigan Press, 2001.

Kane, Leslie. *Weasels and Wisemen: Ethics and Ethnicity in the Work of David Mamet.* New York: Palgrave, 1999.

McDonough, Carla J. *Staging Masculinity: Male Identity in Contemporary American Drama.* Jefferson, NC: McFarland, 1997.

Roudané, Matthew. "Something out of Nothing." *David Mamet in Conversation.* Leslie Kane, ed. Ann Arbor: University of Michigan Press, 2001: 46–53.

Sauer, David K., and Janice A. Sauer. *David Mamet: A Research and Production Sourcebook.* Westport: Praeger, 2003.

Arthur Miller

Bigsby, Christopher, ed. *The Cambridge Companion to Arthur Miller.* Cambridge: Cambridge University Press, 1997.

———, ed. *Arthur Miller and Company.* London: Methuen, 1990.

Bigsby, Christopher. *Modern American Drama, 1945–2000.* Cambridge: Cambridge University Press, 2000.

———. *Arthur Miller: A Critical Study.* Cambridge: Cambridge University Press, 2005.

Bloom, Harold. *Arthur Miller.* Philadelphia: Chelsea, 1999.

———, ed. *Arthur Miller's* Death of a Salesman. New York: Chelsea, 1988.

———. *Willy Loman.* New York: Chelsea, 1990.

Carson, Neil. *Arthur Miller.* London: Macmillan, 1982.

Centola, Steven, ed. *The Achievement of Arthur Miller: New Essays.* Dallas: Contemporary Research Press, 1995.

Corrigan, Robert W., ed. *Arthur Miller: A Collection of Critical Essays.* Englewood Cliffs: Prentice-Hall, 1969.

Goldstein, Laurence, ed. "Arthur Miller." *Michigan Quarterly Review* 37.4 [Special Issue] (1998).

Griffin, Alice. *Understanding Arthur Miller.* Columbia: University of South Carolina Press, 1996.

Hayman, Ronald. *Arthur Miller.* New York: Ungar, 1972.

Huftel, Sheila. *Arthur Miller: The Burning Glass.* New York: Citadel, 1965.

Jenckes, Norma, ed. "Arthur Miller." *American Drama* 6.1 [Special Issue] (1996).

Koon, Helene Wickham. Twentieth Century Interpretations of *Death of a Salesman.* Englewood Cliffs: Prentice-Hall, 1983.

Marino, Stephen A., ed. *The 'Salesman' Has a Birthday.* New York: University Press of America, 2000.

Martin, Robert A., ed. *Arthur Miller: New Perspectives.* Englewood Cliffs: Prentice-Hall, 1982.

Martin, Robert A., and Steven Centola, eds. *The Theater Essays of Arthur Miller.* Ed. and intro., Robert A. Martin. New York: Da Capo, 1996.

Murphy, Brenda. *Miller's Death of a Salesman.* Cambridge: Cambridge University Press, 1995.

Otten, Terry. *The Temptation of Innocence in the Dramas of Arthur Miller.* Columbia: University of Missouri Press, 2002.

Roudané, Matthew C., ed. *Conversations with Arthur Miller.* Jackson: University Press of Mississippi, 1987.

———, ed. *Approaches to Teaching Miller's Death of a Salesman.* New York: MLA, 1995.

Harold Pinter

Billington, Michael. *The Life and Work of Harold Pinter.* London: Faber and Faber, 1996.

Burkman, Katherine H. *The Dramatic World of Harold Pinter.* Columbia: Ohio State University Press, 1971.

Diamond, Elin. *Pinter's Comic Plays.* Lewisburg: Bucknell University Press, 1985.

Gale, Steven H., ed. *Critical Essays on Harold Pinter.* Boston: G. K. Hall, 1990.

Knowles, Ronald. *Understanding Harold Pinter.* Columbia: University of South Carolina Press, 1995.

Quigley, Austin E. *The Pinter Problem.* Princeton: Princeton University Press, 1975.

SUZAN-LORI PARKS

Carr, C. "Review of Imperceptible Mutabilities in the Third Kingdom." *Artforum,* November 1989: 154.

Gussow, Mel. Review of *The Death of the Last Black Man in the Whole Entire World. New York Times* 25 Sept. 1990: C15.

———. Review of Imperceptible Mutabilities in the Third Kingdom. *New York Times* 20 Sept. 1989: C24.

Jiggetts, Shelby. "Interviews with Suzan-Lori Parks." *Callaloo,* 19.2 (1996): 309–17.

WILLIAM SHAKESPEARE

Bamber, Linda. *Comic Women, Tragic Men: A Study of Gender and Genre in Shakespeare.* Stanford: Stanford University Press, 1982.

Bloom, Harold. *Shakespeare: The Invention of the Human.* London: Fourth Estate, 1999.

Bradley, A. C. *Shakespearean Tragedy.* New York: Meridian, 1955.

Drakakis, John, ed. *Alternative Shakespeares.* New York: Methuen, 1985.

Dutton, Richard. *Shakespeare: A Literary Life.* New York: St. Martin's, 1989.

Eagleton, Terry. *William Shakespeare.* New York: Blackwell, 1986.

Erikson, Peter. *Rewriting Shakespeare, Rewriting Ourselves.* Berkeley: University of California Press, 1991.

Frye, Northrop. *On Shakespeare.* New Haven: Yale University Press, 1986.

Grady, Hugh. *The Modernist Shakespeare: Critical Texts in a Material World.* New York: Oxford University Press, 1991.

Hirsh, James. *Shakespeare and the History of Soliloquies.* Madison, NJ: Fairleigh Dickinson University Press, 2003.

———. *The Structure of Shakespearean Scenes.* New Haven: Yale University Press, 1981.

Ioppolo, Grace. *Revising Shakespeare.* Cambridge: Harvard University Press, 1991.

Jacobus, Lee. *Shakespeare and the Dialectic of Certainty.* New York: St. Martin's, 1992.

Jardine, Lisa. *Still Harping on Daughters: Women and Drama in the Age of Shakespeare.* Totowa: Barnes, 1983.

Kiernan, Pauline. *Shakespeare's Theory of Drama.* Cambridge: Cambridge University Press, 1998.

Kiernan, Ryan, ed. *Shakespeare: Texts and Contexts.* New York: St. Martin's, 1999.

Shellard, Dominic. *William Shakespeare.* The British Library Writers' Lives. New York: Oxford University Press, 1998.

Wells, Stanley W., ed. *Shakespeare and Language.* Cambridge: Cambridge University Press, 1997.

______, ed. *Shakespeare in the Theatre: An Anthology of Criticism.* Oxford: Clarendon, 1997.

______. *Shakespeare: The Poet and His Plays.* London: Methuen, 1997.

SOPHOCLES

Bushnell, Rebecca. *Prophesying Tragedy: Sign and Voice in Sophocles' Theban Plays.* Ithaca: Cornell University Press, 1988.

Buxton, R. G. A. *Sophocles.* New York: Clarendon, 1984.

Kitto, H. D. F. *Sophocles: Dramatist and Philosopher.* London: Oxford University Press, 1958.

Knox, Bernard M. *Sophocles at Thebes: Sophocles' Tragic Hero and His Time.* New York: Norton, 1971.

Scodel, Ruth. *Sophocles.* Boston: Twayne, 1984.

Segal, Charles. *Tragedy and Civilization: An Interpretation of Sophocles.* Cambridge: Harvard University Press, 1981.

Wiles, David. *The Masks of Menander: Sign and Meaning in Greek and Roman Performances.* Cambridge: Cambridge University Press, 1991.

Winnington-Ingram, R. P. *Sophocles: An Interpretation.* New York: Cambridge University Press, 1980.

Woodard, T. M, ed. *Sophocles: A Collection of Critical Essays.* Englewood Cliffs: Prentice, 1966.

PAULA VOGEL

Bigsby, Christopher. *Contemporary American Playwrights.* Cambridge: Cambridge University Press, 1999.

Kimbrough, Andrew. "The Pedophile in Me: The Ethics of How I Learned to Drive." *Journal of Dramatic Theory and Criticism* 16.2 (2002): 47–67.

Parker, Mary-Louise. "Paula Vogel." *Bomb* 61 (1997): 44–49.

Savran, David. "Driving Ms. Vogel." *American Theatre* 15.8 (1998): 16–19, 96–106.

Tennessee Williams

Crandell, George W., ed. *The Critical Response to Tennessee Williams.* Westport: Greenwood, 1996.

Devlin, Albert J., ed. *Conversations with Tennessee Williams.* Jackson: University Press of Mississippi, 1986.

Donahue, Francis. *The Dramatic World of Tennessee Williams.* New York: Ungar, 1964.

Falk, Signi Lenea. *Tennessee Williams.* 2nd ed. Boston: Twayne, 1978.

Griffin, Alice. *Understanding Tennessee Williams.* Columbia: University of South Carolina Press, 1995.

Hayman, Ronald. *Tennessee Williams: Everyone Else Is an Audience.* New Haven: Yale University Press, 1993.

Kolin, Philip, ed. *The Tennessee Williams Encyclopedia.* Westport, CT: Greenwood, 2004.

Leavitt, Richard Freeman, ed. *The World of Tennessee Williams.* New York: Putnam's, 1978.

Leverich, Lyle. *Tom: The Unknown Tennessee Williams.* London: Scepter, 1996.

Martin, Robert A., ed. *Critical Essays on Tennessee Williams.* New York: Hall, 1997.

Parker, R. B., ed. *The Glass Menagerie: A Collection of Critical Essays.* Englewood Cliffs: Prentice, 1983.

Roudané, Matthew, ed. *The Cambridge Companion to Tennessee Williams.* Cambridge: Cambridge University Press, 1997.

Savran, David. *Communists, Cowboys and Queers: The Politics of Masculinity in the Work of Arthur Miller and Tennessee Williams.* Minneapolis: University of Minnesota Press, 1992.

Spoto, Donald. *The Kindness of Strangers:* The Life of Tennessee Williams. Boston: Little, Brown, 1985.

Williams, Dakin, with Shepherd Mead. *Tennessee Williams: An Intimate Biography.* New York: Arbor, 1983.

Gao Xingjian

Tam, Kwok-Kan, ed. *The Soul of Chaos: Critical Perspectives on Gao Xingjian.* Hong Kong: The Chinese University Press, 2001.

CREDITS

David Mamet. From *Glengarry Glen Ross* by David Mamet. Copyright © 1982, 1983 by David Mamet. Used by permission of Grove/Atlantic, Inc.

Arthur Miller. From *Death of a Salesman* by Arthur Miller, Copyright 1949, renewed © 1977 by Arthur Miller. Used by permission of Viking Penguin, a division of Penguin Group (USA) Inc.

Suzan-Lori Parks. *Topdog/Underdog* is Copyright © 1999, 2001 by Suzan-Lori Parks. *Topdog/Underdog* is published by Theatre Communications Group. Used by permission of Theatre Communications Group.

Harold Pinter. From *The Dumb Waiter* by Harold Pinter. Copyright © 1960 by Harold Pinter. Used by permission of Grove/Atlantic, Inc.

William Shakespeare. "Hamlet: Prince of Denmark," from *Riverside Shakespeare*, 1997, pp. 1189-1245. Copyright © 1997 by Houghton Mifflin Company. Reprinted with permission.

Paula Vogel. From *The Mammary Plays* by Paula Vogel. Copyright © 1998 by Paula Vogel. *How I Learned to Drive* is Copyright © 1997, 1998 by Paula Vogel. Published by and used by permission of Theatre Communications Group.

Tennessee Williams. *The Glass Menagerie* by Tennessee Williams. Copyright © 1945 by The University of the South. Reprinted by permission of Georges Borchardt, Inc. for the Tennessee Williams Estate.

Gao Xingjian. "Dialogue and Rebuttal" from *The Other Shore: Plays by Gao Xingjian,* translated by Gilbert C. Fong. Reprinted by permission of Chinese University Press, Hong Kong.

INDEX

CPSIA information can be obtained
at www.ICGtesting.com
Printed in the USA
FFHW011806181218
49920467-54540FF